CHARLES ELIOT

LANDSCAPE ARCHITECT

CHARLES ELIOT
LANDSCAPE ARCHITECT

Charles W. Eliot

Introduction by Keith N. Morgan

UNIVERSITY OF MASSACHUSETTS PRESS
AMHERST

IN ASSOCIATION WITH
LIBRARY OF AMERICAN LANDSCAPE HISTORY
AMHERST

This volume is reprinted from the first edition of *Charles Eliot, Landscape Architect*, published by Houghton Mifflin in 1902. In that edition, the second insert map was mistakenly labeled 1910. The correct date is 1901.

The Institute for Cultural Landscape Studies of the Arnold Arboretum of Harvard University is the educational partner for this edition of *Charles Eliot, Landscape Architect* and the sponsor of a lecture series in conjunction with its publication. The Institute supports the management and conservation of cultural landscapes in the northeastern United States. The Institute's programs integrate, develop, and disseminate information across three traditional fields: historic preservation, natural areas conservation, and land use planning.

Printed in the United States of America
LC 99–21373
ISBN 1–55849–212–7
Printed and bound by Quinn-Woodbine, Inc.

Library of Congress Cataloging-in-Publication Data

Eliot, Charles William, 1834–1926.
Charles Eliot, landscape architect / Charles W. Eliot ;
introduction by Keith N. Morgan.
p. cm.
Originally published: Boston : Houghton Mifflin, 1902.
Includes bibliographical references.
ISBN 1–55849–212–7 (cloth : alk. paper)
1. Eliot, Charles, 1859–1897.
2. Landscape architects—United States—Biography.
3. Landscape architecture—United States—History—19th century.
I. Title.
SB470.E6E6 1999
712'.092
[B]—DC21   99–21373
CIP

British Library Cataloguing in Publication data are available.

PREFACE

The ASLA Centennial Reprint Series comprises a small library of influential historical books about American landscape
architecture. The titles were selected by a committee of distinguished editors who identified them as classics, important in
shaping design, planting, planning, and stewardship practices in
the field and still relevant today. Each is reprinted from the original edition and introduced by a new essay that provides historical and contemporary perspective. The project commemorates
the 1999 centennial of the American Society of Landscape Architects and is underwritten by the Viburnum Foundation, Roch-
ester, New York.

We are pleased to inaugurate the series with *Charles Eliot,
Landscape Architect*, the biography of one of the profession's
visionary practitioners, written by Eliot's father a few years after his son's premature death. Charles Eliot emerges from these
pages as a brilliant though melancholy young man with a passion for travel, history, and the natural landscape. The book
traces Eliot's years in solo practice and his partnership with John
Charles Olmsted and Frederick Law Olmsted Sr. Several percep-
tive passages from Eliot's travel writing and an annotated anthology of professional correspondence and public reports bear
witness to the range of his interests and intellect.

"In the natural course of events," wrote Eliot's father after
examining his son's papers, "I should have died without ever
having appreciated his influence." In fact, no one writing at the
turn of the century was in a position to grasp the younger Eliot's
extraordinary achievement. Charles Eliot was the first landscape
architect consciously to analyze landscapes as entities composed
of layers of systems—cultural, economic, and ecological—while
devising scientific methods for recording them, and implement-
ing political measures to conserve them. In this sense, Eliot was

a modern thinker whose work influenced several generations of landscape architects, beginning with Warren Manning, who adopted Eliot's methods as an apprentice in the Olmsted office.

Keith Morgan has written a superb introductory essay that provides the modern reader with an elegant perspective from which to engage the 1902 book. His research findings fill many of the gaps left by Eliot's father and contribute substantially to our growing understanding of this important chapter in American landscape history. Morgan also offers the reader ideas about how best to tackle the historical text and how it might prove most interesting. Through his guidance, the story and its elusive subject assume new significance.

To further vitalize the connection between Eliot's ideas and today's increasingly pressing land use conundrums, we have invited the new Institute for Cultural Landscape Studies of the Arnold Arboretum of Harvard University to join us as an educational partner in creating a public program of lectures, tours, and associated publications. The Institute integrates information from three traditional fields—historic preservation, natural conservation, and land use planning—in the service of managing and conserving cultural landscapes. We are pleased to be working with them to bring the timely perspectives and insights of Charles Eliot to a wide audience.

Robin Karson, Executive Director
Library of American Landscape History
Amherst, Massachusetts

The Library of American Landscape History, Inc., a nonprofit organization, produces books and exhibitions about American landscape history. Its mission is to educate and thereby promote thoughtful stewardship of the land.

LIBRARY of

AMERICAN
LANDSCAPE
HISTORY

INTRODUCTION TO THE 1999 EDITION

CHARLES ELIOT,

THE MAN BEHIND THE MONOGRAPH

Keith N. Morgan

Recently returned to Boston from a year-long study tour of Europe, the young Charles Eliot (fig. 1) set up a landscape architecture practice on Park Street in December 1886. Over the next decade he would make an indelible mark on the physical form of the metropolitan region and beyond. In Eliot's solo practice, and later as a partner in Olmsted, Olmsted and Eliot, he developed many fine public parks and private estates. He became one of the country's most prolific and influential landscape critics and historians, and provided the creative and political impetus for the Trustees of Public Reservations, the first statewide preservation and conservation organization in the country and the precursor to Britain's National Trust. Finally, and most importantly, Eliot directed the early development of the Boston Metropolitan Park System, one of the first and most successful American experiments in regional landscape planning. It is astounding that all this was accomplished in less than eleven years. Eliot's death from spinal meningitis in 1897, at the age of thirty-eight, robbed the country of one of its most talented landscape architects ever.

Eliot envisioned a new type of public landscape and used a distinctive vocabulary to articulate a new set of objectives. His ideas about park making differed from those of Frederick Law Olmsted Sr., the dominant figure in American landscape architecture in the second half of the nineteenth century, Eliot's mentor and eventual partner. Olmsted wrote about green country parks, parkways, and pastoral retreats as places in which modern city dwellers could find spiritual replenishment through passive contemplation of nature. Eliot, on the other hand, discussed reservations, trusteeships, and rural landscape preservation that would provide settings for active enjoyment of nature. In con-

FIGURE 1. Charles Eliot, ca. 1895.
Courtesy of Alexander Y. Goriansky.

trast to Olmsted's Emersonian view, Eliot compared scenery or landscape to other advantages of urban culture, especially books and art. While Olmsted's parks were created through design, Eliot's reservations were products of choice, preservation, and improvement.

Eliot used the word "reservation" often in his articles and lectures. Indeed, he even thought that the Boston Metropolitan Park Commission should really be called the Metropolitan Reservations Commission.[1] He realized that the term "park" had a specific and limited meaning for his contemporaries, so Eliot took a different word—"scenery"—to distinguish his ideas from common assumptions. He had three basic goals: to preserve scenery, make it accessible, and improve it.[2] By Eliot's definition, scenery was land that had been "resumed" or reclaimed for the public benefit. Reservations, Eliot believed, should be "held in trust," and those who preserved and improved scenery were therefore "trustees" of that heritage.[3] Eliot's use of the term "trustee" invoked a legal process by which individuals were designated as the guardians of landscape, as in the Trustees of Public Reservations. It is interesting that he also referred to park users as "trustees." He was convinced that "ordinary people," as trustees, had the potential to appreciate and the right to expect the merits of public reservations.

Charles Eliot, Landscape Architect is the record of this philosophy, the biography of a remarkable career, and a landmark in American writing on landscape architecture. It is a rare example of filial biography, the story of a son's life by his father. Charles's father, President Charles W. Eliot of Harvard College, did not sign the title page because he considered his role to be that of editor and organizer of his son's writings and record. To understand fully the context of this biography and anthology, it is necessary to know more about the subject and the author.[4]

Charles Eliot, Landscape Architect is really three books intertwined. The first is an intimate life story, told as a loving tribute by a devoted father. The second is a species of superb travel literature, written by young Charles from the perspective of a landscape analyst. The third is an annotated, chronological anthology of professional correspondence and public reports. President Eliot's format places these elements in the context of his understanding of his son's life and career. Changes in size of the typeface subtly signal the alternation from the explanatory background text of the father to the voice and cadence of the son.

While his name does not appear on the title page, there is no question of President Eliot's role as Cicerone on this journey of reconstruction. He not only wrote but financed the publication of this book, a print run of one thousand copies.[5] For the spring 1902 Houghton Mifflin catalogue, the senior Eliot provided his publishers with a statement of the contents and purposes of the volume:

It describes (1) the short but fruitful life of a well-born and well-trained American; (2) how he got his training as landscape architect; (3) the enjoyment of landscape at home and in travel; (4) the physical features of enjoyable landscape; (5) the landscape art—what it can do, and what it should aim to do; (6) the means of promoting and carrying on public landscape works; and (7) as illustrations of (6) the methods and achievements of the Metropolitan Park Commission (Boston) to which he was landscape advisor during its first five years.

The things are set forth, not in the above order but in the chronological sequence of Charles Eliot's experiences and labors. I only edit the volume; it is in the main written by Charles Eliot himself.[6]

A labor of deep affection, the book was meant to inform the public of Charles Eliot's extraordinary accomplishments, not to turn a profit. "I am more interested," President Eliot confided to George Mifflin, "in the problem of getting it into the hands of people that will enjoy it, than in getting the cost . . . of the book repaid."[7]

The elder Eliot probably began to consider the project in the days immediately following his son's death. In April of 1897 he told one friend, "I am examining his letters and papers, and I am filled with wonder at what he accomplished in the ten years of professional life. . . . In the natural course of events I should have died without ever having appreciated his influence. His death has shown it to me."[8] In preparing the monograph, the elder Eliot was particularly concerned about the number and quality of illustrations to be used in the book, illustrations that he assembled from various sources or commissioned as new photographs and maps.[9] The scale of the book was also an issue, leaving the editor uncertain whether to publish the material in one or two volumes.[10]

In 1902 no precedent existed for a monograph on an American landscape architect. Frederick Law Olmsted's biography was yet to be written, and no other member of this young profession, or American landscape architecture as a field, had yet attracted book-length analysis.[11] The rich archival collections that survive from both father and son document the multiple-year campaign by President Eliot to assemble the reports, correspondence, and diaries from which he drew this manuscript. The speed at which the book was written and published reflects its author's determination, especially given his other responsibilities as president of Harvard College.

The father presented a very different biography from the one his son would have written about himself. By today's standards, the book is hagiographic; Eliot emerges as the perfect model for the young profession, receiving credit for ideas and projects that were actually the work of many minds and hands. The overstatement of Eliot's achievements is particularly evident in the description of his role at the Metropolitan Park Commission. President Eliot presents his son as the sole creator, but it is clear that the journalist Sylvester Baxter (fig. 2) played a seminal role in conceiving of the metropolitan Boston ideal.[12] Baxter certainly wrote about the idea of a metropolitan park system before Eliot, but the landscape architect had been thinking about issues of regional planning for many years and would prove to have the staying power and political acumen necessary to make it possible to realize Baxter's dream.[13]

Also, President Eliot's narrative emphasizes the importance of heredity and the influential background from which his son had emerged. The Eliots belonged to what Oliver Wendell Holmes had dubbed "the Brahmin caste of Boston." "In their eyes," observed Charles senior's biographer, "their wealth obliged them to strive for personal achievement and social usefulness."[14] So we are treated to glimpses of many family members including President Eliot's first wife and young Charles's mother, Ellen Peabody Eliot.[15] Thus the book is an intimate family portrait, symbolized by the father's always referring to his son as Charles.

Not all of the nearly 750 pages of text will prove interesting to a modern reader. For example, the chapter on the Metropolitan Park Commission projects of 1894 is excessively detailed, of concern only to those thoroughly familiar with the topography of the Boston area parks. But certain sections of the text are true gems of landscape literature.[16] Anyone interested in the history of landscape architecture, regional planning, or city planning will want to read them.

The reaction to this monograph was enthusiastic though genteel.[17] Characteristic was the review in *Nation*, which interpreted the book as a story of personal struggle and achievement. The reviewer emphasized Charles Eliot's early frail health and self-doubt, quoting a letter from the landscape architect written to his father during a tour of European landscapes: "In dealing with men, I am nowhere . . . an unbaked loaf in the human bread

FIGURE 2. Bas-relief of Sylvester Baxter by Bela Pratt, 1913.
Special Collections, Boston Public Library.

batch." But once young Charles began his extraordinary work with the park commission, the author enthusiastically relates, "having discovered his power, he plucked up heart, threw off ill health, and started to persuade first Boston, then Massachusetts and the whole of the United States to procure sites for parks while land was cheap."[18] Rather than critique the book, the reviewer eulogizes Eliot's unselfish leadership.

Despite the book's being privately produced and only moderately distributed, it has become a classic in the literature of American landscape architecture and city planning, just as President Eliot had hoped that the example of his son's brief career would be a standard and a model for the profession.

FATHER AND SON

When Charles Eliot was born in 1859, his father (fig. 3) was a professor of mathematics and chemistry at Harvard College. His mother, Ellen Peabody Eliot, was an amateur artist and lover of nature. She died when he was ten years old. Charles had one younger brother, Samuel Atkins Eliot, who became an important Unitarian minister, presiding over the Arlington Street Church, Boston, and president of the Unitarian Association. The Eliots' home life was characterized by cultural and social prestige and by intellectual stimulation.

Young Charles was a fragile boy, diffident and often given to melancholic moods, while Sam resembled his father. As President Eliot wrote: "His father and brother had very different temperaments from his. They were sanguine, confident, content with present action, and little given to contemplation of either the past or the future; Charles was reticent, self-distrustful, speculative, and dissatisfied with his actual work, though faithful and patient in studies which did not interest him or open to him intellectual pleasures.[19] Charles Eliot seems to have inherited his mother's talents and interests in art and nature. Unfortunately, her death in 1869 coincided with his father's appointment to the presidency of Harvard College: the emotional gulf widened between the busy father and his awkward, shy elder son.

When his father remarried in 1877, the young man resented the intrusion of a stepmother. He recorded his surprise at the speed of the new union in his diary: "Heard rumors of father's wooing a Miss Hopkinson and one day after Sam had gone East was told by father of his engagement."[20] After President Eliot married Grace Mellen Hopkinson (fig. 4) in October, Charles reported that he "tried hard to be pleasant, but felt awkward and

FIGURE 3. President Charles W. Eliot, 1875.
Harvard University Archives.

FIGURE 4. Grace Mellen Hopkinson Eliot, the second
Mrs. Charles W. Eliot. *Courtesy of Alexander Y. Goriansky.*

'queer'." The distance between father and son continued to grow.
Charles secretly complained that he was "distressed by father
never telling Sam & me of his plans & doings as he once did. Also
much annoyed by *many* things at 'home'."[21]

Ironically, it was his stepmother who ultimately became an
anchor in his emotional life. In the summer of 1881, after having
spent three wonderful months camping, sailing, and exploring
Mount Desert Island in Maine, he described a dramatic emotional
transformation:

> After Camp broke up in Aug. joined F[ather]. & M[other]. and
> "broke down" completely—such a flood of thought and feeling as
> I had never experienced swept over me and through me. My head
> was full of memories and dreams—of fearful hopes, dreads, and
> pains. The Beauty and the Wonder of God's earth burst upon me
> like a holy vision—the depths of this hell on earth opened too at
> my feet. I lay awake whole nights. I cried my eyes out and to
> crown it all I fell in love—with mother.[22]

Charles had come to understand how completely his mother's
early death had affected him. He later wrote to his stepmother:
"If mamma had lived perhaps I should never have formed this
'shrinking' habit; for I certainly should have continued to go to
her with all my joys and troubles. As it is, I know that most
people, judging from my conduct, think me 'indifferent' and 'unenthusiastic'."[23] The slow development of friendship and trust
between the teenager and his new stepmother helped Charles
Eliot to find a path to happiness that he had long lost.

President Eliot hoped to improve his firstborn's sense of self
and increase his physical strength by involving him in the
"strenuous life," camping and sailing along the coast of New
England. Young Charles enjoyed these rigorous forays into nature. During the summers of his second and third years at
Harvard, he organized and led a small band of classmates known
as the Champlain Society in scientific exploration of Mount
Desert.[24] Like Theodore Roosevelt, his near-contemporary at
Harvard, young Charles Eliot embraced life in the out-of-doors,
but he was inspired primarily by a delight in viewing nature.[25]
President Eliot had consistently reinforced the benefits of physical activity and knowledge of the wilderness, emphasizing this
experience as a way of counteracting his elder son's melancholic
withdrawals.

Father and elder son differed in their religious beliefs as well
as in temperament. President Eliot concluded the narrative section of his book with a discussion of his son's religious sentiments.
Unlike his brother Sam, who continued the Eliot family clerical

tradition that had its roots in the Colonial era, Charles worshiped in a Transcendental manner, seeking the hand and mind of the Creator in the beauties of humankind and nature. His letters and diaries often express frustration or confusion about religion. "I go to church every Sunday," he once mused, "but somehow it does me very little good. They never preach about anything elementary enough for me. I want to know how to do my daily work & lessons cheerfully, bravely & well, how to quickly see and instantly use any opportunities of being kind, useful & helpful to another person, how to be content with doing little things well."[26]

President Eliot's text touches on his son's early life and alludes to frequent illnesses, but there is a great deal more to know. Young Charles Eliot's nomadic childhood may have contributed to his later emotional struggles. After losing a promotion battle at Harvard in 1863, Eliot senior took his family abroad so that he could study in French and German laboratories.[27] From August of 1863, when young Charles was three, through the summer of 1865, the family traveled between Paris, London, Heidelberg, Marberg, Vienna, Berlin, Switzerland, and Italy.[28] Late in 1864 Ellen Eliot (fig. 5) wrote to her mother of the family's life abroad:

I keep regular school for Charly every morning & it is a pleasure & an interest to him & to me. He learns readily & enjoys it highly—I really sometimes fear the chicks may be spoiled by the entire devotion of their parents to them. They are necessarily with me all day & Charly sews with me & studies with me & paints with me and they generally walk with me, and it is rarely that I can catch Charles—Every day C[harles] gives Charly a regular gymnastic exercise—the child has improved much in the use of his arms & legs.[29]

The exercises were intended to counteract the lingering effects of a bout of typhoid fever that little Charles had suffered during the winter of 1863–64. He was ill for more than a year but eventually recovered fully.[30]

An invitation to teach chemistry from the Massachusetts Institute of Technology brought the senior Eliot and his family back to Cambridge in the fall of 1865, but his wife's lung and throat congestion prompted them to return to Europe in June 1867 through the following June. When they came back, Grandmother Peabody and Aunt Anna Peabody became members of the household to care for the two young boys. Mrs. Eliot died a year later.

Young Charles had loved learning at his mother's knee, but he

FIGURE 5. Ellen Peabody Eliot with Samuel Atkins Eliot on her lap
and Charles Eliot at her side. *Courtesy of Alexander Y. Goriansky.*

found formal education onerous. In 1876 he wrote: "To my dismay was sent to Kendall's School, Appian Way! . . . Disliked most of the boys but liked Kendall. Often dissolved in tears even in schoolroom; much to my despair."[31] Fortunately, his education was supplemented by drawing lessons from Charles H. Moore, which he liked. He made lifelong friends at Kendall's, however, especially Roland Thaxter and John H. Storer, and his preparation there helped him pass the entrance examination for Harvard College in June 1877.

It is important to understand the values that President Eliot tried to instill in his sons. In 1914 he wrote a short but informative article for *The Delineator* titled "Bringing Up a Boy." Although written almost two decades after the death of his son, this essay clearly recalls young Charles: "The alert boy is often troublesome to parents and teachers, but he is the most promising boy, and great pains should be taken to direct his inquiring mind and eager senses to whole objects, like plants, animals, brooks, forests, landscapes and the products and tools of human industry."[32] President Eliot believed that heredity, rather than environment, was the greater determinant, but he emphasized in his article the role that parents can play in providing an appropriate setting for learning. Clearly, Charles Eliot was a child who caused his father grave concern for many years and great pride when success was achieved.

THE EDUCATION OF A LANDSCAPE ARCHITECT

Charles Eliot's preparation for a career in landscape architecture began long before his Harvard years. During the family's travels in Europe, his parents showed him the beauties of many natural and manmade landscapes. After the death of his mother, his father and other family members continued this tradition. In the summer of 1871 the Eliots spent their first summer on Mount Desert Island in Maine, and the following year they acquired a forty-three-and-half-foot sloop, *The Sunshine*.[33] Maine would remain a central and important part of Charles Eliot's life thereafter.

In spring 1874 young Charles accompanied his aunt Anna Peabody on a trip through South Carolina, Georgia, and Florida. A notebook (fig. 6) in which he recorded his impressions of the landscape, people, and local customs provides us early evidence of his response to landscapes. At this time he was sketching frequently (fig. 7), exhibiting the natural talent that would later encourage him to consider a career in landscape architecture.

In shaping his education, Charles had the advantage (or dis-

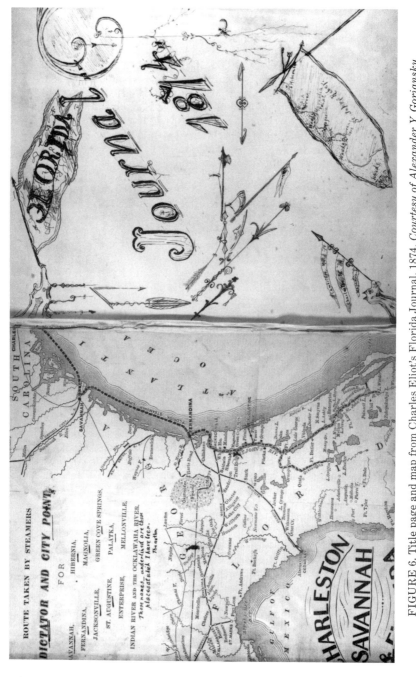

FIGURE 6. Title page and map from Charles Eliot's Florida Journal, 1874. *Courtesy of Alexander Y. Goriansky.*

FIGURE 7. Charles Eliot's drawing of an oak leaf, 1875.
Courtesy of Alexander Y. Goriansky.

FIGURE 8. Charles Eliot's European sketchbook, site and date
not recorded. *Courtesy of Alexander Y. Goriansky.*

advantage) of being the son of one of the era's major educational reformers.[34] Parent and child frequently discussed Charles Eliot's future vocation, although it was Charles's own decision to pursue a career in landscape architecture. Since no professional programs existed at the time, the two men together devised a postgraduate course of study at Harvard's Bussey Institute, a professional apprenticeship with Frederick Law Olmsted, and a period of professional travel in the United States and abroad.

"YOU SEE I AM A WANDERER"

Charles Eliot was a landscape *flâneur*, a constant but attentive wanderer, and a connoisseur of landscape forms.[35] While still a young teenager, he began in 1875 to take a series of walking tours, often tied to public transportation routes, which allowed him to visit natural areas throughout the greater Boston basin in a methodical manner.[36] In his diary for 1878, he provides a "Partial List of Saturday Walks before 1878." Eliot would later recommend many of the sites as additions to the Metropolitan Park system. He also meticulously recorded a short trip that he took with his father in 1875, to a "small manufacturing village" (of which he drew a plan), where there was "a very large woolen mill" and also "a tannery and a stream below the mill."[37] In these notes, one sees an early sensitivity to landscape and to the role of man in reshaping that landscape. Charles's penchant for landscape description and analysis was further nurtured by keeping the log for *The Sunshine*.

During his thirteen-month tour of England and the Continent in 1885–86, Eliot continued to record scenery through detailed narratives and sketches (fig. 8). Chapters 9 and 10 contain a richly annotated collection of excerpts from his diaries and journals. Here Eliot assesses the design, horticulture, and topography of the sites on his self-generated itinerary and offers sharp opinions about the defining characteristics of cultural landscapes—admiring the Scandinavian countryside, expressing contempt for French landscape fashion and suspicion toward the "nabobry" of the aristocratic English landscape.[38] Eliot often used his extensive knowledge of the New England landscape as a touchstone, describing an island near Stockholm, for example, as "roughly, wildly beautiful in a wholly New Englandish manner."[39]

Of all the private estates, public parks, and natural sites that Eliot methodically visited, he was most affected by the former estate of Prince Hermann Pückler at Muskau in Silesia. In one of his last letters to Olmsted before returning in October 1887, Eliot effused about the lessons that Muskau could teach:

His park is probably the finest work of real landscape gardening on a large scale that this century has seen carried out in Europe. It is a work that has made one very proud of the profession—for here was a river valley in great part very barren,
fringed by monstrous woods of p. sylvestric and in no way remarkable for beauty or interest—but now one of the loveliest
vales on earth—and full to the brim, so to speak, of variety or
pleasant change, of quieting and often touching beauty.[40]

In many ways, Muskau served as a prototype for all that Charles
Eliot would do in America. Every element of the landscape—the
pleasure grounds near the Schloss, the village and the alum
factory, the river valley and the surrounding woodlands—was
carefully "improved" with native plants. Pückler presented Eliot
with a lasting lesson on how to capitalize on the inherent qualities of site and celebrate the ability of man to enhance nature.

No landscape architect before Eliot had combined so thorough
a grounding in the literature of the profession with such close
observation of the practice of landscape architecture. Eliot's call
slips from the British Library are evidence of his voracious literary appetite and the methodical manner in which he read everything on the topic in English, French, and German from the
seventeenth century on.[41] Thus Eliot returned to the United
States with a uniquely profound knowledge of the history of his
profession. In the December 1887 issue of *Garden and Forest*,
he included a recommended list of books on landscape architecture, based on his readings in Europe. (This list is found on pages
219–23 of the text.)

Eliot also actively pursued the individuals who could help him
grow professionally.[42] His journals recount his critical reaction
to many of the leading landscape gardeners and nurserymen of
Europe. The biography text often fails to fully identify these
figures or to provide information about them. For example, one
of the most hospitable of his English contacts was James Bryce
(1838–1922), with whom Eliot stayed in both London and Oxford.[43] Bryce was an avid mountaineer (fig. 9), secretary of the
Commons Preservation Society, and the author of the Scottish
Mountains bill and other open space legislation in Parliament.
Thus, he could share with young Charles Eliot his direct knowledge of efforts to legislate landscape preservation in Britain.

Similarly, Eliot's visit to an unnamed secretary of the Lake
District Defense Society needs to be understood as a meeting
with Canon Hardwicke D. Rawnsley, vicar of Crossthwaite,
Keswick. Rawnsley was an activist who advocated protection of
the Lake District, especially from the potential intrusion of rail-

FIGURE 9. James Bryce, British historian, politician, and
conservationist. *Courtesy of the Bodleian Library, Oxford University.*

THIRLMERE FROM RAVEN CRAG.

FIGURE 10. Thirlmere from Raven Crag, illustration for brochure arguing against the construction of reservoirs and railroad lines in the Lake District. *Courtesy of the British Library, London.*

road lines and urban reservoirs (fig. 10). Later, he was one of the
founders of the National Trust for Places of Scenic and Natural
Beauty in Great Britain. It is likely that Eliot was introduced
to Rawnsley by his cousin and former teacher, Charles Eliot
Norton, one of two Harvard faculty members who had become
supporters of the Lake District Defense Society.[44] From their
meeting, Eliot learned about landscape preservation strategies
in England and was able to share his knowledge of parallel
American efforts. It could not have been a better preparation for
the work that lay ahead.

"MR. OLMSTED'S PROFESSION"

Charles Eliot inherited a professional mantle defined in the
United States by Frederick Law Olmsted Sr. After pursuing ca-
reers as a farmer, journalist, publisher, and traveler, Olmsted had
established himself as the country's leading landscape architect
with his 1858 design for Central Park in New York City. He
moved his highly successful practice to Brookline, Massachusetts,
in 1883. One of Olmsted's neighbors in that suburb was Charles
Eliot's uncle, the architect Robert Swain Peabody. It was he who
suggested Olmsted as a potential role model to the young man
in search of a vocation.[45] After a period of self-designed study
at Harvard's Bussey Institute, in 1883 Eliot gladly accepted the
invitation to become the first official unpaid apprentice in the
Olmsted office.[46]

Olmsted soon recognized Charles Eliot's multiple talents and
encouraged their development. While Eliot was in Europe in
1885–86, he wrote frequently to Olmsted about the sites he
visited and people he met, many of them through his mentor.
Olmsted responded, "I have seen no such justly critical notes as
yours on landscape architecture matters from any traveler for a
generation past. You ought to make it a part of your scheme to
write for the public, a little at a time if you please, but methodically, systematically. It is part of your professional duty to do
so."[47] Eliot heeded Olmsted's advice and became one of the most
productive and effective landscape critics of his generation.

Gradually, the professional relationship achieved more equal
footing. While Eliot was in Europe, Olmsted asked him to return
home and join the firm. Olmsted was currently developing plans
for the Stanford University campus in California and was eager
to capitalize on Eliot's fresh knowledge of Mediterranean plant
material and design. President Eliot's opinion of the offer was
characteristically firm: "You can make an excursion to Califor-

nia whenever it is your interest to do so for $300 & I shall be happy to pay for it. I see no inducement whatever in Mr. O's offer of $50 a month. You had better start for yourself in my opinion."[48] In the end, Eliot took his father's advice, finishing his trip as planned and setting up his own office on his return. Instead of working for Olmsted, Eliot asked his former mentor to provide a reference for an advertisement announcing his new business.[49]

Three years later, Eliot asked Henry Codman, who had followed him as an apprentice in the Olmsted office, to join *his* firm as a partner, but Codman declined. Then, in July 1889, in a letter to Olmsted, Eliot proposed yet another plan:

My talk with Codman has led me to imagine a possible general union of forces in which all three of us young men [Eliot, Codman and John Charles Olmsted] might serve as more or less independent captains under you as general. We could perhaps have offices in N.Y. and Phila. as well as in Boston and Brookline . . . and while we should manage all small jobs ourselves we should refer all weighty matters and all persons who distinctly desired your opinion to you.[50]

But his idea never materialized. Codman accepted a position with Olmsted, and Eliot continued to pursue his independent practice until January 1893, when Codman suddenly died from appendicitis while supervising the landscape development of the World's Columbian Exposition in Chicago. Once again, Olmsted, especially eager for help with the Chicago Fair, asked Eliot to join the partnership, and this time the younger man agreed. In March 1893, the office of Olmsted, Olmsted and Eliot was officially announced.

Eliot thoroughly absorbed every lesson on landscape aesthetics and professional practice that Olmsted taught. Much of the younger man's writings was also cast in the mold of his mentor. By the time Eliot had joined the firm in 1893, Olmsted's health had begun to fail, and one of the burdens Eliot could take on for his elder partner was the writing of reports and articles. One of these defended his former mentor. Realizing that Olmsted's work for the Boston Municipal Park Commission was frequently attacked for its "unnaturalness," Eliot responded with an article titled "The Gentle Art of Defeating Nature," in which he stated his (and Olmsted's) belief that landscape architects must alter natural conditions to meet the needs of the public.[51]

On one occasion, Eliot actually wrote an article that was published under Olmsted's name. The senior Eliot states that "Parks,

Parkways, and Pleasure Grounds" in *Engineering Magazine* was "a concise statement—with some new illustrations—of doctrines which Mr. Olmsted had been teaching all his life. It was prepared however by Charles . . . Mr. Olmsted being unable at the time to write it himself."[52] In addition to the standard Olmsted agenda, the article includes new ideas that Eliot was then pursuing and uses language—"reservations of scenery," "Board of Trustees"—typical of Eliot's philosophy in these years. As an ultimate indication of mentor-student closeness, Eliot was invited to draft an obituary for Olmsted in 1896 (several years before Olmsted's death). He submitted the draft "with great diffidence," he wrote in the accompanying letter, having "been too near him to write it rightly." Eliot began the piece: "It is seldom that the death of one man removes a whole profession, but, excepting for a few associates personally inspired by him, this is really what has happened in the case of the death of Frederick Law Olmsted."[53] Eliot was certainly one of those "associates personally inspired by him" and provided a rich and elegant account of his mentor's life and work.

From his apprenticeship days on, when Eliot wrote to his family and friends about Olmsted, he expressed a mixture of both respect and criticism in his letters. He happily told his close friend Roland Thaxter in October 1882 that he had "become apprentice to the leading man in my proposed profession—namely Mr. Fred. Law Olmsted . . . the man who has had a hand in almost every great Park work that has been attempted in this country."[54] But in six years of private practice, Eliot had formed his own distinct opinions and was highly critical of many things that Olmsted did. Eliot also maintained many of his earlier, independent jobs—such as positions on the Metropolitan Park and the Cambridge Park commissions—after he joined the firm. Eliot was neither an extension nor pale reflection of Olmsted; he was his own man, facing important new issues in the profession of landscape architecture.

Olmsted was delighted to have his former apprentice in the firm and the added income from major projects on which Charles was working. In an 1893 letter to his partners, Olmsted effused about the importance of the work currently in the office:

Nothing else compares in importance to us with the Boston work, meaning the Metropolitan quite equally with the city work. The two together will be the most important work in our profession now in hand anywhere in the world. . . . In your probable life-time, Muddy River, Blue Hills, the Fells, Waverley Oaks, Charles River, the Beaches will be points to date from in the his-

FIGURE 11. Photograph by Arthur A. Shurcliff of
Charles Eliot's office desk on the day of Eliot's death.
Courtesy of Mr. and Mrs. William Shurcliff.

tory of American Landscape Architecture, as much as Central
Park. They will be the opening of new chapters in the art.[55]

All but the first of these landmark projects were commissions
that Eliot brought to the firm.

Within the Olmsted, Olmsted and Eliot office, Charles exerted
a major influence, especially among the younger members of the
firm. Warren Manning worked closely with Eliot on the analysis
of the Metropolitan reservations, learning a process of natural
condition data collection and systematic analysis that he would
use frequently later in his practice.[56] Arthur Shurcliff, who with
Frederick Law Olmsted Jr. established the first academic program in landscape architecture at Harvard, wrote extensively
about the lessons he had learned from Eliot.[57] The poignant
vacuum that Charles Eliot's early death left in the firm is haunt-
ingly symbolized by the photograph (fig. 11) that Shurcliff took
of Eliot's desk on the day he died.

ELIOT'S LANDSCAPE PHILOSOPHY AND LANGUAGE

Eliot's highly effective and original landscape ideas were especially apparent in his work for the Metropolitan Park Commission, where he envisioned a new regional approach to planning. In his first letter to Charles Francis Adams, chairman of the temporary commission, Eliot outlined the landscape types he wished to incorporate into the system:

As I conceive it the scientific "park system" for a district such as ours would include

1st Space upon the Ocean front.

2nd As much as possible of the shores and islands of the Bay.

3rd The courses of the larger Tidal estuaries (above their commercial usefulness) because of the value of these courses as pleasant routes to the heart of the City and to the Sea.

4th Two or three large areas of wild forest on the outer rim of the inhabited area.

5th Numerous small squares in the midst of dense populations.

Local and private action can do as much under the 5th head but the four others call loudly for action by the whole metropolitan community. With your approval I shall make my study for the Commission on these lines.[58]

This broad scheme represented a larger landscape analysis than had ever been attempted in America.

To explain these concepts and others, Eliot invoked a landscape language that had not previously been employed. His arena was the physical world at large. In a lecture to a farmer's association in New York State, he explained that he meant "by the term 'landscape' the visible surroundings of men's lives on the surface of the earth." Eliot considered himself an architect and repeatedly referred to the definition of architecture borrowed from the English socialist and art critic William Morris: "Architecture, a great subject truly, for it embraces the consideration of the whole of the external world, for it means the moulding and the altering to human needs the very face of the earth."[59] This broad environmental consciousness is rooted in the lessons he drew from Prince Pückler, a topic about which Eliot frequently both spoke and wrote.[60]

Eliot's proto-environmentalist viewpoint grew naturally out of his contact with the Transcendentalist writers of New England. Ralph Waldo Emerson, for example, is frequently quoted in both Eliot's common book and in the selections his father incorporated in the biography. An uneasy product of Unitarianism, Eliot had been attracted early to the Transcendentalist belief in nature as an allegory for the divinity. In essence, however, Eliot practiced an applied Transcendentalism, actively securing the advantages of nature for the general public, not just urging its passive contemplation.

Onto this literary-philosophical base, Eliot grafted other ideals. He was a Millsian and an environmentalist, long before the term had been coined. He stated that reservations, parks, and parkways must "be placed, without regard to local pressure, solely with a view to securing the greatest good of the greatest number." And he opposed commercial intrusion into this scenery of beauty; he argued against the exploitation of the landscape with giant advertising signs and proposed that telegraph lines be sunk below ground to remove another modern irritant from the reservations. His concern transcended the needs of his contemporary generation. He wrote about hopes for improved water quality in the Charles River and celebrated the increase of "wild birds and animals" which had resulted from improvement in the Stony Brook Reservation.[61] Recently, Ian McHarg, a leader in landscape architecture education, commented in his autobiography: "I have been described as the inventor of ecological planning, the incorporation of natural science within the planning process. Yet Charles Eliot, son of Harvard's president, a landscape architect at Harvard, preceded me by half a century. . . . He invented a new and vastly more comprehensive planning method than any pre-existing, but it was not emulated."[62] McHarg believed that his own education as a landscape architect at Harvard had been deficient because the school had forgotten the planning vision of Charles Eliot in the 1890s.

A persistent theme in Eliot's public writings and professional reports is the principle "What would be fair must be fit." In an article for *Garden and Forest* by that title (which is also the title of chapter 29), Eliot first warned his readers about the three types of landscape designers to avoid: commercial nurserymen who would think only in terms of the plants they could sell, landscape gardeners who laid out everything in curving lines, and former students of the Ecole des Beaux-Arts in Paris, who saw garden design in lockstep geometry. Eliot's distance from these dominant trends reflected his sense that function, or "fitness," should be the guiding principle of design. He was not a proponent of either side of the great debate between the natural and the formal style of landscape design. In his review of *Italian Gardens* by Charles A. Platt, a leader of the formal garden re-

vival, Eliot was enthusiastic about the lessons that the Renaissance garden could teach but warned that the conditions of climate, topography, and needs of the client must all justify this
choice of landscape mode.[63] In his essay "Anglomania in Park
Making," he similarly cautioned against the mindless popularity
of the English or natural landscape style as the only correct manner for public park design. Eliot's philosophy resembles a landscape theory variation on the theme of "form follows function"
—the battle cry of the Chicago architect Louis Sullivan at this
time.[64]

To achieve his broad aims for landscape design preservation,
Eliot lobbied ceaselessly through prolific letter writing, frequent
public speaking, appearances before legislative committees, and
regular contributions to popular magazines and professional journals. His major written contribution to a philosophy of scenery
preservation and enhancement was his report, posthumously
published in 1898, *Scenery and Vegetation in the Metropolitan
Reservations of Boston*. Although specific in its definition of the
basic types of landscapes found in the Boston metropolitan reservations and the appropriate methods for their management and
development, Eliot's report has generic implications as well.

One important message conveyed in the report is that all of
the landscapes of the metropolitan reservations are "artificial"
in that they have been changed through human interaction with
them. Eliot wanted to counter the popular assumption that the
reservations were "wild" and therefore should not be altered in
any way. "Before and after" drawings (figs. 12 and 13) of specific
sites emphasized the importance of improving the scenery
through careful analysis of natural systems and well-conceived
plans of action.[65] Much of this analysis had already been begun
with the surveys of geology, topography, and history of use in
the reservations. The next step would have been the development of general plans for each of the reservations, blueprints for
improving the scenery and providing access to these sites.[66]
Sadly, however, Eliot died before he could convince the Metropolitan Park Commission to move on to this next stage.

Political and social action were two of the tools Eliot wielded
brilliantly to achieve his evolving goals. He worked from the
bases of power and influence that were his birthright. As the son
of the highly visible president of Harvard College and the descendant of well connected and powerful families, Eliot innately
understood how to inform and influence his contemporaries, even
contributing portions of speeches to powerful friends, such as his
Harvard contemporary Governor William Russell, who appointed
Eliot to various commissions. Eliot's network involved a core
group of fellow travelers who could understand and appreciate

FIGURE 12. Arthur A. Shurcliff, Tree-clogged notch in the Middlesex Fells, in Charles Eliot, *Vegetation and Scenery in the Metropolitan Reservations of Boston* (Boston, 1898).

FIGURE 13. Arthur A. Shurcliff, Improved view of a notch in the Middlesex Fells, in Charles Eliot, *Vegetation and Scenery in the Metropolitan Reservations of Boston* (Boston, 1898).

his ideas. For example, Dr. H. P. Walcott, whom Eliot invited to chair the initial meeting in the formation of the Trustees of Public Reservations, was also the chair of the state board of health and would become the chair of the Joint Commission on the Improvement of the Charles River, for which Eliot served as secretary. And Eliot could rely on Frederick Law Olmsted Sr., Charles Sprague Sargent—director of Harvard's Arnold Arboretum—and a host of literary and political lions to come forth in support of many of his efforts. But he did not work primarily for the benefit of an economic and political elite; he deeply appreciated the involvement of an informed public. In 1897, when Warren Manning wrote to him about the possible formation of a professional society for landscape architects, Eliot responded that it was more timely and important to establish a broad-based support group for public landscape causes. The American Park and Outdoor Art Association, founded in 1897, was the result.

CHARLES ELIOT AS A HISTORIAN

Eliot's highly original philosophy of landscape conservation derived, in part, from his interest in the writing of history. Indeed, Charles Eliot may be considered America's first landscape historian. His personal interest parallels the development of the Colonial Revival during the late nineteenth century in New England.[67] One of Eliot's favorite childhood books was Frothingham's *Siege of Boston*, and as a teenager he eagerly participated in the celebration of the centennial of the Battle of Lexington and Concord. His diary records a visit to the site: "Almost every house had some bunting or other decorations, so that the road looked very gay. . . . A pretty, narrow road leads from Monument St. through a pine grove by the granite monument to the bridge which crosses the river on the spot where the old bridge stood in 1775. Across the river is a bronze statue of a minute man, designed by D. C. French, a young Concord artist. . . . Papa says it is very handsome."[68] In this passage, young Charles reveals his sensitivity to history and his growing fascination with the landscape.

One of Eliot's earliest projects as a landscape architect was the design for the Longfellow Memorial Gardens in Cambridge. Here he proposed "a village green in the manner of New England" for the space before the Vassall-Longfellow mansion, a house that had been George Washington's headquarters briefly during the Revolution, which, because of this association, Henry Wadsworth Longfellow's father-in-law, Nathan Appleton, had purchased for his daughter and son-in-law's residence.[69] Eliot was determined to maintain the historical land use pattern of this

Colonial country seat, using the "village green" and a more asymmetrical space beyond as a visual corridor to connect the mansion to the Charles River. Many of the features in Eliot's designs were based on historical prototypes.

Eliot wrote about the historical domestic landscapes of the Boston region and Hudson River valley in a series of articles for *Garden and Forest*.[70] The series, "Six Old Country Places," was inspired by the demise of such resources as a result of urban expansion. But Eliot also showed himself to be an astute analyst of these properties, lauding the functional values expressed in one and criticizing the ostentation of another.[71] Eliot's celebration of these Colonial estates is the equivalent in landscape history of the writings of his uncle, the architect Robert Swain Peabody, on old New England architecture.[72] Yet, Eliot was neither an elitist nor a nativist;[73] he was actively working for the betterment of his contemporaries, not wallowing in nostalgia for past glories.

ELIOT AND CLASS ISSUES

Like Olmsted, Charles Eliot firmly believed in democracy. He assumed that his work with public commissions should and would benefit all levels of society, including "the common people," "the ordinary people," and "the crowded populations," to borrow his terms. His sympathetic attitude toward the poor and their condition in life can be seen in a letter to his stepmother about a walk through the city after viewing an exhibition at the Museum of Fine Arts: "Part way down Hanover St. I visited a market where women were buying their Sunday dinners and loading their little girls with the purchases. The elder sisters and brothers thronged the streets—an orderly enough crowd for the most part—many, no doubt, of a high degree of goodness."[74]

On several occasions, he wrote from Europe about his dawning awareness of the plight of the working class: "The fact seems to be that the wage-earning classes the world over are just waking up to the fact that their lot in life—to work all day for a pittance that will hardly feed them—is a hard lot—and it is no wonder they should try to improve their position by means of their political power or that they should make fearful mistakes in the use of it. It is going to be intensely interesting—this 'tremendous seething' of the labouring world. The London & Chicago and the Belgium riots make a striking beginning certainly."[75] Nearly ten years later, as a mature professional, he wrote to his wife about the people he was designing his parks for:

Last evening after dinner I talked with Mr. Gilder of the "Century" [magazine]. . . . I cross-examined him with reference to his slum clearance in New York City, and the taking down of rear tenements, and so on. Two or three times in each year I am smitten with pity for the slum people—pity and horror mixed. My walk from Cambridge Field through East Cambridge to Charlesbank! Doorsteps crowded with unclean beings, children pushing everywhere, and swarming in every street and alley. What a relief when Charlesbank is reached. The quiet open of the river, the long, long row of twinkling lights on the river wall, the rows upon rows of seats all lined with people resting in the quiet air, and watching the fading light behind the Cambridge towers. The new terrace at the North End is to be another such evening resting-place. It is good to be able to do something, even a little for this battered and soiled humanity.[76]

His being "smitten two or three times per year" might be read as tokenism, but there is no doubting Eliot's social conscience. For example, he joined Sylvester Baxter in promoting legislation for the Metropolitan Park Commission which would require open garden courts in working-class tenements (fig. 14).[77] In discussing the development of Revere Beach, for which he had fought long and hard, Eliot emphasized that the site was "the first that I know of to be set aside and governed by a public body for the enjoyment of the common people." And Eliot supported preservation of the banks of the Charles River so that they might benefit the working class: "If the low lands of the valley should eventually become the seat of a population of well-housed working people, who would find refreshment on the public river bank at the noon hour and in the summer evenings, a most desirable result would be secured."[78]

Neither was Eliot naive in his understanding of basic human nature. When pushing for the construction of a park building at Cambridge Field, he noted: "Without the building and its caretaker, the field will necessarily seem a somewhat unprotected and uncared-for place, to which gentle people will hardly care to resort, and in which the ruder element will see opportunity to display its rudeness."[79] Although Eliot considered himself one of the gentle people, that description was tied not to economic class but to an expectation of self-control and proper deportment on the part of all park users, of all park trustees.

Artisans' Dwellings erected by the Municipality, Liverpool, England.

FIGURE 14. Model working-class tenement, *Metropolitan Park Commission Annual Report* (Boston, 1893).

THE CIVIC PRIDE MONVMENT
IN MEMORY OF

CHARLES ELIOT
LANDSCAPE ARCHITECT

IN ANY CITY, TOWN OR VILLAGE
WHERE MEN AND WOMEN GIVE JOINTLY AND
FREELY OF THEIR WISDOM, STRENGTH AND
SVBSTANCE TO ACHIEVE AND MAINTAIN
APPROPRIATE BEAVTY IN THE SVRROVNDINGS OF PVBLIC
AND PRIVATE BVILDINGS, THE VISIBLE PERFECTIONS OF
A PLACE WHOSE WAYS ARE WAYS OF PLEASANTNESS
AND ALL WHOSE PATHS ARE PEACE, BEAR WITNESS TO
THE ENLIGHTENED CIVIC PRIDE OF ITS INHABITANTS

FIGURE 15. The Civic Pride Monument, St. Louis World's Fair, 1902.
From *Harvard Bulletin*, 25 January 1905, 1.

ELIOT'S LEGACY

Despite, or perhaps because of, his early death, Eliot inspired others to perpetuate his ideals. He had not only expanded the parameters and concerns of the profession of landscape architecture, he had also laid the foundations for the environmental movement and for the professions of city and regional planning. A model village erected at the St. Louis World's Fair of 1902 included a "Civic Pride Monument" (fig. 15), one of many such testimonials to his importance and influence. (Ironically, Eliot would have preferred to be remembered for his belief in metropolitan or regional, rather than civic or municipal, pride.)

Eliot's father became a vocal advocate for the issues his son had embraced. Indeed, President Eliot showed the zeal of a convert. Not only did he write and edit *Charles Eliot, Landscape Architect*, he also began to write articles and speak in public about landscape preservation. From 1905 until 1926, he served on the Standing Committee, the central governing board of the Trustees of Public Reservations.[80] President Eliot carried forward his son's vision of a forest reservation on Mount Desert Island, Maine, now Acadia National Park.[81] Perhaps Charles Eliot's finest legacy was his father's commitment to establishing a professional program in landscape architecture at Harvard, which was inaugurated in 1900 under the direction of Frederick Law Olmsted Jr., Eliot's former colleague, and Arthur Shurcliff, his former protégé.[82] President Eliot's program today maintains his son's name in the Charles Eliot Professorship in Landscape Architecture and the Charles Eliot Traveling Fellowship, which enables promising young landscape architects to benefit from travel study as its namesake had.[83] After his retirement from Harvard College, Charles W. Eliot moved to a house on Fresh Pond Parkway, a green corridor designed by his son. The Parkway, in turn, connects the Fresh Pond Reservation, his son's design for the Cambridge Park Commission, to the Memorial Drive Reservation on the Cambridge side of the Charles River, another of the younger Eliot's early projects for the Cambridge Park Commission. Today the Eliot Bridge (dedicated in 1955 to both father and son) connects the Fresh Pond Parkway to the Soldiers Field Road Reservation on the Boston side of the Charles River.

Even more directly perpetuating the ideals of Charles Eliot was the work of his nephew, Charles W. Eliot II. Born in 1900, three years after his uncle's death, but named for his grandfather, this Eliot was destined from birth to adopt his uncle's profession. "At the time I was born," he reported late in life, "my grandfather came to the house and asked if it was a boy or a girl.

When he was told it was a boy, he said: 'That's good! His name will be Charles like his uncle. He will be a landscape architect like his uncle. He will go on with his uncle's work.'"[84] Trained in landscape architecture and regional planning at Harvard, this Charles became the first field secretary of the Trustees of Public Reservations in 1925.[85] In May of that year, the Trustees sponsored a conference, "The Needs and Uses of Open Spaces in Massachusetts," in which he took a leading role. One result of the conference was a renewed effort to coordinate the activities of private and public conservation organizations in the state. Equally significant was the proposed "Bay Circuit," a new and larger greenbelt for the Greater Boston Basin. The idea for the Bay Circuit may not have been Eliot's alone, but he became its strongest long-term supporter.[86] Like his uncle, Eliot soon saw an opportunity to advance the cause of landscape architecture and regional planning by moving into the public sector. He became the director of the National Capitol Park and Planning Commission under the Roosevelt administration, a position he maintained until 1955. Eliot then returned to Harvard to become the Charles Eliot Professor of Landscape Architecture. He retired in 1968 but remained an active supporter of land conservation and became the conscience of both the Trustees of Reservations and the Metropolitan District Commission until his death in 1992.[87]

The early growth of the Trustees was modest, in part, because Eliot turned his attention so quickly to the Metropolitan Park Commission. By 1897, the year of Charles Eliot's death, only two properties, Rocky Narrows on the Charles River in Canton and Mount Anne Park in Gloucester, had been given to the Trustees. Together they totaled fewer than one hundred acres. Today, the Trustees are stewards of more than twenty thousand acres, "the best of the Massachusetts landscape in all its diversity."[88] The organization has been the inspiration for land trusts both in the United States and abroad, and Eliot's early writings also inspired the formation of other organizations.[89] Most notably, the National Trust for Places of Historic Interest or Natural Beauty in Great Britain was modeled on the Trustees, as was, ultimately, the National Trust for Historic Preservation in the United States.[90]

Soon after his success in forming the Trustees, Eliot turned his attention to the creation of a public authority, the Metropolitan Park Commission. Celebrating its centennial in 1993, the commission now "embraces almost twenty thousand acres of parklands ranging from dense woodlands and wetlands to intensely developed and managed urban parks."[91] One of the most important potential benefits of the centennial celebration was the appointment of the Green Ribbon Commission to suggest improvements to the organization. At the top of its list of priorities was the issue that Charles Eliot had fought hard but unsuccessfully to impress on the early commissioners—the need for careful and persistent maintenance, or what is today called stewardship.[92] The responsibility now rests with the commission's current administration—and with all of us who are "trustees" of the Eliot legacy—to ensure that these resources receive the care and the use they merit.

Despite the enormous challenges posed by increasing traffic and neglected maintenance, the Metropolitan Park system that Eliot envisioned remains his greatest achievement. In a chapter titled "Growth Invincible" in his 1906 book *The Future in America*, H. G. Wells contrasted his recent visits to New York and to Boston:

> If possible it is more impressive, even, than the crowded largeness of New York, to trace the serene preparation Boston has made through this [Metropolitan Park] Commission to be widely and easily vast. New York's humanity has the curious air of being carried along upon a wave of irresistible prosperity, but Boston confesses design. I suppose no city in all the world . . . has ever produced so complete and ample a forecast of its own future as this commission's plan for Boston.[93]

Today, Charles Eliot's ideas "confess design" as clearly as they did a century ago, just as they attempted to forecast a future not only for Boston but for the whole of American landscape architecture.

NOTES

For a research and writing grant that supported the preparation of this introduction, I am deeply grateful to the Graham Foundation for Advanced Studies in the Fine Arts. Katherine Boonin provided invaluable research assistance at an early stage in my explorations of Charles Eliot. Robin Karson, executive director of the Library of American Landscape History, read the manuscript and offered important criticism from her broad knowledge of landscape history. Karl Haglund, senior planner for the Metropolitan District Commission, also read and criticized a draft of this manuscript and improved its arguments in many important ways. His 1998 MIT dissertation, "Inventing the Charles River Basin, Urban Images and Civic Discourse in Boston, 1844–1994," elucidates the centerpiece of Eliot's schemes for the Metropolitan Park Commission.

The Charles Eliot archives are divided between the Special Collections of the Loeb Library at the Graduate School of Design, Harvard University, and the family papers that are maintained in Boston by Alexander Yale Goriansky, a grandson of Charles Eliot. The Charles W. Eliot Papers in Pusey Library at Harvard University are another important source for information on Charles Eliot's parents and early life. For access to the Eliot material in Loeb Library, I am grateful to Mary Daniels, the curator of Special Collections. My deepest debt is to Alec Goriansky, who encouraged my research, generously provided access to the family manuscript collection in his care, and served me lunch more often than he should have. His friendship has been one of the happiest byproducts of my research on Charles Eliot.

1. *Charles Eliot, Landscape Architect* (Boston: Houghton Mifflin, 1902), 600. Hereafter cited as *CELA*.
2. Eliot outlined his goals in the 1894 Metropolitan Park Commission report. Ibid., 492.
3. Ibid., 517, 230.
4. There is a real problem in keeping separate the three Charles Eliots that appear in this introduction. The first is, of course, the landscape architect Charles Eliot (without a middle initial), who is the subject of the book. The second is Charles W. Eliot, who will generally be referred to as President Eliot. To make matters more complicated, Charles W. Eliot II, the son of Samuel Atkins Eliot, Charles Eliot's brother, was named for his grandfather (but followed the career of his uncle with distinction).
5. President Eliot's first correspondence with Houghton Mifflin about this project was a brief explanation of his intentions and a prospectus: "The book I have in preparation is a collection of the writings of my son Charles, the landscape architect, with a sketch of his life and character. It must be amply illustrated, because the book ought to describe what a landscape architect can do through what he has done." Charles W. Eliot to Henry O. Houghton, 3 May 1901, Letters to and from Houghton Mifflin, Charles W. Eliot file, Houghton Mifflin Collection, Houghton Library, Harvard University, Cambridge, Massachusetts (hereafter cited as HMC).
   The book was first published in June 1902, with an initial run of 1,000 copies. President Eliot kept the book in print until 1922, when he accepted the advice of his publisher and let the volume go out of print. Charles W. Eliot to Ferris Greenslet, 13 September 1922, HMC.
6. Charles W. Eliot to publisher, 15 December 1901, HMC.
7. Charles W. Eliot to George Mifflin, 8 August 1902, HMC.
8. Charles W. Eliot to D. C. Gilman, 23 April, 1897, quoted in Henry James, *Charles W. Eliot, President of Harvard University, 1869–1909* (Boston: Houghton Mifflin, 1930), 91–92.
9. In a letter to his publishers concerning methods of advertising this book, President Eliot suggested that the number and variety of illustrations should be emphasized: "3 photogravure portraits, 35 full-page heliotypes, 28 full-page black and white plans and sketches, 45 black and white sketches inserted in the text, and 2 folded maps" included

in pockets in the front and rear covers. Charles W. Eliot to publishers, 7 February 1902, HMC.

10. As late as 7 February 1902, President Eliot was still debating the issue. The following year, he wrote to Houghton Mifflin about advertising a new edition of the book "in its two-volume form." Charles W. Eliot to publisher, 19 February 1903, HMC. I am grateful to Jane LeCompte, archivist for Houghton Mifflin, for information from the printing cards that the 1903 edition of the book was published in two volumes. Readers wishing to consult a two-volume edition of the book will find one in the Avery Architectural and Fine Arts Library, Columbia University, and in the Boston Atheneum. The two-volume edition did not change the page numbering.

11. Even relatively few monographs on American architects had appeared. The earliest was Marianna Schuyler Van Rensselaer's *Henry Hobson Richardson and His Times*, published in 1888, two years after the architect's early death. Mrs. Van Rensselaer was also a prolific writer on landscape issues. See especially her *Art Out of Doors: Hints on Good Taste in Gardening* (New York, 1893).

12. Sylvester Baxter, "Greater Boston's Metropolitan Park System," *Boston Evening Transcript*, Part 5, 29 September 1923, p. 8. As Baxter explained it: "In 1891 a brochure called 'Greater Boston,' by the present writer, was published. . . . The organization of Boston and the surrounding cities and towns into a 'federated metropolis' as a civic entity was advocated, giving a unified administration for various functions of collective concern. . . . Soon after the appearance of 'Greater Boston' . . . the writer met his friend Charles Eliot, the young landscape architect. Eliot, enthusiastic about the suggested metropolitan park system, proposed that they work together for realizing it." I am deeply grateful to Karl Haglund for sharing his research on Baxter with me.

13. Sylvester Baxter, *Greater Boston: A Study for a Federated Metropolis* (Boston, 1891). For a review of Baxter's life and accomplishments, see his autobiography in James Phinney Baxter, "The Baxter Family: A Collection of Genealogies" (1926), 94–102; manuscript in the New England Historic Genealogical Society, Boston.

14. Hugh Hawkins, *Between Harvard and America: The Educational Leadership of Charles W. Eliot* (New York: Oxford University Press, 1972), 3.

15. The only portrait included in the book other than the two of Charles Eliot is the one of Ellen Peabody Eliot. In minor ways, the biography is also a remembrance of President Eliot's first wife, who died at age 33; note especially pages 21–24.

16. See "Vegetation and Scenery in the Metropolitan Reservations," pages 715–32; the 1893 report to the Metropolitan Planning Commission, pages 385–415; and chapter 18, in which the development of the Trustees of Reservations is detailed.

17. Three reviews were published in predictable sources: *Harvard Graduate's Magazine* (11:31); W. W. Ellsworth, *Outlook* (72: 135); and H. Lamont, "A Story of Achievement," *Nation* (75: 47–48).

18. Lamont, "Story of Achievement," 47–48. (For the full context of the letter, see page 91 of the biography.)

19. *CELA*, 16.
20. Commonplace Book, July 1877, Charles Eliot Collection, Graduate School of Design, Harvard University. Eliot continued: "Had often thought of the possibility of this happening for a year past—and took it calmly—much more so than did the Aunts."
21. Ibid., 30 October 1877 and December 1878.
22. Ibid., 1880–81.
23. Charles Eliot to Grace Mellen Hopkinson Eliot, 1881, Charles Eliot Papers, Goriansky Collection, Boston; hereafter cited as GC.
24. See Nan Lincoln, "The Champlain Society," *Bar Harbor Times*, 1 August 1996, B5. Nan Lincoln is a descendant of Charles Eliot's brother. She has placed the Champlain Society logs and the logs from the *Sunshine* and related photographs on deposit at Mount Desert Island Historical Society.
25. For a picture of Harvard in the later 1870s, see David McCullough, *Mornings on Horseback* (New York: Simon and Schuster, 1981), esp. chap. 9.
26. Diary of 1878, GC. This entry continues in the typically self-deprecatory manner that characterized most of his early life.
27. For a discussion of this awkward period in President Eliot's life, see James, *Charles W. Eliot*, 87–158.
28. Winter 1863 was spent in Paris. Summer 1864 was divided among London, Heidelberg, and Switzerland. The Eliots spent the following winter in Marberg, and in summer 1865 they visited Italy, Vienna, and Berlin.
29. Ellen Peabody Eliot to her mother, Marberg, 17 November 1864, Charles W. Eliot Papers, Pusey Library, Harvard University.
30. His father reported to his grandmother Eliot in January 1865: "I have postponed saying anything about Charlie, till the last day, because we hope every day that he will recover from the languid condition in which he has been. He does not seem to have anything the matter with him, but he has a little too quick pulse and is disposed to lie down almost all day—it is apparently what we call slow fever." Charles W. Eliot to his mother, Marberg, 5 January 1865, Charles W. Eliot Papers, Pusey Library.
31. Commonplace Book, October 1876.
32. Charles W. Eliot, "Bringing Up a Boy," *Delineator*, October 1914, republished in Charles W. Eliot, *A Late Harvest: Miscellaneous Papers Written between Eighty and Ninety* (Boston: Atlantic Monthly Press, 1924), 80–81.
33. The Eliots camped with their relatives the Footes; the Rev. Mr. Henry Wilder Foote was Charles's uncle and the minister of King's Chapel in Boston, having succeeded Charles's grandfather Peabody in that position.
34. For further information on Charles W. Eliot and educational reform, see Hawkins, *Between Harvard and America*.
35. The quotation is from a letter Charles Eliot wrote to his wife, Sunday, 20 July 1895, *CELA*, 515. See the writings of Walter Benjamin, especially "Paris: The Capital of the Second Empire," in *Charles Baudelaire: A Lyric Poet in the Era of High Capitalism* (London: Verso Books, 1983), for a discussion of the concept of the *flâneur*. Al-

though Benjamin used this term to describe urban observers, the characterization closely fits Charles Eliot's ceaseless need to walk and view and analyze the landscape.

36. Diary of 1878. This unusual habit may have been another indication of his insecurity and isolation.

37. Diary of 1875, 14 May 1875, Princeton, Mass., GC.

38. For his comments on "nabobry," see *CELA*, 176–77.

39. Charles Eliot to Frederick Law Olmsted, Sunday, 10 October [1887], GC.

40. Ibid. Eliot began the letter, "My travels are over: for I cannot imitate Count Pückler—who journeyed thro' Europe for 5 years or more," and continued, "I spent two whole days there [at Muskau], in the park all the time. In London last winter I had read his little book, and the descriptions written by his foreman after his death and something about the Count's life."

41. These call slips survive in the Charles Eliot Archive at Harvard University's Graduate School of Design. It is, therefore, possible to chart exactly which books he read and in which order.

42. He was greatly assisted in this process by the letters of introduction he brought from his father, Frederick Law Olmsted, Charles Sprague Sargent, and Asa Gray, among others.

43. James Bryce, Viscount Bryce, was both a professor of law and a member of Parliament. He had first met President Eliot and his son in 1879 when he stayed at the Eliot house in Cambridge during a tour of the United States. He later became one of the most respected observers of the American political system; his book *The American Commonwealth* was published in 1888.

44. Charles Eliot Norton, first cousin of President Eliot, inaugurated courses in the history of art at Harvard College, which Charles Eliot took. Norton no doubt became involved with the defense society through John Ruskin, the British social and art critic, who lived in the Lake District and wrote passionately about its preservation. Norton was a close friend of Ruskin's and would later be the literary executor of his estate. See the Rawnsley Papers, Cumbria County Public Records Office, Kendal, WDX/422/2/3 for the May 1884 brochure of the Lake District Defense Society, which lists Norton and Professor Palmer of Harvard University as supporters.

45. *CELA*, 32.

46. Cynthia Zaitzevsky notes that Eliot was the first official apprentice in the Olmsted office, to be joined by Henry Sargent Codman in 1884. By the 1890s, the Olmsted office had become an important training ground for young landscape architects. Zaitzevsky, "Education and Landscape Architecture," in *Architectural Education and Boston: Centennial Publication of the Boston Architectural Center, 1889–1989*, ed. Margaret Henderson Floyd (Boston: Boston Architectural Center, 1989), 25. It is interesting to note the close ties between architects and landscape architects in Boston; Codman was also recommended to Olmsted by an architect uncle, John H. Sturgis.

47. *CELA*, 207.

48. Charles W. Eliot to Charles Eliot, 11 June 1886, Goriansky Collection. President Eliot continued: "Boston Uncle Robert [Swain Peabody]

says that you will know best whether you want to go in again with Mr. O. He thinks that a student who returns in haste for some job generally makes a mistake. . . . My impression is in favor of refusal by cable—'Decline' & by effusive letter."

49. "My latest determination is to 'set up' at once. . . . I must make you what for me is a most important request. If I were to put a modest advertisement in the *Nation* for instance would you allow me to print your name (with 1 or 2 others) as a reference?" Charles Eliot to Frederick Law Olmsted, 10 October 1887, GC.

50. Eliot saw a generational distinction that would either have himself and Codman in charge of offices in Boston, New York, and Philadelphia, with Frederick Law Olmsted and John Charles Olmsted located in Brookline, or Olmsted in charge of the Brookline office and the three young men in partnership at the other sites. Charles Eliot to Frederick Law Olmsted, 20 July 1889, Eliot Correspondence File, 141–42, Loeb Library, Harvard University.

51. *CELA*, 554–56, 543–45.

52. Ibid., 441.

53. Charles Eliot to Mr. Garrison, 2 November 1896, Manuscript Letters, vol. 2, nos. 164 and 165, Charles Eliot Collection, Loeb Library. Ironically, Eliot died before this obituary could be used for Olmsted.

54. Charles Eliot to Roland Thaxter, 13 May 1883, GC. Eliot continued: "The world says I am a lucky fellow—and congratulates me on all sides."

55. Frederick Law Olmsted to his partners, Biltmore, N.C., 28 October 1893, Frederick Law Olmsted Collection, Manuscript Division, Library of Congress, Washington, D.C.

56. For information on Warren H. Manning, see Robin Karson, *The Muses of Gwinn: Art and Nature in a Garden Designed by Warren H. Manning, Charles A. Platt, and Ellen Biddle Shipman* (Sagaponack, N.Y.: Sagapress/Library of American Landscape History, 1995), esp. chap. 3; and Lance Neckar, "Developing Landscape Architecture for the Twentieth Century: The Career of Warren H. Manning," *Landscape Journal* 8 (Fall 1989): 78–91.

57. Shurcliff created a notebook that he titled "What Mr. Eliot said, 1894–7. Notes, original, copied and remembered of a few of the things which Mr. Charles Eliot said to Arthur A. Shurtleff about landscape." Arthur Shurcliff Notebooks, Houghton Library, Harvard University. (Shurtleff changed his name to Shurcliff after he made the notebook.) Here are assembled descriptions of conversations, recommendations for courses to take and books to read, and discussions of sites that the two men had visited together. See also Elizabeth Hope Cushing, "The Life and Work of Arthur A. Shurcliff" (Ph.D. diss., Boston University, 1997).

58. *CELA*, 381.

59. Ibid., 367, 662.

60. For the 28 January 1891 edition of *Garden and Forest*, Eliot contributed "Muskau—A German Country Park," 38–39, the fullest statement of his understanding of and admiration for this site, which he had visited on 22–23 September 1886.

61. *CELA*, 596–97, 303, 377, 562, 680.

62. Ian L. McHarg, *A Quest for Life: An Autobiography* (New York: John Wiley & Sons, 1996), 82.

63. *CELA*, 547–49.

64. Eliot and Sullivan were developing parallel philosophies at the same moment. Eliot published "What Would Be Fair Must First Be Fit" in *Garden and Forest* on 1 April 1896. Sullivan published the clearest expression of his ideas in "The Tall Building Artistically Considered," *Lippincott's* 57 (March 1896) 403–9.

65. These wonderful foldout sepia watercolors were made by Arthur Shurcliff, following Humphrey Repton's practice in his Red Books.

66. *CELA*, 650.

67. For the Colonial Revival movement, see William Rhoads, *The Colonial Revival* (New York: Garland Press, 1977), and James Lindgren, *Preserving Historic New England: Preservation, Progressivism, and the Remaking of Memory* (New York: Oxford University Press, 1995).

68. Diary for 1875, Concord and Lexington, Tuesday, 20 April 1875, GC. This entry also contains a description of the huge traffic jams that were a part of the centennial celebration.

69. *CELA*, 211.

70. Ibid., 241ff.

71. Henry Winthrop Sargent's revised edition of Andrew Jackson Downing's *Treatise on the Theory and Practice of Landscape Gardening* did include a discussion of these country seats, but the descriptions were of active estates rather than historical landscapes.

72. For the development of a Colonial Revival literature in architecture and the early role of Robert Swain Peabody, see Vincent Scully, *The Shingle Style and the Stick Style: Architectural Theory and Design from Richardson to the Origins of Wright* (New Haven: Yale University Press, 1971), 42–46. Peabody had read a paper titled "A Talk about Queen Anne" before the Boston Society of Architects in 1877 which revealed the relationship between the Queen Anne Revival in England and the emerging Colonial Revival in the United States. A decade later his nephew would be demonstrating the value in studying Colonial examples in garden design.

73. Although he was included in *Sons of the Puritans: A Group of Brief Biographies* (Boston: American Unitarian Association, 1908), 219–30. These biographies, reprinted from the *Harvard Graduate's Magazine*, introduced their subjects as "successful men of affairs" who each owed his efficiency to a certain moral idealism, which is part of the Puritan inheritance.

74. Charles Eliot to Grace Hopkinson Eliot, 16 October 1881, GC.

75. Charles Eliot to Eleanor and Katherine Guild, 16 May 1886, GC.

76. *CELA*, 485–86. Cambridge Field was a project Eliot was completing for the Cambridge Park Commission. Charlesbank was an earlier design by the Olmsted office, the first American park to incorporate apparatus for active recreation, divided into different sections by age and sex. The "new terrace at the North End" was Eliot's Copps Hill Terrace, which provided a bathing beach and a promenade for the densely populated North End of Boston.

77. The proposal for model tenements, including mandatory garden courts,

certainly came from Sylvester Baxter, the original secretary of the Metropolitan Park Commission and Eliot's colleague there and at the Trustees of Reservations.

78. *CELA*, 679, 575.

79. Ibid., 521.

80. Gordon Abbott Jr., *Saving Special Places: A Centennial History of the Trustees of Reservations, Pioneer of the Land Trust Movement* (Ipswich, Mass.: Ipswich Press, 1993), 271.

81. Lincoln, "Champlain Society." Eliot first described his vision in an article for *Garden and Forest* in 1889. The dream was realized in 1916 with the establishment of Mount Desert National Park.

82. For a concise review of the early Boston and Cambridge efforts to create academic programs in landscape architecture, see Zaitzevsky, "Education and Landscape Architecture," 20–34, esp. 30–31.

83. Norman Newton, *Design on the Land: The Development of Landscape Architecture* (Cambridge: Harvard University Press, Belknap Press, 1971), discusses the memorialization of Charles Eliot in the establishment of the Program in Landscape Architecture at Harvard: "Thus it was that Harvard in 1900 established the first university course of professional training in landscape architecture in memory of Charles Eliot with a professorship and, a few years later, a traveling fellowship endowed in his name."

84. "From Olmsted's Emerald Necklace to Eliot's Metropolitan Parks," lecture given by Charles W. Eliot II, 27 February 1983, transcript, 1, copy in possession of author.

85. Abbott, *Saving Special Places*, 26–28. This source is rather confusing on the chronology of Charles W. Eliot II's professional life and his involvement with the Trustees.

86. Abbott (ibid., 33) quotes the report of the Committee on the Needs and Uses of Open Spaces, in which the Bay Circuit was "first suggested by Henry M. Channing, Secretary of the Trustees of Reservations." However, in a letter to the author, 24 December 1991, Eliot referred to "'the Bay Circuit Greenbelt'—launched by Charles Eliot's nephew (me) in 1925 as part of my commitment to 'carry on my uncle's work' (as ordained by my grandfather at my birth)."

87. The papers of Charles W. Eliot II are held in the Special Collections of the Loeb Library, Graduate School of Design, Harvard University.

88. Frederic Winthrop Jr., introduction to *The Trustees of Reservations Property Guide* (1996), 9.

89. Abbott, *Saving Special Places*, 310–19.

90. Charles Sprague Sargent, director of the Arnold Arboretum, served as the early representative of the Trustees to the National Trust in Great Britain. Throughout its first century (the Trustees celebrated its centennial in 1991), the Trustees became more of a land trust and less of an organization concerned with land of historic significance, as originally envisioned.

91. *Enhancing the Future of the Metropolitan Park System: Final Report and Recommendations of the Green Ribbon Commission* (Boston: Metropolitan District Commission, 1996), 9. Nine thousand of these acres were acquired in the commission's first ten years. The

Metropolitan Park Commission merged with the Metropolitan Water and Sewer Commission to become the Metropolitan District Commission in 1919.

92. Ibid., 47–49. The Green Ribbon Commission focused on three general areas for improvement: building effective stewardship, linking the parks and the public, and managing, planning, and supporting the public trust. The concerns Eliot expressed in his letters to the commission about general plans are identical. See chapter 34.

93. H. G. Wells, *The Future in America* (New York: Harper & Row, 1906), 49. I thank Cecelia Tichi for bringing this passage to my attention. Sylvester Baxter, Eliot's colleague, was the guide for Wells's tour of the Boston Metropolitan Parks.

CHARLES ELIOT

LANDSCAPE ARCHITECT

FOR THE DEAR SON
WHO DIED IN HIS BRIGHT PRIME
FROM THE FATHER

Æt. 33

Charles Eliot.

CHARLES ELIOT

Landscape Architect

A LOVER OF NATURE
AND OF HIS KIND
WHO TRAINED HIMSELF FOR A NEW PROFESSION
PRACTISED IT HAPPILY
AND THROUGH IT WROUGHT MUCH GOOD

TABLE OF CONTENTS

CHAPTER I

CHAPTER II

CHAPTER III

CHAPTER IV

CHAPTER XIII

CHAPTER XIV

CHAPTER XV

CHAPTER XVI

CHAPTER XVII

CHAPTER XVIII

CHAPTER XIX

CHAPTER XX

CHAPTER XXV

CHAPTER XXVI

CHAPTER XXVII

CHAPTER XXVIII

CHAPTER XXIX

CHAPTER XXX

CHAPTER XL

APPENDIX

I

II

III

IV

V

FULL PAGE ILLUSTRATIONS

ILLUSTRATIONS IN THE TEXT

CHARLES ELIOT
LANDSCAPE ARCHITECT

CHARLES ELIOT

CHAPTER I

INHERITANCES

He hears his daughter's voice,
Singing in the village choir,
And it makes his heart rejoice.
It sounds to him like her mother's voice,
Singing in Paradise! [1]

LONGFELLOW.

CHARLES ELIOT was born in Cambridge, Massachusetts, on the 1st of November, 1859. His father was Charles William Eliot, at that time Assistant Professor of Mathematics and Chemistry in Harvard College; his mother was Ellen Derby (Peabody) Eliot, daughter of Ephraim Peabody, minister of King's Chapel, Boston (1845–1856), and Mary Jane (Derby) Peabody. His father came from a line of Boston Eliots who for several generations had been serviceable and influential people, and on the maternal side from a line of Lymans who in three successive generations had lived at Northampton, Mass., York, Maine, and Waltham, Mass., and had been useful and successful in life. On his mother's side, his grandfather Peabody (Bowdoin College, A. B., 1827), son of a blacksmith at Wilton, N. H., was a man of keen insight, lofty character, and much poetic feeling; while his grandmother was a Salem Derby, at a time when that family had acquired in world-wide commerce a wealth considerable in those days, — the first quarter of the XIXth century. His father and mother, and all four of his grandparents, were carefully educated persons; and among his progenitors were several men who had been rich in their generation, able to support considerable establishments, and to give their children every accessible advantage.

---

[1] The quotations at the heads of chapters are taken from Charles's commonplace books, or from poems he knew by heart.

It is altogether probable that Charles Eliot's tastes for out-of-door nature and art were in part inherited, for some of his ancestors manifested in their day dispositions and likings to which his were akin. Among the Trustees of the Massachusetts Society for Promoting Agriculture, a public-spirited body established in 1792, appear his great-grandfather Theodore Lyman, his great-uncle George W. Lyman, and his great-great-grandfather Elias Hasket Derby; while among the earliest members of the Massachusetts Horticultural Society, which was founded in 1829, appear E. Hersey Derby, of Salem, his grandmother Peabody's uncle, and John Derby, her father, Theodore Lyman, his great-uncle, and Samuel Atkins Eliot, his grandfather. Theodore Lyman of Waltham created one of the handsomest country-seats in New England; E. Hersey Derby introduced and tried various breeds of cattle, sheep, and swine, and different kinds of crops, hedges, trees, and shrubs from foreign parts on his beautiful estate at Salem,[1] and Samuel A. Eliot was one of the first citizens of Boston to build a house at the seaside (Nahant) for summer occupation. In 1825 this same Eliot, Charles's grandfather, planted the greater part of what has since been known in Cambridge as the Norton Woods. Samuel A. Eliot's sister Catherine having married Professor Andrews Norton, her father provided a handsome residence for the newly married pair, and her brother Samuel, who had just returned from a European tour, was allowed to improve both the house and the grounds. More than thirty years afterwards he himself passed a summer with his family in this sister's house, and wrote as follows to her about the result of his efforts : " Being here has reminded me of the part I had in making it a fit residence for you ; and the vision of the old house fronting the wrong way, and with its awkward, bare, comfortless look, has come up to me strongly several times since I have been here ; and I find it hard to recollect how it used to look, without the trees of the avenue and circle, which are now so beautiful, and with a garden full of apple-trees (of which I see some still remain), and without the pines which make so capital a screen on the north and west. My visions of improvement have been largely fulfilled." When in after years Charles was invited

---

[1] Mr. Derby's house was a very hospitable one. There descended to the next generation a tablecloth of his which was eight yards long. His collection of books on rural architecture descended to his grandnephew, Robert S. Peabody, architect.

to write accounts of some of the finest American country-seats for the weekly publication called " Garden and Forest," it turned out that of the six places in different parts of the country which he described, one had been created and another occupied by his kindred.

His training in drawing and sketching began early. His grandmother Peabody had all her life been in the habit of using her pencil, and her two daughters and one of her sons inherited, or imitated, this habit. Charles's mother and her sister Anna used both pencil and brush for pleasure; and they and their mother set Charles drawing and painting at a tender age.

" Charley is making us a little visit just now. Mamma [grandmother Peabody] devotes herself [to him]. They paint from the same picture pattern, and write letters at the same time." . . . (From a note by aunt Anna H. Peabody.)

His childhood was different from that of most American children, in that he had spent nearly three years in Europe before he was ten years old. From the middle of 1863 to the middle of 1865 his father and mother and their two little boys were in Europe for the professional improvement of his father; and the family were again in Europe from June, 1867, to June, 1868, on account of the ill-health of his mother. During these two periods Charles saw many of the most interesting cities, and much of the most beautiful scenery in Europe. He spent the greater part of one summer in Switzerland, and of another in rural England ; and he played in Regent's Park, St. James Park, and Hyde Park, London, on the Champs Elysées in Paris, in the Boboli Gardens at Florence, along the Philosopher's Path at Heidelberg, on the Fincian Hill at Rome, and the Hautes Plantes at Pau. The whole family enjoyed visiting collections of animals ; so that the boys became acquainted with the principal zoölogical gardens in Europe, and found in them stores of delight. In all this foreign residence and travel Charles showed a good sense of locality, a decided fondness for maps, and great enjoyment of scenery. His mother had the keenest enjoyment in travel, and Charles from childhood felt the same pleasurable excitement in change of scene, and in the sight of natural beauty. In 1855, at the age of nineteen, Ellen Derby Peabody spent a week at Niagara Falls in company with some older friends, and this is the way in which she described her enjoyment of it: " I am so happy, and am enjoying it so very, very much that I cannot help writing on and on to tell you about it. I don't believe anybody ever enjoyed

anything more in the world." Thirty-one years afterwards
her son Charles, at the age of twenty-seven, wrote thus to his
father from Florence, — he had been spending a month along
the Riviera: " I have never been quite so happy as I have
been this past month. I have been simply revelling in the
beauty of this fair land. I think my inadequate journal must
have in it some signs of my great pleasure; and now that I am
come to the city of all others where are works of man which
partake of the loveliness of nature, — my heart is more than
full and I am extravagantly happy."

His mother's delight in beautiful scenery found expression
in her letters whenever she was away from home. Thus, in
June, 1858, when she was just twenty-two, she paid a visit
with her sister Anna to some friends of her father and
mother, who lived at Irvington on the Hudson; and this is
her description of the place: " We arrived at this beautiful place just in time to be welcomed by a most glorious
sunset. The river and the hills were all lighted up with
glowing colors, and the birds were singing their loudest. It
is a very pretty stone house with piazzas and pointed windows, and vines climbing all about it, and trees all around,
and a garden filled with roses, and certainly as beautiful
views of the river in every direction as one could well wish
for. It stands very high, but it is nestled in among the trees
so cosily, and if ever there was a happy family, it certainly is
here. . . . Such a morning as we waked up to! I would not
undertake to describe to you all the beauties we saw from our
window. Such an air, and such a sky! The white sails
glancing in the fresh new light, the river lying so still and
calm, and the Palisades lighted up far down the shore with
morning sunshine!" (From a letter written by Ellen Derby
Peabody to Charles W. Eliot, to whom she had become
engaged two months before.)

In March, 1869, his mother died at the age of thirty-three,
and soon after his father was chosen President of Harvard
University. In September, 1869, Charles returned to Cambridge with his father and younger brother, and the President's House on Quincy Street was thereafter his home until
1891. From June, 1867, to September, 1869, grandmother
Peabody and aunt Anna had made one household with the
Eliots, and exercised a strong and precious influence on the
two little boys. The summer of 1868 was spent in Brookline,
that of 1869 at Chestnut Hill, and that of 1870 on Pond
Street, Jamaica Plain. Wherever the family lived, Charles
roamed the country roundabout, and learnt it by heart.

CHAPTER II

GENERAL EDUCATION

Many gardeners assume that before beginning their plantings they must dig up everything that Nature has nursed up ; whereas experience proves that they would accomplish their ends much sooner and better, if they should try to second Nature by making slight changes here and careful additions there. — HIRSCHFELD.

As soon as the family was again settled in Cambridge, Charles began to go to school regularly, which had hardly been possible before. He began Latin just before he was ten years old, and in general followed the usual course of preparation for admission to Harvard College. The languages, except English, were a trial to him, and for mathematics he had no special aptitude; but he patiently accomplished that amount of work in those subjects which was then considered necessary. History was interesting to him; and from the first, even before he could use a pen himself, he showed an unusual capacity for making a clear and concise statement of facts, or giving an accurate description. Here is a short note which he dictated to his mother for his aunt Anna when he was five years old. The dear aunt had been travelling with the Eliot family in Europe during the summer, and had returned to America. "DEAR AUNT ANNA: I love you very much. Papa tells me to look at all the donkeys' and cows' and horses' tails, and see if they are just alike, or not. We have got a new lamp, and it is tin, and papa tells me all about how it is made. On my birthday morning I found it very hard to have to sit in my chair and eat my breakfast, because I wanted so to get down, and play with my new things. Here is a little kiss for Aunty Anna — ○. I have made a windmill for you like what we have seen in the cars. Good-by, dear Aunty Anna — I think every night about you, and wonder how you are getting along — CHARLEY."

Both Charles and his brother Samuel began early to commit to memory hymns and other short poems; and their parents took pains that the poetry they learnt should be worth remembering. Before Charles was fifteen years of age he had in his mind a considerable store of excellent verse, which probably affected favorably his own style in writing English, and certainly heightened his appreciation of rhythm, melody, and poetic imagination. In a note which Charles wrote to his aunt Anna in December, 1869, when he was ten years old, he says: "I have just learned 'The Village Blacksmith' and 'The Rain' from Longfellow, and I am going to learn 'How They Brought the Good News from Ghent to Aix' from Browning." They both learnt early Bryant's "To a Water-Fowl" and "Not in the solitude alone may man commune with Heaven;" and these two poems continued to express for Charles through all his life much of his own philosophy and religion. The first entry in the commonplace book which he began when he was seventeen years old, except a sort of dedication taken from Chaucer, is Sir Henry Wotton's hymn, "How happy is he born or taught," which he had learnt when a little boy.

The following "composition," written February 19, 1870, at the school kept by Miss Sarah Harte Page, further illustrates his early tendency to exact observation and description: —

SNOW, ITS USES, AND THE SPORTS IT GIVES US.

Snow is solid water. Some times it falls six inches thick, and then it makes a warm blanket for the earth. It is good for sledding heavy things, like stone, and timber, and great logs out of the woods. The Esquimaux build their houses of it. Boys can make a great many things of it. They can build forts, and make snow-balls. This winter with Sam's help I built a snow-man; but just as it was finished, it tumbled over and broke all to pieces. I like to coast very much; it is good fun to slide so fast over the frozen snow. We also built a fort; it was on the bank of our house, and was higher than my head, and was very thick indeed. It lasted longer than any of the other snow. This last snow we tried to build another fort, but when the rain came it got beaten all down. It was square, and its walls were about a foot and a half thick; it was made of lumps of snow all plastered together. I like to see the snow-plough making paths through the snow. The deeper the snow is the more men must stand on the plough to press it down.

Another composition, written January 21, 1870, shows how early his predilections for history and natural history were declared : —

A COMPOSITION ABOUT THE BOOKS I LIKE TO READ BEST.

I like to read the Child's History of the United States very much ; it is in three volumes, the first is about the discovery of America, and how it was settled, the second is about the war of the Revolution, and the third about the Rebellion. It has plans and pictures of the battles, and is very interesting. I also like the Natural History of Animals by Rev. J. G. Wood ; it is illustrated, and tells the habits, color, and country where they live, of all the animals in the world, I should think. There are accounts of adventures men have had with wild beasts, and a great many stories. Robinson Crusoe is another book I like — how he was wrecked on a desert island, and fought the savages, and how he did not get home for a great many years. It is very exciting. There is one more book that I like very much, and that is Frothingham's Siege of Boston ; it has accounts of the battles of Lexington, Concord, and Bunker Hill. I have a great many other books, but the ones I have mentioned I like best.

His school work was occasionally interrupted by headaches and short feverish turns, which incapacitated him for a few hours or days. On this account, and also because of his slightness of form, his father was anxious to limit as much as possible his hours of indoor occupation, and to encourage him in all sorts of out-of-door sports. The two boys had a sagacious and competent pony, that could easily keep up with their father's saddle-horse ; and both learned to ride at an early age. In a note to his grandmother Peabody on January 1, 1871, Charles says, " Papa wants me to say that I can ride pretty well. I have got a McClellan saddle ; and yesterday the pony jumped a good deal, and I did not fall off. He stopped short, and dodged round a cart."

In the summer of 1870, when the family were living at Jamaica Plain, the boys and their playmates in the neighborhood organized a band called the " Knights of the Woods," to the imaginative sports of which their aunt Anna contributed many suggestions. This society was continued at Quincy Street, Cambridge, where thirteen boys were enlisted, and equipped with silvered helmets, decorated shields, and wooden swords and spears. Their adventures took place chiefly in the Norton Woods, although their combats extended to the yards and interiors of their fathers' houses. By 1872 another band, called the "Lances of Lancaster," was duly organized, and a pitched battle took place in that year between the "Knights of the Woods" and the "Lances of Lancaster." All the Knights and Lances had names, mainly copied from Scott's novels, which the boys were at that time reading. These bands of knights soon gave place to the Quincy Cricket Club, the Quincy Telegraph Company, the Football Eleven, the Society of Minerals, the Good Fun Club, and the Theatrical Club, in all of which organizations Charles took active part, and of all of which he subsequently (1875) made systematic member-lists which are still preserved.

In the spring of 1871, actuated by a desire to get for their families the most thorough possible open-air life during the summer, Charles's father and uncle (Henry Wilder Foote, minister of King's Chapel, Boston) agreed to live together in tents on an island in Frenchman's Bay (Mount Desert) during the larger part of their vacation. Mr. Eliot provided the sloop yacht Jessie, thirty-three feet long, as means of transportation and of pleasure sailing. The party consisted of Mr. and Mrs. Foote and their little daughter, Mr. Eliot and his two boys, a woman nurse and seamstress, and a man cook. The sailor from the yacht gave assistance at the camp. Here is a note from Charles to his grandmother, in which he describes the camp with characteristic precision.

July 22, 1871.

Dear Grandma, — I got your letter this afternoon, and I am sorry you are not any better. Our Camp is on Calf Island which is farther off than Iron-bound. There are four tents. The tent Sam, and Papa, and I have, is the largest, and has a curtain in the middle to separate it, from the Parlor and Dining-room. Aunt Fannie and Uncle Henry have one tent, Agnes and Mary another, and Kelly sleeps in the kitchen. Here is a plan of the way our tents are placed: they are on a peninsula with water all round except to the right, where it broadens into an island. Kelly built the arbor to wash dishes in and eat. We have little beds with rubber pillows and hay mattresses. On the end of the point

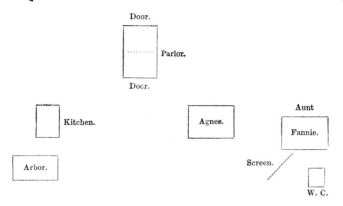

is a flag-pole where we have a flag, and salute all the Boats that go by. It is foggy to day and we cannot see Mount Desert at all.

Your affectionate grandson,

CHARLES ELIOT.

The camp described in the above letter was subsequently moved to a more central position on the island.

This way of passing the summer in camping and yachting combined was continued by the family until 1878 inclusive, excepting the summer of 1877. The children began with imaginative sports in the woods on Calf Island and about the puddles the tide left in the gently sloping ledges which formed part of its shores. They sailed their shingle boats on the puddles, and imagined the sailors, cargoes, and harbors, and the lighthouses and day-marks of the coast. They had caches of treasures at various mysterious points on that larger half of the island which was wooded, and with the help of their elders they made various beloved paths to attractive points of view. The island was more than a mile long, had a considerable variety of surface and of shore, and commanded exquisite views to the northeast, the northwest, and the southwest. The children came into close contact with Nature in all her various moods; the rain beat loudly on the tent-flies right over their heads; the wind shook the canvas shelters and threatened to prostrate them, but never did; the oxen — the only other inhabitants of the island — walked about the tents in the early morning, waking some of the sleepers by their loud breathing; the sun beat fiercely on field and tents, but the double roofs were always an adequate protection ; and from the kitchen-tent the cook produced in all weathers the elements of simple but delicious repasts. They learnt by experience that in summer at least, health, comfort, and great enjoyment can be secured without elaborate apparatus or many costly possessions, and that the real necessaries of healthy and happy existence in warm weather are few.

In notes to his aunt Anna written about this time Charles mentions some of his reading and other mental occupations at Cambridge. Thus in November, 1871, he says: " We write compositions in German now, and read too. There are eleven children and fourteen or fifteen ladies and gentlemen." This was a school conducted in the so-called natural method by Mr. Theodore Heness. In the same note he says: " I have read the ' Pathfinder' and the ' Spy ' lately, and I like them both very much. On Saturday we are going to see ' Guy Mannering' at the Globe. Sam and I have read the story." In the following April, he writes: " We acted our play [Red Ridinghood in German] last Friday at Mr. Houghton's house on Main Street. Willie Putnam was a dog, Sam was a young man just married, George Dunbar was the wolf, and Charlie Cole was a robin. Lulu Parsons was a Grandmother, and Helen Hinckley was Red Ridinghood. Harry Spelman was an old cross farmer, and I was the hunter who killed the wolf. . . . I had to ask Red Ridinghood to give me a kiss."

In the autumn of 1871, when he was only twelve years old, Charles and his playmate George R. Agassiz made a plan of the northwestern portion of the Norton estate, using a compass to get the angles, and a rope marked off in equal parts by knots to measure distances, a knot being the unit of length. On the map so prepared they indicated the different vegetations which occurred in the different parts of the region mapped ; so that the map showed the combination of forest and marsh, the forest without marsh, the grassy portions, and the small sandy desert. They then named each district on the map, the boundaries of the districts being marked by red lines. The names of the districts were Violet, Pine, Pond, Barn, Skunk Cabbage, Wild Cherry, and the Desert. This prophetic plan was duly preserved by his aunt Anna, and marked " C. Eliot, twelve years old." At the same age, after his return from the first camping season at Calf Island, he used to amuse himself by laying out plans of imaginary towns, with their roads, water-courses, houses, wharves, and harbors, the towns being always situated by the sea. The slopes of the sites are always indicated by proper hatching; the harbors are invariably well protected from the sea by islands, points, or promontories, and their approaches are marked by lighthouses and buoys. Three such plans were preserved by his aunt Anna, and on all three of the plans public reservations are indicated. In one sketch this reservation is called " Public Land," in the next " Public Reserve," and in the third " Public Park." These labors were performed entirely spontaneously and in the way of play; but they required a good deal of patience. In the largest of the three plans the sites of over one hundred and forty buildings are indicated, beside wharves and quarries. His spontaneous interest in the subject was strong enough to carry him through a deal of work.

The next year he began to be interested in house-plans, which he took pleasure in drawing with some elaboration and no little ingenuity. In the one plan which has survived, it is interesting to see that he indicated the way in which both the front door and the back door should be approached by the driveway. During his professional life he often had occasion to say that architects seemed to deposit their houses on the ground without considering at all how roads were to be got to the entrances.

In 1871 the small sloop Jessie was for the children the vehicle for half a day's sail only, or for doing errands about the Bay; but in the winter and spring of 1872 Mr. Eliot had built a family cruising sloop $43\frac{1}{2}$ feet long, with a high trunk, and room enough for four adults and two children in the cabin, beside two men forward. Thereafter, the cruises before and after camping became important to the children, and particularly to Charles and Samuel. The Sunshine cruised in successive summers along the shores of New England from Sag Harbor and Fisher's Island on the west to Eastport on the east, going up the principal rivers, and visiting all the bays and harbors, and many of the outlying islands like Shelter Island, Block Island, Nantucket, the Isles of Shoals, Monhegan, and Grand Manan. Parts of the coast were of course visited many times. Thus Charles gradually became acquainted with the whole New England shore. He acquired skill in the use of charts, and of all the other aids to navigation which the government publishes, including the List of Lighthouses, the List of Buoys and other Daymarks, and the admirable Coast Pilot. He also became interested in the history of the coast, and in the adventures of its early explorers, like Cabot, Verrazano, De Monts, Champlain, Weymouth, and Smith. This interest lasted the year round, and gave direction to some of his spontaneous reading at Cambridge.

In 1873 the camp with additional tents was pitched on the island of Nonamesset, Buzzard's Bay, instead of at Calf Island, in order that the children might learn in the warmer water south of Cape Cod how to swim well. This island adjoins Naushon, and Charles there became familiar with the Elizabeth Islands, and particularly with Naushon, the most beautiful of the group. An acquaintance with these islands was the more desirable because their configuration, soil, climate, and flora are different from those of the coast of Maine. Billy, the pony, and a stout horse and wagon added to the resources of the party, Naushon, unlike Calf Island, being large enough for much delightful riding and driving.

Charles had an inherited interest in Naushon ; for through all his mother's childhood the Peabody family had spent a month there every summer as guests of Governor Swain, its then owner ; and she had the strongest affection for it. The following note written from Naushon by his mother to her Grandmother Derby about 1850 shows what the charms of the island were for the Peabody children.

My dear Grandma, — We have no time to write at all except Sundays, but then we have nothing to do till eleven o'clock, when Papa reads a sermon. Last Sunday I wrote a good long letter to Eliza, and Anna wrote one to Aunty. We are having a splendid time, riding, walking, swimming, drawing, fishing, and sailing. I have seen twenty-one deer, and Anna has seen seventeen. We generally go to ride on horseback in the evening, and almost always see one or two deer. When we get home, we unharness the horses, and ride them bare-back to the field. We have been to bathe quite often, and the waves have been splendid. Saturday they were so high, they went over Rob's head all the time. Since Cousin Annie Drinker has been here, we have drawn a good deal. We intend to finish our sketches with Cousin Annie at New Bedford. We have a good many baskets of egg-shell which are very pretty. We knock off the top of the egg and bind it with ribbon. We cover the egg-shell with the pith of rushes. Annie and I have kept a daily journal, which will be very pleasant to look over. I have a great deal more to tell you, but I must save it for another note, because the mail

is going now to Wood's Hole. Please give my best love to
them all.

Your affectionate granddaughter

E. D. PEABODY

Grandma's birthday.

In the summer of 1858 Ellen Derby Peabody and Charles
W. Eliot spent a delightful week together at Naushon as
guests of Mr. and Mrs. John M. Forbes. Governor Swain,
her father Mr. Peabody, and several friends who were intimately associated in Ellen's mind with the lovely island had
died, so that sadness was mingled with the joys of this visit.
In the following October, a few days before her marriage,
Ellen wrote as follows to her betrothed : " Am I not glad I
have had that week at Naushon with you ? It was a strange
kind of pleasure I had. It was more a pleasure of memory,
I think, and the sharing with you the pleasures and the feelings of years now gone, than what we really did and enjoyed
now." Aunt Anna, who had shared with Ellen every Naushon delight, helped to transmit to Charles an interest in the
island. Its hollows full of old wind-clipped beeches, its
breezy uplands, its sheltered harbor — the Gutter — and its
wide sheep pastures were enjoyed by Charles at fourteen as
they had been by his mother and aunt in their happy childhood.

Between the end of January, 1874, and the middle of the
following May, Charles made a journey with his grandmother Peabody and his aunt Anna to Florida, and visited
also Savannah and Charleston, his father going to England
at the same time. This excursion enabled him to observe
sub-tropical vegetation, the mild winter climate of the south
Atlantic shore, a low-lying country without hills, and rivers
and creeks as unlike as possible those of New England. It
distinctly enlarged his experience of landscape. He was
encouraged and helped to draw, paint, and keep a journal ;
and he illustrated the journal with photographs, cuts, and
pen-and-ink drawings of his own. One effect on his mind is
brought out in a letter he wrote his grandmother the following September from Maplewood, in the White Mountains.
" Bethlehem, I think, is very beautiful indeed. I have a very
pretty view out of my window across a wide valley with distant blue hills in the background. There is a swift little
river in the valley which, like all the streams here, have very
rocky beds. I like the streams and brooks very much ; they

are so swift, and seem so jolly and frisky, — much nicer than the sluggish Southern streams."

In the next spring he took a different kind of journey, which again enlarged his observation of scenery. He described it on a postal card written to his aunt Anna, then become Mrs. Henry W. Bellows. " May 14, 1875. Papa and I are on a journey with Jack in the buggy. We left Cambridge at 3.30 Thursday, and drove through Waltham, Weston, Wayland, and Sudbury, to Maynard, formerly Assabet, where we arrived at 6.45, and put up at the only hotel. This morning, came through Stow, Bolton, between Lancaster and Clinton, to Sterling, where, as the hotel was closed, we had dinner at a Mr. Merriam's at 12. At 1.30 left again, and came on to Princeton, arriving here at 3.15, twenty-four hours from home, forty-three miles, about. We have had splendid weather, and the horse gets on very well. We go home by Leominster, Harvard, and Concord, to get home Monday to tea." That little journey showed him some of the fairest of the New England towns at the apple-blossom season.

By 1875 Charles took up a sport which had an important bearing on his professional career. It was suggested to him by his father, who had got much pleasure from it when a boy himself. In company with two or three other boys, Charles would take the steam-cars or horse-cars to some convenient point of departure within easy reach of Cambridge, and then walk from five to ten miles cross country to another point whence there was railroad communication to Boston or Cambridge. These excursions always took half a day, and sometimes more, and it was part of the fun to take luncheon or supper in the open air on the way. At that time there were no contour maps of the vicinity of Boston; so that, in making plans for walks, Charles had only the guidance of the common maps which showed the roads, water-courses, and railroads, and, in a rough way, the hills. From such maps of the region round Boston Charles would make beforehand a small tracing covering the particular portion which he proposed to explore, and this tracing, which was seldom more than six inches square, he carried in his vest pocket on each walk. On every such map he put a scale, and for his guidance he carried a pocket compass. As Charles made all the preparations for such walks, he was invariably the guide. This sport, which he followed for years, made him familiar with the whole of what is now known as the " Metropolitan District " round Boston, and, moreover, afforded a good training in discerning the lay of land, picking out the land-marks, and finding a way over or round obstacles. In a note-book for 1878 he made a "partial list of Saturday walks before 1878." There are sixteen walks enumerated, and they stretch from Quincy on the south of Boston to Lynn on the north. No better preparation in youth for some of his most important work as a man could possibly have been de-vised ; but all was done without the least anticipation of his future profession. It was to him just an interesting though laborious play.

There was another kind of research which interested both the boys before they went to college, namely, the identifica-tion of the localities mentioned in such books as Frothing-ham's " Siege of Boston " and Drake's " Historic Mansions of Middlesex." They sought for all the sites and structures mentioned by these authors, which had not been completely obliterated by streets and buildings, and became acquainted with all such relics of Colonial and Revolutionary times in and about Boston.

All this time he was getting on at school with what were then the regular studies for his age. He writes to his aunt Anna in December, 1875 : " My school I like moderately ; go at 8.30, get out at 1.30; and I am studying Latin, Latin composition, algebra, and Harvard examination papers in arithmetic. I begin Ovid to-morrow. There are some good fellows at school ; but I never see them except in school hours. I ride often, but the best fun is the telegraph line which I joined about a month ago, and the drawing class Tuesdays and Fridays." This drawing class was conducted by Mr. Charles H. Moore, afterwards instructor and pro-fessor in Harvard College. A year later he speaks of this drawing again : " November 25, 1876. I am having draw-ing lessons four hours a week from Mr. Moore. The last things I have done are a twig in profile and also the same foreshortened. I have been in to Uncle Bob's [Robert S. Peabody, architect], and he has given me a whole set of plans, elevations, etc., to copy. I trace them on tracing cloth in India ink with bow pens, and color them, and put in all the dimensions, etc." He was at this time seventeen years old. In a note a few weeks earlier than that from which the last quotation was taken, he writes to his aunt Anna : " I am going to Mr. Kendall's school, as I did last year, and at present I am studying the following subjects : Virgil, one hundred lines daily ; Ovid, last review, seventy-five lines daily ; Cæsar, last review, three paragraphs daily ; Greek grammar or Greek composition, daily; algebra, last review, daily; arithmetic, one examination paper a week; geometry, last review, twice a week; Roman history on Saturday; Botany on Saturday; Latin composition, three times a week. ' Last review ' means that I am going over it the last time before the examination for College next spring." He never really enjoyed his school work; but he liked the master, Mr. Joshua Kendall, and he made two valued friends there, — Roland Thaxter and John H. Storer. He was never confident of success in his studies; so that when in June, 1877, he passed the preliminary examinations for admission to Harvard College in seven subjects, it was a great surprise to him. He was diffident and sensitive, and found it difficult to express his feelings, though they burned within. In the next house but one to the President's house on Quincy Street lived the family of Professor Lane, whose children, one son and two daughters, were not far removed from Charles in age. The companionship of these merry and sympathetic children was a real source of happiness to Charles, who was often lonely and tended to be down-hearted.

At this time, there was no feminine influence in his home; his dear aunt Anna was living in New York; grandmother Eliot had died; his Eliot aunts were all married, and no one of them lived in Cambridge; and grandmother Peabody was crippled by rheumatic gout and could never come to Cambridge, though her house in Boston was always open to Charles and Samuel, who went thither at least once a week. Then his father and brother had very different temperaments from his. They were sanguine, confident, content with present action, and little given to contemplation of either the past or the future; Charles was reticent, self-distrustful, speculative, and dissatisfied with his actual work, though faithful and patient in studies which did not interest him or open to him intellectual pleasures.

In July, 1877, his father was engaged to Grace Mellen Hopkinson of Cambridge. Charles heard the news from his father with calmness but without pleasure; and all summer long, though he was yachting on his beloved Sunshine, he was not cheerful, though well in body. When the marriage took place at the end of the following October, and "mother" — as the boys soon called her — came to live in the President's house, Charles was pleasant and interested, but did not at once open his heart to her, and claim her sympathy and affection. It was not till four years later that an intimate and tender relation was established between these two, a delightful intimacy never afterwards interrupted for a moment.

He rode much on horseback during the year 1877–78, and was active in the " Game Club," which successfully produced in the spring a little play called " Andromeda." With the springtime of 1878 a great delight in natural scenery awoke in him, a conscious love of buds and blossoms, rocks, sky, and sea; and in after years he recalled this spring as an epoch in his reflective life. In June he was admitted to Harvard College, and much to his surprise with only two inconsiderable " conditions," namely, Greek grammar and composition.

At that date the Freshman year in Harvard College was a year of required studies, and these studies were little else than a continuation of his uncongenial school studies. He therefore got little pleasure from his regular work ; but he persevered with it, and finished the year clear of all conditions. He did, however, record a thanksgiving that his " classical education " was at last ended. He had a room in the " Yard " and took his meals at Memorial Hall, coming home for Sundays, like students whose families did not live in Cambridge, but yet were not so far away as to make a weekly visit impossible.

His summer yachting was an important element in Charles's education; and in particular the Sunshine gave him good training in writing condensed English. It was the custom to keep a log on board the boat, mentioning the weather, the winds, and the chief events of each day. Charles was always a careful reader and critic of the log. Moreover he acquired the habit of reading all the year round the brief accounts of marine disasters which appeared almost daily in the newspaper taken by the family, accounts which were usually extracts from the logs of the vessels concerned, or were furnished by their masters. As a rule, no words are wasted in log-books. The first time that he kept the log himself was in 1876, when he was nearly seventeen years old. In the following extract from the log of the Sunshine in that summer, the first two days were written by his father, the rest by Charles. The extract will serve to show the mode of life on the yacht, and the interest it had for the two boys and their friends. One or two boy friends and one older guest were generally on board during cruising. On July 25th the yacht was at Boothbay, Maine : —

July 25. Calm. Waiting for J. E. Cabot who did not

arrive. Telegraphing. In P. M. with fresh S. W. ran up Muscongus Sound (visited New Harbor and Round Pond) to Hockamock Channel.

July 26. Still. Variable. Showers. Wind. Ran by Gull and Friendship Islands, and Herring Gut entrance to Rockland. Beat through Muscle Ridge Channel. F. G. Peabody joined. In evening to Rockport.

July 27. With a light breeze, across West Penobscot Bay to Gilkey's Harbor, C. E., R. W. G., and C. W. E. climbing the hill of 700-Acre Island. Thence to Belfast. Thence with a fresh S. E. wind up the Penobscot as far as Bucksport. Mounted the hill by the Seminary in evening.

July 28. Up river to Bangor, a cracking S. E. wind all the way. Anchored off the Kenduskeag at 11 A. M., but later hauled in to the Brewer wharves to avoid tide and steamers. Explored the city of sawmills and enjoyed view from hill back of Seminary.

July 29. R. W. G. took steamer to Boston. A drizzling mist all day. Down river as far as Winterport, stopping at Hampden to visit sawmills and wait for tide. Climbed the Winterport hill in evening to the beautiful Soldiers' Monument.

July 30. Dropped down river with early tide and fanned over to Castine by noon. Walked to the forts in P. M. Sunday School concert at church in evening.

July 31. Rainy and calm all day. Lay at Castine till 3 P. M., then with tide and light air reached Cape Rosier. Found good bottom in Cove, and anchored after a fine sunset. Visited the lone house near by, and talked with intelligent father of seventeen children.

August 1. Cloudless and lovely morning with light northerly air. Ran very slowly across to North Harbor, N. W. side of N. Haven Island. Thence through " Leadbetters Narrows " and " The Reach " to Carver's Harbor, sweeping her through " The Reach " at its narrowest part. Rambled over the quarries, and watched the polishing of granite.

Aug. 2. Early start. Very little wind. Inside Brimstone Island to Isle au Haut. Climbed the highest hill to Coast Survey Beacon, and piled stones to guide future

comers. After dinner, with fine breeze, beat through " Merchant's Row," but wind
failed before reaching
" Burnt Coat Harbor,"
and it was another case
of sweeps and towing.

Narragansett Bay.

Aug. 3. Beat out the
narrow E. entrance of
"Burnt Coat" with very
light air, past Long Is-
land and by Long Ledge
Buoy up Somes Sound.
Fine run up the Sound.
Shopping at Somesville.
Beat down the Sound,
and being caught by
flood tide and calm an-
chored off Fernald's
Point. Mounted Fer-
nald's Hill [Flying Mt.]
in evening. Superb view.

Narragansett Bay.

Aug. 4. Got under
way at about 9 A. M.
Light air to Great Head,
then more breeze, and
took in topsail. Arrived
at Bar Harbor at 11.45.
In P. M. took aboard
Ernest Lovering and
Willie Thayer, visited
Calf Island and an-
chored at Point Harbor
[Sorrento].

Off Portsmouth, N. H.

A certain felicity of expression is already apparent, and
particularly his choice of simple words that fit.

As the Sunshine was constantly visiting bays, rivers, and
harbors previously unknown to all on board, and as it was
not her custom to take a pilot, she was directed by the admirable charts and Coast-pilots published by the U. S. Coast

Survey. In the use and application of these guides Charles early became an adept. When the yacht was approaching an unknown passage or entrance, and it was desirable to recognize the guiding features of the land, Charles was quicker than anybody else on board to discern the characteristic hill, headland, promontory, or island from comparison with the contour charts, or with the profiles and descriptions of the Pilot. He soon learned to conceive from the contour lines the aspect of the land represented, as it would appear on his line of approach. This practice cultivated his perception of the main features of scenery, and made easy his subsequent professional use of surveyors' plans and contour maps. In yachting Charles had the habit of sketching objects which interested him, such as lighthouses, wharves, old houses, or outlines of hills. Reproductions of a few of his sketches are placed on this page and page 19.

A Pier at Newport.

The accompanying profile of the Mt. Desert hills, taken from an island lying about nine miles south of the Mt. Desert shore under Sargent Mountain, fairly illustrates the accuracy

Mt DESERT HILLS FROM GREAT DUCK IS. ME. SEP 5 1852.

| Western. | Beech. | Robinson and Dog. | Brown. | Sargent. | Pemitic. | Green. | Newport. |

The upper profile is a photograph taken from Little Duck Island; the lower is a pencil sketch made by Charles at sixteen from Great Duck Island, looking over and omitting Little Duck. The sketch looks more like the original than the photograph does.

of his boyish work. In another respect this summer mode
of life cultivated his natural tendency to an admiring observation of nature. His watchfulness of the weather on the
yacht and in camp contributed to the development of his
maturer keen enjoyment of the different aspects of the sky.

In 1877 Charles kept the log altogether, and in that year
and often thereafter he was the captain on board, giving all
orders concerning destination, navigation, and piloting. In
September, 1880, he was captain during a cruise from Mt.
Desert to Eastport and back to Boston, a cruise during which
he encountered fogs, storms, the rushing tides of the Bay of
Fundy, and heavy seas, but also enjoyed much fine weather.
This cruise lasted about four weeks. The following extract
from the log-book will show what the captain's responsibilities and pleasures were. The yacht had been weather-bound
for two days at Grand Manan in a northeaster : —

Sept. 12th. Hauled out from the wharf at 6.45 A. M.
Mr. Gaskell would take no wharfage money. With a little
N. W. air we got under way at 7.30 o'clock bound for Boston. Stood close under Swallowtail, and also followed the
shore close under the Six Days Work, and Ashburton and
Bishop Heads. When the tide began to flood we were
becalmed, and consequently were drifted much up the bay.
With some little S. W. airs we stood over to the N. and
made the shore of Campobello Island about midway of its
length. The air grew thicker and thicker, until about noon
the fog-whistles at Quoddy and N. Head began to blow. At
last a respectable S. W. arose and we made N. Head at about
2.30 o'clock. Here we tacked and laid the course for Quoddy
Head. The tide began to ebb about 4.30, but C. E. was un-
willing to try a night outside, and so at 5 P. M. we anchored
in Quoddy Roads. After an early supper the cabin party
got milk and water ashore at Mr. Wormell's house.

Sept. 13th. At about 7 o'clock got under way with a good
S. by W. wind. Sky was pretty clear at this time, but about
8, when we were laying our course alongshore, a very wet fog
surrounded us very suddenly. We made the land 2 or 3
times, and C. E. made up his mind to get into Little River if
he could find the entrance. We tried to make Little River
Head, but on hearing the fog bell at Little River Light we
headed for that. Here the fog cleared up somewhat, and

C. E. changed his mind and kept on. At 9.15 breakfasted. Took a long tack outside of Libby Island, which we had abeam at noon, and stood towards Mark Island of Moos-a-bec Reach. The island was not to be seen owing to a fog bank which began to envelop us when we were S. by E. from the Brothers. C. E. gave up trying to make the Reach, and kept off, passing the Brothers at about 1 P. M. The fog was not very thick, and we followed up Roques Island, and anchored in Shorey's Cove at about 2 P. M. Dined. During the rest of the day the fog was thick and the winds very variable. Whist, etc., in the evening, and boat-racing in the P. M. S. A. E. and deW. beat R. T. and C. E., and William and Orrin. (For some information about the E. entrance to Englishman's Bay, see C. E.'s journal.)

Sept. 14th. Much rain last night: very calm this morning. Sky looking very rainy. At 9 there came a little air from S. E., and we got under way with gafftopsail set, and stood down to the first black buoy in Moos-a-bec Reach, around which we turned, and after crossing the Bar with a fair tide, we anchored in Jonesport at 11 o'clock. Got some provisions ashore, and mailed letters. At a quarter to 12 we were off again with a very gentle N. E. wind and in a heavy rain. Passed slowly through the Reach and down to Nash Island Light, which we passed at 3.45 o'clock. Here C. E. gave up getting around Petit Manan and headed for Shipstern Island, the most western land to be seen. Soon Pond Island appeared through the rain, and we ran in past its northern end. The sky now began to look windy, and we took in the topsail. Passed slowly into Pigeon Hill Bay between Currant Island and Big Pea Ledge, and anchored under Pigeon Hill, just N. of Chitman's Point, at 5 P. M. C. E. got milk ashore on the Point. At about 9 P. M. got out the second anchor, the N. E. wind having begun to blow quite furiously.

Sept. 15th. We anchored in $2\frac{1}{2}$ fathoms yesterday afternoon, but at 3 o'clock this morning C. E. found the yacht aground and the wind blowing a gale. The bottom all over the Bay is level and eel-grassy, and it being low tide the ledges around the Big Pea kept off all the sea. About 3 ft. of water was around the yacht at this time. Knowing that at high tide the riding would be pretty hard, C. E. had the big mooring hoisted out and prepared. At breakfast time (9.30) the yacht was riding pretty easily at 2 anchors, the tide was high, and the wind blowing very hard indeed from N. E. At 1 o'clock the wind went down somewhat, but the heavy rain continued all day. A. Thorndike departed for home via Mill-bridge.

Sept. 16th. A doubtful looking morning. Wind light S. W. Much low cloud driving over our heads towards the N. E. Breakfasted at 7 A. M. and soon after 8 got under way. The tide was nearly high, but still rising, the wind ahead. We beat down Pigeon Hill Bay, paying close attention to the Pilot's description of the dangers, none of which are marked. Took one tack close to Boisbubert Ledge, which was just awash. Stood towards Petit Manan, leaving the Whale, where the sea was combing, to the eastward. Crossed Petit Manan outer bar at about 10.15 o'clock, having a strong ebb tide in our favor. A big rip all along the bar. Fetched Moulton's Rock on the same tack as that on which we crossed the bar, and then stood off shore. When, at 11.10 A. M., Petit Manan bore E. by N. $\frac{1}{2}$ N., we tacked and laid a course outside of Schoodic Island. Passed the island at 11.55, and continuing across the mouth of Frenchman's Bay on the same tack we passed Bunker's Ledge at 1.20. Great fog banks enveloped Mt. Desert, and stretched away down along the mainland to the eastward. Abreast of Sutton Island we ran into this fog region; and thence into S. W. harbor, where we anchored at about 2 o'clock; we had a very wet time of it. S. A. E. went to the P. O., and C. E. to the store. The barometer was now very low, having been falling constantly since the beginning of the last N. E. storm, and C. E. was doubtful about putting to sea again. However, we got up sail again at 3.45, and beat out the Western Way with a good breeze from S. W. by W. Some very dark clouds came over us, and once or twice we got heavy showers of rain. Had to take 2 tacks to weather Bass Harbor Head, and then put into the harbor, where we anchored at 6 P. M. The sky was very handsome during most of the afternoon, with great rolling clouds, and now and then a rift showing the sunlit blue above. A Fusion celebration took place ashore in the evening.

Besides keeping the log, Charles also kept a journal throughout the summer of 1880, in which he entered many particulars about anchorages, provision-stores, approaches to harbors, geological features, and hospitalities given and received. So he got much practice in good writing during this summer. He had so much to record that his constant effort was to write concisely.

Between seventeen and twenty-one Charles suffered a good deal at times from that mental and moral struggle, that questioning of self and the world, which all thoughtful and reserved boys, who have a good deal in them, have to pass through. They become aware that they are thinking and responsible beings, and find themselves forced to consider questions of conscience, faith, and love, and the meaning of life and death. Sudden floods of emotion overwhelm them, and seasons of uncontrollable doubt, misgiving, and sadness distress them. The struggle is apt to be a lonely one. Nobody will or can answer their deeper questions. " I have trodden the wine-press alone." The struggle in Charles's mind was intensified and prolonged by the nature of his voluntary reading. He read much in Emerson, Carlyle, and Goethe ; in Mill, Ruskin, Spencer, Lecky, and Buckle ; in Huxley, Tyndall, Wallace, and Darwin ; and in Lyell, Le Conte, Geikie, and Lubbock. He preferred poetry and history to fiction ; and in all three of these realms of thought he was more open to the sad than to the cheerful aspects of life. He " browsed " in the original texts of Schiller, Lessing, Rousseau, Montaigne, and Victor Hugo, and in translations of Plato, Herodotus, Lucretius, Plutarch, Dante, and Boccaccio. George Eliot had a strong influence on him. He kept a commonplace book for a time while in college, and the headings in this book suggest the seriousness of his meditations. They are : Duty ; The Law of Righteousness ; Materialism versus Idealism ; Belief in Dogma ; Maggie Tulliver ; The Moral Law ; Darwin's Theory of Morals ; Art and Morality ; Beauty and Goodness ; the Pursuit of the Highest ; The Beautiful and the Useful ; Religion ; Measure not with Words the Immeasurable ; Will ; Virtue and Vice ; The Eternal Life of Humanity. In this book he entered extracts from most of the authors above mentioned, and also from James Russell Lowell, John Robert Seeley, George Henry Lewes, Charles Eliot Norton, Edwin Arnold, Arthur Hugh Clough, John Fiske, David Friedrich

Strauss, and William B. Carpenter. It chanced that two of his most intimate friends at this period were young men of a temperament similar to his own; so that his converse with them did not tend to counteract the depressing effects of much of his reading and meditation. At home, on the other hand, the influences about him were wholesome and cheerful, particularly after the summer of 1877; but even there he sometimes felt lonesome or " left out."

In the spring of 1880 his father and mother decided to spend the summer of that year in Europe, and the question arose how Charles and Samuel should pass the vacation. Thereupon Charles organized a party of friends, all of whom were college students, to make use of the Sunshine and the camping outfit at Mt. Desert during the summer. With slight assistance from his father he made the whole plan, and put it into execution himself. He invited twelve persons to become members of a club, and at a second meeting of the persons thus invited, eleven men agreed " to spend at least the number of weeks set against their names at the camp of which Charles Eliot is to be director," two persons agreeing to stay eight weeks, one six, four four, one three, and three two. It was an important element of the plan that each member of the party should do some work in a branch of natural science. There was a " primary assessment of three dollars per week of stay," payable in advance. An additional assessment was levied on each person actually in camp each week. The number in camp at any one time varied from four to eight, the commonest number being six. The assignment of scientific subjects to the members of the club in 1880 included geology, ornithology, marine invertebrates, meteorology, botany, entomology, ichthyology, and photography; and some work was done in every one of these subjects. Charles selected the place of encampment, managed the camp, gave all directions about the use of the yacht, and kept the accounts; and the successful exercise of these functions had a considerable influence on the development of his character. The camp was pitched on July 5th in a beautiful position on the east side of Somes's Sound, a little to the north of the house of Mr. Asa Smallidge, and opposite Flying Mountain and the cliff of Dog Mountain on the western side of the Sound. A clear and abundant brook which descended from Brown's Mountain just north of the camp furnished an excellent supply of water. The Sunshine was moored on the outer edge of the cove just off the camp. This camp was maintained till August 25th, when the party dis-

persed. The geological work of the party was much aided
by a short visit in August from Professor Davis of Harvard
College. Of the young men who took part in this camp, one
turned out to be a landscape architect, one a professor of
cryptogamic botany, and one a physician, while two others,
who are lawyers by profession, retain keen interest in their
respective subjects, and have an ample amateur knowledge of
them.

The Champlain Society, as the club was called in honor of
Samuel de Champlain who named Mt. Desert, was maintained for several years, and two scientific publications resulted from it, one, an " Outline of the Geology of Mount
Desert," by Professor William M. Davis, and the other, a
book on the " Flora of Mount Desert, Maine," by Edward
L. Rand and John H. Redfield. The Society held occasional meetings in Cambridge during the winters, at which
papers were read by various members on their several specialties. In 1881 the camp was pitched again in the same
place, and was carried on under Charles's direction during
that summer much as before, though it was not continued
after the 13th of August. The Society conducted a camp
again in the summer of 1882, but not under the direction of
Charles Eliot.

This experience in the summers of 1880 and 1881 was
very serviceable to Charles. He found that he could plan
and perform executive work, exercise authority over a considerable party, some of whom were older than himself, and
do business and give orders in a manner which satisfied
the interested persons, and led to success in a somewhat
complicated undertaking. He saw that his authority was
respected, and that the participants all enjoyed the camp
and did some serious work. His previous experience on the
yacht of course helped him in the camp ; but the camp was
decidedly the more complex and difficult thing to manage.
At the time of the first camp, he had just finished his Junior
year in college. It will subsequently appear that the plan of
this enterprise resembled in certain respects plans he afterward made for work in connection with the Metropolitan
Parks about Boston. He began to exhibit at this time a
quality which was of great value to him in his professional
life, — he showed that decision, and that persistence in a
plan once conceived, which prevent waste of time for subor-
dinates.

In spite, however, of the increase of self-confidence which
came to him from these summer camps of 1880 and 1881, he

remembered in after years that when camp broke up in August, 1881, and he joined his father and mother in their new house at Northeast Harbor, he there had days of mingled exaltation and dejection. A flood of thought and feeling, such as he had never experienced before, swept over him. His head was full of memories and dreams, of fearful hopes, dreads, and pains; the beauty and the wonder of God's earthly paradise burst upon him like a holy vision, and the depths of the hell on earth opened at his feet.

The new house at Mt. Desert had resulted from his advice. When his father and mother returned from Europe in late September, 1880, Charles said to them : " If you really wish to build a house at Mt. Desert, you had better examine the coast from our camp-ground on Somes's Sound to Seal Harbor. Somewhere on that line you will find a site that will suit you, — a site with beautiful views of sea and hills, good anchorage, fine rocks and beach, and no flats." The father and mother followed his directions in October, explored the shore he had indicated, — on which at that time not a single summer residence had been built, — and found a site of rare beauty on which the new house was built in the spring and summer of 1881. From that good planting came much subsequent delight to three generations of Charles's kindred and friends, the older, his own, and the younger. From the new house, at the end of that season, Charles sailed away in the Sunshine to return to college work. It happened that his mother stayed on through October at Northeast Harbor ; and from Cambridge Charles wrote her letters expressing the strongest affection and gratitude. The following is an extract from one of these delightful letters : —

MY DEAR MOTHER : This is the second Sunday that we 've been away from you. I met father this morning before church, and said, " Is n't this a wretched business, this leaving mother down East ? " and he said it was a total failure, and that he should never do so again. . . . You asked me the other day if I did n't find it interesting to be growing up, and I must say that I do find it so, — very, — and I 'm particularly glad to find one thing, — that I am growing (though only little by little) out of my habit of shrinking from showing my feelings. . . . I 've come to see what a blessed and helpful thing real human sympathy can be, and what a terrible loss it is to live without it. If Mamma had lived, perhaps

I should never have formed this shrinking habit, for I certainly should have continued to go to her with all my joys and troubles. As it is, I know that most people, judging from my conduct, think me indifferent, unenthusiastic; but the fact is that I have felt the enthusiasm, though I have n't shown it. Though I have enjoyed your singing as I have enjoyed nothing else, ever since I first heard you in Phillips Place, it was only the other day that I began to show you this; and now, somehow, it adds greatly to my pleasure in your singing to know that you know that I enjoy it with you. . . . Grandma Peabody wrote to me when you were engaged to father, — " How delightful it will be when a sweet lady takes you into her heart, sympathizes with your pleasures and your cares," — and now I 'm so glad to have found this delight that I can't help telling the sweet lady of it.

His Senior year was somewhat clouded by uncertainty about his profession. His choice of electives, during the three years when election was permitted, was as follows: In the Sophomore year, physical geography under Professor Davis; descriptive chemistry with laboratory work under Professor Jackson; the principles of design under Professor Moore, with much drawing in pencil, ink, sepia, and water colors; and a rapid reading course in German. All these studies he found interesting and good. The required themes and rhetoric he did not enjoy. For his Junior year he chose qualitative analysis under Professor H. B. Hill; Renaissance and Gothic art under Professor Norton; the constitutional history of England and the United States under Professor Macvane; and a second rapid reading course in German. Forensics he liked better than themes; but still required writing was not agreeable to him. In his Senior year he took Professor Norton's course on the history of ancient art; a course with Professor Dunbar on political economy; a course in mineralogy with much laboratory work; and a rapid reading course in French. All his electives he liked well; but he succeeded best in fine arts, science, history, and forensics. He arrived at the end of his Senior year without having any distinct vision of the profession which awaited him, neither he nor his father having perceived his special gifts. Nevertheless, it turned out, after he had settled with joy on his profession, that, if he had known at the beginning of his Sophomore year what his profession was to be, he could

not have selected his studies better than he did with only the
guidance of his likings and natural interests. He took during his last three years in college all the courses in fine arts
which were open to him ; he subsequently found his French
and German indispensable for wide reading in the best literature of his profession ; his studies in science supplied both
training and information appropriate to his calling ; and history and political economy were useful to him as culture
studies and for their social bearings. In the year of his
graduation Charles pasted into one of his scrap-books these
two lines from the " Taming of the Shrew : " —

> " No profit grows where is no pleasure ta'en ; —
> In brief, sir, study what you most affect,"

— an admirable bit of educational philosophy. One of his
Senior forensics was written on the question : " Is college
life so far analogous to that of the world at large that the
conditions of success are the same ? " It begins as follows :
" I want to define, for the purposes of this discussion, the word
' success.' I define success in college to be the attainment of
two things, namely, high standing as a scholar, and influence
as an example of right living. I define success in the world
at large to be the attainment of a sufficient competency, combined with the largest amount of usefulness to one's fellow-
men." These two definitions are both different from the
common ; they combine a direct practical quality with social
idealism. He seemed while in college to have no desire
whatever for either sociability or popularity. He had a few
intimates and a few more acquaintances ; but apparently no
desire for the society of a large number of his fellows. He
was physically incompetent for the competitive athletic sports.
He was asked to join both the Hasty Pudding Club and the
Pi Eta Society, but declined the invitation to the latter, and
did not rectify a misunderstanding about his invitation to the
former. Most of his classmates knew him only by sight.
He went his way comparatively alone in a crowd, and when
he graduated, neither he nor his classmates knew what there
was in him.

In the early winter of 1881–82 his digestion was somewhat disturbed, and he had more headache than usual. As
a precautionary measure, he and his mother made an enjoyable journey to Canada in December. While he was thus
absent his father wrote to him as follows : " I hope you will
not feel in haste to get through with your education, your
' infancy,' or period of training. There is no reason why you

should, and I want you to enjoy a sense of ease and calm in that matter. It would suit me excellent well if you should quietly study for an A. M. next year, or should spend a year in study and reading without aiming at a degree at all. If you would like to have two Senior years and take your A. B. in 1883, I should be entirely content. You need not feel that you ought to be earning your living, or doing something in the actual market-place. That will come soon enough. There are fields of knowledge and philosophy which you have hardly set foot in. Take time to view them with a disengaged mind. The sense of being driven or hurried is very disagreeable to you; then arrange your life so that you cannot be driven or hurried. Nothing in the way of college rank or college degree is of consequence enough to cause you the loss of enjoyment in study and of tranquillity of mind. I want you to have an intellectual delight in study for the study's sake. You have had a large mental growth during the past two years, but have not been as happy in it as I would like to have you. For the rest of your infancy — and do not shorten it — seek quiet and cultivate contentment." This letter shows that his father had no vision of the calling which Charles was so soon to enter upon.

During his Senior year the indigestion from which Charles occasionally suffered of course affected his spirits. It caused some palpitation of the heart, and a painful sort of nervousness. Once or twice he came near giving up college work. The struggle was hardest in the spring months, when he longed to be in the open air all the time. By means of short absences from Cambridge and a careful use of some free hours in each day for out-of-door exercise, he got through the year. He made visits at the Thaxter place near Kittery, at Mt. Desert, and at Washington, beside taking the Quebec journey. By these means he managed to keep at work, and near the end of June he passed his examinations successfully, and in due course received the degree of Bachelor of Arts *cum laude*. As soon as his examinations were over, without waiting for Class Day or Commencement, he started for Mt. Desert, putting a horse and light wagon, which were to be transported to the Mt. Desert house, on board the Bangor boat, landing at Bucksport, and driving thence, via Ellsworth, to Northeast Harbor. His comment on this drive, made to his friend Thaxter, is as follows: " A very beautiful road. Woods, big hills, and many lakes and ponds. Everything very fresh and green. Apples in blossom, and corn about four inches up."

So ended his general education. Regarded as undesigned preparation for his profession, his plays, sports, and completely voluntary labors had obviously been quite as important as the systematic work of school and college.

Prudence Island Light, Narragansett Bay.

CHAPTER III

PROFESSIONAL TRAINING — APPRENTICESHIP

Whatever contributes to better determine or to emphasize natural character is a resource of the art of landscape ; whatever destroys, enfeebles, or confuses that character the art forbids. — HIRSCHFELD.

CHARLES's choice of profession was practically made during the summer of 1882, which he spent at Mt. Desert, partly on shore and partly on the Sunshine. The Champlain Society conducted its summer campaign in a somewhat different manner from that of 1880 and 1881. In those two years they had not succeeded in extending their explorations all over the island. They had skirted its whole shore, and had explored thoroughly the regions within convenient walking distance of the camp. In 1882 they engaged a number of houses in different parts of the island where the members could pass the night or get meals ; so that they could conveniently travel on foot all about the island, and cover the whole ground for geological and botanical exploration. Charles was again much interested in the work of the Society ; but did not live much at the camp, the new house being close by, and the Sunshine being an appendage of the house. During this summer Charles decided on the first step towards his profession, not without much consultation with his father, but still on his own responsibility, and as a result of his own reflection on the modes of life which were possible and desirable for him. He proceeded by the method of elimination, and rejected one after another of the common professions. Next he decided that there was no form of ordinary business which had the least attraction for him. Having established these comprehensive negative propositions, he asked himself, and his father asked him, what he would best like to do in the world. His uncle Robert S. Peabody was well established in Boston as an architect ; and through him Charles had heard something of landscape architecture, because Mr. Peabody was a near neighbor of Mr. Frederick Law Olmsted in Brookline, and from time to time had professional relations with him. The Boston Department of

Parks was already eight years old, and its great services to the public were beginning to be manifest. The occupation of the landscape architect was probably one which not only permitted but required a good deal of open-air life; and its studies and its results seemed to fall in with Charles's natural tastes and desires. Before the end of September he had decided to try to prepare himself for that profession; although as yet he had no very distinct idea of its functions and prospects. This preliminary decision once reached, he and his father both began to perceive how clearly his whole education and experience up to the age of twenty-three pointed to this occupation. On his return from Mt. Desert, he forthwith entered the Bussey Institution, the Department of Agriculture and Horticulture of Harvard University.

In a letter to Roland Thaxter dated October 15th, Charles thus describes his first experience at the Bussey Institution:

I am at the Bussey, and find it very interesting — quite different from college. We are a class of five, with five instructors, — Storer (agricultural chemistry), very interesting; Watson (horticulture), lectures and garden and greenhouse work, also interesting; Slade (applied zoölogy), anatomy of domestic animals, with dissecting, etc., — pretty dry at present, the subject being bones; Faxon (applied botany) has not appeared yet, but will no doubt be interesting; Burgess (applied entomology) does not begin till the second half year; Motley (farm management), a queer old fellow who lectures and takes us on excursions once a week; Dean (topographical surveying), a course given at Cambridge which only three of us take. The practical gardening work is entertaining and tiresome at once, and the same may be said of the surveying. Mr. Storer is a very able lecturer, and ought to have a class of a hundred men at least.

At this time the profession of landscape architecture was hardly recognized in the United States, and there was no regular process of preparing for it. There was no established school for the profession in any American university, and, indeed, not even a single course of instruction which dealt with the art of improving landscape for human use and enjoyment, or with the practical methods of creating and improving gardens, country-seats, and public parks. The course of instruction at the Bussey Institution did, however, deal both theoretically and practically with several subjects of fundamental importance in the landscape art, and supplied the best preliminary training for the profession which was then accessible; although it offered nothing on the artistic side of large-scale landscape work.

The Bussey Institution is situated on a magnificent estate southwest from Boston proper, and seven miles from the Cambridge site of the University. For greater convenience of access to the Institution, Charles spent the fall and winter of 1882–83 partly at the house of one of his Eliot aunts (Mrs. Charles E. Guild), which was near the Bussey Institution, and partly at his grandmother Peabody's in Boston. Mrs. Guild's house commanded a charming view of the Great Blue Hill, and was close to the beautiful region which afterwards became Franklin Park. The variety of places about Boston in which Charles lived at one time or another was an important element in his preparation for some of his best professional work in after years. During the winter his father had opportunities at the Saturday Club of talking with Mr. Frederick Law Olmsted about the means of preparing a young man for Mr. Olmsted's profession; and Professor Norton, who had formed a good opinion of Charles's capacity, had also opportunities of interesting Mr. Olmsted in him. Finally, on the 22d of April, 1883, his uncle, Robert S. Peabody, introduced him to Mr. Olmsted at Brookline. There resulted from this interview an invitation for Charles to enter Mr. Olmsted's office as an apprentice, an invitation which Charles promptly accepted; for Mr. Olmsted was at the head of his profession, and had had a hand in almost every considerable park-work that had been attempted in the country. He had at the time a large business in landscape designing of many kinds, both public and private. By the 29th of April Charles was established in Mr. Olmsted's office, and on that day he set out with Mr. Olmsted on a short journey of work-inspection. His courses at the Bussey Institution were thus somewhat abruptly interrupted; but he had already got from them much valuable information, and he had assured himself that he wished to be a landscape architect; for he found attractive and interesting all the various knowledges which contributed to the practice of that profession.

Mr. Olmsted was sixty years old, and not very strong in body; so that it was well for him to be accompanied on his frequent journeys by a young man who could relieve him of

all care in travelling, and could make notes and write letters
for him.   Charles writes on May 13th to his friend Thaxter :
" I am to go about with Mr. Olmsted, and am expected to
gather the principles and the practice of the profession in the
course of this going.   I am to be of what service I can, and
this, if I am to judge by ten days' experience, will consist
chiefly in doing draughtsman's work, making working-drawings from preliminary design-plans, etc.   I have already had
a little journey with Mr. Olmsted to Newport and Providence, and learned much and enjoyed more.   I expect to give
two years to this apprentice education, and then hope to
study and travel abroad.   I have a high idea of what a landscape architect should be, and a high ideal of what his art
should be ; and you may believe that I was highly excited by
this sudden plunge into the midst of things.   The world says
I am a lucky fellow, and congratulates me on all sides."

    Charles kept an interesting record of his various trips with
Mr. Olmsted and other persons connected with the firm, a
record which shows how very instructive to him were these
opportunities of observing work in progress.   The work which
Mr. Olmsted had in hand at that time was of great variety.
Thus, on the first excursion Charles made with Mr. Olmsted,
they visited the Town Hall of North Easton, Mass. (by H. H.
Richardson), which is set on craggy rocks made apparently
higher by removing earth at the base.   Broad, easy flights
of steps with ample landings, and well fitted to the jutting
ledges, lead up to the main door of the hall ; a natural growth
of deciduous wood flanks the building on the uphill side ;
while the pockets in the rocks about the building are planted
with Honeysuckles, Prostrate Juniper, Yucca, and Sedums.
A remarkable soldiers' monument (of the Civil War) stands
before the hall at a meeting of three roads.   It consists of an
irregular pile of large boulders brought together from far
and near, and forming a sort of cairn, on the highest point of
which is a flagstaff.   Every chink in the pile is crammed with
peaty soil, and about the foot of the higher rock-walls runs a
deep bed of rich earth.   Here were planted Kalmias, Andro-
medas, Rhodoras, Daphnes, wild Roses, and Honeysuckles,
the tallest plants in the rear of the bed.   From North Easton
they went to a Newport estate, which was originally a completely bare field at the end of a point commanding a wide
sea-view.   Here Charles records that the bare and gentle
slope from the house to the shore is to be left entirely un-
planted, since any elaborate gardening or planting would be
utterly inappropriate.   Another estate in Newport in the

older part of the city was to be improved by Mr. Olmsted by removing trees from the old neglected plantations, and developing the principal lawn. A walling-off of a kitchen and stable court was earnestly recommended by Mr. Olmsted. Thence they went to Providence to study a design for grounds about a new suburban mansion set in one corner of what had been a large village lot. Here the gardener was instructed to plant, always irregularly, three or four of the to-be-large trees together, all but one of which were to come out by and by ; to mix shrubs with the trees ; to use shrubs to break the edges of the plantations ; and to see that there were no sharp lines between groups of this and groups of that. All the walls about the estate were to be vine-clad — English Ivy on the shady side of the house and in other sunless corners, Virginia Creeper on the brick walls, and Japanese Ivy on the stone posts. One can easily see how instructive and interesting such days as these were to the receptive disciple.

Shortly after this excursion Charles spent a delightful day with Mr. Olmsted on Cushing's Island in Portland Harbor, Mr. Olmsted having been called on to advise the owners of the island about laying it out as a seashore resort. Mr. Olmsted's advice included the enlargement of the brick hotel ; the reservation of a considerable area near it for hotel cottages ; the making of play-grounds for common use by all the island people ; the laying out of about fifty house-lots on the island, small on the landward and smooth part of the island, larger on the ocean shore where the building sites are finest ; the reservation of White Head at one end of the island, and of the southwest point at the other end, these two to be connected by a wide strip down the middle of the island along the highest ridge, whence views can be had in both directions at once. The whole shore was to be common to all the inhabitants. The Spruces on the island being badly blighted, Mr. Olmsted recommended that Pine seed should be sown among the dying Spruces, so as to have a growth to fall back on, when the Spruces should necessarily be removed. To clear away the present forest immediately would not be safe ; for the mosses, ferns, and other undergrowth might be lost.

The greater part of Charles's time was of course spent in the office, and his work there consisted in making sketches, enlarging or reducing plans, calculating earth-work, making preliminary studies for laying out grounds, some private, some public, and some belonging to schools and colleges ; and finally, often after repeated reconsideration and revision by the master, in preparing working-drawings, with all their elaborate details of figuring, lettering, and coloring. Before Charles had been six months in the office, he was making sketch-plans and working-drawings in considerable variety, and occasionally freehand drawings to accompany letters which explained designs. He also prepared not infrequently what he called " show maps," that is, maps intended to interest prospective buyers in estates which it was proposed to cut up into house-lots. He acquired considerable skill in both mechanical and freehand drawing; and gradually came to prefer for his own use the least elaborate sort of drawing. A drawing which was clear, easily interpreted, and as accurate as the methods which were to be used in working from it on the ground, always answered his purpose. The preparation of planting-maps was also a part of his work, and, in connection with these designs, he received much instruction from Mr. Olmsted and his assistants, — instruction relating to the kinds of plants which could be advantageously used on the different soils and in the different climates of the United States, and to the best mode of disposing plants in groups. He was taught to distrust specimen planting, — that is, the use of single specimens of plants in an ambitious variety, — and also to be cautious about using plants the hardiness of which had not been demonstrated by the experience of many seasons. While plants of various merits would naturally be used, — as, for example, plants with colored stems, handsome blooms, or foliage remarkably beautiful in spring, summer, or autumn, — preference should always be given to such trees and shrubs as will certainly thrive and come to perfection under the climatic and soil conditions of the places where they are to be put, and the planting should be in masses. The ordering of plants for private places, both in the country and by the seaside, was an instructive part of Charles's practice in the office. He learnt what the most desirable and trustworthy plants were, what appropriate effects could be produced on sites of various kinds, where the plants desired could be most advantageously purchased, and how the satisfaction of proprietors with the planting could be best assured. In making plans for the approaches to private houses, Charles was early initiated into the importance of frankness about the kitchen region. Some proprietors would rather pretend that they had no back door, kitchen garden, or stable; but Mr. Olmsted always advised perfect frankness about the whole service region, the convenience of every household requiring that wagons should be able to stand at the back door, and stables and kitchen gardens being indispensable adjuncts of every large establishment.

By frequent visits, often with some specific object in view, Charles became familiar with the Arnold Arboretum, — a collection of all the trees, shrubs, and herbaceous plants which will thrive in the New England climate, — to which a considerable portion of the Bussey estate had been devoted by an agreement between the University and the City of Boston. Here was a precious opportunity to study the materials available for artificial plantations. It fortunately happened that in the winter of 1884–85 the planting-plans of the Arboretum, which were originally made by Mr. Olmsted, had to be thoroughly revised in view of ultimate extensions of the Arboretum. Charles worked on the new drawings, and it was a great advantage to him that he was thus obliged to study carefully systematic planting in a very large collection, in which not only a great variety of species was to be exhibited, but fine specimens of each species as well.

Sundays and occasional half-holidays Charles contrived to utilize for walks and drives. Under date of Sunday, May 27, 1883, he writes : —

Delightful spring weather. Woods full of delicate tints and shades of color, and soft and feathery with the young leafage. Thickets still more or less transparent, and horse-chestnuts and some maples as yet the only trees that are solid against the sky. This Sunday a delicious drive to Belmont and over Wellington Hill with E. L. B. [one of his Eliot aunts]. Apples in bloom, Judas-trees out, and many flowering shrubs in their glory.

Towards the end of September, 1883, he made a short visit at Mt. Desert, at the end of which he records : —

What with Mother, Sally Norton, and Sam, there was much good music. On last Sunday evening the music — mostly gentle and tender — went straight to my heart of hearts as music seldom has before. I hope that, some day or other, work of mine may give some human being pleasure, pleasure of that helpful kind which beauty of music and of scenery gives me.

Charles continued to profit very much by casual but fruitful suggestions which he received from Mr. Olmsted during the inspection-tours on which he accompanied him. Thus, when visiting Easton's Pond at Newport in 1883, — a shallow lagoon behind the bathing-beach, largely overgrown with sedges, and partly filled with blown sand from the beach, — Mr. Olmsted suggested a treatment of the unsightly pond which foreshadowed the method afterward so admirably used at the Chicago Fair. He proposed to the city to dredge an irregular water-basin, and with the material so obtained to raise the level of the remaining area, thus making land and water of a place then neither the one nor the other. On the same occasion, Mr. Olmsted pointed out that any large structure, like a city bathing-house, on the sandy and surf-beaten beach would appear wholly incongruous and out of place. This hint bore fruit in Charles's mind thirteen years afterward on Revere Beach, one of the Boston Metropolitan reservations. A visit to the Capitol grounds at Washington was very instructive. Charles here noted that an immense, massive building requires visibly firm and broad ground-support, and adequate and dignified approaches ; that curved drives and foot-paths must be justified by some necessity of climbing by easy grades ; that there should be no curves for the curves' sake, unless in absolutely formal gardening on a small scale ; that single conifers tend to betray the small size of a piece of ground, acting as exclamation marks or measuring-poles ; that the scheme of planting round a building should consider the permanent visibility of the best aspects of the building on the one hand, and, on the other, should provide for the obscuring of the necessary spaces of gravel and asphalt.

By reading Mr. Olmsted's printed writings, by listening to his conversation, and going over the letters he wrote about new undertakings, Charles soon absorbed the fundamental principles which had long guided Mr. Olmsted in his landscape work. Mr. Olmsted always desired to emphasize in park-work the antithesis between the objects seen in city streets and the objects of vision in the open country. He thought that trimmed trees, flowers in pots, clipped grass, and variegated flower or foliage beds savored of the city, or at least of the suburb ; and he preferred for the purpose of refreshing a city population, undulating meadows fringed with trees, quiet, far-stretching pastoral scenery, and groves which preserved the underbrush and the rough surface of the natural forest. Paths, roads, resting-places, and restaurants were always to be regarded as the necessary facilities for enabling the population to enjoy the essentially restful elements of park scenery. These artificial features were not the objects of any landscape undertaking, but its necessary impediments.

Although in general Charles had the greatest admiration for his master, and sympathized completely with his general principles in landscape work, he took the liberty of exercising his own independent judgment about some of Mr. Olmsted's designs. A high degree of complication and artificiality in a design never pleased him. Within three months of his entrance into the Olmsted office, he records his objections to the design for a small suburban lot in which stood a house and stable, partly of brick and partly of wood. "The cramped turn at the door, the brick wall around it, the handsome but far-fetched and out-of-place boulders, the equally improbable made valley with its boulder bridge across a dry brook, make it altogether the least pleasing work of Mr. Olmsted's I have yet seen."

In connection with various pieces of work which were in hand during the years 1883 and 1884, Charles had steady guidance towards fundamental principles of landscape work which he was already well prepared to accept and transmit. Thus, in one New England city the owner of a large estate had given the city a tract of land of varied and delightful interest, comprising a steep gravelly shore with its islands and peninsulas of drift all clothed with woods, rocky spots overgrown with wild verdure, and groves of large trees. It commanded also a noble prospect from the top of its hill. The park commissioners appointed by the city expected a general smoothing of everything, — a cutting down of the rough sumacs and brambles, and a making of nicely kept lawns with flower-beds and plantations of fancy trees and shrubs. Mr. Olmsted advised against all such work. He regarded the park-land in its actual condition as a fine piece of rural scenery, to be religiously preserved so far as the use and enjoyment of the place by the public would permit, as a scene of quiet character, graceful and picturesque by turns, in which only such changes and additions should be permitted as would bring out still further the prevailing character of the place, — such work, for instance, as the removal of stone walls and fences, the cutting out of the poorest trees, and the planting of indigenous trees and thickets in furtherance of nature.

One of the important works of which Mr. Olmsted had charge during Charles's apprenticeship was the Belle Isle Park of Detroit. The river is the pleasure resort of Detroit. There are many excursion steamers; there is always a breeze;

and great numbers of lake-craft are to be seen.   Belle Isle itself is a flat, wet island, two miles long by half a mile broad, with a thin soil and a clayey subsoil.   The highest point is but six feet above the level of the river, and many acres are subject to flood.   The interior is well wooded with Elm, Oak, and Hickory, of natural but too close growth.   The chief elements of Mr. Olmsted's plan were drainage by means of a system of canals with tile drains discharging into them, and gates and pumps to keep the canals at the normal level when the river should be in flood.   The shores of the island were wearing away ; so it was a part of the plan to give the exposed parts of the shore a beach form with a grade of one in six. The quality of the natural woods was allowed to determine the character of the park.   The usual park woods were out of the question, owing to the spindling form of the trees ; but the interest of the existing woods was heightened by open-ing glades, by judicious thinning, and by breaking into the edges.   The scheme involved the raising of the roadways by means of the material derived from the canals, in order to ensure the dryness of the driveways even immediately after rain.   On this design, with its landing-pier and other acces-sories, Charles worked a long time as a draughtsman, his interest in the drawings being greatly stimulated by visits to the locality.   The steamboat pier presented many complica-tions of curvature and structure.   It had two decks and a roof, and inclined planes on brackets leading to the second deck.   The line of the eaves was undulating, and the roof was full of curvature.   The ridge rose and fell according to the width of the deck below, and the section of the roof varied with every wave of the eaves-line.   It will easily be seen that such a complicated design cost the draughtsman much labor, particularly as the design was repeatedly modified.   After all, it was never built.

Another very interesting project which was in the office some months, and on which Charles frequently worked as a draughtsman, was the layout of the grounds of the Lawrence-ville School, at Lawrenceville, N. J., the school buildings be-ing simultaneously designed by Messrs. Peabody & Stearns, his uncle's firm.   The designing of these spacious grounds and numerous buildings was an interesting piece of work, such as is very seldom presented to a landscape architect and an architect together.   The estate was handsome and ade-quate ; and the buildings were to be erected simultaneously on a well-studied scheme.

In the autumn of 1883 work was active on the Back Bay

Fens, and Charles had ample opportunities of watching its progress. At the end of November he records the interesting variety of work which was going forward there. The great dredge was digging into the existing marsh across the channel near the gate-house, and the material there obtained was going to fill the promontory which was to carry Westland Avenue across the reservation. Men and teams were carrying marsh-mud from the vicinity of Westland Avenue and spreading it over the bare gravel slopes near Beacon Street. Teams were carrying marsh-sod for the shores and coves between Boylston and Beacon streets. Trains were bringing gravel for filling, and good soil from the new Sudbury River water-basins of the Boston Water Works; and men with barrows were spreading this loam on the finished slopes north of Boylston Street. Carts were bringing quantities of suitable manure to compost heaps which were being prepared for use when planting should begin in the spring; and plants were arriving and being heeled-in close to Beacon Street, so as to be handy in the spring. He noted, also, the quantities of plants received at the Fens for planting at the opening of the season of 1884.

At this time the Boston and Albany Railroad was rebuilding many of its stations, and laying out, under Mr. Olmsted's direction, the grounds about them. With all these plans Charles was familiar, and on many of them he worked. He came to value more and more a good topographical survey of an estate or region for which he was to prepare road-plans or a division into house-lots; and his test of the excellence of the engineer's plan was the amount of revision which his own plans, made in the Brookline office, required when with these plans in hand he visited the ground. On a good topographical survey he maintained that he could do his own work as well in the office as on the ground, and often better, — particularly in the laying out of roads. For owners he thought it a real economy to get a good survey.

During February, 1884, he made some progress in gathering material for a paper on the History of Mount Desert, which he proposed to read before the Champlain Society; and in due time he presented the results of his researches to the society. At times there was not work enough in the office during Mr. Olmsted's absences to keep both Mr. J. C. Olmsted and Charles busy. At such moments Charles turned with pleasure to the study of the best authors on landscape architecture, and to out-of-door excursions. In the spring of 1884 he had leisure to copy many citations from the best authors on his subject. In the winter of 1883–84 Charles worked for some weeks on the City Point design made for the Boston Park Commission, one of the most interesting of the many designs of extraordinary originality and utility which the city of Boston owes to Mr. Olmsted's genius. It included two long piers, facilities for bathing, rowing, and sailing, the improvement of Castle Island, — which belongs to the government of the United States, — a small artificial island as a pier-head, and several buildings for the accommodation of the public. The whole was planned with great forethought and a vivid conception of the needs of the future. On all the details of these plans Charles worked with enthusiasm, in company with Mr. J. C. Olmsted; and when the great design was itself nearly finished, he prepared a reduced map of Boston Bay to serve as a key-map to accompany the City Point design. This public reservation, which is not yet completely executed, though it has long been in use, stands as one of the best monuments of the genius of its designer.

On all the journeys Charles took during his apprenticeship, he made notes of the landscape through which he passed. It was a great pleasure to him just to ride rapidly through fine country, though he could only see the alternating woods and fields, the cultivated valley-bottoms, the fields of buttercup or clover or white-weed, the various shades of green in the growing crops, and the moulding of the hillsides. He always noted, also, the prevailing industries of the regions through which he passed. If it was a coal region, for example, he observed the picturesque, ungainly shaft-houses and breakers, the great waste dumps, and the miserable hovels of the miners. If it was a Western city, he observed the mode of planting the streets, the addition of the radial system of streets to the rectangular, and the quality of the houses, pretentious or simple, commonplace or picturesque, of the Greek portico period or the Queen Anne. Of course he always visited any public parks which lay in his way ; and before long he was familiar with the parks of Baltimore, Philadelphia, New York, Brooklyn, and Buffalo.

In the opening months of 1884 he began to record in his commonplace book the action of the various public bodies with which Mr. Olmsted dealt in carrying on his chief works. He noted the appropriations made, and the conditions attached to the appropriations. On a single day at the end of March, 1884, he records the condition of fourteen different undertakings which were then under way, part of them public parks, part school, college, and railway grounds, part real estate speculations, and part grounds of private owners. He was thus studying the conditions under which both public and private landscape work had to be carried on. By the summer of 1884 he had begun to pay attention to contract prices for dirt roads, stoned roads, drains supplied and laid, silt basins, and stone walls. The prices of such construction varied, of course, in different parts of the country; but as work of this description often enters into landscape work, whether of large scale or small, he found it desirable to inform himself concerning its cost. He began to classify trees and shrubs in his mind according to their uses. For example, he made lists of plants in the summer of 1884 suitable for the following objects : for the seaside, for cascade planting, for covering ground under thick-growing trees, for autumn beauty of foliage or fruit, for autumn flowering, for high exposed places, and for bare or rocky places.

The winter of 1884–85 Charles spent at his father's house in Cambridge, going to and from the Brookline office on horseback or by wagon. His office work during the autumn was chiefly draughting on a variety of private places, all instructive, but less interesting to Charles than public work. Near the end of October, 1884, he took time to lay out a new approach road to his father's house at Mt. Desert, and did a considerable quantity of planting about the roads and the house, using only plants native to the place, such as Birches, Spruces, Ashes, Oaks, Pines, Golden-rod, Blueberry, Huckleberry, wild Roses, wild Asters, Brakes, and Ferns, and carefully avoiding the introduction of grass. The only plants he used which were not absolutely native were Virginia Creeper, Clematis, Honeysuckle, and a Japanese Willow.

The study of the Arboretum planting-plans, which began in January, 1885, continued at intervals during the spring of that year, and was very profitable to Charles. He also worked at this time on the Franklin Park plans, which were then developing in Mr. Olmsted's office. This great project was at that time referred to in Charles's notes as the West Roxbury Park. He labored on the design until the close of his service as an apprentice. The last entries in his diary during his apprenticeship relate to large-scale drawings of what was then called the Corso in the West Roxbury Park, now the Greeting in Franklin Park. On the 1st of April Charles makes the laconic remark in his diary: "No more draughting," and thereupon his service as an apprentice seems to have ceased, although he was frequently at the office during the spring. He also worked at the Arboretum, staking out shrub beds from plans he had helped to prepare. It was not till the 31st of May that he wrote a letter of farewell to Mr. Olmsted thanking him for the instruction he had received and for the great privilege of working under his direction.

After the 1st of April that spring, he renewed his connection with the Bussey Institution by attending there a course of lectures on horticulture and arboriculture by Mr. Benjamin M. Watson. He also began to make a collection of dried plants, confining himself, however, to those trees, shrubs, and other plants which would be useful in his professional work. Mr. Watson's class was often carried through the Arboretum, so that Charles had further opportunities of becoming familiar with this comprehensive collection. During this period of collecting, Charles took many walks with congenial friends through the wild parts of what is now known as the Metropolitan District. He thus completed his knowledge of the flora of the district, not from the point of view of a botanist, but from that of the student of scenery. He covered in these walks the whole half-circle from Nahant, Lynn, and East Saugus, on the north, by the Middlesex Fells, Belmont, Lincoln, and Waltham, through Wellesley and the Newtons, by Dedham, Readville, Hyde Park, Milton, and Quincy, to the south shore. He also spent several days on the upper parts of the Charles River, renewing his acquaintance with the most beautiful parts of that stream. These excursions bore ample fruit in later years.

He travelled during the summer and autumn of 1885 into other States, visiting Newport and Bridgeport, the popular seashore resorts in the vicinity of New York city, Greenwood Cemetery and Prospect Park in Brooklyn, Sandy Hook, and Long Branch. On this journey he spent several profitable days in the Bridgeport Park, which he had visited two years before. His notes of botanical observations on this journey cover thirty-five pages, and relate to the flowers and shrubs in bloom at that season, to the materials of hedges and of vine coverings for walls, to decoration by tub-plants and greenhouse exotics, to the extraordinary defacing of the beaches accessible from New York by badly placed hotels, shops, and pile-work, to the selection of plants in the great parks of Brooklyn, New York, and Philadelphia, to the autumnal condition of the parks as regards flowers and the foliage of the less familiar trees and shrubs. At Sandy Hook he was at pains to make a list of the luxuriant vegetation which covered

the sand. He admired greatly the fine old Cedars of all shapes
and habits, — many intensely blue in color, by reason of great
quantities of berries, — the thrifty Sumacs, the vast quantity
of poison Ivy and Golden-rod, and the interesting sand grasses
or sedges. During his stay at the Beardsley Park at Bridgeport, he made twenty-three pages of notes, relating to plant
hardiness, to changes of color in the course of the season, to
spread, to color of bark, twigs, or foliage, to power of resist-
ance to cold, ice, and drought, and to strength or rankness of
growth, and consequent tendency to kill out weaker plants.

In a letter to his mother he tells how he passed a Sunday
at Bridgeport : —

Yesterday was a delightful day — the sky partly cloudy, so
that it was not too hot for walking. I tramped out over some
pretty roads and lanes, not caring whither, and by and by
came in sight of some church spires rising from a fine mass
of woods. Slowly I travelled towards them, and discovered a
very pretty village hidden under the trees, and hard by the
churches a little inn — the Fairfield Hotel — where I got a
good dinner. In the afternoon I returned by a still crookeder
course than that of the morning, climbed some gentle hills,
got many delightful views of the shadow-flecked country,
investigated many woodsides and shrubberies, and enjoyed
myself highly.

Whenever in his travels he found himself in the vicinity
of a large nursery, he invariably explored its resources, and
made himself acquainted with its prices and its methods of
work.

From Bridgeport, in the midst of these labors, he wrote to
his intimate friend Roland Thaxter : —

Why did n't you come along with me ? . . . I approve less
than ever of travelling alone. I have not had a soul to speak
to for fourteen long days and nights, and I think another
fourteen would probably drive me mad. How in Heaven's
name am I ever to spend nine months in Europe ? I can't.

He allowed himself but a short vacation this year, and that
was spent at beloved Mt. Desert.

On the 14th of September he started for Washington, Virginia, and the southern peaks of the Appalachian range, visiting
with several older friends, Natural Bridge, Roan Mountain,

Burnsville, Marion, Asheville, Charleston, Great Smoky Mountain, Nantahala, Hiawassee, and Highlands, whence he returned to Asheville. On this journey he saw forests of a different character from those of New England, and a population whose history, traditions, and habits were very unlike those of the New England people. From Roan Mountain he wrote thus to his mother : —

Thus far our trip has been very enjoyable. The valley of the Shenandoah is very beautiful in a soft and fertile way, the Natural Bridge is far finer than the Geography picture would lead one to expect, and this mountain, and the approach to it, are grand and lovely at once.

In the limestone gorges near the Bridge grow Cercis and Ptelea and other trees not seen North, beside large and fine specimens of Sassafras, Magnolia, Linden, Beech, and Hemlock, and many fine shrubs. In the mountain passes climbed by the narrow-gauge railroad on its way to the Cranberry Forge and the foot of this mountain, grow acres of Rhododendron and Kalmia, with Holly and Oxydendron and Aralia, and Andromeda in variety. The most beautifully wooded hillsides I ever saw. Then the flanks of the mountain (which it took us seven hours to climb) are clothed with a great forest of large timber trees, among which are nineteen species attaining such size that clean logs fifty feet long can be got from them. None of this is yet cut save the Cherry. Near the top conifers take possession, and — wonderful to relate — the summit, which is some three miles long, is almost wholly in grass, great thickets of Rhododendron and some patches of Fir with occasional Mountain Ash being the only trees of the place. Fine ledges crop out at a few points, and give glorious views over a vast stretch of wooded mountains, only one or two of which are higher than this.

Later he wrote to her about the journey as follows : —

We saw a great deal in our three weeks of travel — much beautiful scenery — some magnificent forests of large trees — innumerable beautiful shrubs and flowers — and a few very interesting human beings — all men ! Much of the country we rode through is but just being settled — we found one new colony made up largely of New Englanders, and in another place a little band of Germans. The few mountain valleys that were occupied before the war have not yet recovered from the killing off of their men. In these parts the war-times still monopolize conversation. The mountains abounded in Unionists, and their trials and adventures make fine stories. Men are now living in the same valley who burned each others' houses in the war-time — and in Swain County almost everybody seems to have shot a man. Everywhere the people are shiftless and ignorant, and have plenty of time to waste in hunting, and in attending Court at the county-seat. Whole families travel to town, and women carry babies into the court-room to watch the progress of the shooting cases. In all the western counties of North Carolina only one man has been hanged since the war.

On his return he spent a week at Natural Bridge, having been recommended by Mr. Olmsted to Colonel Parsons, the proprietor of over 2000 acres of diversified lands, to help him about thinning the woods and making cuttings for roads and vistas. Although Colonel Parsons gave him his board and lodging in consideration of his services, and these were his first professional earnings, he by no means regarded himself as practising his profession, but rather as trying his 'prentice hand. To his mother he described this experience as follows :

My week at Natural Bridge was very pleasant. I was out every morning and afternoon, nearly half the time with Colonel Parsons. As I never had more than two axemen, results are not very tremendous. We attempted only easy work giving immediate effects — breaking up straight edges of woods — opening vistas — clearing to bring out fine trees — and opening lines through the woods for two new roads.

Returning homeward through Philadelphia, he made there a stay of several days to refresh his knowledge of the admirable parks of that city. In a note to his mother he speaks with delight of the Cumberland valley, — "the most ideal farming country I ever saw." By the middle of October he was again in Cambridge. He now began to prepare for a year of travel in Europe, in execution of the purpose he had formed when he first entered Mr. Olmsted's office, — largely on his advice that for the education of a landscape architect much observation of many kinds of scenery was indispensable. On November 5th he took steamer for Liverpool, and on the 14th arrived in England for the third time in his life. His own country was in great part rough and wild, and its large agglomerations of population were but recent; he was going to see what landscape and scenery had become in regions which had been occupied by man for many centuries, and what rural delights remained possible for the population of great cities a thousand years old.

The placing of a new house on top of a high rock close to the sea, too near the public road, and surrounded by rough ledges between which grow Bay, Sumac, Juniper, Huckleberry, and the like. The shore is bold and surf-beaten.

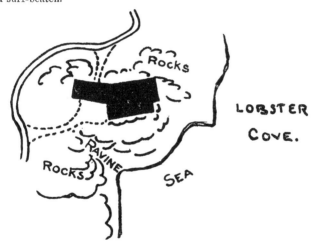

Mr. Olmsted's design for the avenues (1883). The approach-road passes between two big ledges, and goes under one wing of the house. No proper grade could in any way be obtained short of the distance to the other side of the house. The turning space on the seaward side of the house, and the road which leads out across the head of the little ravine are held by low retaining-walls. (C. E.'s note-book.)

CHAPTER IV

LANDSCAPE STUDY IN EUROPE. LONDON AND PARIS

> Invention, strictly speaking, is little more than a new combination
> of those images which have been previously gathered and deposited in
> the memory, — nothing can come from nothing; he who has laid up
> no materials can produce no combinations. — SIR JOSHUA REYNOLDS.

CHARLES went to Europe to study, just as much as if it
had been possible for him to settle down at a university like
a student of languages, history, or philosophy; but his
objects and methods were necessarily very different from
those of the ordinary student. His first object was to examine public parks and gardens, private country-seats and
suburban house-lots, nurseries, and public collections of trees
and plants. Next, he needed to study in the great art-
museums paintings of landscape, that he might learn what
sort of scenes the masters of landscape painting had thought
it worth while to depict. Then, he wanted time to acquaint
himself with the bibliography of his subject, and to read the
works of some of the chief authors, where he could grasp
the European conditions, both climatic and social, under
which they were written. Finally, whenever the weather and
the situation permitted, he observed scenery and studied its
parts and its composition.

From the start, November 5, 1885, to October 7, 1886,
he kept a journal, and he maintained through all the year
of his absence a tolerably regular correspondence with his
father and mother, five female cousins, two male cousins,
and two college friends. He also made lists of plants and
books, and numerous sketches and diagrams as notes of
scenes and designs. This large amount of writing was chiefly
done in the evenings or in bad weather. It proved to be a
very valuable part of his year's work; for it gave him practice in a graphic, condensed, and interesting style of writing
which was subsequently of great advantage to him.

The journal begins with the voyage to Liverpool. "There
never was a smoother or more prosperous voyage." His
letters describe some of his fellow-passengers, most of whom

he found uninteresting. " Sunday I was assailed by my
room-mate on the subject of becoming a ' Christian ; ' and
also by a Methodist gentleman of emotional character who
wept over me." But there was one party from Philadelphia
which engaged his attention, — " a Mrs. Beadle, who was a
Miss Yale, Mr. Beadle her son, and three young ladies, a
Yale and two Pitkins, — all, I believe, of Philadelphia. The
eldest Miss Pitkin is very good to look at, and I must confess that after I was at length (on the fourth day) introduced to her, the voyaging became much more agreeable."

At Liverpool he began at once the study of the parks, and
presented a letter of introduction from Mr. Olmsted to Mr.
Kemp, —

a jovial old Englishman, very cordial and agreeable, — a
man who has worked hard in his profession in his day, and
who seemed interested in my account of the works going on
in our country. He told me that his profession was lan-
guishing in England ; that proprietors were all too ready to
accept the services of nurserymen instead of landscape gardeners proper, and that the results of this practice were
necessarily inartistic and bad. The nurseryman offers his
services as designer for little or no pay, getting his reward
from the plants he supplies. . . . It is impossible for him to
have an eye solely directed to his client's interest and the
interest of good design.

Birkenhead Park he found excellent as regards both
grading and planting ; but Sefton Park seemed to him bad,
and he records his opinion with great candor. After his
inspection of Prince's and Sefton Parks, —

feeling like walking, I kept on towards the country, and
discovered Mossley Hill, a little suburban district of beautifully planted grounds and gardens, which I enjoyed very
much. Most of the places are on the American scale. The
houses are brick or stone, and the grounds, whether large
or small, shut off from the path by high walls grown with
Ivy. Evergreens, such as Hollies, Laurels, Arbutus, and
Laurustinus, make the plantations very beautiful, even at
this season. Primulas, Violets, Wallflowers, and so forth,
are abundantly used in the foregrounds, and under the
shrubs. Then I also had a glimpse of real country, with

hedgerows and farmsteads; and a look at a small village of tenantry, with its church, school, and inn — newish, and looking as if built to order, but very neat, and orderly, and petite.

Another gala day he spent at Chester, a place he had visited when a boy. "Almost the last thing in our walk about the walls, we came upon the so-called Phœnix Tower, which I have remembered well all these years — the Tower from which King Charles saw his army defeated at Rowton Moor." That night he passed at the house of a hospitable Englishman who had visited Harvard University; and the next morning he had the advantage of examining his host's grounds, which had been designed by Mr. Kemp, and were adorned with many plants new to him.

On Saturday, November 20th, he went up to London and took rooms with his steamer acquaintance, Mr. Beadle, in Southampton Row, Russell Square. Then followed a week of sight-seeing in London, some parks being always taken in the daily route. When the weather was too bad for walking, the British Museum, close by his lodgings, was his resort. The whole daylight of one day he gave to the Kensington Museum, where the great collections of architectural casts, sculpture, and stucco work especially interested him.

Thursday, November 26th, was Thanksgiving Day at home; but in London it was "very dark, too dark for collections or interiors. . . . The atmosphere and weather generally are utterly abominable and oppressing. At the Zoo all the morning, and for luncheon. A walk through the Regent's Park and Regent Street in the rain." Of Westminster Abbey he remarks: "Beautiful interior greatly marred by hideous modern monuments." At St. Paul's, too, he says: "More monstrous monuments to unheard-of military and naval gentry."

On the 28th of November he records an "intensely interesting morning at the National Gallery, and the pictures not half seen; . after lunch, across Hyde Park, — glorious skyscape." On Thanksgiving Day he wrote to his mother as follows: —

One year ago Sam and I dined at Aunt Annie Bob's. Since then I believe I have had the best year of my life to date, — the first half of the year with Mr. Olmsted, and this made pleasanter than the preceding eighteen months by the presence of Codman in the office; the latter half spent

in roaming about, observing and enjoying in so many different and interesting places, — the Arboretum, the Botanical
Garden, and New York, Washington, Philadelphia, Bridgeport, and Mt. Desert.   A very rich year, and one that has
been hugely enjoyed by reason of my seeing so much that
was beautiful.   My introduction to the Old World has been
gloomy enough, — dark, sunless weather ever since landing.
Here in London, the yellow darkness is peculiarly disheart-
ening and oppressive.   A young man in our square killed
himself the other day ; and he had eighty pounds and a
check-book with him at the time.   And London is so horribly ugly and so abominably grimy, and poverty and vice
are so conspicuous in the streets, and the darkness of midday is such that the things of beauty in the museums, to
which one goes for relief, are only dimly seen.   On the other
hand, my voyage over here to this dark Old World was a
time to be always remembered with exceeding pleasure.

On the 1st of December he remarks in his journal:
" Yesterday the Tower, — the last sight-seeing for the present.   To-day Kew."   The Kew gardens offer to the student,
not only an immense collection of trees, shrubs, and herbaceous plants in open ground, with extensive plant-houses of
every sort, but also very lovely landscape effects.   It was
always the landscape which most delighted Charles.   Although he found many trees and shrubs of extraordinary
beauty in the grounds, he was chiefly struck with the pleasing effects of distance in the soft English atmosphere, and
with the long shadows cast in a tolerably clear day by the
very low December sun.   On his way back to London, by
Brentford and Hammersmith, he noticed especially " one
extremely picturesque farmstead with old and crooked tile-
roofed barns."   Those were the pictures which remained in
his memory.

The London parks afforded him, even in December, very
interesting resorts.   He contrasts the simple, broad, and dignified character of Hyde Park and Regent's Park with the
recent Battersea Park, made in the American way out of the
whole cloth at great cost, — with its large, well-outlined
lakes, and big cement rock-work, " with springs issuing from
near the summit, — the highest ground anywhere about, —
and this on the extreme end of a longish promontory in the
lake."   Such unnatural features in park or landscape — like

an artificial pond placed on a hill-top and filled by pumping
— Charles always found extremely distasteful. In his view
they were wholly unlike ponds or reservoirs in natural valleys : they were mere engineering necessities, which by good
judgment might be adorned and slightly disguised. His
journal criticises the "clumpish" spaded shrubberies in
Battersea Park, their borders trimmed with some low growing herbaceous edging-plant, and the beds for exotics scattered about everywhere, with other beds of Roses, Pinks,
and Wallflowers. He found the best part of Battersea Park
to be that which was most like the old parks, — "long
stretches of greensward with trees in ranks, or scattered on
the borders." Conspicuous artificiality, and the introduction of flower-garden treatment, he found intolerable in any
large park. For him the flower garden was a thing distinct.
An artificial treatment, appropriate to a small city enclosure
into which many elaborate features might be compressed to
interest and amuse children or childish men and women,
he thought never desirable in spacious country parks. Any
unnatural treatment of the banks of a brook, or of the
shores of a pond or lake, always distressed him. Thus he
writes of the water in Regent's Park as " the miserable ditch,
called the lake, with its shore a wide muddy path, and an
iron fence at the brick edge of the water." The Park Road
at Regent's Park afforded him a profitable study of house-
yards in great variety: some decorated with piles of slag,
white quartz, or blue glass (probably called "rockeries");
and some with statuettes or rustic seats made of iron ; the
best " those in which the path to the door is carried conveniently direct, and simple green grass or Ivy covers most of
the remaining ground. Ivy as a green cover is particularly
useful in the shade of trees or shrubs." Here he notes the
good effect of plantations of low-growing shrubs set under
the windows of the house itself. We shall see hereafter how
he applied these observations at home in the suburbs of
Boston.

On the 8th of December he writes thus in his journal of a
day spent at Hampstead : —

A gloriously bright, cold day, — bright for London. Off
for Hampstead by ten o'clock, by means of a 'bus from
Tottenham Court Road. After some twenty minutes' ride
over stone pavements a third horse was hitched on, and the
ascent of the northern heights began. Open fields appeared between the buildings along the highway ; but the

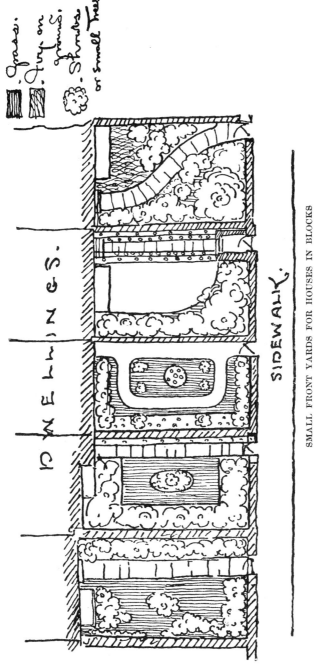

Grass.

Ivy or grass.

Shrubs.

or small trees

DWELLINGS.

SIDEWALK.

SMALL FRONT YARDS FOR HOUSES IN BLOCKS

road itself is now built up all the way to the Heath, — a picturesque road it is, as it winds and struggles up the steep hill. Numerous narrow footpaths and lanes appear, sometimes lined with pollarded trees. Up on the height is an indescribable mixture of tree-planted, private places enclosed by high walls, clusters of tile-roofed cottages, little inns now and then with their hanging signs, a big church, a little old church, and a chapel; and worked in and among and around these the bays, straits, and reaches of the wild, untamed Heath, with its Furze, Gorse, and Bracken, and its innumerable trodden cross-paths leading in every direction. And then the glorious outlook, — southward over all London; westward to Harrow-on-the-Hill; northward over a smiling farming land as green as green can be; and eastward to the companion height of Highgate with its conspicuous church, and its tree-embowered gentlemen's places. After a delightful tramp all through and about Hampstead, I pushed on for the town-end of Highgate by way of the open fields and hills, by the Ponds, and through a big farmyard· with its elaborate ricks, to the beginning of the villa region; then to the top of the hill by a footpath leading between private places. At the top is a confused meeting of many ways, lanes, highroads, and paths, and one wide and straightish ' Broadway ' lined with small irregular buildings, such as cottages, shops, inns, and stable-yards. At one end an (open) toll-gate and an old inn building block the way, — the Old-Gate Inn, 1671.

Letters of introduction brought from home procured for Charles a brief acquaintance with a considerable number of persons interested in forestry and horticulture. At a single dinner of a horticultural club he met a learned horticulturist, editor of a paper devoted to that subject, a white-haired grower of flowers, a fern specialist, a fruit-tree grower, a landscape gardener to some of the nobility, and several notable amateurs in gardening. There was real profit for the young student in intercourse with such men, who showed him much kindness, and manifested an interest in what he had to tell them of the difficulties of the New England garden and landscape work. One evening he listened to the recommendations of a master in the art about shrubs for London

town gardens; and when called upon to contribute something himself to the discussion of the subject, he was able to
tell them that of all the twenty evergreens recommended by
the author of the paper, only one, the Box, would endure the
New England climate.

In the pleasant English fashion, the first professional
acquaintances Charles made in London passed him on to
others, who could give him valuable information or introductions not only in England but also on the Riviera.

On those December days when the weather did not lend
itself to excursions in the open air, Charles had other resources in the Reading-Room of the British Museum and in
the South Kensington Library, where he had access to many
books relative to his profession, and to valuable collections of
photographs and plates illustrating English and Continental
gardens and parks. In the long evenings there was time for
much note-making, journal and letter writing, and for occasional dining or theatre-going with the members of the pleasant Philadelphia family whose acquaintance he had made on
the steamer, or with English friends. Some of the indoor
days were highly profitable, — thus, one was spent at Mr.
Milner's office, looking over plans, and hearing from the
master about his manner of making his charges, and of
carrying out his designs; but the out-of-door days were for
Charles much the more enjoyable. On the 17th of December he spent the best part of the short day on horseback,
going with the superintendent of Epping Forest through that
beautiful reservation of about 6000 acres, which is only
sixteen miles from London. Here he saw the work of thinning coppice, the product being made up in three grades
from poles to fagots. The Forest has immense masses of
coppice and thicket where the trees and shrubs kill each
other, — the result being dangerous quantities of materials
for fires. Yet the superintendent's intelligent efforts to clear
and thin the woods encounter incessant popular opposition,
and it is a useful part of his function to make "explanatory
excursions" with committees. There is no large variety of
vegetation in the Forest; and no large variety is necessary to
produce the finest landscape effects. Gorse, Heather, Broom,
Thorns, Hornbeam, Crabs, Birch, Beech, and Oak are quite
sufficient.

On the 22d of December he had an interesting day in the
country, of which his journal gives the following account: —

Gloomy, as usual; but being thoroughly sick of the town I

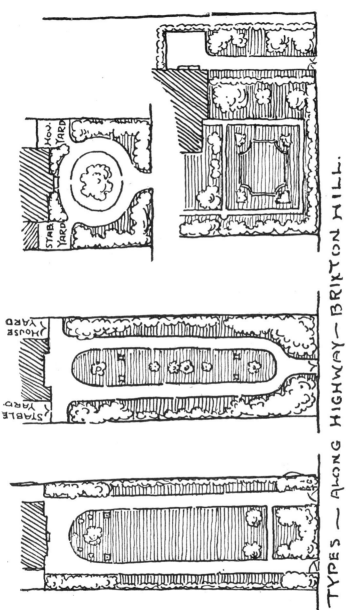

TYPES — ALONG HIGHWAY—BRIXTON HILL.

took train to Bedford Park where I tramped till lunch time. It is a whole town, built of pretty houses of red brick and tile, with picturesque chimneystacks, dormers, and roofs, stoops, porches, and leaded windows, a church, a block of " supply " stores, and a " Tabard Inn." The houses are rather crowded ; but in a few streets there are little gardens, — some extremely well contrived and pretty. The roads are narrow, with curbstones, paved gutters, and street trees throughout. There are no service alleys ; so that in some parts of the town the houses look across the street at the backs of other houses ; but then, the backs are good-looking. There is a pleasing variety of street palings, walls, and fences, and a few houses are well grouped with large elms.

After luncheon in a neat little den, I walked down to the Thames and Chiswick by way of a snarl of narrow lanes, and thence turned cityward by footways and lanes, sometimes on a river wall, sometimes behind factory or wharf properties, — everywhere crookedness and surprises. There were a few regions of pretty, riverside dwellings, one or two boat-landings, groups of large Elms on the river wall, and occasional red-sailed barges drifting by. It was a population of poor folk, living in jumbled cottages, in many parts approached only by footways or by the river.

That day closed with a sharp contrast, — " Faust " at the Lyceum Theatre in company with two young ladies of the Philadelphia family and their male cousin. Of this performance Charles wrote in a letter home : " It was a wonderfully perfect work of art and acting in every particular, — superlatively beautiful and appropriate scenery and costuming, and wholly faultless acting. Not a failing or imperfection or regrettable thing about it anywhere, save that physically Miss Terry is not one's idea of Margaret. It does one good to see work of human skill and thought and taste accomplished in such perfection."

On December 23d, which brought a brightish morning soon changing to cloud, Charles got out to Pinner by a forty-minute journey from Gower Street, his object being to see a true country village, — an object which was completely attained. He found a rambling, uphill street of cottages, farm barns, shops, taverns, yards, and gardens, with a square-towered church built of flints at the top, and old graves about the church. In the neighborhood there were a few very pleasant small country-seats, one or two " half-timbered parks," and many time-worn houses.

Thence I followed a crooked lane past two outlying farms, — with great ricks and tottering tile-roofed barns, — towards the dimly visible church on Harrow-on-the-Hill. Finally, the lane having become untravelled and grassy from hedge to hedge, I took a path across fields and stiles which brought me to the foot of the hill most pleasantly. On the hill — on the London road — I passed many small " parks " pastured by sheep. When I became hungry, the " Mitre " supplied me with a half-bitter and some crackers. At the " Swan " I turned back by another road, and climbed to Harrow itself, — a hill-top village commanding great views, — and there procured beef and potatoes in a little shop frequented by the schoolboys (it is vacation now). In a graveyard on the brink of the hill, with old trees about it, stood the church, built of flints again, and showing some Norman work. Inside the village, maids were busy putting up Christmas green. On the hillside were two or three delightsome views out over the surrounding counties, through openings between tree masses or between great trunks. The school buildings were scattered, and all but the old one which stands on the hill terrace were uninteresting.

The London weather towards the end of December gave Charles some gloomy days. On the 28th of December he writes : " Raining now and then, — miserable weather ; Christmas Day, Boxing Day, and Sunday are three monstrously doleful days for any one who is a stranger in London : the streets are muddy, dark, wet, and slippery, and nearly half of such people as are in the streets are drunk or partly so, the public houses being open, and crowded with men, women, and children on all these days, — drunken men and women being in the omnibuses, in the underground railway, and on the church steps." His best refuge in this weather was in the Reading-Room of the British Museum, where he could always find what was to him very interesting professional reading. On the 29th of December he wrote his father and mother as follows : " I always learn something on my suburban and country excursions ; and from Kemp's books in the Library I have got some good points. I enjoy my country walks exceedingly, as I do the National Gallery, and Henry VII.'s Chapel, and the Elgin Marbles, and the Cast Room at South Kensington; but it is all solitary, self-centred, unexpressed enjoyment; and will it help me at all to create what shall be beautiful when I may get a chance to try my hand?"

On the 30th of December he wrote thus to his brother from the Reading-Room of the British Museum: —

My digestion, about which you inquire, is in good shape most of the time; and I want to assure you that I am not at all gone in the other region you mention.   My heart is sound as ever, though on the Germanic I was really frightened lest I was about to lose it.   I have explored this hateful London pretty thoroughly, finding a monstrous deal of interest mixed up with all the ugliness and foulness.   The streets are always interesting; there are so many more marked types of men and women, houses, vehicles, and buildings, than in our towns. But the suburbs and the country I like so much better, — the great Elms, the Lebanon Cedars, the half-timbered houses, the parish churches, the quaint village streets, the lanes and hedges, the footpaths, the occasional parks, the soft greensward, the soft atmosphere, and the long shadows.   In spring and summer this land must be a very garden of delights. . . . The political situation here has interested me much.   Parnell's almost complete victory throughout Ireland has made home-rule the question of the hour; and only just behind this (to the English mind) momentous question stand the problems of church disestablishment, free schools, and land reform.   Curiously enough, all these were questions settled for us in America some time ago. . . . Such talk as one hears about the Church goes beyond belief, — such cant, bigotry, and intolerance, such crying that disestablishment means the knell of religion in England and the beginning of the end for the Empire.   And then I never realized at all, till now, what a monstrous burden is this almost feudal land-system, and the whole aristocratic concern.

In the worst days of cold, rain, and fog, Charles could always go to the British Museum and study Repton, Kemp, and other masters of his art.   There, also, he made numerous tracings of plans and sketches, and notes on practice. There, too, he found much good reading on landscape gardening of the last century, such as Horace Walpole's "Essay on Gardening," and Thomas Whately's "Observations on Modern Gardening," and the works of Shenstone, another of the discoverers of the beauty of natural scenery. He was often

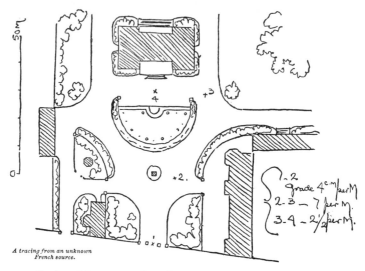

A tracing from an unknown
French source.

Spacious driveways to a large house and four screened out-buildings.
Highway oblique to the buildings.

amused by his companions at the Reading-Room. Here is one of his descriptions of them: "There are all manner of cranks in the Reading-Room, male and female; men with whole walls of books piled about them; men copying and making drawings, and painting in water colors; many very old gentlemen, their noses rubbing the pages of great books; many youthful women in strange dress, most of them reading Ruskin; a few old women hard at work copying or at water colors, and looking as if they had been in the room all their lives. The attendants are very civil; but the time required to get out a book is incredibly long."

In spite of the advantageous use he was making of his time in London, and of his thorough enjoyment of his excursions to the country, he was quite capable of falling into a mood of depression, such as moved him to write as follows to his father: —

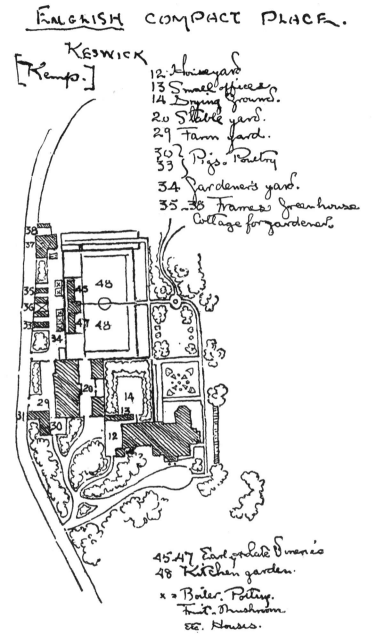

ENGLISH COMPACT PLACE.

KESWICK

[Kemp.]

12. House yard.
13. Small offices.
14. Drying ground.
20. Stable yard.
29. Farm yard.
30 }
33 } Pigs. Poultry.
34. Gardener's yard.
35~38 Frames greenhouse
Cottage for gardener.

45·47 Earl & Lady Simeries
48 Kitchen garden.
x = Boiler. Potting.
Fruit. Mushroom
etc. Houses.

A TRACING FROM KEMP

Sunday, 3 Jan'y, 1886. I am oppressed with a sense of accomplishing little or nothing. Somehow I am getting to think that nothing I can or may do will make much difference in my professional life ; just as Aunt A—— says that she can hardly influence her children's characters at all ; and just as college makes so much less difference in men's lives than it is commonly supposed to. After all, it is what a man is by nature that counts.

On the 7th of January he records his Reading-Room experience thus : "I finished Girardin, — good ; W. Mason's poem, 'The English Garden ;' and another Mason's essay on 'Gardening,' both very interesting, — the first dated 1772 ; the second, 1768, the time of the breaking away from the old formal style. I also discovered a five-volume book in French by one Hirschfeld, published in 1785, and full of the then new spirit." His letters of introduction having procured him admission to certain friendly gatherings of architects and artists, sometimes at clubs, sometimes in private houses, he not infrequently remarks that he had seen the whole thing before in Du Maurier's drawings. He was always much interested in any proof of the accuracy of an artist's representations, whether of landscape or of human society. On the 9th of January he spends the greater part of the day at a winter exhibition of old masters at the Royal Academy. " The day fled all too fast ; a room full of old Italian, another room of Flemish, and a much mixed room of English and Dutch works, Wilkies, Constables, and Teniers, with a great show of ladies' portraits by Gainsborough and Sir Joshua ; but far beyond all these in interest for me was a collection of forty-six water-color landscapes by Turner, — for the most part scenes in England and Scotland, and in the Alps, — every one of them poetic, lovely, enchanting, like the poetry of Shelley ; all the landscape painting I have ever seen is as nothing in comparison with these. These pictures take right hold of my heart, and move me as real landscape sometimes does. I am transported." He refreshed himself also with music occasionally. Thus, on January 11th : " After dinner I went down to St. James's Hall for the Monday ' Pop,' one shilling, which admits one to an unreserved region behind the players, where on a steep grade are arranged a few rows of chairs, and behind them some backless benches. The concert was of chamber music. A new pianist, in whom the audience was much interested, played several bits of Schumann that

E—— plays; and Mr. Lloyd sang, among other things, Schubert's 'Serenade' most beautifully. At Mrs. S.'s invitation I took an omnibus with herself and Mr. B., and at their house partook of a supper, — curry and rice, bread and cheese, and beer. Bed at 12.30." He is often at the Reading-Room of the British Museum, reading Hirschfeld and Hermann Jaeger, and Sir W. Chambers's " Essay on Oriental Gardening," and R. P. Knight's poem " The Landscape," — both good works of the last century, — and Gilpin and Price, of which he says : " After all perhaps the best general works on modern landscape art." There was an inner sanctuary at the Reading-Room where he could look over volumes of plates, such as Adolphe Alphand's superb volumes, " Les Promenades de Paris."

On the 16th of January the sun was actually visible; and he immediately took train for Ashstead Park, a forty-minute ride, to see one of Mr. Milner's places.

The station is in the fields, some distance from a very small hamlet. Beyond this hamlet is a rising ground, covered with great woods, and in the edge thereof stands an old square-towered church. I walked up the hill accompanied by an old fellow in big boots, who told me all about the farms and the gentry of the neighborhood. With him I followed the public way through and across a park to the house of the head-gardener; but the head-gardener had gone away with the owner, so I walked all about the walled gardens and the neighborhood by myself, observing the houses for peaches, pineapples, and grapes, the convenient quarters for the workmen, the very old espalier fruit trees, the standard roses, and the old house of brick, its chimneys clasped by the twisted branches of an old espalier pear planted at one corner. At one o'clock the head-gardener arrived, and walked with me until 3 o'clock, showing me Milner's terrace, and other architectural work about the mansion, his " pleasure-ground," with undulations and evergreen plantings (which harmonized but ill with the surrounding park), his " new pond " and his many " game covers." The deer formerly browsed up to the very walls of the house. A new walled entrance court on one side, and double terraces on the other side, add greatly to the views both of and from the house.

There is a grand view from the terrace front down a long sweep of greensward, having groves of noble trees on both hands, to the wide hills of Ashstead Common on the further side of the intervening valley. I did not like the "pleasure-ground," — some wandering paths in undulating ground, the little swells invariably crowned with close-planted masses of shrubs, mostly evergreens. All this in the edge of the finest possible wood of great Oaks and ancient Elms, where no shrubs ever grew and no undulations ever were. The pond is still worse, though it will appear much better when the plantations are grown. Its position, near the foot of the said long hill, involved a dam on the lower side of its whole length, — a thing very difficult to conceal. The outlines are stiffly curvilinear, and are all neatly sodded and trimmed, and the plantations are too dressy, and such as will never harmonize with the surrounding great woods. These open woods are the glory of the Park, — no undergrowth, numerous trunks, deer browsing among them. The old church is very picturesque, a great yew being crowded into the corner beside the squat tower.

At three o'clock, Mrs. S. having provided me with two buns and three apples, I set out again and walked to Leatherhead, where about four o'clock I got a train for Dorking, and there put up at the White Horse at dark. Dorking is a crooked little place, with narrow streets, save in the centre where a greater breadth gives room for markets. The London road, for instance, is twenty-one feet wide, with one sidewalk twenty-one inches wide; and other streets are even narrower, and with no flags. There are many crooked old buildings, narrow lanes, and small cottages crowded among patches of garden. Over all, rules a tall-spired parish church. I explored the town by moonlight; for the evening, like the day, was gloriously fine. The inn was very comfortable, save for its low ceilings and doorways. In the centre of the building was an inner sanctuary, having sliding small-paned sashes on three sides and the chimney on the fourth side, whence drinkables were supplied to gentlemen in the smoking-room on one side, and to mere men in the hall on the other.

Sunday, 17th of January. As I am the only guest of the house, my meals are served in great state in a good-sized room, with a fire and many newspapers. Chops for breakfast; and for dinner, roast beef, of course, carved by myself, with apple tart, and celery and cheese later. This morning I had a grand tramp, the weather being still clear, eastward through an old park — Betchworth — to a hamlet called Brockham Green, where a number of cottages, an inn, and a church are prettily clustered together. Thence, across the Mole, and by several seats and farms, to the great hill of the North Downs, — Box Hill, — which stands over against Dorking, and commands a most interesting view of one of the many gardens of England, — the county of Surrey. The extent of the woodlands about Dorking, and the great number of country-seats, not counting mere villas, were most surprising to me. The hill itself is really grand; its slopes very steep though rockless, and the groves of Box-trees on the summit very remarkable. Then, the road descending into the valley of the Mole (by which the railway from London reaches Dorking) overlooks a lovely country, well watered and richly cultivated, the great ranges of the surrounding Downs carrying much wood and many mansions on their slopes and summits. I crossed the Mole again at Burford Bridge, where the Guide tells me Keats wrote " Endymion." Between half-past three and dark I wandered close to town among the lovely lanes and woods, and in the mansion grounds of Deepdene, the estate of the Hope family; also through and over several bits of rough common, — where the lord of the manor has set up signs forbidding the cutting of peat or fagots, — and through the highland wood called the " Glory." In the smoking-room I wrote letters, and listened to the village worthies growling about the length of the sermon and the late bad weather for hunting.

18th of January. Weather not so fine, but still too good to think of going back to grimy London. To-day I took the Guildford road, having the hills of the Downs white with frost on my right, and many ridges stretching towards Leith Hill (the top of all this country) on my left. Again there were many seats and many bits of common; and one mile

out a hamlet called Westcott, with a church in the midst of
a Furze-common on a steep hillside. Presently the road
crosses a brook ; and looking upstream I see an ancient
manor-house in a lovely green valley, the hills around it
clothed with great woods. By the side of the brook is an
" avenue " arched with enormous Beeches. Down this road
comes a little cart drawn by two donkeys tandem ; and from
the driver thereof I learn that a public footpath passes the
house, and that the place is the " Rookery." In the Guide I
read that the Rookery was the home of Malthus, translator
of Girardin's " Essay on Landscape," and author of the
" Essay on Population." Therefore I enter said arch of
Beeches, and passing some small mill-buildings, smothered in
vegetation, and the house with its terrace-garden, I reach the
head of the valley, whence the backward view of the house
set on this hillside and backed by woods, with a gentle slope
from terrace to millpond, and then hanging woods again on
the other side, is very lovely. No dressy planting is here, —
nothing out of place or unharmonious, — all is simple, and
yet rich enough. The foot of the pond is shrouded in thick
evergreens. The two or three islands near the head, and the
slopes about a rock-set fall of water from a second pond
above, are clothed with overhanging shrubbery. The pond
shore is not geometrically curved, and the steep hill on the
opposite bank is wooded in part, the trees standing on its
steepest parts only. All in all, this is a spot which art of
man has made more beautiful, and much more characteristically expressive, than ever it could have been in its natural
condition. Is not this the true object of real landscape
gardening ?

A public path beyond the house looked tempting, and I
kept on, — first, over a really wild-wooded hill, and into
another meadow valley, this one with a farmstead in the
midst. Keeping the path which followed the stream, the
valley began to lose its soft character, and finally came to be
narrow and deep, shut in by steep Fir-clad hills, with now
and then open Gorse-covered patches. Suddenly there appeared a cluster of four or five very poorly kept cottages
with thatched or tiled roofs, and small enclosures for vegeta-

bles, — their water drawn only from the streamlet. Thence
I advanced over a high wind-swept common towards an apparently endless Pine forest. No houses were in sight ; but
the sound of a church bell came, striking the quarter hours,
from the great valley between me and the Downs. The Pine
wood had its many paths, and a lovely undergrowth with
many little Beeches ; and by and by I struck a distinct lane
which soon began to dive downhill, sinking itself into the
earth in the process (as roads do in North Carolina) ; and
soon it brought me to cottages, and to the wall of a park.
Then the " great house " appeared, — a very great house,
rambling in the extreme, built of red brick, and in some
parts evidently Elizabethan, at least. From a little hill
before the lodge gates I could overlook the whole place,
lying as it does in a tight little valley surrounded by woods,
most characteristically English, and ancient, and aristocratic.
When I asked the only visible inhabitant — a very old man
in the road — what house this was, he said, " Wotton House,
sir, — Mr. Evelyn's." True enough, — the Guide confirmed
him, and told me this was the house of John Evelyn, the
writer of the " Sylva," in whose family the place has been
since Queen Elizabeth's days. Then I went down and, asking permission at the lodge, I had fifteen minutes' strolling
in the ancient gardens, to my delight. The blue smoke from
the old chimneys rose straight into the air. In the outer
court a young lady was playing with a big dog. There was
not a sound but her voice, and the notes of some birds now
and then. Really, I felt as if I were in a dream. However,
I managed to arouse myself in time to walk back through
Westcott to dinner at the White Horse at 1.30. This time
it was calf's head and bacon ; and I was hungry and tired,
and sat long over it ; and did nothing in the afternoon but
buy three poor photographs, and get myself back to London.

On disagreeable days, towards the end of January, he was
reading the work of Fürst Pückler-Muskau on " The Landscape Art." He found it tough reading, but good ; and
when he had finished it, he notes that " after all it is one of
the best books on the subject." London society was consumed at this time by the home-rule question in Ireland ;

and at almost every breakfast, or dinner, to which Charles was invited, this was the topic of a somewhat exciting conversation. Even his horticultural and landscape friends could hardly keep out of it. Charles was, of course, interested in these discussions, but would have much preferred to hear about English gardens, parks, and scenery. On the 20th of January, after a breakfast with Professor James Bryce, M. P., at which there was a great deal of talk about Ireland, Charles went into the Grosvenor Gallery where are Millais's works. His comment in his journal was that the collection was very interesting, as showing all the stages of Millais's development from his pre-Raphaelite times to the latest of his pretty children pictures. "Interesting, too, to see how throughout all he has held to the central truth of pre-Raphaelitism, — the all-surpassing importance of expression and character." Among the few landscapes, Charles especially noted the wonderfully expressive " Chill October."

All through December and January Charles went with much regularity to hear the preaching of the Rev. Stopford Brooke, finding his discourses unusually interesting and profitable. He is occasionally at pains to enter the substance of the sermon in his journal, and repeatedly expresses his pleasure in the evening services at Mr. Brooke's church. On the 30th of January he records that he had completed, at the Reading-Room of the British Museum, the course of professional reading which he had determined on for the bad weather of the winter; and he celebrated the completion of this undertaking by going to the pantomime at Drury Lane, where he saw " a great show, being a combination of farce, comedy, opera, spectacle, ballet, and old-fashioned columbine and harlequin business."

At the end of January and the first of February, he had a five days' visit to Oxford, where he was very kindly received by English friends of his father, friends who had known him as a boy in New England Cambridge. He was entertained for short periods in Oriel College, at All Souls, and at the house of the Master of Merton. He walked all about the town and through the grounds and buildings under the best and kindest possible guidance, and was presented to a large number of cultivated and interesting strangers. He listened to the talk of a considerable number of young men who had won high standing at the University, and fellowships as the appropriate prizes for such attainment. But the total result of his observation of these young men was a feeling of sadness, — almost of pity: "They strike me — with all their learning, which in things classical and accepted is plainly great — as a monstrously anti-natural product of civilization, — a very much forced crop. They seem to me a set of fellows tightly bound in the bonds of conformity, conservatism, and precedent, and unable to see the narrowness of the education they have all received at the hands of their public school and their college. I like much better the average undergraduate who spends his days at tennis or on the river and just gets through his pass examinations." The general views of Oxford delighted him ; and he says of it : " There is no town of man's building with more character of its own than this." The hospitality of Professor James Bryce, both in London and at Oriel College, was of great advantage to Charles, for he heard at the London house much interesting political talk ; and at Oxford the son was entertained just as the father had been more than twenty years before. At this moment Mr. Bryce was about to receive an appointment in the new government, — the appointment of Under-Secretary of Foreign Affairs.

On February 6th Charles awoke "with a strong desire to get out of London, and away from the ill-managed house in which I have been lodging. The horridness of it seems worse after life at Oxford." That evening he arrived at Canterbury on his way to Paris. Sunday, the 7th of February, he spent in Canterbury, and went to the Cathedral morning service. Here are his comments thereon : " Long, — fit rather for the Dark Ages than for the nineteenth century. Sermon very bad, — a perversion of the meaning of the phrase 'the liberty with which Christ hath made us free.' Shocking ! A carefully arranged seating of the congregation, — the quality, their coachmen in livery, their house servants, the commoners and ordinary townspeople, the charity school children, the strangers, — the latter put behind the reading-desk and pulpit." After the service he walked westward, up a little hill beyond the embattled Westgate and the Stour, whence he gained a good general view of the town lying in a shallow depression, the cathedral rising high from the midst. " Cultivated slopes rise all about the town, crowned by several large windmills, — a dust of snow over all." The next morning he explored the Cathedral, recalling Professor Norton's lectures on the great structure ; but what he most enjoyed was the " lovely intricate region adjoining the Cathedral, — garden mixed with old buildings and ruins." The fresh appearance of the Cathedral surprised him ; it had

" nothing of the ancient look of dirty Westminster." That
evening he reached Paris long after dark; and, having
thoroughly studied the map of Paris beforehand, he walked
from the station to the hotel he had decided to try, — No. 55
Rue de Provence. Supper over, he forthwith walked out
on the boulevards. He had not seen Paris since he was
nine years old. This was his earliest comment: " Interesting
shop windows, lively people, — vast contrast to the gloom
and glumness of London." The next day he made a sort of
general tour of the city, which appeared to him wonderfully
fresh, bright, and cheerful. Almost his first performance
was to mount the tower of Nôtre Dame for the fine view
of the city. Having an extraordinary facility in mastering
the map of any city and all its means of transportation, —
omnibuses, tramways, and steam railways, — he was completely independent of guides, and of the usual resorts of
English-speaking people. His first luncheon in Paris was
taken in a café in the Latin quarter, on which he chanced
at the right hour. " I found I comprehended the geography
very well, and knew many of the buildings at sight." He
also understood the language well enough for the common
purposes of a traveller. In the evening he ordinarily wrote
either in his journal or letters to go homewards; but on
this first day in Paris he took pains to buy a ticket for
" Faust" at the Grand Opera the next night.

On the 11th of February he wrote as follows to his
mother : —

What a sight are Paris shop windows, and how fine are the
new boulevards with their handsome terminations in domes of
Pantheons, and Columns of July, and pediments of Made-
leines. Verily, it is good to see a well-designed city, and one
so superlatively well kept. Our American cities have been
made to order; but how ill in comparison with this made-
over one. I knew that Paris was handsome and cheerful;
but I never realized the degree of its beauty and brightness.
Already I have been to the Louvre, — first to the shrine of
the Venus of Milo (pity to call her a Venus, as if she were
one of the softly pretty creatures) ; and then to stand before
the glorified men and women of Titian. What superb creatures! gifted with the same calm divinity as the Victory;
more than humanly lovely, healthy, and sane. We folk of
to-day — and particularly these French — are the veriest

apes and idiots in comparison. How I wish I might have a drop or two of their rich, warm blood put into my feeble heart. What would n't I give for something of their complete naturalness, their unconsciousness, their magnificent physical perfectness? After a sight of these, the rest of the Louvre counts for little, — at least one cannot care for it the same day.

His journal thus describes his first morning at the Louvre : —

I discovered She of Melos from afar ; and fell down in worship at her shrine like any Pagan. Then in the Salon Carré and the next room I discovered adorable creatures of Titian's, Giorgione's, and Veronese's painting ; and after long gazing on these I found I could not care for the rest of the Louvre, and so left, surprised at finding it three o'clock. The landscape backgrounds of the Titians were not the least interesting parts to me, — some of them being very lovely, and all interesting as first examples of landscape painting in the modern sense. The three or four Raphaels were very sweet and beautiful ; but not nearly so interesting to me as the Titians, beside lacking the richness of color of the Venetian's work. The several reputed da Vincis were very disappointing, — all the same type of gently smiling woman, figuring as " Virgin," " Mistress," or what not. It is impossible to record the innumerable impressions and delights of my four hours.

That evening he visited the Place de l'Etoile, where he used to play when a little boy, and climbed to the top of the arch for the fine view. Thence he went to the little Parc de Monceaux. He says of it : —

The little Parc was interesting, — nearly spoilt by being cut into four quarters by two cross-roads, but possessed of some well-modelled little lawns, shady walks, and some bits of made ruins, set about a pool and elsewhere, that smack of the earlier days of naturalistic gardening, and, being well planted and partly vine-clad, and hidden away in groves, are not unlovely. In summer the whole park is evidently given over to the exhibition of exotics, many strangely shaped and conspicuously placed beds being scattered about.

After dinner I went early to the Grand Opera, loafed in the magnificent foyer, watched the coming of the throngs, and saw several parties I took to be American. From my seat (in the very centre of the parterre, and just in front of the abominable claque) I studied the gorgeous decoration of the room, and the behavior of the demi-nude females in the first circle. "Faust" was very well sung and acted; — as a whole, it was not nearly so interesting or beautiful as the play at the Lyceum, but in parts, by reason of the power of music, exceedingly thrilling and moving. There was a really lovely ballet (in place of Irving's witch-scene of the Brocken), — the first charming one I ever beheld. After a bock bier and a petit pain, to bed considerably weary, it being one o'clock.

He was chiefly bent on seeing the parks and out-of-door recreation-grounds; but when the weather was unfit for such explorations, he resorted to the museums, where the landscapes and seascapes always interested him. On the 13th of February he went to the Parc des Buttes-Chaumont, where he found much good planting, and some very well-executed rock-work. "As a whole, the place is dangerously close to being fantastic and far-fetched: originally, a quarry; now, a recreation-ground for a poor quarter of Paris. A well-planted railway cutting, ingenious concrete brooklets (!), and very good rock-plantings, — too many carriage roads, perhaps." He noticed that the men who were at work pruning were evidently trained hands. On the 14th of February he had a day of great enjoyment which he thus described: —

Pont Royal to Suresnes, by river. The day bright and warmish, the water blue, the company gay. We changed boats at the city line. The heights of Meudon and Mont Valérien were on the left, and low suburban districts on the right bank. We had a glimpse of the architectural cascade of St. Cloud; and in the park of St. Cloud there was a conspicuous mass of pink twigs of Limes (?). At Suresnes I crossed the bridge and entered the Bois de Boulogne. The effect of the great open space of the race-course of Longchamp was grand. The windmill of Longchamp was very pretty, — Ivy-clad, standing on a mound of well-clothed artificial rocks, with moat-like water about it. Near by was much interesting planting. The "Grande Cascade" has a good effect from the distance of the cascade knoll, with its lichen-covered ledges, its Pines and White Birches. The detail of rock-forming and rock-planting is admirable; but the anti-naturalness of the position of the cascade spoils half the charm. I walked to the Carrefour, between the two lakes. Great crowds were hurrying to the Auteuil steeple-chases. The view down the larger lake was very pretty, with swans flying in the distance. At Pré Catelan I had beer and bread and butter; and then strolled by crooked paths through the wood till I came out at the end of the lake. Here was a vast throng of carriages and foot-passengers, a very gay scene, — far beyond anything I ever saw. I walked thence all the way to the Tuileries, meeting the same throngs on the way. The crowd on the Champs-Elysées was very democratic, with many shows in progress, much eating and drinking, crowds at open-air tables as if it were summer, swarms of children and pretty bonnes, — all very amusing.

February 15th was spent at the Botanical Garden, " getting acquainted with unknown evergreens and other strangers lately met with in the parks (Chionanthus [Fringe-tree] and Rhod. Dahuricum, in bloom)." The next day he visited the Jardin d'Acclimatation, " where I loafed away the after-noon, — not very profitably professionally, unless a zoölogical garden should be required of one. There were many amus-ing creatures, — human, and other." February 17th he men-tions that after dinner he had a talk with a Rev. somebody, a Cambridge man, — " my first conversation since Oxford, ex-cept a few words with an American on the Channel steamer. I find the mere riding on tram and omnibus-tops highly interesting, — the people very easy, good tempered, and democratic in their ways. It is strange to see so many women bareheaded, and so few men with overcoats or gloves. The cheerfulness of even the very poor is a great contrast to the desperate glumness of the hideous London poor. Apparently they know better how to live on very little." Another day he called upon the leading French landscape architect, having an excellent letter to him. This gentleman's practice was enormous, as was that of the Eng-lish landscape architect whose acquaintance Charles had made earlier in London. Charles made the same comment on both offices, the English and the French, — " Work of men so much driven, as these men are, can hardly be artistic,

I fear. It is very doubtful if an architect, like U. R. for example, can do artistic work of any excellence under such circumstances; much less can a landscape gardener, whose works cannot be executed from drawings only."

On the 21st of February he wrote to his mother : —

The fine weather fled three days ago. Chill, and cloud, and some wet have succeeded. No more wandering in parks, or riding on tops of omnibuses; and the Louvre, too, is cold; and the Luxembourg remains closed. . . . Last night I was at the Eden Théâtre. Lots of ballet, and a very Parisian audience; innumerable dangerous-looking women; but all well-dressed and well-behaved. I concluded I regarded the ballet dancers (as I do the professional ball-players in America) with much more respect than their audience. At midnight, when the show was over, I adjourned to a café for a bock and a sandwich, and then to the Place de l'Opéra, where a great throng was enjoying the arrival of innumerable maskers, a bal masqué being about to begin at the Grand Opéra, — a strange Sunday morning spectacle! And it was so cold that the half-clothed dancers had to run from their cabs up the great steps, — a brilliant sight under the light of long rows of gas jets on the front of the building and of electrics in the square.

The weather during the last week of February was often bad; but he could always find plenty of occupation at the Louvre or the National Library, or in reading guide-books in anticipation of his proposed Mediterranean journey. On the 22d of February, although the weather was still cold and dreary, he walked to Montsouris, where he was much interested in the artificial hiding of the two railways that cut the land into four quarters. There, too, he found some excellent planting, and more artificial rocks, brooklets, and cascades. Of these he says in a letter to his father: " I am astonished at the French work in the smaller city squares and places. Their formal work — fountains, parterres, etc. — I like well; but artificial rocks, cascades, streams (all edged with concrete!), and cement stalactites in concrete caves, seem somewhat childish." From Montsouris he went again to the Luxembourg to study the cold and dreary gardens, and thence to the Trocadéro, where were more grounds and gardens to be studied. On the 23d he wrote in his journal:

"Another bad day; but I concluded not to go south just yet, considering yesterday was so profitable." On the 24th the clouds partly broke at last, and he was off at once to the western end of the Bois de Vincennes, where he had a pleasant walk about the lake. There he found many very good bits of planting, — Tamarix with Pine and much Mahonia, — delightful rock-plantings, and a lovely bit of shore near the bridge to the island. Thence he walked to the terrace at Gravelle, noting the wide prospect over the Seine and Marne valleys, peaceful as possible save for the incessant rattle of musketry on the practice-ground in the Bois. Then he went on past the race-course, and some great batteries, into the eastern part of the Bois, where were thick woods of trees generally small, meandering, ditch-like, made brooks, a largish lake with islands, — for the most part well handled, — and one especially pretty strait, with steep bank, thickets, overhanging trees, and rushes on the water side. At Porte Jaune Island there is a good bridge.

After such a long day out-of-doors he was generally glad to spend a day in a library. Accordingly, he sought the reading-room of the Bibliothèque Nationale, and, on demanding a book not to be had there, was admitted "exceptionnellement" to the fine Salle de Travail, where he stayed till 4 P. M. "A fine time! Then I crossed the Seine and bought one of the books I had there discovered, — the descriptive catalogue of trees, shrubs, and herbaceous plants used in planting for ornament in the City of Paris, — a book in default of which I have spent much time in making lists of my own." The next day, February 26th, it snowed, with sleet and rain, till nearly 5 o'clock, when the sky suddenly cleared. Immediately he got out for a walk, and noted the "admirable and successful activity of the street-cleaning gangs." On the 27th the sky was partly clear, and he took a tram-car to the Bois de Boulogne. The streets were all perfectly dry, the snow having been swept into the gutters before it hardened. The Bois was all white and bright. "I walked to the Butte near the Auteuil grand-stand, viewing the upper lake, and thence by a woodland path to the Bois gate, seeing many pretty glades on the way. Thence I passed along the edge of the Longchamp, getting glorious views of the snowy heights beyond the Seine, to the Cascade; and into the café there for lunch. On by the gates of the Bagatelle to the Mare de St. James, and so to Porte Maillot and the Arc de Triomphe, — a fine walk in a lonely country, for Paris is apparently kept at home by snow." The next day, February 28th, he

explored again Parc Monceaux, and also the so-called Square
or Place des Batignolles. " Both these are interesting works,
wholly different from any city plots of similar area in England or America, or anywhere but just here in Paris, — such,
at all events, is my present imagining."   In the evenings he
was now studying Italian tours, and narrowing his choice
between several attractive routes.

When he had been in Paris three weeks, he made the following memorandum, headed, "Some curiosities of Paris:"
"Sharp-cracking whips; cabmen's white glazed hats; hatless
women; funeral processions; also les noces; fried potatoes;
public cigar-lighting gas jets; fish-women with a basket on
each arm, and perhaps three fish in each; hand-carts drawn
by harnessed men; women's hand-carts loaded with fruit,
vegetables, beans, and flowers, the women enormous, strong,
wooden-shod; monstrous three-horse omnibuses; long and
narrow high two-wheeled carts; huge horses; processions of
school-children; pack-men who are also bootblacks; funeral
decorations at house doors; countless small newspapers; vast
array of trashy books prettily got up; square yards of photographs of Salon pictures of the nude hung up in shop
windows; acres of sharply worded manifestoes, political and
such, posted up on walls; also whole speeches in the Chamber or the Senate, and innumerable public notices headed
' Liberté, Egalité, Fraternité; ' pretty theatre posters."

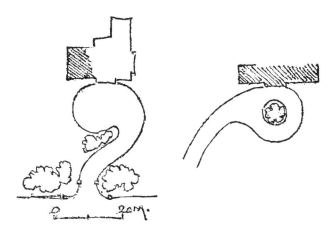

Short driveways — French.

CHAPTER V

LANDSCAPE STUDY IN EUROPE. THE RIVIERA

> Let our artists be those who are gifted to discern the true nature
> of beauty and grace ; then will our youth dwell in a land of health,
> amid fair sights and sounds ; and Beauty, the effluence of fair works,
> will meet the sense like a breeze, and insensibly draw the soul even in
> youth into harmony with the beauty of reason. — PLATO.

> The excessive variety of which some European gardeners are so
> fond in their plantations, the Chinese artists blame ; observing that a
> great diversity of colors, foliage, and direction of branches must create
> confusion and destroy all the masses, — they admit, however, a mod-
> erate variety. — SIR W. CHAMBERS.

ON the 3d of March he left Paris for the south, wishing
that he had left some time earlier. To his mother he wrote
on the 3d of March : —

I have bought my ticket, and propose to take the night
train to Lyons. The continued bad weather, and the " state
of mind " it has got me into, are the reasons of my sudden
fleeing. I have stayed one week too many in Paris. I
wanted to study evergreens, but the weather has prevented
being outdoors ; and I ought to have remembered that the
evergreens will still be here in early May. . . . I vow I do
not know why I did not start off south several days ago.
. . . It is going to be a great treat, — the greatest of the
many I have had in my life; though I am sure I cannot
enjoy it any more than I have enjoyed days and days of our
yachting, camping, and tramping.

4th of March. Comfortable enough ride. . . . I awoke
as the train passed a small town. The snow-sprinkled roofs
were in silhouette against the glow of dawn ; the sky clear
and starry. More sleep. Later, the river Saône; countless
Lombardies; the Jura dimly visible under the rising sun ;
vineyards on hillsides ; higher and higher hills, the valley
narrowing; suddenly two romantic hillside châteaux, with

towers round and towers square, and high terrace walls; then a tunnel and Lyons. I went to the Hôtel de l'Europe for breakfast at 10 o'clock, the quay of Saône and the heights of Fourvières before my window. After breakfast I went up the heights in the bright cold morning. The prospect was vastly wide, with the snowy mountains of Auvergne, winding rivers, and a great city in sight. At the foot of the hills were steep flights of steps, a maze of alleys, and all manner of intricacies; on the top, great fortifications, numerous charity schools, nunneries, barracks, poorhouses, and hospitals, and the far-seen church of strange architecture containing the miraculous image (1,500,000 pilgrims annually); below the church on the hillside, a garden with a toilsome zigzag path having "stations" and many shrines. Here were processions of priests, soldiers, nuns, barefooted brothers, and school-children; and continuous pealing of church bells, and sounding of bugles in the still air. A *champs de manœuvres* lies close behind the church. All these are high in the air. Wide prospects stretch into faint blue distances round every corner, and down every alley.

Descending the hill and crossing the Saône, I took a tram-car, which passed over the rushing Rhone, and brought me to the Parc de la Tête d'Or. I came first to a pretty lake with two islands in it, yellow with the bloom of Alders. Taking a boat, I explored all its shores, studied the plant-ings, and admired the careful designing of the views from the head of the lake, — the long water-perspectives, with the blue heights of Fourvières and the church as termination. There was also a good log bridge, and a pretty châlet. Next, I walked round the skirts of the Parc, — a charming glade, long, rather narrow, and gently hollowed, the bounding woods consisting of Conifers in great variety of species, and presenting interesting and beautiful contrasts of forms and colors, all well grown, evidently planted some thirty years. . . . A small grotto was visible among the evergreens from far down the glade. It was apparently made of cement, on an iron frame; but, being planted about with brambles, etc., had a good effect. Many lovely and delightfully framed views of Fourvières were to be gained from points beyond the head of the lake. The lake-creeks were well planted with rushes, hanging willows, and white birches. Nowhere was there anything gardenesque or presumptuous. The roads were well curved, and not too numerous, and they led to good points of view. They were narrow and without sidewalks. The paths were few and simply curved. There was one good road-bridge of ingenious timberwork frankly shown, with a well-designed roof over it. There was also one shockingly bad bridge of cement concrete, in the form of an arch, but wholly without appearance of keying, so that it had a look of great instability. There was very little underwood or shrubbery in the Parc; and there was no attempt at massing flowering shrubs, — such as Rhododendron or the like. That sort of thing was to be found in a separate garden at one side, together with a very large Palm house and other glass houses. Late in the afternoon I discovered a botanical garden in a corner of the Parc, and therein cleared up several doubts and ignorances. Apparently there is no great change of climate between Paris and Lyons; for the same things were covered-in that were covered-in at Paris. I was much pleased with the Parc as a whole, and thought it about what Cambridge or Worcester ought to have.

To bed early, after reading of papers. No. 1 of my sixty days [excursion ticket], — excellent well spent.

March 6. I set out in the rain, without having determined on an alighting-place; but at 3.30 alighted at Avignon, after a railway journey memorable and exciting by reason of the variety and interest of the scenery. The total effect, as I look back on it to-night, is rather confused, being made up of visions of blue, purple, and snow-white mountains, the yellow-flowing Rhone, wide cultivated plains, vineyards on steep hillsides, hill-climbing towns, hill-crowning ruins of castles, and hilltop churches. There were hillsides of barren whitish rock; slopes of stone chips (like those on Pierce's Head, Mt. Desert); ragged and raw torrent beds and gulches; rocks of fantastic, wildest form (those near Montdragon); rocks, and great steeps clad with evergreens, Pines, Savins, Box, and low-growing Furze and Broom; lands deep covered with débris of torrents; fields separated by high and wide ridges made of small stones picked up from the soil; and irrigated lands also. At length we came to a more open, peaceful country, with Olive-trees both cultivated and wild growing. Some sort of Prunus was in full bloom, pink and white, looking chilly enough in the blast of the fierce mistral. There was one region of bright-colored soils, the mountain sides being pink, orange, and chalky, but clad in part with dark Cedars and Pines. The train reached Avignon at 3.30. I went immediately to the Rocher des Doms. The wind was fairly howling through the narrow streets and round the strange building called "Château des Papes," the Pines on the rock bending low. The view was glorious, including rivers, mountains, and many towns. Across the Rhone were the quaint towers of Villeneuve (what a name!); and at my feet the crowded tile-roofed mass of the houses of Avignon, girt by a wall with many towers. I stayed till sunset on the hill, studied the layout of the terraced garden, measured and sketched, and rejoiced in the wealth of lovely evergreens in the plantations. Photinia serrul. a foot through; Arbutus Unedo the same! Viburnum Tinus coming into bloom, save on exposed corners where frost has killed the buds; Forsythia, Jasminum, and Iberis in bloom; also many Almond-trees, and Pansies. The sun set behind distant hills, the sky but partly clouded, and the stars coming out brightly.

This garden of evergreens and waving Pines, on a terrace on a great 200-foot cliff immediately above the Rhone, with the old church behind crowned by an image of Mary Virgin, with its several shrines, its monument to the discoverer of madder, its memories of Rienzi, and Petrarch, and of Petrarch's "Laura," — the whole a veritable Acropolis. C. E.'s first.

Sunday, March 7. A cloudless sky. The mistral (twin brother of our own northwester) still blowing a very gale. The view from the rock was far wider than last night. In the northeast a vast pile of high mountains rose into dazzling snow peaks. Again, C. E.'s first. I made choice of the direction for my walk, and went down across the Rhone, getting a fine view of Avignon and the Mont Blanc (?) behind. I walked down the river bank, and then turned westward, finally taking a seven-foot lane leading up one of the many semi-wild hills. There were views in all directions, — orchards of small Olive-trees; little terraces for vine-growing; many small, windowless, white-stuccoed cottages and villas. In the distance, westward, were rougher and higher hills, terribly stony, torrent-swept, and soilless. My lesser hill was very barren also, made of gravel full of large pebbles. The bits of vine or olive land had been cleared with great labor. Elsewhere there was a dense, low growth of a very small-leafed Holly, mixed with various Brooms, Euphorbias, Thorns, and a sort of Green Brier bearing red berries. The general effect was much like that of Cape Ann thickets where Myrica (Bayberry) predominates. I found Genista, Periwinkle, and Dandelion in bloom. I returned through more lanes, and finally by a white highway over the long bridges, the suspended bridge rocking violently with a wave-motion from end to end by reason of the gale.

Leaving Avignon by train, we first passed more white rock hills with little Olive orchards in the narrow valleys, then Tarascon, — a castle above the town, and another over the river. This was the home of René and the Troubadours!

Next came Arles, and then the sad country of the Camargue, low, often stony, flat, and dismal. The sun set over the dark green water of the Etang de Berre. Then came more barren hill-country, a three-mile tunnel, darkness, down a long valley a glimpse of the sea, and was that a flashing light? — Marseilles at 6.30. Provence is a sad land, with gray rocks, gray stony soils, little or no grass, gray Olives and almost black Cypresses, dull-colored buildings, and faded tile roofs.

No companionable people have been met with yet. I was alone coming from Avignon, and dreamt of its past; of Hannibal marching up the Isère; of Cæsar marching into Gaul; of Cinq-Mars, and " In His Name; " of Petrarch (whom I read in the Junior year), who loved the wild ravine of Vaucluse; of the minstrels of Beaucaire and Tarascon; of the Roman builders of Arles; and of the fleets of Phœnicians, Greeks, Carthaginians, Romans, Venetians, and Saracens who have harbored in this port of Marseilles.

He was up betimes next morning, and could not help visiting first the ancient port, being " drawn thither as by a magnet, just by the sight of masts and gleaming water." But soon he climbed the great hill of Nôtre-Dame de la Garde, a steep, almost bare rock, above the house line, having on top a high building, — church, fort, and lookout for ships combined.

A glorious prospect: two fifths the blue sea, three fifths a jagged hill horizon, the great city filling the valley, and the hills about it set thick with white villas. Seaward there were long breakwaters, miles of quays, and a coast in both directions rockbound, naked, jagged, high, white, and somewhat indented. Abreast of the city was a group of bare, high islands, clifty, and castle-crowned. Far seaward was a low rock with a tall tower (like Boone Island, Maine). About the islands were many clustered fishing-boats; and here, there, and everywhere the graceful lateens were beating or running free, — lovely to see. The water was blue and purple, flecked with cloud shadows, and ruffled but gently by the warm west wind. Two sorts of flowers were blooming in rocky chinks. I laid me down and basked in the warm sun. Uncle F.'s little field-glass is a great pleasure.

In the afternoon Charles surveyed a portion of the road which winds along the coast, sometimes walled, sometimes carried on arches across valley-mouths. The coast is high, and is broken by little coves with rough beaches. The heights bear Pines and villas; a vast variety of evergreens adorns the way, with gigantic Aloes, Agaves, tree Tamarisks, masses of yellow-flowering Genista, Periwinkle, and a Cactus which hangs over the cliffs. " I kept one eye on the sea and the sails, the other on the cliffs and blooming vales, and watched a lateen run into a tiny cove and land her catch of fish. Finally, the shore near town becoming rather Coney Islandish, I took the tram and rode through the main streets of the city to the hotel."

The next morning he went to the Jardin d'Acclimatation, in hopes of finding the plants named; but labels were few and far between, as usual. Enormous Agaves were flourishing under fine parasol Pines; and there was much interesting, if nameless, vegetation.

Rain coming on, I looked into the Art Museum for an hour, — a poor collection in costly halls. Outside, there is a fountain arrangement like that of the Trocadéro, — more curious than likable. Train for Hyères at 1.20, having seen all of profit in big, busy Marseilles. The population seems remarkably homogeneous and tremendously democratic ; if there are any nabobs, they are careful not to show themselves. No swell turnouts ; hardly a well-dressed person, man or woman, anywhere to be seen. The streets were thronged with chattering humanity, apparently loafing.

The town of Hyères is built on the south slopes of a high, rocky hill which bears many walls, towers, terraces, gardens, and olive orchards. The old town is in a sheltered hollow, and walled ; but the walls are built over with houses. It is a genuine feudal strong-place, with a complication of steep alleys, arched passages, flights of steps, stuccoed houses, terraces, and little gardens. Above the town are the rock and the ruined castle.

I clambered all round the castle rock, observing its hedges of Agaves and Aloes, the blooming Euphorbia and Jasmine, the evergreen Oaks and Olives, and many smaller evergreens making Cape-Ann-like thickets between ledges, filling the crevices in the cliffs, and growing out of the very walls of the castle, — lovely old walls growing, as it were, from the ledges and cliffs. There were round towers and square in all stages of dilapidation, Olives growing out of them, and Ivy, Smilax, and Green Brier clambering over them. On a shelf below a bristling row of Agaves, I met the goatherd and the village flock, behind him the blue sky and the sea, — a perfect picture. I met nobody else. The stillness was wonderful, the air good, and the whole walk delightsome. Next, I went to the Jardin d'Acclimatation, a branch of that of Paris, situated in the plain, but sheltered by plantations of Cypress, Pine, and Eucalyptus. Here were glorious foreign evergreens, a big collection of hardy Cacti, many sorts of Palms, Palmettos, Bamboos, Yuccas, Dracœnas, Acacias in glorious golden bloom, Viburnum Tinus a snowy mass, Templetonia [?] a mass of red ; with Violets, Pansies, Periwinkle, Salvia, and Geranium in prolific bloom ; early Spiræas, Pruni, and Willows coming into full leaf (March 10). Returning to town, I stopped in the Place des Palmiers to study the layout of the terrace and garden. In the evening, very tired, I read a good book bought in Marseilles, — "La Provence Maritime."

11th of March. This morning is gloriously bright, clear as a bell, and rather warmer. I shall stay another day. A very lovable place this, in spite of the English quarter.

The morning he spent at the nursery garden of Huber et Cie., which was filled with all manner of strange and familiar plants, — trees, shrubs, and flowers. He found blooming all the bulbs, Roses, Camellias, Acacias, Viburnum, Templetonia, Vinca, Tritoma, Anemone, Viola, Houstonia, Myosotis, and much else, — Iris of many sorts, for instance. The afternoon was passed —

most happily on the castle rock, where was much lovely mixing of walls, cliffs, jutting crags, and bastions overgrown with Agaves, Wallflower, or Smilax, or crowned with clustered Cypresses, or shrouded in evergreen Oak. . . . The old walls are mostly bare; but like the ledges, richly spotted with Lichens, — orange, brown, and pale green. The summit is exceedingly abrupt, approached by steps built in a narrow cleft; thence a grand prospect, — the sea and the isles, the plain, the presqu'ile of Giens, the wooded ranges of les Maures, the rock-capped hills and mountains back of Toulon, and a glimpse of the Bay of Toulon.

The next day he enjoyed the railway ride to Cannes.

At Fréjus I got a glimpse of a Roman amphitheatre, and saw close to the railway the big stone beacon that once marked the end of the Roman jetty, but is now more than a mile from the sea. A sudden leap of the railway into the red rocks of the Esterelle Mountains, a struggling along, through, and under heights and cliffs, by many tiny coves, and deep, narrow valleys filled with Heath breast high and blooming; under fantastic mountain-topping rocks; by grand headlands, white surf and deep red cliffs, and one little port with a lighthouse and a single lateen at anchor. This is a sparsely inhabited shore, reminding one a little of that between Seal Harbor and Great Head [Mt. Desert]. . . . To-day has been cloudy, — the sea purple, green, and gray.

Two days of stormy weather, and a troublesome ankle hurt at Hyères, intervened. But on the 15th of March he writes : —

I went down to the port and out on the breakwater, where I spent a delicious hour, — the weather bright, blue, warm, and still. I watched the surf, the quaint boats, the bare-legged, red-capped fishermen, and a row of moored trading coasters, their great lateen sails hanging from the long tapering booms to dry. Behind all this was the ancient rock with its old walls and towers; and far in the west, beyond a stretch of sea all topaz and emerald, the shadowy masses of the blue and hazy Esterelles. Next I went along the shore promenade, planted with Palms and Planes, — and Venetian masts with banners. Then slowly, and with many pauses to look at pergolas, water-towers, and other strange constructions, I walked up the height called la Californie, through loveliest winding lanes, bordered by hedges and walls of Roses, Jasmine, Acacia, Mimosa, and Agave, past many charming villas, commanding westward views, through rustling Palms or waving Eucalyptus, the sea spread wide below, the enchanting Esterelles waiting to hide the descending sun.

After calling on two English ladies who have lived at Cannes many winters, presenting to them a letter from Mr. Bryce, and being instructed in respect to the gardens best worth seeing, he walked down the hill, "the rapturous sunset squarely before me. What changeful color of sea! "

The next day was spent in studying the marvellous garden called Vallombrosa, situated on a rather steep slope between the château ("a poor castellated affair thoroughly out of place") and the highroad to Fréjus. This famous garden Charles considered rather a museum of specimen plants than a piece of landscape work. He found its general effect to be fantastic, stagy, astonishing, and exciting, rather than restful or calming. As an exhibition of splendid plants in immense variety it was intensely interesting ; but it reminded him, in its general effect, of the scenery of the pantomime stage rather than of anything in the real world. It was to him a medley of incongruous things, — such as Palms of many sorts and all ages, grouped or standing singly on grass, with brilliant flowers massed at their feet. His journal enumerates a profusion of trees and plants from many different climates and parts of the world all flourishing here together; but he says of the scene as a whole: "There is absolutely no breadth of effect, no landscape gardening save that successfully directed to concealing the bounds. . . . I loafed all the morning here; and in the afternoon walked on wild hills further inland; and concluded I should rather live among Heath and Pines and red rocks than in any Vallombrosa."

The gardens called Larochefoucauld gave Charles much more satisfaction than Vallombrosa.

These lovely grounds are situated between the Fréjus road and the sea. They contain but little specimen gardening. The house is of a sober and somewhat Italian character, white but pleasant, concealed in rich foliage, which yet is not too near the walls. The views from the terrace — over a sunken orange garden in one direction — of sea and sails, and in another direction of the Esterelles, are set in frames of tree masses. The sea-view might have been a wide one; but it is delightfully broken up into bits and glimpses by plantings of a most varied character, — Pines, and particularly Stone Pine, predominating. One little knoll bears a dozen Pines, which reach out seaward and bend low, and break the glare from the water without really concealing anything. In one part there is a steep bank which a path follows, the bank being clothed with a crowded thicket. Ilex and other trees stretch their limbs and trunks over the path. In rough places there are Agaves in shade of Pines, monstrous Sedums on rocks, and an undergrowth of Abutilon and Aralia, and such greenhouse plants, mixed with commoner things. Unfortunately, the railway passes between the garden and the beach; but a sea terrace hides it. Compared with ambitious Vallombrosa, this is a most charming place. Once within it the whole world is shut away, and one can see nothing but loveliest foliage, the sea, and the Esterelles. One is not distracted by "exclamation marks," — Asparagus shoots twenty feet long, and Dracænas like long-handled mops, and glowing carpets of flowers as at Vallombrosa. I have great respect for whoever made this place. Design is discoverable at many points; and it is much to have refrained from turning the place into a museum in a region where the climate offers such temptation to indulge in collecting curiosities.

The Villa Valletta, near Cannes, was a second example of a garden of specimen plants which Charles saw under the most favorable auspices, and thought "probably the most wondrous specimen garden to be seen in Europe." It is said that the place was cleared of 3500 trees in 1878, and then sodded and planted. "No vestige of the original wild hillside now remains. All is shaved, exquisitely trimmed, and 'well kept;' zigzag paths conduct to all parts of the steep sloping ground; and on all sides and everywhere are groups and single specimens of all manner of plants, great and small, beautiful and ugly, from all parts of the world save the cold parts. Nothing is labelled; and I therefore learned but little. I became more than ever convinced of the tiresomeness and the bad taste of these museum-like gardens." He sought consolation, the next day, in a rough scramble for two hours on the wild promontory of Théoule, among ravines and valleys, and along the shore.

Out of Cannes Charles took various excursions, — to Grasse with its Rose farms; to le Bar and Courmes, whence he saw the little town and castle of Jourdon; to Ile Sainte-Marguerite; and to Ile Saint-Honorat. These low, Pine-clad islands interested him very much, as all islands in view of higher shores had always done. One of the excursions, that to le Bar and Courmes, he thus describes: —

In half an hour we reached a high divide [he was with an agreeable English acquaintance], and looked away from the sea down into the deep valley of the Rivière du Loup, and across to high, wild calcareous mountains whose whitish steeps are almost completely bare, and whose broken summits were flecked with snow and partly veiled with cloud. On a spur of the craggy mountain called the "Saut du Loup," and just at the mouth of the gorge from which the river Loup comes down, stands le Bar, a small, compact town of high buildings, which we reached and passed after long following of mountain flanks. The road then turning southward and toward the gorge, we came in sight of the narrow cañon and the great cliffs of Courmes, and of a little town and castle called "Jourdon" on a seemingly inaccessible and almost pointed mountain 800 metres above the sea level, — a most astonishing vision; for I did not know we were coming to anything of the sort. At the Pont du Loup we halted, and walked up the gorge a little way; but time was short, and though I wanted to follow the foaming river to its Alpine springs, I was compelled to turn about and travel back to Grasse, and so to Cannes.

In a letter to his mother he says of himself at Cannes : —

I am loafing horribly on this Riviera. The vegetation is hopelessly strange, and, I suppose, unreproduceable in America unless in Florida or California. The sea, on the other hand, and the blue Esterelles look very familiar ; and I never tire of either. There is one yacht in port here, a creature like this, evidently masted and hulled for Bay of Biscay weather.  . . . Time flies terribly ; and, somehow, I don't learn anything ; but I enjoy myself much, on the whole. It was good to be approved of by Mr. Olmsted and by Mr. Brodrick. I wish I might some day find something in me I could approve of myself.

With some pleasant English acquaintances he visited the Cistercian Monastery on Île de Saint-Honorat, and says of the brothers : —

They farm it a little, and have a walled garden close by the surf to dig in ; and no man could desire a lovelier spot than is theirs. Adjoining the monastery, but set out in the sea on a low ledge, stands a square-built, tower-like fortress, which was the monks' defence against Moorish pirates in the old days (A. D. 1000). This I had seen from far Théoule ; and I was glad of the chance to climb about the place. An interesting thing this, with vastly thick walls, and narrow stairs, and battlements, and an inner court which has been restored. Its position, not on a crag or cliff, but on a very low ledge off a low shore, is peculiar.

In the afternoon of Sunday, March 21st, he left Cannes for Cap d'Antibes. Of this place he wrote to his mother thus : —

Cannes, and my excursions out of it, were good ; but this Cap d'Antibes is better. Here one is set off from the Con-

tinent a little way, so that there is a fine view of said Continent, the coasts and mountains of it; and the place is wholly
quiet and free from crowd and swelldom. There is no town,
only one big, empty hotel, half a dozen scattered villas (most
of them shut up), and a few Orange groves and flower farms.
The rest is wild land, with thickets of evergreens, and shelves
and banks where bloom Anemones, Daisies, Primroses, and
wild Hyacinths. Last night I went to sleep to the sound of
gentle surf. This morning there was a thick haze over all
the sea and hiding all the shores, — just such as I have often
seen in Boston Bay, — and slowly, as the sun came up the
sky, this haze was swept away, and showed first the pale sky,
then the nearer shores, and the big war-ships in Golfe-Jouan,
then Ile Sainte-Marguerite, a dark line of pine woods, and
the Pointe de la Croisette of Cannes; and it was not till
nearly noon that the outline of the Esterelles became dimly
visible.

The sort of problem which was always engaging Charles's
attention is well illustrated by his remarks about some private
grounds at the Cap d'Antibes. The house had before it a
formally modelled lawn, with flower beds on the swells, and
at the foot of this lawn was a long, straight, terrace-wall, and
a balustrade near the brink of rough cliffs.

I could not make up my mind about the wall and balustrade. They serve as dividing line between the dress ground
before the house and the wildness of the cliffs; and probably
they make a good foreground for the grand view when one
looks from the house; but seen from other parts of the shore
one wishes them away. They seem wholly out of place; for
they are not near enough to the house to seem a part of the
building. A row of small palms just within the balustrade
is also of very questionable value. Just below this wall, on
a jutting point of cliff, is an ordinary rockery, with the plants
labelled in little compartments, — this in the foreground of a
sea-view which is only bounded by the Esterelles seen over
Ile Sainte-Marguerite! Too bad! At the gate is a charming lodge, built of stone, low, and of simplest form, with
an "outside room" screened by lattice with creepers. The
flowers — chiefly Cinerarias of magnificent colors and huge

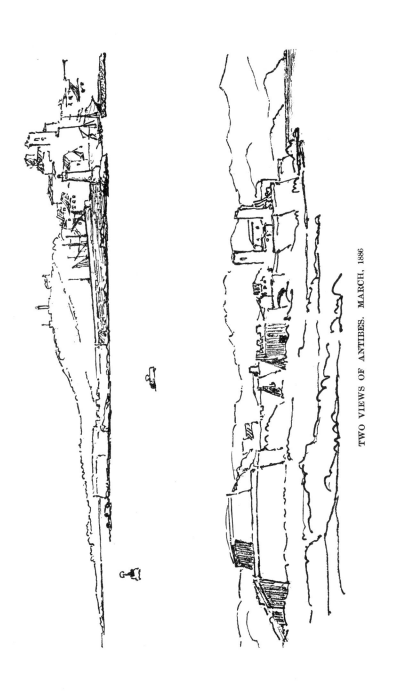

TWO VIEWS OF ANTIBES. MARCH, 1886

Cyclamens — are confined to the immediate neighborhood of this lodge, and to beds of dress ground before the house.

In another private place, which he examined, he speaks of " a region where the original wild shrubbery has been made to make room for a well-chosen variety of plants, which have been naturalized in its midst." The word " naturalized " defines what was, for him, good taste in the artificial treatment of rough and essentially wild regions. Again, concerning the same place, he says : —

On a jutting point of hill is a very pleasant, well-contrived, and pretty sort of arbor, having stone piers and a roof of canes, its irregular ground-plan conformed to the shape of the ledge, the views from within it very wide and well framed. In a hollow, where it is not seen till the hollow is entered, is a small, well-built rockery, — the stones large, with no petty compartments. Some largish trees shut in the whole hollow ; but down a gulch leading to the water is a controlling view. . . . The shore cliffs are made the most of, — rude paths with rude stairs (where necessary) lead to the finest points; and one big gulch has a way down into it, the stairs so well contrived as not to be visible save to one travelling them.

Before going on to Nice, he climbed the hill of Nôtre Dame (March 23).

The air was thick with a smoky haze, all outlines soft, and everything mysterious. Suddenly high in the sky, above a dark headland, something gleaming white, — quick, my glass, — yes, a snow-peak, fine cut, and radiant, seamed with delicate lines of blue shadows ; but in an instant wrapt again in mists. I spent most of two hours on this lighthouse hill. Little feluccas crept in and out from the port of Antibes ; goats and kids frisked about on the rocky hillside ; birds kept up continuous singing in the Pine woods and Olive groves at the foot of the hill ; cloud shadows and flecks of sunlight travelled slowly over shores, mountains, and sea ; and now and then the veil of haze behind the foot-hills was silently rent, and jagged summits and long crests of snow-mountains stood revealed. I believe it was all lovelier than if the day had been wholly bright, and the mountains completely visible. I passed down into the ancient town by the path used by mariner-pilgrims when they go up to the church. The quays were of stone; and about a dozen vessels were moored to them, — one big sloop almost like a Cape Ann stone-sloop. . . . I rambled also in the crooked old town. It is the first place I have seen which has not spread over and out of its walls; but the walls here are modernized. Nice at 3 o'clock.

The next day Charles strolled about the town, along the sea front to the little harbor, and up the high castle hill. A hot sun made the roads very white and glaring. The town he found citified, — a band playing in the public garden. " There is a big cascade on the very summit of castle hill, — how fantastic are some men! There is no view thence to the eastward, a great wooded mountain being in the way. Westward, the view includes the Cap d'Antibes. The hills about Nice are dotted with villas. The mountains behind, to-day, are wrapped in cloud."

Charles's time at Nice was much taken up with social engagements. A few days later he wrote to his father : —

At Nice days disappeared very rapidly. There I saw but one fine garden. I disliked the whole Paris-like place; and there was nothing particular to see in my line. I have, I fear, yielded of late rather much to the softness of this sunny climate. Several days have fled, I hardly know how. . . . Here I am in one of the fairest regions of the earth; and daily I am in want of more strength of limb, of eyes, of heart, — more power of grasping and remembering the beauty that I am here fairly overwhelmed by. I say with Keats : " Now Beauty is the substance of things hoped for; the evidence of things not seen; the shadow of reality to come." The forces of the universe work and work, in affairs human and social, as often towards ends our souls call evil, as towards ends we call good. I find no correspondence between my soul and the world, save in this, — that the natural world is beautiful, and that my soul loves beauty. The fairness of the earth, not the rainbow only, is the " sign set in the sky."

In this letter Charles betrayed some of the gloomy speculations about himself in which he had indulged.

You urge me to count Mr. Olmsted's [favorable] judgment for much ; and I do.   It is, however, not in matters of
theory and taste that I feel myself so utterly incompetent.
It is in the more practical affairs of the profession, and particularly in dealing with men, that I am nowhere.   In matters of design I arrive at definite opinions only with great
difficulty.   I am far from quick in getting new ideas. . . .
But I am most at a loss when thrown with other men.   I
cannot think, and at the same time talk and give attention.
I am never at my ease, — indeed, I am as far as possible
from being so. . . . I know myself to be ill-made, or, as it
were, an unbaked loaf of the human bread-batch.

To this letter both his brother and his father sent hortatory
replies.   " Dear Boss, — What a plum you are !   You seem
to have occasional blue fits, — a most unwarrantable proceeding.   You are the only person that I know who does not
take a very rosy view of your proceedings and prospects.
You 're about the last fellow with reason to growl.   Your
stomach is the only reasonable excuse, and a man who eats
curry at midnight, and seems to be good for all-day tramps
over rough country, had better not make too much capital out
of stomach growls.   The Riviera in April !   Why, man alive,
it 's paradise !   All bright sunshine and flowers ; while here,
— well it 's as much as a fellow's life is worth to get across
the Yard, which is a great lake of dirty slush. . . . It makes
me quite weary to hear of a youth of your capacity, with a
new trade to develop, well equipped and well supported,
sitting down to grumble at his prospects." . . .

CAMBRIDGE, 20 Apr. '86.

DEAR CHARLES, — Don't imagine yourself deficient in
power of dealing with men.   Such dealings as you have thus
far had with boys and men you have conducted very suitably.
There is no mystery about successful business intercourse
with patrons and employés.   Nobody can think, and at the
same time pay attention to another person, as you seem to
expect to do.   On the contrary, exclusive attention to the
person who is speaking to you is a very important point in
business manners.   Nothing is so flattering as that.   Some
audible or visible signs of close attention are of course desirable.   Then there is very seldom any objection to the
statement, " I should like to think that over."   On the contrary, such evidence of deliberation is ordinarily acceptable.

Good judgment is what people are most willing to pay for. Quickness and reputation for speed are much less valuable. . . . I wish you were tough and strong like me. But you have nevertheless an available measure of strength, and within that measure an unusual capacity of enjoyment. In this respect you closely resemble your mother. She enjoyed more in her short life than most people in a long one; and particularly she delighted in natural scenery. You get a great deal more pleasure out of your present journeyings than I ever could have. I should not have your feelings of fatigue and weakness, but neither should I have your perception of the beautiful and your enjoyment of it. When you come to professional work, you will have to be moderate in it. Where other men work eight hours a day, you must be content with five. Take all things easily. Never tire yourself out. If you feel the blues coming upon you, get a book and a glass of wine, or go to bed and rest yourself. The morbid mental condition is of physical origin. Take comfort in the thought that you can have a life of moderate labor, — the best sort of life. You will have a little money of your own, and need not be in haste to earn a large income. I am strong and can work twelve hours a day. Consequently I do; and if it were not for Mt. Desert, I should hardly have more time for reflection and real living than an operative in a cotton mill. For a reasonable mortal, life cannot truly be said to have " terrors," any more than death. [Charles had quoted the lines: —

> I am not one whom death does much dismay.
> Life's terrors all death's terrors far outweigh.]

The love of beauty is a very good and durable correspondence between your soul and the world; but the love of purity, gentleness, and honor is a better one.   [C. W. E. to C. E.]

From Nice Charles returned to the Cap d'Antibes to visit the Garden Thuret; but Sunday, March 28th, was the loveliest possible day; and he devoted it altogether to strolling through lanes and woods and alongshore, and watching the sky and the sea.

At sunset I watched all the changing coloring of sky and sea, — the paling opal pearl and amethyst of the still water, the glowing and the fading of the sky. The sea was very still; the water wondrous clear in deep basins among the whitish rocks. The only sound was the splashing of gentlest surf in the caves and crannies of the low and jagged shore.

Peace here, — Nice with its swarms of knaves, swells, and cocottes, its luxuries, scandals, and all else, is as though it were not. After dinner the stars were out, and extraordinarily bright. Verily this out-of-door life by the sea in the month of March is marvellously good and pleasant.

A letter of introduction from Professor Asa Gray, of Cambridge, caused Charles to be cordially received at the Garden Thuret by Mons. Naudin, — an elderly man with a kindly face, but stone deaf. He showed Charles over the place, spending the whole morning in this way. They communicated by signs and a slate.

It is the most lovely garden I have ever seen. In reality, a small place; but very much made of it. Mons. Thuret had his choice of sites on the cape. The house stands at the summit of the northward slope, commanding views of both bays, with a glimpse of the light-tower close at hand, and from under parasol Pines, a view of the town and towers of Antibes, and of the Alps above, — a perfect picture. All the views and glimpses are beautifully framed by varied foliage ; and the rest of the world is shut out completely. A steep lawn descends from the house, — a field of fresh green, thickly strewn with small Daisies, and with brilliant single Anemones of many colors ; many fine Conifers stand about the edges of the lawn ; Eucalyptus trees of many sorts form the bulk of the plantations ; countless foreign and native evergreens from all parts of the world, mixed together in large masses and thickets, take up most of the ground ; Palms have a region near the house to themselves ; a rockery is hidden away. The general effect from the house is not inharmonious ; although most of the plants used are foreign, and of marked individual character. Mr. Naudin — who is called " director," being appointed to the charge of the place by the government, to which Thuret's relatives gave the garden on his death — is particularly interested in the Eucalyptus tribe ; so he has been cutting down old Olives and Ilexes which Thuret had spared, to make room for his " darlings," of which he has some 130 sorts. He is first a botanist ; and I fear he will sacrifice the beauty of the place to his collecting instinct. Across the road he has large collections of Irises, bulbs, climbers, etc., lists of which, and of the trees and shrubs grown in the main garden, are printed in pamphlet form.

March 30. Again clear and most lovely. The doors of the hotel stand open all day. I sleep with a long French window at least half open. The frogs make a great noise at dawn and at sunset. The country becomes lovelier daily. Fig-trees have leaves about half out of the bud ; Wych-Elms are clad in yellow bloom ; Almonds, Peaches, and others of the Prunus tribe, are blooming pink or white, or pushing fresh green leaves ; Willows are lovely in light green ; a sort of Thyme, which carpets the ground between clumps of Myrtle and Pistacia, is blooming pink ; lovely wild Anemones are almost everywhere ; Primroses on banks, and Narcissi in wet meadows, are much rarer ; but Hyacinth, Forget-me-not, Daisy, and Dandelion are very common.

Another long day was spent in the Garden Thuret and its neighborhood, making notes of the most striking plants, especially of the shrubs. The proprietor of a neighboring nursery gave Charles some information about the indigenous shrubs, twigs of which he had gathered. He went up to the lighthouse to watch the sunset, — a supremely fine one ; and walked back in the dusk, meeting many parties of men and women going home from labor on the flower farms, some singing as they walked.

The next day, March 31st, he contemplated philosophically the Bataille des Fleurs at Nice.

Two interesting young French women were near me in the crowd by the roadside, — one, virtuous, quietly dressed, accompanied by her brother. She threw what flowers she caught always at men, young or old, but got very little in return ; the other, very jauntily dressed, alone, and of doubtful reputation, soon got her parasol full of flowers, and got more and more as time went on. . . . I was three times favored by a certain painted fair one ; but the pretty American at whom I flung what I got, only replied once. I amused myself with imagining what sort of a time I should probably have had that day had Mrs. Beadle not gone. [Mrs. Beadle was the head of the pleasant American family whose acquaintance Charles had made on the Germanic and in

London.] Looking on alone at a thing of this kind is not very interesting.

April 1st was his last day in Nice. He was shown over the garden Vigier by the gardener, to whom Mons. Naudin had given him a card. There was a small green lawn, and a terrace balustrade to hide the road, the sea view being obtained over the balustrade. Charles noted a grove of Palms, — two very large ones in the form of an arbor, — the grove of Yucca Indivisa, the thickets of huge Bamboos (nigra, gracilis, mitis), the Cedars and Acacias, and the masses of blooming Camellias with tree Ferns in a shady corner; and many rarities in the way of Palms, Bananas, and Cocoas. Returning to town, he watched a big lateen's arrival in the port under full sail, " with some astonishment until I saw how quickly headway could be stopped by clewing up the big sail to the yard." In the evening he saw " a big show of fireworks, with lighted boats, etc., — the Fête Venitienne being the termination of the Mid-Lent carnival. This and all Nice fêtes are got up by a committee of subscribers to draw visitors, — quite as at Montreal."

On his way to Mentone Charles stopped at the romantic hill-village of Eze, placed on top of a seemingly inaccessible rock a thousand feet and more in the air, — once a Saracen stronghold. Catching a glimpse of this village from the railway station at the shore, he —

was tempted and yielded, — vowed I would get into said stronghold, and took the first mountain path. It climbed and climbed and twisted; not a house on the way, and a very few scattered Olive terraces, — only gray sunburnt rock and bare baked earth, and clumps of light green Euphorbia, dwarf Pines, yellow-blooming Genista, and Cistus, and Harebells. There was a deep ravine, — where was welcome shade, — and down at the mouth of it, blue sea, and a little jutting isoletta or "thumbcap." Up at the head were utterly bare ridges of gray rock, and on the left cliffs, on top of which must be the invisible Eze. There was continuous beauty of rock and natural rock-planting all along the steep zigzags of the path, — a very rude path, its turns very sharp, no railings even on great precipices, a veritable mountain mule-track, — for centuries and now the only road from Eze to the shore. There was one ruined, overgrown, stone and tile

building at the head of a gulch. From that point up the
path was rudely paved, often becoming a stair. At last I
came in sight of the town, with its high, continuous outer-
walls of cliff-perched houses, Prickly Pear and Fern growing from the walls and rocks. There was a crooked, narrow
gate and entrance passage, passable only by human beings,
donkeys, and goats   Within was a complication of jagged
ledges, walls of dwellings, and steep paved alleys, over which
the roofs nearly met. Then a high rock with ruins, a church
with a campanile, and a most glorious, wide prospect, — indescribable ! The silence of death was all about ; not a
human creature ; not a voice. Sheep in a flock were visible
over across a monstrously deep valley on the slope of another
mountain. Some rude carts were clustered at the end of a
road, that seems to have attempted to get up to the town
from the landward side. At several points on the mountains
round about I could make out the line of the old Corniche
road. Trying to find something of the nineteenth century, —
so weird was the whole place, — a few telegraph poles following the Corniche was veritably all I could see. . . . A most
memorable day : Eze and its mountains, — the most picturesque of places.

Of Mentone and its neighborhood Charles wrote : " I
thought little Mt. Chevalier (Cannes) picturesque ; but this
is incomparably more so. The view from the breakwater is
enchanting, high buildings rising from the very rocks of the
shore, — rocks to which mooring lines are fastened ; a curious
church steeple rises above all." The walk eastward into Italy
especially delighted him, over the winding and climbing Corniche, from several points of which superb views are obtained
westward even as far as the Esterelles, and eastward to Bordighera on its point. The road curves inland into a shady
valley ; and then comes the village of La Mortola, set on an
Olive-clad point of mountain. Close by are the gates of Mr.
Hanbury's villa. The garden around this villa is the most
famous of all the Riviera. " A wonderland of vegetation ; a
garden of Eden. ' C'est le pays du bon Dieu ! ' said a man to
me ; and he was right. That view from the high cape near
Mr. Hanbury's scuola is the most utterly romantic thing mine
eyes have seen." Charles made two visits to this garden,
having a letter of introduction from an English friend. He

took notes of many lovely things; but also "noted much as what not to do." As usual, he was more delighted with the general aspect of the country and the sea than with the details of garden-work, beautiful and rare as they were.

In the afternoon of April 4th, I walked inland; and again was wrought into a sort of ecstasy, — an exaggerated form of the "spring fever" I have had at home. I went up a valley with a torrent bed in it, bounded by steeper and steeper hills, bearing Olives interspersed with groves of Oranges and Lemons, occasional blooming Peach-trees, and bud-bursting figs, with now and then tall spires of Cypress. The dwellings of the peasantry, stuccoed, and colored yellowish or pinkish, were buried in foliage. On the right, above rich woods, was a high-perched town, — Castellar. On the left, a huge mill with three great wheels, set on the steep hillside, the water brought to it from a great distance. Up the valley, a distant church nestled in woods; and behind it great ranges of rock mountains with sharp crests, fantastic pinnacles, and deep gorges. Everywhere fresh plant life was pushing out, — Hornbeams, various Pruni, and the deciduous trees generally were all in loveliest half-burst state, beside many flowers, Ferns, and pretty wall plants. On the 5th of April, beside the time spent in Mr. Hanbury's garden, I took half an hour to look at little La Mortola, — a cluster of houses on a sort of headland above the Corniche road, approached only by footpaths; but possessed of two churches, and of a prospect lovely beyond words. I met many groups of peasants, with faces and costumes thoroughly Italian; lovely children and pretty girls. One of the latter, in an Olive wood, was watching bread-baking in an outdoor oven. Women, bearing great sacks or bundles, were travelling the one road, or climbing the paths leading mountainwards; mules, decked out with all manner of tassels and finery, passed in procession, each with his laden paniers; little mule carts were freighted with jars, such as the Forty Thieves got into; flocks of sheep and goats were attended by the conventional herder; wall frescoes of "Virgo Potens" and other subjects were painted on the walls of the humble dwellings; there were wayside inns with little pergolas; . . . men with what I have always supposed to be the fisherman's hat, — red woollen and tall so that the top hangs over; men with bright scarfs around their hips; and half-naked children running after the few travellers' carriages. I have been coming to Italy very slowly, and the changes have been very gradual; but, verily, I have now arrived. On the Italian end of Pont de Saint-Louis (near Mentone) sits a haggard beggar; and on a rock near by is written " *E viva Garibaldi!* "

From Mentone Charles made an excursion to Monte Carlo, where he spent a whole morning in the famous gardens designed by André of Paris. His journal describes its broad terraces, with balustrades and vases of stucco; its steep, pebble-paved walks; the rich verdure of its formal thickets; its smooth green lawns, set with specimens in great variety; and its concrete brook, planted with even more fantastic plants than are used, or can be used, in Paris.

On the land side of the Casino there is handsome formal work; ample gravel spaces; a circle with a fountain; a long, narrow sunk parterre with Palms at the corners, borders of Ivy, massed Roses in the borders, and brilliant flowers in raised beds in the centre, — all exquisitely kept and very costly. It is a strange contrast to the barren mountain sides which tower immediately behind, culminating in the mountain headland of the Tête du Chien, and the high ridge, where, seen against the sky, stands a great ruined tower — the Tropæa of Augustus Cæsar.

He looked into the gambling hells in the afternoon, noticing "the continuous shoving about of money in big sums and little; the extreme silence; the odd faces; the many queer folk: and some wild behavior, — a monstrous curious spectacle altogether."

Thence he walked round the "Port of Hercules," and up into Monaco, "a place I have always much desired to see, having had some photographs of it at home." He enjoyed the magnificent views east and west along the coasts from the open place before the palace, and the cliff walk all around the old town, and the Pine-grove garden at the extremity of the point; but when he reached this grove, what he did was to watch two brigs in the offing, and two feluccas, close at hand, beating round the point.

. . . In the palace square, near the wall at the edge of the west cliff, I came upon a row of old cannon, among them two of the same pattern as those on Cambridge Common, and with the same monogram, — " G. R." . . . By train back to Mentone for table d'hôte. Weary, and to bed early. This climate, though divinely fair, is weakening. I am too easily tired; and, when tired, I see and learn little or nothing. What a curious life I am leading! Day after day do I come upon some new beauty; and daily I say, " Here is something more picturesque than ever." To-day I swear I never saw a picturesque town until I saw Mentone; and never a paintable mill until I saw that of the Grimaldis in the Val di Castellar. By the time I am back in Paris I shall be utterly spoilt. How miserable will seem the vegetation of the north, how hard and unlovely my New England!

He wrote to his mother, on the 12th of April, —

I live nowadays in a sort of dream — a very lovely dream the Riviera has been — wholly indescribable in any wretched journal that I have time or wits to write. I have slept many nights close to the surf; and several times, on first waking I have thought myself at Manchester [Mass.]. That this sea is veritably the Mediterranean I find it hard to believe; and how incapable I find myself of taking in and really in any way assimilating the much that I see. I have felt a little rushed since those quiet days at Antibes, so many and so quick-succeeding have been the new scenes, new experiences, and new ideas. Mentone I really came to know something of; but of Bordighera, San Remo, and Alassio, I got only glimpses — all lovely and different places, and any one of them containing food for a week for a hungry and raw Yankee like me. I set out from Paris with the notion that these weeks of March and April were to be given to a pleasure trip almost pure and simple; that eight weeks would be as much time as I ought to give to this purpose; and that it was my bounden duty to be back in Paris in very early May. Now I have learned, I think, that I should have started earlier, and planned to stay longer; for I find and now believe that it would be well worth while to study Italian gardening with some thoroughness — particularly as Mr. Olmsted seems to think so too. . . . Perhaps it will be well to come back here in the autumn; though by that time, Heaven knows, I shall be wanting to get home pretty badly.

His glimpse of Bordighera included an exploration of the old walled town, and a walk up the hillside, through narrow lanes between large Palm gardens — Palms leaning out of and over the walls, and forming large groves, very beautiful when seen against sky or sea. At San Remo he was delighted with a picturesque Olive mill in the first valley east of the town hill, with the sluices carried on slender arches, and a high "flying bridge" for the footpath, its parapets crumbled away, and other slender bridges of great span to carry the waste water to stone settling-tanks built in the side of the gulch. "Thence I climbed through Olives to the church at the top of the town, then down through old narrow staircases, alleys, and tunnels, to luncheon in the restaurant of the new town. The alleys were the narrowest, darkest, and dirtiest of any yet seen — a veritable ant-hill." He took an omnibus thence to the east end of the route; and then followed a winding mountain road up a long ascent.

A turn in my road; and suddenly, close at hand, a little town on the slope of my mountain, close packed as possible — not one straggling building; a church with a high, false front, and a campanile in the midst. Suddenly the sound of a deep, distant bell from beyond the great valley. I looked hard, and discovered another small ant-hill town, perched on a steep bluff over across the valley. It was approached only by zigzags through low Pine woods and Olives, or across bare, torrent-washed slopes. At a ruined church on the top of the ridge — a smithy in it — I took a road leading seaward . . . on high land and presently arrived at the Cape Madonna della Guardia — which I had seen in the morning from the port of San Remo — in time to see the final closing-down of the clouds upon the mountains towards Bordighera and the heights back of San Remo. I was on a high point, barren to a degree, a bleak, white chapel on the summit, in which I took refuge from the first shower of rain. A storm was evidently brewing. I hurried down, and followed a dull shore road back to San Remo, which town seemed astonishingly far

away.　A second shower fell with vigor; but I hid in the
house of a railway gate-keeper; and finally arrived at the
hotel, dry, just before the continuous downpour began.　This
was of importance, because my clothes had gone to Genoa.
I made a short evening over plant-notes, weary but happy,
being fairly drenched with picturesqueness if not with rain.
I met much semi-costume to-day and yesterday.　Why need
these women carry such burdens?　In the towns everybody
is lugging something; and what loads they pile on mules and
donkeys; and what a good time they seem to have gathering
olives; and how unblushingly the pretty and healthy children
run after one and beg.

Riviera journeying is almost at an end for me.　The best
of it has been the seeing of real picturesqueness — a sight for
which mine eyes have been hungering many years.　I have
also got a good idea of what can be accomplished in the way
of plant-growing in a climate of this character; have made
long lists of the trees and shrubs best worth remembering;
have learned to recognize very many sorts (but shall forget
them); have copies of the printed lists of plants at Monte
Carlo and Cap d'Antibes; and have got together some ideas
as to what general design in landscape gardening should be
in similar countries.

At Alassio Charles visited the garden of General Sir M.
McMurdo, to whom Mr. Bryce had given him a letter, — a
small but very delightful place, made on a very steep hillside
as at La Mortola.　It was formerly in Olive terraces; but
these are now partly done away with, and partly disguised.
There was a pleasantly intricate series of along-hill paths,
close thickets, rude flights of steps, a less rude but handsome
flight, with a turn, made of red tufa rock with a terra-cotta
balustrade.　In many directions, glimpses of sea and mountains were obtained; but there was only one point of general
widespread view.　General McMurdo had been the engineer
of the place; and Mrs. McMurdo the gardener.　The engineering was conspicuously good, the walks having an adequate
appearance of support on the downhill side — an unusual
merit.

At six o'clock, in loveliest evening light, I set out alone
from the hotel; and walked westward over the sand beach,

along which is built the old town. . . . The old town is
crowded at the water's edge, the railway passing behind it —
an altogether unusual arrangement on this coast. There was
one short stone pier; but all the boats were drawn up on
the sands. The calm was delicious, with lovely reflections;

Two Riviera arrangements for a drive and sea-wall along a beach.

and a gentle white surf played all around the great sweep of
the beach. The boats were loading with empty fish-barrels,
for a small steamer at anchor outside to carry to the fishing-
grounds. There was a pretty scene at the launching of the
last boat-load, — crowds of bare-legged boys helping shove off,
their backs against the stem of the big seine-boat-like craft.
Many children and their mothers were out for air on the
beach, — building sand castles and so forth.

Sunday, April 12th. The railroad ride to Genoa offered a
succession of small bays, valleys, and grand mountain capes,
with many charmingly placed towns, and many castles more
or less ruined set on romantic heights. There were also
glimpses of snow mountains, continuous blue sea, and fine
masses of cumuli over both the Rivieras. This ride, however,
impaired somewhat Charles's enjoyment of the next day, for
it was a succession of black tunnels and bright openings, very
trying to the eyes. The countless Renaissance palaces with
their courts, loggias, and staircases in many architectural
styles, were the chief objects of interest in the city; but the
well-devised promenade Acquasola and the public garden of
Villetta di Negro, which offered fine views over the city, port,
and environs, were also instructive. The Villa Pallavicini
lies a little outside of Genoa; and was carefully examined by
Charles; but he did not find it very instructive, although it
is a famous garden. There were some pleasant shaded walks,
some very successful rock-work made of stones from the sea-

shore, some well-devised streamlets, a large stalactite grotto, and a lakelet from which, by taking a boat, fine views are to be had of the Genoa light-tower and the sea. Many fanciful pavilions and summer-houses, Turkish, Chinese, and other, diversified the garden; also temples of Flora and Vesta; and a building which, on one side, is a triumphal arch, and on the other, a rustic cottage! Many odd water squirts entertained the visitors. Among the unusual decorations are the imitation ruins of two fortresses, with a tomb of a general supposed to have died in defence of one of them; and even a sort of imitation shrine of the Virgin in one corner, with an inscription granting certain indulgences to whoever may salute her image.

The Villa Rostan, which Charles also visited, is a less puerile place, although there are several squirts, and a hermit's cabin with a stuffed hermit, also a grotto with Diana bathing, and other illustrations of classical legend. Most of this place is a wood with underbrush, through which there are occasional very long vistas — one of the distant light-tower very effective. In the depth of the wood is a paved, moss-carpeted dancing-floor, with stone seats in the shrubbery round about, and an overlooking stone gallery; also a little open-air theatre, all mossy, and (like all else in the place) with an air of neglect, or romantic dilapidation, about it which is not unpleasing.

The next day Charles spent much time over photographs in an attractive shop; but, as had often happened to him before, he found but few worth buying. " They are verily a snare and a delusion except for buildings and architectural details." Throughout all Europe he found it very difficult to get pleasing and instructive photographs of scenery. Either the objects which interested him had never been photographed, or the photographs which had been taken gave no just idea of the real scenes. He came to the conclusion that one who desired to bring away from Europe photographic memoranda of landscape which had interested him must be his own photographer. His last remark before leaving Genoa was, " I looked into two fine palaces. What nabobs these merchant princes of Genoa were; and what ingenious architects built them their palaces! "

In the afternoon of April 14th he went on to Santa Margherita, enjoying intensely, as usual, the railroad ride by the small crowded towns, the many villas, the lemon groves, and the bits of castles in all sorts of positions, — in torrent beds, on top of heights, on the sea beach, or on slopes of mountains

The hotel at Santa Margherita stood on the edge of the water of the port, almost as close as at Alassio, where the surf on the sand beach seemed about to roll into the hall and dining-room. The outlook eastward from the hotel presented a grand succession of mountains, very many of the height of Mt. Desert's highest (1527 feet), rising directly from the sea; and behind these others rising to 3000 feet and more — none quite so fine, however, as those which hang over Monaco and Mentone.

April 15. A divine morning, still, bright, and fresh. I took the shore road toward the end of the cape, bound to see Portofino. The road was very winding, always close to the water, and having now heights and cliffs, and now mountain-descended valleys on the right hand. There were many deep coves, many short bits of beach, and many wild cliffs and fantastic forms of coarse, conglomerate rocks. Everywhere were Pines, Arbutus, blooming Coronilla, Heath, and Myrtle, and now and then steep slopes of Olive woods. For three miles there were no houses, save a group at Paraggi; but a monastery on the flank of the mountain (with one Palm reared above the enclosing walls), and a quaint rectangular castle, set on a jutting rock of the shore at the mouth of a cove, its battered base partly hidden by Pines which also reached down over the shore rocks, its upper parts curiously broken into bays and groups of windows. At the head of one rock-bound cove, in a cleft of the cliffs, were a spring and cistern, where groups of women were washing. Around the next headland the wagon road suddenly ended against the close-built buildings of the town of Portofino. Hence was one of the quaint-est pictures ever seen, — a deep hill-piercing cove, the shores opposite wooded and reflected in water; small vessels were moored in the inmost corners, their yards almost touching the trees, and the steep wooded heights of the long promontory opposite were crowned by castles of varying form, partly hidden in verdure. The little port was headed by a wide, short beach, with high buildings close about it, and strung in a block along the hither shore. Olive-clad heights close behind rise further off into Pine-clad summits of some two thousand feet. The road having ended, I got down into the

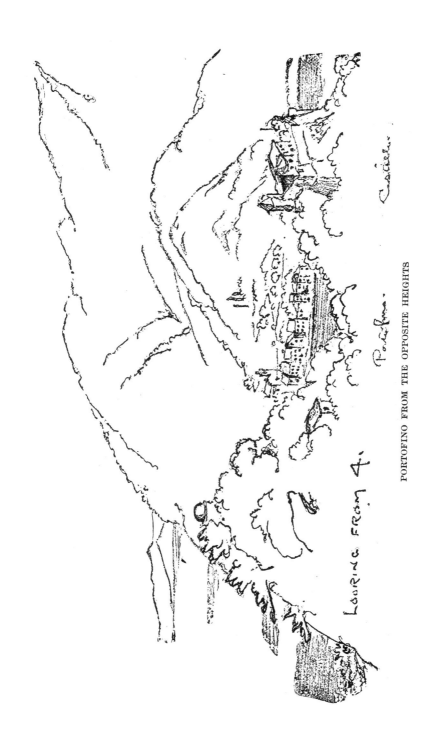

LOOKING FROM 4.

Portofino.

Castle.

PORTOFINO FROM THE OPPOSITE HEIGHTS

piazza at the beach by poking down a steep staircase under buildings. From the beach, looking outward, the view was more striking. At the right, the wooded castle-crowned heights ; at the left, a little quay and the blocked buildings under the mountain, the opening between crossed in the far distance by the coast line of the mainland.

Next I climbed round the cape to the church visible at point No. 1 in the map, using a little path and staircase which winds among cliffs and under mossy boulders, and to my great surprise found myself on the brink of great cliffs of open sea, with white surf dashing far below at their base. I pushed on by a footpath along the harbor side of the promontory, past the first strange castle, — or, rather, stronghold house, — between lovely thickets, under Olives, past one or two little hidden cottages, and up an exceedingly steep but little trodden

zigzag to the ruined tower and walls on the highest peak of this much-peaked headland. Here were vastly fine seaward cliffs, where, under a big Pine, I lunched off stuff from my pockets, while far below, and often hidden by Pines, two boats slowly dragged nets close to the rocks, and in the far distance two feluccas and one steamship sailed east towards Genoa. I loafed long on this height, and found many lovely wild flowers, and rescued an earthworm from a centipede. Then I returned to the little piazza (No. 2 on the map), and took a mountain-ward path, which led me up a succession of valleys different from anything yet seen, — a sort of fairyland of fresh green grass and Ferns, moss, Ivy, and countless flowers, with new-budding trees and singing birds, and cottages hidden away in corners, and steep side-hills of Olives. Much stairs and much winding among verdurous walls and boulders, the path often but two feet wide between crags, with sudden turns between rude vine-clad trellises. At last a ridge, wholly open, a tremendous wild valley going down into the sea just beyond; a jutting rock close by; a little shrine; a view of sea and near mountains, and little Portofino. . . . Hence I discovered a tempting rock over across a deep gulch-like valley, and an Olive wood with a cottage not far from it; so I went round the head of the valley by a little footpath, meeting a little girl driving cows, and passing the dooryard of the cottage, gained the high rock easily, and was well repaid; for in addition to all else I got here a view of the fine snow mountains not far back of Rapallo, and also a far better look at the really stupendous cliffs of the coast close at hand at the west, whence a sound of surf in caves came faintly to the ear. This cottage was the highest on all the mountain. Above all is Pine and wildness up to the summit at about two thousand feet. I went down by a new way, through other fairylands, offering surprising views of the sea through trees from a great distance, the hills being exceeding steep. I met a few beautifully dressed peasant women, toiling up the hill, two little boys carrying big sacks, and three sweet-looking nuns, also climbing. At the piazza of Portofino at 3 o'clock (I had set out at 8.15), finding myself weary, for 4 lire I got a boatman to carry me back to Santa Margherita. We rowed and we sailed and I steered, and it was sport! Then, at 4.30, after a hurried cup of tea and a roll, I took train again and travelled the superb coast to Spezia, where the sun set in great glory; and on in moonlight through Tuscany to Pisa, dining off roast chicken, bread, and wine on the way. My heart on fire! What a glorious day!

April 16. Yesterday's five-hours' journey to Pisa was largely underground while daylight lasted. . . . A flash of daylight, and you cross a narrow gulch or valley, surf on the one hand, falls in the torrent stream on the other, then blackness again and another mountain overhead. The close-built towns are packed in the mouths of valleys, the railway sometimes behind, but unfortunately oftener in front. This is sad, because the railway's high embankment often cuts off the town's view of the sea and the view of the town from the sea. The coast is more precipitous, ruder, and wilder than any part of the western shore. After la Spezia, darkness came soon, but moonlight, the ghostly white mountains of Carrara gleaming in the distance, and the marble ballasting of the railway gleaming too. The night was so bright that the Pisan Duomo was visible from afar.

Pisa. This morning I looked out on the Arno and its grand, sweeping curve through the town. I rambled out without guide, and discovered a beautiful brick palace on Lung Arno; admired the wide eaves of the houses; took side streets, and presently, at the end of one of these, the Leaning Tower. . . . Like the rest of the world, I stood amazed at the Tower, the Baptistery, and the Church, — three marble wonders. . . . Next I got into the Campo Santo, and there stayed long. These were my first old frescoes, — hells, heavens, and so on; also many fine monuments, Roman, early Christian, and Renaissance; some excellent heraldic work in the stones of the floor, and graves of college teachers, — the whole enclosure with its neglected court, its faded wall paintings, its light arched tracery, its long roofed aisles, its quiet and seclusion, most utterly expressive of peace and the dead past. From within, through an iron grating, I watched the folk pour out of the Duomo; and when the preacher appeared, the crowd clapped and cheered — a strange scene. Then I wandered through the emptied church, looking at the rich marbles, the splendid pillars (brought home by Pisan conquerors), and the many peasant women kneeling at shrines — how beautiful are their faded gowns and kerchiefs and their dark faces! I could not get into the Baptistery, but climbed the Leaning Tower, and said farewell to the Mediterranean — my one true friend since Marseilles. After lunch I went out again to see the famous botanical garden, where I spent two profitable hours. It was an interesting opportunity of comparing the vegetation growable here with that of the western Riviera. I

noticed, among many other things, a huge Magnolia and a
Yankee Shadbush in bloom. . . . At 5.30 I was off for Florence, a two-hours' ride through fertile, highly cultivated
country, and one narrow defile. Heavy showers were falling
on the surrounding mountains. The effects of bursting sunlight on the new leafage in distant parts of the plains, on
the hill-set towns, and on the winding Arno, were startling.
Near sunset the light-effects were most marvellous. Clouds
everywhere, yet much sunlight too; bright gleams of rainbows; dark rain-clouds behind gleaming snow-mountains;
white, billowy cumuli over shadowed hills — altogether wondrous and Turneresque. . . . Actually in Florence, city of
my dreams!

Charles stayed six days in Florence. His visit was considerably impaired by heavy rains, which interfered with out-
of-door excursions. The following summing up made April
22d will serve as introduction : —

End of my present looking on Florence and her treasures :
six daylights have fled, and I have seen much; but sixty
would not suffice. Here is not only beauty of situation, and
of city as a whole, and of plain and mountain round about it,
and of vegetation, and of winding river, — but also beauty
in abundance within the town, in the very streets, in broad
day. Palaces, churches, fortress-houses, bell-towers, loggias,
and bridges are full of character and meaning. The iron-
work, bronze-work, mosaic, and sculpture are spirited, quaint,
or exquisite. There are precious frescoes on the walls of
courts in the open air, and bits of della Robbia's terra-cotta
in street-corner shrines. The fine arts are not hidden away
in museums, but set into every-day life.

In Florence he was looking more than usual at the main
objects of tourists' interest, because these main objects are in
high degree artistic ; but he also visited the surrounding heights
to enjoy the setting of the city.

The afternoon (April 17) was given to rambling on the
heights of San Miniato, whence an entrancing view was made
doubly lovely by effects of cloud-broken light. The winding
Arno; the soft colors of new leafage in fertile plains, all

flooded with golden light; the purple and azure mountains stretching to far distance, and backed by snow crests at many points; and clouds, clouds, clouds, of such variety of form, mass, and color as is seldom seen. The city in the midst of the valley is a perfect thing too — a comprehendable place — a composition in the painter's sense. Rich brown roofs, from which rise the white walls of the Duomo and the Campanile, and the high stem tower of the town house, — towers and church all rising against exquisite coloring of plain and mountains beyond.

He liked the handsome carriage " concourse " with Angelo's " David " in the centre; and noted the Wistaria, Lilacs, Roses, and Spiræas in bloom on the 17th of April. He noted also

the absurd stucco caves within the arches of terrace walls. Another day he visited the Boboli Garden, where he had played every day for a fortnight when he was a boy of five. He explored it thoroughly, and got from it " an idea or two," but found it a dreary place. The Pitti Gallery, however, was close at hand. The Florence galleries invited him strongly, and as the weather was showery, he made frequent visits to them. At these galleries he " was vastly disappointed in some pictures familiar in engravings and photographs, and was delightedly surprised at others. The Venetian work, particularly, cannot be reproduced in photographs. The print of Titian's ' Flora,' compared with the original, is but a blot of ink; and the lovely Madonna, like that yet lovelier in the Louvre, is in photograph almost nought." He cared

little for any of the famous pictures in the Tribuna at the
Uffizi; but greatly enjoyed the Angelicos and Botticellis, and
every one of the Venetians; "and liked the small picture of
'Tobias and the Angel' by Granacci, and others unheard of."
Of his visit to the San Marco monastery, now museum, he
writes: "Here, as at Bargello, and as in Piazza della Signo-
ria, and many side streets of the city, a mighty flavor of
mediæval days. Walls of faded frescoes, angel hosts, Madon-
nas, saints, martyrs, pagan Aphrodites, Christs, — what creatures of imagination are these!" On the 21st, —

in despair of better weather, I took an omnibus to the park,
where I was rained on vigorously for half an hour, and was
then rewarded by a lovely clear-up. Sunlight through trees
and thickets, all in young leaf. Very joyous and refreshing,
particularly as I have hardly seen anything of the kind in all
the Riviera region. . . . This park is wholly flat, and lies
along the Arno. It is mostly woodland with underbrush, the
trees large, and close-grown; but in one part lately thinned
and cut back. There are some shrubless groves of Ilex
among prevailing deciduous wood; and Ilex, also, now and
then stands singly, — with big Poplars, for instance, near the
river-side. On the few straight-edged grass lawns, or rather
plots, the grass is uncut and poor. The roads and paths run
in straight lines through woods and grasslands, and are everywhere bordered by at least one row of avenue trees; a ditch
lies outside these trees, and then comes the wild wood, or
sometimes a hedge beside the ditch. The edges of the woods
towards the river and about the grass spaces are always a
straight, unbroken wall, usually with a dense ten-foot Ilex
hedge hiding the trunks of the trees, — a hedge over the top
of which trees stretch bigger branches. There are many fine
vista effects, excellent hedges with bays and stone seats; and
good stone terminals; and corner posts; and posts with hanging chains to define footpaths; and curbs around the planting-spaces along the chief avenue where a footpath is carried
alongside the drive. The woods with shrubbery are very
pretty (when not stupidly hidden by hedges); but there is
no landscape design in Mr. Olmsted's sense. I actually had
to go outside of the park about fifty yards to get a lovely
distant view of the city towers and Duomo, which might
easily have been had within the park.

Charles thought no day well spent unless he was roving about on foot at least ten hours of it. Thus, on the 22d of April he visited in the morning the famous Viale dei Colli

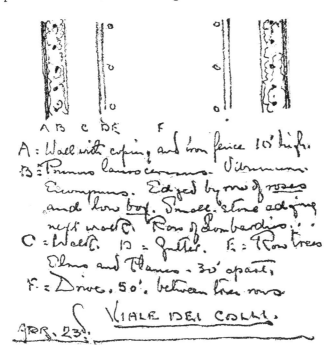

and the grounds along it. The morning was fresh and fair, and the views lovely as possible; the gardens pleasant, but not instructive. There he watched the country carts and the country people. Then he drifted about the streets of Florence, in which there were crowds abroad, apparently going from church to church. He went into the Duomo, where some great function was going on, which culminated in the archbishop washing the feet of a dozen white-clothed ruffians. Great crowds were constantly moving in and out, — all sorts and conditions of men. In the —

Baptistery I saw a baptism. The old priest and his assistant straight out of a Giotto picture. There was a long rigmarole, through which the mother of the child had to stand, the baby in her arms. Then came the sousing of the little head with water, — what a heathen institution! The little crowd from the street that looked on was interesting, — children who, after the ceremony, crowded to see the baby, and three costumed peasant women, amid rich marbles and gilding, and under high, shadowy vaulting. In the church of SS. Annunziata was a great array of candles, and a crowd apparently awaiting some ceremony. In the cloister adjacent I happened on del Sarto's " Madonna of the Sack " in the lunette over the door. Then outside, to my great surprise, I discovered della Robbia's charming bambinos set into the street wall of the Spedale degli Innocenti. I took an opportunity to say farewell to Bargello and the Ponte Vecchio, and the Campanile; and, a shower coming on, and my feet being almost sore, I put back to the hotel at the ignominious hour of 4.30.

On the 23d of April Charles crossed the Apennines on the railroad route to Venice. The ascent offered "many wondrous views of the plain of Arno and Pistoja's domes and towers seen from a great height; but the mountains seemed brown, steep, and often bare, wooded only with scarcely started low scrub." The crooked descent to Bologna was more interesting, the mountains being more clifty, with many deep ravines and some valleys gay with fresh green.

I got a good look at the leaning towers and strange domes of Bologna at the beginning of the great plain of the Po; and then came long rushing over fertile plains, — small fields ditched about, rows of strangely trained fruit trees, and white oxen ploughing. A strange land altogether, where rivers flow on ridges, and railways and wagon roads have to climb long grades to get over them. The towers and domes of Ferrara, Rovigo, and Padua were visible from great distances across a plain of freshest green. The train passed close under one group of blue hills, — Colli Euganei, — whence Shelley once looked over the great plain, "islanded with cities fair;" and eastward —

> " Where beneath Day's azure eyes,
> Ocean's nursling, Venice lies."

After Padua, the plain grows wetter and wetter, — becomes, indeed, a marsh with creeks; a bridge is entered on, and the marsh becomes flats; and Venice appears ahead. At four o'clock the sun was behind a cloud for us, but was beaming bright on the walls and towers of the floating town. In the distance great stretches of sands shone golden, while the nearer flats and channels and grass patches were dullest gray. Strange boats and barges were about; and westward rose the Euganeans. Soon a hubbub of gondolas at the station; and then silent, lonely floating through water alleys, twice across the Grand Canal, and into a narrow crack beside the Giardino Reale to the steps of the Hotel la Lune. I got a room high up, with a view, over the rich foliage of the garden, to the east end of the Canal, and the churched and towered Isola di S. Giorgio Maggiore. Blue sky, blue water, colored sails, shooting gondolas, a big ship between buoys, off the Piazzetta, — Venice! and this morning I was on the bridge over Arno!

After washing, I went out into the Piazza. The low sun was shining full on the front of St. Mark's, and in at the open doors. I went in, and out again; and in, and out. What a wonder of earth is this! I strolled about the Piazzetta and the quays adjoining; and concluded that for a man of my tastes, and my sea education, this must ever be the perfectest spot."

Charles spent four days in Venice, — days fully occupied with a delighted study of the city, — its churches, pictures, and prospects, — in the pleasant company of Cambridge friends.

Again into the Piazza on Good Friday evening, — the Church front and the Palace very lovely by the light of gas-lamps. Within the Church, shadows and darkness, a few taper lights, quiet moving crowds, — the singing most touching. I sat in a corner till all was done. Life more a dream than ever.

Easter Sunday, April 25. Bright as possible! From the great Campanile, I was surprised to see so many little Venices round about. The Piazza was very gay with huge flags on the masts and St. Mark's banners at the corners of the Church. . . . In the evening with A. G—— drifted an hour in the Grand Canal. About perfect this!

From Venice he went to Lake Como and Bellagio, stopping on the way for a hasty look at Verona, and the cathedral and public garden of Milan.

Once embarked [on Lake Como], the rain ceased, and the clouds lifted and broke just enough to let the sun through in spots. What heights, what verdurous gulches, and high-set houses and hamlets; what fresh, soft greens, shaded off upwards into strange browns and golds; white snow on the top ridges, and in the deep gullies of the mountain flanks. On the lake shore itself was an infinite variety of wall and arching and bridging. There were little ports, bits of beach and of wild rock, and cliffs, and strings of towns, scattered villas, boathouses, and roofed ports; strange boats with high sails; steps leading down into the water; and landings in under houses. The sky was very glorious. Scraps of cloud lay about the sunlit snow peaks. There were showers in many directions, and wreaths of mist about the flanks of green mountains. There was sunlight on soft, green summits; and great shadows under the western shores.

The next day was misty and rainy; but in the afternoon the showers ceased, and he " watched the breaking up of the heavy clouds, snow peaks shining with sunlight appearing now and then through gaps in the clouds; the wind rising out of the north, and tall sails coming down the lake before it; the clouds, too, sailing fast." The afternoon voyage to Como was delightful.

I spied diligently at the strange, beautiful lakeside, different from anything I ever imagined. There were walls of every conceivable form and device, with piers, with high or low supporting arches, with crannies, crooks, and caves for boats, and complications with beaches and brook-mouths. There were bridges, jutting rocks, waterfalls, mills at mouths of gulleys, and little walled ports. Houses rose from the water, as at Venice, with water doors. Garden things hung down to the water from over garden walls. There were lovely church towers, sometimes on low points of beach, or on top of cliffs, or high-set on spur or shelf of mountain. Villages and hamlets were charmingly scattered along the shores, and along the mountain flanks. Of the villas, some few were staringly ugly and pretentious; but many, to American eyes, very original and fine. One, on the tip of a long point, had three arched loggie entirely open, separating its two wings. Another stood at the head of a wide cove, with wooded mountain shores. A great house stood at the water's very edge, with woods close about it, and no visible means of arriving thither save by water.

In the hotel at Bellagio was nobody but two young Germans, and a French party of three. These latter could see no beauty in rain-swept lakes; although one of them was an amateur photographer.

For lovers of landscape or of word-painting it is interesting to compare this description of Lake Como — one of the most beautiful pieces of scenery in Europe — with a description of Goat Island, Niagara Falls, which Charles wrote three years earlier when an apprentice at Mr. Olmsted's office. It occurs in an irregular journal or note-book which he kept during that period.

July 8, 1883. I am writing to the sound of the rapids of Niagara after a really worshipful Sunday. A beautiful gray morning. To Goat Island alone as a "passionate pilgrim."

The shore is generally regular in its curves, but in detail delightfully intricate with numberless little water-filled chasms, crooks, and caves. There are hanging trees, old gnarled Cedars clutching the rocks, overhanging verdure of much variety, rich masses of Bitter-sweet and Virginia Creeper, the young sprays often trailing in the rushing water, and quiet pools behind old stranded logs with Iris in bloom therein. Within is much ancient forest — old and tall Beeches. In the open spaces are luxuriant masses of Sumac, Wild Rose, and Gooseberry, Rubus odoratus, Poison Ivy, Virginia Creeper, and Bitter-sweet, the latter often in masses on the ground and twisted about itself.

Delightful narrow wood-roads, and " unimproved " trails and footpaths. Everywhere is the sound of the surrounding rapids, like surf on a shore of broken rocks.

To the Sisters, the great Rapids, the brink of the Horseshoe, and Luna Island. The sun broke through the clouds;

a mist-bow spanned the spray-filled gulf; and the Gorge and
its delicate suspension bridge were marvellously illumined.

In the evening of May 2d Charles reached Paris, having
enjoyed very much his quick ride by the Pass of St. Gotthard
and across France. "Saturday's journey (May 1) over the
St. Gotthard was of course the most interesting of all my
life," he wrote to his mother May 3. He invariably enjoyed
a long ride by railway, whether through a wild or a cultivated
country, whether through mountains or over great plains;
but this day's ride was unique, — he was seeing at once stupendous scenery and a marvellous feat of engineering. It
was a cloudy day, —

but the sun came out now and then in beauteous fashion.
The train passed through the fresh green valleys of Breggia,
past the torrents of Laveggio and the great crags of Monte
Generoso; crossed the crooked Lago di Lugano on bridges,
causeways, and islands, twisting along the western shore;
climbed slowly the narrowing Val d'Agno; passed through a
tunnel under Monte Cenere; and burst suddenly into the
sunshine of the wide valley of Ticino. Here, from a high
position on the mountain side, there was a great view northward into Alpland, and southward to green meadows and

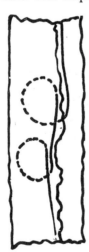

blue waters at the head of Lago Maggiore.
. . . Soon the train followed constantly the
river Ticino up a valley shut in by higher
and higher mountains, which were very steep
and rocky, yet inhabited almost to the summits. Countless waterfalls were in sight, —
some exceeding high, — and many chains of
falls coming from great heights. Beyond
Bodio, the valley, which hitherto had some
flat land in it, contracted; and soon the train
passed a bridge over the river, then suddenly
jumped back again, and plunged straight
into the mountain side, to come out again
at a point downstream from the point of
entrance, but at a higher level. The same
tactics were repeated again immediately, the
result being the attainment of a sort of higher valley above a
steep, narrow river gorge. Here Firs first appeared high on

the mountain sides ; and here also were the first signs of Swiss
builders' work.   After more slow climbing, there appeared
below Faido a hillside of pastures dotted
with dark brown log barns, — altogether
Swiss. Superb waterfalls were in sight.
The railway plunged into a huge preci-
pice mountain to take another upward
spiral; then crossed a river gulch, and
another, and so pulled up through the
now slender valley to Airolo, — a little hamlet where all river meadow-land
ceases, and the snow mass of Mt. St.
Gotthard blocks the way.   The snow-
piled zigzags of the carriage road were
plainly visible high on the mountain.
I slept profoundly all through the nine-
mile tunnel ; but was told that the
passage took twenty-two minutes.   The
train came out into wet cloudland, and
looked down the steep torrent of Rense,
— quite undescendable in appearance.
The down grade was tremendous, through
a very wild ravine differing from everything in the Italian side.   Firs were
everywhere.   The principal descent was
accomplished   thus, — the   round   dot
stands for a village.   The first view of
it is from a great height above it; but,
after long travelling, the train passes at
last far below it.   The side torrent near
the village is crossed three times at
different levels ; and the extraordinary
changes in the apparent position of the
village are exceedingly confusing.   Down
we went into Switzerland, out of cloudland and rockland into fresh greenland
about Altdorf and the head of the lake
of Vierwaldstätter, . . . the lake very dark, and the air full
of wet.

Of Lucerne and its lake he says : —

It was good to see hillsides of mixed woods, fresh pastures, great apple orchards, big barns, and other almost Yankee-like things. I hunted up the great Lion, and admired the strange bridges and the Northcountrymen's towers, so utterly different from those of the morning. Here are steep roofs of many stories. It is a marvellous transformation in architecture. And this dark, gloomy, cold lake, — how different from fair Como, lovely in spite of rain.

His brief comment on the ride from Lucerne to Paris (May 2) is as follows : —

The country is very beautiful. A charming mixing of hills and valleys, lakes and streams, ravines and intervales. The buildings become thoroughly German, then beyond Bâle, slowly French. The long ride across France is really interesting. Farms everywhere, and not a fence or a wall ; not a dozen pastured cattle were in sight all day. There were occasional preserved woodlands, the coppice-cutting lately completed, and some woods for growing large timber ; all large forests were intersected by straight alleys. Paris at seven o'clock.

His sixty days' absence from Paris had cost him on the average $4.60 a day, including the purchase of a trunk, photographs, and some books, — not much more than it would cost a young man just to live in a good hotel in an American city without travel. Nevertheless, he wrote to his mother on May 3d : " I am, in fact, becoming a confirmed spendthrift." To his father he wrote May 11th : —

I have to confess to five days of comparative do-nothing-ness, — the five following my arrival in Paris. Verily I was a good deal fagged out in body ; and in mind I was in a state of chaos and confusion : such a whirl of new sights, impressions, and experiences had I been through. Sometimes I wish I were mentally and emotionally duller than I am! There must be a great peace in unawakedness. But, rather, I wish my mental as well as my bodily digestive powers were stronger than they are, — so that I might make some use of the rich food that has come to me in the last two months.

CHAPTER VI

LANDSCAPE STUDY IN EUROPE. PARIS AGAIN

I think there are as many kinds of gardening as of poetry: your
makers of parterres and flower gardens are the epigrammatists and
sonneteers in this art; contrivers of bowers and grottoes, treillages and
cascades, are romance writers; Wise and Loudon are our heroic poets;
. . . as for myself, you will find that my compositions in gardening
are altogether after the Pindaric manner, and run into the beautiful
wildness of nature, without affecting the nicer elegancies of art. —
ADDISON.

HAVING spent two months on the Riviera, and in Italy,
amid great natural beauty and much picturesqueness of
man's creation, Charles was now to study artificial park and
garden work in a comparatively flat country, mostly cultivated, and repeatedly injured, within the lifetime of many
species of trees, by invading and defending armies. The
writing of letters and notes of his journey, of course, occupied a considerable portion of his time; and the art collections of Paris could not be neglected. Thus, he spent the
whole day, on the 7th of May, in the Salon.

A monstrous big show, with some interesting architectural
drawings; some queer, original sculpture; and endless walls
of paintings. There was an infinite variety of subject and
treatment, — horrors, dramatics, mythologies, nudities, portraits, landscapes, peasantics (after Millet), butcheries, pots
and pans, cheeses and old books, all jumbled together in
distressing and wearying confusion. A portrait of a great
hog, life-size, adjoined "Love Disarmed;" a scene of battle
slaughter was placed beside a group of "Sirens" or choir of
angels. There were six different "Judiths," as many mur-
ders of differing kinds, endless, realistic imitation of old
books, glassware, preserves in jars, roast beef, and raw
meats; endless painting of death, — dead soldiery, dead old
men, dead girls; much realistic copying of every-day life, —
a yachting party in a steam launch, for example, the figures

life-size, — ball-rooms, weddings, funerals, street scenes, family dinner parties, scenes at the theatre or in restaurants; every sort and kind of nakedness, from most unreal, conventional creatures to completest imitation of even ugly women; many fairly loathsome creatures, and hardly a respectable creature among them all, — men or women; though many of a pretty or sentimental kind. Many pictures entitled "La Misère" represented all the ugliness of poverty most faithfully, and sometimes touchingly. There were numerous archæological pictures, cold artificial renderings of supposed life and costuming of the Greeks and Romans; many detailed portrayals of crime with all manner of blood and thunder; in fact, a wholly riotous and chaotic collection, — individualism run mad. Amid all these, the few good landscapes and seascapes were exceedingly refreshing; and, in fact, played the same part that landscape plays in real life. Some coast of Norway scenes were especially good in spirit; though I detested the manner of their painting, — the manner of their execution.

He found at Paris the Philadelphia family with whom he had enjoyed intercourse in London several months before. Twice he had sought them on the Riviera, and had been much disappointed to find each time that they had gone on before him. "Mrs. Beadle was kindly as ever; Miss Pitkin as fresh and fair and pretty (I believe it is Louisa L—— that she is like); Miss Yale as wise and quiet. They made me talk; then I quarrelled a bit with ——, a Harvard man, over the inevitable Irish question; and at 9.15 departed, Miss Pitkin desiring me to come in again very soon."

He reëxamined the Paris squares, which he had before seen in mid-winter, finding them to look far better, when the grass was green and the plantings showed the designed colors of their foliage, than in their bare winter state. He was much interested also in the use made of these squares by the children and women of their neighborhood. One Sunday afternoon spent in the Parc Monceaux was especially delightful to him, because of the countless "children and gayly dressed bonnes, with a band of music between 4 and 5 o'clock, the whole driveway occupied by a crowd seated in chairs. The crowd was very quiet and well dressed, — not a sign of a 'mucker,' — as different as possible from the scene at the

Boston Common Sunday band concerts."   He noted, also,
the " very green grass, good even in the shade ; gracefully
modelled surfaces ; open groves ; Ivied tree-trunks ; and
thicket plantings, edged with Euonymus, Veronica, and
Euonymus radicans, or even with formal rows of Geraniums.
All the paths were edged by 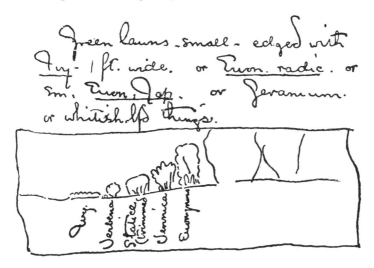."

Mons. André, the eminent landscape architect, gave him
much valuable information, directing him to old and interesting places in the neighborhood of Paris which it would be
worth while for him to see, and explaining to him his own
business arrangements, which seemed to Charles admirable.

Of late years, Mons. André has undertaken the designing
of country-houses, as well as of grounds ; and he has always
kept to himself, as far as possible, the designing of all acces-
sory buildings, walls, bridges, terraces, etc., — things which
Mr. Olmsted gives up to the architect. . . .   His landscape-
gardening work is sometimes executed by contract for a lump
sum, there being men in Paris who will undertake work in all
departments in this way ; oftener by contract at fixed prices
for the different kinds of work ; and oftener still by day
labor.   In the latter case, the men at work are overseen by a
foreman employed by André, whose services are afterwards
charged as an item in his bill.   These foremen make reports

every week in writing. I saw many of the reports ; and inferred that these must be men of a very superior sort. When André visits a work in progress, and directs such and such things to be done, the foreman, who has taken notes in his book, on the next day sends up to Paris a memorandum of the things commanded. These memoranda are preserved, and the items checked off as the weekly reports warrant.

Charles was also allowed to look over many colored plans of work already executed ; so that he obtained a clear idea of Mons. André's methods and results.

The fine annual Exhibition d'Horticulture was in progress at the Champs Elysées ; and there Charles spent many hours studying not only the annuals, hardy flowers, and greenhouse plants, but the exhibits of garden tools, iron and terra-cotta vases, railings, fences of wire and wood, plant tubs and boxes, rustic bridges, cement-work in imitation of wood, — even a rustic-work summerhouse with a thatched roof all of cement. The plant collections were especially useful to him, because the specimens were all labelled ; and he could thus get the names of many plants which he had seen on the Riviera and in the French gardens.

TREE GUARDS.

He found the Bois de Boulogne much more beautiful than in winter ; although he still objected to much of the artificial water and rock work. He could never enjoy a fall or cascade unnaturally placed, so that the water

"issues from the top of the highest mound in the neighborhood," unless, indeed, it was a completely architectural series
of falls and cisterns, like that at St. Cloud. The thing which
most pleased him at the Bois de Boulogne was the view over
the great open Longchamp, —

as there is no large or even largish stretch of grassland in all
the Bois, this is very valuable. I examined the Moulins, the
arrangements about the grand-stand, the pretty little lakes
near the Suresnes gate, and the partly open country of this
part of the Bois, — the prettiest part of all. The scrub wood
of the major part, and the wide roads lined with rows of ugly-
colored planes are too monotonous, particularly as many of
the roads are straight.

In all his excursions about Paris, at this season, he noticed
the careful way in which the railroad embankments were
treated. "No raw banks. Grass, and Ivy, and thickets of
small trees, chiefly Maples and Locusts, evidently often cut
down, but as evidently encouraged to grow, at least on the
upper parts of the banks in the cuts."

At Versailles he gave hardly any attention to the palace
and its contents, —

but passed straight through to Le Nôtre's great gardens,
where I soon discovered there was very much to be seen. I
looked at numbers of varied parterres, and walked round and
about for two hours; but then found my way into the gardens
of the Petit Trianon. What pleasantness, what delight, what
romantic charm is here, particularly to one coming directly
from the formalities and eccentricities of the great gardens.
Plainly, this Petit Trianon is the better sort; but what a
simple sort, — nothing but grass and trees, and a little water,
and a very little undulation of surface; but grassland and
woodland run in and out of each other; and water appears
unexpectedly; and there is the charm of not knowing what
the next turn may bring you to; and the great trees are of
many sorts. The mixing of them is ever varied; and sometimes the wood is open and grassy, and sometimes dense with
low branches and shrub thickets. The roads and paths are
no longer parts of the scene; but only the means of arriving
on the scene. They go about unobtrusively. In this little

space, — perhaps a tenth or twentieth of the area of the large garden, — there is a great variety of quiet, peaceful, soul-refreshing scenery. I think it the best thing of its sort I have seen on the Continent. Whoever designed the few buildings in it did well. The hamlet where the Court and Marie Antoinette used to play at being peasants is very pretty; so is a group of buildings called the Swiss cow-house; and the farm gate behind these. The picturesqueness of these things is a little too much that of the stage, but only a little; most of it is a real, that is a reasonable, picturesqueness. Here I lingered long, admiring. Three dark clouds came up and delivered as many heavy showers. The effects of light were very lovely. I passed out to the head of the long water in the main gardens. This is a very grand perspective, the country being flat as far as eye can reach, and nothing hindering looking to the very uttermost horizon. I walked up to the palace front again, and got the effect of change of level on this immensely long, narrow view. It is very fine — finer far than the similar thing at Hampton Court. I took note, during the afternoon, of various handsome  forms of " avenues " and alleys, some where trees are clipped part way up and then grow freely, some in which the whole tree is clipped and trained, and some where the trees are as free as on Boston Common; of various designs for parterres and Boxedging work, and of pattern gardening in three elements — gravel, grass, and Box. The account of the interior of the palace does not sound interesting. The inscription says, — " To all the Glories of France " — war glory chiefly, I fear.

Charles visited with pleasure the Baron Rothschild's great park Ferrières, originally designed by Paxton, and later by André. The place contains every element of an expensive country-seat: splendid glass-houses admirably stocked, formal gardening about the huge château, flower gardens, and a park wholly English in style, but too recent to have any fine trees as yet. From the windows and terraces of the château there

FRENCH TREES AND AVENUES

are many long vistas — apparently a limitless property; yet the
boundary is really very near at some points. There are great
stretches of greensward running far into woodlands at many
points, two or three keepers' houses seen at the ends of long
vistas, a long, crooked lake, and at its head a brand-new
concrete stream (Paris contractors make these at so much a
metre). The plantations are exceedingly varied in outline,
and many species are used. Everywhere is dense-planted
underbrush, chiefly Berberis, Ruscus, and Box. There are
too many sensational bits of planting, — such as silver Poplars
against dark Conifers, white Negundos beside purple Beeches,
and huge banks of purple Pansies far off in corners of the
dress-ground. This sort of thing becomes tiresome when
often repeated. The great lawns are cut by hand machines,
and become brown in summer in spite of constant watering.
The more distant parts of the park are pastured by sheep,
and by a fenced-in herd of deer kept to supply beasts for
hunting. In one corner is a "faisanderie," where birds are
hatched and raised to stock the woods for fall shooting.
There were many good points about the formal gardening
near the château, especially some exceedingly pretty "spring
bedding" made with yellow and purple Pansies, red and
white Daisies, and pink Silene. The glass-houses were extra
fine, of course, all extra well stocked too; although the boy
complained that "the decorator from Paris took away all the
best plants." Heavy showers fell while we were in the
houses. About one o'clock I completed the long round, and
got lunch at a small country inn in the village, in company
with the driver of a fancy biscuit wagon which was hitched
at the door, — a man in a white cotton gown, with a pencil
behind his ear. He had asparagus, some sort of cheese, nuts,
and wine; I two eggs, an entrecôte of something, cheese, and
wine. The horse munched his oats just outside the window.
Across the narrow road the children of the village school
were playing very noisily. In one corner an old woman sat
knitting.

An omnibus was to start back for the railway station Lagny
at 3.15; but I strolled out into the fields and lanes, and by
and by came to a highway skirting the great park. There I

saw a gentleman in gray, with a coat on his arm, walking fast away from the village; and, remembering that a map I had seen showed a railway rather nearer Ferrières than that at Lagny, I chased said gentleman and inquired if he were bound for a railway and Paris. Yes, he was; so I fell in. We walked fast round the walled park, and then down a long, straight road through the " forêt " belonging on the one hand to Rothschild and on the other to the Commune. There were no houses at all in sight, and the station itself stood alone in the depths of the woods; but villages were reported all about. We walkers started up two pheasants and a rabbit. The wood was carpeted with Lily-of-the-Valley and with Strawberry Blossoms. My companion was very silent; but we took the train at half past three, and reached Paris before five."

The ancient park of Ermenonville, the first French place made in the landscape style, the home of Girardin, and the abode of Rousseau, was restored a few years ago by André. Charles rode to it, an hour by train, through the tamest possible country, — some gentlemen's parks the only oases, — and an hour by omnibus over a straight, treeless, paved road across a gently rolling plain, with few trees, and no visible houses, but one or two church spires far off. " A rattling, tiresome ride, with many packages but only one fellow-traveller — the woman mail-carrier. At length, there rose above an intervening swell of ground a cream stone tower. Then came a twisting descent into a suddenly disclosed valley sunk in the plateau, — a pleasant valley with much wood and also a gleam of water, — and immediately arrival in the inn yard of a close-built village — Ermenonville." The park gates are close beside the inn; and the old woman at the Lodge gave Charles cordial permission to walk anywhere about the place, the family not being at home.

I first inspected the curious arrangements by which the public road is carried close past the château without interfering with the view up the valley beyond the said road. The road is here " fenced " by ditches of water derived from a stream which comes down the valley with two falls, and then fills the wide moats about the château, and flows on for a long distance in sight of the château between low banks, through flat, green meadows, and around some wooded islands, its waters made to go slowly, and to spread, by means of several low dams. The long water perspective is very striking. Woods (of disappointing stature) are on every hand ; far in the distance a glimpse of the famous mill figured in Laborde. Some white fences were very intrusive ; and some high earth beds far off on the points of otherwise good islands caught the eye — beds for scarlet Geraniums, I fear. The château walls rise directly from the water, one arched bridge leading into the court. The terrace on the park front has a boat-landing. The banks of the irregular moat are very finely wooded, the trees hanging over the water, and reaching towards the cream stone building. Pleasant walks lead along these banks off through the wet meadows over many bridges, and, on the other side, to the new orangery. The stables and gardens are hidden behind a thick screen. I walked all about the place ; and discovered a view of a charming wild-shored pond beyond the highway, — a view obtained by the substitution of ditches for high walls along the road. I found, also, two or three traces of the romantic buildings with which Laborde describes the place to have been adorned.

At noon I lunched in the inn, the entrance being through the kitchen. A group of three men out of a story-book, or painting, sat at the adjoining table — one blue blouse, one green corduroy with leggings, one very aged nondescript sleeveless garment and a crumpled white collar about five inches high.

In the afternoon I explored the upper park which possesses an unsuspectable pond dam, an island with Rousseau's tomb ("Ici repose l'homme de la nature et de la vérité"), small-wooded slopes and coppice Beech wood, and an old archery ground with buildings. Then I walked down the highway for another look at the really wild pond, which was like Had-lock's Lower Pond [Mt. Desert] without the mountains. In a tame land like this part of France, no wonder this feature was exceedingly admired.

Charles spent a long half day (May 19) at the Buttes-Chaumont, a remarkable Paris public ground which he had visited in the winter. He admired " the much excellent detailed work in the plantings along the artificial brooks, on the rocks generally, and in wildish thickets;" but he could not like the tree-planting, for he found numerous ugly species mixed in an ugly way, the masses being too regularly outlined, or too formally shaped. To save the many striking views from the higher ground, the trees had been planted too sparingly, so that there was hardly a shady path in all the park. "Fundamentally, the whole thing is too fantastic, too theatrical, too mimic romantic."

May 20th he spent a very good day in the gallery and gardens of the Luxembourg. "I enjoyed many of the pictures and detested many. The old Renaissance garden and the side gardens in 'English style' are interesting, and the avenue of the Observatory very fine; and the whole thing is much more appropriate for a town garden than the Buttes-Chaumont; but the latter was a rough region of quarries and rubbish heaps, and I know not what else could have been done with it, save that its new character need not have been so much exaggerated — so caricatured." What pleased him most in the Parisian open grounds was the "countless children of all styles."

May 21st, by train and omnibus, he went in two hours to Mortefontaine, a very small hamlet at the gates of the great château bearing this name. Across the road lay the nursery gardens of Chantrier Frères, to whom Charles brought a note of introduction from M. André. This famous nursery he wished to examine with a business object, as well as for the pleasure of seeing its products. The firm had just won a medal of honor at the Paris Horticultural Exposition for Crotons and Dracænas, specialties of theirs. Charles was cordially received, and shown all over the nursery and through the glass-houses; he was then invited to déjeuner with another stranger, — a gardener come to make some purchases.

Madame was in black cap and gown; Monsieur in a black coat, but his blue apron was tucked up round his waist. A young boy completed the party. The menu was — eggs, fish, greens with eggs, steak (provided especially for me), plum preserve with little cakes, an ample supply of good claret, and an especially fine sort to top off with, and then the inevitable café avec cognac, which I wanted to refuse but could not. Next we had some discussion on the catalogue and prices; and then, with the above-mentioned strange gardener, and under the guidance of Chantrier, I made the grand tour through the park of Mortefontaine, — a long and very enjoyable walk. The property is extensive, cut by several highways, one of which passes close by the château and between the château and the grand park; but this road is concealed by woods, and — where it crosses the open — by being slightly sunk and fenced by ditches only. The access to the park from the château is by a tunnel under the public road, the approach-gullies and steep rocks about the openings being shaded by largish hanging trees — the whole exceedingly well done. Then came a view of large lakes, high-shored on one side, intricate in outline, containing several islands, and held by long, but hardly suspectable dams. We passed down along the low banks under pendant trees, getting many charming glimpses across water, and one long view down a second lake to a high, wild hill, showing much bare rock (where thousands of Pinus maritima had been winter-killed). Finally there came into view a third lake, yet larger and longer, in reality held by a low dam along almost the whole of one side; but this dam is concealed by thick plantings which hide the fact that the land is a little lower just beyond. (This successful hiding of a dam is not accomplished at the Bois de Boulogne, where, at the dammed end of the lake, the woods are open, and strange sights may be seen, — such as the upper halves of carriages and the heads of men moving apparently along the ground among tree-trunks.) In this largest lake are some rocky islets, and many bits of rock shore, as at Spot Pond [Middlesex Fells]. Issuing from the farther end, two narrow channels are seen which surround a hilly, rocky island of a hundred acres. The whole park is on this grand scale.

We walked back by the high, wild woods of the hill country above the chain of lakes, with much Pine and many boulders in some parts, and evergreen Fern, and other homelike things. Rabbit holes were abundant; and many trees were gnawed by stags and rabbits, and there were great ploughings under Oak-trees, said to be the work of the wild boar. On one high point was the ruin of a guard-house, which I think is figured in Laborde. The whole place possesses no interest but of the landscape sort; and in this it is very rich, particularly when compared with the tame uniformity of ordinary French country. There is not a rare tree in the place, as

Monsieur Chantrier dolefully remarked ; and not a flower bed save in the garden by the château. Long years of neglect have increased the landscape charm. Planted and roughly made before the Revolution, the place was afterwards taken by Napoleon, and inhabited by " King Joseph," who, when he went to America, carried the predecessor of the Chantriers with him. It has since been owned by a Prince de Condé, who gave it to a person who has no money to spend on it. I had much good talk with Adolphe Chantrier, and, after a drink of wine and water all round and farewell to Madame, I took the omnibus at 4.30, and reached dinner in Paris at seven.

The next day he visited St. Denis, which he found very stupid. " An ugly town, and a Viollet-le-Duc church, and countless restored tombs." He made this excursion, however, by appointment, in company with Mrs. Beadle's interesting nieces ; and the following was the part of the excursion which he enjoyed : " Lunched in best discoverable restaurant, and talked long." With the same young ladies he visited Versailles again ; looked through the palace ; walked through the great gardens and the Petit Trianon ; hid from a couple of showers ; and returned with them to Paris. In the same pleasant company, on Sunday, May 30th, he heard a fine performance of Gounod's " Mors et Vita," conducted by Gounod in the superb hall at the Trocadéro. " After it we walked to Boulevard Haussmann. Farewell! The family goes to London to-morrow to meet Mr. Pitkin. Monday, May 31. Midnight bed last night, late up this morning. I looked into Boulevard Haussmann and discovered a railway omnibus before No. 52 bis. Mrs. Beadle and the Misses depart for London — all with flowers in hand. Bon voyage. C. E. again solus." It was a great evening fête which had kept him up late on the 30th. The garden of the Tuileries, the Place de la Concorde, the Champs Elysées, and the great avenue up to the Arc de Triomphe were illuminated with lanterns in the trees, colored fires, and colored glass lamps strung on wire ropes, or forming designs on light wooden frames. The parterres also were prettily illuminated. Charles observed especially the " huge, well-ordered crowds " enjoying not only the fireworks and illuminations, but the free pantomimes, ballet, merry-go-rounds, gymnastic exhibitions, and music.

His attention was now distracted from professional study for a few days by the people in the hotel, who were curiosities in a way, by the necessity of making some calls, and, besides, by a troublesome tooth, which cost him two or three days of precious time. Rain and rather cold weather also impaired his enjoyment of the late days in May and the early ones in June. Thus, when he visited St. Germain, the drive along the terrace, through the forest, and over the fine avenues of the Château Lafitte was impaired by low clouds which limited the prospects. On the 4th of June he says, "As yet I have not seen Fontainebleau or half what I wanted to see;" but it rained steadily on the 5th, 6th, and 7th of June, and Fontainebleau was impossible. On the 8th it was rainy as ever, and he took train for Rouen, on his way to England. On the ride to Rouen he noted wide intervale lands along the Seine, wooded hills, Poppies and Corn flowers, very few towns or scattered houses — yet cultivation everywhere and everything intensely green. Cattle were feeding in ranks across fodder fields. At Rouen he saw, in intervals of rain, the cathedral, and St. Maclou and St. Ouen, and the garden about the latter; but after a six o'clock dinner, he sought the quays, which always attracted him. "Stern-wheel steam canal-boats were loading even for Lyons; and English coal steamers lay at the quays." The next morning, "under an umbrella, I went to see the beautiful Palais de Justice and Jeanne's monument; a big flag was in her hand, and many wreaths were hung on her spear, her arms, and all about — some from 'les Positivistes du Havre.'"

Arrived at Havre, he first placed his effects on the steamer for Southampton, then took a chop in a little English place on the quay, inspected the fine jetty and docks, and watched the passing in and out of the narrow entrance to the port. The rain had stopped, but fog lay over the sea, and the fog trumpet blew now and then. Next he took a tram-car from the city to the foot of the great wooded height visible from the jetty. "I climbed up by stairs between gardens, through a sort of Milton Hill or Longwood region [neighborhood of Boston] commanding grand views over the great misty sea, and over the city from a ridge running along the crest. Taking the bearings of two public gardens visible in the city, I descended by other stairs, and inspected the said gardens, finding a botanic collection in one where I got the names of several striking common plants — to my considerable pleasure. At six o'clock, finding myself at the door of a certain Hôtel d'Angleterre, I entered, and partook of the table d'hôte dinner, — 3.75 fr. vin compris. The bill of fare was very Frenchy, including vegetable soup, eels, some sort of brains, beef à la mode, peas, the inevitable veal, salad, etc." This last day in France well illustrated the energy, ease, and economy of time with which he travelled, and the variety of observations and impressions he would accumulate within the hours of a single day. He reached Southampton in rain on June 10th.

Just before landing in England, when his proposed year abroad was more than half over, Charles wrote to his father about the extreme difficulty of getting advice as to the prosecution of his studies. He had felt that difficulty at home, even in the office of Mr. Olmsted; but he felt it more abroad, where the men whose advice would have been valuable were "too busy to give much real help to a wandering chap like me; and the people who had time to talk — well, had nothing valuable to say." Influential letters of introduction from home procured him, at a few points, some useful hints; but his conclusion was "that the only way is to keep moving, and to keep my eyes open, and to trust to chance to show me something interesting and professionally instructive." On the whole, he found the books he had read, and the catalogues, guides, and directories he had procured, the most trustworthy sources of preliminary information — in short, he experienced to the full the difficulty of studying a profession in preparation for which there is no recognized school or course of study.

ERMENON-
VILLE

CHAPTER VII

LANDSCAPE STUDY IN EUROPE. THE SOUTH OF ENGLAND

Gardening, in the perfection to which it has been lately brought in England, is entitled to a place of considerable rank among the liberal arts — it is an exertion of fancy, a subject for taste ; and being released now from the restraints of regularity and enlarged beyond the limits of domestic convenience, the most beautiful, the most simple, the most noble scenes of nature are all within its province. — WHATELY.

His first act, when the weather cleared in Southampton, was to visit the parks, — which are many and large in comparison with the size of the town, — and a great contrast to French public gardens. As for the townspeople, the contrast is greater still. " Again I see rags and dirt, and hobble-de-hoy girls and men, and drunkenness, and servile manners. Vive la République ! " He was invited to stay at the house of Mr. and Mrs. William Darwin, Mrs. Darwin being the sister of the wife of Professor Charles Eliot Norton. There he enjoyed an easy hospitality, and friendly guidance to much which he desired to see in Southampton and its vicinity. One of the most beautiful of the gardens he visited he thus describes : " A lovely wilderness for the most part, — Rhododendrons as in North Carolina, Azaleas, Kalmias, Amelanchiers [Shadbush], and so forth." With Mr. Darwin he walked through an adjoining wild park which was in chancery. Here were many fine Oaks and Spanish Chestnuts, and an ugly mansion ; but very good dammed waters, and much variety of scene all round about. He walked, too, with Mr. Darwin across country, through a large Fir wood with a Roman camp in it, to another private place in a charming situation at the head of a valley, — its approach road, along the side of the valley, very fine, but its near slopes spotted all over with round flower beds, single specimen Azaleas, etc. There was afternoon tea at a hospitable house, and a walk back across fields. " A very pleasant day (June 13): no rain for a wonder." A drizzling foggy day, closed by a heavy rain, was spent at Winchester, examining the charming old Hospital, the big trees in the fields beside the river

Itchen, the courts and cloisters of the Winchester school, and the Cathedral with its Saxon kings' boxes, Templars' monuments, and grand Norman work in the transepts.

On the 15th of June, after a day spent in London on an errand for Harvard College, at 6 P. M. he reached the Crown Inn at Lyndhurst, a small village, the capital of New Forest. After dinner he strolled about the village, it being broad daylight till 9 o'clock. Between 9 and 10 he was reading inscriptions in the churchyard. At 10 it was full moon, — a very fine sight from the wide, open moor near the village.

The next day, which was bright, cold, and windy, he first looked into Verderers' Hall, in the quaint house called Queen's House (the Queen is the lady of Lyndhurst Manor), and then walked off by a charming road into the Forest; and did not return till 6 o'clock. " I walked a great square, and ·saw every type of scenery the Forest affords, — glades, greensward with scattered Oaks and Beeches, groves of monster trees, wild and wide heaths and moors on the high ridge of Stoney Cross, and a pretty oasis of farming lands in the Manor of Minstead. I lunched in a far-viewing old inn at Stoney Cross, where I saw Rufus's Stone." He reached Basset (Mr. Darwin's) again in the evening.

Another day, his host, Mr. Darwin, took him on an excursion contrived for members of the Hampshire Field Club. The party consisted of about fifty persons, some of whom were ladies. There was first a railroad ride through much very English country; then the party walked up lanes, finally reaching open heaths rising up to a high, rounded summit called Hindhead.

This highland country looked Scotch. The air was cloudy and misty; and so we could not see very far. It was a pity; for we were 900 feet above the sea, and should have seen much. We could see Leith Hill and the North Downs near Dorking, where I was in the winter. The geologist of the party explained how the chalk had been washed off from the country between the North and South Downs; and a parson-antiquary also addressed the party. Then we marched down in long procession, first over moors, then through Fir woods, next through a charming valley holding ponds, and then across a private park to Liphook, whence the party returned to Southampton by train. This was a great day. I saw a variety of country, and true English scenery; and met some

pleasant folk (and some unpleasant). Mr. Darwin is A No.
1. It will appear that my Southampton stay was altogether
very agreeable, — thanks to Mr. and Mrs. Darwin.

From Southampton Charles went to ˙ Salisbury, and thence
to Wilton, where, the park of Wilton House being closed,
he got but glimpses of the old Cedars which Sir Philip Sid-
ney planted when he was writing " Arcadia."   He saw much
prettiness, however.   " The gentle river, the village with its
many tree-shaded triangles, and a surprising view of Salisbury's spire far in the distance, across rich water meadows
between masses of heavy Elms."   The railway ride on this
day (June 19th) showed him some soft green valleys, hedges
with many large trees set along them, and wild Roses, Honeysuckle, Elder, Barberry, and wild Geranium crowded in the
hedge-rows.   " Occasionally great rounded uplifts of treeless chalk down appeared ; but no heath or moor of the sort
seen at Hindhead.   Thatched cottages were frequent, as all
about Southampton and in the New Forest.   Luxuriant
climbers of many sorts abounded, — such as Roses, red and
white and yellow, Virginia Creeper, Ivy, Cotoneasters, and
blue-flowered Ceanothus."   At Salisbury he found the Cathedral " a great treat, particularly the cloisters, and the tower
seen from them, and the gardens of the Bishop's Palace
adjoining."   He notes a cuckoo, a " lover and his lass," and
two girls planting box on a little grave under one of two
Cedars in the cloister court.   " The rambling old place is
charming, with a balustrade dividing the little house garden
from the general garden beyond, a bit of water in which the
spire is reflected, trees both scattered and grouped, and a
nearly level greensward pastured by one cow !   On the town
side of the long house was gravel, then some level grass, and
a dwarf wall dividing it from the irregular shrubberies and
lawns beyond."

In the late afternoon he went on by express to Exeter
through a smooth cultivated country ; but in some parts (on
the Devon border) very high and smoothly hilly.   " There
were grand views˙ up and down river valleys, pretty water
meadows with lazy, twisting streams, a few largish bodies of
woodland, one or two striking ' seats,' and an exceedingly
picturesque old priory with many outbuildings all grouped
with fine trees.   After seven o'clock dinner I strolled to the
wondrously rich front of the little Cathedral and through the
thronged High Street.   As to forming a plan of a tour, I
have given it up.   I shall proceed as on the Riviera, trusting
to luck and previously acquired information."

Sunday, June 20th, was hot and sultry, like the several preceding days; and Charles began to feel the relaxing effects of the climate. He did not get out of doors till two in the afternoon; but once started got a good walk

up on the high ground north of the town, — a villa region on a slope called Pennsylvania, offering wide views seawards and inland towards Tiverton. There was much hill country and but little wood. Everywhere were green fields, hedges, and countless Elms. I turned west, and descended rapidly into the deep valley of the River Exe, passing several small "seats;" and finally came through a villa region to town. I saw two very good, quiet, not over-ornamented small villa grounds; but the general run was very bad indeed. A bit of greensward would be dotted all over with about equally spaced specimen shrubs, cut by a too much twisted path, and fenced with ugly iron. In the evening I viewed the throng in High Street — a sight to behold — all in Sunday rig; and a more utterly provincial-looking lot could not be imagined. Down by the river were some red-coat soldiery, very tipsy. In the bay of a side street was a little crowd singing minor-key hymns of infinite length, accompanied by an organ on wheels, a fiddle, and a cornet. A very mild preacher was saying he had "only one thing to talk about; and that was Jesus," etc. The evening was hot, and the hotel dreary, — hardly anybody in it. Usually there is somebody conversing with the bar-maid. Nobody else to talk to in the whole great house; and I am not yet educated up to bar-maids.

He spent a morning at the well-known nursery of Lucomb, Pince & Co., over across the Exe, a large establishment, but not on the American scale. "It is an old and famous place; yet I was disappointed. The large Conifers mentioned by Sargent had been cut down, because the hired land must be put to more profitable use. There were millions of fruit trees, many glass-houses, and a fine walk a quarter of a mile long, planted with specimen Conifers and evergreens of small size. There were gorgeous golden Yews, Junipers, Retinosporas, fine matched Wellingtonias, many fine Abies, big Pinus Insignis, big purple Beech, grand Hornbeam shelter hedges, and so on. A bit of formal Yew planting was very perfect. I was surprised to hear that seedlings are imported from France as by American nurserymen." In the afternoon Charles visited Robert Veitch's nursery, finding a less fine Conifer walk; but many things not noticed at Lucomb's. From these nurseries, with his pockets full of catalogues, he went to the Cathedral, where he was much interested in the interior, with its fine windows, chantries, tombs and effigies of knights, and battle-flags. From Exeter he wrote to his mother : —

I am off again, as you see, fled from the too pleasant, quiet house at Basset, and again "looking for ideas" in earnest and in solitude. Salisbury cathedral and its immediate surroundings were all my fancy dreamed it, as you know was Canterbury. This Exeter I know less of; and as yet have seen nought of save its marvellous west front. My excursions from Basset and my rail ride hither have given me a good notion of rural England. What a soft, green, gentle, human land it is; and how strangely different from the France I saw on my excursions out of Paris. Southampton — what a contrast to Havre : a far greater contrast than that between Marseilles and Genoa. I was on the broad grin on my first walk in the English-Indian port. What strangely awkward and ingenuous-looking creatures are the lower class of English girls, — and boys too. There was a band playing on the green, the evening of my arrival; and the manners and customs of the assembled natives were very amusing. Mr. Darwin I took to mightily, — no coldness or holding-aloofness about him, — and the result was that I talked more than was becoming. Mrs. Darwin seemed frail in body, but very active and Nortonesque in mind. . . . The house — ugly outside — inside is very good indeed; the pictures and books are only the very best of their sorts; and there is absolutely no useless bric-à-brac. [Letter to G. H. E.]

Tuesday, the 22d of June, out of Exeter by the 8 A. M. train, down river to Exmouth, passing close to the seat of the family of Sir Francis Drake. . . . A stage mounted the hills behind Exmouth; and descended after one hour to the coast village Budleigh Salterton, where there was a brook running down the main street, an exposed pebble beach, and a red rock point beyond the mouth of the Otter at the east. I walked inland by a road up the Otter valley, in sight of much high swelling hill country and by two little villages, thatched and whitewashed, on to Bicton Park. . . . There I met nobody; but explored alone the lower garden, a bit old-fashioned but good, with formal water. At last I met a frowning head-gardener; and was attached to a party that was being ·shown round by an ignoramus who could answer none of my questions. We saw the curious walled gardens, the famous Pinetum, the largest specimens of Conifers ever seen — very fine — and the old plantation admired by Loudon; and came out by the water garden again in two hours. At an old cross at the cross roads I turned westward again to see the farmhouse called Hayes Barton, Sir Walter Raleigh's

Hays Barton. Raleigh's birthplace. Garden.

birthplace. I found it, at last, thatched, white walled, many gabled, and with oddly mullioned windows. Thence with some difficulties I found my way back to Salterton across country through very beautiful wood, and over a high Furze-covered hill whence a wide view, — the finest part that towards the big hills and sea-cut cliffs, somewhere between which is Sidmouth.

The next day he wrote in his journal : —

The beauty of the evening and the band playing on the sea-wall tempted me out last night ; though I was weary. The bulk of the town lies on a flat spit ; but the cliff of the mainland is wooded and is a public ground.   On top are a beacon, and a hotel with a fine view.   The entrance from the sea is tortuous and narrow, with vast sandbanks and a two-mile-long Sandy Hook reaching from the west shore.   At the end of the town spit is a little dock full of craft.   This morning there is a big breeze down the river.   The view from the breakfast-room is of the estuary with wooded parks and the high (800 feet) ridge of Haldon Hills behind, and the red clifty coast, topped now with smooth fields now with woods, stretching off to Berry Head.   I took a small two-sailed boat, and sailed rapidly to Dawlish, coasting along a Hook called the Warren.   A cutter yacht was running out under a jib. A shot from the big guns in a practice battery was skipping across the water just outside of our course.   There was no swell at all ; and I landed easily on the sloping stone pier at Dawlish.   It is a queer village, wholly composed of villas. A stream with parked banks runs down the middle, and a railway accompanies the esplanade.   At the west is a high cliff, with a little breakwater at the foot thereof.   I climbed said cliff ; and found a public ground.   Then I went inland by a footpath ; and returned by the stream valley.   It is a public garden all along the latter on both sides ; but it is not good save in a general way.   Taking a train one station towards Exeter by the root of the Warren sand-spit, I went one mile beyond to the gate of the park of Powderham Castle, belonging to the Earl of Devonshire.   I prowled about alone ; and found my way up a big hill, and up a tower at the top of it.   Exeter and Exmouth and the almost waterless Exe were in view.   Then I prowled some more, finding lovely slopes and swells, very large Oaks, Beeches, Ashes, and Cedars, occasional thickets of Bracken, and many deer.   I swung round past a cottage or two, seeing Roses in profusion and Pansies used as edging along the path through a potato patch, — standard Roses rising from potatoes !   The group ing of cottages with large trees was charming.　A red sandstone church sat on the bank of the Exe.　Thence I drifted

into the park again; and before long found myself close to the castle with its dry moats, high-walled courts, corner towers, and iron gates, and a large towered mass of main building.　I retreated to a respectful distance; and then took a bee-line back to Starcross, through the park most of the way.　The effect of the great castle with its surrounding walls seen through groves of great trunks, or terminating open glades, was fine.　It was low water in the Exe; and some fishery or other was going on, — men wading and dragging nets.　Big ships below were aground and keeled over, their spars looking strange seen between big trees.

That evening, by train

past Dawlish to Teignmouth; and a look around the town after supper.　This is another town on a spit, with a sand dune on the sea front, lately " parked," but not badly, being chiefly in grass.　The rock-raised corners of paths were planted prettily with Tamarix kept low, and stout perennials.　There was a sea pier, a squat light-tower, a life-boat house, and a yacht-club house out on the spit.　Opposite, forming the west point of the river-mouth, was a high, red headland wooded — the Ness.　Shipping was moored in a crowd in the stream behind the spit.　From a long wooden bridge, just above, were charming views up and down the stream (at 8.30

P. M.). The light effects on the moving river tide, on the green hillsides (whence came the sound of mowing of grass), on the black clustered shipping, and the high tree-topped Ness, were exquisite. Very weary to bed. Second rather tremendous day.

The next day he went to Torquay. "Here were high villa-crowned and verdurous hills; and, at the foot of three of them, a little port and shops on its quays. Here were also yachts of all sorts; and the fine, wide, moon-shaped, high-shored Tor Bay." After lunch on the quay he had

a grand climb through walled lanes, between steep terraced gardens, up to Daddy Hole Plain — a public ground on the cliff with views over sea and bay. Here I fell asleep for half an hour. The verdure of the cliffs was wonderful: pink with Cheiranthus, yellow with Sedum and some sort of Mustard — Ivy everywhere. I went back by other lanes through another public ground to the foot of the cliffs beside the port. Fuchsias and Mesembryanthemums reminded one of the Riviera. Fine effects were produced with large perennials, such as Canterbury Bells and white and pink Cistus: the cliff itself was very beautiful; the fine sea-wall rough and strong, its joints much weathered, its parapet 4 feet high by 4 feet thick. By train at five o'clock along the shore; then across the valley of the Dart to hotel and dinner at Kingswear, opposite Dartmouth, at seven o'clock. This is the loveliest place yet — a narrow, deep, high-shored estuary; a town op-

Sea-wall at Torquay.

posite, set on a steep slope; downstream on the high rocky shores, woods, an old church and a castle on one point, and a narrow entrance from the sea; upstream, high, green, and partly wooded hills. Yachts and brigs were at anchor, and two big hulks — a schoolship. Many rowboats were flitting about. The beauty of the long evening, after the late and glorious sunset, was very great. I walked along a shaded lane seawards. The hillside is as steep as that at Northeast Harbor, the green water being seen far below through Ivy-clad trees.

June 25th. The next morning Charles watched people
going on board a big steamship bound for South Africa; and
at noon the firing of heavy guns announced that the ship was
off. He climbed a hill behind the hotel, and saw the great
ship put out from the narrow, high-shored river. In the early
afternoon he crossed by ferry to Dartmouth, and walked
down to the western entrance point where is Dartmouth
Castle, Kingswear fort being opposite.

Here were more harbor-shore woods, and near the town
some irregularly walled shore with steps, arches, and even
buildings at the water's edge in Lake-of-Como fashion. The
walls were draped very prettily — Centranthus everywhere,
even on the top of high walls. Under the tree-covered hillside of Warfleet Cove were picturesque old lime-kilns. There
were high rocks about the Castle point, an old church and
graveyard, and a sea-cliff path leading westward. Small
craft were running in and out of the hidden river-mouth.
Children were swarming about; and boys were bathing far
below in a tiny cove. I spent an hour on a bench scribbling
in my note-book; and then walked back by way of the highland country behind, passing down into crooked Dartmouth
by an unusually pretty, small " place," the banks being richly
clothed in Ivy mixed with various Ferns, such as I have seen
on the back walls of greenhouses at home. The town and its
outskirts are set on very steep slopes with long stairs and
high terrace walls, as on the Riviera. At 7.45 I took a small
steamer for " up river," a ten-miles' run up the high-shored,
lovely river Dart, in the soft and fading evening light. The
river is now very narrow, now a mile wide. At the narrowest
place, between high wooded banks, is a rock in mid-channel
where Raleigh once landed to smoke. Just beyond is the birthplace of John Davis, the navigator; then comes the lovely
seat of the Gilbert family where Sir Humphrey was born.
We passed the village of Dittisham, the Ivy-covered church
of Stoke Gabriel, many inlets, branches, and twistings, and
the grand wooded bank of Sharpham. The trees send down
their branches so as to touch the water when the tide is up.
Under them was a curious straight-edged shadow, the tide
being three feet out when we passed. Next came a rapid

narrowing, much salt marsh, a little quay just below a stone bridge, and the inn of Totnes. A delicious evening! The gas was just being lighted as we arrived at Totnes at something past nine o'clock.

From Totnes he explored the exceedingly pretty ravine of the river Erme, which divides a manufacturing village, and has been preserved in a wild state. Above the railway the stream is full of falls, pools, and big ledges, and a path follows it northward seven miles, — indeed, to its head in Dartmoor.

He next went on by train, through Plymouth, to St. Germans, where he found close to the station the old church of St. Germans, strangely placed just at the foot of a steep bank.

It has two towers and no chancel. The third aisle is almost gone. It contains monuments of many Eliots, a grand family pew, an old font, and an ancient monastery choir. The great house of the Eliot tribe is close beside the church, the seat being called Port Eliot. At the lodge I got permission to walk about the park, which is very large, but not fine compared with Powderham, for instance. I took note of the even, swelling hills where hay-making was going on, and the fringing woods. At the east was a salt-marsh creek, — huge evergreen Oaks on its banks, and a little steam yacht moored under the shade of one of them. I walked back close past the house, which is partly old and partly new, one side having a big Ivy-clad bay, the other sides very plain. The entrance front, which shows much gravel, is ugly; and the whole is set very low, — but little above the marsh land. It is backed by a wood of large trees on rising ground. It has views across grasslands, up grassy hills to woods rambling along near the crests, and of water through a fringe of trees on the creek-side at the east. In the village I found an inn — the Eliot Arms — and from the bar-maid got a vague tale of how the Eliots once lived in Devon and came to St. Germans by exchanging lands with the Champernownes (it was a Champernowne who once owned Cutts Island (near Portsmouth, N. H.) and a large territory in that vicinity). I should like to be instructed in these antiquities.

In the evening at Plymouth he found his way, after dinner, to the famous Hoe, whence is a fine view over wide open sea, with high capes at the east and west, and a long breakwater half-way between.   Many large vessels were at anchor; many war-ships; and just at the foot of the Hoe a fleet of yachts.

The great wooded heights of Mt. Edgcumbe Park were across the estuary at the right, and more woods beyond the estuary at the left.   The citadel was on the left, and the great dockyards below on the right.   On the steep green slopes of the Hoe itself were several stone terraces, and bastions, and staircase paths.   Many people were lying on the grass watching the life on the water.   I went back past a great shabby drill-shed where Mr. Parnell was addressing a vast crowd.   As I was reading the papers an hour later at the hotel, a huge approaching cheering announced Mr. Parnell's coming in a cab.   I saw his arrival, and the rush of the mob up the steps after him.

When Charles first passed through Plymouth, he received a letter from Mr. Olmsted proposing that he go to California about the middle of August, with Mr. Olmsted and General Francis A. Walker, who were to advise Governor Leland Stanford about the grounds and buildings of his proposed university.   Mr. Olmsted pointed out that during the excursion a great variety of climatic and landscape conditions could be observed, and spoke of the great interest of the California problem, — which was really nothing less than the designing of characteristic and appropriate landscape work for a rich soil in a hot and arid climate.   He thought that Charles's recent observations in Italy might be in some measure applicable.   The proposition, which was a liberal one, involved Charles's working at least three months in Mr. Olmsted's office after the return from California.   Charles reflected on this proposition for twenty-four hours, and then declined it, writing to his father on Sunday, June 27th, —

Here yesterday I got your two business letters with Mr. Olmsted's enclosed; and I was somewhat disturbed thereby at first.   I went out to see Port Eliot yesterday afternoon, and the California problem kept presenting itself in all manner of lights; and I could not make up my mind to decline until this morning.   It might lead to work in California for me on my own account; it might ensure my falling co-heir to some of Mr. Olmsted's many big works, as H. H. Richardson's head men have fallen heirs to his — and more " mights " innumerable. . . . On the whole, I prefer to stay out my stay hereabouts in Europe, and then, in a quiet sort of way if you please, to " set up." . . . To-morrow morning I shall cable " Decline," as you suggest.   I told Mr. Olmsted I was thinking of hanging out a shingle for myself. . . . I think he really likes me; and I hope thinks me better fitted than most.   If he should disapprove I should feel badly.[1]

I am going no further into Cornwall; though there are reputed to be wondrous gardens down by Penzance.   I found at Torquay the sort of thing it must be — a faint reflection of the Riviera: places that I should have gone wild over had I not seen the perfection of their type on the Mediterranean shore.

That same Sunday, which was a very hot day, he strolled into the Plymouth streets late in the afternoon.

The Salvation Army was parading with flags and bands. Among their tunes were " Marching through Georgia," " The Union Forever," and the " Marseillaise."   Strange!

Monday, June 28.   To and all through grand Mt. Edgcumbe.   A great house half-way up the hill; sea views from the swelling park hilltop; a very lovely steep shore; evergreen Oaks; Rhododendrons in thickets like North Carolina;

---

[1] " His observations are keen and sound, and show (without looking further) that he can easily be a better critic and commentator on landscape-gardening works than any whom we have had for a long time." (F. L. O. to C. W. E., 2 March, 1886.)

" I did not much suppose that you would take a vacation from your European school for a visit to the Pacific, but . . . thought it best to propose it.   I don't doubt that you are right.   What you said in your note of 5th June about the charm of some of the old gardening work and the folly of some of the new English work in Italy pleased me very much.   I suppose that in at least half of our country the conditions are much less favorable to English gardening than in northern Italy, yet nobody cares for any other.   I find Governor Stanford bent on giving his university New England scenery, New England trees and turf, to be obtained only by the lavish use of water."   (F. L. O. to C. E., 20 July, 1886.)

frequent glimpses of the sea, the breakwater, and the road-stead; at the water-side, gardens in the Italian and French styles. The shipping was gay with bunting; and there were big guns at noon in honor of the Queen's coronation day.

From Plymouth he went to Bideford; and thence to Clovelly, going by coach to Bude by hot and dusty roads over high ground, all in hedged fields, by woods and much twisting of narrow lanes, to the end of the road on the brink of a great steep. The descent thence was by a footpath, the luggage being placed on a sort of sled which two men held back.

Section of a Devon lane — earth fence — Hawthorn hedge. Banks densely clothed with young Maples, Oaks, and Elms, and with Woodbine, Privet, wild Roses, Ferns, Geraniums, Poppies, Bayberry, Ivy, Hazel, Holly, and all manner of crowded herbs.

At a sharp turn we came out of the woods, and saw the sea straight down far below — 400 feet. A chain of cottages, no two on one level, was strung along the steep path which now and then became a staircase. Half-way down was an inn, then more jumbled cottages, bits of gardens, stairs and walls, climbing Roses and Fuchsias, and a little platform with a seat where old salts were surveying the tiny port and the sea. The path was carried through a house, and then, steeper than ever, down to the sea level and a high stone pier, behind which a few smacks were aground. The Red Lion Inn is at the root of the pier, and from the pierhead a good view of the strange village is obtained. I never saw anything more quaint and amusing, — in its homelier fashion it is as picturesque as anything on the Riviera. I explored the few short branches out of the main street, admired the charming cottage gardening, and loafed on the pier till half-past nine.

June 30. This inn is half on one side of the "street," and half on the other, neighbors' houses adjoining it above and below. Folks clattering down the street, or toiling up, pass within four feet of the window of my six-feet-six-inches-high bedroom, and even closer to the window of the coffee-room. All the windows are open, so that conversation in the neigh-

borhood is very audible.   I walked westward a mile or two
along the ridge of the high steep of the coast.   Inland were
the open and be-groved grasslands
of the deer park of the manor
house ; and alongshore much Oak
wood.   Wild ferny combes opened
down to the stony beach at the
foot of the verdurous cliffs.   At
length I mounted a heath and a
Gorse-grown hill to the brink of
the great cliff called Gallantry
Bower (300 feet and more).   A
few Thorn-trees supplied the only
shade, and these were strangely
wind-pruned by the southwest
wind, so that they bent towards
instead of away from the sea.

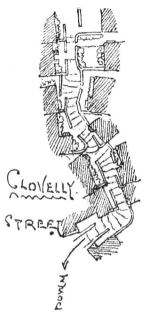

The same day Charles returned
to Bideford, took a train to Barnstable, and at 3.30 a coach for
Lynton.

I was the only passenger.   It
was a grand drive of three hours
up the valley of Yeo, over the thousand-feet-high spurs of
Exmoor, and down the valley of West Lyn, wild with
coppice wood and a brawling stream.   The hotel overhangs
the sea at the height of 300 to 400 feet, the shore being very
high in both directions.   After supper I went down the said
400 feet by a twisting path through the woods of the cliffside
to Lynmouth — an ecstatic spot.   There are three high, steep,
wild hills ; the two Lyns pour swiftly down leafy combes
between these hills, and meet just above a boulder beach on
the seashore.   A tiny village is crowded about this meeting ;
and below are a bit of stone pier and a smack or two.

Thursday, July 1st.   I walked along the shore path westward, the path being about 450 feet above the sea, on the
steep slope of a mountain which rises as much again above it.
The slope is now and then broken into rock ; but generally it
is covered with Bracken, Heather, yellow-blooming Lotus, and

grass. After a mile of this I arrived at a region of high pin-
nacle rocks, commanding charming views westward along the
high and varied coast, and inland up a treeless valley of rocks.
Among the rocks I found a sort of low Blueberry, Thyme, a
blue Scabious, a thriving and blooming Cotyledon; and of
shrubs only Privet, Thorn, and Furze. After lunch I strolled
down shady paths — the vegetation most luxuriant, the walls
wondrously clothed — into little Lynmouth, and out on the
pier to see how it looks at low water. Then I went inland by
a footpath, up the bank of the stream of East Lyn. There
was the solitude of a narrow, deep, mountain valley, a rushing
stream, Oak woods, rocks, and bits of cliffs, Ferns, and much
fine detail of stream-side planting. I came to " Watersmeet "
— the union of two large brooks to form the main stream.
. . . There were some folk to talk to at dinner, for a change.
I afterwards walked to big Castle Rock with one of them, to
see the sunset. The colors of the water under the great red,
gray, and green cliffs were very wonderful. Two steamers
were moving up the channel far offshore. Gulls were flying
and screaming far below — otherwise complete quiet.

Walking on the shore path this morning, I sang loud and
long. Since Southampton I had met nobody to speak with —
and so had to do something to let off pent-up enthusiasm at
finding myself in so superb a region.

2d of July. Box seat on a coach at 8 o'clock. Down a
tremendous hill, across little Lyn bridge, and with five horses
up a long, steep road on the ridge between " Watersmeet "
and the sea, with views now of one, now of the other. The
coast was very fine; the hill curves very simple and grand.
On the high open country for many miles were Heather and
Gorse, sheep, rabbits, and partridges. Far inland, in the
midst of the Exmoor hills, is the valley of Doone. The road
now and then circles the head of some deep and steep combe,
leading down into the sea; now sweeps inland around some
high moorland ridge; finally the height of 1500 feet is attained, and a grand view opens eastward along the shore with
Porlock Bay and a fertile valley immediately below. By a
long, steep hill we descend thither to a lovely vale, the cottage
gardens in two villages more ravishing than ever, and Elms

in hedge-rows again as in South Devon. We pass over a low
watershed, and descend to Minehead station, the railway
terminus on the seashore. I took train to the first station
beyond — Dunster, where I was induced to stop by the report
given me by a gentleman met at Lynton, who had never been
there! On walking up the road from the station I discovered
the village — a very quaint one — at the foot of the hill
country, and a big castle on the wooded hill at the end of the
main street. The old inn where I lunched had a porch pierced
for crossbows, and very old woodwork in the gables. There
was an ancient shed-like "yarn market" in the street adjacent,
and also several half-timbered houses. Very luckily I found
the castle grounds open (Tuesdays and Fridays). The castle
had a high knoll and a Norman keep, an Ivy-mantled gate-
house, and Edwardian towers. There was a Yew hedge probably 800 years old, and much most lovely vegetation. . . . I
walked along the stream at the foot of the castle hill, and
came to a picturesque mill. In the village was a church in
perpendicular Gothic, and an ancient tithing barn. Thence
I took train to Taunton, where I dined at seven, and wrote
this. Weary.

The next day was hot. He travelled on to Wells, and
remained quiet in the Swan Hotel till the midday heat was
past, then he explored the Close, the moated bishop's garden,
and the Cathedral. He walked beside the moat with its large
pollarded Elms reaching over the water, and so out into the
open country beyond the bishop's palace. July 4th. "Sunday,
and only one train out of Wells, which I took and travelled to
Bath." He disposed of this famous watering-place in nine
lines, as follows : —

Biggish hills surround the place ; and there is one good-
sized park, pastured by cattle and sheep, the nicer parts of
it fenced off with iron. It contains nothing remarkable. A
new corner with a small, crooked, slope-side pond was planted
in the flashiest style with golden Yews and Elders, purple
Hazels and Beeches, silver Negundos, etc. In the town
were many crescents and squares, of which the simplest
were the best. The architecture is heavy, same, and unat-
tractive.

He went on the same evening to Chippenham, in order to be able to walk to Bowood before hot noon.   July 5th : —

It was a hot four miles to the park gates.   Then a lovely mile through great Beech woods to the large, low-spreading house.   The distant view of the house was very striking, its irregular terraces coming down into the rough pasture grass of the deer park.   Deer were browsing close to the foot of the steps.   A herd of some sixty deer ran close past me in the woods.   In the lake, at the foot of the slope, were many wild ducks.   Rabbits were plenty, of course.   I hunted up the stew-

ard in a remote corner of the manor buildings, and got leave to see the gardens.   There was a large Pinetum ; but the trees were not very large as yet.   I rambled about a delightful wood-land at the foot of the lake.   The lakeside was very, very good, wild with all manner of shrubbery, Water-Lilies, and rushes ; and the dam of the lake is well treated.   There is a pretty region of wooded mounds, where no doubt earth from the lake excavation was dumped.   All this was done very long ago. Finally, the ancient terrace gardens before the house are kept up in the old-fashioned manner, and are very quaint, with stone-edged parterres, much balustrading, walks on different levels, Yews, etc.

Writing to his father the next day he says, " Yesterday I saw splendid Bowood — Lansdowne place — which Mr. Henry

Winthrop Sargent pronounced the second best in all England."

That evening he took train for London, where he arrived "with but eight pence in pocket." His letter of credit on Baring Brothers, being intended for the Continent, was of no use in British provincial towns.

English barns.

CHAPTER VIII

LANDSCAPE STUDY IN EUROPE. LONDON AND THE NORTH

True taste is forever growing, learning, reading, worshipping, laying its hand upon its mouth because it is astonished, casting its shoes from off its feet because it finds all ground holy, and testing itself by the way that it fits things. And it finds whereof to feed and whereby to grow in all things; for there is that to be seen in every street and lane of every city, that to be felt and found in every human heart and countenance, that to be loved in every roadside weed and moss-grown wall, which in the hands of faithful men may convey emotions of glory and sublimity continual and exalted. — RUSKIN.

HE next took lodgings at Kew, in order to have convenient access to the gardens at all times of day. The weather was extraordinarily hot for England. He writes to his father, "Weather shockingly hot for some days past. 87 degrees in the coolest part of last night, according to the newspaper. I have not met a drop of rain since leaving Southampton — a great contrast to the soaking I had in my last weeks in Paris. . . . I am just now very ambitious to see cold and hot St. Petersburg."

He now collected nurserymen's catalogues with energy and success; sought for books about Sweden, Finland, and Russia; and was forced to attend to some matters of business, — such as the replenishing of his wardrobe. Every day, however, he found time for some study of parks and gardens. He could not walk across a London park without seeing much that he wished to take note of, the whole aspect of the parks being utterly different from what it was in mid-winter. If he had a few minutes in London before train time, he would go into the Turner water-color room of the National Gallery. In the long afternoons he could spend an hour or two in Kew gardens "working over herbaceous things." July 7th: "Supped in a place on the river-bank by Kew bridge, and watched the pretty boating. Thermometer 90 degrees to-day." The river sights fixed themselves in his memory; and, in his view, justified the urgency with which he advocated in later years the devotion of the Charles River (Boston) to purposes

of popular enjoyment. For more than a week at Kew,
"every day was divided between plant-inspecting and note-
taking in Kew gardens, and study of plant-books in the
house. Some little progress made; but what a limitless
field!" One evening he took a look at Bedford Park gardening, and a Sunday evening he spent at Richmond, watching the boating thereabouts. On a cool northwest day he
visited Eton and Windsor Castle, and took a long tramp
through the great park, taking special note of the Long
Walk, Cumberland Lodge, the cricket ground, and the lovely
Virginia water. "The water is very, very fine, with good
plantings, and a pretty treatment of the outlet and of the
long dam. The evening was very lovely — showers and rainbow, with sunset and moon.'

On the 17th of July Charles had the pleasure of lunching
by appointment with Mr. Harry Milner, the direct inheritor
of the principles of Paxton and Mr. Milner, Senior. Charles
intimates in his journal that, according to Mr. Milner, "there
is no landscape gardening anywhere save in England; and
no styles or principles at all other than English." In the
afternoon Charles looked at the magnificent but ill-kept gardens of the Crystal Palace, and then sought at the British
Museum for books which might guide him on his proposed
Scandinavian and Russian journey. Another day he visited
the nursery of Mr. Waterer at Woking.

From the station I went afoot to Mr. Waterer's — very
crookedly, being misdirected twice. Everybody in England
says right hand for left, and vice versâ. The country was
full of nursery grounds; and almost every cottage had golden
Yews about it. Two little showers occurred; and the air
was very, very muggy. I stopped under a canal bridge during one shower, with four young fellows who were cruising
in a wherry. When I reached Mr. Waterer's house, Mr.
Waterer was at "the farm" dining two Americans introduced
by Mr. Sargent! I walked through the nursery to said farm,
and found that Mr. and Mrs. John L. Gardner, of Boston,
had just gone. Mr. Waterer talked with me, over cham-
pagne and biscuit, about Sargent, Kemp, Thomas Milner,
and American planting. We walked in the nursery, seeing
wonderful weeping Beeches, and acres of "American plants."
I was introduced to a son — Antony Waterer, Jr., who
showed me all about the place, and took me to tea with his

aunt at six o'clock. The whole establishment is very interesting. Getting from Mr. Waterer a plain direction for
reaching the station, and walking fast a distance of two miles
and a half, I caught a train which carried me to Mortlake,
whence I walked in the dark to Kew, where I arrived about
ten o'clock.

The next day Charles visited Mr. Ware's herbaceous nursery near Tottenham — a very rich and interesting collection,
and had a long talk with the head man, Mr. Ware being
away. " He says that their small American trade has never
been satisfactory, the American nurserymen being hard to
deal with ; and the American amateurs very particular. He
thinks the climate opposed to horticulture in America, as it
is in Russia. In England there is a continuous ever-growing
demand for good perennials."

On the 21st of July Charles returned to London. Calls in
London, and necessary preparations for his journey to Russia,
took up two or three days. One of his visits in London was
to the office of the secretary of the Commons Preservation
Society, where he learned about its work, and got a set of its
reports. The success of this society encouraged Charles in
later years to attempt the organization of a somewhat similar
society in Massachusetts. In the afternoon of the 24th, having stored his heavy luggage, he took train for Cambridge
with two small pieces, an overcoat, and an umbrella. The
next day being Sunday, he wrote letters, and rested. Nevertheless, after lunch he " strolled about the town. The Backs
are very pretty, but very damp. I discovered Emmanuel
College by the coat of arms, entered, and watched the swans
in ' the pool.' " The next day, July 26th, he tried in vain to
find Professor Alfred Marshall, who had stayed at his father's
house at Harvard University in 1875. To console himself,
he visited the Botanic Garden for an hour, and then walked
in and out through the colleges along the river. Observing
on a bulletin board the name of a lecturer, " Dr. Cunningham, D. M. D., Harvard," he sought him out to ask about a
discolored front tooth. Dr. Cunningham " pronounced the
tooth practically dead, and proceeded to get out the ' pulp ; '
but I going off into fainting, he had to stop and postpone the
operation till to-morrow." Dr. Cunningham, who was a graduate of the Harvard Dental School in 1876, was at pains to
procure various courtesies for Charles during the next two
days; but these days were much interfered with by the necessity of repeated operations upon the damaged front tooth.

On Charles's last day in London he had tried in vain to
find Mrs. Beadle and her young ladies at the Hotel Metropole, having received a note from Mrs. Beadle to the effect
that her party had returned from Scotland, and was at that
hotel.   At Cambridge he now received a second note from
Mrs. Beadle, to say good-by; for she expected to sail for
home very shortly.

From Cambridge Charles went to Derby, hoping to see
Elvaston Castle grounds; but he found there was " no admission on any account."   He saw, however, the Arboretum first
planted by Loudon, now a public garden.

From Cambridge he wrote to his father as follows : —

It rained all day yesterday ; and I only got a damp stroll
along the Backs and into Emmanuel Quad.   For three or four
days I have been feeble and blue.   Damp heat does not suit
me at all.   To-day I believe I feel better, and shall sally out
to hunt up Mr. Marshall or somebody, and on to Derby to-
night.   Here follows a financial report.   I believe you have
had none since I arrived in Paris from the south : —

Paris, 34 days, 1. Ordinary expenses	$2.53 a day
2. Extras, for dentistry, books, and	
photographs	39.00
Moving from Paris to Southampton, and expenses	
at the latter place	35.00
South of England, 18 days, expenses	5.12 a day
Kew and London, 19 days, 1. Ordinary expenses .	2.86 a day
2. Extra expenses, for	
clothing, books,	
and passport . .	88.00

From Matlock Bath he wrote an amusing letter to his
mother, on July 30th, in the main about what he called " my
second series of dentistry adventures," but he added : " It
seems ages since I last saw any landscape gardening.   I have
a feeling of having passed a very unprofitable month of July.
I vow I do not know where the time has gone to.   At Kew I
picked up something; but not very much, for hardly anything
is growable with us.   London days were dismal — very —
being full of journeyings on omnibuses and in the Underground, and little anxieties about clothes and other purchases,
and some weariness and stupidity.   The latter kept me from
making the evening journey to the Metropole to see the Pit-
kin-Yale-Beadle party."

Considering that Charles had seen in July Lynton, Lynmouth, Dunster, Wells, Bath, and Bowood, and had restudied Kew gardens and London parks and the Thames, beside visiting Windsor, the Crystal Palace Gardens, the Waterer nursery, and Cambridge, his lament that he had seen no landscape gardening in July seems but ill-founded. The fact seems to have been that hot, sultry weather, his dental experiences, and some social disappointments in London, had combined to depress him somewhat. He wrote to his friend Roland Thaxter from Derby on the wet, dismal afternoon of July 29th, telling him of his varied experiences at Cambridge: " All this (and indeed all going about in this land) makes our College and our New England seem exceedingly youthful and provincial, — but none the less exceedingly dear to this C. E. . . . Some day I must come again for a regular pleasure trip in this old world. This time I am continually torn by contending forces — one of pure pleasure urging me this way — the other of assumed or imagined professional advantage pulling me the other. I long for Alps, for instance, but I go to flat Russia."

On Friday, July 30th, he took the train at Derby to Matlock Bath, and thoroughly enjoyed the ride. He always liked going up hills; and rough rocky places were, on the whole, more delightful to him than smooth cultivated country. So he writes in his journal: —

Up grades into higher country, narrow valleys, tunnels, the twisting Derwent, rocks good to see, the railway walls wondrously beverdured. I tramped along the village street with luggage in hand, and lit upon a small inn between the road and the rushing river. After supper, uphill into the Pavilion Gardens soon after seven. Thence I had a view of the narrow valley with the village street on one side of the stream, and cliffs, woods, and " lovers' walks " on the other. The " gardens " were made out of wild coppice woods strewn with Ivied boulders. The Pavilion was of glass — a concert-room. The terraces before it were not bad.

The next day, July 31st, he took the train up Derwent Valley to Rowsley.

A lovely country, — the swelling hills bearing woods, distant summits of bare moor in view, and valleys of luscious green with scattered trees. It rained heavily on arriving; but after an hour came a grand clear-off, and a fine ride to Chatsworth House. There was a crowd of excursionists at the gate; but I got in at last. The showing round through the great house was tedious; but there are fine views from the windows, including terraces before the house, a vista with formal water, and a slope behind stretching up under high woods. Out of doors we were hurried round past a "French garden," a cascade, a rock garden (where rocks are handled on a larger scale than I have ever seen), and a fine Palm house; and back by the water, a fountain, and the terraces. I strolled over the bridge, and to the inn at Edensor for lunch, and got most lovely outlooks in every direction. There were cattle in the river as in all the photographs, and great sweeps of green land edged and broken by woods. The village of Edensor is a fancy one; the houses too villa-like. Taking the omnibus back to Rowsley, I set off on foot for Haddon Hall, passing the charming "Peacock" and through the valley meadows. At length, the old towers and familiar bridge appeared at the right. I crossed the bridge, and went up to the low door, a young man and his wife just before me. With them I saw the interior, shown in a well-devised order, ending with the beautiful ball-room, and then the throwing open of Dorothy Vernon's door — "Oh, no, it is 300 years since Dorothy left." The other folks marched off immediately; and I was left alone under old Yews, Dorothy's door having closed. It was a dark and damp nook between the house and the wall against the hill. At the right, sunlight was entering from the open ground of the lower terrace. At the top of the terrace stairs I sat long — enchanted, verily. A small boy was weeding the path against the battlement of the lower terrace. I went down and talked to said boy, who showed me a way down past the buttresses of the terrace wall to the stream and the ruined foot bridge at the foot; whence I went back to Rowsley by a path along the stream. The evening light was soft; and two fair maids were strolling, arms locked. How wise was I to go to Chatsworth before Haddon.

Sunday, August 1st, he spent the whole afternoon, until late, in the Pavilion Gardens of Matlock, which he found particularly instructive as being developed chiefly from New

England-like copse wood. On the 2d of August he went on to Buxton, where he explored the Pavilion Gardens made by Edward Milner. They are owned by a company, as at Matlock. Admission four-pence. Concerts are given in the glass Pavilion ; and there are tennis grounds, a bowling green, a "lake" for boating, a Rose garden, a rockery, and so forth, — too many features, for the ground is taken up with them to the destruction of breadth of effect.

I found out many names of plants from an old gardener ; and took note of much in a small way. Herbaceous plants are well used here in the edges of shrubberies ; not in bands as in France, but irregularly. Crowds gathered, — people from Manchester and other cities. There was very fine tennis playing, — one girl a "terror." Buxton is a town of stone villas, hydropathical establishments, etc. The crescent and the terraced hill before it were rather daringly, but success-fully, designed. I took a walk out of town into the country visible from the gardens. There were few or no hedges ; but rude stone walls. The surface of the country was hilly and tossed, with patches of small wood, and bits of roughish pasture, — altogether, rather New England-like. A beauty Valerian along the roadsides.

He went on to Manchester that evening ; and had no sooner dined than he strolled into the street, and took a tram-car marked "Alexandra Park." "A long road through the ugly, smoky town ; but the park well worth seeing, being of peculiar design, consisting chiefly of playgrounds with a long, low terrace along one side." The next morning he visited Peel Park.

An ugly, nondescript sort of place in the hideous region called Salford. Back into town again ; and another tram out to the Botanic Gardens, so called, where was no botany, but a pretty place enough, owned by a body of subscribers. I took note of the flowers in bloom, and of the general arrange-ment. There was an iron frame for a tent, wherein to give big horticultural shows ; a band-stand green, and a twisting, hidden swan-water. Back again to town ; and an afternoon train for Preston, where I had almost two hours in the rather large parks which stretch along the river. These are Edward

Milner's work again, and good.   The best features are the
natural terrace, and the slopes to river meadows and the river,
large open lawns, well-massed woods, a loggia whence views
over distant open country, a well-made ravine, an excellent
treatment of two crossing railways, a good terrace with a
statue above backed by foliage and a fountain below, and
Milner's regulation spiral and sun-dial.   At 7 o'clock I took
train for Windermere.   Fewer and fewer were the tall chimneys ; and at length, no more smoke.   At sunset there was
a lovely look across a bay of salt flats at the soft mountains
of Westmoreland.   The train was delayed, — up grades and
rising hills.   At Kendal, an influx of lads and lassies from a
"gala."   Reached a small inn at Windermere at 9 o'clock.
No lake visible yet ; but a young moon in the sky.

On the 4th of August : —

My hotel was a little one with a small girl to wait, and no
other lodger ; but a crowd always in the bar.   I was rather
late getting up the hill near the station by a path through
private grounds ; but finally got on to the open " Fell ; " and
then had a delightful view of the whole of Windermere and
the mountains roundabout.   It was a scene of tenderest
beauty, wrapt in softest haze.   Helvellyn was very dim, and
Langdale Pikes also.   The lake was smooth and palely blue,
its two long reaches separated by the island-dotted narrows
about Bowness.   I went downhill again, and on to Bowness ;
then by steamer, at 3.30, first down the lake to the foot
thereof, where I strolled to old Newby Bridge by a road
chiefly bordered by coppice ; then, in the late afternoon, back
by steamer to the very head of the lake, and to Bowness
again after seven.   All delicious.   The next day (August
5th), I left the little hotel at 9 o'clock on a coach for Keswick, where I arrived before one.   First, we went up the
shore of Windermere by a gently hilly road through much
wildish small wood, past many " seats," — a region of the
Beverly [Mass.] type.   Then to Ambleside ; and so past
Rydal Water ; on past Grasmere, and up into wholly open
land in the pass called " the Raise " at the west foot of Helvellyn.   Then on, and down past Thirlmere and the works

just begun for taking water hence to Manchester. There was a look down the Vale of St. John. Then we went over a low pass, and down a long hill into Keswick Vale, and to the George Hotel in Keswick just as a shower came down smartly. In the afternoon, between showers, I got out to the foot of Derwentwater, whence was a beauteous view of the lakeside mountains, ranged in lovely perspective of silvery, showery distance. I also strolled about the neighborhood of the village; and, towards evening, enjoyed the striking effects of sunlight bursting from between clouds, and gleaming golden on emerald slopes of purple-shadowed and silver-misted hills, — a sight to make one hold one's breath with wonder. At my late supper I had a little talk with a young man and his wife, — the first talk since Cambridge.

August 6. The morning was cloudy, but clearing; so I took coach at 10 o'clock, with nameless acquaintances of last evening and others, for an all-day trip. We went out along Derwentwater, through rich woods at the foot of ferny heights, past wet meadows and fields of rushes at the head of the lake, past the foot of almost waterless Lodore, through a low pass at the foot of the fine Castle Crag, past Bowder Stone, and into fair Borrowdale. There were meadows and hay-making, one or two tiny hamlets, little stone bridges over clear streams, the mountains around wooded below and rising above in exquisite forms of crag and scar, and steeps of golden green mottled with the deep green of Bracken, and higher up with the brown and bronze of Heather. There were many silver threads of streamlets, and many wet and glistening bits of ledge. About the high peaks were much broken fog and cloud. The walk up the ascent of Honister Pass was long and steep, — a hard struggle for the horses, — first along the wooded course of a rocky stream, and then along the same stream in an open land of rock, Fern, and Heather. At the summit was a corner and an impressive view down the steep and narrow valley at the foot of the Crag of Honister, by which we proceeded on and down, and so to Buttermere and an inn for lunch about one o'clock. Next, I went by boat, with some others, over a bit of Crummock Water close by, and walked part way up the open val-

ley to see a high, slender waterfall, — Scale Force, — issuing
from a corner in a grassy mountain, and falling in a narrow,
verdurous rock-cleft about six feet wide.   At four we took a
coach again, passing first over a higher but less imposing
pass, then down the Vale of Newlands, and round the foot of
Derwentwater into Keswick.   Fog and cloud were thicken-
ing fast, — no glory from low sun to-night; but an ever
memorable day.

This lovely country is just what I imagined it, — mountains of friendliest character, of exquisite highly-wrought
sculpturing, of subtlest, gracefullest form, and of marvellous
fitful color under this watery sky.   The scenery is of a very
distinct type, and of its sort the perfectest imaginable.

The next day was dark and rainy.

Just as well, perhaps; for fine weather would have persuaded this sybarite to linger and linger on.   I looked at
some absurdly inadequate photographs ; and then bethought
me of the secretary and prime mover in the Lakeland Defence Association, which has fought off two railway schemes
and done other service.   I got directions ; walked a little
way from town ; and fortunately found him at home.   I introduced myself as an American much interested in the work of
the Association.   He told me that the closing of ancient footways was the chief trouble at present.   It was done right and
left by new proprietors newly rich ; and was hard to prevent,
because the burden of proof lay strangely enough with the
public ; it was also a disagreeable sort of quarrel, because it
seemed, in some measure, personal.   A new law was wanted
to enable the local authorities to fight the battles, instead of
the secretary and his Association.   Parliament will soon take
this matter up along with Mr. Bryce's " Scottish Mountains "
bill ; Parliament has already affirmed in other matters the
principle of the real value of scenery ; has refused to charter
railways which would have injured scenery ; and has required
the Manchester Water Works people to save soil wherewith
to re-cover their masses of tunnel débris.   Mr. R—— asked
about my work in America, — if I were in the Law or what ;
and on hearing my trade, made me sit down again and tell

him about the Yellowstone, Niagara, and so forth. Then
we looked at his old vicarage garden, — and I fled for the
noon train.

Out of the mountains and to Carlisle. The day was
clearing up ; so that, on crossing the low land at the head of
Solway Firth, I could see the fine group of Cumberland
Mountains very well. We crossed some wet moorlands, —
very bleak. There was a long ascent through bare hill
country with not much cultivation, but occasional plantations
of Spruce. In the hedge-rows were Scotch Pines instead of
Elms. The Scotch names of stations seemed familiar. Once
" Ecclefechan " flashed past, — Craigenputtock must be
somewhere behind these dreary hills, thinks C. E. Two or
three castles, with plantations around them, appeared in valleys of these moors. We went up and over a dull pass near
the source of the Clyde and Tweed ; and on, down into a
country of chimneys, and to smoky Glasgow. After dinner
I took a short stroll about the cold, windy, and deserted
streets, empty because the shops were closed. It was Saturday afternoon, and the dismal pall of Sunday had fallen
already.

On Monday he went by tram-car to the south verge of the
smoky city to Queen's Park.

I had been urged to be sure and see it; but I found
nothing worth while, — much carpet bedding, every plant
numbered, and a printed list under glass set alongside! I
journeyed back again, and out another way to the Botanic
Garden. It is chiefly a pleasure garden, with much bedding again, and shrubberies stiffly edged. A small plant
collection in one corner I looked over thoroughly, since it
afforded a review of some of my labors at Kew. Next, I
looked at the outside of the University buildings, and at the
park below it. During a shower I looked into a museum.
Rain coming on, I discovered an interesting photograph
exhibition in the Public Galleries. I am weary of mists and
showers; and believe I have seen enough of British gardening. . . . I shall skip to Edinburgh to-morrow. Glasgow is
unprofitable and ugly.

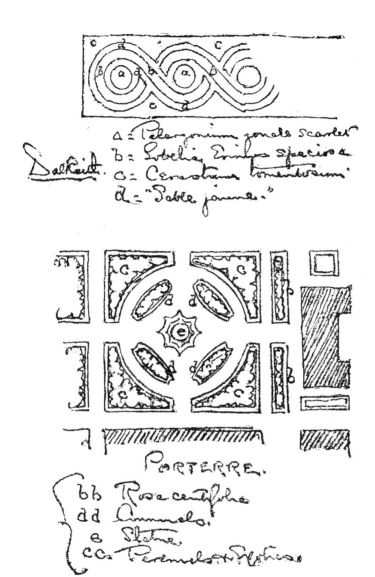

a = Pelargonium zonale scarlet
b = Lobelia Emilia speciosa
c = Cerastrum tomentosum
d = "Sable jaunes."

Dalkeith.

PARTERRE.

bb Rosa centifolia
dd Annuals.
e Statue.
cc Perennials or Alpines

The ride to Edinburgh, on the 10th of August, was through a dull open country of hilly pasture, broken by dirty mining villages and smoking chimney stacks of huge "works." His enjoyment of Edinburgh was interfered with by very bad weather. On his one fine day he explored the Castle, High Street, Arthur's Seat, and the Crag, "finding the prospects finer in every way than I anticipated, the effect heightened by the Turneresque atmosphere, and by cloud, haze, and smoke." As usual, he also visited and explored thoroughly the Botanic Garden. With his characteristic love of the seaside, he took a tram-car to Newhaven, where he saw with pleasure the queer fishing-boats and the fish-wives in costume. He also looked into an exhibition which was "called International; but was not. As a Scotch show it was good, the ship-builders' exhibits being particularly interesting." On an afternoon which was only cloudy instead of rainy, he found his way to the long, shabby village of Dalkeith, and to the park gates at the end of its main street.

Explored the said park of Dalkeith, which is curiously different in quality from English places of the same general character. Many of the trees were large and old; but, seen from the house, not effectively arranged. The house stands on the brink of the deep valley of Esk, the opposite bank being richly wooded with old trees. A cove in the bank, at one side of the house, is treated as a " pleasure garden," showing steep banks of Laurel and scattered Yews, and of massed Rhododendrons. A very high, stone-arched bridge is carried over Esk just below, springing from a natural bluff on one side to the made bank on the other, its abutments finely hidden in foliage. Through the high arch one gets a pretty glimpse of the splashing river.

That evening he took the steamer to Hamburg at 9.30 from Leith docks. The passengers were chiefly German tourists going home.

All the persons to whom Charles had letters in Edinburgh were absent at the time of his visit. He was particularly sorry not to find Mr. McPherson, of the Scottish Footpaths Society; for he was already interested in the work of that society, and had seen the need of some similar work at home.

CHAPTER IX

LANDSCAPE STUDY IN EUROPE. HAMBURG, DENMARK, SWEDEN, AND RUSSIA

The more extensive, therefore, your acquaintance with the works of those who have excelled, the more extensive will be your powers of invention, and what will appear still more like a paradox, the more original will be your conceptions. — SIR JOSHUA REYNOLDS.

FOR twenty-four hours, from Sunday noon to Monday noon, the sea was very rough, and I was sick; but Monday afternoon I got on deck (wet with water shipped in the night), and, as the sea fell rapidly, I soon recovered. We passed red-clifted Helgoland about four o'clock, and a lightship marked " Elbe " two hours later; but saw no land till about seven. It was Cuxhaven with its wooden piers and docks. Thence we proceeded slowly up the river, many odd fishing-smacks coming down with sidelights burning. The evening was very warm, but wettish. When I went to bed the ship was still proceeding against a strong tide. This morning (Tuesday, August 17) I took a cab up-town to the hotel on Binner-Alster. In the streets were women and dogs harnessed in carts, and other queer things. Sad to say, rain and smut as ever.

In the afternoon of the same day the weather cleared, and Charles walked out countrywards along the inner and outer Alsters.

Water parks such as Boston should have made of the Back Bay. I got out into a villa region — Longwood-like — whence a view of the high city spires across long green-edged water alive with boats, small steamers, and fleets of swans. When sunset came and the lighting of lamps, I returned by steamer under the fine Lombards Bridge, across the inner basin to the quay in the heart of the town. There I took an ice in a water pavilion. Hamburg is a delightful town !

These water parks interested Charles greatly. He inspected repeatedly their shores, the landing-stages, and the planta- tions; and, as usual, took great delight in the intelligent pro- vision for public enjoyment upon the water. " I followed

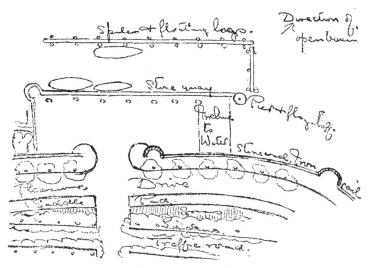

A water-side arrangement — Hamburg.

the good public gardens which run all round the lines of the old walls to the Botanic Garden and the Zoölogical Garden, both of which are interesting and instructive." He walked through the river-side of the town, observing the old canals and the high gabled buildings; and thence to the steamer- landing just below the mooring-ground of the crowded ships. Here he took a steamer down the Elbe seven or eight miles to Blankenese landing.

The banks are rather high, and wooded and villaed all along, the houses looking westward over the river and the low salt- creeked country beyond. The river is full of small shipping, with quaint rigs and colored sails. Blankenese is very odd, having steep, crooked, paved footways, — a bigger and Ger- manified Clovelly. Close by is a large park. I entered and rambled in it long. It is a very fine piece of landscape work. Thence I turned towards town, along the high road. Many people were out pleasure-driving; the whole road and the bordering, largish places very Brooklinesque [Brookline,

Mass.], — new telephone poles and all.   A steamer from the
landing Teufelsbrücke brought me to the hotel just in time
for dinner.   Very odd soup to-night, having the appearance
of broth; but containing, beside numerous vegetables, slices
of eels, doughballs, prunes, and much vinegar.

The next morning, August 20th, he spent on Alster steamers, taking notes of the excellent water-side arrangements,
and of the water-side villa gardens, the public walks, and the
beer gardens.   In the afternoon he took the train for Kiel;
but found the country dull till near Kiel.   There was much
open moor, Heather, small Birches, peat-diggings, and fields
of grain; few hedges or wooden fences divided the fields, but
mainly walls of earth.   The houses were steep-thatched, and
planted close about with small trees for shelter, making thus
islands in the flat expanse.   The train passed one large Beech
forest and one of Pines.   Birches, Alders, Poplars, Wych-
Elms, and Mountain Ashes with bright berries were visible.
The cottage gardens were full of Dahlias.   Charles had
stopped at Kiel to see the Botanic Garden, but he found it
locked up, and no porter's lodge was visible, the university
being in vacation.   He visited, however, the Schloss Garden
on the shore of the harbor, finding a water-side avenue of
Elms and Lindens, a soldiers' monument, and stretches of
greensward and massed shrubs, — a homelike scene.

In the market square before a very odd brick church, a
throng of country-women were selling produce to towns-
women, the country-folk wearing one sort of straw hat, and
the townsfolk another.   Beyond the Botanic Garden, and still
close to the shore of the bay, I found a region of detached
houses in Cambridge-like yards, the streets quiet and tree-
planted, leading down to the old avenue along the shore,
whence were pretty pictures of coasters, ironclads, and small
boats on blue water.

At eleven o'clock, August 21, I took the steamer " Au-
gusta-Victoria," bound for Scandinavia.   The craft was excellent, and the passengers very civilized, — chiefly tourists,
Germans going to see Scandinavia, and Scandinavians going
home.   There were several pretty girls of the Swedish type,
and one couple speaking French, in whom everybody was soon
much interested.   He was dark and Spanish-looking; she

fair and beautiful, like the pictures of Nielson. Their behavior was rather "pronounced," — he lay with his head on her knee; and at table he put a piece of paper in her pretty ear. How the sober, quiet-faced, smooth-haired womenkind looked and looked, and how the men admired! In the Kieler Fjord I saw a navy yard and twelve ironclads in the stream. The shores were very like those of Narragansett Bay. Very soon the open sea appeared ahead, and a tall, white light-tower, and a string of white buoys. The water was utterly smooth and blue; colored sails were becalmed here and there; and the sun was very hot. After midday dinner there was no land in sight. I wrote a letter home, and read. Happy as a clam! Nothing agrees with this child like sailing in smooth water. We were some hours coasting Langeland. It showed low gravel bluffs and beaches, much grain inland, scattered groves, stumpy spires, and stray windmills. Thence we passed into the wide waters of Grosser Belt, Seeland rapidly rising, and showing gravel bluffs and low hills — Long Island Sound scenery. Soon a cluster of red roofs, a narrow entrance to a port, a big railway ferry steamer, a quay, and a custom-house — Korsör. . . . The port is very small, merely an embarking-place, reminding me of Warwick, R. I.; then sunset, and we were off in the train. . . . Through a soft, pretty country — fine Beech woods now and then — but soon dark. Kjöbenhavn [Copenhagen] at 9.45.

Sunday, August 22. Clear and warm. I walked through this town generally. Its streets are stone paved, its sidewalks likewise, with no curbstones. In the old streets is some very quaint architecture; some canals come into the town from the harbor. . . . I followed the fortification promenades northeastward, and came to the salt water side below the harbor quays. Here was a large fort surrounded by a moat — a shaded promenade on a narrow strip between the moat and the water of the harbor, the strip containing a drive, a saddle pad, and a footpath. The banks of the moat were all covered with verdure, and the fort was hidden. Small boats and yachts were moored all along the seaside, and just beyond this was the main channel with big vessels, an island with a harbor lighthouse, and the open water of the Sound each side thereof. . . . There were many seats, and much people enjoying the harbor scene and each other's appearance. I returned through the aristocratic quarter, which lies strangely near the shipping and the warehouses. . . . From a large irregular " square " in the heart of the town, thirteen streets went out, several with tramways in them. Thence I went to the Botanic Garden, which I found rather large, with trees as well as herbs, and irregular planting. The trees were generally small, and crowded in groups of orders. The herbaceous. plants were in scattered beds, and in one corner in a formal arrangement. There were water-side boxes for water plants, and stream plants were similarly grown. There was a special space for Danish plants. . . . Evidently this is no climate for evergreens. The grass, too, was very weedy and brown — quite American. I was twice ordered off it by Garden officers when poking to find labels. What use in labels, if one may not get to read them?

The next day he greatly enjoyed a visit to the Frederiksberg-Have, formerly a royal park, the château now a military school.

This park is unlike anything I have ever seen. Its woods are cut by straightish grass alleys. Its paths twist and curve about, crossing vistas and much crooked water very irregularly. The ground is flat, and comparatively very little of it is in grass. The woods consist of Beech, Oak, Elm, Ash, and a few other trees; and are much trodden by the populace; yet they are generally green with sprouting from the base of the trunks, and pushing of seedlings. The Renaissance château is on an overlooking elevation. Old Linden alleys lead up to it; and immediately in front of it are grass terraces and hedges of Hawthorn. There was a poor zoölogical garden alongside; but I crossed over the road into the park of Söndermarken, where was a water reservoir in place of a château; but otherwise it was like Frederiksberg. There were some masses of very fine woods, and a good Linden avenue; but the grassed vistas were too straight and too parallel-sided.

After dinner I sauntered on the lovely Lange Linie. There were yachts about and much people; soldiers in blue, all Christy's first cousins [Christy — a Dane — was his father's coachman for several years]; old ladies, very old-fashioned; all sorts of young women, — countrified with flat black straw hats and ribbon hanging behind, to stylish creatures almost Parisian. The great majority were soberly dressed, hearty, and good-faced; the children were of very American appearance, — young boys in unbound felt hats, sailor-suits, and so forth. . . . There were people driving in barouches, and on horseback, as well as walking; but these were few.

He was out early the next morning, walking along the empty pavements across the canal, past the ruin of the burnt palace, past the Egyptian (!) (or Etruscan) Thorwaldsen Museum, through the thronged market-place, and along the fish quay of the canal. " It was a very quaint scene, — the crowd of a general mixed color with their blue aprons, straw hats and white handkerchiefs tied over, and the odd gabled buildings around, one of which had a spire of four alligators, their tails twisted up to a great height." At eight o'clock he went on to Helsingör, a pleasant two-hour ride through " a gently undulating grain-growing country in which reaping was going on. The cottages were long and low, and thatched or red-tiled, and white-walled, the outbuildings being often of wood, — the first since Boston. Fences, hedges, or stone walls were few. There were groves and some large woods, chiefly of Beech; but also Norway Spruce, Larch, Birch, and Mountain Ash. There was no rock save boulders. The train passed two or three châteaux of Western Europe architecture set in simple parks." The general aspect of Helsingör is thus described : " The buildings are low and white-walled, — apparently of yellow brick whitewashed; the roofs are of red tile, but some of thatch; the shops are very small; the windows are white-framed, and they open outward in four pieces ; and as most of the windows are open, the effect is odd." He went down to the small breakwater port where there was nothing going on; but the Sound outside was full of large vessels.

Here I got sight of a large castle on the extreme end of the point towards the Swedish coast; and to it I went over three several moats and through a complication of military buildings, gates, and shaded moat-side walks. The great building was very striking ; its architecture, particularly that of the roof, very picturesque and characteristic. Following some signs, which I managed to comprehend, I arrived at a small jutting brick bastion, at the angle of a small water battery mounted with a row of small guns. There was a view all up and down the Sound. One guardsman was using a mounted telescope to make out the flags of passing vessels; and the red and white crossed banner of Denmark fluttered from a staff. This was the Platform before the Castle of Elsinore! There were ten barques under full sail standing north, and many smaller craft, some tacking under the Swedish coast, some close at hand. A great fleet was coming up from the far south. A very beautiful sight. The guard had already recorded ten Danish vessels, six Norwegian, one Russian, three Swedish, two German, etc., as having passed this morning. The water was as blue as possible. Thought I should not object to standing watch at Elsinore myself! This is one of the few famous straits of the world. I lingered long, alone with the silent sentinel; no sound but the ripple of water on the boulders below and the gentle slatting of the flag halliards. Presently came the heavy tramping of two large companies of infantry passing out to the drill-ground. I went out after them; and along the north-looking shore to a bathing-beach, hotel, casino, and so forth, called Marienlyst. Here I examined some very unsuccessful recent planting of shore grounds; and then went slowly back through town to the port, passing many high, paintless wooden fences with Lilacs and Virginia Creeper hanging over them, — very American. Next I took steamer to Skodsborg through a small water-side villa region. Helsingör is very quaint from the water: a red-roofed town with a big Slot (palace) and five windmills waving their arms over it. Behind Skodsborg I viewed the large royal forest. It has Beeches young and old, pretty paths and thickets, a Godthaab and a mill-pond with a mill in the midst; then a high open part, and a royal hunting-lodge with a view of the blue Sound over the woods of the shore, big ships appearing above trees. This part of the forest is wholly English-park-like, with broad but browned stretches of grass, deer, and masses of very large trees. I saw Hawthorns, but no Hollies. I reached the

shore again at Klampenborg. All manner of summer houses
are strung for miles along the shore road. I looked into
many places hereabout; supped under some trees on the
shore; and at dark took a steam tramway and a horse-car
which brought me to my hotel in Copenhagen at half past
nine.

The next day he looked through the Thorwaldsen Museum.

There is sculpture enough for five men's life-work, one
would think. Some of large, heroic creatures, very fine;
many portrait busts also; but most of the work on rather a
small scale, and all in imitation Greek, — even a Pan-
Athenaic frieze! What a curious genius out of the land of
the Vikings. His body lies buried in the court of the building, which building is Pseudo-Egyptian in design, — Pseudo-
Greek sculpture in a Pseudo-Egyptian temple, — and in the
same town with such admirable native architecture as that of
the Börsen and the Rosenborg Slot. In the afternoon I took
tram-cars out on the northern shore road to the Royal Park,
Charlottenlund; but there was no admittance to the park, so
I inspected the neighborhood, which was partly open forest,
partly small summer places, and partly all-the-year-round villages. The summer villas were generally small, low, and
pretty, a door in the middle of the long side leading into a
large middle room-hall. The front yards had little greensward, but much shrubbery, with a variety of deciduous
things; sometimes some Conifers, but these were seldom successful; and not much flower gardening. Indian Corn was
used with other foliage plants; Ivy was rare; but Virginia
Creeper and Dutchman's Pipe were very common. The
Creeper on wire fencing made high, dense hedges; but
there were also hedges of Hawthorn, Privet, and Lilac, and
of Norway Spruce clipped. Painted wooden fences were
everywhere, of several sorts, — pickets, round sticks, and
fancy sawed boarding, — all as about Boston; also American twirling water-sprinklers and hand mowing-machines
abounded. There is no green grass now unless watered.
. . . The alongshore road is Copenhagen's chief pleasure-
drive, and yet there is a steam tram in it. . . . The long road

is all tree-planted and watered, and bordered now by villas, now by open fields for sale, now by bits of fishing village, now by the large Royal Park at the left, and always the Sound close at the right.   There are also regions of beer gardens and bathing establishments.   For six kilometres the Beech forests of Jaegersborg and Dyrehave are just behind the roadside places at the left.

That evening Charles crossed the ferry to Sweden, making a breakwater port just at dark after a delicious hour and a half crossing the Sound, through much shipping and in the glow of sunset.   The train started at ten o'clock.   In the roomy compartment, which resembled the Swiss second-class carriage, Charles could lie at full length.   The night was warm, and he slept well; but whenever he woke, he looked out to see the country.

I woke at three odd.   A young moon shone over moving Spruce tops.   There was some light when next I woke.   We were passing through forests of Spruce, Pine, and small Junipers; the surface was irregular; and there were rocks and boulders everywhere; white mists were spread far over heathy flats between hills.   At my next waking the sky was clear, and the sun was rising; woods and hummocky open land were all twinkling with dewdrops; soon many ponds appeared, quiet, with rocked and wooded shores, and islets, and perhaps a clearing or two (the first time this word has been applicable in my European travel).   By and by there was more and more open country; but into Stockholm wild land still predominated.   There were rough pastures, woods of small Birches, Poplars, Alders, Mountain Ashes, Pines, and Spruces; small fields of Barley and Oats now reaping, and often big boulders in the fields, — all irregularly bounded by rockiness.   The houses were small and low, made of hewn logs; the roofs shingled, thatched, tiled, or slated; the walls colored dark red; and when, as sometimes, finishing-boards were used, these and the window-sashes were painted white. There were big red and unpainted wooden barns; and about the crop lands split-log fences.   The little farmsteads looked comfortable.   The railway cuts showed barren glacial gravel; and there were big glaciated rocks, mossy and partly bever-

dured. Put me anywhere out of sight of the houses and
fences, and I should say I was in Maine. There were whole
beds of low Blueberry, and also much mountain Cranberry;
crowded young Spruces, some sawmills, and much piled cordwood; but not one town of any size, and not a sign of
nabobry anywhere, — what a contrast to dogcart-at-every-
station England! Stockholm at 12.30. Bath and lunch.

August 26. At the breakfast station on the railroad this
morning there entered three brothers, all in broadcloth, and
all in good spirits. The eldest, a sea captain, told me that
he and his brothers had united in a visit to their old father,
somewhere about Gotenburg, the family not having come
together for many years, and that now they were going back
to work, — one in the far north of Sweden, one in Stockholm,
and one at sea. . . . He said the land thereabout was owned
chiefly by the men in occupation thereof, yet there were some
very large tenanted estates; that very few were rich, and
equally few were poor; that a man with $50,000 was very
well off, and one with $100,000 or $200,000 very rich. After
establishing myself at the Hotel Rydberg, I bought a map
and guide-book, and conned the same with great interest; but
had to take a nap, being fagged with fourteen hours' rail. In
the afternoon I strolled out to get my bearings, and to take a
general survey. My hotel is at the end of the North Bridge,
which is the centre of the town, with the King's Palace,
(stupid Renaissance) at the other end. There is a tree-planted
sort of bastion in the stream beside the bridge, whence steam-
boats may be taken to other parts of the town. The palace
and the old town are on an island and islets, whence the North
Bridge leads to the northern new town, and by drawbridges
to the southern new town, which latter is built high on a
rocky bluff. There is a lock between the drawbridges for the
passage of vessels from the salt water fjord below to the fresh
Riddarfjärde above. There are quays all about the island of
the old town; a mass of wood-boats at one, large sloops with
standing gaffs. On this quay are wooden frames, in which
cordwood is piled and so measured, people buying it out of
the frames. Fishing-boats lie in another part; and one long
quay is lined by the bows of as many as thirty small iron

steamers, all with their steam up, and their destination and hour of departure placarded. Country folk were going on board with empty produce baskets, and odds and ends of freight for country stores. These boats navigate the intricate inland waters of Lake Mälaren. I further discovered the Kungsträdgarden (" Tuileries ") — rather originally designed with rows of trees and Hawthorn hedge parterres.

The next morning Charles took a small omnibus-steamer at a neighboring quay, and sped out of town.

Pine-clad rocks were in sight from the very North Bridge, and the steamer took me towards them. A tall wood-sloop was coming down through a dark, wooded strait in the west. My boat soon entered a narrow passage ; made many stops at tiny landings ; put a " bloated capitalist " ashore on his own float, where children met him under big willows ; made a call at the gate of the big State Prison ; turned sharply around several rocky points of partly behoused islands ; passed a ship-yard or two hidden in coves, and landed me at the end of the route. Fare, three cents. There are such voyages in countless directions from the old town. Seeing a rocky, piney hill not far off, I went for it, the road passing over rough ground with wooden houses often set on rocks, a plank walk from ledge to ledge at the roadside ; a factory or two near by, — the sort of rawness and awkward newness such as I have not seen since I left Boston. I arrived at unfenced Pine woods — delicious. Going up, I came out on the ledgy top. The Blueberry bushes were already turned scarlet in places. There were beds of Mountain Cranberry, mosses, and in shallow hollows in the ledges and clefts (where low Blueberry and Lambkill grow at Mt. Desert) there were crowded plants of pink-blooming dwarf Heath. I noticed Pines and a few Spruces, Birches, tree Elders, Poplars, richly fruited Mountain Ashes, and a Wild Cherry ; also Barberries, Privets, wild Roses, Elders, Hazels, Hawthorns, Scrub Oaks, Willows, Gooseberries ; and on open ledges, Raspberries, Harebells, blue Scabious, golden St. Johnswort, and a pink Geranium. From the upper ledges there was a view of the water-girt and water-cut town, and of the dark, sombre girdle

of Pine forest all round about. "The Venice of the North!"
The North indeed it is. Descending from the ledges into a
narrow road, I passed a long, narrow pond between hills, and
so, by aid of the map, to a hamlet with a wooden church,
a variety store, a house of battened boarding, and another
omnibus-boat landing. After a sail of one minute and a half
I landed again on an island, whence I walked over two bridges
to the Prison landing, and took another boat to town. All
these islets and shores have the character of, say, West Manchester [Mass.] ; the rocks often high, with buildings scattered about in odd places. A little further from town, but in
sight, the shores are more wooded, and resemble, say, Bartlett
Island Narrows [Mt. Desert]. It being now half past five, I
crossed to the east quay of the old town, and took a boat on
the Saltsjön. Here in the stream between high, partly-built
shores, are large vessels at moorings and along the quays.
We passed two islands with public buildings and villas, which
are reached from the north town by bridges, and in five
minutes landed on Djurgarden. There were lumber-yards at
the shore; but just behind, on higher ground, a string of
pleasant restaurants, beer gardens, etc. This is Stockholm's
chief pleasure ground. I selected the very swellest, where a
big band was playing good music, and on the piazza dined
handsomely. A heavy shower now coming on, I spent the
evening in an adjacent circus-theatre, taking a boat to town
just after ten o'clock. The night effect of the city was glorious, — lights on the shipping and on many islands, on the
heights of South new town, and on the shores of lower North
town ; bright electrics on the bridges of the old town quays
between. My omnibus-boat was full of theatre-goers; but
others had taken an open horse-car, which arrives at North
new town by going round and over bridges.

The next morning, August 28th, was spent in study of the
interesting plantations of the Kungsträdgarden. Here was
much Willow of several sorts, and other hardy things. In
the Humlegarden and along a new boulevard in a new quarter, he found excellent shrub masses of a decorative sort, suitable for a town way. The arrangement of the whole island
of Djurgarden interested him very much, the interior and

much of the shore being wholly public; but parts of the shore still commercial, and other parts, further from town, set with gardened villas. At this extreme end was a sort of fishing hamlet. The ground was of a rough, wild sort, with grassy bits among ledges, and big boulders now and then, —

the West Roxbury Park [Boston] sort, with the addition of water views of great interest. Schooners were beating up the channel; a brig or two was running out; the opposite shore was high and piney, with a few summer houses on steep rocky sides or at the head of coves (as if on Harbor Hill at Northeast Harbor, or on Mr. Curtis's shore, and but twenty minutes from town by boat!). Eastward there was a charming wild scene, — blue water, breezy, and a few sails in the distance among grouped and scattered islands and rocks, — for all the world like the east end of the Fox Island Thoroughfare or Edgemoggin Reach [Maine]. Some of the summer houses were approached from their landings by a tower, thus:

 there being, apparently, an elevator inside the tower. At the extremity of the island I found a little quay which looked like a steamer-landing; so I waited awhile, watching the struggles of a big sloop with a square sail which was trying to beat up the channel; and, sure enough, a mite of a steamer shortly appeared from behind a rock point, stuck her nose against my quay, and carried me off along the shore of Djurgarden back to Stockholm.

The next day, Sunday, he took a steamer at nine o'clock for Upsala, — normally a five-hour voyage; really a voyage of six hours and a half.

The bow was piled with country freight. The upper deck was full of passengers quite of the coast of Maine description, including young sailors going home. Within fifteen minutes from the quay we were passing among scarcely inhabited, rocky, and spruce-clad islands. An endless succession of them; through straits of all widths. We passed through two floating bridges; picked up passengers out of rowboats, — sometimes when no houses were in sight; entered a cul-de-sac, to all appearance, with a low reedy shore ahead ; but, lo, a channel through the reeds into another arm of the lake. At the head of one large island was a big four-domed building, and an excursion steamer at the quay flying Norse, Danish, German, French, English, and American flags. Pine woods stretch all round the horizon. At length we came into a narrow river, which at last was little more than a ditch. The country was now flattish and cultivated. A big ugly schloss, and the odd towers of a church appeared above trees and roofs, — Upsala.

The rainy afternoon was spent in viewing the old-fashioned Botanic Garden of Linnæus with its clipped hedges of pyramidal Conifers, the large new building of the University, the ugly but famous brick Cathedral, several public gardens of a very simple sort, and a promenade along the ditch-like river. "There were many students in the streets, wholly American-esque. The voyage of the morning was very pleasant; but the scenery rather same, having not nearly the variety of that from Rockland [Maine] eastward." After dark he took train for Stockholm again.

The next day he took steamer for Helsingfors ; but before he left Stockholm he made the following entry in his journal: "Hurrah for the North and Stockholm. Here is no archi-tecture, — not nearly so much as in Copenhagen, or in Bos-ton for that matter, — except the bridges. Nothing great in the way of fine art in any sort. No Parisian fashions ; no conspicuous nabobry ; no smoke or smut ; no rags, dirt, or drunkenness ; but men and women of a most sterling appear-ance."

The voyage to Helsingfors (Aug. 30th) was very prosperous.

The afternoon among the sea islands off Stockholm was extremely interesting and amusing. We twisted and turned in this manner, often pass-ing through passages of extreme narrowness, the islands rocky, darkly wooded, and very sparsely inhabited. The steamer did not get fairly to sea 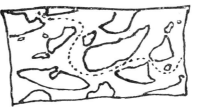 till almost sunset, having started at 3 P. M. We passed through one narrow crack between two modern forts, and

later, just before putting to sea, through a gulch between two
islets only just wide enough to admit the ship, — a red fishing village on the southern isle.   Out in the open water were
some bad ledges, an island with a big day-mark, and another
with a lighthouse.   All the inner islands were wooded and
scarcely inhabited.   'A few were occupied by summer houses
half-hidden away under trees or beside big rocks.   We met
a few vessels towing up, several wood-boats under sail, a big
one-masted craft with no bowsprit, and one pretty sloop
yacht.   There were very many pretty views up open reaches,
with complicated side-scenes of jutting points and woods,
and perhaps a sail or two in the far distance.   The night
was good, and the water smooth ; and at breakfast time the
low Finnish coast was in sight, with three Russian iron-clads
on the horizon.   Rounding an outlying rock the ship headed
shorewards about ten o'clock ; passed an islet with a lighthouse, and slowed down to pass a very narrow passage between the islands of Sweaborg, — high, white-rocked, and
covered with strong forts.   Helsingfors with two big Greek
churches came in sight on rocky ground at the head of the
bay, well sheltered by islands.   There was a blue-turnip
church on Sweaborg itself.   We landed on the quay in the
midst of a market. . . .   The people had rather a cadaverous
and villainous look, being plainly very poor.   The men wore
colored shirts not tucked in, with perhaps a waistcoat or coat
over same, — odd effect.   The women had a meek, mild
appearance, and a very light complexion.   Swarms of children were almost white-haired.   These were the Finns.   The
townspeople were chiefly Swedes.   Russians were not so
common ; but were generally more barbarous-looking than
the Finns, being short legged, and short necked, and having
snub noses.

After lunch I explored the broad and straight, cobble-
paved streets, with sidewalks rudely paved with stone, but
having no curbs.   The streets had a bleak, cold, and ugly look
altogether, and all were very empty of people.   One planted
boulevard was more cheerful, being lined with coldly ambitious Frenchy buildings.   The suburban parts were very
dishevelled.   The streets pushed out with difficulty among

raw ledges.   There were views up and down the ragged coast, which was low, with many rocks and islets and occasional fishermen's hovels.   The whole had the rather dismal character of the region about our Carver's Harbor [Penobscot Bay], for instance.   On the water-side, at the back of the town, I found a public garden, with groves of Birch, Poplar, and Alder in swales among rocks, and some groupings of hardy shrubs.   The Botanical Garden of the university was close beside and decidedly interesting ; small and soon explored, but surrounded by a superb hedge of American Crataegus coccinea.   I made note of the trees and shrubs which looked thriving, — a short but hardy list. . . . The climate must be rougher than ours of Boston, — probably much like that of our northwest, — and some Siberian things should be of use to us in those parts.   The glass-houses were on a small scale, hardly up to little Harvard's.   I walked thence to the villa region at the extremity of the town point towards Sweaborg islands.   Here were wooden houses, battened or made of matched boards, some with much jig-saw work, — all with piazzas and canvas shades.   The more modern houses were rather good, of bright wood, — these being in the latest Russian style, as an architectural picture-book in a shop window showed me.   There were painted fences of too fancy patterns, and rather desperate shrubberies ; and hardly any trees but white Birches and Mountain Ashes.   There was much bare ledge about ; and from the top of one I saw a cold sunset.   How these cold shores must shiver in winter, when they say there is a regular road across the gulf to invisible Reval on the Russian side opposite. Turning back, I followed the shore into town, getting the last reflections of the sun from the gilt turnips of the big church, and from a sort of minaret in the town behind.

September 1st.   I rattled over the cobblestones to the station for a 9 A. M. train in a droshky, driven by a villain of the deepest dye.   It was a strange vehicle, with no traces and no breeching to the harness.   The train passed slowly through what the guide-book calls the most thriving part of all Finland, — that is, the best settled part ; but it is a poor enough country, more like some of the interior of New

Brunswick than anything I have ever seen. Then we came to wilder parts, to stations where there was no house in sight, — only a few muddy carts, perhaps, with the horses hitched to the fence, — to endless forests of dwarf trees, — mostly Spruces and Pines, — to great mosslands where no trees grow, and now and then to ponds, to rocky regions, and rarely to some poor farms with small weather-stained log-houses, the people harvesting the dwarf grain. So on all day. . . . I read " Vanity Fair " most of the way, and was glad enough to arrive at Wiborg at 7.25. A droshky carried me into a very uninviting sort of town, — cobbles and rawness in the main street even, and many houses of logs. At the hotel I was shown to a room through a stable-yard, several store-rooms, and a kitchen ; but it was good when I got there. The house was only one story high, like most of the town ; and the rooms were arranged round an interior court, there being no such thing as a hall or entry.

The next day Charles wished to see the Nicolai place ; and started to do so in spite of low clouds and a high wind ; but finding himself somewhat ill, he turned back, and took the next train for St. Petersburg through more wilderness. His first remarks about that city are as follows : " Long, cobble-paved streets, wide Neva, not enough people to fill the frame of the city, — a huge, long-distance town."

Having taken a general view of the city, and presented certain letters of introduction, on the cool and bright 4th of September Charles took a horse-car over long, straight roads, across a semi-suburban region, over a bridge or two crossing branches of the Neva, and arrived within a short walk of the Botanical Gardens, which proved exceedingly interesting.

Arriving at the apparent headquarters of the garden, I marched up and asked for Dr. Regel, having a letter to him from Professor Sargent. He was within ; and proved to be engaged in sorting apples. He talked to me briefly in French, and on learning that I was a landscape architect, he gave me an introduction to a person at the Park of Pavlofsk, and then handed me over to a youth who conducted me through endless greenhouses, and finally into a big botanical library. Here I met Maximowicz, who was cordial and

talked English remarkably.   Here also appeared the younger
Dr. Regel, presumably sent by his father, who showed me
more greenhouses, and, at length, something of the outdoor
garden.   But it was now half past five; and I bade farewell
to get back to half past six dinner by another tram and a
rather long walk.

The distances here are enormous; the streets straight and
wide, with many and large open squares; the buildings are
brick, but stuccoed and tinted, and generally covered with
big signs, quite in the New York manner.   The outer parts
of the city are very poorly built, — log buildings are now and
then mixed up with brick blocks, and open land, mud-holes,
and board houses abound; so that the general effect is very
like that of some squalid American suburbs.   Beyond St.
Isaac's and one or two other churches, and a Florentine palace or two, there is no architecture worth looking at.

The next day, in accordance with an invitation from one
of the gentlemen to whom he had a letter in St. Petersburg,
Charles took a ten o'clock train from the Baltic station
(reached by a droshky over endless cobbles in half an hour),
and was met by his new friend at the first station out.   The
country was flat and dreary, and sparsely peopled; but
there were some summer villas near this first station.   They
went together two or three stations further to Peterhof, the
railway thus far being patrolled by infantry, because the
Czar was in Peterhof.

We alighted, and in a rickety vehicle drove about the imperial domain.   There were many made ponds; and in one
of these a stucco Roman villa on one island, and an Ionic
ruin on another.   On a little hill, at a distance, was a sort of
Parthenon, built on top of an ordinary dwelling; and here
were terraces, and Greek statuary, and a very distant view
of the Gulf and of the gilt dome of St. Isaac's.   There was
only one other small hill in sight.   We visited various parts
of the large park, finding a birch cottage, a thatch cottage,
and an " English palace in an English park," and so down
towards the Gulf side by way of a made " ravine; " and to
lunch in a restaurant.   We walked in the afternoon in the
inner park, roundabout the big, ugly palace, seeing more toy

buildings, — Monplaisir, Marly, and so forth, — and a great many elaborate fountains and step-cascades scattered about in the scrub woods on the plain between the palace and the Gulf shore. Finally we went up to the palace front on a terraced bluff, and through more stupid pseudo-Versailles gardens behind it, to the station for the train back to Ligowo; whence a half-hour's walk through a brick avenue brought us to a little wooden house hired for the summer by my friend's cousin.

Here Charles was pleasantly entertained by a small colony of English people. The region was characterized by Birch woods and a mill-pond, one side of which was a region of villas all built to let.

September 6. Still bright and cool. A morning of prowling in the poor public gardens of the inner town. In one were many labelled specimens. Another was made by Peter the Great in the formal manner; but its trees are now in a wretched condition. A third was in English taste; and the best. . . . In the afternoon I took notes in the garden of the Admiralty. I find the interpretation of Russian lettering difficult but amusing; though frequently impossible. It is the first land I have got into where signs on horse-cars are of no use to me. Words that are Greek are decipherable; but much of the alphabet is not Greek, and the combinations have a strange appearance.

On three different days in St. Petersburg Charles sought diligently for an entomological paper by a Russian savant, which was much desired by his friend Roland Thaxter at Cambridge. Through the kindly assistance of two or three Russian men of science, he at last procured the desired article. He gave part of every day, however, to the gardens. Thus, on the 7th of September, he explored again the Botanical Garden, but was disappointed, finding little of profit to him. On the next day he took a long journey by tram across the " islands," and then walked through the park of Yelagin Island, —

where water was all around, and also much within the island ; so that the effect was unique. Evidently it was once a flat, boggy ground, which has been made usable by digging deeper the wettest parts, and raising the roads and paths with the material so obtained. The roads of this park were unusually well planned; and the trees are the best I have seen about St. Petersburg. The general effect of the mixed water, greensward, and wood is very pleasing; and there are pretty outlooks up and down arms of the Neva and across the same to occasional villa regions. Also, there is a yacht-club house; and a fleet of craft.

He visited the Hermitage picture gallery for the greater part of a rainy day.

A glorious collection, with good representatives of every school. No end of fine Rembrandts, and Dutch and Spanish pictures in quantity; but for me the Italians are better than all else. There were two or three very poetic Salvator Rosas, only one Angelico and one Botticelli, but both good. Some supposed da Vincis were no more pleasing than others I have seen; but there was a lovely Luini, good Tintorettos, and a Veronese.

On September 7th Charles wrote to his mother: —

The droshkies are the life of the streets. They are driven very fast, even in the Nevsky Prospekt, where they are thickest, — there being nothing in the way. A big bearded officer alone in one of these, his great winter coat always on his shoulders, and he being rushed and rattled over the endless cobbles — this is typical St. Petersburg. The army is everywhere; and a shabbily uniformed and dirty lot are the common soldiers, but good fighters evidently. The common people are dirty and of strangely primeval appearance, so to speak. They might be Cave men, most of them — long-haired, and completely unkempt, and hungry-looking.

Friday, September 10. Bright, blue day. Visit to Pavlofsk. The first forty-five minutes by train were through an open, flat, wet, almost useless country; but the low hill land of Pulkova was in sight at the right. I got a strange view of the clustered domes of the many Greek churches in St. Petersburg, and of one or two huge domed structures out of town set in swamp. The terminal station is in the midst of the Imperial park.   The park village is at a short distance, all being the private property of the Czar.   The park lies on the first upland, a stream descending to the swamp level through a winding hollow.   There is no rock anywhere; yet this valley is picturesque.   The highway is carried over the valley on a granite bridge, a low dam under the bridge hold- ing back water which forms an irregular pond.   This pond is surrounded by country places; and there is much boating on the pond.   Below the bridge, on the brink of the valley, is the Palace, flying a big Imperial banner.   There is no ad- mittance to the grounds close about it; but all of the large park behind is freely opened.   I walked far through this park, and returned to the valley some distance downstream. The park is exceedingly good.   It is very flat, and the soil is rather poor; yet, as a whole, it is a very charming piece of scenery — incomparably more interesting than any wholly natural scenery to be found about St. Petersburg.   There are but few sorts of trees and shrubs; but these are admirably grouped and massed, and great intricacy results therefrom. The water is carried about in an irregular way, running now into green meadow, now into wood, and is often come upon with surprise.   This water is held, occasionally, by low dams hidden under bridges, as in the case of the main stream in the valley.   Finally there is a rather deep gulch in the woods by which the park water runs down to meet the main stream, and flows into the lowland.   The lowland and all the exterior country is shut out of view; but there are amply long vistas and varied perspectives within the park itself.   The roads and walks are few and narrow; but they are well and always reasonably curved, and all appear to have definite destina- tions.   Near the palace is a formal park with straight hedged alleys, a "rondpoint" with statues at terminations, and massed wood.   There are dark alleys with openings at the ends into the light of the valley; and stone, shaded seats on the brink of the valley bluff, with pretty views up and down the stream.

After lunch I rambled about a village of villas; but saw little that was good.   The small yards were cut up by very unreasonable paths, and were dotted all over with separate

young Birches, Mountain Ashes, Poplars, Spruces, or Pines.
There were too many mirror-balls and flagpoles, and very
little good keeping. The houses were mostly one storied and
wide spreading, with large windows and large panes, and cool-
looking rooms within. . . . The park had many people in it;
and the train to St. Petersburg was full of excursionists; but
the people from the train were soon lost in the city's wide, dusty
spaces among these cold, stupid blocks of stuccoed buildings.
The emptiness of St. Petersburg's endless streets is strange.
There are soldiers' barracks and engine houses all about, and
many domed churches, and elaborately roofed and glazed
shrines, before which people stop to bow and bow and cross
themselves many times over — even men on the tops of
horse-cars. Everybody is dirty, including the soldiery and
the long-haired priests; and a great many are almost shaggy
and wild-man like. People of the upper classes are very
scarce. In the public garden of the Admiralty young ladies
may be seen smoking cigarettes in the late afternoon. There
seems to be very little heavy carting, — or perhaps the distances dissolve it; what there is goes on in very rude carts
hauled by single horses more or less barbarously adorned,
which carts always proceed through the streets in caravans.
. . . As I write, I can see such a procession full half a mile
away, crawling along a straight, cobble street, and nothing
between here and there save three or four foot-passengers
moving like ants at the foot of the long salmon-colored walls.

It must be obvious to any one who compares Charles's description of the state of the French population with that of
the English, or of the Swedish with that of the Russian, that
his feelings toward any given community were much influenced by its physical surroundings, or in other words by
its architecture, landscape, and climate. This was no new
thing with him; as the following description of an American
city bears witness : —

July, 1883. The city and people are very interesting to
me. The system of streets is rectangular, but also radial.
Most streets and all avenues are planted with trees — chiefly
Maples — and there is considerable variety in the plans of
planting. Very few dwellings are built in blocks. There

are miles upon miles of cheap but decent houses, each within its little plot of land. A few streets contain more pretentious houses ; but these are also of an appalling architectural sameness — French-roofed, square, brick, stone-trimmed dwellings, unhomelike and " stuck-up." No Greek-portico houses, and as yet no Queen Anne. It is a commonplace and very communistic-looking city, but, I suppose, a fair type of many cities in the West.

The dull flatness of the country in which the city lies, the oppressive lack of interest and variety in the city itself, and the sameness of the people — here are three phenomena to be set down as closely connected.

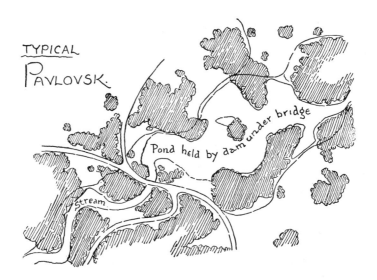

TYPICAL
PAVLOVSK.

Pond held by dam under bridge

Stream

CHAPTER X

LANDSCAPE STUDY IN EUROPE. GERMANY, HOLLAND, AND HOMEWARD

I believe it is no wrong observation, that persons of genius and those who are most capable of art are always most fond of nature : on the contrary, people of the common level of understanding are principally delighted with little niceties and fantastical operations of art, and constantly think that finest which is the least natural. — THE GUARDIAN, 1713.

CHARLES mailed no part of his journal in Russia, fearing that it might be taken for newspaper correspondence and so be detained. From St. Petersburg he rode straight to Berlin, the journey requiring about thirty-four hours. The first day's ride was

as dull as possible. Interminable small wood, wet heath or mossland, with occasional open spaces, partly in grass and partly in grain. There were small villages of primitive appearance now and then; but they were scarce. At dusk I noticed small camp-fires at short distances along the line, a sentinel at every bridge and culvert, and other soldiers along the line, their bayonets gleaming in the light of the full moon. Doubtless the Czar is to pass this way to-night. There were only four cars in the train — one sleeper, one first-class, one second-class, and a luggage van ; and this is the great express between Paris, Berlin, and St. Petersburg.

The ride through Prussia on the second day was still very dull ; but there were more towns, and some of picturesque aspect. The Vistula and Oder were stupid and slow rivers where the railroad bridges crossed. There were miles of browney, whitey stubble on light sandy soil ; and the dust was horrible — fine and suffocating. Berlin, with its brilliant lights and good pavements, seemed a great contrast to St. Petersburg. Charles's first object of interest in Berlin, apart from a general survey of the great city, was the Botanical Garden, which he found very rich and fine ; glass-house plants set out in groups by continents, collections of annuals and biennials specially arranged, and great numbers of new-planted trees and shrubs sadly crowded. The Conifers were very prettily grouped ; the Sequoia gigantea large, but covered in winter. The garden was adorned with some fine old trees. The city squares — for example, the Königs Platz, Pariser Platz, and the older-planted Leipziger Platz — were very good indeed. The streets were smooth and clean, as in Paris ; and there was a general air of great prosperity. Most of the gentlemen to whom Charles had letters of introduction being out of town, he took refuge at the opera and in an art exhibition — the Centennial of the Berlin Academy.

The finest collection of moderns I have ever seen. All countries but France are represented ; and it offers an encouraging contrast to the Salon. Here are very few sensational pictures, very few horrible, and no low realistic. There is landscape from " China to Peru," and North Cape to Sahara, and human life from huts to courts, and from babyhood to death — a sort of summary of life and of the scenes that life is lived in. It is more educative than any school, and in America it would be impossible. There is no end of patriotic cartoons for town halls ; Kaiser Wilhelm, Bismarck, and Moltke glorified in all ways. Here were Makart's lunettes from the Academy at Vienna ; some striking symbolical friezes ; and a few pleasing fanciful pictures, — such as one called " The Loves of the Waves."

At Berlin Charles enjoyed for two days the company of Dr. Carl Bolle, who was good enough to guide him personally through much of the government park and forest work about Berlin.

September 17th, with pleasant Dr. Bolle I had a long tram ride out to Dorf Tegel, Schloss Tegel, and the graves of the Humboldts. We walked along a lake-side through Pine woods on sandy soil, with government forests all about, and the Berlin Water Works on the further shore, to the charmingly wooded and very secluded island owned by Dr. Bolle. Here in a new brick villa we had a primitive déjeuner prepared by a sort of " Laura " [of Northeast Harbor] in charge. Then we had a long and interesting inspection of

Dr. Bolle's plantations. There were numbers of rare trees, among them many Americans, planted during the last twenty years. Dr. Bolle's talk about his trees was highly instructive. The climate is evidently milder than Boston's; but less favorable than Hamburg's. After coffee in a garden, we took a rowboat around the island, and down the lake, and came as the sun was setting to Tegel again; and thence I went to town, while Dr. Bolle went back to his island.

In a letter of the 24th of September Charles wrote to his mother : —

You should have seen me going about with that completely bald-headed and very kindly Dr. Bolle, — short-legged, and with a very old coat and a black slouch hat. He ambled along, and I continually had to stop my headway, because of his halting to finish a sentence. We talked about trees and shrubs chiefly; and he seemed to like it, for he spent one whole day and two half days in taking me about. . . . His knowledge of trees and plants was something marvellous. I could hardly name an American plant that he had not had growing in his island of Scharlenberg. I know he showed me what was best worth seeing near Berlin. . . . But my time was very short. I begin to feel driven. . . . I am sorry if my letters from the North of England gave an impression of illness; but I was only "feeble;" and since then, save a few very hot days, I have been very well, but I shall come home corporeally, at least, the same creature you last saw, — very thin, the right shoulder higher than the left, long-footed, and all. People stop outside my door to view my boots, and exclaim, " Wunderbar."

Charles had the usual varieties of fortune with regard to letters of introduction. Sometimes the persons to whom his letters were addressed were out of town; sometimes they received him politely, but gave him but little time and few valuable directions; sometimes they put him into the hands of incompetent guides about gardens, nurseries, or parks; sometimes they took the pains to copy out for him extracts from printed books which he had in his trunk; and sometimes he was indebted to them for instructive guidance at their own homes, and for invaluable indications as to what he

had better search for in places near his future route.   To the
end Charles remained in doubt as to whether it was profitable
to be conducted through interesting places, even by experts
or owners.   He needed no one to point out to him the merits
or defects of scenery ; and in any garden or park where the
plants were named he always thought he could learn more
alone than in company.   His experience, however, might not
be a very good guide for other people ; for he had an extraordinary facility in the use of maps, guide-books, and
time-tables, and found his own way about very easily in
any country where he could speak and understand a little of
the language.

From fine Berlin Charles rode, on the 21st of September,
by rail through a much cultivated country, occasional government forests, and the pretty region of Spreewald, — green
meadows with haycocks, much branching of the river, red-
tiled villages, dark-stained old windmills built to be turned
bodily about, many idyllic groups of peasants at work in
fenceless fields, barefooted women digging potatoes, and oxen
at work.   Towards night he took a branch road to the station
Muskau, and landed there in great darkness with woods all
about.

A small boy showed the way to the Hotel Hermannsbad,
— woods — at length a building with one light ; much pounding, but nobody comes ; small boy smiles much, and I sus-
pect him of wanting to take me to some other hotel ; more
pounding on door and windows, but all dark and still, and
rain beginning.   Finally I commanded the boy to take me to
Hotel Stadt Berlin, whose omnibus I had seen at the station.
More dark woods, then a narrow, cobbled street, an ox-cart
blocking the way, a little square with an ambitious lamp-post
in the centre by a water tank, an archway and a door indicated by the boy.   The door was open and — behold, men
beering and smoking.   A pleasant woman in black exhibited
astonishment at my not having taken the omnibus.   A little
supper upstairs was served by Marie in friendliest fashion.

The next morning was lost through a heavy rain ; but in
the afternoon, —

the clouds breaking, I went out with an umbrella, having
first planned my walk by the aid of a map in the hotel.   The
village is surrounded by a park, the Schloss standing close

beside the village, near the river Neisse. My walk was long and most interesting. This is landscape gardening on a grand scale, and the resulting scenery is extremely lovely. Altogether it is the most remarkable and lovable park I have seen on the Continent. There are no ledges; but steep irregular slopes of river bluffs, and hills beyond. The woods have an almost American variety of species, and many American plants are very common, — such as wild Cherry, Acacia, and Cornel. I found even Clethra, Hamamelis, and Diervilla. There are many large Oaks, and much Juglans (walnuts), Liriodendron, Magnolia, Negundo, Tilia, etc. One valley is all Conifers. A long stream, derived from the river, is exceedingly well treated; its varied banks are covered with Cornus, etc., and masses of American Asters, Eupatorium and Golden-rod. The water about the Schloss is also most exquisite with a tiny island or two, a water terrace, and a landing under a far-reaching Negundo. The distant parts are wholly naturalesque, with well-designed roads and paths, and charming views from capes of highland over the river valley and the almost hidden Muskau village. By sunset the clouds were all broken, and the light from the low sun was very beautiful. The hotel at dark, weary but happy. This work of Fürst Pückler is of a sort to make me very proud of my profession! For here in a land of dull, almost stupid scenery, Nature has been induced to make a region of great beauty, great variety, and wonderful charm.

Charles spent the whole of the next morning in the park and in the Muskau Baumschule; and in the afternoon went to Dresden. Ever since Stockholm, the letters Charles wrote home had shown a strong desire to turn homewards himself. On the 27th of September he wrote to his father: " To tell the truth I am now in a hurry to get home, and wish I was going on the 12th of October instead of the 19th." Dresden, September 24 —

An almost frosty night. In Muskau there had been a severe frost on the 17th of September. This morning I found the Botanical Garden here dilapidated by the same fiend. Many of the greenhouse plants set out were utterly lost, and the whole place was very dismal. I explored the

Bürgerwiese, a strip of park running into the city; and looked about the Grosse Garten. And after lunch, just as a heavy shower came down, I turned into the picture gallery. Again glorious Italians, and a vast collection of Dutch things, and Raphael's "Sistine Madonna" and "Santa Barbara." . . . My hotel is almost empty but good, my room looking on the Augustus Brücke and the river Elbe. The centre of the roadway of the bridge is given over to the use of little carts drawn by girls and dogs, to country women carrying great baskets strapped to their backs, and to frequent squads of soldiery.

The next day he took a horse-car to the river-side suburb of Waldschlösschen, where he examined many private grounds, the houses being finely placed on a hillside above the Elbe. He noted many good pergolas and some excellent terrace gardens. Parts of the hillsides were used for vines on terraces. The distant views were good; and the showery sky very lovely. In the afternoon he searched for photographs; but found "naught of professional value. I bought a few picture photographs; but, as usual, found photographs a snare and delusion." Sunday, September 26th: —

I took a steamer from the quay below Brühl Terrace for a voyage up the river. There were few passengers, for Dresden's season is evidently over. Rafts of logs and many long canal boats were drifting down the stream. Long tows were being pulled up by chain-winding craft. The ferries were queer, and the rowboats queerer with a long oar fixed at the  stern for rudder. The river is winding, the bank sometimes high and "villaed," oftener low and set with willows. The hills at the east are pretty high and wildish; and at Pillnitz where I landed (told to by Dr. Bolle), not far off. There is a water-side Schloss, a part of its grounds pseudo-Japanese, enclosing a formal Renaissance garden with old oranges in tubs, high hedges of the labyrinth variety, and a good avenue of Horse-Chestnuts. Between the Schloss and the foot of the high hills is an arboretum of moderate-sized specimens, mostly well grown and including all the

modern introductions. Here I rambled long. After lunch
in a river-side restaurant, whence was a charming view over
river meadows to the distant blue hills and the fantastic rock
forms of the foot-hills of the " Saxon Switzerland," I went
back through gardens again, and alongshore past several
country-seats to the steamer, which took me back to Dresden.

That evening Charles went on to Leipsic, where, on the next
afternoon (September 27th) he examined carefully two parks,
Rosenthal and Johanna Park.   " The first is large and very
simple ; flat, with woods, winding roads and paths, some long,
narrow vistas, and much broad, open grass.   American Oaks
were set out from wood masses, and looked well.   The
Johanna Park is small, with a circular tour-drive, a small
irregular pond, and some good intricacies of shrubbery.
Children and maids were everywhere in flocks."   Leipsic
happened to be full of commercial men.   A fair was going
on.   Every square was filled with booths, — one given over
to shows, candy booths, and merry-go-rounds; another full of
Jews.   The hotels were full of advertisements, and exhibitions of products were numerous.   " The booksellers' windows were also very interesting.   Plainly Germany excels
the world in quantity and variety of printed books."

September 28.   Heavy rain.   In a big bookstore I looked
through catalogues for landscape-gardening books, and bought
two.   After a long table d'hôte I marched out to the Botanic
Garden.   It is a small garden, and not over interesting ; but
there has been no such frost here as at Muskau and Dresden.
I came back through the town fair, where crowds were trying to enjoy themselves over beer, cake, and candy, and all
manner of shows, including a " grand American theatre."
The " Star-spangled Banner " once more !   Last seen on the
clown in a circus at Stockholm, and before that on a quack
doctor's van in the town square of Wells.

Wednesday, September 29.   I took a ten o'clock train on
the Thuringian Railway for Weimar.   There was not much
scenery save along the river Saale.   Now and then the river
had been undermining hills of gray and soft rock, verdurous cliffs being thus formed.   Two ruined castles appeared
on high rocks.   The small, brown-roofed, crowded villages
were often placed just under wooded hills at the edge of

the cultivated plain, each with some sort of quaint church steeple. In the afternoon I explored Weimar during a clearing of the sky, enjoying the old church, the good Markt Platz with its old, decorated houses, the quaint old Schloss with its trees and tower, making a charming group, and several old-German streets. The valley of the river Ilm is close beside, and all open as a park. There is one formal part, but almost all is irregular. It includes a winding stream, a few rocky slopes well shaded, some romantic paths at the foot of wooded banks, a künstliche Ruine in a wood, and Goethe's gardenhouse and Römishes Haus, the latter with old American Cedars beside it. There were Tulips, Poplars, and Birches, and American Oaks and Maples in abundance ; and some of these had already turned handsomely. Rhus Cotinus and Rhus typhina were turned too. Plainly the summer is over, and this child must put for home. I spent the evening over Jaeger's book — good.

September 30.. I looked through the small public gardens of Weimar on my way to the station to take a train which brought me to Eisenach at 11.30. The ride was charming. Castles and views of the Thuringian hills. In the afternoon I explored the town of Eisenach, which is small, crooked, and in parts very quaint. I happened on "Luther's house," and the house in which Bach first saw the light. There is a monument to the latter in the Markt Platz, and also a good war monument behind the old church. On a slope commanding views of the town, the valley, and Wartburg, I found Mr. Eichel's garden planted largely with American trees and shrubs, and arranged to show off Wartburg, which appears as a high, wooded, and in parts steep hill, crowned by an irregular group of buildings and towers. Other lesser hills fall towards a cultivated country lying northward, and become densely wooded with the Thuringian forest towards the south. The garden contains all manner of tree-framings and foregrounds for the picture of Wartburg. The town in the deep valley is mostly planted out. The garden, on the whole, is good, although some very bad use is made of brilliant flowers. I passed down into the town again, and up a valley out of it towards the forest. Here is the charming Marienthal, an

open glade with a stream.   At the sides are high, and sometimes bare-rock hills, and also much wood.   At first many
villas are set on hill-slopes at the sides ; but the bottom of
the valley is always open and park-like.   There are many
side paths to view-points and to distant parts, signs being
set up by the Waldverein, and seats being provided by the
Verschönerungs Verein.   Finally the valley grows very narrow, and a path leads up a brook bed into a strange cleft
two feet or so wide, long, crooked, and from twenty to fifty
feet deep.   Here I turned back, the sun having set.

October 1.   "Ach du lieber Gott!"   The first words from
some feminine in the next room this morning.   So say I,
when I look at the above date.   I started out early.   The
air was very misty ; but while I climbed the pretty path up
the slopes of Wartburg the mists were dissolving, and all was
clear when I reached the top.   A delightful climb — the
woods fresh and dewy, many birds, and up, high ahead, the
walls of the Burg, a square tower, with a big cross against
the˙sky.   I arrived on the platform before the drawbridge
about ten o'clock.   There were two soldiers under the arch,
but nobody else was about, and all was intensely still.   There
were grand views over plains, and over the rough wooded
mountains of Thuringia — for Wartburg is some 600 feet
above Eisenach town.   The exterior of the Burg itself is very
well worth looking at, — part is half-timber work, part rude
masonry, part handsome Romanesque.   There is also, alas ! a
modern part for the residence of some Herzog.   On the spur
of the mountain is a little inn, very pretty in mediæval style,
and most excellently planned to fit its position on the ledge.
With two other lone men I was shown all about the Burg in
too hurried fashion.   There are many buildings on different
levels of the ledge, and of different dates and styles.   The
Romanesque Schloss is very fine, well restored in this century. . . . From grouped, round-arched windows of every
room are wondrous views over hills and woods down into deep
valleys immediately below.   Luther's room — his table and so
on — is in a small side building.   In one court was a particularly picturesque grouping of the buildings, old copper gar-
goyles, and wrought-iron flowery bell-pulls — very good to see.

In the afternoon I set out in a carriage to see Wilhelmsthal, a park in the midst of the Thuringian forest, first made
in 1700, and in this century partly remade by Fürst Pückler.
It is the summer residence of Gross Herzog von Sachsen.   I
drove in state out by the Marienthal, on up the narrow Anna-
thal, to the pass called the Hohe Sonne, whence was a distant
view of Wartburg through a narrow cutting in dense woods.
Thence I went down a skilfully designed road on the further
slope to Wilhelmsthal, which is only an inn and a very plain
château with outbuildings, in a " park " entirely unfenced
and undefined as to boundaries, — the fact being that the
whole forest roundabout belongs to the same Herzog.   Its
principal features are a good made pond, pleasant green
slopes running up into the edges of the forest which comes
down from surrounding high hills, some fine groups of old
trees, some good water-side planting, and a quaint water tank
near the house in a grove of very large Norway Spruces.   It
is a very simple and very quiet sort of place, not more than
any well-off American might have — the whole situation being
extremely American.   I returned to the hotel at 5.30 in part
by another and lesser road, leading through the forest and to
a grand view-point called Marienblick.   Who the " Marie "
so often honored here may be does not appear.

That evening Charles went on to Cassel; and the next day
(October 2d) was almost all spent at Wilhelmshöhe, an extraordinarily elaborate and artificial hillside park, full of a
great variety of curious, interesting objects.   He observed the
artificial waterfalls, architectural and natural, the sham mediæval castle of great size, the huge nondescript construction at
the head of the fine cascades crowned by a big statue of
Hercules, one thousand steps leading up thereto from the
basin at the foot of the cascades, and a grand " perspective "
down these cascades over a long, narrow green, over the
château, and on some five miles across the plain at the foot of
the hill into distant, faintly seen Cassel.

Altogether this is the hugest work of " landscape gardening " — if such it must be called — I have seen, more impressive through its vastness than Versailles, Peterhof, or Windsor.   It is a work, one would say, such as only a despot could
have carried out.   A high ridge, almost a mountain, is made

use of in bold fashion. Everywhere are steep slopes of forest; and then this semi-architectural alley runs from the château straight up to the crest, with Hercules at the top, almost a thousand feet above the Schloss. Cascades start from his feet! and a huge jet fountain (not playing for me) is in the foreground before the Schloss. There is no end of other water works and "temples," and several "lakes" and caves; and flower gardens are scattered about in the big woods on each side.

Of course Charles needed to see this largest thing in Europe of its kind; but, to his thinking, it was not a good kind. The next day, which was dark and gloomy, he went on to Arnhem, on the Rhine in Holland. The ride of the morning was very pretty, up the vale of Diemel, across the water-shed at noon, and then down the vale of Ruhr. . . .

Wednesday, October 4. "The Hotel of the Sun," immediately upon the Hafen, which holds a heavy barge or two. Beyond is the muddy Rhine, or so much thereof as has not been turned off into other channels, and the green bank of the further side. Now and then a boat passes. I took a tram-car out of the dull, narrow streets — all brick walls, sidewalks, curbs, and roadway, — along an eastward road of villas. I alighted at the end of the route, and explored on foot, finding two larger places having oddish brick châteaux with moats around them, one girt about with straight rows of young Quercus palustris, which are going to be fine. The moats were made more or less irregular with little islands, and were decorated with swans. On the main road was a fine quadruple row of Beeches, the nuts pattering down. The country beyond was very open and green, but not so very wet, and not bewindmilled, as I had expected to see it. Even the side roads were paved with small bricks, and swept of leaves, which are beginning to fall. Going back the car was full of folks, — ladies returning from making calls, and children from an afternoon in the country. These were queer and old-fashioned-appearing people, their bonnets worse than English. Most of them were left at their doors, the houses looking on to the quay of the Rhine. The streets were narrow and very quiet, the clatter of wooden shoes the only noise, save (curious contrast) the occasional clanging of the bell of the steam tram-car which starts from the door of the hotel.

October 5.   I took the steam tram some four miles to the open villa-garden of Hemelsche Berg; and through this to a sort of public ground called Oorsprong — a gully with water and old Beeches.   This region is reputed the most varied and agreeable in Holland ; but it is very tame and un-remarkable, save for the number of small villas in small gardens.   These, however, are not peculiarly Dutch.   There are no canals and no particular trimness.   Most of the gardens, or rather door-plots, are in a Frenchy style, with a semicir-cular driveway never used as such, and standard Roses along the driveway with shrubs grouped in corners and strung along the fence.   The houses also are Frenchy.   Only in one sort of dorp did I find Dutch cottages.   These were brick and very plain, and the door-plot was all clean gravel with a row of clipped Lindens close to the house wall, and some plants in tubs set about.

After dinner I examined the park of Sonsbeek behind the town.   Here are some well-wooded hills, a chain of dammed ponds with old trees en masse about them, and bits of meadow coming to the water here and there.   Between the ponds were some poor rockery waterfalls.   The woods were thickened with successful undergrowth, and carpeted with Ivy, this treatment being very good.   The neighborhood of the house, too, was good.   A court between the house and the deer park was formal Dutch, with trees in tubs.   In front of the house all was English — a slope to the stream, greensward, massed large trees, and the town of Arnhem only agreeably seen in the distance.

An evening train brought him to the Hague by eight o'clock.

While I could see, we were crossing sandy, heathery coun-try, which the guide-book says extends to the Zuider-Zee. This is not my idea of Holland.

October 6.   I first looked about the town, which is really Hollandish this time with its canals and basins, the roads alongside hardly ever railed or parapeted, and the house windows often not two feet above the water level. There is one basin with green islets; formally arranged trees stand about the straight edges of the water. Soon I rode out to Scheveningen through a long tree avenue, which passes through the royal wood; so I came to the narrow fishing-town "high street." At the end thereof were two huge, brown, lubberly hulls of tub fishing-craft set up against the sky at the top of the sea beach. Eastward were several big closed hotels and some villas, and a huge ruin of a great hotel recently burnt. The sea promenade on the face of the dune is paved with brick; it winds, and travels up and down, and is drifted over with sand. The beach is wide and flat and "unterminated," the coast being here convex. The sea was roughish and hazy. Half a dozen "tub fishermen" were aground in the midst of the surf; and I watched one new arrival put ashore. The fish were unloaded by baskets borne by men wading up to their necks. The fish were then spread in little piles on the beach, and were at once surrounded by a small mob of fishwives, to whom an imperturbable official, armed with an old red, white, and blue staff, sold the fish at auction. There was hot squabbling and jabbering such as I have never heard. I could not see how any one woman knew what she was buying. Indeed, I saw much quarrelling after the departure of the auctioneer. This was a scene as mysterious as that at Monte Carlo; but that is all silent as a church. The women were most picturesquely dressed — tight white caps with pin-like or plate-like side and front fixings, very full skirts, crossed shawls, black stockings (the legs often shown to the knee), and big and white wooden shoes. The men, too, were very odd fellows with loose trousers, hands in their pockets, a sort of short-sleeved over-jacket, and a very small hat — the latter particularly funny on many very old men who were loafing about. I have seen nothing more amusing than these crowds about the fish. Everybody was so utterly unconscious, too; though most of them knew they were being sketched by a Frenchman who was on one knee a little way off. . . . After dinner at the Hague I walked into het Bosch (the wood), a formal arrangement of trees becoming forest beyond. The avenues of old

Beeches were grand.   At four o'clock I took the train with a
ticket for London.   We passed through real Dutch land,
green meadows with rows of pollarded Willows, canals above
the general level, houses strung along the canals, masts often
visible above low roofs or low trees, tanned sails and big hulls
apparently sailing over grassland, countless windmills whirl-
ing rapidly, in groups and scattered here, there, and everywhere, black and white cattle feeding or drinking from tubs,
wooden-shoed children waddling home from school — all merry
and delightful.   Delft, Schiedam, Rotterdam — a short ride.
An omnibus took me through the edge of Rotterdam to the
steamer.   I supped after the glory of a red sunset was over.
The river was full of shipping — after all there is nothing
like the picturesqueness of water and water life.   The fading
light was followed by a pale moonlight.   The river is crooked,
but well lighted by range lights.   There was much slowing
of engines, and cautious management to avoid all manner
of craft.

The next morning (October 7th) at eight he was in London.
"The weather all smut and rain — England."   At the end
of his journal he gives the reckoning of the seventy-four days
spent in Germany, Denmark, Sweden, Finland, Russia, Germany again, and Holland, and makes the cost, including his
purchases, $5.63 per day.   On the 14th of October he wrote
to his father : —

I am in the midst of complications of packing.   Books are
coming in, and clothes, and so on daily.   I managed to spend
some ten pounds ten yesterday — awful.   I have been out to
the village in Essex where Repton, a great landscaper of the
last century, lived, this excursion being at Mr. Olmsted's
request, who wrote me he would like a photograph of the
house if it could be found.[1]   In the British Museum I learned

[1] "When you are in England again, if you can find the village of
Hanstreet, and it is not much out of the way, you might like to see the
present condition of the cottage and its garden that Repton says, at the
close of his book, has been the most interesting place in the world to
him.   The house in which he died a few weeks later.   If there happens
to be a local photographer there, I shall be glad if you can order a picture of it taken for me."   (F. L. O. to C. E., February 25, 1886.)   Repton
published his excellent treatises from 1794 to 1803.   Mr. Olmsted was

Naught from 172 St.? — where you must have arrived in the week previous: — you were however very busy. of course.

R.T advises me to <u>elope</u> — as the easiest way of accomplishing the publication of an engagement. He wrote me from the midst of "congress."

I arrive very soon after this — unless Parrnia imitates Anchona., In case my luggage, but not I, should be landed in Boston — send my professional books to the Coll. Lib. this is the whole of my "last Will and Testament."

Goodbye — for some 2 weeks: a long time I'm afraid it will seem to me. Affectionately

C.E!

from a this-century edition of Repton that the house existed fifty years ago; so I set out, and find it I did. The village has not a new building anywhere in it; and Repton's cottage, as the people still call it, stands between two big Lindens at one end of the street. But nobody seemed to know who Repton might have been, — not even the family living in the said cottage.

His last professional visit in England was to Dropmore and the garden of Mr. Theodore Waterhouse, whom he had met agreeably on the Riviera.

The Pavonia sailed from Liverpool on the 19th of October. On the morning of the 29th, after being in the fog for three or four days without getting observations, she ran on to High Pine Ledge off the shore of Scituate, Mass., ten miles south of the entrance to Boston Harbor. The captain sent a boat ashore to summon assistance from Boston. The tide was rising; and in a few hours her own engines backed the ship off the Ledge. The rocks had, however, broken the skin of the ship enough to admit water to one or more of the forward compartments. The captain being firmly persuaded that he was north of Boston entrance, proceeded southward. Charles had seen and recognized the shore while the ship was fast on the rocks, and had told one of the officers of the deck what land it was. The wind was northeast, and a storm threatened. The captain, clinging to his idea that he was north of Boston, kept on going south towards Barnstable Bay. Fortunately two men in a fishing-boat at anchor shouted to him as he passed that if he went on two minutes longer he would be ashore. From them he learnt where he was, and turned his ship to the northward. But precious time had been wasted. Water was coming slowly into the forward part of the ship, and she settled more and more by the head. The wind increased, and the prospect darkened; for night was approaching. When the ship got within seven or eight miles of Boston entrance, a pilot boat suddenly hove in sight. Thereupon, the first-class passengers were notified by the ship's surgeon that, if they chose, they might go to the pilot boat. The great majority of the first-cabin passengers chose to go, and were set upon the pilot boat by the steamer's boats. Charles remained on the steamer. He had made friends with

not born till 1822; so that two far-away Americans of the second and third generation after Repton were interesting themselves in his local surroundings.

some of the younger officers of the ship, and with some of the Swedish steerage passengers, men, women, and children, whose appearance and manners he had very much liked. The distinction made between the first-cabin passengers and the others, when the pilot boat presented herself, went very much against his grain. Moreover, there were some old and delicate persons of his acquaintance among the first-class passengers who could not be transferred to the little schooner. When his father asked him afterwards why he did not seek safety on the pilot boat, his only answer was that the suggestion did not agree with him. The steamer now proceeded very slowly towards Boston light, her screw coming more and more out of the water as the vessel settled forward. At last it became impossible to steer her; and she was forced to anchor in deep water three or four miles from the entrance to the harbor. The situation was extremely forlorn; and every person on board was filled with the gravest apprehensions. Suddenly from out the fog there appeared a powerful towboat which had been sent from Boston to seek for the Pavonia, in answer to a telegram from the officer of the boat which had landed near Scituate in the morning. This towboat had sought for the Pavonia several hours unsuccessfully, and in despair of finding her was returning to port just before dark. She at once took the Pavonia in tow, and attempted to pull her towards the entrance; but with all her efforts she could effect nothing. The Pavonia could not be steered, and yawed wildly about. At last the captain of the towboat conceived the idea of towing her stern foremost; and this method succeeded. Very slowly in the rising wind and increasing darkness the great steamer was pulled into the narrow entrance. She struck again upon a rock near the lighthouse, but did not stick there. At last she was dragged into the President's Roads, where the water was comparatively shoal. The passengers had been some hours on deck with their life-preservers on. When at last she sank, the water just came over the main deck; so that the whole cargo and all the passengers' luggage, except some small pieces, were submerged.

Charles's family heard early in the morning that the Pavonia had gone ashore; and they had no more intelligence until he arrived late at night at his father's house. At the end of a year's solitary travel, he had run his greatest risk, and passed the day of greatest emotion and most serious meditation, almost within sight of home. All his precious books and photographs remained at the bottom of the Bay for three

days ; but by careful treatment after their recovery they
were saved in fair condition. A few books had to be re-
bound ; but there was no irreparable damage — even illustrations printed in colors in some of the books on landscape
art came out unhurt.

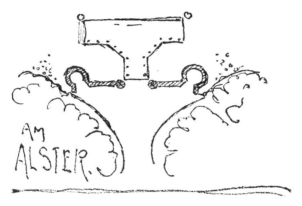

A bastion and landing on the Alster Basin, Hamburg.

CHAPTER XI

STARTING IN PRACTICE. FIRST WRITING

Consult the genius of the place in all :
That tells the waters or to rise or fall,
Or helps the ambitious hill the heavens to scale,
Or scoops in circling theatres the vale ;
Calls in the country, catches opening glades,
Joins willing woods, and varies shades from shades.
Now breaks or now directs the intending lines,
Paints as you plant, and, as you work, designs.

POPE.

THE very name of Charles's profession was still undetermined in the United States, when in December, 1886, he hired an office in Boston, and offered his services to the public. Mr. Olmsted had always used the term Landscape Architect in preference to Landscape Gardener; because the word architect conveyed clearly the professional idea, and distinguished the designer of landscape from the nurseryman or florist. English custom was rather in favor of Gardener, but French and Italian were on the side of Architect. Charles decided to call himself a Landscape Architect.

A much greater difficulty in his path was the almost universal ignorance as to the function of the profession. Few persons knew what a landscape architect could do that was desirable and worth paying for. People knew that it was profitable to employ architects; for that profession had been recognized, even in the United States, for nearly a hundred years. But what is this so-called landscape designing? they asked. Does not Nature make the broad landscape, and the gardener decorate the house-lot? A building should doubtless be designed; but can the building's surroundings and approaches also be designed? Moreover, there was no established method of charging for the services of a landscape architect. A physician received a fee for each visit, a lawyer charged a lump sum for his services in each case, a sum bearing some proportion to the values at stake ; and the architect charged a percentage on the total of the contracts made and executed under his supervision. Should a landscape architect charge for his time by the day or hour, or for a design by the number of acres it covered, or should he proportion his charges in a general way to the importance of the work planned by him ? A still graver question was this : Shall the landscape architect take contracts for executing the work he has himself planned, and so add the profits of a business to the income of a profession ? Of this last method Charles had seen successful examples, pecuniarily considered, both at home and abroad ; but it had seemed to him that in all these examples the artist had been well-nigh lost in the man of business. Charles, therefore, resolved to follow the example of his master, Mr. Olmsted ; he decided not to undertake surveying of any sort, not to take contracts for the execution of his plans, and not to take commissions on labor or materials, or on the amount of a contract, as architects habitually do, but to be in all cases strictly a professional adviser like a lawyer. After an experience of about two years, he described his function, and his way of charging for his services, in the following concise circular : —

Mr. Eliot offers his services to owners of suburban and country estates, trustees of institutions, park commissioners, hotel proprietors, and persons or corporations desiring to lay out or improve villages, suburban neighborhoods, and summer resorts. He is consulted as to the placing of buildings, the laying out of roads, the grading of surfaces, and the treatment of new and old plantations. He designs the arrangement and planting of public grounds, of private parks and gardens, of house-lots and streets.

A visit and consultation is the first step in all cases. Verbal suggestions and rough sketches, embodying a satisfactory solution of the immediate problem, can sometimes be made on the spot ; while if plans, designs, or written reports are required, the preliminary visit supplies the information upon which these can be based and their cost estimated. In case a plan drawn to scale is obviously necessary, a surveyor's plat should be obtained before the visit of the landscape architect.

The usual charge for a day visit, made from any principal railroad centre not more remote from Boston than the following named points, is fifty dollars : —

| Bar Harbor, Me. | Binghamton, N. Y. | Wilkesbarre, Pa. |
| Montreal, P. Q. | Rochester, N. Y. | Philadelphia, Pa. |

The usual charge for a day visit made from the office in Boston is twenty-five dollars. The expense of the round trip from the chosen centre is in all cases to be added. The charge for designs, and for plans based upon surveys previously obtained, depends upon the amount of detail called for, and cannot be fixed before the problem is examined.

The railroad points mentioned are about a night's ride from Boston.

The first paragraph of this circular simply describes the things he himself did as a landscape architect; but it defines perfectly the function of this new profession. A little later he used a somewhat longer circular, which gave a few more particulars, and was better suited to his enlarging practice at a distance from Boston; but he never changed his general method of work, or his method of charging for his services. (See Appendix I.)

Charles's first office was in the southwest upper corner of the southern half of the square house on the corner of Beacon and Park streets, the half which had been the home of his great-aunt, Mrs. George Ticknor. The rooms commanded a broad view over Boston Common to the west and south, and were as sunny and out-of-door-like as any lover of fine landscape could desire. The first decoration he pinned to the walls was a large coast survey chart of eastern Massachusetts and the coast of Maine. That old love warmed the new purpose. Naturally his clients were few at first, and he had some leisure, which he devoted to visiting his relatives, old and young, to making notes on the pioneer voyages to the coast of Maine and the early trading-posts along that shore (notes which he first used in a paper read to the Champlain Society at a meeting held at his office February 9, 1887), and to occasional work on a descriptive catalogue of the plants in the Arnold Arboretum.

To write for the press was a part of his plan of life; for he had accepted in some measure the opinion expressed repeatedly by Mr. Olmsted and his father that he had a gift of expression which ought to be utilized. Thus, Mr. Olmsted wrote to him on October 28, 1886, a letter to be received on landing from his homeward voyage, in which the following passage occurred: " I know that you will feel more than most men what you owe to your profession, — that is, to 'the cause.' I mean [something] beyond the zealous pursuit of it. In one way I wish to give you my opinion, derived from reading your letters chiefly, that you are able to serve it

MR. JOHN PARKINSON'S ESTATE AT BOURNE, MASSACHUSETTS, 1887

The bare field with some of the first plantings

MR. PARKINSON'S ESTATE AT BOURNE, MASSACHUSETTS, 1901

This view is taken from about the same direction as the preceding one

MR. PARKINSON'S ESTATE AT BOURNE, MASSACHUSETTS, 1901

From the doorstep.   All the near plantations are artificial

better than any living English-writing man. . . . You will
not think it flattery, if I say that you can easily give the public what the public most needs much better than any other
man now writing." In an earlier letter Mr. Olmsted had
written : " I have seen no such justly critical notes as yours
on landscape architecture matters from any traveller for a
generation past. You ought to make it a part of your scheme
to write for the public, a little at a time if you please, but
methodically, systematically. It is a part of your professional
duty to do so."

The first private place for which Charles made a design
was the estate of Mr. John Parkinson at Bourne, on Buz-
zards Bay, Massachusetts. The house was already built
close to the shore, and about it was a bare, wind-swept, sandy
field of pleasing surface, covered with an old sod and low
bushes. From the front door of the house one looked
straight into the broad stable door, four hundred feet away.
Charles planted at various distances from the house, in front
and on the right and left, masses of small Willow, Maple,
Linden, cork-barked Elm, Poplar, and Sumac, with some
Stone Pines ; but reserved about three acres between these
detached groups for an open lawn. These plantings were all
made in the spring of 1887 ; and the general plan has never
been changed, although some of the groups have been somewhat increased in size, and additional nurse trees have been
planted to secure effectual protection against the heavy winds.
The first of the three accompanying illustrations shows the
aspect of the field when the plantings were just made. The
next illustration was taken from the same point of view
fourteen years later ; while the third, taken from the doorstep of the house, shows the lawn as bounded on the north
and west by the plantations as they appeared in June, 1901.

All the plantations have been assiduously tended ; but no
wooden shelters have ever been provided against the formida-
ble winds. When the house was built, there was only one
tree on the field (it appears on the left of the first illustration), so that the owners thought of naming the place
" Single-Tree." They did name it " Plainfield." The transformation of the scene from the house within fourteen years
is remarkable.

Charles's first article for the press, dated March 12,
1887, appeared in the Boston " Transcript " on March 16th,
under the title, " The Duty of the Season." In the following March the same article, recast and shortened, appeared
in " Garden and Forest," under the title, " The Suburbs in

March." The doctrine set forth was of course applied by its author in all the suburban plantings of which he had charge; and in the spring and fall of 1887 he had the opportunity of giving a conspicuous example of the effect of his principle in suburban planting; for he was employed by the Treasurer of Harvard University to direct the expenditure of five hundred dollars on shrub plantations in the College Yard at Cambridge. It was the first time that any considerable amount of decorative planting had been attempted in those much frequented grounds, — except indeed with trees.[1] The gist of the advice is not to dot the ground with single plants, but to plant thick masses along the fences and close about the house. His teaching of this old and simple method seemed to have a quick and widespread effect in the vicinity of Boston, where the planting of front yards and other small enclosures soon afterwards showed great improvement. The article is here printed as it appeared in the "Transcript," but with four emendations, including the title, drawn from the revision in "Garden and Forest."

THE SUBURBS IN MARCH.

In the suburbs this is the ugliest season of the year. The snow lies only in dirty patches; the bare earth is alternately frozen and thawed; the grass is colorless; the houses in their forsaken enclosures stand cold and forlorn.

Large districts of Dorchester, Jamaica Plain, Brookline, Newton, Brighton, Cambridge, and Somerville are now in this dishevelled state, more accurately described as this disgracefully naked state. For it is not our pitiless climate (as we commonly persuade ourselves) that is chiefly responsible for this bleakness. If we will walk out into the country, we shall have to recognize this: there March is not ugly — far from it. If our surroundings are unhappy, we ourselves are to blame; we who have built streets and houses all through the fields and woodlands which once were beautiful the year round, and, having by so doing destroyed that original beauty, have as yet done nothing at all to win back what we may of it.

---

[1] By 1901 much of the planting against the low fence about the Yard had been destroyed; but the plantings against the buildings have for the most part survived, although never properly tended for lack of money.

In these woods and pastures grew a great variety of trees, shrubs, and herbs; some which attained their perfection only in summer, others which were especially the delight of winter. Of the former our public and private grounds, our front yards and back yards, hold far too few — our sins of omission in this respect are surprising — but of the latter almost none. Where can be seen planted about houses the richly colored red Cedar, or the Arbor Vitæ (except rarely as a hedge), or the prostrate Juniper, or Bayberry with its clustered gray fruit, or red-twigged wild Roses, or yet redder Cornels, or the golden-barked shrub-Willows? How seldom appear white Birches, or any of the American Firs and Spruces? Where about Boston do any of the trailing evergreens cover the ground at the edges of shrubberies? Where are the houses which have bushes crowded about their bays and corners (as the field-bushes crowd the stone walls) till they seem to be fairly grown to the ground? Where is any suggestion of those thickets of mingled twiggery and evergreen which once adorned the very fields our houses stand in? We have destroyed, and we have made no reparation. Speaking generally, we have reduced our bits of ground to mere planes of shaven grass, from which the house walls rise stiff and unclothed. We expend from $3000 to $20,000 and upwards upon the shell of our abode, and indefinite sums upon its interior appointments and deco-rations, but outside we leave it all bare and unbeautiful, and spend only for the gaudy brightness of geraniums in summer. No wonder March is ugly in the suburbs.

Let us look to ourselves and see if this year we cannot better things a little. The remedy is the planting of appro-priate and numerous shrubs and small trees. Between this writing and the coming May are the weeks of later April, during which trees and shrubs can be moved with safety. Now is the time to plan our plantings. Close at hand are the tree nurseries crowded with plants — our native species and those of all similar climates. Here are a hundred sorts of trees, not counting the forest kinds which grow large, species and varieties of every form, habit, and color; among them such fine-blooming sorts as the Yellow-wood and Locust, the Tulip-tree and the Magnolias, the double Apples and Cherries, the Catalpas, the Redbud, and the flowering Dogwood. Of shrubs there are some two hundred sorts, including about a dozen really hardy broad-leaf evergreens, and another dozen coniferous evergreens; beside some fifty fine-blooming deciduous varieties. Beware of the nurseryman's " choice specimens," many of which will need to be protected by boards during five months of the year; and do not make the common mistake of dotting the ground with single plants. This, at any rate, is not the way to make March dooryards less bleak. Rather may we spend the same money in planting mixed and somewhat crowded thickets, here of high and there of dwarf bushes, along the fences and close about the house. To clothe the nakedness of the ground and of the fences and buildings should be our aim. Large trees, such as our suburbs are full of, cannot do this; neither can scattered specimens of smaller sorts; neither can sparse, stalky shrubberies: we must plant our bushes thickly, so as to hide the dirt beneath them, and we must carry the grass under them as far as possible. Then, even though we use few evergreens, our yards will appear well furnished and sheltered, and no coming March will ever seem so bleak as this has been. Moreover, when summer comes, we shall find we have exchanged our geraniums for varied banks of foliage set with a succession of flowers of vastly greater interest, which too will bloom season after season without further expense to us. The twentieth part of the cost of a house will do thoroughly well such planting as I mean. Where house-lots are very small, we can form " planting clubs " of our neighbors, and so get shrubs enough for all at wholesale prices; but under any circumstances the cost of such planting is by no means so great as to excuse us from attempting it.

9 PARK STREET, BOSTON, 12 March, 1887.

In June, 1887, The Directors of the Longfellow Memorial Association called upon Charles to present a plan for laying out their grounds, lying between Brattle and Mt. Auburn streets, Cambridge, directly in front of the Longfellow house. Within ten days Charles prepared a plan, a descriptive letter, and estimates of the cost of executing the work he suggested. The essential parts of his design are described in the following passages of the letter to the President and Directors : —

Your land is sharply divided into upland and lowland by a steep terrace-like bank. The brink of this bank commands a pleasing prospect over the Charles River marshes to the hills beyond. It is plain that whatever memorial monument you may determine upon should be placed here.

By the terms of the deed of your land you are required to build certain roadways leading from Brattle Street to a point about 80 feet from the spot just mentioned as the fittest for a monument. Houses will in time occupy the lands abutting on these roads, and grocers' carts as well as pleasure carriages will use the driveways. Thus this part of your property is destined to be a wholly public place, — not a highway to be sure, but a long court with a road about it and a grassy space in the middle.

I suggest that the grass space be made 55 feet wide, the roadways 20 feet, the sidewalks 10 feet, — the latter including a strip of turf 3 feet wide between the walk and driveway. In this strip I would set a row of Elms or Sugar Maples (the latter would live the longer in your gravel soil). Their tall trunks and their boughs bending over the roadways would frame to its advantage the Southward prospect from Brattle Street. If you may not plant trees on your land, perhaps the adjoining private owners would permit them to be set close to the bounding line. The edge of the sidewalk I place three feet from your line to allow of the widening of the sidewalk by so much whenever increase of population may demand it. On the roadway I would have no curbstones; except at the termination near the monument, where carriages will stop. Along Brattle Street I have thought a dwarf wall of stone necessary, to keep people off the central grass space and to make a handsome finish. So much for the portion of your land which on my plan is called " the green," — from its approximate resemblance to the village green of old times.

From the end of the green to Mt. Auburn Street the land is yours to treat it as you may please, and certainly you can do nothing better than to adapt it to the use and enjoyment of all orderly citizens, and of women and children in particular. On my plan this part is called " the garden," and because a public garden (unless it be expensively lighted by electric light) had best be closed soon after sunset, I propose a wall with a gate in it at the end of the green, and another wall with a gate on Mt. Auburn Street. But the larger part of this portion of your land is at present very wet, — water now stands upon it at ground level. The city dumped much gravel upon it some years ago, but its level is still some 4 feet below Mt. Auburn Street, and about 10 feet below Brattle Street. To make it usable as a pleasure garden, its drainage must be improved and its surface somewhat raised.

After showing how the drainage could be effected, and how the material needed to raise the level of the lowland could be advantageously taken from the upland, the letter proceeded : —

On my plan I have assumed an exedra and placed it facing squarely South. From its terrace-like Southern edge you will overlook the lower garden, and, Mt. Auburn Street being screened by bushes, you will look off across the marshes.

At the foot of the wall there is a gravel walk connecting the two main walks of the garden, — so that promenaders may not have to pass through the exedra. This bit of walk, under the sunny wall of the exedra terrace, will be a warm spot in Spring and Autumn, and two buttress-like wing-walls, jutting from the main wall as shown on the plan, will shelter it yet more completely and make it a favorite " children's corner." People sitting on the exedra terrace will look over the heads of those standing on this path, — and will not see them unless they stand close to the parapet. All this the long section shows plainly.

The lower garden I would treat extremely simply. Let the water of the spring be led across it as a little brook, — its edges set with the wild plants of brooksides ; let the nearly level grass-land spread away from the brook to the edges of scattered masses of shrubs ; let Mt. Auburn Street be hidden by dense shrubbery, and let trees rise from behind shrubs on the East and West boundaries ; for here there can be no question of interfering with the view from Brattle Street.

A single wide path, its gravel generally hidden by the shrubs, will lead one all about the place. It must be wide enough to permit of couples of promenaders passing each other easily, and there will be baby-carriages to be avoided too. Ten feet will do.

Two sheltered corners may be given up to children's play-grounds; a third corner should some day contain a small building provided with closets, for the use of which a woman in charge might collect a small fee, as is done in Paris. The fourth corner of the garden is high, being part of the terrace bank, and the prospect hence over the river marshes is love-lier than that from the proposed exedra because the wooded hills and the tower of Mt. Auburn are included in the scene. If you owned more of the high land at this point, perhaps this would be the site for the exedra or other monument, but your boundary line on the Northeast is only 20 feet from the brink of the bank, and on the East it is still closer to the finest point of view. I propose, however, that this point be made accessible for the sake of the view alone. A broad level walk will lead to it from the exedra, and at its termina-tion in a dwarf terrace of boulders a flight of steps will de-scend to the lower ground. This walk will be nearly 100 feet long, and every foot of it will have command of the river view. It will be immediately overlooked by the house which will some day rise on the lot of land just behind, but the owner of the latter will doubtless see the advantage to him-self of shutting out the sight (if not the sound) of the walk in question, and it will not be difficult to do so.

My plan makes no provision for flower gardening, save in the bit of land between the exedra and the gate which opens on the green. The lower garden, as I at present conceive it, would be spoilt by flower beds. It is to be a very quiet and restful little scene. Near the gate back of the exedra, where the path branches in a formal manner, there is opportunity for flower gardening if you desire it, though it is not at all required there.

This scheme commended itself to the President and Direc-tors ; and considerable portions of the work were executed before winter set in. Later the Directors decided to build

at the descent from the brink of the terrace to the garden
below a more considerable structure of masonry than Charles
had imagined. This work was designed by Messrs. Walker
& Best, architects, and was executed under their direction.
Some of the details of Charles's plan for the low garden
have never been carried out from lack of money; but the
principal features of this memorial to Longfellow are as he
designed them.

Charles was well content with the variety of his work during the first year of his practice. He made designs and gave
advice for private places in Bourne, Cambridge, Brookline,
Winchester, New Bedford, Gardner, Lenox, and Waltham,
and for public grounds in Cambridge, Newburyport, and
Concord, N. H. On the 23d of November he wrote thus to
Miss Mary Yale Pitkin, the young lady from Philadelphia
and New Hartford, Conn., whom he had met with great
pleasure a few times in Europe, and again a few times during the recent summer: "Professionally speaking, my works
of this season are about done. I am neither disappointed
nor much encouraged. I enjoy the work and it suits me,—
and this is more to me than money-making. Perhaps this
is because I know I was not made to be a money-maker."

The year had been one of some family and social perturbation and excitement. His father and mother were travelling
about the Mediterranean from January till September; his
brother was also away from Cambridge the greater part of
the year, but announced his engagement to Miss Frances
Stone Hopkinson as soon as the family was reunited in September; and Charles was himself keenly on the watch for
opportunities to meet Miss Pitkin, opportunities which came
but rarely because both her winter and her summer home
were at a distance from Boston, and the families had few
common friends. At last, in January, 1888, after an acquaintance of more than two years, these two young people became
engaged to each other, just as Miss Pitkin was leaving Philadelphia to spend the winter in California for the benefit of an
invalid sister. The course of true love had already been
much impeded, and now the whole wide continent was to
divide the lovers.

In the late autumn of 1887 and the winter of 1888 Charles
made plans for laying out the Norton estate in Cambridge in
lots suitable for a good class of houses. It was a fine estate
of irregular shape and varied surface containing about thirty-
three acres, on which at that time only five houses stood. He
knew it by heart. The problem was to divide it into salable

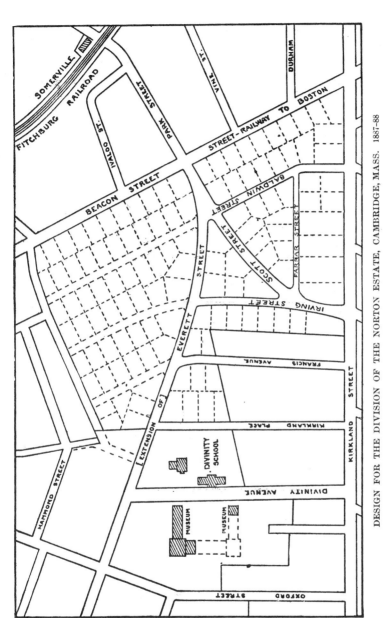

DESIGN FOR THE DIVISION OF THE NORTON ESTATE, CAMBRIDGE, MASS. 1887-88

The portion of the map divided into house-lots represents the estate

lots of moderate size and with desirable exposures, by streets
that should lead well towards the existing lines of railway and
the other quarters of Cambridge. Charles rejected the ordinary American method of dividing unoccupied land into rectangular lots parallel to the line of some selected highway, and
designed the three principal streets, Irving, Scott, and Everett, in gentle curves, as appears in the accompanying map.
These three streets give natural and pleasing means of communication with the steam railway in Somerville, the street
railways of Cambridge, and the most important highways in
the vicinity. Professor William James, the psychologist,
after having lived some years at the junction of Irving and
Scott streets, said that the daily sight of the curve of Scott
Street added much to the pleasure of living in his house, or
indeed in the neighborhood. There are now (1902) twenty-
one houses on the estate. Charles always disliked a lay-out
of streets in squares or rectangles, without diagonals or curved
intersecting avenues. He maintained that such a disposition
yielded no sightly positions for buildings which needed to be
seen from a distance, and inflicted on all the inhabitants and
their animals a perpetual waste of effort in passing over the
two sides of a right triangle instead of the hypothenuse. He
held that the rectangular layout, made without regard to the
natural surface of the ground, was responsible for the permanent disfigurement of several important cities at the West.

At the end of December, 1887, Charles wrote the following
article to illustrate and enforce an idea which was always a
favorite one with him, — the idea, namely, that park work
should conform to the climatal and soil conditions of the place
where it is situated, and should never attempt to produce an
exotic and unnatural beauty.

ANGLOMANIA IN PARK MAKING.

Within the area of the United States we have many types
of scenery and many climates, but in designing the surroundings of dwellings, in working upon the landscape, we too often
take no account of these facts. On the rocky coast of Maine
each summer sees money worse than wasted in endeavoring
to make Newport lawns on ground which naturally bears
countless lichen-covered rocks, dwarf Pines and Spruces, and
thickets of Sweet Fern, Bayberry, and wild Rose. The owners of this particular type of country spend thousands in destroying its natural beauty, with the intention of attaining to

a foreign beauty, which, in point of fact, is unattainable in anything like perfection by reason of the shallow soil and the frequent droughts.

I know too many of these unhappy " lawns." Ledges too large to be buried or blasted protrude here and there. They are bare and bleached now, though they were once half smothered in all manner of mixed shrubbery ; the grass is brown and poor wherever the underlying rock is near the surface, — all is ugliness where once was only beauty.

Moreover, if the lawn were perfect and " truly English," would it harmonize with the Pitch Pines and scrub Birches and dwarf Junipers which clothe the lands around ? No. The English park, with its great trees and velvet turf, is supremely beautiful in England, where it is simply the natural scenery perfected ; but save in those favored parts of North America where the natural conditions are approximately those of the Old Country, the beauty of it cannot be had and should not be attempted.

To be sure, the countries of the continent of Europe all have their so-called English parks, but the best of these possess little or none of the real English character and charm. The really beautiful parks of Europe are those which have a character of their own, derived from their own conditions of climate and scene. The parks of Pavlovsk, near St. Petersburg, of Muskau in Silesia, of the Villa Thuret on the Cape of Antibes in the Mediterranean, are none of them English, except as England was the mother of the natural as distinguished from the architectural in gardening. The Thuret park, if I may cite an illustration of my meaning, is a wonderland of crowded vegetation, of deep ways shaded by rich and countless evergreens, and of steep open slopes aglow with bright Anemones. Between high masses of Eucalyptus and Acacia are had glimpses of the sea, and of the purple foothills and gleaming snow-peaks of the Maritime Alps. In the thickets are Laurels, Pittosporums, Gardenias, etc., from the ends of the earth ; but Ilex, Phillyrea, and Oleander are natives of the country, and Myrtle and Pistacia are the common shrubs of the seashore, so that the foreigners are only additions to an original wealth of evergreens. The garden also has its Palms

of many species, with Cycads, Yuccas, Aloes, and the like;
but the Agaves are common hedge-plants of the country, and
strange Euphorbias grow everywhere about; moreover, the
more monstrous of these creatures are given a space apart
from the main garden, so that they may not disturb the quiet
of the scene.   M. Thuret saved the Olives and the Ilexes of
the original hillside.   He did not try to imitate the gardening
of another and different country or climate, but simply worked
to enhance the beauty natural to the region of his choice.

At the other end of Europe all this is equally true of Pavlovsk.   Here, at the edge of the wet and dismal plain on
which St. Petersburg is built, is a stretch of upland naturally
almost featureless, but which, thanks to a careful helping of
nature, is now the most interesting and beautiful bit of scenery the neighborhood of the Tsar's capital can show.   A considerable brook, in falling from the plateau to the plain, has
worn in the gravel of the country a crooked and steep-sided
valley, and this, the only natural advantage of the park-site,
with its banks darkly wooded and the stream shining out
now and then in the bottom, is the chief beauty of the completed park.   The dead level of the plateau itself is broken
up into irregular strips and spaces given to water, meadow,
shrub-land, or woodland, — a pleasing intricacy.   The grass
is only roughly cut, the edges of the waterways are unkempt,
the woods are often carelessly beset with Cornus, Caragana,
or Siberian Spiræa.   In the woods are only hardy and appropriate trees — Oaks, Alders, Poplars, Pines, and the like; —
few trees are handsome enough to stand alone, but there are
Spruces, pushing up through Scarlet Oaks, and White Birches
set off against dark Firs, and Prostrate Junipers spreading
about Birch-clumps, and no end to the variety of similar thoroughly native and appropriate beauties.   Here is no futile
striving after the loveliness of England or any other foreign
land; no attempting the beauty of a mountain country, or a
rocky country, or a warm country, or any other country than
just this country which lies about St. Petersburg; here also
is no planting of incongruous specimens and no out-of-place
flower-bedding.

The park of Muskau teaches the same lesson, and under

conditions closely resembling those of our Middle States. Indeed, American trees, shrubs, and herbaceous plants are very
numerous in this noble park ; the Tulip-tree, Magnolia, Wild
Cherry, Witch Hazel, Withe-rod, Bush Honeysuckle, Golden-
rods, and Asters are harmonized with native plants on every
hand. It would be next to impossible to find an American
park in which these things have been planted as freely.

Our country has her Russias, her Silesias, her Rivieras ;
and many types of scenery which are all her own besides.
Are we to attempt to bring all to the English smoothness?
Rather let us try to perfect each type in its own place.

This article illustrates very well Charles's method of contributing to the adoption by thinking people of an old and
sound, but to them unfamiliar idea. The fundamental idea
is well expressed in the following passage from Fürst von
Pückler-Muskau's Andeutungen über Landschafts-gärtnerei,
Stuttgart, 1834, which Charles copied into his commonplace-
book at the British Museum in 1886: "In the park I make
it a point to use only native or thoroughly acclimated trees
and shrubs, and avoid entirely all foreign decorative plants.
For nature beautified must still preserve the character of the
country and climate in which the park is situated ; so that its
beauty may seem to have grown spontaneously, and without
betraying the pains which have been spent on it." Charles
first cites a conspicuous American example of the violation
of this principle, and calls this wrong method Anglomania,
and then describes vividly and with sufficient detail three
examples on the continent of Europe of happy conformity to
the true principle. The reader feels as if he had himself
seen all three of these famous parks, and is much disposed to
accept forthwith the conclusion, — " Rather let us try to perfect each type in its own place." In the same sense he wrote
to a gentleman in Michigan for whom he had made planting-
plans and lists, and who was disappointed that the plants
ordered were not larger, showier, and less common.

I cannot possibly prescribe plantations made up of fancy
trees. My plan and my lists suggested backgrounds of massed
and harmonious foliage against which the rarer and more
striking plants of the list should stand. Quicker growing
trees were suggested for these masses. Among them were
many natives of Michigan, and the lists were sent to you

before any order was given to Temple expressly that you might strike out from them or add to them what you pleased. When you wrote me to order the whole list called for by the plan, I gladly did so, believing as I do that "natives" on the whole do vastly better if taken not from the woods but from a nursery row; and by "do better" I mean get established quicker, and grow quicker, and last longer. I also believe that for quick effect it is generally far wiser to plant smallish trees thickly rather than large trees thinly or thickly. Small trees will almost surely get a good start at once, and will continue to thrive, while trees of ten feet and upwards are almost sure to remain in an unhappy state for a long time before they can establish themselves to grow. Massed shrubs give quickest effect of all.

Nobody was better aware than Charles that the founders of the modern landscape art from Thomas Whately to Hermann von Pückler-Muskau had in the course of two generations (1770–1834) laid down all its fundamental principles. He knew that his own function could only be to make intelligent application of their principles under the new and various American conditions, and to persuade some of his countrymen of the significance and value of those principles. Accordingly in December, 1887, he prepared a short list of books and papers by the founders of the art, and introduced the list to the readers of "Garden and Forest" with some observations of his own.

Sir, — I send you a short list of books and papers which influenced, or recorded, the beginnings of the modern art of landscape gardening.

The list is headed by Bacon's familiar Essay, in which some directions for the making of a wild garden are given; but long before Bacon there were plain signs of the coming of the day of naturalistic gardening. The poetry of Dante (1321) is full of sympathetic feeling for the beauty of the natural world, — for meadows, woods, streams, and flowers, even for the sea and the distant mountains. Petrarch, Boccaccio, Ariosto, and Tasso betray no such fresh feeling for Nature as does their great predecessor. Yet in Tasso's "Jerusalem Delivered" (1595) is the following remarkable description of a garden scene: —

" Everything that could be desired in gardens was presented to their eyes in one landscape, and yet without contra-
diction or confusion — flowers, fruits, water, sunny hills,
descending woods, retreats into corners and grottoes — and
what put the last loveliness upon the scene was that the art
which did it was nowhere discernible. You might have supposed (so exquisitely were the wild and the cultivated united)
that all had somehow happened, not been contrived. It
seemed to be the art of Nature herself, as though in a fit of
playfulness she had imitated her imitator." (Leigh Hunt's
translation.)

But it was in England that the love of Nature took firmest
root. Chaucer (1400) and Spenser (1599) sang of the things
of nature with a very fresh delight; and Milton, in the fourth
book of " Paradise Lost," imagined a garden which was an
Eden indeed. England also raised up Shakespeare, whose
love embraced the

> .   .   .   .   " daffodils
> That come before the swallow dares, and take
> The winds of March with beauty;"

and Cowley, whose delight was that characteristic one for an
Englishman, " a small house and a large garden; " and, later,
Thomson, Cowper, Gray, and Wordsworth.

Meanwhile the art of landscape painting had been growing
up. Titian, its founder, composed the first landscapes upon
canvas in the days when Tasso was imagining the garden of
Armida; Claude Lorraine, Salvator Rosa, and Poussin were
contemporaries of John Milton. Well might Wordsworth
write (1805) to Sir George Beaumont: " Painters and poets
have had the credit of being reckoned the fathers of English
gardening; " and he adds, " they will also have, hereafter,
the better praise of being fathers of a better taste."

" Bacon was the prophet, Milton the herald, of modern
gardening; and Addison, Pope, and Kent the champions of
true taste," — thus the Rev. William Mason in 1772, when
the sort of landscape beauty long imagined by the poets was
beginning to be realized in the English parks. Addison
and Pope, each in his few acres, practised what he preached
— Addison at Bilton near Rugby, Pope at Twickenham near

London. Bridgeman, a professional gardener of the period, is said to have been converted by Pope's paper in "The Guardian," and thenceforth to have abandoned the clipping of trees; while Kent, a painter, gave up his art to become the first landscape gardener.

The first complete treatise on the new art was Whately's still indispensable "Observations," published in 1770, and immediately translated into French and German. A few years later appeared Girardin's excellent French work, and Hirschfeld's six volumes printed in German and French. Later came Gilpin's delightful accounts of his English tours, which had great influence in waking the popular interest in natural scenery, and Knight's and Price's vigorous attacks on the smooth monotony which characterized the landscape work of Brown and his imitators.

Shenstone, Whately, Girardin, Walpole, Knight, Price, and Laborde, all worked out their ideas on their own estates; and it is interesting to know that Rousseau, the contemporary of Gray, who yet was the first modern Continental author to write feelingly of natural scenery, was a frequent guest of Girardin's at his Ermenonville.

To close the list we have the writings of a few of the first landscape gardeners themselves, — Repton and Loudon for England, Viart and Thouin for France, Sckell and Pückler-Muskau for Germany.

I hope to see printed in "Garden and Forest" numerous extracts chosen from these books. I am sure you can do us Americans no better service than thus to advance "the better praise" of the founders of the art and their principles.

Boston, March 1, 1888.

A LIST OF BOOKS ON LANDSCAPE GARDENING.

1625. Francis Bacon, Lord Verulam. — "On Gardens," one of his "Essayes or Counsels Civill and Morall."

1712. Joseph Addison, essayist, Secretary of State. — "On the Causes of the Pleasures of the Imagination arising from the works of Nature, and their superiority over those of Art." In "The Spectator," No. 414. — "A Description of a Garden in the Natural Style." In "The Spectator," No. 477.

1713. Alexander Pope, poet and essayist. — On Verdant Sculpture. In "The Guardian," No. 173.

1731. ALEXANDER POPE. — " An Epistle to the Right Honourable Richard, Earl of Burlington." London, fol.

1764. WILLIAM SHENSTONE, poet and essayist. — " Unconnected Thoughts on Gardening." In his collected works. London, 8vo.

1768. GEORGE MASON, " a classical scholar and critic." — " An Essay on Design in Gardening." London, 8vo. — An enlarged edition, 1795. London, 8vo.

1770. THOMAS WHATELY, Secretary to the Earl of Suffolk. — " Observations on Modern Gardening, illustrated by Descriptions." London, 8vo.

1772. REV. WILLIAM MASON, poet, Canon of York. — " The English Garden : A Poem in four books." London, 4to. A new edition, 1785. London, 8vo.

1773. CH. CAI. L. HIRSCHFELD, " Counselor to his Danish Majesty, Professor of the Fine Arts at Kiel." — " Anmerkungen über Landhaüser und Gartenkunst." Leipzig, 12mo.

1774. CLAUDE HENRI WATELET, Receiver-General of Finance, Member of the Academy of Sciences. — " Essai sur les Jardins." Paris, 8vo.

1774. SIR WILLIAM CHAMBERS, F. R. S., architect. — " Dissertations on Oriental Gardening." London, 4to.

1776. J. M. MOREL, architect. — " Théorie des Jardins, ou l'Art des Jardins de la Nature." Paris.

1777. L. R. GIRARDIN, Vicomte d'Ermenonville. — " La Composition des Paysages sur le terrain, etc." Geneva, 8vo.

1777. CH. CAI. L. HIRSCHFELD. — " Theorie der Gartenkunst." Leipzig, 6 vols., 4to.

1780. HORACE WALPOLE, Earl of Orford. — " On Modern Gardening." In his " Anecdotes of Painting."

1783. DANIEL MALTHUS. — An Introduction to a Translation of Girardin's " Essay on Landscape." London, 8vo.

1783-1809. REV. WILLIAM GILPIN, M. A. — " Observations relative chiefly to Picturesque Beauty in many parts of Great Britain." London, 8 vols., 8vo.

1785. WILLIAM MARSHALL, estate agent. — " Planting and Rural Ornament." London, 8vo. — A second edition in 2 vols., 1796. London, 8vo.

1791. REV. WILLIAM GILPIN. — " Remarks on Forest Scenery, etc." London, 2 vols., 8vo.

1792. —— — ——. " Three Essays : On Picturesque Beauty, On Picturesque Travel, On Sketching Landscape, etc." London, 8vo.

1794. RICHARD PAYNE KNIGHT, " a gentleman of great classical attainments." — " The Landscape : A didactic poem." London, 4to.

1794. SIR UVEDALE PRICE, " a gentleman and scholar of great taste, who has greatly improved and beautified his own estate." — " An Essay on the Picturesque, etc." London, 8vo.

1794. HUMPHREY REPTON, landscape gardener. — " Letter to Uvedale Price, Esq., on Landscape Gardening." London, 4to.

1795. —— —— ——. " Sketches and Hints on Landscape Gardening, etc." London, fol.

1803. —— —— ——. " Observations on the Theory and Practice of Landscape Gardening, etc." London, 4to.

1803. JOHN CLAUDIUS LOUDON, landscape gardener. — " Observations on Laying out the Public Squares of London." In " The Literary Journal."

1804. JOHN CLAUDIUS LOUDON. " Observations on the Theory and Practice of Landscape Gardening, etc." Edinburgh, 8vo.

1806. —— —— ——. " A Treatise on forming, improving, and managing Country Residences." London, 2 vols., 4to.

1808. ALEXANDRE LOUIS JOSEPH, Comte de Laborde. — " Descriptions des Nouveaux Jardins de la France." Paris, folio.

1812. JOHN CLAUDIUS LOUDON. — " Hints on the Formation of Gardens and Pleasure Grounds." London, 4to.

1818. F. L. VON SCKELL, Landschafts-gärtner. — " Beitrage zur bildenden Gartenkunst." Munich, 8vo.

1819. GABRIEL THOUIN, architecte-paysagiste. — " Plans raisonnés de toutes les Espèces de Jardins." Paris, folio.

1819. —— VIART, architecte-paysagiste. — " Le Jardiniste Moderne, etc." Paris, 12mo.

1822. JOHN CLAUDIUS LOUDON. — " An Encyclopædia of Gardening, etc." London, 8vo.

1832. WILLIAM S. GILPIN. — " Practical Hints on Landscape Gardening."

1834. FÜRST HERMANN LUDWIG HEINRICH VON PÜCKLER-MUSKAU. " Andeutungen über Landschafts-gärtnerei." Stuttgart, folio.

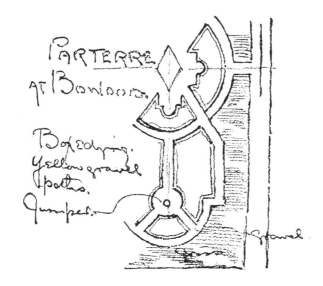

CHAPTER XII

THREE CONGENIAL UNDERTAKINGS. TWO PARKS AND A CHURCH SITE

> Laying out grounds, as it is called, may be considered as a liberal
> art, in some sort like poetry and painting : and its object, like that of
> all the liberal arts, is, or ought to be, to move the affections under the
> control of good sense ; that is, of the best and wisest. . . . No liberal
> art aims merely at the gratification of an individual or a class ; the
> painter or poet is degraded in proportion as he does so : the true ser-
> vants of the Arts pay homage to the human kind as impersonated in
> unwarped and enlightened minds. — WORDSWORTH.

IN September, 1887, Charles prepared a plan for the improvement of the ancient Common at Newburyport, the town
from which came his great-grandmother, Catherine Atkins,
the second wife of Samuel Eliot of Boston. This Common
included a deep pond of variable level, sunk between steep
banks. On one side of it, at the top of the bank, was the
Bartlet Mall, dating from 1800, and this Mall was adorned
with two rows of trees, still handsome, though much injured
by ice storms. In general, the pond and its surroundings
had been defaced and neglected ; so that the whole Common
was an eyesore. An association, called the Mall Improvement Association, was organized to reform the place ; and
this association procured plans from Charles. His general
scheme was to contract the pond somewhat by filling parts
of its lowest shores ; to leave about it a broad, clean, gravel
beach, because the changing level of the pond made any other
shore impracticable ; to provide an adequate number of flights
of steps down the steep banks, and two sloping approaches
to the beach, one a footpath, the other a driveway ; to repair
and protect the grass-banks ; and to plant out the ugly rear
of the Court House, which rose directly from the beach on
the side of the Mall. These changes involved a good deal of
gravel cutting and filling, and the regrading of considerable
areas, some with loam and some with gravel. The plans
made in September, 1887, were accepted, and were but
slightly modified in 1888 ; the work was actually begun in
1889, and was finished, in its main features, during that sea-

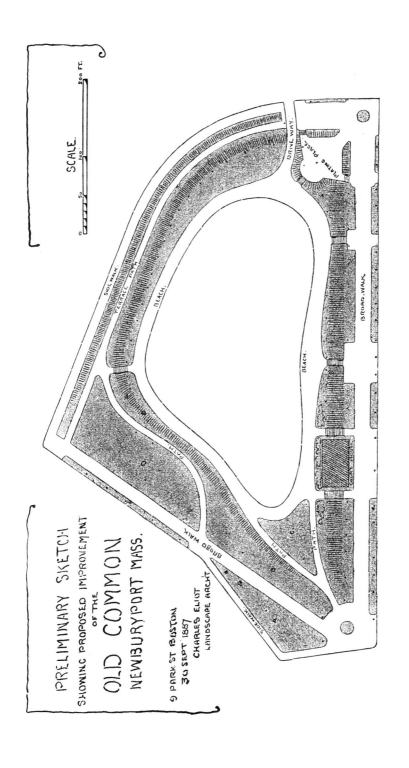

SCALE.

0 50 100 200 FT.

PRELIMINARY SKETCH
SHOWING PROPOSED IMPROVEMENT
of the
OLD COMMON
NEWBURYPORT MASS.

9 PARK ST BOSTON
30 SEPT 1887
CHARLES ELIOT
LANDSCAPE ARCHT

SIDE WALK.

TERRACE PATH.

BEACH.

DRIVE WAY.

PLAYING PLACE.

BROAD WALK.

BEACH.

PATH.

PATH.

PATH

BROAD WALK.

BROAD WALK.

SIDEWALK.

THE COMMON AT NEWBURYPORT, NOW WASHINGTON PARK

son. There was not money enough to make all the improvements which Charles had suggested ; but enough work was done to effect a conspicuous reformation. The city has added to the area of the park on the southern side, but is as yet unable to make an adequate appropriation for care and maintenance, and the water of the pond cannot be renewed as frequently as is desirable ; but the reservation as a whole, from being an eyesore and a nuisance, has become a beautiful object, and a healthful resort for the people of the city. The Association spent about $3500 on the improvements, and Charles received for his advice and plans the modest sum of $88. The first of the following illustrations represents the design, the second depicts imperfectly a portion of the agreeable result.

Until April, 1888, Charles had no assistant in his office. He made all drawings and tracings himself, and wrote and copied all letters and order lists. At that date he procured an assistant whom he taught to draw and letter somewhat in his own rapid and effective style. The spring months this year were very busy ; and thereafter he had so much strictly professional work that he had difficulty in carrying out his purpose of writing for the press. Two jobs on which he entered at this time gave him much pleasure from the beginning, — one was the grading and planting of the grounds about the village church at Weston, and the other the laying out of the new White Park at Concord, N. H. The first letters he wrote on these two congenial undertakings are here given in full; because the principles he enunciates in them are characteristic, and are of general application.

26 April, '88.

The following should be the order of work at the church. All of it is work quite necessary to the proper finishing of what has so far been accomplished with such marked success :

1st. Slopes to be so corrected that water will flow away from the building at all points.

2d. Slopes to be brought down to stakes set to mark the curved lines dividing the church land from the surrounding roadways, and to grades to be marked on said stakes.

3d. Paths to be graded to correspond with the slopes of the adjacent plots and to unite with the roadways. Paths to be surfaced with 6 inches of good binding gravel.

4th. After the rough grading, all the grass-plots to be ploughed or otherwise broken up, and 4 inches of fine loam to be spread on the surface.

5th. Pits 4 feet in diameter and 3 feet deep to be dug at points marked for trees [perhaps 3], and loam to be prepared for the filling of the same. A depth of 2 feet of loam to be provided at points marked for shrubs.

6th. After the planting of the trees and shrubs, all the grass-plots to be raked off smooth, and to be sown thickly with a mixture of blue grass and red-top.

If you can make any arrangement for the handling of the job as above outlined, I will give all verbal directions, will set all necessary stakes, will supply you with a sketch plan, will select for you the necessary plants, and will personally superintend their planting, — my fee to be $25 plus $2 an hour for time spent on the ground.

I think the plants might cost you delivered $40 to $50. They will greatly set off the building, and will practically take care of themselves.

The cost of the grading work it is hard to foresee, but it could not be much.

In the following September he wrote a short article entitled " A Village Church," and illustrated it by a plan and a sketch. The article and plan are here reproduced, and a photograph of the church and grounds approximately in their present (1902) state is given instead of the sketch.

A VILLAGE CHURCH.

Sept. 18, '88.

In the heart of the township of Weston, Massachusetts, four country roads meet at the town flagstaff. Beside the flagstaff stands the village church, and just across the way are the town hall, and a country store, and the sheds for the vehicles which bring the townsmen to Sunday and town meeting. The accompanying plan shows the irregular arrangement of the buildings, the curves of the roadways as they were determined by " the lay of the land," the bounding field walls, the grassy spaces at the roadsides, and the trees and shrubberies which break and partly hide the stiffness of the

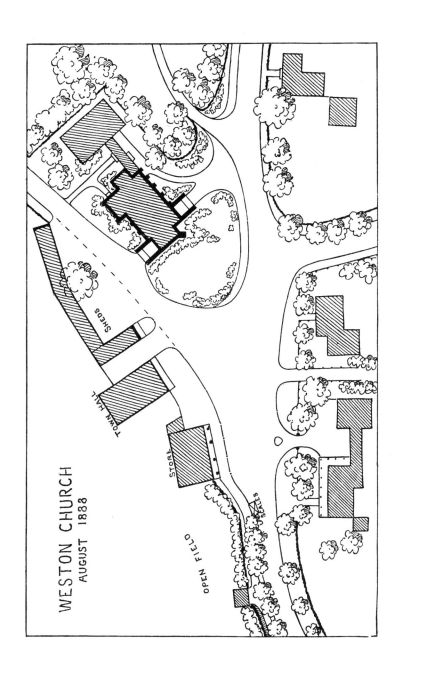

WESTON CHURCH
AUGUST 1888

TOWN HALL

SHEDS

STORE

SCALES

OPEN FIELD

THE VILLAGE CHURCH AT WESTON. MASSACHUSETTS

buildings.   The new church, built of rough field stone, is only recently completed, and the gentle slopes about it are as yet only grassed, but the next planting season will see masses of Mountain Laurel, and of wild Roses, Sumacs, and Barberries, set about the foot of the walls, — native plants beside the native boulders.   Our sketch and plan, taken together, well show what happy results can be attained when wise design works to complete what chance and nature have well begun. The latter fixed here the cross-roads and fixed them thus and so ; but design placed the church upon the rise of ground and built it of the rough stones of the New England fields.   Many a village, both within and without this New England, might draw a useful lesson from Weston.

THE WHITE PARK.

10 May, '88.

DEAR SIR, — At your suggestion I have looked over the White land, and I find I shall have to congratulate Concord on her new possession.   For the uses and purposes to which Concord must wish to dedicate this gift from Mrs. White, a more attractive piece of ground it would be hard to find. What are these uses and purposes ? or, first, what are they not ?

Your city is not so large but that all who take pleasure in driving or tramping in the open country may easily get out of the town and into the woods and fields.   You have nothing of the great city's need of large country parks.   Again, because your city is not large, she would be foolishly extravagant if she desired to make her park a costly flower garden. Public spaces in the style of the Boston Public Garden can only pay for themselves in the largest cities, and even there I should maintain that the large sums spent upon them were wrongly spent unless ample playgrounds and country parks were already provided.

A small park for Concord, then, should have in it no carriage drives, and no decorative gardening.   So far, so good ; for drives or carpet-beds upon the White land, because of the steep slopes, would be expensive to arrange and construct, and altogether inappropriate.

The park for Concord should be a place of quiet resort for people who cannot take the time, or who have not the strength, to go often to find refreshment in the open country. The tired workers of the city should be able to reach it easily. Women and children should find it near their homes, a pleasant place in which to spend the afternoon or the day in rest or play. Within it there should be all possible quiet, together with everything which may call to mind the happy peace of the country, and make us forget the town. To this end the ground should possess as much natural charm as may be, — some pleasant variety of surface, with both wood and open ground, some water if possible, and perhaps some one point from which to view the world around and outside.

In short, such a park should be a bit of New England country, as beautiful and typical as may be, set aside to be preserved as such, close to the city for the enjoyment of all orderly townspeople.

Looked at with this reasonable end and purpose in view, I am sure it would be difficult to find a piece of land so near the town which presents so many natural advantages as does the White land. Here is a steep ridge, the summit of which commands (through the trees) broad views of the Merrimac valley ; here is a flourishing natural wood containing many trees of considerable size and dignity, and many wild flowers from Mayflower to Golden-rod ; here, in fact, is that very bit of typical New England scenery which Concord should preserve for her stay-at-home citizens, — which 50 years from now she will pride herself upon exceedingly, provided that meanwhile she does not forget herself, and allow incongruous "gardening" to get a foothold in the reservation. Every city of the new West may have its carpet-bed park, — the capital of old New Hampshire should make good use of this present opportunity to provide for her children something better far.

Park-work is commonly supposed to be extravagantly expensive ; and it is so, when (as is too often the case) it consists in destroying nature's scenery to make place for formal lawns and carpet-beds. Not that it will not cost something to make White Park safely usable, and to enhance, as we may, its natural character and beauty. To make the land serve the purposes indicated above, you will have to make paths through it, else the trampling of people crossing it and wandering in it will wear away too much of the surface foliage. You will also have to drain parts of it, and change the grades here and there. To add to its beauty, you will make a pond in the hollow, which too will in winter give a chance for good skating. To bring out new beauty, you will cut some few parts of the wood, in order to lead greensward into it in places, and you will introduce and plant many trees, shrubs, and herbs not now upon the ground.

To properly set out upon the development of the park in accordance with the purposes dwelt upon above, the first thing required is a survey upon which to base a scheme of draining, path-building, etc. A wise general plan once adopted, work can proceed year by year as money may be appropriated, — the plan being thus worked out part by part. This, of course, is the only way to make sure of a harmonious result in the end.

The survey should be drawn out as a contour-line plan on a scale of 50 feet to an inch, — contours at every 2 feet difference of level. The adjacent streets and their established grades should be shown. Now, before the leaves open, is the time to make this survey.

7 March, '90.

My Dear Sir, — I have your check, — very prompt payment, indeed.[1]

I do recommend a fence. It prevents much destructive cross-cutting, and saves woods and lawns from damage. In every possible way the people should be taught that the park is a bit of New England scenery which is held, close to their homes, in trust for the enjoyment not only of themselves but of all future generations. It can be so preserved only by a public opinion which will condemn all injurious practices like peeling bark, breaking trees, and trampling grass.

The paths offer a means of enjoying the scene without injuring it, — this is the reason they are made. I would have a plain fence of stout pickets, or better of strong boards of

---

[1] Charles's entire charge for his own work on White Park was $300.

even width, and spaced evenly, and sawed off to give a flowing upper line. The "flows" of this line should be long, —

30–50 feet each. Then I would post a notice to the following effect, though not necessarily in these words : —

City of Concord.   Park Commission, White Park.

Notice.

This Woodland — the gift of Armenia S. White — is held in trust for the enjoyment of the citizens of Concord in their successive generations. All who enter here will bear in mind that they are fellow-trustees in this trust, and they will consequently avoid, and, if necessary, prevent any injury to the banks, lawns, trees, shrubs, or flowering plants.

Here might follow in smaller type whatever ordinance you may frame to cover offences of this sort.

I hope your interesting undertaking may move on prosperously.

In August, 1890, when the work on White Park was well advanced, he wrote for " Garden and Forest " the following description of the Park, taking the opportunity to urge that every American city and town preserve for its citizens' enjoyment some characteristic portion of its neighboring country : —

WHITE PARK, CONCORD, NEW HAMPSHIRE.

The capital of New Hampshire is a pleasant city of some 15,000 inhabitants. Its main street lies near the bank of the River Merrimac, and its residence streets stretch along the slopes of hills which rise irregularly west of the stream. Beyond the older streets, but surrounded by modern ways, is a small tract of land which is in part so precipitous and in part so swampy that all the new roads have avoided it. On this rough land is a fine growth of large trees of many sorts, and although it lies only half a mile from the centre of the town, many of the most interesting New England wild flowers bloom in the shelter of its woods and hollows.

This tract of about twenty-five acres has been presented to the city of Concord, and is named White Park for the donor. A commission of well-known citizens has been placed in charge of the work of fitting the ground for the use and enjoyment of the people, and they have wisely begun their labors by devising and adopting the general plan which is reproduced herewith.

The Commission intends to make the park a place of quiet resort for people who cannot take the time, or who have not the strength, to go often to find refreshment in the open country. No carriages are to be admitted ; not only because the acreage is small and the slopes steep, but also because it seems unfair to injure the park for the use of children and pedestrians while innumerable pleasant country-drives are close at hand. No elaborate gardening will be admitted, not only because it is costly, but also because it would be incongruous. Every city of the new West may have its carpet-bed "park" if it so wishes, but Concord proposes to seize her opportunity to provide for her citizens and their posterity something very much more valuable. She will set aside and preserve, for the enjoyment of all orderly townspeople, a typical, strikingly beautiful, and very easily accessible bit of New England landscape. Would that every American city and town might thus save for its citizens some characteristic portion of its neighboring country ! We should then possess public places which would exhibit something more refreshing than a monotony of clipped grass and scattered flower beds.

The plan adopted by the Commission provides for the enhancement of the natural beauty of the park by spreading water in the lowland where nature made a marsh, by making grassy glades in two or three hollow parts where nature grew Alders and Birches, by planting a thicket of Mountain Laurel here and opening a vista to the Merrimac there; and then the plan leads paths in such directions and by such routes as will best display the beauty of the place while injuring it least. In the opinion of the Concord Commission, a path, far from being a chief beauty of a park, is only an instrument by means of which it is possible for large numbers of people to pass through the midst of beautiful landscape without seriously injuring it.

The variety of limited scenery which White Park will present when it is finished is great. Just within the main gate (at the end of the plan on the left) will be a level of greensward, bounded on three sides by rising banks, from which hang thick woods of deciduous trees. At one end the banks draw close together, and here is a deeply shaded dell, from the head of which a path climbs by steps to the street. Two other paths lead up from the green, by little hollows in the skirting bank, to a plateau where Pitch Pines stand in open order, and the ground is carpeted with their needles. A steep-sided, curved, and densely wooded ridge in turn bounds this plateau, and beyond it, and nestled in the curve at its base, is a tiny pond, fed by strong springs, and overhung by tall White Pines. Its waters overflow, by way of a steep and stony channel, into a much larger pond, with shores but little raised above the water, which occupies the southern third of a long level, through which a slow brook meanders. The shore of this pond and all the flat land near the brook are scatteringly wooded with large deciduous trees. Paths reach little beaches on the shore at several points. Beyond the head of the pond a path leads to a " shelter " on a knoll in the midst of deep woods, and thence by a sharp ascent to a high point on the very edge of the park, whence a pretty view will be had of the pond at one's feet and the Merrimac Valley beyond, with the state-house dome in the middle distance and near the middle of the picture. All things considered, Concord is in a fair way to possess one of the most charming small parks in America.

Why are gifts like this of Mrs. White to Concord not more common? Can any more valuable present to posterity be imagined? Perhaps they may be commoner when it comes

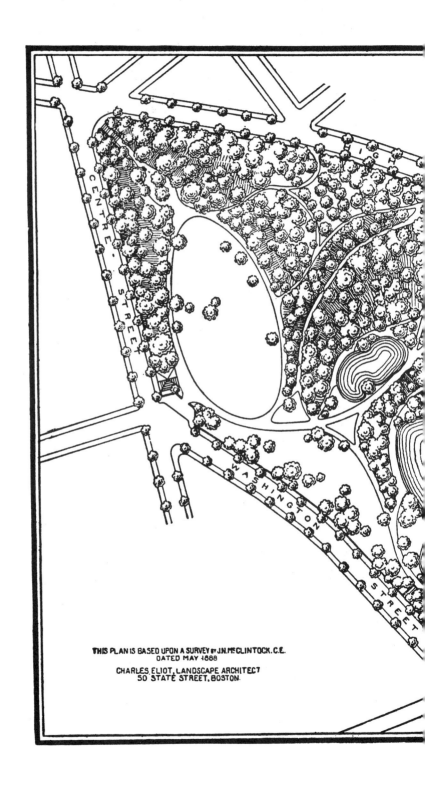

THIS PLAN IS BASED UPON A SURVEY by J.N.M^cCLINTOCK.C.E.
DATED MAY 1888

CHARLES ELIOT, LANDSCAPE ARCHITECT
50 STATE STREET, BOSTON.

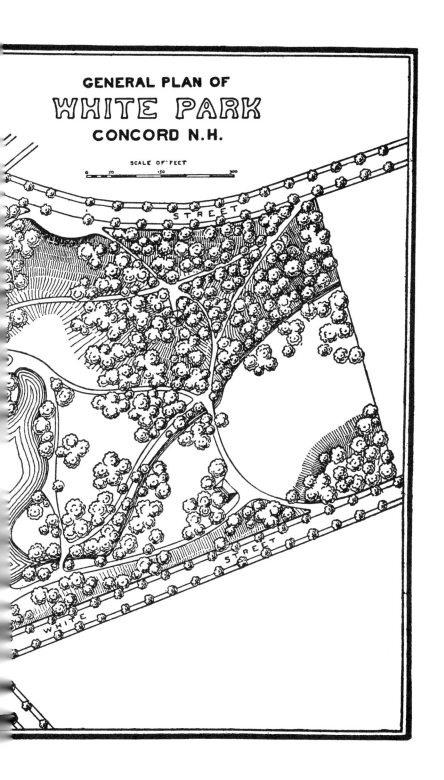

GENERAL PLAN OF
WHITE PARK
CONCORD N.H.

SCALE OF FEET

STREET

STREET

WHITE

to be known that there are now several park commissioners in this country who do not consider it their first duty to destroy the beauty which nature provides. Real landscape art is nothing if it is not broad, simple, and conservative of natural beauty. It is elaborate and gardenesque only in special circumstances. Its old name of " landscape garden-ing " must be discarded at once, if the definition in the new Century Dictionary is correct. Landscape art does not con-sist in arranging trees, shrubs, borders, lawns, ponds, bridges, fountains, paths, or any other things " so as to produce a picturesque effect." It is rather the fitting of landscape to human use and enjoyment in such manner as may be most appropriate and most beautiful in any given spot or region. When this is generally understood by the public and prac-tised by the profession, parks and country-seats will be so designed as to be not only well arranged and beautiful, but beautiful in some distinctive and characteristic way, as is White Park at Concord.

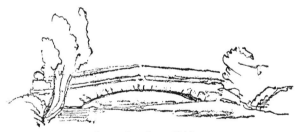

A very low Stone Bridge.

CHAPTER XIII

TWO SCENERY PROBLEMS — MARRIAGE

> With regard to improving, that alone I should call art in a good sense which was employed in collecting from the infinite varieties of accident (which is commonly called nature in opposition to what is called art) such circumstances as may happily be introduced, according to the real capabilities of the place to be improved. This is what painters have done in their art. He therefore, in my mind, will show most art in improving, who leaves (a very material point) or who creates the greatest variety of pictures, of such different compositions as painters would least like to alter. — PRICE.

To illustrate Charles's way of dealing with some of the practical problems which owners of New England country-places may bring to a landscape architect, two actual cases are here given, taken from his letter-book for 1888. The first case is an avenue entrance in stone; and the second a new approach-road to the house on a large estate, with a new lawn and an improvement of the prospect from the house.

The following letter to Mr. Thomas M. Stetson of New Bedford relates to the avenue entrance in stone. The simplicity of the design is noticeable, and its reliance on plantings rather than on masonry. After thirteen years, the result is interesting and handsome, as may be seen in the illustrations (see below, pp. 278, 279) made from photographs taken in 1901.

31 May: '88.

I send you a sketch of an entrance way — with apologies for my delay. I think the sketch explains itself pretty well. Of course the perspective is guess-work, and only intended to help show my idea.

The curved walls should swell a little and attain extra height (without becoming " piers ") at the point where the chain is fastened : then the wall should break away in height by degrees and according to the stones that come to hand, till it is finally lost in the grass. Grass should be carried round between the gravel and the wall as far as may be, and creeping evergreens and such-like plants should here clamber up the stones.

For the wall in general I think of no instructions save that I would set the stones in " stable equilibrium " (*not* on end), and would have no long-continued horizontal joints : no " courses."

The map opposite p. 236 shows on a small scale the new approach-road made to the main house on Mr. Rowland Hazard's estate, called Oakwoods, at Peace Dale, R. I., the new lawn, and the improvement wrought in the view over the South Field from the house, by abolishing the old approach-road, and cutting back the woods on the left of the prospect. For the former avenue Charles substituted the winding road marked " The Water Way " on the plan ; and this new avenue is now a great ornament of the estate — almost its chief beauty.   It was Mrs. Hazard who imagined it, and Charles who showed how to do it.   The Water Way passes with pleasing grades and curves through and under fine Oaks, and gives charming glimpses of the sluice-way and cove on the left and one full view up the mill-pond.   As it nears the house, it has on the left the new westerly lawn, and on the right the broad, open South Field.   If a landscape artist had been inventing good features for an avenue to the mansion on a great estate, he could hardly have devised more interesting features than Charles utilized in the Water Way to Oakwoods.

The trees which had to be removed in order to widen the South Field on the east were forest trees, and many of them had probably stood there since the early part of the 18th century.   When Charles first proposed to sacrifice them, in order to broaden the southerly view from the house, the family felt that such a course was out of the question.   They began, however, with much circumspection to remove a few trees at a time ; and since each cutting resulted in a manifest improvement of the prospect from the house, they gradually carried the edge of the woods back to the line which Charles had originally indicated on his drawing.

The two letters to Mrs. Hazard which follow are early letters in a series written to her between 1888 and 1894 concerning improvements she contemplated on this noble estate.

Nov. '88.

DEAR MRS. HAZARD, — I write to you because I have previously done so.

My enclosed sketch shows what you can have in the way of a new approach. Your old way from your house to the bridge near the mills is about 2300 feet long. This new way measures only about 1550 feet, and at the same time is fully 75 per cent. handsomer. It also brings you to your door without throwing dust upon the Acorns! and it might draw the driving public away from the same as well.

You will see I have imagined that all the land between the new Hall and the old house will become part of Peace Park, and that the pond-shore, up at least as far as the brook which enters the cove, will be included. I have also suggested the removal of the barn behind the old house, and the making of a terrace-like point of view or place for seats, on the brink of the high bank near said barn-site.

At two points only will there be any difficulty in building your new approach — at the head of the pond cove, where some filling should be done, and at the high bank by the cove-side near the mill-dam — which bank the road should pass on a level about half-way up from the water level and wholly below and on the water-side of two Oaks which adorn the high place.

The way up to the lawn from the crossing of the brook is intended to pass between two considerable trees which there stand behind the Rhododendrons.

Would it not be well to get the surveyor to set some stakes to represent the centre line of the road-curves I have sketched — he can find it by measuring from the various buildings and the tennis court — and then we can see what modifications, if any, it will be best to make.

27 Aug. '88.

DEAR MRS. HAZARD, — I send you a rough sketch showing what I would do for the improvement of the prospect from your new drawing-room. The changes suggested will give you a fair sweep of house-lawn and a look westward through the Oak trunks to the water — two things you have not commanded before. The rear approach-road will be removed to

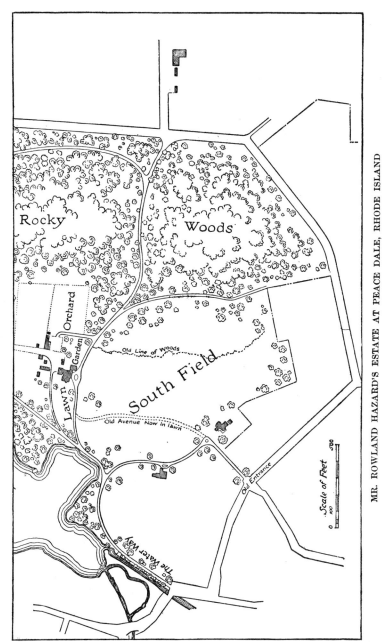

Rocky

Woods

Orchard

Garden

Old Line of Woods

Lawn

South Field

Old Avenue Now in Lawn

Old Entrance

Scale of Feet

The Water Way

MR. ROWLAND HAZARD'S ESTATE AT PEACE DALE, RHODE ISLAND

Change of avenue and enlargement of the South Field

a safe distance, and will serve to define the kept lawn. Not all of the old hedge need go. A new piece should be set for the screening of the kitchen yard.

At the edges of the new lawn put some massed bushes; at the corners of the new wing some dwarf shrubs; in the edge of the Oak wood open and thicken the Rhododendrons here and there; through the Oaks get some glimpses of the water.

When you come to start upon your delightful scheme of a village park in connection with the Memorial building, you will be sure to feel the need of a plan of the neighborhood. A plan would also help to solve many problems on your several adjoining estates. I should like to urge Mr. Hazard to procure a thorough survey. An excellent engineer in Newport — Cotton by name — does such work at very low rates.

The first step in the carrying out of the scheme shown by the sketch might be the building of the new road — supposing you should prefer to keep the hedge, for this season. It will take some courage to remove the hedge, and you will choose between seeing it done or having it done in your absence. In one case we would plant this Fall, in the other next Spring.

All through the year 1888 a new flood of happiness was pouring into Charles's heart. For the first six months there flowed between the separated lovers a stream of intimate letters, Charles writing every two or three days and sometimes oftener. In early July Miss Pitkin returned with her father to Philadelphia; and on the 13th the lovers met at Jersey City and went together to New Hartford, Conn., where her maternal grandfather, Rev. Cyrus Yale, had been the minister of a hill-top church 1100 feet above the sea for forty years (with the exception of an excursion of about two years to Ware, Mass.). He was the first scholar in the class which graduated at Williams College in 1811, and spent his life in the Congregational ministry. At his death in 1854, he left to his children his pleasant house and farm near the top of the hill; and they continued to make it the family summer resort. Here Mary Pitkin had always passed her summers with delight; and this was the first place she visited in the company of her lover. After four days in this dear home they went to Boston, and sailed thence in company with one of Charles's aunts to Mt. Desert, where they spent a month at

Northeast Harbor with Charles's family. The large Eliot connection chanced to be rather numerously represented on the island that summer, and they were all glad to be introduced at the same time to Miss Pitkin, and to Miss Hopkinson, Samuel's fiancée. In passing through Boston, Charles managed to write one business letter at his office — the only one in his letter-book between July 10th and August 27th. It was a delight to Charles to show Mary the scenes at Mt. Desert that he most loved, and to take her driving and sailing through and about the beautiful island. Great was the joy of such companionship amid such scenes.

Mr. Pitkin spent a few days at Northeast Harbor at the close of his daughter's visit; and on the 20th of August Mary, Charles, and Mr. Pitkin sailed for Boston, where on the 22d the lovers parted, Mary going with her father to New Hartford. Twice they were together again for three days at New Hartford; but on the 10th of September Mary returned to Colorado Springs, where her sister had spent the summer in the company of their brother.

By October plans for marriage were being actively discussed by mail, Charles meanwhile doing a large amount of professional work and some writing for the press. He found time enough, however, to invent and advocate a plan of going himself to Colorado near the end of November; so that the marriage might take place there about Thanksgiving Day in the presence of Mary's immediate family. This plan ultimately commended itself to all those most nearly concerned; and Mary's dear "Aunt Ruth" (Mrs. Beadle, the matron of the interesting party in Europe in 1885–86) also went to Colorado to attend the wedding. Charles met with two railroad accidents on the way to Colorado Springs, one somewhat east of Chicago which only delayed him, the second a serious collision on the road from Denver to Colorado Springs, in which several persons were injured, and the baggage car was burnt. He arrived at the Antlers, Colorado Springs, several hours late, and with no clothing except the travelling suit he was wearing. Two days later, on Wednesday, November 28th, the simple, happy wedding took place at the house of Miss Price, where the Pitkins had been living.

Before Christmas the pair arrived at President Eliot's house in Cambridge, where they were to pass the winter. There were rejoicings and congratulations at Christmas and at the bride's receptions on Tuesdays in January, and festivities through the winter, in which the Eliot, Peabody, and Hopkinson families took active part.

Charles's first work on returning to his office was the preparation of some articles on "Old American Country-seats,"
for "Garden and Forest." The seats he selected for description were all eighty years old or more, — that is, they were
old enough to have developed completely their original designs,
and to have been enriched by the care of successive owners in
at least three generations. They showed what was lastingly
desirable in landscape design. They had dignity, harmony,
and loveliness. To commemorate them was for Charles a labor
of love. He visited each place he described, and procured
at least one picture of each, and drew a sketch plan of each.
With the first three of the six he had been long familiar.
These articles constitute the next chapter.

CHAPTER XIV

SIX OLD AMERICAN COUNTRY-SEATS

Any hard fist can draw iron railings ; a hedge is a task for the greatest. Those therefore who want their gardens or grounds or any place
beautiful must get that greatest of geniuses, Nature, to help them. —
RICHARD JEFFRIES.

I. — THE GORE PLACE.

JOHN WINTHROP, first Governor of Massachusetts, had
his country-place. It lay upon Mystic River, and was called
Ten Hills. The pleasures of life there were certainly peculiar, wolves and prowling Indians being frequent visitors ; but
now that several of the ten hills even have been destroyed,
Winthrop's frontier "paradise" can only be imagined, not
described. Unfortunately the same must now be said of
almost all the mansions and gardens of the later aristocratic
time which preceded the Revolution. The rising tide of population has swallowed up the handsome establishments of
Tories and patriots alike. The Craigie house, which the
Longfellow family preserves in Cambridge, is now almost the
sole surviving representative of the terraced and high-walled
stateliness of the colonial days.

Boston and her surrounding sister cities grow continually.
Farm after farm and garden after garden are invaded by
streets, sewers, and water-pipes, owners being fairly compelled
to sell lands which are taxed more and more heavily. Before
destruction overtakes the few old seats now remaining, it will
be well to make some sort of record of their character and
beauty.

About eight miles from the State House, one of the roads
of the Charles River valley, after passing through a somewhat
squalid manufacturing district, suddenly becomes a rural lane,
which winds its shady way first past the low-roofed farmhouse

and then past the lawn and mansion of what is plainly an old
estate. . . . [The accompanying plan shows the general arrangement of the estate.]   The grass sweeps up to the walls

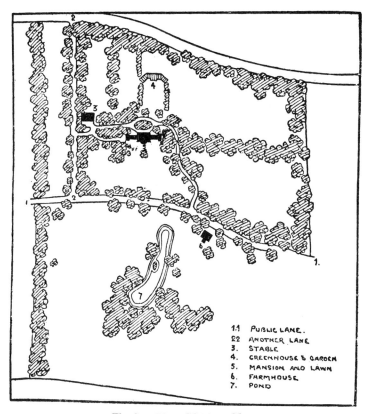

1.1 PUBLIC LANE.
2.2 ANOTHER LANE
3.   STABLE
4.   GREENHOUSE & GARDEN
5.   MANSION AND LAWN
6.   FARMHOUSE
7.   POND

The Gore Place, Waltham, Mass.

of this long south front.   No line of any sort breaks the flowing breadth of the lawn, for the approach-road, which leaves
the lane near the farmhouse, goes around through the trees
to the door in the north front of the house.   The simple but
well-proportioned building is set off against a background of
foliage, and the ends of the low wings are shadowed by tall
Pines and Chestnuts, whose brothers, forming noble masses
at the sides of the lawn, support and frame the house, and,

joined with it, compose one satisfying picture. On the further side of the lane is an open field and a winding pond, whose distant further end is lost in the shadow of a Pine wood, from out the edge of which a White Birch leans over the water. Larches, too, and small Beeches grow in the edge of this distant wood, and enliven the darkness of the Pines in spring and autumn, while here and there above the tops of the trees appear the crests of low hills, a mile or two away beyond the river.

This strikingly peaceful and lovely scene, so religiously preserved by its present owner that he can say that only the gales have harmed it since he came into possession more than thirty years ago, impresses the most casual passer-by, and teaches owners of country-seats a lesson of first importance. Here is not one rare tree, not a single vegetable or architectural wonder, not one flower bed or ribbon-border; only common trees, grass, and water, smooth ground, and a plain building. The scene is interesting, impressive, and lovable, and it is this solely by reason of the simplicity, breadth, and harmony of its composition. This is real landscape architecture of the purest type, in comparison with which all modern arrangements of specimen fancy trees must always appear ineffective as well as inappropriate.

The lands about this mansion, once a part of the so-called Beaver Brook Plowlands, were first owned by the beloved first minister of the colonial church of Watertown, the Reverend George Phillips. After his death, in 1644, certain of the Garfield family became the owners, and when Mr. Christopher Gore bought "the forty-acre lot," about 1791, he entered upon lands which had been the home of excellent people during a full century and a half. Mr. Gore was sent to England in 1796 as one of the Commissioners under Jay's treaty, and one wing of his house having been burned in his absence, he caused the present mansion to be built of brick and made ready for his return in 1804. It is said that he brought with him an English landscape gardener; and certainly the old place bears every mark of the distinctive style of Humphrey Repton, whose book on landscape gardening was published just before Gore's visit to Europe. The brick

house, which is painted white, contains many finely proportioned rooms. Two doorways open upon a long platform on
the north front. Between these doors stretches a hall dining-
room, with a marble floor, and fireplaces at each end. The
large bay in the south front contains an oval drawing-room;
on one side of this room is a breakfast-room, and on the
other a parlor; the east wing contains a billiard-room, the
west the kitchen and offices.

The carriage-turn, and the whole north side of the house, is
crowded with large trees; many Hemlocks, whose soft boughs
sweep the ground at the edge of the drive, several Umbrella
Magnolias among the Hemlocks, some large Lindens, and
many very tall White Pines. Just beyond is the flower
garden, carefully sheltered and quaintly laid out in geometric
fashion, with great banks of shrubs at the sides, plenty of
smooth grass, and large beds crowded with perennials in rich,
old-fashioned array. A small enclosure for deer adjoins the
garden; two smooth and open hay-fields are close at hand,
and around all this forty-acre home-lot stands a dense belt of
forest trees, shutting out the commonplace world and affording a pleasantly shady walk of something like a mile in
length.

Mr. Gore lived to be Governor of Massachusetts and
United States Senator. One of the later owners of the place,
Mr. Theodore Lyman, 2d, made the pond beyond the lane,
and built the present approach-road, and both he and the
present owner planted many trees; but every proprietor since
Mr. Gore's time has respected the character which was impressed upon the scene in the beginning; nothing to-day
appears incongruous or out of place. If Governor Gore himself could walk about this country-seat to-morrow, he would
certainly be very proud to own it his.

II. — THE LYMAN PLACE

Beyond Cambridge and Somerville and about seven miles
from Boston Common rises a range of irregular and sometimes rocky hills, from whose summits one may see on the
west Wachusett and on the east the ocean. At the southern
end of this highland two considerable brooks issue from the

hills and, joining their waters, flow as one stream across about a mile of smoother country to Charles River. Between the western brook and the foot of the rocks is a warm slope having a southern exposure, and here one of the colonists of 1634, by name John Livermore, built his house and cleared the land for a farm. Other Livermores — Nathaniel, Samuel, and Elijah — in turn succeeded to the property; of whom Samuel came to most honor, for he married four times, and served his fellow-townsmen as their clerk, assessor, and captain of the company, and also as deacon of the church, which was built about 1722 " within twenty rods of Nathaniel Livermore's dwelling." Elijah Livermore became the founder of a town in Maine, and sold the farm to Mr. Jonas Dix, of the class of 1769 at Harvard College, who brought his bride to the Livermore homestead, and there lived the quiet life of a schoolmaster and selectman until his death in 1796.

It would be very interesting to know what was the condition of the neighborhood at this time, whether the sheltering hills behind the farm were wooded or no, and what sort of a channel the Chester brook ran in. The place must have been decidedly attractive in some way; for its next owner, Theodore Lyman, a merchant of Boston, bought it with the express intention of making it a country-seat, and forthwith built a mansion which was valued by the assessors of 1798 at the vast sum of eight thousand dollars! This substantial house he placed not upon the highland, where the popular taste of to-day would set it, but upon the flat, and from one to two hundred feet south of the southernmost rocks. Here it was sufficiently high above the brook, which flowed in front about 400 feet away, while behind it space was obtained for a well-sheltered garden. The east wing was built close to a little knoll, which, with the trees upon it, helped to make the house appear firmly and comfortably planted. The west wing also had its supporting trees. The smooth lawn before the house was made with material dug from beside the brook, which was then induced, by the help of a low dam, to flow more quietly and broadly. Plainly, English books on landscape gardening, like Repton's or Whately's, had made part of this American gentleman's reading — the low setting of the house and the

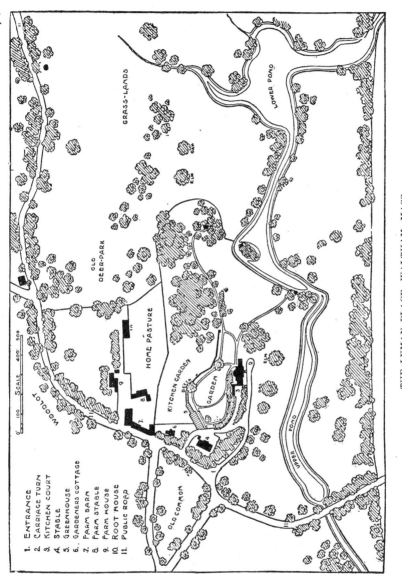

1. ENTRANCE
2. CARRIAGE TURN
3. KITCHEN COURT
4. STABLE
5. GREENHOUSE
6. GARDENER'S COTTAGE
7. FARM BARN
8. FARM STABLE
9. FARM HOUSE
10. ROOT HOUSE
11. PUBLIC ROAD

SCALE
0 100   400 500

WOODLOT

OLD DEER-PARK

GRASS-LANDS

LOWER POND

HOME PASTURE

KITCHEN GARDEN

GARDEN

OLD COMMON

UPPER POND

THE LYMAN PLACE, WALTHAM, MASS.

serpentine curves given to the grass-edged shore of the stream furnish proof of this.

At first, the approach-road entered the estate from the southeast and crossed the brook on a stone bridge of three arches, but in after years a new entrance was made in the position shown upon our plan, and then the older way was discontinued, with the unfortunate effect of bringing the driveway to a sudden ending at the house door. No other important alterations of the original plan have been attempted since the designer himself made this change. To be sure, the second Lyman, probably in haste to provide shade in certain parts, planted many Norway spruces; but these his son is now gradually removing, to the great improvement of the general scene; for the deciduous forest trees which these quick-growing conifers hid from sight have now attained a handsome stature and, leaning forward or hanging from the steep banks behind the house and from the knolls, compose a harmonious and striking scene, which the cone-shaped Spruces at present confuse and obscure. A few of the native trees are uncommonly large; for instance, an Oak and an Elm, which stand alone in the grass-field east of the pleasure-ground; and, just before the house, a fine swamp White Oak, which was, doubtless, an aboriginal inhabitant of the Chester Brook valley — its horizontal branches spread 100 feet. Here, too, is an English Elm of uncommonly widespread habit, its many large limbs supported by a trunk which measures fifteen and a quarter feet in circumference.

But the most remarkable tree upon the place — a Purple Beech — stands in the garden behind the house. This little level space is curiously irregular in ground plan. It is bounded on the north by a short range of glass-houses and by a high brick wall, which curves in and out in order to avoid the ledges of the rocky bank behind it. Peach and Pear trees are trained all over this old wall; an ancient hedge of Box accompanies it at some six feet from its base; and many forest trees rise behind it. The garden ground is all one slightly varied level of soft grass, with a few trees of chosen kinds near the edges, a few Rhododendrons and Roses, and one giant White Pine, which seems to guard the open end of the ground where the simple but picturesque enclosure expands into the still simpler ground outside. With its soft shadows at all hours of the day, its sheltered quietness, its intricacy in one part, and its open outlook in another part, this is a charming spot — a scene which would be lovely enough without its crowning glory, the gnarled Purple Beech. The tree stands close against the brick wall; the circumference of its embossed and tortuous trunk is more than thirteen feet, and its branches extend eighty-five feet. This is a large Beech to be only ninety years old, and it is just possible that Mr. Dix may have planted it and the great Elm before the house; but their stature is more probably to be accounted for by the good soil and shelter.

Many photographs . . . could only partially illustrate the beauty and variety of the larger scenery of the estate — the gentle slopes of grass-land, in the hollow of which lie the ponds, the wide stretches of moist meadow, the occasional passages along the stream where Elms or Willows overhang the water, the sheltering banks and knolls clothed with dense woods, or dotted, as in the remote parts, with dark Junipers and outcrops of rock. The landscape is more appropriate to human use and occupation, and at the same time it is more beautiful than was the original natural scene. The meadows are more meadow-like than they were, the stream reflects more sky, the trees are nobler trees, and they stand in ordered masses, not in uniformly dense array. Here is abundant proof that if Nature is helped and not forced, she will make for us scenery which shall grow to more and more loveliness and character as the years pass.

III. — BELMONT.

Beyond Fresh Pond the road from Cambridge to Waverley ascends a gentle swell of smoothly surfaced upland, enters the shade of arching Elms, and presently discloses on the right hand a green lawn of an extent that is uncommon near Boston. The ground has a beautiful form. It descends a little from the road towards a gentle hollow which holds a small pond, and thence it rises very gradually, and with many slight irregularities of slope, to the wood which bounds the scene at the north, and to the house at the northwest. The western border of the open ground is a wood of native, deciduous trees through which the approach-road goes to the house. In many places the grass runs in between the surrounding groves, so that only the lower or eastern boundary of the lawn appears in the least degree formal or stiff. A few Hickories rise in the midst of the grass. They are quite in keeping with their surroundings; but this cannot be said for the group of White Pines, or the two or three Norway Spruces, or the big Larch encircled by old plants of Arbor Vitæ, which are the companions of the Hickories in the open ground. Our picture [not reproduced here], taken from a point near the little pond, shows only the upper half of the lawn and but one of these incongruous trees — the Spruce, which appears behind the two Hickories — in the foreground. This Norway is a fine specimen of its kind. Its lower limbs rest upon the ground on all sides; but it should never have been planted where it is, for its formal shape is quite the opposite of every shape around it, and attracts the eye to itself at once in a way which confuses the effect of the otherwise harmonious scene. The stiffly circular clump of Arbor Vitæ is a still more obtrusive object. Thoughtless planting like this has too often injured scenes which Nature made harmoniously beautiful, and to which Nature would gladly add more and more of character and beauty, if she were helped and not thwarted by man.

The house is approached through a wood of trees which arch overhead to form a handsome informal avenue within which the road curves very gently; but as the whole length of the road is visible at once from the beginning, it had better have been made straight. [See the accompanying plan.] At the house is a wide gravel space for the accommodation of waiting carriages, and here a junction is made with the service road, a branch of which leads to the stable. Thus all the necessary gravel spaces are provided at this one side of the house, so that the grass is free to sweep up to the very walls on two sides, — a point of great merit in the plan. The fourth, or north, side is occupied by a walled kitchen-court and a laundry-yard.

The house is a substantial structure of brick, with verandas built of stone. Its rooms command a view of the ten acres of lawn, on one hand, and of the interior of the wood, on the other. Over the tops of the trees at the foot of the lawn appears the shining dome of the State House on Beacon Hill, five miles away.

A broad walk leads eastward from the house to a point of view which commands Fresh Pond and the intervening diversified farms. Six Purple Beeches stand in a row beside this path near the house, but formality ceases at the view point, and the walk wanders off along the brink of the gentle eastward slope, passes among scattered Oaks of large size and around the small deer-park, and after sending off a branch to a knoll which offers a yet wider prospect over the Mystic River basin, returns to the rear of the garden. . . .

The garden behind the house is an enclosed square measuring 300 feet each way, level, and formally divided by broad gravel paths, as shown upon the plan. A conservatory and two long graperies, behind which are the potting-sheds and plant-houses, front upon the northern side of the garden, while two Peach-houses and many well-trained Pear-trees occupy the east and west walls. Most of the ground is smoothly grassed. There are two large masses of Rhododendrons mixed with similar shrubs; at the sides are long beds of perennials and foliage plants, and grouped upon the grass near the angles of the walks are specimens of such trees as the Flowering Magnolias, the Red-flowering Horse-chestnut, the Weeping Elm, the Swamp Cypress, the Ginkgo, the Oriental Spruce, the Swiss Stone Pine, and the Mountain Pine (P. Mughus). Such specimen plants are certainly quite in place in a formal garden intended to be decorative. They should, however, be chosen for their appropriateness, and grouped with due regard to the effect upon their neighbors. The Mountain Pine just mentioned is too roughly picturesque to appear in a garden like this where elegance is the end and aim.

A glance at the sketch plan will explain the arrangement of the numerous minor buildings and enclosures of the estate. The completeness of the equipment is remarkable. There

are buildings for all purposes, — they are not all named
upon the plan, — and elaborate facilities for the growing of
everything from the Parsnip and the Potato to the Chrysan-

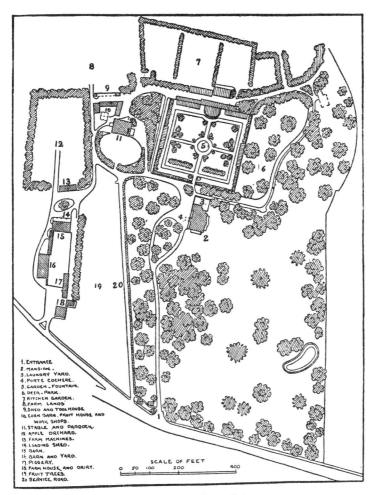

1. ENTRANCE
2. MANSION.
3. LAUNDRY YARD.
4. PORTE COCHERE.
5. GARDEN - FOUNTAIN.
6. DEER - PARK.
7. KITCHEN GARDEN.
8. FARM LANDS.
9. SHED AND TOOL HOUSE.
10. CORN BARN, FRUIT HOUSE AND
        WORK SHOPS.
11. STABLE AND PADDOCK.
12. APPLE ORCHARD.
13. FARM MACHINES.
14. LOADING SHED.
15. BARN.
16. BARN AND YARD.
17. PIGGERY.
18. FARM HOUSE AND DAIRY.
19. FRUIT TREES.
20. SERVICE ROAD.

SCALE OF FEET
0   50 100   200   400

The Cushing-Payson Place, Belmont.

themum and the Orchid. The land company which is now
in possession has cut off the farm-lands, but offers the remaining parts for sale quite intact. These lands made a

country-seat, at least as long ago as 1800, when the owner was a brother of Commodore Preble.   One of the daughters of the house married Mr. Nathaniel Amory, who became the next owner, and he sold the property to Mr. R. D. Shepherd, and he to Mr. J. P. Cushing.   Mr. Cushing spent many thousand dollars every year upon the place, and made it, thirty-six years ago, the most famous seat near Boston.   Mr. S. R. Payson, the last owner, maintained and increased this fame.

To-day the place possesses something of that priceless and poetic charm which so distinguishes the Gore Place and the Lyman Place ; it is felt in the deer-park and among the Oaks, but the spell is not so potent, nor does it pervade the whole scene as at Waltham.   To define the difference is a little difficult; but it is in part accounted for by the fact that a certain unavoidable suspicion of display attaches to this place, — to the great expanse of clipped lawn, the specimen trees, and the elaborate gardening.   On the other hand, the gardening and the specimen planting are generally good in their way, and are placed where they belong, namely, in the garden, and not in the landscape.

IV. — CLERMONT.

New England, in the old days before the growing up of the great cities, possessed many towns in and near which dwelt people of polite cultivation and polished manners, whose sober, but often stately, mansions yet remain.   In the seaboard towns especially, such as Portsmouth, Newburyport, Salem, and New Bedford, still stand numerous examples of this appropriate urban architecture, substantial buildings, with light and some space about them, and sometimes a courtyard enclosed by a high wall in the English fashion.   At Kittery, at New Bedford, and elsewhere, not to speak of numerous, but fast disappearing examples near Boston, mansions of this character may be seen standing well out of town in small parks of their own.   It should be noted that the three old Bostonian country-seats, already described in this series of brief papers, have been chosen only because of their exhibiting more than usual breadth of landscape setting, combined with more than usual excellence of general design.

CLERMONT ON THE HUDSON

Passing now from New England to New York, from the region of small hills, ponds, and streams which surrounds Boston to the prospect-commanding banks of the broad Hudson, and again selecting ancient country-seats which excel in point of design, we come first to Montgomery Place, at Barrytown.

Barrytown is itself but a very small village, about ninety miles from New York and some fifty from Albany; and it is so surprising to find here an old seat of the first class, that this number of the series must be devoted to an explanation of the fact. The Hudson River naturally attracted settlers very early. The Dutch established a trading-post at Beaverwyck even before they built their fort at New Amsterdam; and here the Van Rensselaers held sway as Patroons during many years. After the English gained possession of the country, and renamed the chief towns New York and Albany, the river lands began to be parcelled out among such persons as applied for them, and could persuade the Indians to sell their hunting-grounds for coats, hatchets, or beads. Among others who thus obtained a manor was Robert Livingston, an immigrant of 1674, son of a clergyman who had been exiled to Holland for non-conformity. This gentleman married the widow of the Patroon, and was made lord of the manor of Livingston in 1685 by Governor Dongan, who granted him title to 150,000 acres with a frontage of about fifteen miles on the east bank of the Hudson River, opposite the Catskill Mountains. After a younger son of his, also named Robert, had distinguished himself by frustrating an Indian plot, he set off the southern part of his ample domain beside the river, and gave it to his son, making him lord of a new manor, which he named Clermont. The Clermont manor-house stands intact, its stout walls having survived the fire set by British raiders just before Burgoyne surrendered in 1777. It is approached by a long winding road, which descends from the highway through a wild woodland. Near the house the road divides to send a branch to the kitchen door and to the stable, and the main road ends with a turn placed most unfortunately between the house and the river. The house is a square building with two low wings, and stands on a natural terrace within half a stone's throw of the low bluff which here makes the river's shore. Immediately behind it rises a bank of forest trees, the edge of Clermont Woods, and before it, in an irregular row on the brink of the bluff, stand a dozen huge Locust-trees, doubtless the ancestors of many others which adorn the numerous Livingston properties along the river. One of these great trunks measures six yards in circumference, and shows to this day the marks of British cannon-shot.

From Clermont a short walk southward through an avenue of tall and crowded Locusts brings one to another and more elaborate mansion, situated upon the same natural terrace, backed by the same hanging woods, and commanding the same view of the river and the Catskills. This house was built by that Robert R. Livingston who was a delegate from New York to the Congress of 1776, and became first Chancellor of the State of New York, Minister to France, and a patron of Robert Fulton. The ground plan of his house is in the form of an H. The central hall in the middle of the H is entered from either court; and a long corridor, which looks on the river court, and is hung with family portraits, connects the drawing-room in one wing with the dining-room in the other. The external walls of the house are white, the great rooms in the low wings have long windows opening nearly to the ground, and the two stories of the central block are crowned by an elaborate white railing. Across the ends of the wings and the river court extends a platform at which carriages may draw up, and a carriage-road makes a rectangle about the whole house. A more interesting example of domestic architecture in the formal style does not exist in America. Its owners, men who were conspicuous in the political struggles of the young Republic, were often compelled to make the long journey to New York; but they always returned to Clermont as to their one permanent home, — so strong, even after manorial privileges had been abandoned, was their old English liking for country life and country leisure. Montgomery Place, at Barrytown, was an offshoot of these manorial seats at Clermont. Like several other old seats upon the Hudson, it would never have been created had not Governor Dongan and his superiors in England attempted to plant in America the English manorial system.

V. — MONTGOMERY PLACE.

Janet Livingston, a sister of the Chancellor, grew up in the quiet elegance of Clermont; but after her gallant young husband, General Richard Montgomery, was killed at Quebec, she chose and purchased for her home a tract of three hundred acres lying upon the river by the mouth of the Saw Kill and a few miles south of the southern limits of Clermont Manor. Here, with the help of plans which are said to have been sent from Ireland by Montgomery's sister, a Lady Ranelagh, a mansion remarkable for its simple but elegant architecture was built, and the new seat was named Montgomery Place. Here in later years the eminent jurist, Edward Livingston, was wont to retire from the cares of office to enjoy the beauties of nature.

Approaching the estate to-day from Rhinebeck or from Red Hook, the way lies through a charming farming country crossed by numerous lane-like roads and by the one highway which leads to Albany. The approach to the house at Montgomery Place parts from the high-road at right angles, and leads, at first straight, toward the river through an avenue of noble trees of various sorts, planted in rows, yet not in pairs. Indeed, not only is there no precise symmetry, but a giant Locust may here be seen standing opposite a Linden, or a great Horse-chestnut opposite a Beech; and in one place, where the road is carried on a stone-walled causeway over a little gully, great Willows throw large limbs across the vista. Beyond the rows of trees, on either hand, lie gently undulating pasture-lands, bounded in the distance by woods. Drawing nearer now to the house, the straight avenue ends just as the roadway passes through a tall hedge into the inner park. Here is a wood of fine forest trees standing well apart, and, as the road curves gently to the right between the trees, a little valley on the left begins to fall away quite rapidly toward the Hudson. The sides of this valley are richly wooded, and serve to frame a first glimpse of the river, where it is disclosed by the broadening of the valley's mouth. As the road swings still farther to the right, the house comes into view ahead, and branch roads lead on the left to the stable, and to the kitchen-yard, which is concealed by shrubbery and by being sunk to the basement level at the southern end of the house. The main road ends with an ample turn, placed symmetrically before the semicircular portico which marks the entrance. The guest of the house who turns here looks eastward back toward the Albany road across a gently rising lawn bounded, on one hand, by the same dense wood which he before saw limiting the northern pasture, and, on the other, by the more open groves through which he has just travelled. Formerly this sheltered open ground contained the flower garden and an elaborate conservatory; and, on the gentle rise behind this structure, a considerable arboretum once existed, where now only a few scattered specimens are to be seen; but from the point of view of design and general effect the substitution of the existing simple but well-framed lawn in place of the old garden and conservatory is by no means to be regretted. The entrance front of the house, as it now appears, when viewed from the site of the conservatory, may be seen in the accompanying picture; but though the building and the great Locusts near the porch are well shown, the picture gives no hint of the blue distance of hills and mountains which in reality appears through the tree-trunks just north of the house.

If, tempted by this glimpse of distance, the visitor turns the corner of the building and steps into the round-arched pavilion which is attached to the north side of the house, the whole broad panorama of the river and the Catskills is spread before him to the westward; but even here the wide prospect is broken into scenes and framed by the solid piers and arches of the pavilion itself, and by the trunks and branches of great trees, chiefly Locusts, standing on the brink of the irregular grassy slope which falls steeply to a narrow wood on the bluff at the river's edge. "To attempt to describe the scenery which bewitches the eye as it wanders over the wide expanse to the west from this pavilion would be an idle effort," wrote Mr. Downing in 1847. "As a foreground, imagine a large

MONTGOMERY PLACE ON THE HUDSON

lawn waving in undulations of soft verdure, varied with fine groups, and margined with rich belts of foliage. Its base is washed by the river, which is here a broad sheet of water, lying like a long lake beneath the eye. . . . On the opposite shores, more than a mile distant, is seen a rich mingling of woods and corn-fields. But the crowning glory of the landscape is the background of mountains. The Kaatskills, as seen from this part of the Hudson, are, it seems to us, more beautiful than any mountain scenery in the Middle States. It is not merely that their outline is bold, and that the summit of Roundtop, rising three thousand feet above the surrounding country, gives an air of more grandeur than is usually seen even in the Highlands; but it is the color which renders the Kaatskills so captivating a feature in the landscape here. . . . Morning and noon the shade only varies from softer to deeper blue. But the hour of sunset is the magical time for the fantasies of the color-genii of these mountains. Seen at this period, from the terrace of the pavilion of Montgomery Place, the eye is filled with wonder at the various dyes that bathe the receding hills — the most distant of which are twenty or thirty miles away. . . . It is a spectacle of rare beauty, and he who loves tones of color, soft and dreamy as one of the mystical airs of a German maestro, should see the sunset fade into twilight from the seats on this part of the Hudson."

Mr. Downing did well to sing the praises of the Catskill sunsets, and he might have added that this favored pavilion of Montgomery Place spreads its prospects before the visitor to the delightful accompaniment of the music of waterfalls sounding from the depths of the wood near by. Upon entering this wood it is seen to occupy a large and long valley curiously broken into lesser ravines and hollows. Numerous paths lead through the dark shadows of the wood to all the finest parts, and to the falls, — one of them forty feet high — by which the Saw Kill plunges down to join the Hudson. Here are wildness and extreme picturesqueness in sharp contrast with the stately breadth and quietness of the lawns and groves about the house, and the majestic panorama of the river. Well may Mr. Downing have called Montgomery Place second to no seat in America for its combination of attractions; and it may be added that its makers and owners — all of them Livingstons, or close connections of the family — have been second to none in the taste and skill which took advantage of glorious opportunities, and in the care which has preserved the essential features of the original design until this day.

VI. — HYDE PARK.

In the days of the Revolution, Dr. Samuel Bard was a leading physician of New York. He was a decided Tory in feeling, yet he was a friend of Washington, and when the war was over, instead of migrating, he retired to a country-house by the Hudson. He purchased his lands of the famous " nine partners," and named his seat in honor of Sir Edward Hyde, one of the Colonial governors of New York.

Hyde Park is to-day the name of a station on the Hudson River Railroad, the first stop above Poughkeepsie. The traveller who alights here looks in vain for any village, and after following the one road a little way, he finds himself beside a foaming waterfall, and sees beyond the stream a widespread and apparently unoccupied country-side, composed of woods, grass-lands, hills, and vales, which he rightly conjectures to be Hyde Park proper. If the public road be followed as it winds up the valley to its junction with the old Albany post-road at Hyde Park Corner, and then the post-road be taken northward, the main gate of the park will be reached; but the park may also be entered from the river-side below the waterfall in Crown Elbow Creek. A bridge, which leads to a landing on the bank of the Hudson, here spans the creek, and a narrow road enters the park in very modest fashion just beyond the bridge. Beginning at this gate, a belt of woodland stretches northward for perhaps a mile along the bank of the river, occupying the summits of the little crags and knolls which here make the rocky shore, and enclosing many charming bits of rocky woodland scenery. Parallel with the river, and just east of the wood, lies a gently hollowed valley of smooth grass-land, beautifully fringed by the waving edge of the dense wood, on the one hand, and on the

other rising with concave lines to meet the sharply ascending
curves of a high, steep, and grassy bank, which, with the great
trees near its summit, bounds the scene on the east.

The little road which enters by the bridge commands one
or two views of this bank and the long, green glade at its
foot, and then it turns to follow the windings of the stream
which comes dashing down over rough ledges and under
shadowy Hemlocks on the right. The valley narrows until
there is only just room enough for the stream and the road;
and here a footpath breaks off to the left, and taking a rapidly rising open ridge, plainly indicates its intention to gain
the summit of the high bank with the great trees which was
lately in view. The road continues up the winding glen,
passing by several pretty waterfalls; and, by and by, where
the valley broadens and the stream is held back by a low
dam, it joins the main approach-road, which here bridges the
creek on its way from the Albany highway to the house.
The united roads next ascend by one easy zigzag to a broad
plateau of grass-land, set with numerous and variously grouped
and scattered trees of noble age and stature, between the
trunks of which the house soon appears in the distance. This
level ground is both wide and long, and its strikingly simple,
open, and stately effect is greatly heightened by the fact that
from every part of it is visible in the west, beyond and behind
all the massive tree-trunks, an indefinite expanse of blue
distance. (See the accompanying illustration). When the
house is reached, by the road just described, or by the footpath before mentioned, it is seen to stand close to the brink
of the plateau; in other words, upon the verge of the irregular, mile-long grassy bank the visitor saw first from below.
The descent of this bank is sudden, and some of the largest
trees upon it — chiefly Chestnuts and Oaks — lean outward
from the bank, and most of them grip the ground with a
vigor befitting veterans that have long wrestled with the
gales.

The view from the bank near the house embraces perhaps
ten miles up and down the mighty river, with the varied
opposite bank, and the wooded promontories near Staats-
burg, and, in the far distance, the blue ridges of the high-

lands below Newburgh, the dark outlines of the Shawangunks in the west, and the pale summits of the Catskills in the north. Foreground, middle distance, and distance are presented here with sharp definition. This is a scene not surpassed on the upper Hudson, unless the better composition of the river view from Ellerslie should place that wonderful picture first.

As the illustration shows, the house at Hyde Park is of a somewhat stiff and cold type; but it is simple and dignified, and in this respect is well fitted to its imposing site. Its south and west sides meet the grass of the park, its east side is the entrance front, and to its northeast corner is attached an ample kitchen and laundry yard, reached by a special road from the Albany highway, which, abreast of the house, has gained the level of the upland. The stables stand apart a little to the north, and the greenhouses, with an enclosed garden attached to them, lie in a similar position on the plateau to the south. Both are entirely surrounded by the open groves of the park.

According to Mr. Downing, André Parmentier of Long Island — the first landscape architect who practised in America — arranged the roads, buildings, and plantations of the estate, under the patronage of Dr. Hosack, who succeeded Dr. Bard as proprietor. No man ever undertook a more responsible service in the realm of taste applied to landscape, nor one in which it would have been easier to fail by spoiling what Nature had so magnificently provided. What a contrast is his work to the usual practice of the modern amateur, who, being a cultivated gentleman, considers himself quite able to lay out his own place. With the help of a jobbing gardener, he too often first despoils the natural scene of much that makes its character and beauty, for the sake of introducing supposedly decorative elements, such as strange trees and the short-lived brilliancy of flower beds. Montgomery Place and Hyde Park should teach us better. The soft and tranquil beauty of the gentle landscape of the first named, and the broad stateliness of the upland scenery of the second, must impress all sensitive minds, as no splendor of embellishment can. Decorative gardening, as it is often introduced in mod-

HYDE PARK ON THE HUDSON

ern country-seats, — that is, in patches scattered here and
there, — would at once kill the effectiveness of these old seats.
Their power over the mind and heart consists chiefly in the
unity of the impression which they make.   Their scenery is
artificial in the sense that Nature, working alone, would never
have produced it ; but the art which has here " mended nature," to use Shakespeare's phrase, has worked with Nature
and not against her.   It has, by judicious thinning, helped
Nature to grow great trees ; it has spread wide carpets of
green where Nature hinted she was willing grass should grow ;
it has in one place induced a screen of foliage to grow thickly,
and in another place it has disclosed a hidden vision of blue
distance ; and so, while it has adapted Nature's landscape to
human use, it has also, as it were, concentrated and intensified the expression of each scene.   " Almost all natural landscapes are redundant sources of more or less confused beauty,
out of which the human instinct of invention can by just
choice arrange, not a better treasure, but one infinitely more
fitted to human sight and emotion, infinitely narrower, infinitely less lovely in detail, but having this great virtue, that
there shall be nothing which does not contribute to the effect
of the whole."   Montgomery Place and Hyde Park on the
Hudson may serve as illustrations of these good words of Mr.
Ruskin.

Two other excellencies of these old seats remain to be mentioned, so that they may perhaps be imitated.   First, the roads
and paths, instead of displaying themselves and their curves
as if they were the chief elements of beauty in park scenery,
are rightly made subordinate and inconspicuous, as befits the
mere instruments of convenience they really are.   When they
run straight across level country they are shaded by trees in
rows ; when they curve, as they do only for good reason,
formality of planting instantly stops.   They lead to their
objective points with directness and without superfluous flour-
ish.   Secondly, the makers of these old seats were wise in
their generation in that they chose sites for their houses where
ample space was obtainable, and where fine trees already
existed.   Prevailing custom places fine houses on lots of land
much too small for them, and many a mansion, architecturally

excellent, is foredoomed to rise in some bare field where it must stand naked during many years.   And yet, New England, not to speak of other parts of the country, abounds in accessible park-sites, crying to be occupied, where, if there is no such mighty river as the Hudson, there is great variety of lake, hill, and mountain scenery adorned by fine trees and woods.

CHAPTER XV

THE FUNCTION OF THE LANDSCAPE ARCHITECT

It seems to be universally allowed that the habitation of man should be distinct from that of the cattle that graze around him. We see this principle acted upon from the palace to the cottage, which with its dwarf wall or garden pales, broken and enriched with the simple creepers of honeysuckle, ivy, etc., is an object pleasing to every eye as well as to that of the painter. . . . "What such rustic embellishments are to the cottage," says Sir Uvedale Price, "terraces, urns, vases, statues, and fountains are to the palace and palace-like mansion." — GILPIN.

CHARLES was always trying, both in public and in private, to explain and illustrate the objects of his profession, and its appropriate services to the community; and he was especially anxious to set forth the relations of the work of the landscape artist to that of the engineer, the architect, and the gardener. This chapter contains a selection from his writings on these subjects.

"WHEN TO EMPLOY THE LANDSCAPE GARDENER."

TO THE EDITOR OF "GARDEN AND FOREST:"

Sir, — May I add a postscript to your recent editorial? It is not long since the American public first began to give thought and money to securing well-designed houses. We had first to realize that our dwellings were not what they might be; and, secondly, to learn that if we would do better, we must ask the help of men specially trained to design happily and to build well. As respects the surroundings of our houses, even most of us who have employed architects are still in the first or unawakened stage. We simply have not perceived that our surroundings might be pleasanter or more in keeping with our abode. While we spend freely to fill the house with things of beauty, we probably leave the spaces round about it wholly bare, or if we attempt something better than nakedness, we do so without thought of general effect —

without regard to any such principles of design as guided the architect in his shaping of the house. Not until we come to see that the surroundings of the house as well as the house itself should be designed — that house, approaches, and surroundings should be planned together — shall we be likely to call upon the landscape-gardener.

February 6, 1889.

THE LANDSCAPE GARDENER.

Irresistible forces are drawing vast populations into the cities. Here, in the busy centres of the great towns, life is lived at high pressure — at such pressure that men are continually compelled to seek rest and refreshment, either in suburban home life, or in frequent flights to the country, the mountains, or the sea. It is to meet this want that millions of dollars are spent upon public country parks, and other millions upon country-seats and seaside-seats, summer hotels, and summer cottage neighborhoods; while, near the cities, the same want causes the region of detached and gardened houses to continually expand. This modern crowding into cities results in a counter invasion of the country; and it is just here that the special modern need of an art and profession of landscape gardening is first felt. How can we add roads, and many or large buildings, to natural landscape, without destroying the very thing in search of which we left the city? How shall we establish ourselves as conveniently as may be, and at the same time preserve all the charms of the scene we have chosen to dwell in? How may we rightly work to bring more and more beauty into that scene?

Questions like these are not easily answered, and many other problems arise equally difficult of solution. How shall we arrange the roads and buildings of a new suburb so as to make it a thoroughly pleasant place to live in? How shall we secure all possible convenience and beauty in the dooryards and gardens of a neighborhood? How shall the railroad station-yard and the church-yard, the public school-yard and the public square, be made as pleasant as possible to look at, to linger in, or to play in? How shall the public park, to which many hundreds or thousands will resort at one time,

be so made and preserved as to be to all city dwellers a reve-
lation of nature's beauty and peace?

Only special study and long observation will fit a man
to solve successfully these problems of landscape gardening. Says Mr. Ruskin : " Art, properly so called, cannot be
learned in spare moments nor pursued when we have nothing
better to do. To advance it men's lives must be given, and
to receive it, their hearts." To the art of preserving, enhancing, or creating out-of-doors beauty, whether natural or
formal, the landscape gardener gives his days. One week
will find him plotting the half-formal ways and plantings of
a city square, and the next may see him working to bring out
and to emphasize all the beauty a piece of park land can be
induced to yield. One day he is designing a garden terrace
for a stately country-seat; another day finds him suggesting
ways of perfecting the charm of a rocky wilderness by the
seashore, or the beauty of a meadow or pondside or woodside
in the country; while a third day may be given to the planning of the plantations which are to make some ugly, wind-
swept field a pleasant place. He shares with the architect
the designing of homesteads — fits the part called the house
to the surrounding parts, plans the necessary approaches, and
works out such appropriate changes in the surrounding scene
as trained taste and experience suggest. He plans, with care,
the roadways and the footpaths by means of which the people shall enjoy their country park without harming it ; he
studies sites and surveys, preparatory to laying out new suburbs or new neighborhoods of summer cottages; he devises
the surroundings of hotels, hospitals, and public buildings —
everywhere endeavoring to supply every convenience of arrangement, and, at the same time, to preserve or to create as
much as possible of beauty, be it picturesque or formal.
[Garden and Forest, February 13, 1889.]

HORTICULTURE AND DESIGN IN THE SURROUNDINGS OF
HOUSES.

The recent enormous increase in the variety of the products
of the plant nursery has supplied the designer of house surroundings with much new material, but has not affected the

main principles of his art. Without counting fruit trees, an ordinary American nursery catalogue now offers for sale some five hundred sorts of trees and shrubs and an equal number of herbaceous perennials. The demand for nursery-grown plants — that is for plants trained to bear moving — is great and growing.

Possibly the time may come when thousands of trees will be wanted for timber plantations; but at present in America the first and foremost use for nursery-grown trees is the provision of shelter from cold wind, or hot sun, for men's houses and crops. Almost two thirds of our country must plant trees for this purpose, and Western nurserymen will be called upon to grow vast numbers of quick and hardy sorts. To shade and adorn streets trees must also be wanted. In the more or less arid West they are particularly needed, and there they will be planted even though irrigation must be introduced to support them. In moister climates trees which do not shade a road too darkly will prove best.

A second source of the demand upon the nurseryman is the desire for table fruits. In spite of adverse climates, black rot, and curculio, men will doubtless continue to grow apples, pears, peaches, and berries of ever better sorts and in ever larger quantities. In the West experiment must go on for many years, before the kinds best adapted to the various climates can be discovered and proved; and in the East the limit of improvement is by no means reached.

A third great source of the demand for plants springs neither from the need of shelter nor the desire for pleasant food, but from the love of plants as beautiful or curious objects. Beginning in this country with the introduction of Lombardy Poplars, Lilacs, a few Roses, and a few perennials, the desire for beautiful or striking plants has grown continuously and prodigiously, encouraging nurserymen to discover and grow trees, shrubs, and herbs from every temperate climate of the earth, and prompting them, as each new thing becomes in its turn common or well known, to offer some yet more striking novelty, derived perhaps from Asia or Japan, or else developed from a rare form of some old friend. Fine bloom has been most desired; accordingly sorts which produce striking flowers have been introduced from abroad in great numbers, and these have then been improved by zealous cultivators, until the parent species has come to seem commonplace.   Fine flowering perennials are now offered in innumerable varieties, and the number of conspicuously blooming trees and shrubs exceeds one hundred.   Remarkable foliage has also been sought out and developed.   Fifty or more sorts of cut-leafed and colored-leafed trees and shrubs appear in the catalogues; many coniferous evergreens are grown for their colors; and the foliage plants of the herbaceous tribes number hundreds.   Uncommon form or habit too has its admirers.   The so-called weeping and fastigiate trees now number more than thirty, and some of these add fine bloom and pretty foliage to their more or less graceful or graceless shape.

I must leave the horticultural journals and the catalogues themselves to describe, as best they may, the marvellous wealth of beautiful forms and colors which a great plant nursery now contains.   Progress in arboriculture and horticulture has become amazingly rapid; and if just now the growing of the familiar but handsome native trees, shrubs, and herbs is sadly neglected, this is the one regrettable tendency to be noted.   I know it is often maintained that the growing of "dwarfs," "fastigiates," "weepers," and purple leafed and colored trees is itself a regrettable, not to say a shocking violation of good taste and of nature.   It would seem, however, as if these critics of the nurserymen must be ignorant of the fact that all these so-called monstrous forms were somewhere originated by Nature herself, and that it is in the use which is made of them, and not in the art of propagating them, that the possibility of gross sin against good taste is to be found.

Turn now to the scenes which the treasures of the plant nursery are to shelter or adorn.   Late years have witnessed great movements of city population to the suburbs and the country.   An out-of-town house may be surrounded by something of that country quiet which the tired workers of the cities find so refreshing.   It may, moreover, have light and air on all its sides.   Once so-called rapid transit is provided, it is no wonder that thousands make their homes in the suburbs; and it is equally natural that those who can afford it should spend the hot summers in the open country or by the sea. To the architect the country house and the suburban house present problems very different from those he is called upon to grapple with in the city. Out of town he meets with endlessly differing conditions of situation, of exposure, of prospect, and of aspect; and he finds almost unlimited opportunities for the exercise of ingenuity and taste. That American citizens and architects are taking advantage of these opportunities does not need to be said. One well-designed house built in a given neighborhood becomes the forerunner of a dozen others. Such a new birth of interest in architecture and in the principles of architectural design as has been witnessed in America in the last few years, the world has seen only once or twice before.

The out-of-town house has more or less land about it, — land which the city man buys presumably not only in order to keep other houses at a distance, but also for the purpose of providing something pleasant for his eyes to look upon. This ground about the house, whatever be its character or area, must necessarily be more or less altered from its natural state as soon as the house is set upon it. At the very least, its undulations must be brought to meet the rigid ground line of the architectural structure, and its surface must be crossed by the path to the house door. Generally the natural scene must undergo other and more considerable changes. Trees must be felled to make a way for the approach-road or to admit sunlight to the house; slopes must be cut into to allow the road to pass along them and hollows filled so as to remove standing waters; grounds must be made smooth for the growing of fruits and vegetables, and so forth.

If, now, a man desires that his surroundings, after suffering these necessary changes from their natural state, should be, like his house, convenient and at the same time beautiful as possible, he has upon his hands, whether he knows it or not, a problem of very considerable difficulty. When his house is finished, his house scene is by no means complete; and unless his house has been designed as a part of the house scene, —

that is, with careful reference to the parts surrounding it, — the final effect is almost sure to be disappointingly fragmentary and ineffective. Few architects and fewer house-owners yet realize this. Indeed, the ordinary practice is to design and build suburban and country houses without much thought of the surrounding scene, — often without consideration of so practical a matter as the grade of the way of approach. Commonly such necessary appendages as the laundry-yard and the carriage-turn are not thought of until the house is up; when it is likely that they cannot be so conveniently arranged as they might have been, had they been thought of earlier. As for the beauty of the house scene, although it is so generally desired, it is very seldom planned or arranged for. It seems commonly to be regarded as something to be added to the scene, after the house and roads or paths are built, — probably by making a lawn and inserting flower beds and specimen plants, no matter what may be the nature of the ground.

The growing appreciation of design in architecture must work a reform here in time; meanwhile it will be well to insist upon two fundamental facts, — first, that real beauty of scene is never derived from added decorations, but must spring directly from the shape and character of the scene itself; and secondly, that this true beauty can be attained only when the house and its appendages and its surroundings are studied and thought out together as one design — one composition.

Both the country-seat and the suburban lot may illustrate the truth of these propositions. A suburb is a district in which roads and houses dominate the landscape. In the typical case the ground is smooth and flat, the streets and boundaries straight, the separate ownerships by no means large. In such neighborhoods the architect's share in the making of the scene is so predominant that an error in the choice of the style of the house is almost necessarily fatal to the effect of the house scene. Where the surroundings are mostly formal, much irregularity either of building or of ground always seems out of place and affected; unless, indeed, nature has by chance supplied a site which by its steep slopes or its rockiness conquers the surrounding formality and compels to the picturesque. A many angled and many gabled building on a smooth site in a straight-bounded enclosure is out of keeping ; and so also, in the same situation, are a tangle of bushes and boulders, and a sharply curved approach-road. This does not mean that where the streets are curved, or for any reason a house door is easiest reached by a curved line, the curve must be forbidden and the path or road made straight ; but it does mean the shunning of all purposeless curvature, such as is often to be seen in most suburbs. Awkward and breadth-destroying lines of approach are the rule in the suburbs, and the architect is often responsible for them ; for he frequently places the house door in such a position that the path or road leading to it must necessarily cut the ground before the house into lamentably small pieces, and he does this, too, when a little thought might perhaps have brought about that happiest of all arrangements, in which a stretch of grass as long or longer than the building is brought without a break up to the house wall itself. No subsequent planting can obliterate mistakes in these controlling elements of the suburban house scene, — the house and the approach ; and no planting can accomplish what it otherwise might, if by reason of unmindfulness of the effect of the house scene as a whole, the framework of the scene is wrongly put together.

It is seldom that a suburban lot, after the house and approaches are built, retains much of its former vegetation. A few large trees may survive the necessary gradings, but the natural ground covering is generally killed out. On the completion of the grading grass is sown, and from the resulting sheet of green the house walls and the boundary walls or fences rise abruptly. It is exceedingly surprising to see, as one may everywhere, well-designed houses, adorned within with much rich ornament and probably inhabited by people who appreciate art and nature, standing thus naked in naked enclosures. The contrast between a handsome building and bare surroundings is sufficiently obvious in summer, but in winter, in this New England climate, it becomes positively startling; so that it is difficult to understand how educated people can fail to be impressed by it, and how they can longer refuse to comprehend that the house and the house grounds should be treated in the same spirit.

From another point of view this miserable nakedness is equally surprising. Here in the suburbs is an opportunity for adding to all the usual advantages and ornaments of city life the new and delightful pleasantness of verdure, fragrance, and bloom. As a matter of fact, it is an appreciation of this opportunity that causes the first plantings in most suburban grounds. Trees and shrubs, selected for their profuse flowering or their striking habit, are set out here and there, and brilliant beds of flowers are perhaps added. Desire for ornament of this sort, like some other desires, grows by what it feeds on, and causes the pressing demand on the nurseryman for plants of the marked appearance of which I spoke before. The effect upon house grounds resulting from planting undertaken in this spirit is everywhere to be seen, and is generally unfortunate. Specimens of many sorts planted promiscuously on a lawn compose an interesting though ill-arranged museum, but not an appropriate setting for a house. They wholly destroy all that breadth of effect which it is so difficult but so important to preserve in small grounds ; if they grow large they interfere with the prospect and the aspect of the house, and whatever their size, they give the scene the appearance of having been adorned to make a show, and remind one of the saying of the Greek sculptor, who charged his pupil with having richly ornamented a statue, because he knew not how to make it beautiful.

An ambition to possess a collection of handsome, curious, and rare plants, like the similar passions for shells, or minerals, or precious stones, is entirely praiseworthy and honorable, and may well be indulged *ad libitum*, provided a place can be set apart and fittingly arranged for the purpose, as cabinets are prepared indoors for collections of curios of all sorts. Out of doors, a flower garden is such a cabinet, and there is no reason that tree and shrub gardens should not be similarly arranged by those who desire to grow many striking sorts. In formal and highly decorated pleasure grounds specimen trees are already used in this way, and with good effect. Before stately buildings and in connection with terraces and formal avenues, appropriate specimens are always in keeping ; but in New England house scenes, not especially arranged to receive them, they destroy the last hope of good general effect.

With what object, then, should the planting of the suburban house ground be planned?

I answer, with the object of helping the building and the other controlling parts of the scene to form an appropriate and pleasing whole. In the very smallest front yards one thing, which should seldom or never be omitted, can be accomplished just as well as it can be in grounds of larger area — that is the connecting of the house walls with the ground by means of some sort of massing of verdure. Shrubs planted near the base of the house wall remove at once all appearance of isolation and nakedness, and nothing can help a building more than this. There, if nowhere else, some evergreens should be used; and it is fortunate that in a climate in which hardy evergreens are few, the stiff sorts like the Box, the Arbor Vitæs, and the Junipers are all entirely appropriate in close connection with a building. The more irregular the structure, the more varied in detail may be these wall plantings, but if the house is of formal design, a hedge-like row of bushes may be best. The older houses in many New England villages often have bushes set thus along their walls; and at the Longfellow mansion in Cambridge the same purpose is accomplished by a low terrace balustrade, half covered by creepers.

In grounds a little larger than the smallest, the securing of some breadth of effect by means of grass should be attended to next after the wall plantings. If there is space enough to get this openness, and at the same time to have some bushes near the street line as well as next the house, so much the better. Plant nothing which will grow to a size disproportionate to the scene. Large trees on small lots are not only inappropriate, but they shade the ground excessively and make it difficult to grow the indispensable ground-covering of shrubs. Maintaining sufficient openness, plant shrubs against the naked fences, or grow climbers on them if space does not permit of anything more. In larger grounds give the house a setting or background of appropriate trees. Where, as in New England, climate keeps deciduous plants leafless half the

year, plant for effect in winter as carefully as for the summer ;
use all possible broad-leafed evergreens and all the cheerful
fruit-bearing and colored stemmed shrubs, and for summer
add various sorts of foliage and bloom, but keep the whole
scene to its own appropriate style, admitting brilliant decoration only in detail, and conspicuous single objects only rarely,
if at all. If many flowers are desired, they should be grown
in a garden, or in formal beds close beside the formal building. The permanent scene can be helped only in its details
by the temporary beauty of bulbs and herbs.

To appreciate that a house scene depends for real effectiveness upon its general design and not upon decoration, one need
only look upon some such ground as that of the Longfellow
place before mentioned, where the planting consists of two
Elms supporting the sides of the house, creepers covering the
balustrade at its base, and Lilacs flanking the balustrade and
forming a hedge along the street wall. The open space of
grass is well proportioned, and the whole scene is one which
— in its formal, symmetrical style — is not surpassed for
effectiveness in all New England. Suitable general design
is just as effective in any other conceivable style.

Space forbids further dwelling upon the suburban lot, and
I must close with a few words about the country-seat. All
that has been said of the importance of care for the house
scene on the part of the architect is just as applicable here as
in the suburbs. Approach-roads may be rightly or wrongly
placed, and much depends upon this. The house, if it stands
in wild scenery, should either be made to harmonize with
the scenery, or it should distinctly contrast with surrounding
nature. In this latter case it should be given a setting of
its own, divided by terrace, wall, or hedge from the scenery
around. Within this setting the rarest and strangest specimens may be handsomely and fittingly displayed, even though
the neighborhood be extremely wild and rough. On the other
hand, if specimen planting generally works mischief in the
suburbs, it is absolutely monstrous in a broader landscape.
Small or large scenery can be "improved" by one method
only : it may be induced to take on more and more of appropriate beauty and character. What Nature hints at she may

be led to express fully; and, if the genius of the place be continually consulted, there is no scene the natural beauties of which may not be heightened by landscape art. [Proceedings of the Massachusetts Horticultural Society, March 23, 1889.]

The following letter was written to Mrs. Schuyler Van Rennselaer, whose writings in the public press on various topics connected with landscape art Charles found unusually discriminating and attractive.

3 Dec. '90.

I have just heard that you are writing on "Landscape Gardening and Architecture," and I write because I think you may perhaps like to think over certain notions of mine on your subject, which notions I proceed to lay before you — without ceremony: — you will treat them accordingly!

The scope and breadth of my profession is not often recognized — it is not comprehended even by architects, much less by the public.

As I understand it, all conscious arranging of visible things for man's convenience and for man's delight is architecture. " A great subject truly, for it embraces the consideration of the whole of the external surroundings of the life of man: we cannot escape from it if we would, for it means the moulding and altering to human needs of the very face of the earth itself." Morris.

The building of convenient and beautiful structures is thus but a part of the art of architecture. The arranging of these structures in streets, in neighborhoods, on sea-coasts, in the valleys of the hills, the careful adjustment of the structure to its site and its landscape, the devising of ways and roads so that they may be either impressive through order and formality, or charming through their subordination to natural conditions, the development of appropriate beauty in the surroundings of buildings, whether by adding terraces and avenues or by enhancing natural beauty — all this is, or ought to be, at least one half of the art and profession of architecture. This is the landscape architect's part: for the field is so wide that it can hardly be comprehended by one man, and two professions seem necessary, each approaching and helping the other.

Landscape gardening is that part of the landscape architect's labor which is directed to the development of formal or natural beauty by means of removing or setting out plants. As a matter of fact, I find it but a secondary part of the profession : the devising of general schemes which shall combine convenience with preserved, increased, or created beauty is the most important part of our work. I know that Mr. Olmsted would agree to this. Felling or planting is generally necessary to the completion of such schemes; but neither can ever cure the defects resulting from ill-considered fundamental arrangements.

Many architects have never conceived of their art in its real breadth and height. Many still build houses in the abstract, with little regard to site and aspect. Many set doors where the necessary approaches must greatly mar the foreground of the prospect — and so on. They " wash in " supporting foliage in their drawings, which they take no pains to secure in practice. They seldom conceive of the house and its surroundings as a whole — their education has fixed their attention too exclusively upon the structure alone.

On the other hand, the broader minded among them are the men who will lead the way to a better general appreciation of Mr. Olmsted's profession. As the value of design applied to structures comes to be understood, the appreciation of design applied to the inter-arrangement and the surroundings of structures must follow. The architects ought to be the chief missionaries of this cause.

In a letter written December 2, 1896, to Mrs. Mary C. Robbins, who had just contributed to " The Atlantic " an excellent article on the function of the landscape artist, but had confounded landscape architecture with landscape gardening, Charles said : —

Landscape architecture includes and covers landscape engineering, landscape gardening, and landscape forestry. A formal avenue or parkway is a work of landscape architecture; so is a well-designed picturesque park. The engineer and the gardener will each have his share in both pieces of work; but each must labor for the perfecting of the general design, if a successful result is to be achieved.

In some undated notes for an article or essay on American landscape architecture, Charles defines landscape architecture to be the art of arranging land and landscape for human use, convenience, and enjoyment; and then proceeds to indicate the conditions under which landscape is evolved. These conditions are first, geological or physiographical — mountains, narrow valleys, wide plains, river-banks, coasts, gaps, notches, cañons; secondly, climatal — arctic, temperate, tropical, wet, dry, windy, cyclonic; thirdly, vegetal, following climate — forests, prairies, arable and pasture lands, and deserts; and fourthly, human — effects of land tenures, building habits, social customs, and prevailing industries. For him, therefore, landscape architecture included the designing of a farmstead, plantation, or ranch, of a country-seat or seaside-seat, of a suburban colony, of the grounds about a railway station or a factory, of a city, or of city squares, playgrounds, parks, and parkways; and American landscape architecture would include all these arrangements of land for human use and enjoyment through a wide range of climate, and under a great variety of physiographical conditions.

CHAPTER XVI

SELECTED[1] LETTERS TO PRIVATE OWNERS, TRUSTEES, OR CORPORATIONS

> To range the shrubs and small trees so that they may mutually set off the beauties and conceal the blemishes of each — to aim at no effects which depend on nicety for success and which the soil, the exposure, or the season may destroy — to attend more to the groups than to the individuals — and to consider the whole as a plantation, not as a collection of plants, are the best general rules that can be given. — WHATELY.

A PLANTING-PLAN FOR HOUSE GROUNDS. — The planting-plan described in the next two letters was made for an area about 600 feet square, on which stood a large house and a stable. About sixty kinds of trees and shrubs were used in the design, all of them being native or thoroughly domesticated varieties. They yielded a delightful succession of bloom and fruitage, and a pleasing variety of foliage; and they were expected to require much less care and annual expenditure than the beds of exotics, which at that time were commonly used for the decoration of house grounds. These plantations were all successful, and have been and are much enjoyed by the family. The accompanying photographic illustrations represent in an imperfect way some of their present (1901) aspects. The accompanying plan is a reduced copy of Charles's design for the shrubberies, the original having been all made by his own hand.

Prior to the plantings of 1889 there was little or no grass on these grounds. The surface was covered with Alders, Catbriars, wild Cherries, Tupelos, and Maple coppice with a liberal admixture of stones and rocks. There were, however, a few large Oaks. Round each Maple stump stood from four to eight sprouts twelve or fifteen feet high. These unsightly

---

[1] The selection of letters is perforce a limited one. As a rule, many letters were written concerning each undertaking; from such a series only one or two can ordinarily be given. It has been necessary to choose among many pieces of work a few which seemed to be types, or which represented the variety of a landscape architect's labors.

KEY TO THE PLAN OPPOSITE

1. Pinus sylvestris 5. Betula alba 2. Caragana. Cornus.
2. [Populus Bolleana 3.] Cornus. Corylus. Sambucus aurea.
3. [Pinus Strobus 3.] Pinus sylvestris 10. Pinus Mugho 2. Tsuga 10. Caragana. Cotoneaster. Colutea. Cornus. Salix. Ligustrum.
4. Betula alba 1. Pinus Mugho 3. Berberis. Eleagnus.
5. Betula alba 1. Forsythia.
6. [Populus Bolleana 3.] Colutea. Forsythia.
7. Pinus Mugho 3. Cornus Mas. Cornus.
8. Ligustrum. Cydonia. Calycanthus. Berberis purpurea.
9. [Tsuga 3.] Tsuga 15. Kalmia 10. Ligustrum. Forsythia. Rhus.
10. [Pinus Strobus 3.] Pinus Mugho 2. Pinus Sylvestris 10. Tsuga 10. Ligustrum. Salix. Chionanthus. Calycanthus.
11. Spiræa van Houttei. Rhus. Berberis.
12. [Pinus Austriaca 3.] Pinus Sylvestris 10. Rhododendron 10. Ligustrum. Chionanthus. Cornus. Calycanthus.
13. [Picea alba 3]. Tsuga 15. Cotoneaster. Cornus Mas. Caragana. Halesia.
14. [Cratægus coccinea.] Corylus. Hamamelis. Forsythia.
15. [Liriodendron 3.] Kalmia 10. Chionanthus. Azalea. Calycanthus.
16. Berberis. Berberis purpurea. Colutea.
17. Salix. Ligustrum. Forsythia.
18. Leucothoë 20. Euonymus 10.
19. Mahonia 20. Euonymus 10.
20. Salix. Cotoneaster. Forsythia.
21. Ligustrum. Hamamelis. Chionanthus. Spiræa sorbifolia.
22. Sambucus. Sambucus aurea. Rhus. Rhus typhina.
23. Hamamelis. Corylus. Cydonia.
24. Cotoneaster. Cydonia. Spiræa Thunbergii.
25. Ligustrum. Berberis. Ribes. Spiræa Thunbergii. [Sophora 2.]
26. Pyrus aucuparia. Spiræa sorbifolia. Zanthoceras. [Koelreuteria 2.]
27. Cratægus. Cratægus pyracantha. Ligustrum. Berberis. Eleagnus. Berberis purpurea. Colutea. Rhus.
28. Tsuga 5. Betula. Cornus. Rhus.
29. Kalmia 10. Azalea.
30. Tsuga 5. Rhododendron 10. Cornus florida. Cercis.
31. Tsuga 5. Betula. Cornus. Forsythia.
32. Cotoneaster. Berberis. Berberis purpurea. Eleagnus.
33. [Cornus florida.] Caragana. Colutea. Calycanthus.
34. [Prunus Pissardi.] Prunus. Ligustrum. Forsythia.
35. Ligustrum. Cornus. Cornus Mas. Caragana. Berberis.
36. [Populus Bolleana 3.] Salix. Cornus. Thuja Wareana 10.
37. Thuja Wareana 3. Thuja pyramidalis 2. Thuja Hoveyi 5. Berberis purpurea 5. Forsythia 5. Deutzia gracilis 10.
38. Thuja Wareana 1. Kerria Japonica 5.
39. Thuja Wareana 1. Rhodotypos 5. Thuja pyramidalis 2. Thuja Hoveyi 5. Berberis purpurea. Berberis Thunbergii. Spiræa Thunbergii. Aralia spinosa.
40. Thuja pyramidalis 1. Buxus 5. Mahonia. Spiræa Thunbergii. Cydonia. Aralia.
41. Rhododendron. Kalmia. Azalea.
42. Kerria. Spiraea van Houttei. Spiræa Thunbergii.
43. Thuja Wareana, pyramidalis, and Hoveyi. Tsuga. Buxus. Cornus.
44. Berberis Thunbergii 2.
45. Caragana. Berberis.
46. Berberis. Berberis Thunbergii.
47. Picea excelsa. Populus Bolleana. Salix. Cornus. Caragana.

[Plots 1 and 2 are not on the accompanying plan: they lay to the left of 3 and 6.]

PLANTING-PLAN FOR
THOMAS M. STETSON, ESQ.
NEW BEDFORD, MASS., 1889

Scale of Feet

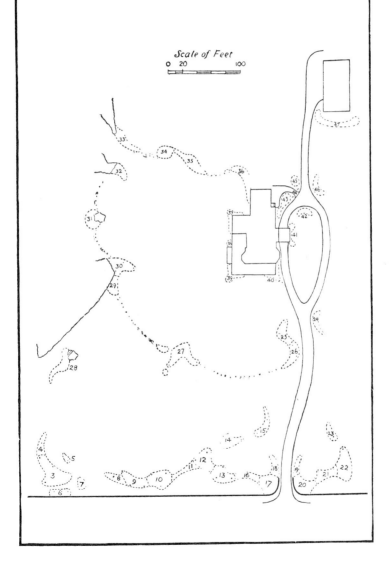

rings were reduced gradually, that is in three or four years, to one surviving stem. The soil was fairly good, for additional loam was carted in to perfect grades, and take the place of stones and rocks removed. On the whole, the present aspect of the estate, though apparently natural in the best sense, is really the result of artistic design in the beginning, and intelligent maintenance for twelve years.

21 Feb. '89.

I send a planting-plan [for shrubs] and a price list. The dotted lines outline the proposed shrubberies — the ground within the lines is to be made ready. The black dots show some of the trees of my tree-plan, the crossed dots [not legible on the reduced plan] denote such of the trees as are evergreen. In the list upon the plan these trees are named in brackets. The evergreens in the list are underlined.

I keep the shrubs back from the street wall because you have plenty of room, and they will look so much better from the street. The plantations are arranged to make a pleasing rather than a very picturesque or striking scene, and the plants are chosen accordingly. The small trees are mostly fine flowering sorts. The large shrubs are mostly for foliage. Among them the Privets (Ligustrum) and the Coloneasters are partly evergreen. I can get Laurels (Kalmia) dug from the woods for $3.50 per hundred, and Rhododendrons for $4, and I should much like to try to use them. It would be an experiment — they are not easy plants to handle — shall we try it? You could not possibly wish for better evergreen shelter than they furnish, where they succeed.

The smaller shrubs are mostly for bloom and fine foliage, and they will go in the fronts of the shrubberies. They are not always mentioned in the plan list — neither are the " small trees " — they will be planted as seems best after the main masses are set out.

The Pines and Hemlocks are for shelter and screening. They will generally occupy the centres of the masses near the coniferous trees of last year's tree-plan. They are intended to be removed as may seem best after a few years.

About the terrace walls the plantations are to be low, with an occasional upright shaft of green. Something is needed

MR. THOMAS M. STETSON'S ESTATE AT NEW BEDFORD, MASSACHUSETTS

View of the avenue (1901) approaching the Porte Cochère

MR. STETSON'S ESTATE AT NEW BEDFORD, MASSACHUSETTS

The entrance from the highway

ANOTHER VIEW OF THE WALLED ENTRANCE FROM THE HIGHWAY

MR. STETSON'S ESTATE AT NEW BEDFORD, MASSACHUSETTS

A view of the plantations near the house (1889–1901)

here to connect the house with the ground. The somewhat formal Thujas and the Tree Box are quite in place in such situations.

I shall answer any inquiries you may wish to make and hear any suggestions — both with pleasure. The prices I quote are for small plants — only such can be obtained at such low figures — but shrubs grow fast. The lists in Scott's "Suburban Grounds" and Long's "Ornamental Gardening" contain some information about shrubs. I am sorry I can name nothing better.

25 Feb. '89.

I answer your questions in order.

The dotted line indicates a proposed limit of the cut lawn. The plantations are arranged in part to make this right. It is usually an awkward line — we must not allow it to be.

The planting-spaces should be dug precisely as you describe. I will come down and stick in the outline sticks if you say so. I should probably modify the lines a little if I were upon the actual ground.

Decidedly you want climbers on the wall. I put fifty on the list, but did not name them in detail. I do name them on the new list I send to-night.

We can manage the planting very easily, I think, without any more detailed plan. It will cost you less to have me on the ground for a day or so than to get a detailed plan. I propose that the plants be ordered of the men whose names appear on my list — the conifers from Hooper, who makes a specialty of such things — and so on. Of the four nurseries I would call upon, three are beyond New York (that is, all but Temple). Might not these men express their three boxes to the New Bedford steamer in New York?

If you can prepare the ground, the planting will not take long, and you had best order the whole list. The dug beds will not be kept weeded permanently. The Periwinkle is intended to cover the ground under the shrubs in those masses and groups which are near the drive and about the house. It is a great addition to the appearance of such groups.

Another plant — the fragrant Sumac — is intended for a like purpose — the connecting of tall masses with the grass.

The purposes of all the list of smaller shrubs it would take too long to tell. The Angelicas are to rise through the Japan Barberries near the house — the Sumacs through the Elders — the silver Thorn is to set off the purple Barberry — the formal Arbor Vitæs are to stand with the house walls — so is the Box — and so on.

The sooner I can have authority to order the plants, the better. First come first served in Nurseries!

I hope the list is decipherable this time!

AN IMPROVEMENT OF STATION GROUNDS. — An Improvement Society, which had been formed in Beverly, Mass., interested itself in improving the unkempt grounds about the North Beverly Station of the unsympathetic Railway Company; and a member of the executive committee, charged with that part of their undertakings, sought Charles's advice. He described the work to be done in the following letter, the first of a series, for many difficulties arose in getting the plan executed by the three bodies concerned : —

14 Feb. '90.

MY DEAR MRS. ——, — I have visited North Beverly, and am now prepared to recommend the following order of procedure in improving the Station grounds : —

1. The whole area should be ploughed. 2. The roads should be staked out, and the stakes marked to show the finished grades. 3. The loam now lying in the proposed roadways should be moved to the proposed plots and spread there in accordance with the stakes. 4. The proposed roadways should then be filled up to grade with coarse material and finished off with binding gravel. 5. The few shrubs which the lawns will require should be planted. 6. The Town should complete the work by constructing the sidewalks near the street-railway track, and placing proper quarter-circle curbstones at the entrances to the Station ground from the main road.

This work could be done very cheaply by the railroad if it were equipped, as it ought to be, with a special gang of men used to such work. As things are, I suppose the most economical way of accomplishing the object will be by dividing the labor something as follows : —

The ploughing, staking, and removing of loam from the roadways, together with the finishing touches of grass-sowing and shrub-planting to be undertaken by the Improvement Society, or other local forces.

The hauling, delivering, and spreading of material to fill the roadways to be undertaken by the railroad, which can command a gravel train with ease.

If the work were divided in this manner, I think $250 would pay the Society's part of it. The material and road gravel to be delivered by the railroad would amount to about 600 cubic yards.

The western proposed grass-patch lies beyond the stone bounds, and so I suppose belongs to the Town. If the Society should leave this to be graded by the Town, it would save money.

The gravel-bank across the tracks from the Station can easily be covered with loam by the railroad. Nobody else can get at it. It is not included in what I have written above. Neither are the sidewalks mentioned under No. 6, which should be built by the Town.

Much of the ground is at present too low. This must account for the considerable amount of filling I propose.

Charles's suggestions could not be carried out completely; but through the persistence of the agent of the Improvement Society enough was done to make the station grounds tidy and pleasing. The careful arrangement and decoration of railroad grounds has now become much more common than it was in 1890.

In the summer of 1889 Charles began to advise Dr. Carroll Dunham, of Irvington-on-Hudson, about the grading of his new estate, the disposition of its roads and paths, and its planting-plan. The place was of limited extent, — about six and a quarter acres, — but it was to be the site of a large house and stable, the ridgepole of the house, on a line nearly east and west, being ninety-two feet long. The available dimensions of the rough, bare field were 460 feet from north to south by 325 from east to west; and the house site was about twenty-two and one half feet above the highest available point of the contiguous highway, which runs approximately north and south. The lot was therefore too small for the house: and its elevation gave it a full view of the highway and of the neighboring structures.   The first problem was to construct from the highway to the house an approach-road which should not have too steep grades or too sharp turns. The next was to regrade the field which sloped southward from the house, so as to give the future lawn slightly concave curves.   The following extracts from two letters from Charles to Dr. Dunham show how these problems were approached : —

26 July, '89.

Your first problem seems to be that of the turn in the approach, and then that of the service-road and the turn-round. If you still think the turn [near the rock on the plan] in the approach too sharp, you can of course do some more deep cutting and give the turn a radius of twenty feet instead of fifteen — but I don't think I would do more than this, else the bank between the house and the road at the east end of the house will be so sharp as to be ugly, and it will be impossible to make it blend southward into the natural bank, as my contours were intended to suggest that it should.   On the sketch I send I have drawn the turn with a twenty foot radius, and the reverse towards the house door with a thirty foot radius — and I think this will seem about right to you.   The "falling off" feeling can, you know, be greatly alleviated by making the outside edge of the turn in the manner I previously suggested in section thus : —

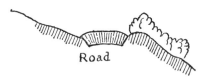

Road

By all means I would hollow the lawn to the south — preserving always a flowing surface — no sharpness at the sides. These sides I would design to be planted in the way we at first spoke of.   A narrow path might certainly wander through this planting, and I will consider its lines when I come to take up the planting. . . .

I hardly like your suggested way of starting these lawn paths from the house, and I feel a little shaky about the height of the water-table above finished grade.   Perhaps I do not quite understand you on this head.   I would have the building set as low as may be, and the piazzas as near the ground as may be.   Then I would if possible lead the paths

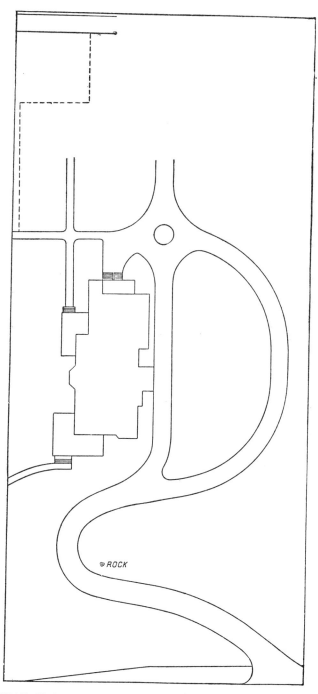

PLAN OF DR. CARROLL DUNHAM'S HOUSE AND APPROACH
ROAD, AT IRVINGTON ON HUDSON

from the piazzas without bringing them between the house and the lawn. The more intimate the connection between a building and a lawn of your gentle sort, the more pleasing the scene — to my eye, at least. . . .

25 Sept. '89.

. . . The cuts necessitated by the roadway you will probably find deeper and longer than you expected, and the cutting required to make an easy lawn south of the house surprised me, and may perhaps alarm you. If you, however, will regard my figures as indicating extremes of cut, and will proceed with the work gradually and evenly, you may be able to get a good surface short of the figures of my plan. I think it likely that you can. . . .

You will have an interesting problem also in saving handling of material by preparing successive portions of completed sub-grades upon which loam from portions to be cut can be placed at first hauling. I am assuming you are to be your own " boss " !

Then it remained to conceal the boundaries of the estate by plantations; to plant out undesirable objects; and to connect, to all appearance, the plantations on these six acres with the groves and thickets on the neighboring estates, so that the eye should be carried easily far beyond the boundaries of the house-lot, towards pleasing objects at a distance. These problems were all successfully solved. The easterly gable of the house was only 160 feet from the highway, and the front door was only 125 feet from the northerly border of the estate; yet the approach-road, leaving the highway at the northeastern corner of the estate, rose gently with a grade of only 7 per cent. to the front door, before which an ample turn-round enclosed a grass-plot larger than the entire area of the house. Dr. Dunham himself superintended all the road-making, grading, and planting required by the design, and has ever since taken assiduous care of the plantations, rejecting the shrubs which did not accommodate themselves to the soil and the climate, replacing feeble plants with strong ones, and paying attention to the preservation of the original curves and surfaces of the avenues, paths, and grassed areas. In March, 1890, sixty-two kinds of trees and shrubs were set out on the estate; and in the following autumn Charles provided another list of 725 plants, this list embracing fifty-two kinds, many of which were, however, included in the preceding sixty-two kinds. The following spring another list of 520 plants was used by Dr. Dunham.

The results obtained in about ten years are certainly surprising, and very pleasing. In driving down the avenue there is no sense of danger, — no apprehension of falling off on the down side. The accompanying cut shows the descent at the

turn below the house. The surface of the lawn is singularly pleasing, as it descends towards a natural grove of trees on a steep bank at its southern extremity; and from the house and its vicinity one does not perceive at all the boundaries of the place. The accompanying illustrations represent but imperfectly the results achieved. The first one exhibits the entrance and the ascending avenue with planted slopes on either hand; the second depicts the house and stable when the first plantings were made; the third the present aspect looking towards the house. The fourth illustration shows how plantations not far from the house lead the eye across the broad sunken highway to the woods and thickets on the neighbors' lands. Yet it is only 160 feet from the house to the highway. All the surfaces and plantings depicted in these photographs are artificial, yet their effect is natural and altogether pleasing.

DR. CARROLL DUNHAM'S ESTATE AT IRVINGTON-ON-HUDSON

The avenue seen from the highway

DR. CARROLL DUNHAM'S ESTATE AT IRVINGTON-ON-HUDSON

The bare house and stable in 1890

VIEW OF THE HOUSE AND STABLE FROM NEARLY THE SAME POINT IN 1901

DR. CARROLL DUNHAM'S ESTATE AT IRVINGTON-ON-HUDSON

View from the lawn over the invisible highway

The making of this beautiful residence on a site originally unpromising illustrates the resources of landscape designing when applied year after year by an owner of intelligence with a real love for out-of-door art.

A NEW COUNTRY-SEAT NEAR BOSTON. — In 1889, while Charles's office was still at No. 9 Park Street, he began to give advice about his new country-place to Mr. Henry S. Hunnewell, of the firm of Shaw & Hunnewell, architects, whose office was in the same building.   Mr. Hunnewell proposed to make a handsome place gradually out of a rough, rocky, and rather barren wooded tract in Wellesley.   The house site was to be selected, the approach-road laid out, all the lesser buildings and enclosures provided for, the gardens designed, the woods improved, and new plantations made. Mr. Hunnewell, being an architect, was accustomed to the use of drawings and to superintending work.   Charles's way of attacking this complex problem would have been to get first an accurate topographical survey of the estate with contours at intervals of five feet of elevation, and then on this survey to plan simultaneously all the principal features of the finished seat.   But Mr. Hunnewell preferred to solve each problem as it arose, and chiefly by study on the ground.   He liked to get Charles's ideas by consultations on the spot.   In that way Charles gave advice without any engineer's plan, about placing the house and laying out the roads, grading the lawn (made out of a "burnt swamp"), felling trees, opening vistas through the woods, and setting out shrubs and trees.   For nearly five years Charles gave such advice at intervals, and also supplied planting-lists almost every spring and fall.   He was studying successive garden plans for Mr. Hunnewell in March, 1891, in October of the same year, and again in January, 1892.   The following letter, written after Charles had become a member of the Olmsted firm, and therefore signed Olmsted, Olmsted & Eliot, describes the garden which was ultimately made, and the tracing therein mentioned is reproduced in the next illustration.

21 December, 1893.

The accompanying tracing shows a suggestion for a hollow grading for your new garden glade which we should like to see carried out.   The circuit path is made to follow the outside edge of the gentle hollow.   Shrubbery and gardenesque trees would fringe the path on the outside.   Garden shrubs and perennials would border it on the inside.   Inside of all would be a glade of grass of varying width.   To effect the hollow appearance it will be necessary to excavate about a foot in the middle in some places, and to pile up at the sides a little here and there. The perennial beds should be rounded up a little, so that the path will generally be in a very slight depression.

This treatment will give a pleasing effect, and furnish ample room for perennials. If you would prefer to make a jumble of the whole place, — not a bad thing to do, — we, of course, cannot assist you further.

The making of this garden proved to be a long affair, so that it was only finished in 1899. The upper garden, marked " flower garden " on the plan, is larger than there shown and circular; the lower garden is almost exactly as drawn. The few trees in the latter were really planted without the plan in hand; but when, later, the sites of the trees were compared with the plan, they were found to correspond to the drawing.

This is a favorable example of the creation of an interesting country-seat in ten years of steady labor under the direction of an owner able to give much time and thought to the subject, and unusually competent to make good use of slight sketches, and of oral advice given by an expert on the spot. Charles was glad to take part in such a delightful work on his friend's terms; but he always thought the method employed extravagant, and unsafe even in professional hands. This is the only case in his practice where he coöperated in large work carried on in this manner.

A TOWN-SITE ON SALT LAKE, UTAH. — On the 23d of July, 1890, Mr. Charles Francis Adams, President of the Union Pacific Railroad, asked Charles to go to Utah with him to advise the railroad company about a town site and hotel at Garfield beach on Salt Lake. The job had been offered to Mr. Olmsted, and declined on account of other engagements; but Mr. Olmsted advised Charles to accept it. The expedition was entirely congenial, and the work to be done looked attractive; so Charles postponed his appointments in Boston, notified his wife at New Hartford and his nearest relatives, and on the 24th started in pursuit of Mr. Adams, who had already left Boston. On the 30th he solved to his satisfaction the problem presented to him, gave two days more to the study of its details, and on the morning of August 2d started for home. The engineers of the railroad made the surveys required by Charles's preliminary design, and their drawings reached him in the middle of September.

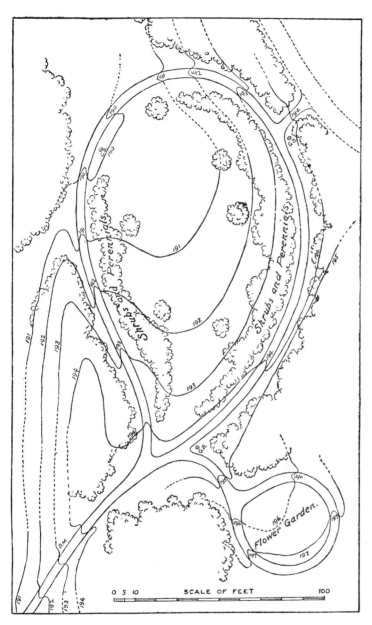

Shrubs and Perennials

Shrubs and Perennials

Flower Garden.

SCALE OF FEET
0 5 10   100

MR. HENRY S. HUNNEWELL'S GARDEN-PLAN

1 November, 1890.

C. F. ADAMS, ESQ., PRESIDENT UNION PACIFIC RAILROAD CO.

Sir, — I beg leave to report upon the plan for the development of your Company's property at Garfield, Utah, devised by me at your request, during the past summer.

A few words will describe the general situation.

The Great Salt Lake extends about ninety miles in a northwest and southeast direction. At right angles to this line of its greatest length, the southern shore of the lake stretches northeast and southwest for thirty miles, having at either extremity a wide and very low-shored bay, but in the middle of its length a distinctly bold, rocky, and projecting swell of coast, immediately behind which rises the exceedingly steep Oquirrh Mountain. The total length of this bold and handsome portion of the southern shore is about three miles ; and all this stretch of shore, with what inhabitable land lies back of it and much of the mountain side which towers over it, is the property of the Union Pacific Railroad.

The surface of this tract, like that of all the land about the lake, is full of salt ; it bears little or no vegetation except sage-brush ; it is in parts exceedingly stony and in other parts exceedingly steep, and the steep parts are subject to destructive gullying whenever a cloud-burst strikes the mountain overhead. On the other hand, this shore commands the finest possible view of the surface of that Great Lake which, in the almost waterless region of the Great Basin, must always be a wonderful and moving spectacle. The prospect is both very broad and very far. Most of the lake-shore is so low and flat as to be indistinguishable at a distance, so that the blue waters appear to stretch from the foot of the lofty and notched Wahsatch Mountains twenty miles away in the east, to the foot of the similar Desert Range as many miles distant in the west, while northward, between the parallel ranges which form the islands called Antelope and Stansbury, the lake appears to stretch into infinity, no land being in sight. The mountains and the reflecting lake are daily decked in changing colors under the influence of shifting lights and shadows, haze, and sunset glow ; but the unique glory of the prospect from Garfield must always be the grandeur of its perspective of mountains retreating towards a vanishing-point where water meets with sky.

Your company already operates a railroad along this favored shore. At present the line runs upon the upland at varying distances from the water's edge, but it must obviously be moved elsewhere if the narrow strip of land between the lake and the mountain is to be developed into a handsome pleasure resort. Left where it is, the railroad would not only cut the usable land into awkward pieces, but it would cut off access to the shore except by dangerous grade crossings; moreover it would be an eyesore throughout the whole length of the foreground of the lake view. To move the line to the rear of the site of the proposed pleasure town would make it very inconvenient for the thousands of would-be bathers in the lake which the railroad will bring daily from Salt Lake City. Therefore the plan of the new Garfield shows the railroad shifted to the only other possible position, namely the foot of the lake bluff, in which location it will be easily crossed above grade by means of light bridges springing from the brink of the bluff and reaching the beach on the water-side of the tracks by stairs. Thus all grade crossings will be avoided, and the tracks will be put comparatively out of sight. The principal station will stand at the top of the bathing-beach between the tracks and the water, and from this station direct access will be had to the bath-houses, and to the pier or piers from which the crowd will view the bathing. Stairs and bridges will lead over the tracks to the brink of the bluff, where will be found a long, straight, and level esplanade from which the grand view over the lake will best be had. The same view and the same breezes will also be had in the second story of the station building, where a half-open hall or loggia may be made the principal restaurant for excursionists. Immediately behind the middle of the esplanade, and separated from it only by the roadway which is necessary to enable carriages to approach the station, will be a large reservation, extending to the county road at the foot of the mountain, and so preserving a view of the steep and shadowy slopes thereof which will be appreciated by all who stand upon the

esplanade or the piers.   The mountain rises so close at hand
and so steep that low buildings may occupy this reservation
without hiding any appreciable part of its great mass, and so
the plan shows a shelter building for the use of excursionists
and picnickers, to consist of a gallery or pergola surrounding
the four sides of an irrigated garden, and in the rear of this
a court surrounded by carriage sheds and such stables as may
be required.   East and west of this reservation, and extending from the county road to the esplanade, the plan shows
streets of summer villas so arranged as to ensure for all direct
access to the esplanade and the station.

Such is an outline of the scheme for the development of
the central or bathing-beach section of the new Garfield, — a
section planned particularly for the enjoyment of excursionists from the city.   For the accommodation of others who
may wish to spend more than a day in the presence of the
grand panorama of the Salt Lake, our scheme must include
a Hotel which shall be set beyond the reach of the excursionists and as removed as possible from the railroad.

At first sight it might seem that some point upon the mountain side would best fill these conditions, but the mountain is
everywhere so steep that it would be very difficult to place
an accessible hotel upon it.   It would also be extremely difficult to provide the view from a hotel so placed with any
sufficiently strong and handsome foreground: moreover, even
if site and foreground could be arranged, the unavoidable
overlooking of the whole pleasure colony below would detract
from the impressiveness of the prospect over the lake.   For
these reasons it seems best to place the hotel upon the immediate lake-shore rather than upon the heights, and if upon
the shore, then upon that part of it where it is possible to
place the building in front of the railroad, that is, between
the tracks and the water.   With the waves playing immediately below the terrace or piazza on the one side, and an
unobstructed view of the threatening mountain wall upon the
other, the hotel will be well placed.

Most fortunately, a situation of this sort presents itself about
one third of a mile west of the bathing-beach.   Here a long
hotel building may rise at the edge of the water, having the

railroad in a cut in its rear. The principal rooms will occupy the whole width of the structure, thus commanding the lake in one direction and the mountain side on the other. Two low wings in the rear may contain the laundry and the billiard departments respectively, and stretching towards the county road these wings will help to enclose a rectangular court or irrigated garden, which will add much to the attractiveness of the house. No buildings should be allowed upon the mountain behind this hotel site, and it would be well if the Company could buy the whole slope in this part. The widest gulch in all this side of the Oquirrh Mountain is here in full view, having at present a growth of Pine on its upper slopes, and presenting as each day passes a succession of ever changing effects of light and shadow. The view up this steep-sided channel in the mountain side, with its parched ledges, and its naked slopes of débris contrasting with the luxuriance of the hotel garden below, will be as striking in its way as the broad panorama of the lake in the other direction. A well-planned house built on this site cannot fail of being an attractive and refreshing resting-place.

West of the hotel site the mountain wall approaches the shore more and more closely, until there is no more than room for the one county road and the railroad, and then it again retreats so as to leave a narrow strip of usable land along the highway. Throughout this mile and a half of the Company's property no other road than the county road will be required, for when villa lots are sold here, they will all front upon it necessarily.

Returning now and going east from the central or bathing-beach section, we come first to a somewhat elevated yet sufficiently smooth region having a slightly irregular shore line, in front of which stands a solitary bare rock called Black Rock. Several small and crumbling buttes rise above the general level of this section, and the main body of it is considerably higher than any other part of the habitable area between the lake and the mountain. This is obviously the best site for a handsome colony of summer villas. Accordingly the plan shows a broad avenue sweeping nearly at one level around this swell of upland, and connecting with the county road at both ends. Another avenue will bisect the curve of the first named, and will lead straight down the slope to the railroad station at the water's edge. This arrangement will provide many fine house sites commanding good views; it will ensure a handsome general effect when the houses shall be built; and it will secure this effect with no sacrifice of convenience.

Further east again, your Company's property increases rapidly in breadth, at the same time becoming rather low, flat, and monotonous. The mountain has here begun its retreat towards the south, and the lake-shore has begun its long sweep towards the northeast. At one point your land extends more than three fourths of a mile back from the lake. Here also the railroad leaves the shore, and strikes off across the plain for Salt Lake City.

This is a site for a considerable town, if people shall ever flock to the lake-side in such numbers as to demand a town; and the plan shows a system of streets arranged as concentric half-circles with their ends upon the lake-shore. Every main street leads by a tempting curve to the lake front; that is, to the prospect and the breeze which will ever be the pleasures of the possible town.

The foregoing are the principal considerations governing the arrangement of my plan for the proposed development of the several natural divisions of the property at Garfield, namely, the eastern town section, the Black Rock villa section, the bathing-beach section, the Hotel, and the western strip of shore.

The survey upon which the plan was based, together with a survey of the proposed new railroad location, was made in the summer by the Division Engineer's office. The new plan was then drawn out in his office from my directions, then sent to me and slightly altered, then submitted to you and returned to Salt Lake, where I understand it may soon be necessary to make copies for filing.

Nothing came of this project, for Mr. Adams, soon after the date of this report, retired from the presidency of the Union Pacific Railroad Co.

THE YARD OF HARVARD COLLEGE. In 1887 Charles was

employed to design some new plantations of shrubs for the College Yard at Cambridge, and this work went on slowly for three years; but Charles was not satisfied with the results obtained, although the aspect of the grounds and buildings was decidedly improved. The soil was thin, the beds for shrubs were not thoroughly prepared for lack of money to spend in that way, large trees standing near sent their roots quickly through the beds, and the growing shrubs were not kept in shape by competent pruning, or properly fed with fresh soil and manure. A more serious difficulty, in Charles's view, was the lack of a general plan for roads and building-sites on the twenty-two acres of ground lying between the bounding streets. He expressed his views in the following letter to the Treasurer of Harvard College on December 31, 1890.

In sending you this bill, let me report that I am ignorant as to how much of the $500 appropriation remains. I suppose it is a large part, for the Arboretum could supply but few shrubs and little was done. Eveleth [the foreman], I think, was puzzled to know how to draw a line between his regular and my special work. If in the new year I am to be allowed $500 plus what remains from this year, what are your desires as to its expenditure?

You are, I think, aware of my hope that the Corporation may adopt some fundamental scheme for the development of the Cambridge property. Shapes and areas of buildings cannot be foreseen, but main lines of roads and sites can be established; and no fine general effect can be reached unless they are. This permitting donors of buildings and gates to choose their sites is fatal to general effect. Outside the quadrangle the Yard is already a jumble of badly placed buildings and roads which are first formal and then natural. To contrive a practicable scheme which might, if it were adhered to, bring some sort of order and organization into the scene will be difficult; but if the Corporation really saw the value of order and fine general effect, they would not hesitate about attempting to contrive one.

As respects planting, you know I think the outer edges of the Yard should be much more richly planted, and that with many evergreens of moderate size and many spring blooming and autumn coloring shrubs. I can do something in this line if I may go beyond the Arboretum for plants; but I should still better like to see first the adoption of some fixed conception or skeleton-plan of the Yard of the future. Planting ought to be the decoration of some systematic fundamental arrangement: not a helter-skelter addition to no arrangement at all.

PERFECTING AN OLD CEMETERY. — The following letter is practically a report made to a member of the corporation of the Springfield cemetery on the best means of enhancing the beauty of the grounds, and keeping them appropriately beautiful, when the use of the cemetery as a burial place should come almost to an end through the sale of all the land suitable for interments. The Springfield, Mass., cemetery was among the earliest of the American garden cemeteries, and had at the beginning a very diversified surface and many fine forest trees. The advice given was conservative; yet it outlined a distinct policy for the future which would in time produce valuable results.

27 June, '91.

At your request I have studied the condition and circumstances of your Springfield Cemetery, and I now beg to report briefly as follows: —

Your ground was originally a steep-sided and branching hollow drained by several brooklets and shaded by fine forest trees. Year by year the slopes have been terraced and sold as lots; until there is now but little ground belonging to the corporation, except such as is either too wet or too steep for burial purposes. Again, such salable land as still remains in your hands is all easily accessible by existing roads, so that there is no need of planning any new arrangements on this account. In other words, the roads within the Cemetery are as numerous as they need ever be. They are not all laid on the best possible lines; but to alter their few bad lines is now impracticable because of the graves in the adjacent private lots.

After careful study I have reached the conclusion that the amount of alteration which it is still possible for you to make for the sake of improvement is very small. Most of your land is so completely occupied that you are tied down hand

and foot ; while in those few parts where you seem, at first sight, to be free to act, you are in fact almost as closely hampered by surrounding conditions.

Thus the result of my study is largely negative. I do not find that there is much for you to do. The occupied parts of your land might certainly be better kept and planted. There is great need, it seems to me, of more low shrubbery, particularly in the level upland parts where the monuments stand close together, and tend to remind one of a stone-cutter's yard. Many shady spots, also, where grass fails, might better be clothed with Moneywort or Periwinkle, or even with masses of shade-loving bushes, such as Indian Currant, Flowering Raspberry, and the like. Shrubs used intelligently will add variety and interest. Among the monuments only nice sorts should appear ; but on some of the steep banks a wide variety of wilder plants might advantageously be used. Much work of this sort will soon suggest itself to an intelligent superintendent, and to him I must leave it.

You will perceive that I have concluded that most of your work is to be the perfecting of the Cemetery on its present lines. In this I think you should be controlled in great measure by the evident fact that the resort to the Cemetery is hereafter to be chiefly for its quiet and peacefulness. Your new parks will draw away the mere holiday-makers. You should, I think, do all that may be possible to emphasize the retired and restful character of the place. To this end you will avoid all appearance of endeavoring to make a show. To the same end I would, if I were you, obtain and preserve in the hollows the greatest possible extent of uninterrupted turf. These hollows are too wet for graves. You have in them your one golden opportunity for the development of an effective bit of scenery of the peaceful sort. I strongly advise you not to fill these hollow glades for the purpose of providing lots. I would put in new lots in any and all of the other available places, before I would permit a single lot within the valleys. Indeed, I hope they may never be permitted there. The valleys should be gently graded at their sides. To relieve the existing likeness to railroad banks, shrubbery should be scattered along the brink of the hollow

slopes, and the moist levels of the bottoms should be preserved as rich and unbroken sheets of greensward. If this is
done, the Cemetery will possess a central feature of remarkable though quieting interest and influence, — a bit of scenery
upon the beauty of which every entering visitor will look with
pleasure and relief.

The plan is an endeavor to indicate the form and character
of these reserved lands in the hollows. Placing it over the
plan of the Cemetery as it exists, every alteration that I propose will appear at a glance.

It will appear that I would do away with the cross-paths
and the beds which destroy the unity of the open grass near
the gate. For the same reason I would shift the main road,
and I would break the stiff line of elms, where they, as I
think, obscure the effectiveness of the open valley.

Similarly I would abolish the rigmarole of paths near the
fountain basin. I would abandon the practice of spotting
garden beds about the grass, and I would rely for pleasing
effect upon the simple openness of the green framed by
shrubbery on the brinks and the trees hanging from the
banks above. I am convinced that this would be the happiest possible treatment of these valleys, and I hope to convince you of the same.

Near Pine Street the plan shows a straightening of the
boundary road and the resulting removal of a projecting knoll
which is now found there. Also the parking of a smaller
and a larger triangle in this neighborhood is shown on the
plan, both spots being at present unoccupied lands. These
triangles I would put into grass, with the addition of some
such arrangement of trees and shrubs as I have indicated.

At the main gate I would certainly set the road into the
hill as was suggested when I was with you on the ground,
and I would reserve a large part of the wooded bank at this
point. The proposed reserved lands are colored green on the
plan. I will only add that I would rather see every other
inch of your land sold in lots than see one foot of these
reserved areas given up to private occupation. Upon their
preservation rests the effect of the Cemetery as a whole.

You will perhaps be surprised that I propose nothing more

radical or revolutionary. I can only reply that I find the Cemetery in very fair condition indeed, and endowed by Nature with an unusually interesting shape and character. Most of it is occupied. The institution approaches the limits of its growth. The people who visit it are henceforth to be chiefly of the serious-minded sort. Moreover a Cemetery is a serious place, and ought to express and awaken serious rather than frivolous emotion. For these reasons I think your course should be that which I have tried to indicate.

Lastly, let me say that after my study I find that you stand much more in need of a good superintendent than of any plans or advice from me or any architect. If I can help you at all, I think it must be through discussion and consultation with your superintendent. This is often the case upon gentlemen's private places. It is distinctly your case.

17 Oct. '91.

SELECTING A SITE FOR A COLLEGE OR ACADEMY. — MY DEAR SIR, — As you know, I am filled with enthusiasm over your comprehensive scheme for the Academy and its friends. The idea is so excellent, and its future is so far-reaching, that we ought to go slowly and carefully at the beginning, perfecting our notions of what we want to attain before we act.

What would be the ideal situation and appearance of a New Church college and its attendant colony, in the climate and country of the neighborhood of Philadelphia? Without citing reasons, I think I may safely summarize an answer as follows : —

The situation should be high enough to be airy in summer without being bleak in winter. The land should slope sufficiently to drain easily, but not so much as to incommode travel over it, and cause the necessary ways to gash the hillsides. The general slope should tend southward rather than northward. The land should possess, if possible, some unity of topographic character. It should not be a jumble of unrelated slopes and shapes. It should possess some pleasing central feature, such as a sheet of water, a stream, or a valley, so that an effect of composition may be attainable. Its boundaries should be scientific, — that is, they should conform

to the topography in such a way as will tend to enhance the
effect of unity.   If woods or fine trees assist in framing and
adorning the central scene, so much the better.

The college proper should stand upon nearly level land in
a situation accessible from all parts of the colony.   The
buildings should be low rather than high, sober and quiet in
design, of good proportions rather than rich in ornament;
and they should be arranged somewhat formally, and so as to
relate themselves to the principal or administration building
in pleasing composition..   The tributary colony of dwellings
should in turn bear a similar relation to the college as its
centre and the reason of its being.   On favorable ground and
with careful planning a most pleasing and effective result
could be attained; and I believe that such a well-composed
result is much more worth trying for than is anything which
can be reached by sheer elaboration of design and ornament
in handsome but ill-related buildings.

With this ideal in mind, let us look at the lands which I
visited with you last week.   [The letter describes tract No.
1, and rejects it on the grounds that the sloping parts are too
steep for building purposes, the plateau too bleak, and the
whole lacking in unity; and then rejects tract No. 2 also,
for the reason that it " falls generally towards the northeast,"
although suitable in other respects.]

I think I must urge you to look farther before purchasing.
I have at last obtained a copy of the U. S. Geological survey
of your region, and I send you with this a tracing of a part
of the same, showing roads in black, streams in blue, and 20-
feet contours in red.   I can see upon this sheet several parcels of land which have a promising appearance, and perhaps
you will like to have a look at the few I have marked.   They
may indeed all prove valueless or unobtainable, yet I would
investigate them if I were you.   It will be well worth while
to give plenty of time to your undertaking at this early stage,
even if we revert in the end to either tract 1 or tract 2!

24 May, '92.

A SUBURBAN GARDEN. — MY DEAR MRS. ——, I am happy to hear that the general arrangement about your house is a success in your eyes. You can bring the details of the garden into harmony with your wishes at any time. The ground-work is the fundamental and important thing.

Referring to my letter-book, I find that I suggested holly-hocks and the like plants along the wall of the terrace, and a long strip of mixed perennials around the circuit of the outer part of the garden. In the sunk garden we had intricate beds and box edging. It is true the edging must be defended from the adjacent grass, but just as the grass edges of the walks have to be tended and trimmed, so the grass edge next the box can be. It is only a question of care. Box can be set now, and can be had in good form from Hooper Bros., West Chester, Pa., for 20 cents a yard.

As to the contents of the trefoils, if you will be so venture-some as to attempt something a little different from the usual florist's beds, I think you can have something very pleasing, — particularly if you will establish the reserve garden you write of, from which you can bring out at any time whatever you please to decorate your terrace and sunk panel.

The sunk panel with its trefoil beds is to be looked down upon as a rule, and the trefoils should be filled with this in mind. One lobe of a trefoil might for example be filled with blue Campanula carpatica, surrounded by yellow Œno-thera missouriensis: another with Lobelia fulgens growing up through Tussilago variegata: another with Ajuga dotted with Sedum spectabile. This sort of thing can be arranged for you, and the plants grown for you, by any florist who will take the trouble to be a little original and enterprising. It is not so easy as the ordinary bedding with tender gera-niums; but it is vastly more interesting. I think you will have to work gradually. It is impossible to get just the right thing at once.

AN OHIO TOWNSHIP PARK. — The park at Youngstown, Ohio, was thus described by Charles in a note to his wife of May 11, 1891, on the occasion of his first visit: "A fine river glen with numerous side ravines and some cliffs, — a really good reservation, and the work of a single energetic young lawyer, an enthusiast, — and he has done a fine thing." The following letter was addressed to the young lawyer : —

26 May, '91.

I think I can answer your specific question in a few words.

For appearance it is best to keep the roadways fairly low. To make them causeways is ugly, but is sometimes necessary on account of wet land. In ordinary situations I suppose you will remove the top-soil at any rate. This will drop the road a little, and the shaping which will follow will generally bring the crown or centre about on a level with the un- 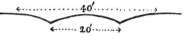 disturbed surfaces at each side.

Here is a usual method. Strip off top-soil forty feet wide. If the sub-soil found in the ten-foot side strips is good enough material for road-surfacing, scrape it up to raise the roadway to the original surface grade. Then loam the side strips with some of the top-soil first removed.

In case of side-hill work, one side strip may well become a grass gutter, or if the wash is very great, a stone gutter; while the other side strip becomes the retaining bank, thus:

For appearance it is very desirable to have this re- taining bank on the down side; 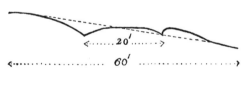 but on very steep side-hills it is of course expensive to get much of it. When the slope is thus abrupt, however, a fence will be required for safety, and this will satisfy appearances.

This beautiful park is a winding gorge, with bluffs on each side which vary from sixty to more than a hundred feet in height. A rapid stream flows through it; and within the park area several tributaries enter this stream through deep wooded ravines. Cascades adorn both the main stream and its tributaries. In the valley are two small lakes, — ponds they would be called in New England, — one having a water surface of about forty-three acres, the other of about twenty-

six.   It was desirable to have a drive on each side of the
gorge its full length, — about two miles and a quarter in a
straight line, — and these drives, because of the winding of the
gorge, would be four miles long on one side, and five miles on
the other.   Around the smaller lake the bluffs were so steep
that the drives were apparently forced on to the heights.   At
the head of this lake, on the more abrupt side, the valley suddenly rose about twenty feet above the water, pushed back the
bluffs, and formed a level amphitheatrical meadow of about
five acres girt by wooded hills.   The entrance from the water-
side was by a fine grove upon the terrace ; and here between
the stream and the meadow was placed a pavilion with shaded
pleasure grounds adjoining.   Access to these grounds by boat
and walks was easy ; but to reach them by driveways, without leaving permanent scars on picturesque and lovely scenes,
seemed at first next to impossible.   The above description is
taken from a letter written January 8, 1902, by Mr. Volney
Rogers, the young lawyer mentioned above.

The letter proceeds : " This was one question.   The other
was, how to get a water drive along a portion of the smaller
lake.   There was an opportunity here to keep entirely on the
bluffs, and bridge a deep ravine . . . but then the visitor
would not reach the shore of the lake at any point by driveway, which all agreed was very desirable.   Mr. Eliot worked
out a plan that accomplished the desired result by the use of
two long retaining-walls. . . . This access to the lake accomplished, the shore of the lake was followed quite a distance ;
and then the original, higher location of the driveway was
reached by the ' Cascade Ravine,' a ravine unexcelled in
natural attractions in any park the writer has ever visited.
This solution of the lake-side problem led to the solution of
the other problem.   In the summer of 1891, a topographical
survey and contour map were made of the entire park area ;
and with this map in his hands Mr. Eliot was asked to indicate the best way to carry a driveway to the amphitheatre.
The next day Mr. Eliot came to me with the result of his
study.   He proposed to continue his lake-shore drive from
the point where it reached Cascade Ravine up the main valley
until farther progress in that direction was cut off by a cliff.
He was now on the side of the stream opposite the amphitheatre and some distance above.   Here he crossed the main
stream with a bridge, returned on the opposite bank of that
stream to the foot of the hill near the amphitheatre, and
passed along the foot of this hill to the site of the proposed
pavilion.   A drive was also planned from the bridge just

THE YOUNGSTOWN GORGE—THE DRIVE ALONG THE SMALLER LAKE

mentioned, after crossing the stream, up the main valley and connecting with the principal drive on that side. A new drive through the valley was thus devised, in addition to those on the bluffs.

" These drives are now all constructed ; and those who traverse them do not know to whom they are indebted for the pleasure the drives afford. The fact is that Charles Eliot is entitled to the credit above given."

A letter which Charles sent a year later to the Youngstown Park Commissioners after one of his visits to the Gorge closes thus : " Your Gorge is one of the finest park scenes of America, and deserves most careful handling ; and all who work in or for it have my very best wishes."

A SEASIDE VILLAGE.

1 March, 1893.

To the Chairman of the Selectmen, and the Town Forester, Nahant.

Gentlemen, — As requested by you, I submit the following brief notes on your township as it appears to a professional designer of the arrangement of land for human purposes.

Nahant is a rock-bound and sea-girt island, about two miles long from east to west, half a mile wide from north to south, and connected with the mainland by a narrow causeway beach two miles in length. The surface of the island is irregular, the coast line is broken and picturesque, the views over the ocean and the adjacent bays are grand or beautiful according to the changeful moods of sky and sea. As nature and the early settlers left it, the place possessed a special charm for modern city-bred men, a few of whom built villas on the island as many as sixty years ago. Even to-day, when almost every part of the peninsula is dotted with buildings, something of the old charm remains ; for it is fortunately impossible to mar the sky and the sea. Land surfaces, however, are very easily made ugly, and the surface of Nahant has not escaped. Indeed, if regard is had to its rare opportunities and possibilities, few places so disappoint, discourage, and alarm careful students of my profession as does the Nahant of to-day.

To put the case very briefly, it is true that while that beauty of the wild island, which first led to Nahant such men as Messrs. Cary, Robbins, and Eliot of Boston, has been gradually destroyed by the building up of the place, no attempt has been made to secure for the township that good general arrangement, adapted to the topography and the circumstances, which is the foundation of permanent beauty and convenience in populous places. The general plan of the highways of Nahant is almost as bad as it could possibly be. The roads, except the main Nahant Road, have been laid out upon the division lines of estates; they generally end abruptly at the shore; and their straight, parallel, and rectangular courses are peculiarly ill-fitted to the varying forms of the island's surface. Moreover, most of the roads have been made very narrow — so narrow that when the increasing population has demanded sidewalks it has been necessary to make them of diminutive width, and to edge them with granite curbstones like those of city streets. Within these pinched and ill-placed public ways there is no room for those green spaces and those banks of wild Roses which would add so much to the attractiveness of the town. Moreover, these existing ways are really worse than no provision for the development of a closely built town in a handsome way. That the township must become a closely built place is admitted by all; and the question is, shall the new Nahant be an attractive and beautiful place of its kind, where intelligent people will desire to live and real estate will possess high values, or shall the town be allowed to drift into that gradual loss of attractiveness and consequent diminution of values to which its present general arrangement inevitably consigns it? For Nahant to permit her shore front to be owned by private persons and her interior ways to remain the ugly things they are is simply to bind herself hand and foot — it is to commit township suicide.

I have often been asked to perform that ineffectual act called shutting the door after the horse has been stolen; but never have I encountered a more pronounced case of this sort than that to which you invited me last summer. The road over the Long Beach, to which you called my particular attention, is not built upon the beautiful curve of the beach, but upon non-conforming and therefore ugly lines of its own.

Moreover, it is accompanied by a hideous procession of telegraph, telephone, and electric-light poles and wires.   No
bordering thickets of dwarf bushes and clambering vines can
do away with the ugliness which has been inflicted on this
road.   Similarly no decorative planting in the few corners of
the Nahant streets which are not gravel can hide the obvious
fact that the streets are wrongly placed and wrongly shaped.
Nahant is rich and strong, and whatever her voters will to do
can be done.   The town's case seems to me to call for radical treatment.   It is for the voters to determine whether the
painful but beneficial operation shall be performed now, when
it will hurt and cost comparatively little, or later, when it
must hurt and cost much.   As palliatives for the present condition of things, I recommend : —

1st. The burial of the wires on the Long Beach, the correction of the road lines there, and the planting of a strip
along each side of the road with dwarf bushes.

2d. The acquisition by the town of outlying points like
Castle Rock, of beaches, and of sea front generally, so far as
may be possible.

3d. The opening of shore roads to connect the outer ends
of the present streets wherever and whenever such action is
possible.

CHAPTER XVII

ADEQUATE OPEN SPACES FOR URBAN POPULATIONS, AND PUBLIC OWNERSHIP OF COAST SCENERY

> Meantime there is one duty obvious to us all: it is that we should set ourselves to guard the natural beauty of the earth: we ought to look upon it as a crime, an injury to our fellows, only excusable because of ignorance, to mar that natural beauty which is the property of all men. — MORRIS.

CHARLES had not been in practice two years before he began to study the problem of securing for American towns and cities an adequate number of public squares, gardens, and parks. He had seen in Europe how liberal a provision of this sort was there made for the health and enjoyment of urban populations; and he had learnt that the provision of public grounds made by American towns and cities was comparatively scanty. To demonstrate this neglect of one of the most important public interests was his first contribution to the discussion of the subject. The following article, which appeared in "Garden and Forest" in October, 1888, was written in September of that year, when Charles had been in practice only twenty months: —

PARKS AND SQUARES OF UNITED STATES CITIES.

The nineteenth volume of the Final Reports of the Census of 1880, only lately distributed, completes the "Statistics of the Cities of the United States," and enables us to view the condition of 180 cities of the Union in respect to those necessities of modern town life — public parks and squares.

Two hundred and ten cities are enumerated. Of these thirty make no report concerning their public spaces, and may perhaps be presumed to own none, while forty state outright that they possess no public grounds whatever. Some surprisingly large towns appear in this latter class; for instance, Paterson, New Jersey (population, 51,000), Scranton, Pennsylvania (46,000), Wilmington, Delaware (42,500), Wheeling,

West Virginia (31,000), Trenton, New Jersey (30,000), and many smaller but bustling places like Fort Wayne, Indiana, Poughkeepsie, New York, and Topeka, Kansas. Since the Census year, several of these forty cities have taken steps to provide themselves with public spaces of one sort or another.

Turning now to the 140 cities which report one or more public grounds, we notice first the universal abuse of the word park. It is applied to every sort of public space, from the minutest grass-plot to the race-track or the fair-ground. The strict meaning of the word is completely lost. Hereafter we shall have to speak of country parks when we wish to designate those public lands which the word park alone ought by rights to describe — namely, "lands intended and appropriated for the recreation of the people by means of their rural, sylvan, and natural scenery and character."

Country parks are sometimes of small area, as when some striking glen, or river-bank, or cañon is preserved in its natural state (would this were oftener done!) — but generally an area of at least fifty or one hundred acres is required to provide a natural aspect. Smaller spaces can satisfy many of the desires of the crowded city people — can supply fresh air and ample play-room, and shade of trees, and brightness of grass and flowers — but the occasionally so pressing want of that quiet and peculiar refreshment which comes from contemplation of scenery — the want which the rich satisfy by fleeing from town at certain seasons, but which the poor (who are trespassers in the country) can seldom fill — is only to be met by the country park. If a few of the twenty-six cities, which reported themselves in 1880 as possessed of large tracts of land, have put these lands to uses for which small areas would have served as well or better — if they have given them over to decorative gardening, to statuary and buildings, or to other town-like things — they have made (unless the circumstances are peculiar) an extravagant mistake. For large open spaces close to cities are excessively costly, and one such interferes with traffic in far greater degree than do many small areas, so that no town can properly afford to own a large tract, unless for the express purpose of providing refreshing natural scenery.

The accompanying table of the twenty-six cities which reported park lands of fifty acres and upwards presents curious
contrasts.   The first column gives the number of inhabitants
per acre of park, which is the basis of the order of the names,
the other columns the population and the park acreage : —

18	Macon	13,000	720
22	Council Bluffs	18,000	600 + 104 + 90
166	Detroit	116,500	700
172	St. Paul	41,500	240
175	New Britain	13,000	74
176	St. Louis	350,500	1,372 + 276 + 180 + 158
182	Binghamton	17,500	96
222	San Francisco	234,000	1,050
280	Bridgeport	28,000	50 + 50
281	Chicago	503,500	593 + 372 + 250 + 200 + 185 + 180
309	Philadelphia	847,000	2,740
310	Baltimore	232,500	693 + 56
410	San Antonio	20,500	50
417	Omaha	30,500	73
442	Buffalo	155,000	350
508	New Orleans	216,000	250 + 175
680	Portland, Me.	34,000	50
685	Cincinnati	255,000	206 + 164
833	Indianapolis	75,000	90
907	Fall River	49,000	54
940	Allegheny	79,000	84
1019	Providence	105,000	103
1122	Brooklyn	567,000	505
1213	Albany	91,000	75
1400	New York	1,206,500	862
3424	Boston	363,000	106

Little Macon's large park was the gift of the State.   It is
mostly in large forest trees.   Boston, at the other end of the
list, boasts uncommonly attractive suburbs, which have served
some of the purposes of a park ; but she has lately begun
work upon a real park of more than 600 acres.

Of small public grounds there appears to be an equally
various provision.   In New England many cities possess the
remains of old town commons — for instance, Nashua (13,000)
has forty acres in North and South Commons, and Newburyport (13,500) has the same ; while Boston, Salem, Lynn, and
other places own larger or smaller areas of like origin.

At the founding of Philadelphia, five public squares of about six acres each were carefully reserved ; but the example of the founders has been woefully forgotten by the builders of the great city of to-day. Savannah has done better, for she has continued the city plan devised by her first colonists, and in 1880, with a population of 31,000, she had thirty acres in twenty-three public spaces, besides a ten-acre park and a twenty-acre parade-ground. About the worst case reported is that of Pittsburg, a city of 156,000 inhabitants, and yet possessed of less than one and one third public acres — a contrast to Buffalo (population, 155,000), which reported, in addition to the Park, fifty-six acres in the Parade, thirty-two acres in the Front, and forty-two acres in eight pieces. Compare also the following : —

Troy, New York (57,000), one acre. Richmond (64,000), sixty-five acres in five pieces.

Kansas City (56,000), two acres. Akron, Ohio (16,500), twenty-five acres in seven pieces.

Auburn, New York (22,000), one acre. Salt Lake (21,000), forty acres in four pieces.

And the remarkable case of Lawrence, Kansas (8,500), seventy-three acres in five pieces.

We have no fixed rule for the proper ratio to population of the acreage or number of public squares ; but it is safe to say that while a few of our cities are well provided for, a majority are still very badly off. New York is now tearing down buildings to make room for public gardens. Philadelphia, also, is endeavoring to make up for her past carelessness. Smaller places should secure the necessary lands before the cost becomes intolerable.

A word in conclusion as to the laying out of public squares and gardens. The problem is wholly distinct from that of the country park. Here and there, to be sure, is found a small public ground of such strongly marked shape and character that it by right rules its surroundings, whatever they may be, — as the Back Bay Fens in Boston call a halt to the city structures, — but small grounds in general are necessarily dominated by the formal lines of the streets and buildings which enclose them, and they must generally be shaped to a correspondingly formal plan. Every hope of a fine general effect hangs on the securing of a good general plan. The famous Public Garden of Boston, recently criticised in this paper, fails of fine general effect because its framework or ground plan was never thought out as a whole — as a design. The handsome and costly gardening which is to be seen there, the gorgeous beds, and the fine specimen plants, cannot be fittingly displayed — can only be promiscuously scattered as they are — so long as the ground plan of the garden remains the mongrel thing it is.

A little more than a year later, after his usual summer's visit to the coast of Maine, he wrote the following description of the natural features of that beautiful coast, and of its preëminent merits as a summer resort ; but he gave one third of the paper to a statement of the way in which the inroad of humanity is destroying, or rendering inaccessible to the public, much of the wild beauty of the coast, and to the suggestion of means of averting such a calamity, or at least of preserving from degradation some of the finest scenery. The suggested means are local associations, and action by the Commonwealth. Neither of these means has been (1901) adopted in Maine, but Massachusetts has adopted both.

THE COAST OF MAINE.

From Cape Cod, Massachusetts, to Cape Sable, Nova Scotia, the broad entrance of the Gulf of Maine is two hundred miles wide, and it is one hundred miles from each of these capes to the corresponding ends of the coast of Maine at Kittery and Quoddy. Thus Maine squarely faces the wide opening between the capes, while to the east and west, beyond her limits, stretch two great offshoots of the gulf, the bays of Fundy and of Massachusetts. The latter and lesser bay presents a south shore built mostly of sands and gravels in beaches and bluffs, and a north shore of bold and enduring rocks, both already overgrown with seaside hotels and cottages. The Bay of Fundy, on the other hand, is little resorted to for pleasure. Its shores in many parts are grandly high and bold ; but its waters are moved by such rushing tides, and its coasts are so frequently wrapt in cold fogs, that it will doubtless remain comparatively an unfrequented region.

Along the coast of Maine, stretched for two hundred miles from bay to bay, scenery and climate change from the Massachusetts to the Fundy type. At Boston the average temperature of July is 70°; at Eastport, at the farther end of Maine, it is 61°. No such coolness is to be found along the thousand miles of monotonous sand beach which front the Atlantic south of the Gulf of Maine; and though the coolness of the waters of the gulf precludes most persons from sea-bathing, this freshness of the air will always be an irresistible attraction to many thousands of dwellers in hot cities. Again, in contrast with the southern sea-beaches, the scenery of the Maine coast is exceedingly interesting and refreshing. The mere map of it is most attractive. Beginning at Piscataqua River, a deep estuary whose swift tides flow through an archipelago of rocks and small islands, the shore is at first made up of low ledges forming ragged points, connected by sand or pebble beaches, where farmers gather rock-weed after storms. Seaward lies a group of dangerous rocks, the Isles of Shoals. Beyond the tortuous outlet of York River and the Short and Long Sands of York, Cape Neddick and Bald Head lift high rocks toward the sea, and behind them rises Agamenticus Hill, a conspicuous blue landmark sometimes visible from Cape Ann in Massachusetts. Low and sandy coasts succeed, fronting the old towns of Wells and Kennebunk. Cape Porpoise follows, a confused mass of rocky islets, salt marshes, and tidal flats; then more long and short beaches, a lagoon called Biddeford Pool, the mouth of Saco River, barred by its washings from the White Hills, more beaches, and so to Cape Elizabeth, a broad wedge of rock pushed out to sea as if to mark the entrance to the land-locked harbor of Portland.

Thus far the coast is sufficiently rich in varied scenery — in shores now high, now low, now wooded and now bare, now gentle and now rough; first thrust seaward in rocky capes, then swept inland in curving beaches, and now and again broken by the outlets of small rivers. Cape Elizabeth ends this scenery, and introduces the voyager to a type still more intricate, picturesque, and distinctive. Casco Bay, with its many branches running inland and its peninsulas and islands stretching seaward, is the first of a succession of bays, " thor-

oughfares," and " reaches," which line the coast almost all the
rest of the way to Quoddy.   The ragged edge of the mainland
becomes lost behind a maze of rock-bound islands, and appears but seldom where the surf can strike it.   The salt water
penetrates in deep and narrow channels into the very woods,
ebbs and flows in hundreds of frequented and unfrequented
harbors, and enters into countless hidden nooks, coves, and
narrows.   Sand beaches become rare, and great and small
" sea walls " of worn stones or pebbles take their place.
Islands, islets, and ledges, both dry and sunken, are strewn
on every hand.   The tides flow among them with increasing
force, and the fog wraps them from sight more and more frequently as the Bay of Fundy is approached.   Great cliffs are
rare until Grand Manan is reached, and high hills come down
to the sea only by Penobscot Bay and at Mt. Desert; but,
on the other hand, the variety of lesser topographic forms is
very great.   In Casco Bay, for instance, the rocks trend northeast and southwest, and all the crowded islands run out into
reefs in these directions.   Penobscot Bay presents wide
stretches of open water divided by well-massed islands, but
still preserves a fine breadth of effect; and these islands differ
greatly in form and character, according as they are built of
hard and glaciated granite or of altered stratified rocks.   The
border bay of Passamaquoddy is distinguished by fine headlands, which terminate in islands, generally lower than the
heads.   In like manner the sounds and fiord-like rivers differ
much from each other.   For instance, the Kennebec River is
extremely narrow, and many bold knobs of rock turn it this
way and that; but the neighboring Sheepscot is fully three
miles broad at its mouth, and this noble width contracts but
slowly; while the Penobscot above the Narrows takes on such
a gentle appearance as to be hardly recognizable as a river of
eastern Maine, the general aspect of this part of the coast
being distinctly wild and untamable.

Doubtless the raggedness of the rocky shore is the first
cause of the almost forbidding aspect of the region, but the
changed character of the sea-coast woods is a second cause.
Beyond Cape Elizabeth, if capes and islands are wooded at
all, it is with the dark, stiff cresting of Spruce, Fir, or Pine,

fringed perhaps with Birch and Mountain Ash. Near Kittery fine Elms and even Hickories may be seen on the open shore, but there is a gradual dying out of many familiar species as the coast is traversed eastward. Thus Holly and Inkberry, together with Prickly Ash, Flowering Dogwood, and Sassafras, are not seen near the sea north of Massachusetts Bay. White Cedar, after following the coast all the way from the Gulf of Mexico, dies out near Kittery. York River is said to see the last Buttonwoods, Saco River the last Chestnuts, and the Kennebec the last Tupelos and Hickories. Conversely, this coast has its many forerunners of the flora of the far north. While the White Pine is met with all alongshore north of New Jersey, the Red Pine first appears by Massachusetts Bay and the Gray Pine by Mt. Desert. The Arbor Vitæ is first met with near the Kennebec. The Balsam Fir and the Black and White Spruces show themselves on no coasts south of Cape Ann, and do not abound until Cape Elizabeth is passed. It is the blackness of these dwarf coniferous woods which, with the desolation of the surf-beaten ledges and the frequent coming of the fog, impresses the traveller with the fact that this is a really wild and sub-arctic shore, where strange red-men's names for islands, capes, and rivers — names such as Medomak, Muscongus, Pemaquid, Megunticook, Eggemoggin, Moosabec, and Schoodic — seem altogether fitting.

The human story of the coast of Maine is almost as picturesque and varied as its scenery. This coast was first frequented by stray French fishing vessels, and first scientifically explored by Samuel de Champlain, whose narrative of his adventures is still delightful reading. Fruitless attempts at settlement followed, led by French knights at Saint Croix, by English cavaliers at Sagadahoc, and by French Jesuits at Mt. Desert; all of them years in advance of the English Colony of New Plymouth. Then followed a long period of fishing and fur trading, during which Maine belonged to neither New France nor New England, and a genuine border warfare was the result. Two rival Frenchmen also fought and besieged each other in truly feudal fashion at Penobscot and Saint John. Again, while the long French and Indian

wars lasted, this coast saw more fighting. The older settlements west of Cape Elizabeth were sacked several times, and
even the English stronghold at Pemaquid was captured; but
the forest allies of the French Baron Saint Castin were beaten
in the end.   The numerous French names for points on the
eastern coast bear witness to the long French occupation; as
for instance Grand and Petit Manan, Bois Bubert, Monts
Déserts and Isle au Hault, and Burnt Coat, apparently English, but really a mistranslation of the French Côte Brulé.

No Englishmen settled beyond Penobscot until after the
capture of Quebec; and when they did, they, as Yankees, had
to take part in still more fighting in the wars of the Revolution and of 1812.   The settlers first fished and hunted, then
cut hay on the salt marshes and timber in the great woods,
and in later years took to ship-building, and later still to
stone-quarrying and ice-harvesting, and, near Rockland, to
lime-burning.   These works are still the business of the coast.
Even hunting is carried on at certain seasons in the eastern
counties, where deer are still numerous.   All the large Pine
and Spruce of the shore woods have been cut; but Bangor
still sends down Penobscot Bay a fleet of lumber schooners
every time the wind blows from the north; and as for fishing,
fleets of more than two hundred graceful vessels may often
be seen in port together, waiting the end of a storm.

It was about 1860 that what may be called the discovery
of the picturesqueness and the summer-time healthfulness of
the coast of Maine took place.   Only the beaches of the
western quarter of the shore were at first occupied by hotels;
but when the poor hamlet of Bar Harbor leaped into fame
through the resort to it of a few well-known landscape painters, it became evident that the whole coast was destined to
be a much frequented summer resort.   At present, York,
Kennebunkport, Biddeford Pool, and Old Orchard Beach,
together with the Casco Islands, Boothbay, Camden, Mt.
Desert, and Campobello, are a few of the more populous
neighborhoods; but summer hotels are now scattered all
along the shore, and colonies of summer villas of all grades
of costliness occupy many of the more accessible capes and
islands. Thus there are many cottages at York, and the

islands near Portland are fairly covered with cheap structures. Squirrel Island in Boothbay is another nest of small houses, and Bar Harbor is a summer city surrounded by a multitude of very costly and elaborate wooden palaces. The finest parts of the coast are already controlled by land companies and speculators, while the natives' minds are inflamed by the high prices which the once worthless shore lands are now supposed to command.

The spectacle of thousands upon thousands of people able to spend annually several weeks or months of summer in healthful life by the seashore is very American and very pleasant; and the impartial observer can find but two points about it which are in any considerable degree discouraging or dangerous. The lamentable feature of the situation is the small amount of thought and attention given to considerations of appropriateness and beauty by the builders and inhabitants of the summer colonies of the coast. Indifference in these matters works ill results everywhere, but nowhere is lack of taste quite so conspicuous as on the seashore. Both corporations and individuals are guilty on this head. More than one booming land company has hastily divided and sold its rough ledges in rectangular lots, whose lines bear no relation to the forms of the ground, so that houses cannot be well placed. The squalid aspect of the public parts of these settlements, the shabby plank walks, and the unkempt roadways are other causes of reproach. The houses themselves, if cheap, are too often vulgarly ornamented, and if costly, are generally absurdly pretentious. Even the government, which has lately been rebuilding many of the lighthouse-keepers' dwellings, has substituted for the simple, low, and entirely fitting structures of a former generation, a thin-walled and small-chimneyed type of house, such as is common in the suburbs of our cities. One of these perched on a sea cliff is an abomination, and might well have illustrated the mournful remark of a recent writer in "The Atlantic Monthly," who pointed out that American indifference to beauty cannot be caused by the newness of our civilization, for when this was still newer we built both more appropriately and picturesquely than we commonly do now. Again, in the treatment of the ground about their houses, the millionaires of Bar Harbor are quite as apt to err as are the humbler cottagers of Squirrel Island. Smooth lawns, made of imported soil, and kept green only by continual watering, furnish a means of displaying wealth, but they cannot be fittingly united with scenery which is characterized by rough ledges and scrubby woods. On this rough coast level grass will please when it is joined to a house and enclosed by walls. In the open ground it can hardly ever be in keeping. Similarly incongruous are flower beds scattered over rocky and uneven ground, set between the trunks of Pitch Pines, or perched on the tops of whaleback ledges ; and yet such things are common sights at Bar Harbor.

The real danger of the present situation is that this annual flood of humanity, with its permanent structures for shelter, may so completely overflow and occupy the limited stretch of coast which it invades, as to rob it of that flavor of wildness and remoteness which hitherto has hung about it, and which in great measure constitutes its refreshing charm. A surf-beaten headland may be crowned by a lighthouse tower without losing its dignity and impressiveness, but it cannot be dotted with frail cottages without suffering a woeful fall. A lonely fiord shut in by dark woods, where the fog lingers in wreaths, as it comes and goes, loses its charm whenever even one bank is stripped naked, and streets of buildings are substituted for the Spruces and Pines. A few rich men, realizing this danger, have surrounded themselves with considerable tracts of land solely with the intention of preserving the natural aspect; and at least one hotel company, by buying almost the whole of the wild island of Campobello, has saved for the patrons of its houses a large region of unspoiled scenery. The readers of " Garden and Forest " stand in need of no argument to prove the importance to human happiness of that refreshing antidote to city life which fine natural scenery supplies, nor is it necessary to remind them that love of beauty and of art must surely die, if it be cut at its roots by destroying or vulgarizing the beauty of nature. " Men cannot love Art well until they love what she mirrors better," says Mr. Ruskin.

The United States have but this one short stretch of Atlan-

tic sea-coast, where a pleasant summer climate and real picturesqueness of scenery are to be found together.   Can nothing
be done to preserve for the use and enjoyment of the great
unorganized body of the common people some fine parts, at
least, of this seaside wilderness of Maine?   It would seem as
if the mere self-interest of hotel proprietors and land-owners
would have accomplished much more in this direction than it
yet has.   If, for instance, East Point near York, or Dice's
Head at Castine, or Great Head near Bar Harbor should be
fenced off as private property, all the other property-owners of
the neighborhood would have to subtract something from the
value of their estates.   And, conversely, if these or other
like points of vantage, or any of the ancient border forts, were
preserved to public uses by local associations or by the commonwealth, every estate and every form of property in the
neighborhood would gain in value.   Public-spirited men would
doubtless give to such associations rights of way, and even
lands occasionally, and the raising of money for the purchase
of favorite points might not prove to be so difficult as at first
it seems.   The present year should see, all up and down the
shore, the beginning of a movement in the direction here
indicated.   In many parts of the coast it is full time decisive
action was taken ; and if the State of Maine should by suitable
legislation encourage the formation of associations for the
purpose of preserving chosen parts of her coast scenery, she
would not only do herself honor, but would secure for the
future an important element in her material prosperity.

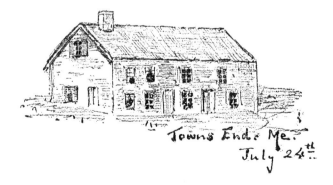

Towns End. Me.
July 24th

CHAPTER XVIII

THE TRUSTEES OF PUBLIC RESERVATIONS

Doch der den Augenblick ergreift
Das ist der rechte Man.
                    GOETHE (*Faust*).

HAVING finished in January, 1890, the series of articles
on Old American Country-seats, Charles wrote on the 22d
of February a letter to the Editor of " Garden and Forest "
which bore the title " The Waverley Oaks," but was really a
plan for preserving fine bits of natural scenery near Boston,
and for obtaining an adequate number of properly distributed
open spaces for the use of the public.

THE WAVERLEY OAKS: A PLAN FOR THEIR PRESERVATION
FOR THE PEOPLE.

Your recent editorial on the Waverley Oaks, with its plea
for the preservation of the charming scene in which they
stand, prompts me to lay before you an imperfect outline of
a scheme by which, not the scene at Waverley only, but
others of the finest bits of natural scenery near Boston, might
perhaps be saved to delight many future generations.

But first a few words on another pressing problem. It
is everywhere agreed that a great and growing population,
such as now inhabits Boston and her widespreading suburbs,
should, for its own best health, provide itself with all possible open spaces in the form of public squares and playgrounds. Boston (including now the various municipalities
which surround her) is far behindhand in this matter. Large
areas outside of the old city are wholly unprovided with public open spaces ; and while the various municipalities which
compose this larger Boston continue to be fearful of spending money for the enjoyment of their neighbors, there can be

little hope for much improvement. The difficulty arising from the conflicting interests and desires of these many towns and cities delayed the construction of a proper sewerage system for the suburbs, until the danger and the scandal which the lack of such a system caused fairly compelled the State to create a metropolitan drainage commission, with power to plan and to build a complete main drainage and to assess the cost thereof upon the towns and cities benefited. It looks now as if the acquisition of a suitable number of well-distributed open spaces must wait for the appointment of a similar commission. Meanwhile the available open ground is being rapidly occupied, and Boston, like New York, may yet be compelled to tear down whole blocks of buildings to provide herself with the needed oases of light and air.

But a crowded population thirsts, occasionally at least, for the sight of something very different from the public garden, square, or ball-field. The railroads and the new electric street railways which radiate from the Hub carry many thousands every pleasant Sunday through the suburbs to the real country, and hundreds out of these thousands make the journey for the sake of the refreshment which an occasional hour or two spent in the country brings to them. Within ten miles of the State House there still remain several bits of scenery which possess uncommon beauty and more than usual refreshing power. Moreover, each of these scenes is, in its way, characteristic of the primitive wilderness of New England, of which, indeed, they are surviving fragments. At Waverley is a steep moraine set with a group of mighty Oaks. At the Upper Falls of Charles River the stream flows darkly between rocky and broken banks, from which hang ranks upon ranks of graceful Hemlocks. These two remarkable scenes have been described in " Garden and Forest ; " and I shall name no others, though several are well known to all lovers of nature near Boston. One is the solemn interior of a wood of tall white Pines — the tree the forefathers blazoned on their flag. Another is a Pine grove on a group of knolls in the bend of a small river, where it first meets the tide and the salt marshes. Still another is a hillside strewn with great boulders, and commanding, by a bowl-shaped hol low of the hills, a distant view of the ocean and its far horizon. At present all these beautiful scenes, excepting such as are included in the Franklin Park and the adjacent Arnold Arboretum, are in private hands; and many of them are in daily danger of utter destruction — some of the finest spots have been destroyed within the last ten years. Most of them lie outside the municipality of Boston proper. They are scattered in different townships or along the border lines, and only an authority which can disregard township limits can properly select and establish the needed reservations.

The end to be held in view in securing reservations of this class is wholly different from that which should guide the State Commission already suggested, and the writer believes this different end might better be attained by an incorporated association, composed of citizens of all the Boston towns, and empowered by the State to hold small and well-distributed parcels of land free of taxes, just as the Public Library holds books and the Art Museum pictures — for the use and enjoyment of the public. If an association of this sort were once established, generous men and women would be ready to buy and give into its keeping some of these fine and strongly characterized works of Nature; just as others buy and give to a museum fine works of art. Indeed, the association might even become embarrassed, as so many museums are, by offerings which might not commend themselves to its directors.

Purely natural scenery supplies an education in the love of beauty, and a means of human enjoyment at least as valuable as that afforded by pictures and casts; and if, as we are taught, feeling for artistic beauty has its roots in feeling for natural beauty, opportunities of beholding natural beauty will certainly be needed and prized by the successive generations which are to throng the area within ten miles of the State House. As Boston's lovers of art united to found the Art Museum, so her lovers of Nature should now rally to preserve for themselves and all the people as many as possible of these scenes of natural beauty which, by great good fortune, still exist near their doors.

On the day this letter was printed (March 5th), Charles set to work to get such an association established, although he was much occupied with plans for private places. His first steps are described in the following letters to Professor Charles S. Sargent, Director of the Arnold Arboretum, and Mr. George C. Mann, President of the Appalachian Mountain Club : —

March 5, 1890.

MY DEAR PROFESSOR SARGENT, — What think you of making an attempt in the direction indicated by my letter to G. & F. ? (I assume you have seen the letter; if not, you will see it soon.)

I am one of the Council of the Appalachian Mountain Club. I propose to try to get ten of the best men in said Club to invite to meet with them at the Club-room another ten or more men from outside for the purpose of discussing ways and means of accomplishing the establishment of an association, or board of trustees, with power to hold such " bits " of scenery near Boston as may be given into their keeping.

I think I can get of the Club members, A. Agassiz, T. W. Higginson, Edward C. Pickering, S. H. Scudder, and so on — and of outsiders should ask Dr. Walcott, yourself, and other names that will occur to you.

The meeting should talk over the various ways of attempting such an organization. I think it should be modelled after the Art Museum — and consist of a board of trustees to be composed say of the Director of the Art Museum and the Director of the Arboretum ; with a representative from the Horticultural Society, the Agricultural Society, and the Appalachian Club — for instance. These trustees would be also a board of directors, with power to accept or refuse gifts of lands, and so on.

This scheme would require a small endowment fund to pay small expenses (the reservations must be accepted only when offered with a fund for maintenance) ; or perhaps an organization having a membership which should elect the trustees and supply an annual income for office expenses would seem more suitable to some persons. These are problems which would come up at the proposed meeting.

The President of the Appalachian Club is the only man

beside yourself to whom I have yet suggested this scher
so if you cannot think well of it, it is not too late to giv'
fatal dose.

If you do think well of it, let me hear from you at your
convenience. . . .

March 5, 1890.

MY DEAR MR. MANN, — I have in my head a scheme for
an attempt at preserving some of the finest bits of Nature
near Boston.   I want, if possible, to interest you in the
scheme, my idea being that it might be well to interest perhaps a dozen of the more distinguished Appalachians, who
might then call a meeting of another dozen or so outsiders —
men like Professor Sargent and Francis Parkman. . . . I
open the subject by a letter to " Garden and Forest " which
will appear this week; and if you happen to be in town
within a day or two, I hope you will come to see me here. . . .
Meanwhile, can you call to mind ten Appalachians who would
make good fathers for such a scheme?   Higginson, Scudder,
and Fay might perhaps be three.   I should like to have them
hail from different suburbs. . . .

Ever since his return from Europe Charles had taken a
strong interest in the affairs of the Appalachian Mountain
Club ; he had been elected a member of the Council, and had
commended himself to the leading members of the Club by
disinterested and effective service in connection with the publication by the Club of an excellent contour map of the country about Boston.   He was therefore in position to secure the
coöperation of the officers of the Club in his new enterprise.
Professor Sargent and the President of the Club having given
prompt approval (Mr. Mann called at Charles's office on the
same day that the above letter was written), Charles immediately took counsel with an intimate friend and frequent companion in country walks, who was a lawyer, and on March
8th drew up the following statement of reasons for the action
he proposed, to be presented to the Council of the Club as a
suggestion of preliminary action : —

8 March, 1890.

Whereas — it is everywhere agreed that it is important to
the education, health, and happiness of crowded populations

that they should not be deprived of opportunities of beholding beautiful natural scenery.

Whereas — the cities of Massachusetts are continually growing both in number and in population, so that it is increasingly needful, and at the same time increasingly difficult, for the inhabitants of said cities to obtain the peculiar pleasure and refreshment which the contemplation of natural scenery alone affords them.

Whereas — many scenes near the cities of this State, which once possessed uncommon beauty and refreshing power, have been despoiled within the last ten years, while many scenes of similar value are at the present time in similar danger.

Whereas — it is highly probable that individuals and bodies of subscribers would gladly purchase scenes of this valuable character for dedication to the use and enjoyment of the public, provided they were fully assured that their intentions in so doing would be lastingly respected, and the lands presented by them carefully preserved for the purpose just recited.

RESOLVED — that in the opinion of this Council, the facts above recited call for the creation by the State of a Board of Trustees endowed with power to hold real estate in any part of the Commonwealth for the purpose already set forth. . . .

This paper was not adopted by the Council; but served as a clear statement of the objects Charles had in view.

The Council met on March 10th, and appointed Messrs. Eliot and Mann a committee "to draw up an invitation to societies and individuals to meet and consider a plan for preserving natural scenery." The next day Charles prepared the following circular letter, and on the 12th began sending it to influential persons who he thought would be interested in the project.

March 11, 1890.

MY DEAR SIR, — In view of the recent and the threatened destruction of some of the most beautiful scenes within the State of Massachusetts, it is suggested that it would be well to procure from the legislature a special act creating a Board of Trustees with power to hold lands free of taxes in any part of the Commonwealth for the use and enjoyment of the public.

It seems likely that the existence of such a board, into whose keeping lands might be committed, would stimulate individuals and bodies of subscribers to obtain possession of bits of scenery here and there, while men who happened to own suitable lands would occasionally pass them to the Trustees by will. It is further suggested that the Trustees had best be appointed in part by the Governor of the State (as is the case with the Trustees of the Massachusetts General Hospital), and in part by certain designated societies and corporations (as is provided in the act of incorporation of the Boston Museum of Fine Arts). Such societies as the Appalachian Mountain Club, the Massachusetts Horticultural Society, the Massachusetts Historical Society, the Essex Institute, and perhaps the various colleges, should be represented in the Board of Trustees ; and each Society should pledge itself, on first naming its representative, to pay into a common fund say $100 a year for five or ten years in order thereby to form a nucleus for the endowment of the Trust — an endowment which would be increased by individual benefactors.

Funds for the maintenance of particular reservations would have to be provided at the same time that lands were given.

If you are interested by these suggestions — they are no more than that — will you not kindly inform me of your interest, and at the same time send me the names of persons belonging in your part of the State who ought to be invited to a conference which it is proposed should be called in Boston some time in May. I should also be glad to be informed of the name and address of the secretary of any society or institution, other than those I have named, which in your opinion should be represented in the proposed Board of Trustees.

Encouraging answers at once began to come in from persons living in different parts of the State, and representing different occupations. Almost immediately it became clear that the precise work to be done was to give effect to a public sentiment already in existence. Many persons had seen the urgent need of preserving from imminent destruction this or that beautiful scene ; many had suggested, or even persistently advocated, the preservation of particular pieces of wild nature which had thus far escaped destruction. Thus, Elizur Wright, the eminent insurance actuary, had for nearly twenty years (1867–1885) made well-directed and patient efforts to enlist the interest of nature-loving individuals, and of the towns of Malden, Medford, Winchester, Stoneham, and Melrose, in a large tract of woods, rocks, marshes, and ponds lying in those towns, and since known as the Middlesex Fells; and these efforts had really borne fruit; although his ends were apparently far from attainment at the time of his death in 1885. Mr. Wright also foresaw that great parks would be needed for the dense population occupying Boston and the country immediately around; and in 1867 he used these prophetic words: "If Boston makes a park that will only do for the present municipality of that name, a larger Boston will soon have to make another."

When Mr. H. W. S. Cleveland of Minneapolis, the oldest landscape artist in the country, who was in early life thoroughly acquainted with the vicinity of Boston, read in "Garden and Forest" Charles's letter of March 5th, he at once wrote to him as follows: " I was rather surprised that you made no mention of the Middlesex Fells as a desirable locality for preservation. I do not know its present condition ; but it formerly comprised very picturesque scenes and much fine wood. I remember once spending most of a day there with George S. Hillard, when he was President of the Massachusetts Senate (some thirty years ago),[1] and urging upon him the preservation of a large area there either by the State or the City." Indeed, the love of beautiful scenery, or of particular scenes of natural beauty, had long been cherished and had become widespread ; but it was helpless. It had not been given an organized body and an executive hand. Nevertheless, strong influences had been at work towards preservative action. The artistic and financial success of Central Park in New York City had taught all large American municipalities an invaluable lesson. Since 1875 Boston had been developing a park system within her own boundaries, which more and more commended itself to the popular mind. The Commonwealth had adopted in 1882 a general law providing for the laying out of Public Parks by towns and cities within their own limits. In the vicinity of Boston, the weekly excursions of the Appalachian Mountain Club to places interesting for their scenery, or their historical associations, had made many persons familiar with the places and scenes which ought to be preserved, and with the destruction already

---

[1] Mr. Hillard was a member of the Senate in 1849-50.

wrought by the rapid and unguided growth of the suburbs. In the publication of the same Club entitled " Appalachia," Mr. Roswell B. Lawrence had printed in 1886 an excellent account of the Middlesex Fells, accompanied by a map showing the paths and wood-roads, the hills, brooks, swamps, and ponds of the whole district, and rehearsing the arguments in favor of public ownership. The Lynn Woods on the north of Boston afforded an admirable example of a great public forest (2000 acres) obtained by the coöperation of public-spirited citizens with the municipality. A few journalists, chief among whom was Mr. Sylvester Baxter of Malden, had written frequently and earnestly about the park needs of the million people within twelve miles of the State House, and had pointed out the opportunities for effective action, and the obstacles which prevented it. These sympathetic writings had helped to form an expectant public opinion on the subject. Finally, the genius of Frederick Law Olmsted had gradually been informing cultivated Americans concerning the nature and uses of public reservations.

In anticipation of a meeting of the Council of the Appalachian Mountain Club on April 2d, Charles wrote out on March 30th what he called a " Preservation Scheme." It was his habit to go to any meeting, in the work of which he was strongly interested, with something already well considered and put into writing, in order to supply a definite basis for discussion, and a preliminary framework for action by the meeting. This habit was a thoughtful and helpful one ; it gave evidence that he had studied the subject, and undoubtedly added to the influence which his quiet but persuasive speech gave him in all meetings of committees or boards for the discussion of subjects he had at heart.

At a meeting of the Council of the Appalachian Mountain Club on April 2d, it was unanimously voted " to add Mr. Lawrence to the committee, and that the committee call a meeting of persons interested in the preservation of natural scenery and historical sites in Massachusetts ; and that fifty dollars be appropriated for the purpose of such meeting." In this vote historical sites appear as well as scenery ; hitherto, scenery only had been mentioned.

Charles now had a good piece of machinery in his hands, and he promptly set it in motion. In a week the Committee adopted a preliminary letter, a letter of invitation to the proposed meeting, and part of a statement of the reasons for the creation of a Board of Trustees with power to hold lands for the use and enjoyment of the public. The preparation of lists of addresses of persons to be invited to the meeting was a considerable labor; and Charles did most of it with his own hand.   The membership of the Historical, Antiquarian, Horticultural, Natural History, and Village Improvement societies, and of the College Faculties in the State served as a basis; but many names were added on the recommendation of interested persons to whom Charles had written asking for lists.   (See Appendix II.)   April and May were Charles's busiest months; but he found time for " Preservation work." Not content with sending out about two thousand copies of the following invitation, he personally wrote to many influential persons whose presence he thought would be especially valuable, and made all the arrangements for officers and speakers at the meeting, and for letters to be read there. From May 19th to May 24th he gave all his time to preparations for the meeting on the 24th.   Mr. Mann, the president of the Appalachian Club, was frequently in helpful consultation with him in April and May.

APPALACHIAN MOUNTAIN CLUB,
9 PARK STREET, BOSTON, May 10, 1890.

DEAR SIR, — At a meeting of the Council of the Appalachian Mountain Club held on Wednesday, April 2, 1890, it was unanimously —

Voted, That Messrs. Eliot, Mann, and Lawrence be a committee to call a meeting of persons interested in the preservation of scenery and historical sites in Massachusetts.

In accordance with this vote, you are hereby invited, with friends who may be interested in the subject, to take part in a conference to be held in Boston, at the Massachusetts Institute of Technology, Boylston Street, at 12 o'clock, on Saturday, May 24, 1890.   Hon. Henry H. Sprague will preside, and among those who will either attend the meeting, or send letters, are Governor Brackett, General Francis A. Walker, Dr. O. W. Holmes, Colonel T. W. Higginson, Mr. Francis Parkman, and Mr. Frederick Law Olmsted.

Please use the enclosed postal-card to inform the committee whether or not they may expect you.

You are also requested to examine and consider the statements and proposals of the circular which accompanies this letter, and if you cannot attend the conference, you are respectfully urged to communicate your opinions and suggestions in writing to Charles Eliot, 50 State Street, Boston, before the day of the meeting.

AN OUTLINE OF A SCHEME FOR FACILITATING THE PRESERVATION AND DEDICATION TO PUBLIC ENJOYMENT OF SUCH SCENES AND SITES IN MASSACHUSETTS AS POSSESS EITHER UNCOMMON BEAUTY OR HISTORICAL INTEREST.

There is no need of argument to prove that opportunities for beholding the beauty of Nature are of great importance to the health and happiness of crowded populations. As respects large masses of the population of Massachusetts, these opportunities are rapidly vanishing. Many remarkable natural scenes near Boston have been despoiled of their beauty during the last few years. Similar spots near other cities of the Commonwealth have likewise suffered. Throughout the State, scenes which future generations of townspeople would certainly prize for their refreshing power are to-day in danger of destruction. Unless some steps towards their effectual protection can be taken quickly, the beauty of these spots will have disappeared, and the opportunity for generous action will have passed. Scattered throughout the State are other places made interesting and valuable by historical or literary associations ; and many of these also are in danger.

What public or private, general or local, action in aid of the preservation of fine natural scenes and historical sites will it be best to attempt under existing circumstances in Massachusetts ? This is the problem which will be the subject of debate at the conference called by the Council of the Appalachian Mountain Club ; and it is only for the purpose of provoking discussion that the Committee which has been authorized to call the meeting makes the following proposals : —

1. The establishment of a Board of Trustees to be appointed as follows : Some to be named in the act of incorporation : their successors to be elected by the full Board as vacancies occur. Some to be named by the governing bodies of several designated incorporated societies, such as the Massachusetts Historical Society, the Essex Institute, the Appalachian Mountain Club, etc. Some to be appointed by the Governor and Council.

2. The Trustees to be empowered to acquire by gift from individuals, or bodies of subscribers, parcels of real estate possessing natural beauty or historical interest, and to hold the same, together with funds for the maintenance thereof, free of all taxes.

3. The Trustees to be required to open to the public, under suitable regulations, all such parcels of their real estate as lie within the limits of those towns and cities which may provide police protection for the same.

4. The Trustees to be prohibited from conveying real estate once accepted by them, except to towns and cities for public uses.

In order to effect the creation of this proposed Board of Trustees, the Committee suggests : —

5. The appointment by the meeting of May 24 of a Standing Committee of twenty-five, to be provided by the meeting with a working fund, and empowered —

a. To draught and present to the General Court at its next session an act of incorporation.

b. To correspond with societies and individuals for the purpose of deciding upon two or three parcels of suitable real estate which, with endowments for maintenance, may be offered to the Trustees immediately upon their incorporation.

c. To secure subscriptions to an endowment fund with the income of which the Trustees may meet their general expenses.

In further preparation for intelligent and productive discussion of the subject, Charles informed himself about the statutes or acts under which most of the existing national, state, and municipal reservations were held, such as the Yosemite and Yellowstone Parks among national reservations, Niagara and the Adirondacks among state reservations, Montreal, Belle Isle (Detroit), and Lynn Woods among municipal reservations. He wished to be familiar with the precedents on the subject; and in a few weeks he made fortunate use of the information he had acquired.

The meeting took place as appointed. The following account of the meeting written by Charles is taken from his "First Annual Report of the Trustees of Public Reservations:" —

About one hundred persons were present, representing most parts of the State. Hon. Henry H. Sprague, President of the State Senate, presided, and Mr. William Clarence Burrage, Secretary of the Bostonian Society, acted as clerk. Mr. Mann, of the Committee of Arrangements, gave an account of the four hundred cordial letters received from persons who were unable to attend the meeting. The letters from Governor Brackett, Mr. Whittier, Mr. John Boyle O'Reilly, Dr. Holmes, Mr. Francis Parkman, and other well-known persons were heartily applauded by those present. Mr. Eliot followed with a statement of the reasons which led to the calling of the meeting, and after mentioning the occasional special Acts by which the General Court has authorized the preservation of a few remarkably interesting monuments, such as the Old South Church in Boston, he advocated the establishment of a central Board of Trustees, as follows : —

" This necessity for special Acts, combined with the trouble involved in organizing special societies and boards of trustees, naturally discourages and hinders those who might otherwise do much for the cause we have at heart. I say those who might do much, because I believe that this worthy cause of ours, like most other noble causes, must, under our democratic government, be fostered in its beginnings, at least, by the individuals who may be interested in it. Some day, perhaps, the State may create a commission, and assume the charge of a large number of scattered spots, to be held for the enjoyment of the people. But that day is not yet. Those of the people who feel and know the great value of such reservations must first prove their value by actual experiment ; in other words, by opening many such places and managing them for the public good.

" The way our committee would propose to do this must now be clear to you all. Scattered throughout the State are many thriving historical and antiquarian societies, and many other associations which may be grouped as being interested in the world out-of-doors. Some of these societies have already accomplished the saving of memorable or striking spots. The Essex Institute has purchased the great boulder in Danvers called Ship Rock, the Old Colony Historical Society owns Dighton Rock, and the Worcester Natural History Society owns a part of the shore of Lake Quinsigamond. Many others would like to do something of this kind, and more would like to, if the way were easier. Let these societies, with all individuals who may be interested, unite in asking the legislature to establish one strong Board of Trustees, to be empowered to hold for the benefit of the public the desired sort of property in any part of the State. There seems to be no need of any new society or association: what is needed is concerted and coöperative action on the part of the many interested existing societies. Such action can probably effect the creation of the Trustees, who will in turn facilitate and stimulate the acquiring and giving of the desired scenes and sites. The necessity for zealous local action will not be done away with: it will be provided with a definite end for which to work."

Mr. J. B. Harrison, of Franklin Falls, N. H., made an appeal for prompt action of some sort, in view of the fact that population is increasing at a tremendous rate, while the space which is open to it grows less and less. He dwelt more particularly upon the future of the seashore, and the general physical and moral suffocation which must attend the exclusion of the coming multitude from the free light and air, without which no people can exist. A day or two later one of the most influential of the Boston newspapers said of this address: " It touched upon the most vital concerns of the people and coming generations. It was the most forcible and most wisely and wittily spoken address, without any sort or shadow of exception, which has been delivered in Boston in several years."

The chairman next called for remarks from the floor, and the Hon. Leverett Saltonstall, Professor C. E. Norton, and Judge William S. Shurtleff followed one another with stirring speeches. After some further discussion, a vote was passed asking the chairman to appoint a committee " to promote in such ways as may seem to it advisable the establishment of a Board of Trustees to be made capable of acquiring and holding, for the benefit of the public, beautiful and historical places in Massachusetts." This committee, after adding to its members by election, organized itself for work as follows : —

Henry P. Walcott, Cambridge, Chairman; George Wigglesworth, Boston, Treasurer; Charles Eliot, Boston, Secretary.

Francis A. Walker, Boston; Sarah H. Crocker, Boston; Marion Talbot, Boston; William C. Burrage, Boston; C. S. Rackemann, Milton; George C. Mann, Jamaica Plain; L. Saltonstall, Chestnut Hill; F. L. Olmsted, Brookline; C. S. Sargent, Brookline; Moses Williams, Brookline; Sylvester Baxter, Malden; Elizabeth Howe, Cambridge; William S. Shurtleff, Springfield; Joseph Tucker, Pittsfield; Christopher Clarke, Northampton; Richard Goodman, Lenox; Franklin Carter, Williamstown; George Sheldon, Deerfield; Henry M. Dexter, New Bedford; Henry M. Lovering, Taunton; George R. Briggs, Plymouth; J. Evarts Greene, Worcester; Henry L. Parker, Worcester; Philip A. Chase, Lynn; W. C. Endicott, Jr., Salem; John S. Brayton, Fall River.

Another and better piece of machinery was now at Charles's disposition. The new committee met within a week, Charles preparing with Mr. Burrage, the secretary of the meeting, the letters of notification, and making beforehand studies of circulars to be issued in the name of the new committee. On June 5th the chairman of the committee, Dr. Henry P. Walcott, appointed a sub-committee, consisting of Messrs. Greene, Olmsted, Williams, Wigglesworth, and Eliot, to prepare a scheme of organization for the proposed Board of Trustees. Charles attended to the correspondence of the sub-committee, called their meeting, draughted their report, and consulted with the members who could not attend the meeting. On July 17th the sub-committee reported to the whole committee an organization for the proposed Board of Trustees, and advised the establishment of a companion board with the powers of a Board of Visitors. (See Appendix III.) This report was referred to a new sub-committee on legislation consisting of Messrs. Shurtleff, Parker, and Williams. In August two circulars, written in the first instance by Charles, were freely sent out with the request that they be brought to the attention of the people throughout the State. The first circular was intended for posting; it rehearsed the facts about the appointment of the committee and their purpose to ask the legislature to establish a Board of Trustees capable of holding lands for the use and enjoyment of the public, and ended as follows : —

The Committee desires to hear from the officers of all societies which may wish to send Delegates to the proposed Board [of Visitors], and also from the officers or members of any societies which may see fit to assist the Committee by adopting resolutions favoring the establishment of the proposed Board of Trustees for public places.

The Committee hopes to be informed of all movements now on foot looking to the opening to the public of any beautiful or historical places, as also of all lands which it may be desirable and possible to obtain for the proposed Trustees. Letters may be addressed to the nearest member of the Committee, or to the Secretary, Charles Eliot, 50 State Street, Boston.

Lastly, the Committee requests all persons who may feel interested in this attempt to facilitate the preservation of natural scenery and of historical memorials to send contributions for this purpose to the Treasurer of the Committee, George Wigglesworth, Esq., 89 State Street, Boston. If the working fund can be made large enough, the work of the Committee can go on prosperously; otherwise it must languish.

The second circular recited the reasons for the establishment of the proposed "Trustees of Public Reservations," gave a list of existing reservations, some national, some state, and some municipal, and others established by corporate or individual action, and then described as follows the proposed action of the committee, and the reasons for it : —

It is proposed to establish in Massachusetts a corporation to be called the "Trustees of Public Reservations." It is proposed to give these Trustees the power to acquire, by gift or purchase, beautiful or historical places in any part of the State, to arrange with cities and towns for the necessary policing of the reservations so acquired, and to open the reservations to the public when such arrangements have been made. This Board of Trustees should be established without further delay, and for the following reasons : —

(1) Because the existing means of securing and preserving public reservations are not sufficiently effective. Every year sees the exclusion of the public from more and more scenes of interest and beauty, and every year sees the irreparable destruction of others.

(2) Because, if it is desirable to supplement the existing means of securing and preserving the scenes in question, no method can be found which will more surely serve the desired end than that by means of which Massachusetts has established her successful hospitals, colleges, and art museums: namely, the method which consists in setting up a respected Board of Trustees, and leaving all the rest to the munificence of public-spirited men and women. When the necessary organization is provided, the lovers of Nature and History will rally to endow the Trustees with the care of their favorite scenes, precisely as the lovers of Art have so liberally endowed the Art Museums.

(3) Because a general Board of Trustees established with power to accept or reject whatever property may be offered it in any part of the State will be able to act for the benefit of the whole people, and without regard to the principal cause of the ineffectiveness of present methods, namely, the local jealousies felt by townships and parts of townships towards each other.

(4) Because the beautiful and historical Commonwealth of Massachusetts can no longer afford to refrain from applying to the preservation of her remarkable places every method which experience in other fields has approved. The State is rapidly losing her great opportunity to ensure for the future an important source of material as well as moral prosperity.

Newspapers throughout the State were informed of the doings of the committee, and made frequent favorable mention of the project. Mr. Sylvester Baxter, a member of the committee, had access to influential newspapers, either as an editorial writer or a correspondent, and had been for many years warmly in favor of any and all measures which promised to secure for the future dense population of Boston and the vicinity the benefits of public reservations, large and small. He lost no opportunity of furthering the new project. Charles had the firm belief that parks ought to be created and maintained in the moral and physical interest of the great popular majority of a democratic community ; and he therefore welcomed every means of commending public reservations to the goodwill and favoring care of the great mass of the people.

The autumn was filled with active professional labors ; but as a new session of the legislature approached, Charles's mind turned again to " Preservation work." Having learnt that Judge Shurtleff, the chairman of the sub-committee on legislation, was in Europe, he wrote as follows to the next member of the sub-committee : —

11 Dec. '90.

H. L. PARKER, ESQ.

My dear Sir, — Judge Shurtleff being in Europe, you are the senior member of our sub-committee on the preservation of beautiful and historical places — our legislation sub-committee, I mean.

I hope you will allow me to call upon you some day before Xmas. I want to hear your view of the situation, and your opinion as to the form of our petition to the legislature — if petition it should be.

I suppose that having obtained a draught of a bill, the general committee should meet and approve the same, and then address a petition to the General Court — but I hope you can name an hour in the middle of the day or afternoon some time next week when I can find you.

As to a bill, I find the following old bills are interesting reading : —

Massachusetts General Hospital	Feb. 25, 1811.
Pilgrim Society	Jan. 24, 1820.
Mission Park Association	Feb. 16, 1857.
Museum of Fine Arts	Feb. 4, 1870.
Pocumtuck Valley Association	May 9, 1870.
Standish Monument Association	May 4, 1872.
Longfellow Memorial Association	May 23, 1882.
Greylock Park Association	April 15, 1885.

I append the following not because I have any notion it is anywhere near right, but only to set the ball rolling a little : —

Sec. 1. —— and their successors, are hereby made a body corporate by the name of The Trustees of Public Reservations, for the purpose of acquiring, preserving, and opening to the public beautiful and historical places within this Commonwealth, with the powers and privileges, and subject to the duties, set forth in all general laws which now or hereafter may be in force relating to like corporations.

Sec. 2. The said corporation may take and hold by grant, gift, devise, or purchase such real estate as may seem worthy of preservation, and such personal property as may be necessary or convenient to promote the objects of the corporation.

Sec. 3. The said corporation shall not sell, convey, grant, mortgage, or lease any real estate accepted and owned by it (except that it may sell the same when it is compelled so to do by the exercise of eminent domain on the part of the Commonwealth or other authorized power).

Sec. 4. The personal property held by said corporation, and all such real estate as it shall cause to be opened to the use and enjoyment of the public under suitable regulations, shall be exempt from taxation in the same manner and to the same extent as the property of literary, benevolent, charitable, and scientific institutions incorporated within this Commonwealth is now exempt by law.

This is, it seems to me, "lowest terms." If we must introduce State representatives and a Board of Delegates, they must be added.

It appears in the last sentence of this letter that Charles himself did not care to have any Board of Delegates or Visitors. At the third meeting of the general committee, held January 31, 1891, the sub-committee reported a draught of an act of incorporation which was approved by the committee. Thereupon a petition praying for the passage of the act was signed and addressed to the General Court, the name of one person from every county in the State, except Nantucket, being inserted in the act. It fell to Charles to procure the assent of the persons named in the first section of the act. Most of those whom he asked to serve gave their consent, and the list of names was deservedly an influential one with the legislature.

The measures taken to interest large numbers of persons in the undertaking proved to have been effective; for when a hearing was held on the proposed act before the Judiciary Committee of the Senate, on March 10, 1891, hundreds of persons attended the hearing, and the speakers in favor of the act were numerous. Charles, however, left as little as possible to chance. Four days before the hearing he sent a circular invitation to be present to all the persons who had expressed to him decided interest in the undertaking — about seven hundred in number. At the hearing, he stated the purpose of the committee in asking for the proposed act. On March 14th he wrote to the members of the committee appointed at the meeting of May 24, 1890, and to the proposed incorporators, asking them to write in favor of the bill to members of the House of Representatives.

The act passed both Houses without difficulty, and was approved by Governor William Eustis Russell, May 21, 1891.

Thus was accomplished within fifteen months the undertaking about which Charles wrote so modestly to Professor Sargent on the 5th of March, 1890. The qualities which brought this quick success were capacity for rapid and yet accurate work, persuasiveness, and good judgment about both men and measures. The personal quality of the officers and members of the corporation created with the title Trustees of Public Reservations was remarkable. Senator George F. Hoar, General Francis A. Walker, Professors N. S. Shaler and Charles S. Sargent, Mr. Philip A. Chase of Lynn, Mr. Frederick L. Ames of North Easton, and Mr. Leverett Saltonstall of Newton were among the original incorporators, and Dr. Henry P. Walcott, chairman of the State Board of Health, President Franklin Carter of Williams College, Mr. Charles H. Dalton of Boston, Mr. William C. Endicott of Salem, and Mr. Augustus Hemenway of Canton were among those soon added to the Board. The selection of persons was well adapted to commend the new Board and its undertakings to the people of Massachusetts.

While the act was on its easy passage through the legislature, Charles made a short address on the evening of May 9th before the Advance Club of Providence on " The Need of Parks." The whole address, as he subsequently wrote it out for publication, is given here; because it reveals the underlying convictions which induced Charles to give so much of his time to the advocacy of various measures for providing squares, gardens, beaches, and parks — the best means of out-of-door enjoyment — for the masses of the urban population. He was a genuine democrat; and he wanted the democracy to have every chance of attaining a real well-being.

THE NEED OF PARKS.

Very naturally the American Colonists gave little thought to parks. Only where their captains were extraordinarily far-sighted was any action taken to provide permanent open spaces in their towns. Philadelphia possesses to-day four considerable public squares placed symmetrically by William Penn in a plain which has now become the heart of the city. Savannah has twenty-three small squares, for unlike Philadelphia she has continued the excellent city plan devised by her founder Oglethorpe. Boston has her Common. These and the like exceptions only prove the rule that our predecessors gave small thought to parks. I ask now — why should we? Why should we tax ourselves for parks? Can we afford the expense, and is this the time to provide them? Let us see what answers can be found for these questions. To this end we must glance for a moment at the progress of population and civilization here in New England. After our ancestors had conquered the woods and the Indians, they settled down in numerous scattered villages of farmers, each with its meeting-house, inn, store, and blacksmith shop. Every little neighborhood, almost every separate farm, was sufficient unto itself, — supplied itself with the necessaries of life, raised its own crops, and made its own shoes, clothes, boats, and carts. In every village lived people of refinement who visited about the country, read good books, and were the leaders of the people. Providence was once such a village, and New England was made up of the like. Gradually the seaport villages, with their natural advantages for commerce, drew away from the inland communities. Trade became the source of fortunes. Trade began to draw men from the country to the seaboard. Then suddenly came the railroads. By their help many interior villages became trade centres, where labor was in demand, where countrymen found they could gain more than their farms had ever offered them. Then followed the rise of manufacturing. The first mills were operated by men and girls from the farms. Beside every considerable water power rose towns, as by magic ; and where water power proved scanty, coal hauled by the railroad took its place.

From farming through trading to manufacturing. Such has been the story of all the considerable New England towns of to-day.

And what of the inconsiderable places, — the places which have remained rural? They have been steadily losing population : As soon as a town becomes large enough and rich enough to provide itself with water and sewers, and lighted streets, and the multiplied conveniences which are only to be found in towns, — as soon as this is the case, it begins to draw in people from the surrounding country as by a mighty magnet. And this is only natural and proper. As the intelligence of the people is wakened, their thirst for congenial society, and for books, music, and art, grows importunate. Even those who resist these attractions of the town, and continue to live in the country, are compelled to depend upon the town. Their children probably take the train to school. They purchase everything, from hats to boots, in the town. Their very flour and meat is probably delivered to them from a Chicago car at their railroad station.

A curious thing is the disgust of the country-bred for the country, after they have once tasted the exciting town life. The girl who stands all day behind a dry-goods counter will tell you she would rather starve or faint in the city than go back home. Even the wretched beings of East London, whom General Booth is trying to move to clean and fresh country quarters, assure him that they will run away back to town as soon as they get the chance.

Now it has been the fashion to attribute the depopulation of the country districts of New England to the opening of the cheap and fertile lands of the West; and this undoubtedly is in a measure true. But what shall we say when we read, as we do in the returns of the new census, that many of the rural counties of fertile Iowa have lost population in the last ten years; that the same thing has been going on in other fertile parts of the country; that New York State, above Harlem River, outside the towns of 10,000 inhabitants, has lost 13,000 people? Evidently the causes of the depopulation of the country districts and the great growth of the cities lie deep. To me they appear to be inherent in the progress of our race, — to be permanent elements in that which we call the progress of civilization. In England the six largest cities add as many persons to their population in any given period as the rest of the nation, counting all the other bustling towns; and the same is true in all the highly civilized parts of Europe. It is evident that modern civilization is to have its home in cities, in cities of vastly greater population than any the world has yet seen.

If this be so, — if "the further progress of civilization is to depend mainly upon the influences by which men's minds and characters are affected while living in great cities," — with what zeal should we not endeavor to make these influences such as shall be elevating? If this be so, — if the human race is destined to be more and more closely crowded into towns and suburbs — with what seriousness should we not endeavor to make these towns and suburbs as decent, as healthful, and as refreshingly beautiful as possible? Our race has already learned by sad experience that this crowding into cities is attended by grave dangers. It is well known that the average length of human life is very much less in the town than in the country. Disease is more prevalent in town than out. Cholera infantum, that fearful scourge which in August and September kills our young children by the thousands, is preëminently a town disease.

And physical ills are not the only ills of town life. Our cities are our hotbeds of vice and crime. The herding of the very poor in city slums breeds a degraded race. The lack of opportunity for innocent recreation drives hundreds to amuse themselves in ways that are not innocent. The tremendous competition for the opportunity to work breeds that discontent, and anger, and despair, which lead to anarchy, and feed the fires of that volcano under the city which the alarmists tell us is so soon to break forth. Even if the volcano does not belch forth, civilization is not safe so long as any large part of the population is morally or physically degraded; and if such degradation is increasing in our great towns (and who will say that it is not?), it is plainly the duty and the interest of all who love their country to do what they can to check the drift.

This question is squarely put to us: Shall the forces of darkness, the forces which drag men down, the forces which push men into the arms of ignorance, sin, and death, be allowed a free field in our cities, or shall they be opposed at every point and even routed, if it be possible, from their strongholds by the forces of enlightenment and progress?

Gentlemen, who are to be the captains of the army of light here in Providence, if not yourselves? Our cities can be saved to civilization only by the vigorous and united action of their citizens. There exists no outside power which can help you. The future of your city and the happiness or misery of the thousands upon thousands who are to succeed you here, lie very largely in your hands. Can there be any question as to what your course should be? Are you not bound by every consideration of honor and of financial interest to do for Providence everything that modern science has discovered to be of value to the physical, moral, and financial prosperity of large cities? How can you any longer ask: "Can we afford this or that public improvement?" If the experience of other cities has scientifically proved that certain improvements are sources of physical and financial advantage to the cities which introduce them, you cannot longer afford to do without them. Already you vote to tax yourselves severely for police, light, paving, sewers, scavengers, and a host of other costly public agencies, because you are convinced that the public health and safety require these things. You know that these things are necessary to the preservation of that civilization upon which your own prosperity and that of your neighbors and successors must be based.

Now I think I can prove to you in a very few words that just as you can no longer afford not to tax yourselves, let us say for pure water, so you can no longer afford not to tax yourselves for pure air and open spaces.

Any city physician will tell you that air-poisoning kills a hundred human beings where food-poisoning kills one; yet you pay for food inspection, and do little or nothing to provide your crowded quarters with fresh air. All authorities on the diseases of children prescribe fresh air and plenty of it for cholera infantum. Says Dr. Bell of Philadelphia:

" The restorative effects of fresh air are strikingly evinced in the relief procured by many hundreds of children every summer by simply crossing the Delaware River in the ferry-boats once or twice a day." Dr. Clark of Boston says : " A few hours' exposure of a child on a mother's lap or in a basket or carriage, to the freshness of a park, will produce a sleep such as never follows opium, chloral, or ether, and will yield a chance for health such as no drug can give." Philadelphia had long been a healthy city, but in 1874, when the death rate dropped to the extraordinarily low figure of 19.3 per thousand, Dr. William Pepper reported as follows: "This very favorable result is largely due to the abundant and cheap water supply, and to the opportunities given even the very poorest citizens for the enjoyment of pure air in Fairmount Park. The extent to which this is valued by the citizens may be inferred from the fact that the park was visited in 1874 by 11,000,000 persons."

Similar reports are constantly appearing from the sanitarians of the large towns where parks have been established. All are agreed that convenient playgrounds must be opened for the children and open-air parlors for their parents, if a decent physical standard is to be maintained ; and all are agreed that where these are opened, a visible improvement is the result. And the improvement is not physical only. The removal of the children from the crowded streets to the quiet playgrounds, and the gathering of the neighbors from their narrow homes into the neat public squares when the labor of the day is over, has worked in many places something like a moral revolution. Whoever has visited even one of the numerous public squares of Paris, Berlin, or Vienna, and has there watched the bearing and behavior of the common people, will ever afterwards be an earnest advocate of public gardens. London has converted almost a hundred small open spaces — many of them ancient graveyards — into children's playgrounds and old folks' resting grounds. Even New York has waked to the vital importance of providing accessible breathing-places for a crowded population, and is spending this year the second million of dollars out of an appropriation of ten million, which is to be expended in ten years in purchasing small open spaces in her crowded wards.

Doubtless the necessity is less imperative in Providence than it is in New York or London, but it will soon be upon you, and you will never be able to obtain these outdoor parlors as cheaply as now. It is very poor economy of human life, it is very poor economy of money, to postpone their purchase any further. "Nothing is so costly," it has been well said, "as sickness, disease, and vice; nothing so cheap as health and virtue. Whatever promotes the former is the worst sort of extravagance; whatever fosters the latter is the truest economy."

And now every argument that has been thus far adduced bears with at least equal force upon the question of the country park — or the public park proper. In the town squares and boulevards, men and women will find fresh air and shade and decent surroundings for their hours of sociability, and safe playgrounds for the children, and fresh nurseries for the babies. But there is an important element in human nature which the town square cannot satisfy. This is that conscious or unconscious sensibility to the beauty of the natural world which in many men becomes a passion, and in almost all men plays a part.

When you who are prosperous, as this world goes, move your families to the seaside or the mountains for the summer, it is not wholly for the fresh air and the freedom that you go. Whether you realize it or not, it is largely for the sake of the subtle influence which skies and seas, clouds and shadows, woods and fields, and all that mingling of the natural and the human which we call landscape shed upon human life — and the life of childhood and youth in particular. This is an influence which is almost indefinable; but it is very real. It is best understood by the poets, and has been sung by them ever since the Greeks invented that delightful phrase — the spirit of the place. It is an influence which has a most peculiar value as an antidote to the poisonous struggling and excitement of city life. Whenever a busy man is over-worried, the doctor prescribes the country; and when any of us are brought into depression by care or trouble, our cure is the sight of our chosen hills.

This if we have money wherewith to fly the town; but if

we have none of that valuable commodity to spare, what can
we do when the thirst for the hills burns in us? If we walk
through miles and miles of brick and mortar, or through other
miles of wooden suburbs, we may be at last rewarded by a
glimpse of a woodside or a meadow; but it is ten to one that
the sign "No Trespassing" confronts us when we reach the
fence. Very naturally the farmer regards us as a pest. We
tramp home again sadder and wiser boys and girls, and if
our cup of life is not seriously soured, it is not because the
fathers of our city have tried to make it sweet.

Gentlemen, the providing of what I call country parks to
distinguish them from squares and the like is as necessary
for the preservation of the civilization of cities as are sewers
or street lights. As our towns grow, the spots of remarkable
natural beauty, which were once as the gems embroidered upon
the fair robe of Nature, are one by one destroyed to make
room for railroads, streets, factories, and the rest. The time
is coming when it will be hard to find within a day's journey
of our large cities a single spot capable of stirring the soul of
man to speak in poetry. Think of what this will mean for the
race, and start to-morrow to secure for your children and your
children's children some of those scenes of special natural
beauty which I trust are still to be found within a reasonable
distance of this hall. For the purposes of the country park a
tract of land upon which Nature herself has framed a scene
of beauty is always to be desired. To buy a commonplace
piece of territory, when anything more effective is obtainable,
is a sad waste of opportunities. Similarly it is a waste of
money to make a large park merely an enlarged copy of a
town square. The tax-payer's money is worse than wasted if
it is spent in the large area of the park for anything which
could be equally well obtained within the small area of the
square or garden. The square is the place for decoration,
for monuments, for ribbon gardening. The park should be
kept free from town-like things. Indeed, if park scenery is
not kept free from decoration, or if the works which make it
possible for the public to enjoy the scenery without harming
it are not devised with religious regard to the promptings of
the spirit of the place, the highest usefulness and main pur-

pose of the park are frustrated. The large area and the large cost of the country park cannot be justified, if its simple but lofty purpose of providing refreshing scenery is lost sight of.

Gentlemen, these are all very obvious considerations, and yet they are very seldom regarded in practice. As yet but few of our communities own sufficient land for the making of a country park. Much of what is owned is, by nature, either dull or ugly. Much that was originally interesting has been spoiled by the mistaken zeal of the park commissioners in charge. The number of really great and noble American country parks may yet be counted on the fingers. Montreal has her Mount Royal, a lofty and craggy hill behind the city, most interesting in itself, and commanding from its jutting cliffs superb views of the St. Lawrence valley. Detroit has her Belle Isle, a low and long green island, clothed with an open forest, and surrounded by waters bearing the concentrated commerce of the Lakes. Baltimore has her Druid Hill, where the deer browse in soft, shady glades. Minneapolis has the gorge of the Mississippi. Lynn has two thousand acres of woods and ponds, and rocks which overlook the ocean. Such are some of the characteristic types of landscape which a few wise American cities have made free to all the world. May Providence soon follow her younger sisters!

Charles was immediately made Secretary of the new Corporation, and three years later Chairman of the Standing Committee. During the summer of 1891 he draughted the by-laws of the Trustees, — a matter requiring study and foresight, — and obtained the contributions which enabled the Trustees to meet their expenses, and to employ Mr. J. B. Harrison temporarily as their agent. He also coöperated with Mr. Harrison in his researches. He was careful to submit to the other members of the Standing Committee all papers which he drew for the committee, and was always ready to revise and rewrite his first draughts in accordance with their suggestions. He wrote the first three annual reports of the Standing Committee (always with the advantage of criticism from his colleagues), reports which went far towards determining the permanent policy of the Trustees and their early functions.

The Trustees had important matters before them in the very first year of their existence. A beautiful tract of diversified woodland in Stoneham, containing about twenty acres, was offered to the Board, but could not be accepted until a fund of $2000 had been raised by public-spirited persons in Melrose, Malden, and Medford to ensure its maintenance and protection. This is the Virginia Wood, so named in memory of a daughter of the giver, Mrs. Fanny Foster Tudor, formerly of Stoneham. This first gift to the Trustees had, therefore, a memorial purpose ; and two others, out of the six gifts thus far (1901) received by the Trustees, have had a similar purpose. They answer a question asked by Charles in his First Annual Report for the Standing Committee of the Trustees, — " Is not a religiously guarded, living landscape a finer monument than any ordinary work in marble or stained glass ? "

Many spots and buildings were suggested to the Trustees as desirable for preservation ; but the Board was obliged to answer such suggestions in the manner indicated in the following passage from the report just cited : —

All these places and many more are doubtless worthy of preservation in the collection of Massachusetts landscapes and memorials which this Board has been empowered to establish and maintain. On the other hand, this Board does not possess either the money or the authority to enable it to snatch real estate out of the hands of anybody. Like the trustees of a public art museum, this Board stands ready to undertake the care of such precious things as may be placed in its charge. It exists " to facilitate the preservation of beautiful and historical places in Massachusetts," by providing an efficient and permanent organization through which individuals and bodies of subscribers may accomplish their several desires.

Another passage from the same report describes concisely certain fruitful activities which he recommended to the Trustees and personally superintended.

In addition to the sympathetic study of the several suggested projects just mentioned, the Committee has from the first given serious attention to certain broad questions from which it found itself unable to escape. Massachusetts, as a whole, is shamefully lacking in open spaces reserved expressly for enjoyment by the public. The mountain-tops of the in-

VIRGINIA WOOD — HEMLOCK KNOLL

terior, the cliffs and beaches of the seashore, and most of the intervening scenes of special beauty are rapidly passing into the possession of private owners, who hold these places either for their own private pleasure, or for the profit which may be reaped from fees collected from the public. Moreover, as population increases, the final destruction of the finest remaining bits of scenery goes on more and more rapidly. Thus the prospect for the future is in many ways a gloomy one, particularly upon the seashore and in the neighborhood of Boston.

Impressed by these considerations, the Committee determined to take action in four directions : first, to thoroughly investigate, and then to publish, the present facts in respect to the provision of public open spaces; secondly, to collect and publish the laws of Massachusetts which permit, or otherwise affect, the acquisition and maintenance of public open spaces; thirdly, to call together the numerous park commissioners and park committees of the metropolitan district surrounding Boston, in the hope that mutual acquaintance may encourage coöperative action in the taking of land for public open spaces ; fourthly, to ask the legislature of 1892 to institute an inquiry into the whole subject.

The first action determined on led to the preparation of two admirable reports by Mr. J. B. Harrison, the first on " The Public Holdings of the Shore Towns of Massachusetts," and the second on " The Province Lands at Provincetown." These two valuable papers were published in the Appendix to the First Annual Report to the Trustees. The second action led to the compilation and publication in the same Appendix of all the Massachusetts statutes relating to public open spaces. The third and fourth actions led to the creation within two years of the Metropolitan Park Commission, as will be hereafter set forth in some detail. Thus the Trustees of Public Reservations became immediately, through Charles's inspiration, an instrumentality for public service outside of its original field.

The report of their agent, Mr. Harrison, on the Province lands led the Standing Committee of the Trustees to petition the legislature of 1892 for better management of the State's large domain (more than 4000 acres) ; whereupon the legislature directed the Trustees to investigate the con-

dition of the lands in question, make a map of them, and
report in 1893. The Standing Committee of the Trustees
did this unexpected and troublesome piece of work, and filed
their report in January, 1893. Charles personally examined
the lands,[1] gave the directions for the making of the map,
decided on the photographic illustrations for the report,
arranged a hearing at Provincetown before the Committee,
and finally wrote the report. Two passages in this paper
are especially interesting because of their clear and vigorous
descriptions of the physical nature of the Province lands and
their condition.

As to the physical nature of the Province lands, the facts are
these : The highlands of Cape Cod terminate abruptly at High
Head in the township of Truro ; north and west of this point
the remainder of Truro and the whole of Provincetown is a
region of sand dunes bounded by beaches, the curves of which
enclose a perfect harbor at the very extremity of Cape Cod.
There is evidence that the tides and waves have built one
beach after another, each further north than the last; and
that the so-called Peaked Hill bar is a new beach now in
process of formation. The sand dunes of the old beaches, as
they were one by one protected by new beaches to the north,
gradually became clothed with the surprisingly beautiful
vegetation which adorns them to-day ; while the hollows between the ridges, each of which was in its day a race run,
have gradually been filled, as the race run is now filling.
Many of these hollows among the sandhills contain fresh-water

[1] The out-of-door part of the work he thoroughly enjoyed — witness
this note to his wife, August 7, 1892 : " My one hour of harbor and three
hours of ocean voyaging yesterday were smooth and pleasant ; and my
afternoon of tramping was full of interest. Marshes skirted by steep
hills of bushes, narrow hollows in the hills crammed full of Ink-berry,
Huckleberry, and Bearberry, wider openings containing green meadows
of grass or rushes, and patches of deep-blue water, and around and outside of all, the shining, threatening sand dune, piled so high in some
places that it looks as if the next gale would upset it upon the trees and
ponds and bushes at its feet ! I tramped round the edge of the dunes at
the west all yesterday afternoon — a good deal of hard walking — and
having got halfway round the whole affair, I cut for supper by an old
road through the centre of the wooded region. I am trying, you know,
to get sufficiently familiar with the lay of the land to be able to direct a
surveyor as to what we want done here. . . . It is a glorious day." . . .

ponds, the shores of which support a charming growth of Tupelo, sweet Azalea, Clethra, and the like ; and in the shelter of the ridges, and even upon their crests, grow Oaks, Maples, Beeches, and Pitch Pines. The layer of surface soil upon the hills is nowhere more than three or four inches deep ; but the underlying sand is wonderfully retentive of moisture, so that this peculiar terminus of the cape presents in its uninjured parts a more verdurous landscape than the main body of the outer cape can show.

There follows this passage a comprehensive statement of all the previous legislation on these lands, none of which had fulfilled its purpose. The report proceeds : —

What manner of destruction is going on meanwhile in the rear of the village of Provincetown the pictures herewith submitted will serve to show. Half of the Province land is already a treeless waste. The commissioners of 1825 reported to the General Court that this desert was the result of the stripping of vegetation from the seaward sandhills. We find to-day that, once the mat of plant-roots is removed from a windward slope, the northwest gales cut into the wounded places and proceed to undermine the adjacent plant-covered slopes. The sands blown out of such places are dumped in the lee, in the nearest hollow, burying the trees and bushes and stifling them to death. Once rid of the trees, the sands are drifted by the winds like snow. The beach grass planted by the government seems to have stayed the destruction of the ridges in some measure ; but the wheels of carts continually crossing the sand-drifts in the direction of the worst gales soon broke the grassed surface so that the wind got hold, " blew out " great areas, and dumped the sand in such steep drifts in the edges of the woods that many cart-paths became impassable, so that new routes were sought, where the operation was repeated. Within the Province lands the grassy Snake Hills and the wooded ridge called Nigger Head have bravely withstood the gales without serious change since Mayor Graham surveyed the field in 1833–35 ; but between these two points the winds have made great havoc. Wooded knolls have been cut in two, ponds filled up, and much wood-

land buried. East of Nigger Head and towards Eastern Harbor, beyond the bounds of the Province lands, the changes
have been even more violent. Several salt creeks have been
wholly filled up, and former sand ridges levelled, so that the
hulls of vessels on the ocean are now visible from the harbor.

The report recommended that the Province lands should
be placed in charge of the Board of Harbor and Land Commissioners already established, and that this Board should
appoint a paid superintendent, and fix the amount which may
be annually expended by him. These recommendations were
adopted by the legislature, and have resulted in an improved
condition of the State's large domain.

In 1892 Charles wrote and issued two circulars on behalf
of the Trustees, the first of which was intended to induce persons to put lands or money into the hands of the Trustees,
while the second asked for information about existing open
spaces in Massachusetts cities and towns, available for public
recreation. The valuable information procured through this
second circular was printed in good statistical form in the
second annual report to the Trustees. This table provides a
firm basis for comparisons which later generations may institute in 1922, 1952, and so forth.

The annual reports to the Trustees of Public Reservations
record the successive gifts made to the Board, and the measures taken to carry out the memorial purposes of some of the
gifts; but they also offer suggestions as to the further use of
the Trustees by intending givers of reservations for public
enjoyment, and they repeatedly discuss the defacement of
natural scenery, highways, and parkways, by obtrusive advertisements. The legislature, in response to representations
made by the Trustees, has begun to repress this offence, but
has not yet (1901) made up its mind to give the public effective protection. One of the most interesting and widely
applicable suggestions is the following from the report of
1896 : —

Much of the most charming and most easily destroyed
scenery of Massachusetts is found along the banks of ponds
and streams; and the Committee believes it would be for the
advantage of the Commonwealth if narrow strips of such
water-side lands could be secured by interested and generous
citizens and given into its charge for safe-keeping. Many
such strips are found between country roads and streams or

THE PROVINCE LANDS — THE EDGE OF THE NAKED SANDS

THE PROVINCE LANDS — A SAND DRIFT FILLING A LILY POND

ponds ; and many other strips of similarly useless but beautiful land are to be found bordering roads in rocky or steep places. Nothing could more directly help to keep the State a pleasant and beautiful place to live in than such preserving of the most interesting parts of the local roadside scenery. Such strips, as well as hill-tops, ravines, bits of seashore, and any remarkably beautiful spots, will always be gladly taken charge of by this Board, provided some little money to form a maintenance fund comes with each gift.

It was a gratification to the Trustees of Public Reservations, and especially to Charles, to learn that the organization of this Massachusetts Trust in 1891 had contributed to the creation in 1893–94 of a similar association in England under the title of " The National Trust for Places of Historic Interest or Natural Beauty." The English Association already holds more properties than the Massachusetts Trust, and is in receipt of a much larger income from money gifts and annual subscriptions. Yet the English Association says (1899–1900) : " It is essential to the success of the Trust that its funds should be very largely increased." In like manner, large permanent funds are the great need of the Massachusetts Trustees of Public Reservations.

The Trustees hold (1901) 431 acres of land, in six tracts, — Virginia Wood, now a part of Middlesex Fells Reservation, Mt. Anne Park, the highest point in Gloucester, Goodwill Park in Falmouth, Rocky Narrows on the upper Charles River, Governor Hutchinson's Field in Milton, and Monument Mountain in Stockbridge and Great Barrington, — and these are all valuable possessions for the present and future generations ; but as Charles wrote in the Annual Report to the Trustees for 1893, —

if Massachusetts possesses no such richly historical treasures as will gradually pass into the keeping of the English Board, she does possess a great wealth of beautiful, though now threatened, natural scenery, and an interesting, though rapidly disappearing, store of archæological and historical sites, such as Indian camps and graves, border forts, and colonial and literary landmarks. Your Board is empowered, and is fully prepared, to assume the legal title, and, if need be, the whole care of such places. It remains for those who really desire the preservation of these places to come forward to their rescue at once.

In some remarks which Charles made at a meeting held by the Trustees at Northampton on the 31st of May, 1895, to promote the acquisition of Mt. Tom as a public park, a passage occurs which clearly indicates what he hoped individuals, or families, or bodies of subscribers might do for the Commonwealth through the Trustees : —

In Massachusetts the variety of these choicest local scenes is very great. One is the curving beach of a tiny cove of the sea, enclosed by granite headlands. Another is itself a headland, or a rugged bit of the ocean bluff of Cape Cod. Another a lily-pond set in an amphitheatre of woods. Another a wild ravine, or a quiet grove, or a hill-top, or a strip of land between a highway and a lake. It often happens that a public road follows a stream, or the shore of a pond. The pleasantness and beauty of the way consist in the appearance and disappearance of the water amid the foliage. How easily is this pleasantness destroyed, — how easily and how cheaply it might be permanently preserved! Those strips and bodies of land which ought to be thus held in trust for the enjoyment of all are seldom of much value to their owners. They are too steep or too rocky for agriculture, too inaccessible for house-building.

Low Rustic. Ermenonville
Span 30'. Railing 3' at centre.

CHAPTER XIX

THE CREATION OF THE PRELIMINARY METROPOLITAN PARK COMMISSION OF 1892-93

That which befits us, embosomed in beauty and wonder as we are, is
cheerfulness and courage, and the endeavor to realize our aspirations.
— RALPH WALDO EMERSON.

THE meeting of the park commissions and committees of
Boston and the surrounding towns and cities, which the Trustees of Public Reservations had determined to call, was held
on December 16, 1891, in the office of the Boston Park Commission, General Francis A. Walker, a member of that Commission, in the chair. Charles was made secretary. He made
the opening speech, explaining the purpose of the Trustees of
Public Reservations in calling the meeting, showing maps
of the country within eleven miles of the State House, contrasting the provision of public open spaces here with that
near Paris and London, and contrasting also the opportunity
for delightful parks around Boston with the "miserable present." The brief he wrote the day before for this speech
illustrates so well his ordinary method of preparing for such
occasions that the last quarter of it is here given just as it
was written : —

Here is a rapidly growing metropolis planted by the sea,
and yet possessed of no portion of the sea-front except what
Boston has provided at City Point. Here is a city interwoven
with tidal marshes and controlling none of them ; so that the
way is open for the construction upon them of cheap buildings for the housing of the lowest poor and the nastiest
trades. Here is a district possessed of a charming river already much resorted to for pleasure, the banks of which are
continually in danger of spoliation at the hands of their private owners.

Here is a community which must have pure drinking water,
which yet up to this time has failed to secure even one water
basin from danger of pollution. Lynn has come nearest to

it. In the Fells they are working towards it, but the ridiculous town boundary difficulty there prevents concerted action.

Here is a community, said to be the richest and most enlightened in America, which yet allows its finest scenes of natural beauty to be destroyed one by one, regardless of the fact that the great city of the future which is to fill this land would certainly prize every such scene exceedingly, and would gladly help to pay the cost of preserving them to-day.

Compare the two maps — one showing the opportunity, the other the miserable present result.

Do not the facts speak for themselves? Is it not evident that present methods are too slow and inefficient? Can this community afford to go so slowly? Is not some form of joint or concerted action advisable at once?

Thirteen other gentlemen addressed the meeting, all of them in favor of concerted action. The following vote was unanimously adopted: "That the chairman and secretary with five others whom they may join with them be a committee to prepare a memorial to the legislature calling attention to the needs of the Boston district as respects the provision of public open spaces, and to report the same to a new meeting of this body." The chairman announced the committee as follows: The chairman and secretary, and Messrs. Philip A. Chase of Lynn, Robert T. Paine of Waltham, F. P. Bennett of Everett, Desmond Fitzgerald of Brookline, and Horace E. Ware of Milton. Mr. Ware subsequently resigned from the committee, and Mr. A. J. Bailey of Boston was chosen in his place. The committee was a strong one. Before the end of December it had agreed that the object to be aimed at should be a commission to inquire and report. A month later Charles wrote thus of this meeting: "A majority of the towns and cities within eleven miles of Boston were represented by their park commissioners or other officers; and so general was the desire for immediate, effective, and comprehensive action towards the reservation of ample public open spaces, that a committee was appointed to draft a memorial to the legislature, asking for prompt action in this direction." (From the First Annual Report of the Trustees of Public Reservations.)

The Trustees themselves by their Standing Committee sent the following petition to the General Court: —

The undersigned petitioners respectfully represent that the seashores, the river-banks, the mountain-tops, and almost all the finest parts of the natural scenery of Massachusetts are possessed by private persons, whose private interests often dictate the destruction of said scenery or the exclusion of the public from the enjoyment thereof. In the opinion of the undersigned, the scenes of natural beauty to which the people of the Commonwealth are to-day of right entitled to resort for pleasure and refreshment are both too few in number and too small in area ; and, therefore, your petitioners respectfully ask that an inquiry be instituted by your honorable bodies for the purpose of ascertaining what action, if any, may be advisable in the circumstances.

The next step was to procure numerous petitions from citizens of the metropolitan district, in aid of the petitions sent in by the Trustees of Public Reservations and by the associated Park Commissions and committees. In consultation with his associates on the Trustees' Standing Committee and the committee appointed at the meeting of December 16th, Charles prepared printed blank petitions, and sent them to all town and city officers in the metropolitan district, and to one hundred interested persons, with a note asking for signatures. The result was that several thousand citizens supported the application to the legislature. The legislature appointed a " Joint Special Committee on Public Reservations," and this committee ordered a public hearing on March 8th. It fell to Charles to make the preparations for this hearing ; as appears from the following passage in a note to his wife written at the end of February : " Yesterday my committee meeting was a farce, — nobody agreeing with anybody else, — and finally resulted as usual, namely, in an appeal to me to invite speakers to appear at the hearing on March 8th, to speak myself, and to make sure of an attendance by sending out postal cards." Charles made the opening address, and among other good arguments brought out with great distinctness the two principal difficulties which beset the subject, as follows : —

. . . Massachusetts as a whole is a beautiful land. Its surface is diversified, its seashore is picturesque, its ponds and streams are clear, its air is good. Already the world is well acquainted with these facts, and citizens of the great cities of the less favored parts of our country are coming in ever greater numbers to enjoy the beauty of the land and to build houses in the Berkshire hills and by the sea.

Moreover, the numerous cities of Massachusetts are grown so large and crowded, that all of our citizens who can afford it seek the country or the seashore for a month or more every year. All these people invariably purchase for their new houses just the prettiest spots they can find, and when they have bought them, they naturally want them for their very own; and they seek to prevent, as they have a perfect right to do, the intrusion of other people.

Thus we find a state of things which may be summarized as follows: 1st. The great towns are rapidly overgrowing and destroying the scenes of natural beauty adjacent to them; and 2d. People escaping from the towns are as rapidly occupying for private purposes the remoter spots of special beauty.

The result is that the great mass of the townspeople of the State, and they will always be much the larger part of the State's population, are more and more shut out from the beauty and the healing influence of Nature's scenery, and are more and more shut up in their tenements and shops. Is this for the advantage of the State?

. . . It has been pointed out that the location of large public reserves should be determined chiefly with reference to the inclusion therein of the finest scenery of each region or district. Now, the park act limits the field of action of our park commissioners to the bounds of their respective towns and cities, while it is self-evident that these boundaries bear no relation to the scenery of the district they divide. Indeed, the boundaries of our towns are very apt to bisect the prettiest passages of scenery, as where the line follows the channel of a river or brook the banks of which are beautiful. In these cases it is at present practically certain that neither town will act to take the banks, for it would be senseless for one to act without the other, and one or the other is almost sure to feel that its burden of expense is out of proportion to the benefit to accrue to it. Under the park act, a board of park commissioners will seldom make open spaces near the boundary of their town or city, even though the best lands for the purpose are to be found there, and even though a dense population needs them there. Under the park act, no park board can take lands outside the arbitrary town boundary, even though a fine site for a park lies adjacent to the boundary near their own centre of population, and so remote from the population of the adjacent township that its park board will never want to buy or take the place.

The appointment of a temporary commission to inquire what was most needful and practicable, and to report a plan of operations to the next General Court, was advocated by many speakers at the hearing, and no opposition to the general project was developed. It was evident to the Committee that action by the legislature was desired by a large body of intelligent and public-spirited citizens, many of whom might fairly be called leaders of the people. On March 11th Charles attended by request a meeting of the Joint Committee of the legislature, and on the 15th he wrote a letter to Senator Fernald enclosing a first draught of the desired act. He kept in communication with the promoters of the bill both within and outside the legislature. The Metropolitan Park Commission bill first passed the Senate April 12, but was finally enacted by the House May 27, and by the Senate June 1, and was approved by the Governor, June 2, 1892.

Thereupon Charles wrote repeatedly to Governor Russell, and called upon him, suggesting names for the commission. Two out of the three persons first selected by the Governor declining to serve, Charles sounded on the subject four other gentlemen in succession, all of whom found themselves unable to undertake the work. On the 5th of July he proposed the function to Mr. Charles Francis Adams, who on the next day consented to serve. The Commission was named on July 9th as follows: Charles Francis Adams of Quincy, Philip A. Chase of Lynn, and William B. de las Casas of Malden. The Board was a strong one, and immediately commanded public confidence.

It was not yet nineteen months since Charles made his first assault on a public official in favor of legislative action to procure a scheme for a metropolitan system of public reservations. Governor William E. Russell was a fellow-townsman of Charles, and both had grown up as boys in Cambridge, and been educated at Harvard College. It was by reason of this long acquaintance, and of friendly relations between the two families, that Charles ventured to write Governor Russell the following letter : —

19 Dec. '90.

HON. W. E. RUSSELL.

My dear Sir, — Let me, with no bumptious or presuming intentions, suggest a topic for your Address : and, if I cast my notes into the form of a paragraph of the Address, you will understand it is only because that seems the easiest way to write them out.

Within five miles of Beacon Hill is seated much the largest body of population in Massachusetts. This population is rapidly growing, and as it grows it becomes more and more crowded. The best building-ground is already occupied, and much wet and unhealthy land is being built upon. Within a comparatively few years there will be a continuous dense city between the State House and the Neponset River, the Chestnut Hill Reservoir, the Fresh Pond Reservoir, Medford, and Malden : and if nothing is done to prevent, much of this great city will consist of low-lying and badly drained slums.

What provision is being made within this metropolitan district for securing those public open spaces which the experience of all great cities has proved to be essential to the welfare of crowded populations? It is obvious that no adequate provision of this sort is either thought of or attempted. The City of Boston is creating a limited system of public pleasure drives and parks, but the other municipalities within the metropolitan district are allowing their few remaining open estates to be divided and built upon one by one and year by year. The excellent public park Act of 1882 remains for these cities and towns a dead letter : and why ? Largely because of local jealousies. One city refuses to seize its opportunity to obtain for all time a charming natural park which the loving care of an old family has preserved, because it fears that the people of the adjoining city will enjoy what it has paid for. The towns are influenced by similar selfish fears, and the very wards within the cities are similarly jealous of each other.

There seems to be no remedy for this state of things except the establishment of some central and impartial body capable of disregarding municipal boundaries and all local considerations, and empowered to create a system of public reservations for the benefit of the metropolitan district as a whole. This central body need do no more at first than acquire the necessary lands. Future generations will "improve" them as they may be needed : and they will be glad of the opportunity.

The planning of the similarly difficult undertaking which the Metropolitan Sewerage Commissioners now have in hand was entrusted by the General Court to the State Board of Health, and I earnestly recommend that the same efficient Board be requested by the present legislature to report a plan or scheme for a metropolitan system of public reservations. The Board of Health will undoubtedly be able to devise a scheme which, while providing suitable, well-arranged, and convenient open spaces, shall at the same time forefend the district from much of the danger to which the building of cheap structures on wet lands might expose it. No question more nearly affects the welfare of that large part of the population of the Commonwealth which is seated in sight of this State House.

Much more might be said and said better, as to the opportunity for the creation of characteristic and therefore interesting open spaces afforded by the many salt creeks, rivers, and marshes of the district, etc. ; but I refrain from assaulting you further!

The objects set forth in this letter and the arguments for legislative action are the same as those which determined the appointment of the Metropolitan Park Commission of 1892 ; only the agent in the inquiry is different.

This quick achievement of a public object by the efforts, in the main, of one public-spirited, well-informed, and zealous young man, availing himself of a strong sentiment already in existence, combining the various resources of a few persons who were already thoroughly awake to the importance of the interests at stake, taking counsel with judicious and thoughtful friends, winning the support and personal help of busy men in high stations, and concentrating at each vital point the influence of thousands of good citizens, is an encouraging example of legitimate efforts to procure beneficent legislation under republican institutions.

CHAPTER XX

WRITINGS IN 1891 AND 1892

Readers of poetry see the factory village and the railway, and fancy that the poetry of the landscape is broken up by these; but the poet sees them fall into the great order not less than the beehive or the spider's geometrical web. Nature adopts them very fast into her vital circles, and the gliding train of cars she loves like her own. — RALPH WALDO EMERSON.

DURING the two years and a quarter occupied by the campaign for the Trustees of Public Reservations and that for the Metropolitan Park Commission, Charles did not altogether give over his writing for the press. The first of the papers which constitute this chapter was written in the period of the agitation for the Trustees, the next four while he was urging a Metropolitan Park inquiry, and the last two just after the appointment of the preliminary Metropolitan Park Commission. Taken together, they undoubtedly enhanced Charles's reputation as an expert in landscape, and a writer on landscape subjects.

MUSKAU — A GERMAN COUNTRY PARK.

Jan. 28, '91.

The River Neisse flows with no great rapidity from its source in the highlands which divide Germany from Austria to its meeting with the Oder in the plains southeast of Berlin. Its total length is perhaps one hundred miles, or about that of our New England Merrimac or Housatonic. In the lower half of its course it traverses an exceedingly sandy region, out of which the river has carved a shallow and crooked valley. Occasionally a cheerful meadow lies along the stream, but the banks or hills which bound the valley, and all the uplands beyond, are covered with a dismal and monotonous forest of Pines. The region has few natural advantages and little natural beauty.

In 1785, in the moated house of the Count or Lord of a

part of this forest-country, was born a boy who was destined
to work a wonderful revolution in the scenery of his native
valley, and by so doing to awaken throughout Germany an
interest in designed landscape which is still active and growing. This boy, Ludwig Heinrich Hermann von Pückler,
became a restless youth, who first attempted at Leipsic the
study of law, then tried and abandoned the military life, and
finally declined to enter even the civil service of his country,
because, as he said, " my liberty is too dear to me."

At the age of twenty-one he set out on a round of travels
which occupied four years. He saw Vienna, Munich, Switzerland, Venice, Rome, Naples, southern France, Paris, and
the lands between, for all his journeying was done either on
foot or on horseback. In 1812 he was cordially received by
Goethe in Weimar ; and in the following year, under the
Duke of Saxe-Weimar, he was military governor of a post in
the Netherlands. When peace was established, he made his
first visit to England, where he saw the landscape works of
Brown and Repton ; and in 1815, his father having died, he
at last turned homeward to his Standesherrschaft of Muskau,
on the River Neisse.

There is every reason to believe that the idea of improving
the surroundings of his home and village had been cherished
by Pückler during all his wanderings. His letters show his
intense interest in both natural and humanized scenery ; and
they make it evident that the sight of the great works then
lately accomplished in England had only made him the more
eager to begin the arduous task he had set himself.

This task was nothing less than the transformation of the
almost ugly valley of the Neisse into a vale of beauty and
delight ; and the great distinction of his idea lay in the fact
that he proposed to accomplish this transformation not by
extending architectural works throughout the valley, — not
by constructing mighty terraces, mile-long avenues, or great
formal water-basins, such as he had seen in Italy, at Versailles and at Wilhelmshöhe, — but by quietly inducing Nature to transform herself. He would not force upon his native
landscape any foreign type of beauty ; on the contrary, his
aim was the transfiguration, the idealization of such beauty
as was indigenous.

In the picture galleries of Europe he had seen the first-fruits of the young art of landscape painting. In common with the painter, he had found in the study of the beauty of Nature a source of pure joy which the men of the Renaissance had failed to discover. Somewhere and somehow he had learned the landscape painter's secret, that deepest interest and finest beauty spring from landscape character — character strongly marked and never contradicted. In England he had seen this truth illustrated by actual living landscape, for Repton's parks were simply the idealization of characteristic English scenery.

Accordingly we find Pückler, on his return to Muskau, intent upon including in one great landscape scheme his Schloss, his village, his mill, his alum works, and all the slopes and levels which enclose them — intent upon evolving from out the confused natural situation a composition in which all that was fundamentally characteristic of the scenery, the history, and the industry of his estate should be harmoniously and beautifully united.

One circumstance greatly favored the happy accomplishment of his design — namely, the very fact that he had to do with a valley, and not with a plain or plateau. The irregularly rising land skirting the river-levels supplied a frame for his picture; the considerable stream, flowing through the midst of the level, with here and there a sweep toward the enclosing hills, became the all-connecting and controlling element in his landscape. Well he knew that what artists call "breadth" and "unity of effect" would be fully assured if only he abstained from inserting impertinent structures or other objects in the midst of this hill-bounded intervale.

On the other hand, his difficulties were many and great. To restore the unity of the river-level just mentioned, he had to buy and remove a whole street of village houses which extended from the town square to the mill. To perfect the levels themselves required the removal of the wild growth from many acres and the cultivation and improvement of the soil. To carry the park lands completely around the village, so as to make the latter a part of the perfected scene, and to otherwise rectify the boundaries of his estate, required the purchase of some 2000 Morgen of land. Moreover, the hill-slopes behind the village, where the Count particularly wanted a background of rich verdure, were so barren they would hardly grow even Pines, so that these and many of the other upland slopes of the estate had to be improved at much cost and trouble.

In the valley the preëxisting but confused elements of breadth and peace and dignity were to be developed and enhanced. In the thickets of the lowlands and along the bases of the hills were found many large Oaks and Lindens which helped much to give character to the intervale. In the upland regions the original tangle of knolls, dells, and glades was to be made still more pleasantly intricate by opening the wood here and closing it there, and by breaking and fringing the original Pine forest with a great variety of appropriate trees and shrubs. This work of introducing more cheerfulness and variety proceeded gradually with the happiest results. To-day the crooked ways which follow the hidden dells in the woods are as charming in their way as is the central valley of the Neisse, while the roads which lead along the edges of the heights and command views of the valley are the most delightful of all. It would be difficult to make choice between the view from the low-lying Schloss over the quiet meadows to the semicircle of hills beyond the river, and the reverse view from these hills looking across the stream and the intervale to where the turrets of the Schloss and the long row of village roofs lie close together under the edge of the dark woods which crown the western range of heights. When his thirty years of pleasant toil were passed, Pückler tells us he was one day showing his results to a very intelligent and discriminating lady of his acquaintance, who told him " very modestly " that she had little knowledge of the art of designing parks, and that she could recall many scenes grander and more picturesque than the one now before her ; " but here," she said, " what strikes one first and gives one most delight is the repose which pervades the whole scene ; " and the Count adds that no praise ever pleased him more.

The accompanying plan (for the original draught of which I am indebted to Dr. Carl Bolle of Berlin) must serve to explain the general arrangement of the estate. Within the park are included not only the château and its gardens, pleasure grounds, and appurtenances of all sorts, but also the very ancient castle hill, the old Schloss of the Count's more immediate predecessors, the close-built village of Muskau, with its churches, schools, shops, etc., many acres of ploughed land owned and cultivated by the villagers with other acres farmed by the Count, a Pine woods hotel and sanitarium, an arboretum and nursery, a woodland cottage called "the English house," used as a holiday resort by the townspeople, a large grist-mill, an alum mine, the ruin of the oldest church in Lausitz, and more than one ancient graveyard. In most directions the park has no definite boundary. It flows into the ordinary Pine forest on many sides, and in several directions the country roads are "parked" for many miles.

Always keeping in mind his general scheme, Pückler was occupied during thirty years in extending his works and developing the details. At the end of that time he suddenly sold his creation! Muskau passed to Prince Frederick of the Netherlands. He who had become Prince Pückler-Muskau was obliged, like many a landscape painter, to confess himself a victim of his love of beauty. In his zeal for his art he had outrun his resources. At the age of sixty he retired to his lesser manor of Branitz, where he wrote his invaluable books and passed a peaceful old age, varied by many journeys and many visits to the country-seats of friends. He died in 1873.

All Germany has long held him in high honor. In England, the "Letters of a German Prince," as the translation of his "Briefe eines Verstorbenen" was entitled, passed through several editions, and remains to this day the best foreign delineation of the England of his early manhood. His essays on landscape were long since translated into French, and it is to be hoped that they may yet appear in English, for they contain a very clear presentation of the elements of landscape design, as well as many lively descriptions of his work at Muskau.

The significance for us Americans of this work at Muskau is very obvious. To be sure, at least one third of our great country is so arid that luxuriant vegetation must depend on

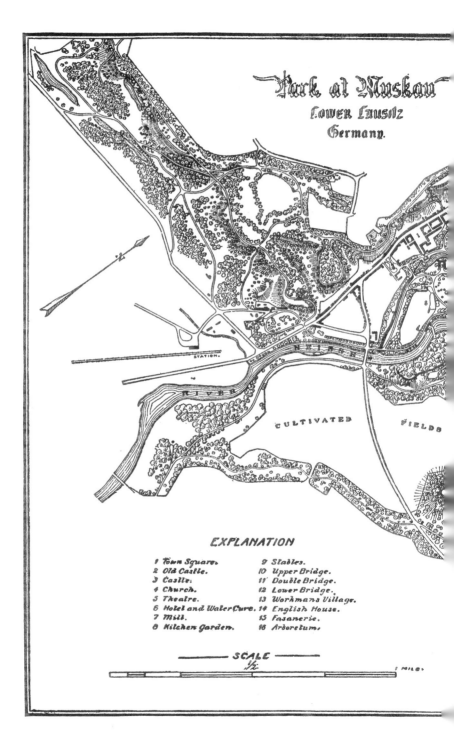

Park at Muskau
Lower Lausitz
Germany.

EXPLANATION

1 Town Square.	9 Stables.
2 Old Castle.	10 Upper Bridge.
3 Castle.	11 Double Bridge.
4 Church.	12 Lower Bridge.
5 Theatre.	13 Workmans Village.
6 Hotel and Water Cure.	14 English House.
7 Mill.	15 Fasanerie.
8 Kitchen Garden.	16 Arboretum.

SCALE
½

1 MILE.

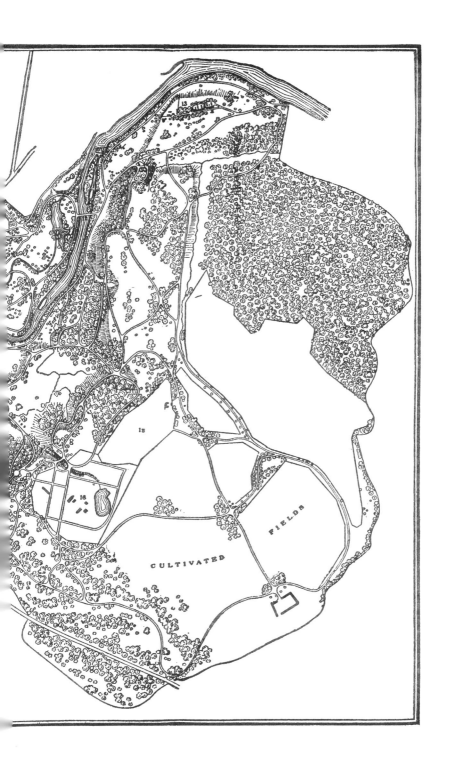

CULTIVATED FIELDS

irrigation; and, where this is the case, a pleasure ground becomes an oasis to be sharply marked off from, and contrasted with, the surrounding waste. Spanish models will help us here. But the other half of our continent presents verdurous scenery of many differing types, from the rocky Pine woods of Quebec to the Palmetto thickets of Florida. Throughout this varied region there is a woeful tendency to reduce to one conventional form all such too meagre portions of the original landscape as are preserved in private country-seats and public parks. What shall check this tiresome repetition of one landscape theme? When shall a rich man or a club of citizens, an enlightened town or a pleasure resort, do for some quiet lake-shore of New England, some long valley of the Alleghanies, some forest-bordered prairie of Louisiana, what Pückler did for his valley of the Neisse? He preserved everything that was distinctive. He destroyed neither his farm nor his mill, nor yet his alum works; for he understood that these industries, together with all the human history of the valley, contributed to the general effect a characteristic element only second in importance to the quality of the natural scene itself.

Our countrymen are beginning to manifest an appreciation of landscape painting; let them show the genuineness of their appreciation by preserving and enhancing the beauty of the actual landscape in which their lives are passed.

[*Paper before the Boston Society of Architects, October 2, 1891.*]

LANDSCAPE GARDENING IN ITS RELATIONS TO ARCHITECTURE.

Gardening and Building are sister arts, but in their progress towards the perfectness of the fine arts, Building is ever in the lead. " Men learn to build stately sooner than to garden finely, as if gardening were the greater perfection," wrote Bacon, centuries ago; and so true is this to-day that most persons are wholly ignorant of the possibilities of artistic work with earth and grass and foliage. Even our professors of artistic building seem slow to perceive the full stature and dignity of the sister art. I have heard a famous architect speak of gardening as the " handmaid " of fine building, and another great man has quoted to me with approval the saying

of the French, that fine gardening is the " sauce " of architecture, — a saying which would be insulting, if it did not so
plainly reveal the speaker's ignorance and prejudice.

If we would perceive with clearness the real sisterhood of
the arts in question, it is only necessary to take one's stand
at a certain point of view, — a point which some men find
hard to reach, because a journey back towards childhood is
involved. We must forget for the time our narrow technical
knowledge and our acquired ideas concerning art and architecture. We must try to look upon the world with the eyes
of youth. If we can do this, what a glorious prospect unrolls
itself before us ! A world of scenery of indescribable variety,
interest, and beauty ; oceans, mountains, hills, valleys, and
running waters transfigured daily by the glory of the rising
and the setting sun. In the midst of this wonderland stands
man, and we are more astonished at him than at all the rest.
We find him in primitive ages apparently unconscious of the
beauty around him, living precariously upon wild nature, and
causing little or no change in the appearance of the wilderness around him. When at last he is forced to increase his
food supply, he takes some wild thing like maize and plants
it in the glades of the forest, and stores the crop in granaries
set up on stakes. When he desires to shelter himself, he
contrives frail tents like the Bedouins or the Indians, or he
walls the mouths of cañon caves, or he builds earthen pueblos,
hardly to be distinguished from the arid soil on which they
stand. When he is awed by death and the forces of nature,
he sets up Druid stones, and raises long, serpent mounds, and
builds the Pyramids. As he comes to cultivate the earth, he
works marked changes in scenery. He fells the woods, and
marks off fields, and draws lines of roads across the country.
He builds farmsteads of as many types as there are different
climates, and different social circumstances. He quarrels
with his neighbors, and builds castles. He trades with his
neighbors, and builds towns. He prospers, and builds palaces. He glows with faith, and builds cathedrals. Fields,
orchards, roads, bridges, farmsteads, villages, towns, palaces,
temples, all play their part in the new scenery — the humanized scenery — of the earth ; and mother Nature, adopting as

her own all these works of her wonderful child, makes with
them landscapes vastly richer in meaning and pathos than
any she can show us in her primeval wildernesses.

> " Know'st thou what wove yon woodbird's nest
> Of leaves and feathers from her breast ?
> Or how the sacred pine-tree adds
> To her old leaves new myriads ?
> Such and so grew these holy piles,
> While love and terror laid the tiles.
> Earth proudly bears the Parthenon
> As the best gem upon her zone,
> And morning opes in haste her lids
> To gaze upon the Pyramids.
> O'er England's abbeys bends the sky
> As on its friends with kindred eye.
> For Nature gladly gave these place,
> Adopted them into her race,
> And granted them an equal date
> With Andes and with Ararat."

Here we reach the point of view of which I spoke. Standing here, we perceive that of all man's works upon the surface
of the earth, — his useful fields, his orchards, his lanes and
cottages, his avenues and palaces, his temples of the gods, —
none can be separated from the natural and historical conditions which give birth to them and surround them. None
can be cut out, and then adjudged to be either beautiful or
ugly. We cannot separate them if we would. The humble
cottages of the English lanes, the towered villages of the
Italian hills, and the red farmsteads of Sweden, are all beautiful ; each in its own place, under its own sky, set in its own
landscape. And the same is true of even the loftiest works
of architecture, such as the Pyramids, the Parthenon, and the
Abbey. None of these noble or charming buildings are beautiful in and of themselves alone, although the world and the
architects have sometimes seemed to think so. On the contrary, the truth is that these works of men are of necessity
but parts of landscape ; and they are beautiful just as the
works of pure nature are beautiful, according as they express
their origin, their growth, and their purpose, and as they help
or harm the expression of the particular landscape of which
they are a part.

If this is true, much of importance follows. We of the modern world, with our inevitable self-consciousness and our world-wide view, can no longer build and garden according to traditional and inherited types as did our fathers. We discover new and strange types in foreign lands, and we want to try them in our own land. Thus men have built Greek temples in the moist English park-lands, and have made pleasure grounds in the Chinese style. We make a series of similar experiments, and then at last we see our folly, and we turn with a new eagerness to discover, if we can, the essential, the vital, the permanent elements in the scenes which most delight us. What is it, we ask, which moves us when we call to mind the churchyard and church of Lincolnshire, the park and mansion of Devon, or the green and the elms and the simple buildings of our own Hadley or Deerfield? I think there can be but one answer. The beauty of such scenes — for each remembrance is the remembrance of a scene, and not of a building only — lies in their unity and harmony of expression.

Such beauty will hardly grow of itself for us in this New World and in this modern day. If we want it, we shall have to work for it through that arduous process which is called designing. At the beginning we must try to picture to ourselves the end, and our constant aim must be to make all that we do contribute to the effect of the whole; and the whole which we aim to produce can nevermore be a building only. The site, the scene, the "landscape," and the building must be studied as one design and composition. No other course is open to those who have once seen what we have seen. There is no other way of winning the beauty we desire.

Here again we stand where we cannot avoid seeing behind the fair figures of Gardening and Building a third figure of still nobler aspect, — the seldom-recognized mother of all that is best in the sisters, — the art which, for want of a better name, is sometimes called Landscape Architecture. If it be true that the art which arranges for use and beauty that part of a scene or landscape which is not a building is fully as important as the art which devises the building itself, — if it be true that Gardening which works with gravel, soil, grass, herbs, and trees is the sister of Building which works with stones, bricks, and wood, — then it follows that the art which conceives of the product of Gardening and Building as a unified scene or landscape is an art which is of even greater moment than either of the assisting sisters.   Evidently Landscape Architecture must rightly conceive the whole before Gardening and Building can rightly conceive or design their respective parts.   The mother art must lay out the main lines before the sister arts can work to their best advantage.

Does it not behoove artist builders to think of these things oftener ?   Should they not be ever ready to assist the slow progress of the artist gardeners, and in company with the latter should they not strive always for that perfect unity of general effect which is the flower of landscape architecture ? And for our encouragement let it be understood that whoever designs the arrangement of the buildings, ways, and green things of a farmstead, a country-seat, a village, a college, a world's fair, or any other scene of human activity in such a way that beauty shall in the end spring forth from the happy marriage of the natural and the needful, is a successful landscape architect, whether he calls himself by that long name or not.

At a meeting of the New York Farmers, January 19, 1892, the subject for the evening was " Arboriculture for the Farm, the Village, and the Highway."   Charles said : —

MR. PRESIDENT AND GENTLEMEN, — Arboriculture is a long word and a long subject.   I suppose it is the whole science and art of growing trees for timber, for firewood, for shelter, for the prevention of destructive erosion, and last but not least, for the beauty of trees individually and in masses. I must, of course, choose some one section of this wide field ; and so I shall, by your leave, give my time to a brief discussion of arboriculture in its relations with landscape — meaning by the term " landscape " the visible surroundings of men's lives on the surface of the earth.

It sometimes seems as if beauty in the surroundings of life were not appreciated, or even desired, here in our America. The man who goes so far as to paint his house and to " fix up " his place is reviled as a "dude" in many parts of our country. A certain brave scorn of beauty seems to characterize most of the people of our new West.

On the other hand we see, when we come to study the matter, that if the experience of the past counts for anything, there is a power in beauty which works for joy and for good as nothing else in this naughty world does or can. And when we come to see this clearly, we are at once compelled to abandon our indifference and to substitute therefor the eager desire of old Plato, "that our youth might dwell in a land of health amid fair sights and sounds." Alas, that "fair sights" do not spring up spontaneously around our modern lives as they seem to have done in the Old World. In the long settled corners of Europe, men's fields, lanes, roads, houses, churches, and even whole villages and towns, seem to combine with nature to produce scenery of a more lovable type than nature working alone can offer us. With us the contrary is too often the fact. Our buildings, fences, highways, and railroads, not to speak of our towns, are often scars which mar the face of nature without possessing any compensating beauty of their own. It is evident that beauty in the surroundings of life is not to be had in this modern day without taking thought, and exercising vigilance. And our thought and our vigilance must be rightly directed, or it will defeat our purpose. Many a man, becoming suddenly conscious of a desire for beauty, has attempted to attain his heart's wish by forbidden and impossible ways. Thus country roadsides have been "slicked up" until all beauty has been "slicked" out of them. Noble growths of native trees have fallen victims to the desire for the beauty of exotics. Village mansions of the dignified old style have given place to the frivolities which are named for Queen Anne. Trim formal flower gardens have been rooted up to make way for the modern gardener's curves and scattered beds. Men seem slow to learn the truth of the old saying, "All's fair that's fit," or that corollary thereof which best expresses the truth of my subject, "All that would be fair must be fit."

This is the principle which ought to govern us in our tree-planting as well as in all else which affects the scenery of our lives. Fields, lanes, and roads should be laid out so as to fulfil the requirements of convenience, while conforming to the facts of topography. Buildings should be designed so as to fulfil and express their several purposes. Ground about buildings should be similarly and straightforwardly adapted to the uses and enjoyments of real life, with no regard to any fanciful or a priori notions of what such ground should look like or contain. So when we come to the most effective means of modifying the scenery about us, the felling, preserving, or planting of trees, our principle will constrain us to cut, and save, and plant for good reasons only, and not from consideration for mere passing fashion or foolish love of display.

Let me illustrate this fundamental principle by briefly noting the main points in regard to the way in which trees and shrubs have been used in a typical New England valley where the eyes of the inhabitants have been opened. I shall describe nothing imaginary, although I may put together things which are to be seen in two or three separate places.

Of course we arrive at our valley by the railroad ; and the railroad banks themselves herald the approach to our station, for behold, they are actually planted ! Not with Forsythias and Japan Quinces, — how absurd such plants would look upon these gravel banks, — but with shrubby Cinquefoil, Dyer's Greenweed, Bayberry, Sweet Fern, and other humble, but tough and hardy plants. When we reach the station, we find not only a decent unpretentious building with substantial platforms, and neat driveways and gravel spaces, but also a fair spread of grass with three or four great Sugar Maples for shade — a contrast, indeed, to the usual North American station-yard, which commonly resembles a cattle-pen more than anything else ; a contrast also to that other type of station ground in which the station master sets out Geraniums supplied by the company, although the fundamental separation of grass-land from gravel space has not yet been made.

From the railroad platform we at once command a view of our valley. The village, with a mill or two, lies below us at the mouth of a gap in the northern hills. Southward the valley widens to contain a fresh green intervale. Opposite us the west wall of the valley is an irregular steep slope of rising woods with numerous hill farms scattered along the more level heights above. The eastern wall upon which we stand consists below the railroad of a long and dense wood, and, above the tracks, of rolling and airy uplands which have been occupied by city men for country houses. The central intervale, the flanking woods, the village gathered at the valley's head, the whole scene before us possesses unity and beauty to a degree which interests us at once. And how was this delightful general effect produced? Simply by intelligent obedience to the requirements of human life in this valley. The village was placed where it is for the sake of using the great water power which rushes from the gap in the hills. The intervale was cleared and smoothed for raising perfect hay. The steep side-hills have been maintained in woods because they are too steep for agriculture, and because if they were cleared of trees, their sands and gravels would be washed down upon the fertile land of the intervale. It is in such ways as these that the every-day forces of convenience, use, and economy conspire to produce beauty, and beauty of a higher and more satisfying type than that which founds itself upon caprice, or pomp, or fashion.

The truth of all this is well illustrated by the details as well as by the total effect of the valley before us. ʻIf we descend towards the village, we find the footpath leaving the highway, and following a swift brook down through the wood, while the road, in order to find an easier grade, makes a long zigzag through the woods to the south. Trees and bushes crowd the sides of the road thus freed from the stiff accompanying sidewalk, while the footpath gains exemption from the dust of the road, and has all the beauty of the brookside in addition. We learn incidentally that all this wooded slope is the property of the township, that it is called the Town Wood, and that it was the gift of some of the men who live above the railroad.

At the foot of the slope, footpath and highway join again, and proceed across the level valley as a straight village street, adorned with rows of trees, and broad grass strips, and sidewalks which conform themselves to the slight ups and downs of the ground. Here is just as much stiffness and straight-

ness as is necessary and fitting, and not a bit more.   Here is
no mimicking of the curbings, and the strict grades which are
necessities only in city streets.   Here, also, the street trees
are neither Gingkoes, nor Koelreuterias, nor Magnolias, but
American Elms.

In the heart of the village we find a town square planted
with Elms in symmetrical rows.   Fronting on the square is
the town hall, — a respectable building, — and back of it rises
a steep rocky slope with a high rock at the top, where a bon-
fire burns every 4th of July.   The rocky bank has recently
been planted with Pines and Hemlocks, which in a few years
will make a dense, dark background for the town hall.   Then
straight away south from the hall and the square runs the
broad main street of the town, an avenue of Rock Maples,
young as yet, but promising a noble vista in twenty years or
less; for the southern end of the long avenue opens upon the
sunny meadows of the intervale; so that a man standing in
the public square will look under the boughs of the trees
away to the south for miles.   Until lately there was a barn
standing in the line of this vista and hiding the open intervale.   The removal of the barn by a public-spirited man has
established the permanence of the outlook, because the lands
beyond are so moist that they can never be built upon.

I should like to speak of the generally sensible and simple
planting of the house grounds, of the good specimen trees in
the yard of the principal school, of the fine gorge above the
gap in the hills, where the mill company has preserved the
woods for the protection they afford to the canal and its re-
taining-banks, of the way in which the intelligent preservation of trees along even the tiniest brooks of the neighboring
hill farms has resulted in unusual beauty of farm scenery, as
well as in the prevention of that extravagant washing away
of soil which results from carrying ploughing to the edges of
watercourses.   All through this district it is most interesting
to note how beauty has resulted from the exercise of common
sense and intelligence.

When we turn the other way, and climb the hill above the
railroad station, we find a charming winding road, the sides of
which are irregularly overgrown with trees, shrubs, climbers,

and herbaceous plants. The footpath is there; but it dodges in and out, and goes here below a knoll and there on top, and does not stick to the roadside like a city sidewalk by any manner of means. Every now and then we pass the entrance of some city man's country estate, — there must be a dozen or twenty such estates in this fine hillside, — and in the course of a summer afternoon we make the round of them. Presumably all these gentlemen have distinctly intended to preserve or create beauty in the surroundings of their country homes. It is very interesting to see the several methods they have followed, and the various results obtained. Some of these estates seem very beautiful to us, while others are far less interesting. After allowing for all differences of natural opportunity, can any general reason for this contrast in results be found? It is obvious at once that the most beautiful of these places are not those upon which the most money has been spent, not those in which natural conditions have been most completely revolutionized, not those which display the greatest number of kinds of trees, shrubs, and herbs, not those in which the gardener has scattered flower beds in all directions. After studying these places, it is plain that the most beautiful are those in which the general arrangement, and the saving and planting of trees, have been made to depend upon those same considerations of convenience, easiness, and fitness which we found produced the beauty of the valley. Arboriculture, when it is practised to produce timber, to prevent erosion, or to form collections of all growable species, is an interesting and noble occupation for mind and for capital; but when it is practised to enhance the beauty of the scenery of every-day life, it must consent to be guided by that keen feeling for fitness which is the essence of what is called good taste.

[From The Nation, May 5, 1892.]

The Formal Garden in England. By Reginald Blomfield and F. Inigo Thomas. Macmillan & Co. 1892.

This is an awakening book. Its plea is for design in the surroundings of houses. It insists that the house and the ground around the house should be arranged in relation to each other.   It maintains the irrefutable proposition that really satisfying beauty in the immediate surroundings of men's lives upon this earth must spring, not from any imitated likeness to wild nature, nor yet from any impracticable conformity to the ideals of landscape painters, but simply from the harmonious adaptation of land and buildings to the uses and enjoyments of real life.

It seems strange that an obvious truth, now universally accepted as respects buildings, should still need to be preached in its application to the ground surrounding buildings.   Ground near a house must generally be devoted to purposes of use and enjoyment quite like the purposes which the house itself is designed to serve.   If the house has its hall, its drawing-room, its billiard-room, and its laundry, the ground near the house must have its approach-road, its garden, its tennis-court, and its drying-yard.   These are all artificial things, demanding formal lines and the subjugation of nature as emphatically as a building.   They ought to be planned so as to make with the building one design and composition.

In the book before us these ideas are deduced and illustrated from a study of the old gardens of England.   The writer and the draughtsman, who are the joint authors of the book, have evidently travelled widely in search of good examples of the ancient style of house grounds, and they have been rewarded for their pains by the discovery of many charming places, possessing fore-courts, house-courts, base-courts, terraces, bowling-greens, and walled gardens composed of " knots," parterres, pleaching, arbors, " palisades," and hedges.   In these gardens grow Gillyflowers, Columbines, Sweet Williams, Hollyhocks, and Marigolds, Lady's Slippers, London Pride, Bachelor's Buttons, Love-in-a-Mist, and Apple-of-Love; peacocks parade their Ivied walls, and Daisies stud their velvet lawns.   The seclusion, the repose, the mingling light and shade, the blending colors, the sweet odors, and, above all, the perfect fitness of these old gardens, conspire to make them lovable and delectable beyond compare. They are well described and happily illustrated in this book, so that the reader can but sympathize with the righteous

wrath which the authors vent upon the men who destroyed
hundreds of such places in the last years of the last century.

What was the origin of the mood or fashion which occasioned this lamentable destruction, and gave birth to the
pseudo-naturalistic style of treating ground about houses that
is even yet in vogue ? Our authors do not attempt a philo-
sophical answer to this question ; but they give us an instructive sketch of the history of garden design from the days of
the mediæval " Romance of the Rose," through the fresh and
simple style of the English Renaissance, to the elaborate
extravagances of the Restoration, and the consequent reaction which assisted in the establishment of the self-styled
" art of landscape gardening."

The prophets and practitioners of the naturalistic school,
from Whately, Uvedale Price, and Repton of the last century, to Messrs. Robinson and Milner of the present day, are
here handled without gloves. They are, indeed, too sweep-
ingly assailed ; for beyond the vicinity of the house and garden lies a broad field in which only naturalistic treatment is
appropriate. Yet, as respects gardens, what follows is true
enough : —

" Presumably, Mr. Robinson's dictum, that ' walks should
be concealed as much as possible and reduced to the most
modest dimensions,' is based on the state of a virgin forest;
the argument perhaps running thus : Because in a virgin
forest there are no paths at all, let us in our acre and a half
of garden make as little of the paths as possible." " But it
is not easy to state the landscape gardener's principles, for
his system consists in the absence of any, and most modern
writers lead off with hearty abuse of formal gardening, after
which they incontinently drop the question of design and go
off at a tangent on horticulture ; and yet it is evident that to
plan out a garden the knowledge necessary is that of design,
not that of growing a gigantic Gooseberry."

Even the latest books on landscape gardening, the English
Milner's and the American Parsons's, treat of trees, shrubs,
herbs, and other things, rather than of design in the surroundings of houses. Our private and public gardens also,
with their necessarily unnatural and yet studiously informal

arrangements, betray the same lack of feeling for design. Our time is certainly out of joint as respects this art, and for this reason this straightforward book is peculiarly valuable and welcome.

[*From the Youth's Companion, June 2, 1892.*]

BEAUTIFUL VILLAGES.

Every part of our great country has its own type of ugly village. " Down East " there is the " rough and ready " kind of settlement, where ledges protrude in the highways and plank walks straggle from rock to rock. " Down South " there are roads of deep sand, dooryards full of weeds, and stray hogs and chickens all about. "Out West" there is the abominable " sham front," and the bleak emptiness of the wide, straight, and windy dirt road.

It would be easy to particularize the many disorderly and unbeautiful elements in our small towns. It would be possible to specify the causes of all this ugliness, and the excuses which may be made for it ; but I propose to pass by all this, and ·dwell on the direct question, " What may be done to improve the appearance of our villages ? "

In the first place, as the village is made up of the estates of individuals, each owner should do as well as he can with his own portion of the general scene. Reform must begin at home. The smallest lot betrays its owner's tidiness or shiftlessness. Its gravel ways may or may not be neatly kept. Its grass may or may not be tended, and its buildings may or may not be clean and fresh. The smallest house and houseyard also shows at a glance its occupant's good sense or folly. The sensible villager will not imitate the narrow houses, the stone curbings, and the paved paths of cities. If a farmer, he will not try to hide his barns as though ashamed of them. If he seldom needs to drive to his house door, he will not make a gravel road for show alone, but drive on the grass.

In improving his place he will be guided by his special needs and his sense of fitness. No real beauty of building, village, city, or of any product of man's art, is attained in any other way. Generally the simplest arrangement of roads and paths is the best possible. When these are nicely built, you, my reader, may next see what you can do to improve the appearance of your lot by means of planting.

If the place has a naked appearance, a few bushes massed about the angles of the buildings, along the base of the piazza or along the boundary of the property, will change the scene at once. Many owners of small places plant trees when they should plant shrubs. Tall trees do not clothe the nakedness of the earth; but the evergreen, the berry-bearing, and the bright-twigged shrubs clothe the ground even in winter. The shrubs should not be dotted all over the lot. For the best effect they should be massed about the edges of the grass spaces, generally with the plants of each kind together. A single place treated skilfully in this manner has often led to the transformation of a neighborhood.

After your private lot is thus set in order, you will attend to your frontage on the street. Probably you will need to begin by forbidding the abuse of the public way before your house. Do not allow the road to be used as a dumping-ground for cans and ashes, or as a rooting-ground for pigs. If a sidewalk is necessary, make it of good and lasting materials. Lay down between it and the travelled way a grass strip of as great width as possible. This travelled way, the central part of the highway, should be no wider than is absolutely necessary, for the care of a wide way is expensive, and the glare and dust from it are disagreeable. If the ground is uneven, the road grade may need to be eased by some cutting or filling, but the footpath and the grass strip should rise above the road or fall below it, if the natural surface of the ground can be more closely followed by so doing.

If any fine trees, bushes, or rocks chance to stand upon your frontage, you should preserve them if possible. If you must plant new trees, you should set them in a row, if your grass strip is straight and level; if it is curved or rough, you should scatter them.

In short, you should treat your frontage as well as your lot according to the teachings of common sense, and not according to the dictates of " fashion " or the advice of the friend who may tell you that a stone curb, an asphalt walk, a retaining-wall, and a gilt iron fence will be " the proper thing."

By the time you have completed these unpretentious and inexpensive improvements, your neighbors will, perhaps, be filled with zeal to do likewise; and you and they may soon be forming a village society to encourage the like good work throughout the place. This society may well assist in the planting of the roadsides where the land-owners are too poor to do much. It may offer prizes for neatness and good design in house grounds. It may occasionally save from destruction a fine tree, or a bold ledge, or some other landmark of the neighborhood. It may help the town or village officers to spend the appropriations for "roads and bridges" in ways which will enhance, and not destroy, the characteristic beauty of the place.

About the post-office and "the store," or along the street of shops, it may be necessary to have considerable level gravel spaces and somewhat broad sidewalks, but in the rest of the village you are fortunately free from the bondage of straight lines and straight grades. The roads and footpaths should turn, broaden, contract, rise, or fall as may be easiest in each particular locality; for it is just this pliant conformity to natural conditions which is the vital element in the beauty of all the loveliest villages in the world.

The village society may well protect the neighborhood from that monstrous form of advertising which defaces buildings, fences, rocks, and ledges. The people should be educated to forbid advertisers the use of their structures, and all who ply the brush without legal right should be summarily dealt with. Villages which are ambitious to attract summer visitors should be particularly careful to suppress this increasing nuisance.

In Massachusetts, and presumably in other States, the village society is privileged to attend to the improvement and decoration of public grounds owned by the township. Here again is work which calls for the exercise of the nicest sense of fitness. Nothing is beautiful which is not fitting. If the ground to be treated is a quiet resting-place or a "lover's lane," it should be dealt with in a style quite different from that fitting a place for band concerts. In our villages the value of public open spaces is hardly realized as yet; perhaps because we have so few which are attractive. Let our village societies show us what pleasing outdoor parlors our village commons can be made, what delightful public footpaths we may have along our streams, and what attractive possessions public hill-tops are.

Under our democratic township and village systems, whatever the people will to do can be done. If a village lies along a lake, and the people come to wish to own the bank, so that they and their guests may there enjoy the loveliest walk in all the neighborhood, nothing can prevent the consummation of their wish, when it is once expressed by vote in town or village meeting. Several sea-coast townships of New England have lately laid out "ocean drives." Several Western townships have reserved their river-bluffs for public use. Several Southern villages cherish old groves of Live Oaks or of Pines. But the movement toward providing public reservations at the public charge is really only just now beginning.

Many town meetings are still frightened at the word "park," and some have been known to reject proffered gifts of land. Opposition to parks will die away as the people learn that public groves, river-banks, glens, and hill-tops are, when rightly handled, exceedingly inexpensive in proportion to their yield of pleasure to the native-born, their attractiveness to outsiders, and their consequent return of money to the township.

On the 17th of August, 1892, Charles spoke on Public Reservations before the Boston Boot and Shoe Club at a meeting the Club held in Lynn Woods, and made one point which he did not often urge: —

. . . Within the district to be covered by the investigations of the Metropolitan Park Commission I have seen a dozen supremely delightful places wholly destroyed within the last few years. In these cases our opportunity for action has not only come, but it has gone and gone forever. Meanwhile, another and only less distressing fate awaits or falls to such spots of beauty as escape the destroyer. They become enclosed for private gain or pleasure. You and I and all of us are shut out, in order that one man may enjoy the beauty of this sea beach, or this pond shore, or this hill-top, or else that we may pay him for the privilege of viewing that which he has fenced in.   How long can we afford to allow the finest of nature's pictures here in Massachusetts to be thus destroyed or enclosed?

Without stopping to consider the evil effects upon civilization, the wounds, as I may say, to art, and morals, and religion, which must follow this blotting out of beauty from the surroundings of life, let me, since I am speaking to business men, call your attention to the business aspect of this question.   In the country and seaside districts of Massachusetts, the summer resort business is the best business of the year.   Now the history of our summer resorts has been decidedly peculiar.   Nahant over here once possessed large hotels.   Newport was also a hotel town.   Bar Harbor, in Maine, filled many huge hotels every year for a considerable period of years; but last year and this year the large hotels of that town have been entirely closed, and I very much doubt if they ever open again.   Who wants to visit any resort where the seashore, or such other scenery as there may be in the neighborhood, is owned and occupied by private citizens who, if they admit you to their lands, do so grumblingly, or for a fee?   It is evident that our hotel men, and all people interested in the development of this great business of the summer resort, must go to work to preserve their goose of the golden egg, that is to say, the fine scenery in their neighborhood.   Even in the case of towns of cottages, would not every estate owner be the richer, if it were possible for him to have access at any time to every finest spot within his neighborhood?   As a matter of business, the proprietors and projectors of summer colonies ought to take account of this.

The bookstores are filled with books in praise of the beauty of nature, and the picture galleries are full of pictures thereof. Meanwhile we are destroying and losing every day the real pictures which the Almighty painted; although we have no longer any excuse for that form of destruction.

CHAPTER XXI

THE WORK OF THE METROPOLITAN PARK COMMISSION
OF 1892

> You will hear that the first duty is to get land and money, place and name. . . . If, nevertheless, God have called any of you to explore truth and beauty, be bold, be firm, be true. — RALPH WALDO EMERSON.

CHARLES was appointed landscape architect to the Commission in August. He was not quite thirty-three years old; but he had been in practice five years and a half, and had given public evidence of possessing business capacity, artistic skill, an interesting style in writing, and an unexampled knowledge of the metropolitan district. Mr. Adams had seen a sample of his professional work in his report on the proposed new town of Garfield, Utah; Mr. Chase had been intimately associated with him in all the work of the Standing Committee of the Trustees of Public Reservations; both these gentlemen manifested great confidence in him from the first, and came to feel for him a sort of paternal admiration and affection.

When the chairman of the Commission asked him in August to describe his conception of the organization and work of the Commission, Charles wrote briefly about the duties of the secretary and the legal adviser, and of his own function as follows: "Your landscape architect will view and map the existing public areas of your district, and the works proposed by the local boards. . . . You will expect from him a preliminary report descriptive of the areas which in his opinion should be 'resumed' (to use the Australian phrase) by the public. This report will cover the whole of your district, no account being taken of the municipal boundaries, and it will be illustrated by a general map on a small scale." This map, and others that he had in mind, were from the beginning important in Charles's eyes; he suggested in this letter to the chairman that $1000 be reserved for printing the map or maps.

From the middle of September through the autumn, the

Commission in company with Secretary Baxter and Charles
visited every point of landscape or park interest within ten
miles of Boston, Charles planning most of the trips, and setting forth in an unobtrusive and attractive way his thoughts
about the merits and value of each scene or prospect, and the
possible serviceableness of each proposed reservation.

On October 6th, in another letter to the chairman, he wrote
as follows : —

. . . As I conceive it, the scientific " Park system " for a
district such as ours would include — (1) Spaces on the
ocean front. (2) As much as possible of the shores and
islands of the Bay. (3) The courses of the larger tidal
estuaries (above their commercial usefulness), because of the
value of these courses as pleasant routes to the heart of the
city and to the sea. (4) Two or three large areas of wild
forest on the outer rim of the inhabited area. (5) Numerous small squares, playgrounds, and parks in the midst of the
dense populations.

Local and private action can do much under the fifth head ;
but the four other heads call loudly for action by the whole
metropolitan community. With your approval, I shall make
my study for the Commission on these lines.

He soon saw that it would be very important that the Report of the Commission should present forcibly to the eye, (1)
specimens of the beautiful scenes in the district which might
still be preserved or restored ; (2) specimens of the accomplished destruction of natural beauty ; (3) maps and diagrams
to exhibit the nature and relations of each reservation proposed, and the equitable distribution of the reservations over
the district. He began to seek appropriate photographs on
the 3d of October ; but finding that many of the objects he
most wanted to represent had not been photographed, or at
least that photographs of them were not in the market, he
sent out the following notice : —

METROPOLITAN PARK COMMISSION.

The undersigned is collecting for the above named Commission one hundred representative views of landscape near
Boston. Pictures of the following localities are particularly
desired : —

A. Nahant Rocks, Revere Beach, the Outer Islands, Nantasket Beach, and Cohasset Rocks.

B. The Inner Islands of the Bay, and the yachting.

C. The salt marshes, and the fresh-water reaches of the Saugus, Mystic, Charles, and Neponset rivers.

D. The rocks, hills, and woods of the Fells and the Blue Hills.

Prints from obtainable negatives should be sent to the undersigned before the end of November. All prints received will be returned, and those the negatives of which are desired for the Commission's report will be designated. The cost of sending and returning prints and negatives will be paid, and every picture in the report will be credited to its maker.

This measure not yielding negatives enough, he wrote many letters to friends who were amateur photographers, and to professional photographers as well, asking for photographs of particular objects. His efforts had but very moderate success. It was especially difficult to get "uglifications;" for nobody had photographed them or wanted to. The report of the Commission contained thirty-one illustrative plates, with three fifths of which Charles was measurably content.

For the maps and diagrams he already possessed the materials, or knew where to find them; and under his direction fourteen such illustrations were prepared for the Report. The map of the metropolitan district to accompany his own report was begun in his office on November 7th. His experience with the Map of the Country about Boston, published by the Appalachian Mountain Club in 1890, facilitated his present task. The new map was on the same scale as that of 1890, and extended a little farther to the north, but not so far to the west. To include all the reservations that Charles proposed to recommend, it was not necessary that the map should extend farther west than Waltham and Wellesley. This map, on which the existing and the proposed reservations were entered, was the strongest argument the Commission had in support of their general scheme. It showed convincingly that the scheme was equitable, economical, and adequate. It remains to this day (1902) a recognized authority on the subject of the Metropolitan Reservations.

Charles had his own part of the Commission's work well started by the middle of November; but his interest in the work extended quite beyond his own function as landscape architect. He talked much with Secretary Baxter, and Mr. Reno, the legal adviser of the Board, and with the members of the Commission separately, and he attended by invitation all the meetings of the Commission itself, — not only the field meetings, but the later ones at which the act to be recommended to the legislature was under discussion.

On the 14th of November he sent to the chairman memoranda on the " machinery " problem which covered the following points : the name, — Metropolitan Open Spaces Commission ; the number of members, — seven, one to be appointed each year ; appointment by the Governor ; no salary for members of the Commission ; powers, — to employ needed officials and servants, to coöperate with local boards, to exercise the right of eminent domain; resources, — (1) for purchase and original construction, State bonds with provision for interest and sinking fund through an annual levy on each city and town, fixed by commissioners appointed every five years by the Supreme Court, — (2) for maintenance and other annual charges, the Commission to estimate these expenses in advance for a period of three years, and the State Treasurer to collect annually from each city and town of the district its percentage of the total annual levy for this object, the percentage to be the same as that decreed for interest and sinking fund. These memoranda suggest a more decided distinction between first cost and maintenance than found favor with the Commission and the legislature. Charles's suggestion was more conservative than the Act which became law ; and in after years he felt great concern at the delay in levying the assessments on the municipalities of the district. As a matter of fact, no collection of money for Metropolitan Park purposes has been made from the towns and cities of the district up to January 1, 1902. The closing paragraph of Charles's letter to the chairman was as follows : " All this I know is outside my proper field, and I submit it only for what it may be worth. My special work I take to be the picturing by printed words, photographs, and maps of those open spaces which are still obtainable near Boston. If this picturing cannot be made vivid enough to command the attention of the people and the legislature, there will be no use in fussing over the details of the legal machinery."

To this " picturing " he gave the greater part of his time for the next ten weeks. He had in hand, however, several other pieces of work which demanded attention during the same busy weeks. He wrote the principal parts of the Second Annual Report to the Trustees of Public Reservations, and edited the whole document of 63 pages, and also wrote the Report of the Trustees of Public Reservations on the Province Lands (House, No. 339, February, 1893). The Second Annual Report, just mentioned, contained a valuable list of all the public open spaces of Massachusetts, arranged alphabetically by the names of the cities and towns, and including statistics of population and area, the source of each reservation, and the nature of the title.

At the request of Mr. Charles Francis Adams, as chairman of the Park Commissioners of the city of Quincy, he had studied during the autumn the interests of Quincy as regards shore reservations; and he now sent in an interesting report on that subject dated January 2, 1893. At the same time he was making plans for several private places, and was giving advice on others. He also gave days to the preparation of a map of New England which the Appalachian Mountain Club thought to publish. The amount of work he did in these months would be very surprising, were it not evident that for much of it he was thoroughly prepared long beforehand. He was putting into practice principles and methods mastered years before, or he was applying knowledge and skill long since acquired.

Charles's report to the Metropolitan Park Commission of 1892 is dated January 2, 1893; but the report of the Commission was not presented until February 1st. The text of his report occupied only twenty-five pages. It was subsequently reprinted in a separate edition with all the diagrams, maps, and photographic illustrations to which the text referred. It is reproduced here in full except that the photographic illustrations are omitted : —

To the Metropolitan Park Commission.

Gentlemen, — You have asked me to report to you upon the opportunities presented by the neighborhood of Boston for the creation of such public open spaces as may best promote the health and happiness of the inhabitants of the metropolitan district. I have given my best attention to the problem, and now beg leave to submit the following paper, asking you to excuse its manifest shortcomings, in view of the great breadth of the field it essays to cover.

PARIS

LONDON

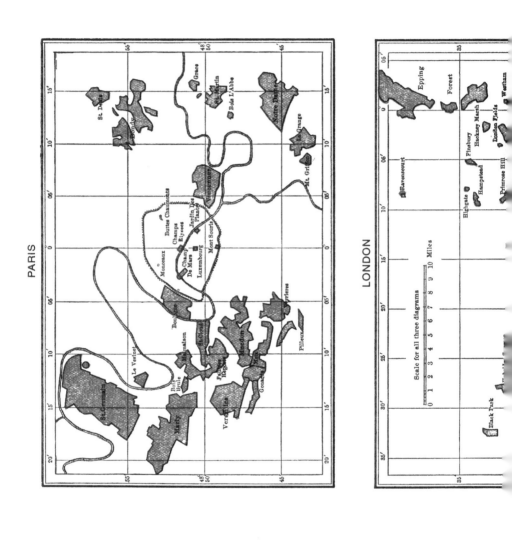

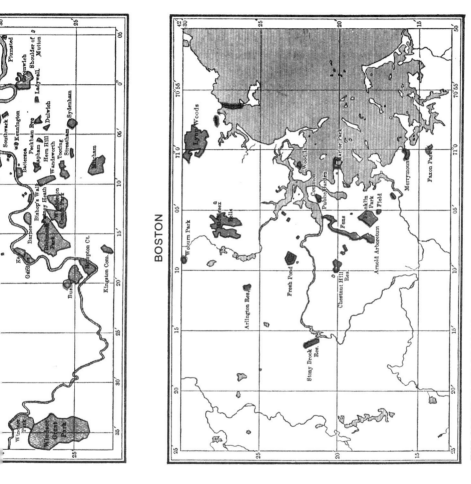

BOSTON

THE OPEN SPACES OF PARIS, LONDON, AND BOSTON (1892), DRAWN TO THE SAME SCALE

INTRODUCTION.

The life history of humanity has proved nothing more clearly than that crowded populations, if they would live in health and happiness, must have space for air, for light, for exercise, for rest, and for the enjoyment of that peaceful beauty of nature which, because it is the opposite of the noisy ugliness of towns, is so wonderfully refreshing to the tired souls of townspeople.

Most of the greatest centres of the population of the world have now accepted the teachings of bitter experience, and have provided themselves with the necessary and desirable open areas, albeit at immense expense and with great difficulty. The accompanying diagrams show the extent of the public open spaces now existing in the neighborhood of Paris and of London, in comparison with those now existing near Boston. "Experience keeps a dear school, but fools will learn in no other," said Benjamin Franklin. Shall Franklin's birthplace play the fool's part? Presumably this is the question which the Metropolitan Park Commission and the people of the metropolitan district will ask the General Court to answer.

If, then, it be determined that the metropolitan district of Boston shall be wise, and shall provide itself with ample open spaces while it may yet do so at small expense, upon what considerations should the selection of lands for public open spaces be based? Obviously this question cannot be answered intelligently without a somewhat detailed study both of the natural or geographical features of the district in question, and of the manner in which crowded settlement has affected these natural features to the advantage or injury of the population concerned. When such a study shall have brought forth the facts in the case, it will be possible to deduce therefrom the considerations which should govern the scientific selection of lands for public open spaces; and it will then only remain to review the existing open spaces, and to propose new reservations in the light of the considerations so established. In other words, this report falls naturally into three parts, as follows : —

PART I. — A summary of the physical and historical geography of the metropolitan district.

PART II. — A study of the way in which the peculiar geography of the metropolitan district ought to
govern the selection of the sites of public
open spaces.

PART III. — A review of the opportunities which still present themselves for creating new open spaces
in accordance with the governing considerations just laid down.

PART FIRST.

The Rock Foundation. — Underneath the whole region —
under the sea, the rivers, the woods — lie the rocks of the
crust of the earth. The oldest and hardest of these rocks,
beside underlying the whole district, stand up in two conspicuous though broken ridges, — that which extends from
Waltham to Cape Ann, sometimes called the Wellington
Hills, and that which from the earliest settlement has borne
the name of the Blue Hills. The northern mass of rock,
though broken in many places by deep transverse valleys,
such as those of the Mystic, Malden, and Saugus rivers, generally presents to the south a steep, wall-like front, about one
hundred feet in elevation. In its eastern extension its highland surface is exceedingly rough, broken into rocky knobs
and narrow hollows, now and then rising into exceptionally
high summits, such as Bear Hill (three hundred and twenty-
five feet) in Stoneham, and Burrill's Hill (two hundred and
eighty-five feet) in Lynn. The southern rock-mass of the
Blue Hills differs from the northern in that it is carved into
a dozen rounded and partially separated hills, steepest on
their south sides, and varying in elevation above the sea
from three hundred to more than six hundred feet, being the
highest hills standing thus near the coast of the continent
from Maine to Mexico.

Between these much-worn stumps or roots of ancient mountains — the Wellington Hills and the Blue Hills — lies a
region some fifteen miles wide, in which the primitive rocks
which form these mountain stumps have been depressed so

far, and the secondary rocks which lie upon the primitive
rocks have been worn down so deep, that the sea has flowed
over both and formed Boston Bay. Not that the waters of
the bay wash against shores of rock. On the contrary, the
points within this region where the sea meets the rocks are
very few, the most conspicuous being the ocean fronts of
Swampscott and Cohasset, Nahant, the outer islands, and
Squantum. Such rocks as do appear above the surface within
the Boston basin are of mixed kinds ; among them the various
slates of Quincy, Cambridge, and Somerville, and the conglomerate or pudding-stone which forms Squaw Rock at
Squantum and the great bosses of ledge which protrude in
spots in Roxbury and elsewhere. But generally throughout
this depressed region there is no solid rock in sight. Even
the rivers rarely discover any, except at their several so-called
" falls." Another material, which must next be examined,
forms almost all the seashore, the river-banks, and the dry
land of the space between the massive uplifts of the Wellington and the Blue Hills.

The Glacial Rubbish. — Dumped in various sorts of heaps,
alike upon the uplifted and the depressed parts of the rock
foundation of the district, lies an enormous quantity of clay,
gravel, and stones of all sizes and kinds, — stuff which the
moving ice-sheets of successive glacial periods bore away from
northern regions. The largest of these heaps form very conspicuous objects in the scenery of the district, being great
rounded hills of symmetrical form, such as are numerous in
the neighborhood of Chelsea and all about Boston harbor.
Lesser heaps take the form of steep mounds and narrow and
long ridges, often enclosing bowl-like hollows from which
there is only an underground escape for water. More important are the large areas in which the glacial material has been
worked over by running waters in such a way as to produce
almost level plains, which, in sharp contrast to the steep hills,
are almost free from boulders of large size. It is with this
material, dumped in these various forms, that the region
where the ledge rocks are sunk is filled and brought above
the level of the sea.

The Fresh Waters. — Upon the surfaces already described

— the well-rubbed rocks and the rounded heaps of glacial wreckage — fall rain and snow, which gathers itself into streams, and sets out for the sea. But the course of the waters throughout all this region is difficult and tortuous in the extreme. Turned this way and that by the accumulations of glacial stuff, the streams follow few sharply defined valleys, but wander about in an unusually aimless manner. In the highland parts of the district rain-waters are caught in rock-rimmed hollows, or in basins formed by dams of glacial drift, from which they can escape only by overflowing the rim or dam. Thus almost every hollow, even at two hundred feet above the sea, contains a pond, or a swamp which is a clogged pond, while along the courses of the brooks and rivers similar morasses appear at frequent intervals. Even the Charles River, the largest stream of the region, suffers in its course from just these difficulties. At Dedham it is suddenly turned aside from a short route to the sea by way of the Neponset valley; and then at Newton Upper Falls the hard rock which it has there chanced to hit upon serves as a dam, which makes a great swamp of all the lowlands for several miles up-stream. It need hardly be added that, however it may be with respect to healthfulness, with respect to scenery these retardations of the waters in ponds and swamps are a very valuable and charming addition to a landscape already wonderfully varied and picturesque.

The Sea. — Eastward on a clear day, from almost any of the numerous rock or gravel hill-tops of the district, is seen the distant horizon of the sea, — sometimes a long field of blue spread across the whole fifteen miles from the Roaring Bull of Marblehead to the Black Rock of Cohasset, and sometimes only a bowl-shaped patch lying between some near or distant elevations of the mainland.

The ocean rocks of Marblehead and Cohasset guard the entrance to Boston Bay. Sweeping between them with an unbroken surface, the salt waters presently meet with many and various obstructions, which everywhere betray the marks of the destructive or constructive energy of the waves. The rock island of Nahant has been gnawed into by the surf until its coast is ragged and picturesque in the extreme; but, in return, the sea has formed out of the waste of the land a beautiful beach, which makes a perfect causeway connecting the island with the main. One step further inland, and similar evidences of the work of the sea appear on every hand. Here the waters meet the foremost of those great hills of clay and stones which the ice age bequeathed to the present. Grover's Cliff, Winthrop Great Head, Great Brewster Island, Point Allerton, and Strawberry Hill still stand boldly in the front against the sea, although they are now but fragments of their originally symmetrical masses. From the feet of their steep bluffs, long curving beaches, built by the sea, stretch away to unite themselves with the next adjacent mounds or hills, or else to join in never-ending conflict with some strong tidal current, as at Shirley and Hull guts.

The waves as they roll inland along the converging coasts of the bay are ever bringing fresh material wherewith to close the remaining gaps and shut up the port of Boston ; but the flowing and ebbing tides are fortunately as constantly at work to keep the entrance open, so that no appreciable narrowing of the passages is accomplished. Once inside Point Shirley and Point Pemberton, the now stilled waters play around numerous other hills of the kind geologists call drumlins, here cutting a steep bluff out of the side or end of one of them ; here, by building beaches, linking two or three together to form an island or a stretch of coast ; or here again reaching far inland between the hills to receive the fresh waters of brooks and rivers. Finally, behind the beaches and in all the stillest parts of the tidal region, the growth of grasses on the muddy flats has resulted in the building up of widespread and open levels of salt marsh, in which the tidal currents are able to keep open only a few sinuous channels. On the north the marshes and the salt creeks extend to the very feet of the rock highlands. Westward the salt water of Charles River reaches inland six miles from the State House. On the south the estuaries and marshes of the Neponset and of Weymouth Fore and Back rivers present beautiful pictures of mingled land and water. This flowing of the sea about the half-sunken drumlins has produced scenery which, were it not so familiar, would be considered wonderfully varied and fine.

The Effects of Human Occupancy. — Into this region of
marvellously commingled waters, marshes, gravel-banks, and
rocks came the English colonists of the seventeenth century;
and, from Miles Standish of Plymouth to Thomas Morton
of Merrymount, every man among them had only praise for
the scenery. To Standish, after he had landed at Squantum
and voyaged up Mystic River, the region seemed "the paradise of all these parts," and he very naturally wished the
Plymouth people "had there been seated." For Morton the
educated sportsman, the blue waters, the salt meadows, and
the great woods which framed the coves of marsh grass with
a wall of varied verdure composed a great free hunting-park,
the like of which all England could not boast.

The annihilation of the native red men by a plague had left
the country comparatively safe, and, although the first houses
of Boston were built on the peninsula of Shawmut, because
of its advantages in case of attack, Governor Winthrop and
the other leaders soon took up large outlying estates, while
outlying settlements were also made very early. The steep
drumlin hills of Shawmut, surrounded and even divided as
they were by the tides, afforded but little opportunity for
tillage, and compelled a scattering of the people; and when
this took place, it was to the most accessible of the few smooth
parts of the neighborhood that they went. Wherever a navigable river or creek swept past a gentle slope of the glacial
drift, there a settlement was made; and from such settlements grew Lynn, Medford, Cambridge, Watertown, and the
other older townships of the colony. The creeks were the
first roads and the marshes the first hay-fields. So reluctant
were the colonists to attempt the subjugation of the great
woods and the slopes of boulders that, when the open spots
near at hand had been occupied, hundreds of people braved
the dangers of a long march over Indian trails, to reach and
settle in the soft intervales of the Connecticut valley. Had
the prairies of the West been accessible, the rougher parts of
the district would hardly yet have been tamed. As it was,
when population increased, men were forced to take up axe
and crowbar in grim earnest. The great hills of boulder
clay had to be made cultivable; generation after generation

labored with the trees and stones, and at last the rounded
hills stood forth as mounds of green, marked and divided by
walls of field stones, and sometimes crowned, as at Clapboard-
tree Corner in Dedham, with the white churches of the victors.
Naturally the bounding hills of rock were only entered for
their timber; nothing else was to be won from their wild
crags. After two hundred years of these arduous labors, the
neighborhood of Boston was a lovely land. The broad or
narrow marshes still lay open to the sun and air, through
them the salt creeks wound inland twice a day, about them
lay fields and pastures backed by woods upon the steeper
slopes, and across their sunny levels looked the windows of
many scattered houses and many separate villages.

What causes brought into this land that ever-increasing
body of population, the coming of which has so shattered the
idyllic landscape of the earlier days, it is not for me to attempt to determine. Whatever its causes, a flood of population, gathered from Europe, Canada, and the country districts
of New England, has poured itself into the Boston basin, and
here among the marshes and the steep hills it is trying to
build for itself a healthful and beautiful city. The undertaking is one of enormous difficulty. Add to the problem of
Venice a tide that flows and ebbs from nine to eleven feet
instead of two, a jumble of hills each of which rises steeply
to more than one hundred feet of elevation, and a winter
climate which locks even the salt waters with ice, and you
have the problem of the central parts of greater Boston.

The peculiar intricacy of the topography caused all the first
streets and country roads to follow very crooked courses; and
when a city began to grow here, one of the first necessities
was better means of communication than the old ways which
wound around the hills and marshes could afford. Accordingly long bridges and causeways were thrust out across the
flats in all directions, and from their terminations turnpike
roads were carried far into the inland country. In order to
eke out the scanty building land in the heart of the district,
the flats along the causeways and in the coves of the marshes
had next to be filled with gravel taken from the nearest hills,
or brought in later days from distant hills by railroad. Upon

these filled lands all structures, from buildings to sewers, must be founded on driven piles or otherwise " floated ; " from these lands there is no fall for the draining off of storm-water, except when the tide is out; from them there can be no way of removing sewage except by pumping its whole volume up to such a level as will deliver it to the ebb tide. In view of the great cost of all these works, it is no wonder that population and manufacturing have in many places crowded upon even unfilled marshes, trusting to dikes to keep the waters out; neither is it any wonder that the regions in which these wet lands are at present but partly filled and but partly built upon should be both ugly and unwholesome.

In the inland parts it is unfortunate but equally natural that the wet lands along the streams tend to become built upon in the same cheap and unsightly ways. Factories have placed themselves along the rivers and brooks; and near the factories, and always with their backs to the stream, are built the houses or tenements of the employees. Thus a once pure stream is at one blow made both foul and ugly. So also with the many areas of ill-drained upland. Wet land being cheap, it is cheaply built upon, to the detriment of both the healthfulness and the beauty of the district.

As to the original drumlin hills of the district, some have been wholly dug away for filling, others have had great holes cut out of them, others have had streets run up them at steep grades, and houses possessed of extra floors on their lower sides stuck all over them. A few hills of this difficult kind in the upland regions of Brookline have been so skilfully laid out that the roads are easy and the general result pleasing; but most of the old drumlins have been badly treated, and the result is ugliness and inconvenience.

Lastly, the same rock-hills, which baffled the men who cleared the drumlins, are now found to present most serious obstacles to the easy construction of cities. In addition to their exceeding roughness, the very hardness of their rocks makes the necessary excavations for streets, cellars, water-pipes, and sewers very expensive; and accordingly the larger rocky regions of the district have not yet been seriously invaded by the waves of population flowing against their feet.

PART SECOND.

Assuming now a thorough acquaintance with this strange city of the marshes and the hills, we must next inquire in what manner the peculiar facts of the situation about Boston should influence the selection of permanent open spaces.

We have found that the metropolitan district of Boston lies, even at this late day, between two wildernesses; on the one hand the untamed heights of the rock-hills, on the other the untamable sea. If it be true that easy access to the refreshing beauty of the natural world is of the greatest benefit to crowded townspeople, the people of this favored district have only to say the word, and to pay out a little money annually during a term of years, and this best of possessions will be theirs at once and forever. Here the busy and the poor can find near home that best of antidotes to the poisonous excitement of city life, which the rich win by travel or by living in luxurious country-seats. From every one of the greater of the encircling hills, even from the inland Prospect Hill of Waltham, the ocean is in sight; and, even if these wild hills were not interesting in themselves, this fact alone would make them valuable to the public. In the other direction the open sea and the surf on the shore are but four miles from the State House: on a quiet night after a storm its note can be heard in the streets; its flowing tide " twice every day takes Boston in its arms."

Thus has nature placed and preserved at the very gates of Boston riches of scenery such as Chicago, or Denver, or many another American city would give millions to create, if it were possible. Stupid indeed will be the people of greater Boston if they fail to perceive and attend to their interests in this matter before the opportunity is lost.

We have further found that the inhabited district is invaded in many crooked directions by the tides, and swamped in many other parts by the fresh waters. What does the greatest good of the greatest number, if not the self-interest of the landowners of such parts, demand?

In view of the fact that good building land is scarce in the heart of the district, it is obviously necessary that all the lesser areas of mud-flat, marsh, and swamp, as yet remaining unfilled, should be filled as soon as may be, thus preventing whatever nuisance may tend to arise from their presence in the midst of the city, while at the same time increasing the area of taxable real estate. On the other hand, such filling, with the accompanying obliteration or covering of ancient waterways, must not be carried too far, for it has its great dangers. The large watercourses, both salt and fresh, cannot safely be meddled with. As has been pointed out already, it is only when the tide is out of the Mystic and Charles rivers that extensive areas of natural and artificial lowland can be drained of storm-waters; if their natural outlets were filled up, these areas, with all their streets and houses, would inevitably become swampy. As to the fresh-water streams, they are subject to floods which cannot be confined within any ordinary conduits or covered channels, as one or two disastrous experiments in this line have proved.

If, then, these larger waterways must be preserved even in the midst of dense populations, how shall they best be treated? Shall they continue in the future, as in the past and present, to be abused, polluted, and defaced by the population living on their banks or near them? Is this for the public advantage? Shall factory waste, sewage, and rubbish of all sorts be continually poured into them, and then allowed to rot in the sun when the tide goes out, or the water is drawn off to turn the wheels of factories? Such practices can hardly be conducive to the public health of a region already more than threatened with malaria. Such practices should indeed be impossible in every civilized community.

Fortunately for greater Boston, most of her streams and ponds may still be rescued, and converted from evil to good uses. Public control or ownership of the banks of the streams will work their cure, and ensure their permanent preservation as the most charming of the many charming features of Boston scenery. For such public control will not only tend negatively to prevent the dangers to health already mentioned, but it will also have many positive good results. It will give an added value to adjacent real estate, which will ensure its occupation by good houses having their fronts, and not their back yards, turned towards water-side roads. It will eventually provide a whole series of public promenades and playgrounds for the use of the population which tends to crowd into the valleys. It will restore and preserve the attractiveness of the streams for that large class of citizens who take pleasure in boating. It will also provide, since the main streams flow towards the heart of the city, a series of sorely needed pleasant routes leading from the country, through the suburbs, to the city, and even to the bay or ocean side beyond.

Thus we find that the rock-hills, the stream banks, and the bay and the sea shores are the available and the valuable sites for public open spaces; available because they are still generally unoccupied and cheap, valuable because they present both the grandest and the fairest scenery to be found within the district.

After what has been said, it hardly needs to be added that the metropolitan district can no longer afford not to take possession of its inheritance in these lands. Private ownership of the lands referred to is not only detrimental to the public welfare in the ways already mentioned, but it is also thoroughly bad as a measure of public financial policy. Private ownership of such lands, because of the need of quick returns, inevitably tends to their occupation by cheap makeshift structures of small taxable value; whereas public ownership will so enhance values that the whole community will reap a profit in the end. Once the lands in question are owned by the public, the work of development may safely wait.

Only one other word needs to be said before passing to a review in detail of the existing and the proposed open spaces. Playgrounds for children and youth are among the necessities of modern town life. Large or continuous open spaces, like those about to be suggested, will provide ample playground for the children of the population seated near them; so that smaller squares, gardens, and open-air sitting-rooms and nurseries will need to be provided only in those crowded districts which the larger spaces do not serve. All scientific planning of open spaces for large cities proceeds thus from the greater to the less. The greater spaces are of first account, because

if they are not acquired at the right time they can never be
had, and because they afford not only fresh air and play-room,
which is all that small spaces can offer, but also those free
pleasures of the open world of which small spaces can give
no hint. Moreover, in the case under consideration, the peculiar subdivision of the metropolitan district of Boston into
thirty-six separate political units makes it unreasonable, and
indeed impossible, to expect that these units should act as one
body, or pay as one body, for more than the principal, leading,
or trunk-line open spaces of the district. Such small spaces
as will be needed after the larger spaces are provided will
have to be acquired by the action of local authorities, or by
the cooperative action of two or more such bodies; and, since
small spaces are almost entirely of local benefit, this seems to
be quite as it should be.

PART THIRD.

The foregoing studies have led to the conclusion that those
large or continuous open spaces which will most benefit the
whole population of the metropolitan district are situated on
the rock-hills, along the stream banks, and on the sea and bay
shores. Now, therefore, it becomes a pleasant duty to examine each of these special sections of the district in some detail,
in order that we may learn to what extent these hills and
shores are already dedicated to public uses, and in order that
we may determine what particular parts thereof can, with the
greatest economy and advantage, be forthwith added to the
public domain.

The Rock-hills. — In the whole length of the northern
rock-hills, only one crowded town is really founded upon them,
— namely, Marblehead, which had to twist its crooked lanes
between the ledges in order to avail itself of a good harbor.
From several public points of vantage on the rocks of the
shore the townspeople, with great numbers of visitors from a
distance, annually view the beautiful pageants of the yacht
fleets of New England.

In Swampscott, the next township, the rock-hills are beginning to be occupied by houses which look southward to
the blue waters of Nahant Bay, over the narrow strip of drift
lands upon which stood the fishing village of the past.

In Lynn the original settlers occupied a somewhat wider strip of coast lands, and during many years held the rocks in their rear as " commons." When at last they were divided, they were used as wood-lots. Even when a few years ago Lynn had become a city of fifty thousand inhabitants, the hills were still as uninhabited as ever; so that when the need of a public water supply arose, the city had only to collect, by means of a few dams in the valleys, the uncontaminated rainfall of her own wooded highlands. Meanwhile many citizens had come to appreciate the great value to a crowded population of these neighboring wild rocks with their broad views over the ocean, the ponds, and the woods; and soon whatever lands remained between the tracts acquired by the water board were given to or purchased by the Lynn park board, and through it dedicated to the enjoyment of the public. To-day the Lynn Woods embrace some two thousand acres, and constitute the largest and most interesting, because the wildest, public domain in all New England. On the other hand, if we exclude the expenditures of the water board, the woods have cost the public treasury of Lynn only thirty-five thousand dollars. About one hundred public-spirited private citizens have contributed in gifts of land and money the equivalent of another thirty-five thousand dollars. Thus for the small sum of seventy thousand dollars the " city of shoes " has obtained a permanent and increasingly beautiful possession, which is already bringing to her a new and precious renown.

Westward again, beyond the deep-cut valley of Saugus River, the next great body of the highlands contains many fine parts, such as the rough hills in northern Saugus, the bold frontal elevations which overlook the great marshes, the charming hollow of Swain's Pond, and the pretty valleys of the brooks which flow towards Pranker's Pond. It is to be hoped that the real-estate dealers, who will soon be cutting up this region, and the townships which include it in their limits, will unite upon a sensible scheme of development, by which the courses of the brooks and the highest rocks will be secured to the public, thus ensuring the perpetual continuance of that picturesque attractiveness which is sure to lead population into this region before long. Such laying out of lands for sale as has been done here has been done badly, except at Pine Banks on the edge of the next cross valley — that of Malden River — where a single land-owner has built many roads, in a particularly charming locality, upon lines which properly conform to the topography. But even here it will be necessary, when the selling of house-lots begins, to reserve long strips and blocks of open ground, if that beauty of situation which gives a special value to the house sites is to be preserved.

Just beyond the once charming but now populous vale of Malden River we must climb a rocky cliff in order to enter the next wild region, once called the Five Mile Woods, but now generally known as the Middlesex Fells. Unlike the two preceding plateaux, this elevated region is entirely surrounded by rapidly growing towns and cities, whose boundary lines meet among the rocks. Four of the surrounding municipalities draw water from its valleys, and for the protection of the purity of the waters large areas of land have lately been converted from private to public ownership. Other public holdings of the region are Bear Hill, the highest summit, controlled by the park board of Stoneham, and Virginia Wood, the gift of the late Mrs. Fanny H. Tudor to the Trustees of Public Reservations. In short, this region of wild rocks and dells is now in the same condition in which the Lynn Woods lay before the park board knit together the disjointed preexisting reservations by acquiring the intervening and surrounding lands. On the other hand, the Middlesex Fells cannot, under existing conditions, be broadly united into one great reservation, because they lie within the bounds, not of one municipality, but of five. When new legislation shall have provided an instrument by which the unifying work which has been done in Lynn may be accomplished in the divided Fells, the people of Boston, Cambridge, Somerville, and the nearer municipalities will soon find themselves possessed of a common domain which, with its Spot Pond, its Bear Hill, its Pine Hill, and its many less conspicuous but delightful ponds, pools, brooks, and crags, will rival, if it will not surpass, Lynn Woods.

Westward once more, beyond the Mystic River valley, the swelling highlands of Winchester, Arlington, and Belmont are far less rugged than those of Lynn, Saugus, Melrose, and the Fells. They are cultivable in most parts, while in Arlington the so-called Heights have become a suburban colony, the inhabitants of which can see the New Hampshire mountains in one direction and the ocean in the other. Two thirds of the way over to the Charles River valley, Beaver Brook issues from the highlands through a miniature gorge, and then flows among some glacial ridges upon which stand the largest surviving Oak-trees of our district. The waterfall in the little gorge and this famous grove of Oaks should certainly be preserved ; but this cannot be accomplished under any statutes now in force, because the brook is the dividing line between Belmont and Waltham. Again, as in the case of the Fells, an instrumentality new to our community is needed.

Still following along the front of the highlands, past Owl Hill and Cedar Hill, it is not until the heart of Waltham is reached that any present need of a large open space appears. Here is a rapidly increasing community, which is fortunate in finding at its very doors both a pretty river and a great and rugged hill. The river's surface is perhaps twenty feet above the average level of the sea ; the hill-top one mile distant from the river rises to an elevation of four hundred and sixty feet. One who stands upon it looks eastward down the Charles River valley to where the golden dome of the State House glistens against the distant blue horizon of the sea. The slopes of the hill, still preserved from ugly scars, present several particularly attractive spots, and the neighboring but lesser Bear Hill has a distinct beauty of its own. The whole tract lies within the bounds of Waltham, so that there is nothing to prevent the opening of a reservation on this hill through local action. The hill, however, is so well placed, both with reference to the view up and down the Charles valley, and with respect to its position in the metropolitan district, that it would merit the attention of whatever metropolitan parks board may be established.

Leaving Prospect Hill and Bear Hill, it is but a short distance to the large collecting reservoir owned by the city of

Cambridge. Here the waters of Stony Brook are held in a long narrow valley before setting out for Cambridge or escaping to the Charles. At the mouth of the stream is the stone tower built by Professor Horsford to mark his conception of the site of a Norse city; and at the valley's head is a rocky passage through which the brook enters the reservoir with a rush.

The point now reached is just halfway around the inland circuit of the metropolitan district; in other words, it is ten miles due west from the State House. Moreover, it is at the meeting-place of the Charles River and the northern highlands. The lower reaches of the river, and the easy roads of its valley, lead thence through populous regions to the city, while the upper river valley leads southeastward along the border of the metropolitan district towards the southern highland of the Blue Hills. So central a situation should, if possible, afford a large and interesting public recreation ground, and it is most fortunate that nature has here provided all the elements and placed them ready to our hands. If to the charming water park of Charles River and Stony Brook there be added not only Prospect Hill to the north of the reservoir but also Doublet Hill on the south, a very satisfactory reservation will be obtained. The latter hill, while not so high as Prospect, commands more pleasing views of the river valley, while from the surface of the stream it is itself an attractive, and sometimes an imposing, object.

Passing now up the Charles River valley toward the southern highlands, it is well to stop for a moment at the wonderful little gorge of Newton Upper Falls, where the river cuts its way through ledges clothed with hemlocks. The narrow stream flows swift and dark between quaintly broken rocks, and the great stone arch which bears the Sudbury River aqueduct leaps boldly across from bank to bank. Like the brook and the Oaks at Waverley, this is a spot of uncommon interest and beauty, which, because it lies within the bounds of three municipalities, can be preserved for the delight of the public only by some coöperative or metropolitan agency.

Where Charles River makes its great bend in Dedham, we leave the stream in order to discover the southern counterpart of the Fells. As Bear Hill in Stoneham is eight miles north northwest from the State House and three hundred and twenty-five feet high, so Bellevue Hill in West Roxbury is seven miles south southwest and of practically the same elevation. The growing suburbs of West Roxbury, Dedham, and Hyde Park surround it, and town streets are even now climbing its slopes ; but, on the Hyde Park side, there still remains a large area of exceedingly rough and steep land, in the midst of which is concealed a low-lying pool called Muddy Pond. From the summit of Bellevue, whence the sea is in full view, to the shore of this pond is half a mile, but the descent is more than two hundred feet. Halfway down, if we pause for a moment on the Dedham turnpike, or on one of the many jutting ledges of rock, we shall see over the pond, the pine woods of the valley, and the half-concealed town of Hyde Park, the range of the Blue Hills, — no longer the pale blue masses which we saw from Lynn Woods and the Fells, but near by and sharply cut. This striking view, the panorama from the hill-top, and the sheltered wildness of the deep valley of the pond, render Bellevue Hill with the Muddy Pond woods the most valuable open space now obtainable in this section of the metropolitan district. This is, however, another case for metropolitan action, for the boundary which divides Hyde Park from Boston also divides these woods.

Crossing the Neponset valley, we at last reach the Blue Hills, — the "mountains" of the metropolitan district. Although they extend hardly one fourth the length of the northern range of rock-hills, their average elevation is three times as great. So considerable a barrier do they present, that the railroads, the creators of suburbs, have avoided them entirely, — with the result that in all the five miles from the eastern base of Rattlesnake Hill to the western foot of the Big Blue, there are not yet a half-dozen buildings standing on the hills above the contour of two hundred feet. There are, indeed, in all this distance only two roads which cross the range. From end to end the wilderness is still practically continuous.

The hunting of foxes and raccoons is still carried on in it. Its separated hills are far larger, if no bolder, than the others we have seen. The notches or passes between the hills are often deep and steep-sided, and the views down the side valleys to the sea, or out over the seeming plain of southeastern Massachusetts, are surprising and grand. It is true that the original forest was swept away years ago, and its substitute of Oak and Chestnut is a little monotonous; on the other hand, the highest parts of all the hills are variously clothed with scrub Oaks, Cedars, Pines, and other toughest growths, while the many narrow and shady defiles shelter other species of their own, among them the Mountain Laurel, which is very rare near Boston. If the people of metropolitan Boston care to possess in common a park such as any king would be proud to call his own, a public forest possessed of vastly finer scenery than any of the great public woods of Paris can show, a recreation ground far surpassing in its refreshing value even London's Epping Forest, they have only to possess themselves of the still cheap lands of the Blue Hills. Like the other highlands which have been mentioned, these hills stand wholly within the sweep of the eleven-mile radius from the State House. They lie south of Boston as the Lynn Woods lie north; and if it is well for the public to possess the northern reservation, it will be even better for it to own the grander southern heights.

Lastly, and speaking with reference to all the open spaces thus far mentioned, it only remains to point out that, once they are acquired, they need cost little for maintenance and nothing for improvement, at least for many years. They are all of a kind which, if forest fires are prevented, will take care of themselves. Moreover, their first cost need not at all alarm the taxpayers of the district. A study of valuations and acreage would seem to warrant an estimate that one million dollars will more than suffice to-day to purchase all the highlands herein named. In other words, there are needed only as many dollars as there are inhabitants of the metropolitan district. This being so, it ought not to be long before the combined action of the metropolitan population shall make the hills their own.

The Ponds and Streams. — When it comes to examining the little lakes and rivers of the metropolitan district, their case is found to be different from that of the rock-hills. Population, which has everywhere avoided the heights, has, like the waters, settled in the valleys. Indeed, most of the centres of suburban populations are crowded, like Hyde Park and Waltham, upon the very banks of streams. Thus at first sight it seems as if the proposed resumption of the banks by the public were already impracticable, if not impossible, so great must be the expenditure which the work of rescue must entail. On the other hand, as already pointed out, the advantages the whole community would reap from public ownership of the waterways are so many and great that the endeavor to secure them cannot be abandoned hastily or without a careful study of the facts and the possibilities.

The streams as they flow through the district on their way to the sea must, therefore, next be followed; and for this purpose the Mystic, Charles, and Neponset had better be taken, rather than their more rural mates, the streams of Saugus and Weymouth.

The Abbajona, as the upper Mystic River is called in Winchester, is already by no means a clean stream; and yet, below the last of the tanneries which pollute it, the appearance of the winding rivulet and its banks is quite delightful, particularly where it passes under a quaint little bridge to find its outlet in the upper Mystic Lake. Here is a natural pond converted by a dam into a collecting reservoir of the Boston water works. Its shores are intricate in outline and attractively wooded, but much of this attractiveness may be destroyed at any time, for the city of Boston owns hardly anything more than the land under water. Below the dam, the lower lake lies so low that its waters feel the ebb and flow of the tide. We are still eight miles in a straight line from the sea, and in the mouth of one of the gaps in the northern range of rock-hills; yet just after the Mystic River has quitted this lower lake, there appears a little flat of salt marsh upon either hand, and from this point to the river's mouth this green border of meadow is never absent. Down to Medford the marsh on the left bank is bounded by a fine tree-clad bluff of upland,

from which some of the solid mansions of a hundred years
ago still look southward across the sunny open of the river.
At Cradock bridge buildings are crowded to the water's edge,
and just below the bridge is the head of navigation, where
ships were built, while there was still ship timber in the Fells,
and where now an occasional schooner discharges a freight of
coal, lime, or lumber. From the lower wharf the view southeastward and Boston-ward includes what seems an ever-widen-
ing salt marsh, through which the channel widens in broadening loops, one of which swings out of the sunlight of the
meadows into the shadow of the steep Winter Hill of Somerville. Three or four manufacturing concerns, of the sort
which require cheap lands and no near neighbors, have set up
buildings on the marsh; but there is no considerable settlement upon the river-bank until after the lesser Malden River
has entered from the north and the long railroad bridges
have been passed. Here the channel becomes deep enough to
float considerable vessels, and a huge chemical factory and
many coal " pockets " are seen. Thus far, excepting for a
short distance near Cradock bridge, there is really nothing to
prevent the reservation of the banks for public use, and ultimately, though perhaps many years hence, the construction of
a river road which would provide the pleasantest possible
route to Boston from Medford, Arlington, and Winchester
and all the towns beyond. Below the railroad bridges commerce should undoubtedly possess the river; so that travellers
by the river road, if bound to Boston, will have to make their
way through Charlestown, or over that boulevard terminating
in Haymarket Square which the consolidation of the railroads will make it possible to lay out, approximately on the
present location of the old Boston and Maine line.

If, on the other hand, the traveller from up the river is
bent on pleasure and desires to drive to the sea, it will not be
difficult to provide him with an easy and pleasant way crossing Malden River near its mouth, passing by the head of
Island End Creek, and so down Snake Creek and by a branch
of Belle Isle Creek, to the southern end of Revere Beach.
This route will bring the ocean beach within six and one half
miles of Cradock bridge, Medford, within seven miles of

Harvard Square, Cambridge, and within correspondingly short distances of many other places whose inhabitants at present never think of driving to the sea because of the miles of pavement which must be traversed on the way.

Doubtless the feasibility of reserving so continuous an open space will largely depend upon the temper of the owners of the river lands. If they can see their own advantage, the needed reservation will be obtained almost as soon as a metropolitan parks board can be created. If, however, for any reason the continuous space should prove out of the question, the metropolitan board should at all events possess itself of the valley and mouth of Island End Creek, which lies within the bounds of Chelsea and Everett, and is the only space which now remains convenient to the populations of those two growing cities.

Proceeding now to Waltham, Charles River should be followed in its course through the very middle of the metropolitan district. As far as Watertown the stream is of fresh water, flowing tranquilly through lowlands. A few large mills are seated on its banks, but outside of the closely built parts of Waltham and Watertown the shores are generally quite free from buildings. Halfway between the towns is the mouth of Cheese-Cake Brook, where the city of Newton is practically illustrating the treatment which, with local modifications, should be applied to all the larger waterways of the district, as soon as the lands about them are demanded for building purposes. Instead of covering the stream with back yards or a street, the watercourse is placed in an open strip of grassy or bushy ground, upon each side of which is constructed a roadway affording access to houses built facing the stream. In this way three results are brought about at once. The pollution of the stream is effectually prevented, a handsome thoroughfare is created, and the value of adjacent real estate is so enhanced that it much more than makes good the subtraction of the brook banks which have been given to the public. The treasury of the city of Newton will soon be more than reimbursed by the increase of the taxable values along the stream.

Below the dam at Watertown Charles River is salt, and

bordered by salt marshes backed by more or less distant uplands. Out of a total length of sixteen miles of bank, from
Watertown bridge to Craigie bridge and back again, almost
four miles are already controlled by public or semi-public
agencies. Among the rest the United States Arsenal, the
Cambridge Cemetery, the Corporation of Harvard College,
and the City of Boston all own long frontages, — a part of
Boston's river front has already become a popular promenade
and playground, known as the Charlesbank. Moreover, the
percentage of the remaining frontage occupied by costly structures is very small. Most of the marginal proprietors are
still at liberty to do what they choose with their own. It
must be evident to them that the use of the river for shipping
purposes is almost at an end. Navigation by masted vessels
cannot be continued much longer, because of the intolerable
interruption to traffic caused by the opening of the draws of
the crowded bridges. This being admitted, the question arises
whether the most profit will in the end be reaped by offering
the river lands to the builders of factories and slums, or by
drawing to them the builders of good private and apartment
houses. One numerous body of marsh and flat owners has
already staked its money on the belief that the most profit
is to be derived from the last-named method of procedure.
Acting on this conviction, the Charles River Embankment
Company has given the city of Cambridge a river-side esplanade two hundred feet wide and five thousand feet long, in
the rear of which it is building a series of fine streets which
converge upon Harvard bridge. In Watertown another company of land-owners is about to lay out a large tract of river-
side upland upon a similar, though a more rural, plan. In
Boston around the so-called Fens, and in Brookline and Boston along the improved Muddy River, real estate is already
reaping the advantages arising from the successful conver-
sion of a damaging nuisance into a profit-making attraction.
What has been done in these last-named places can gradually
be done in less expensive ways along Charles River, whenever
a metropolitan commission, free to act in several cities and
towns, shall be empowered to coöperate with the local land-
owners in pushing forward a work which cannot fail to profit
both the land-owners and the public.

For the descent of our third river — the Neponset — the start should be made from Dedham. A small tributary of the Neponset, called Mother Brook, has here been artificially supplied by means of a canal with an overflow of water from the meandering Charles, so that we find a good canoe stream, which, in the course of two charming miles, brings us among the factories of the town of Hyde Park. The brook flows crookedly between high banks of trees in a valley surprisingly little injured by the occasional factories which use the water power. The mills are still half concealed by trees, and by the very narrowness and crookedness of the valley. In some parts there are already brookside roads having fringes of trees between them and the water. In other parts, the banks afford beautiful views down the descending valley to the Great Blue Hill and its mates. On the other hand, in Hyde Park, where the brook joins the river, we have a striking exhibition of the abuse of streams. The river is here a sewer, and its bank a rubbish dump and continuous back yard.

Passing through Mattapan to the head of the tide at the foot of Milton Hill, several long-established factories are met, but no very evil places. Along most of the way the banks are beautifully fringed with trees and bushy thickets, and in some parts the desirable river roads already exist. At length, with a rush between two great brick chocolate mills, the freshwater river makes a sudden turn, and, sweeping around a last Pine-clad point, flows out to join the tide of the salt marshes. Just here is one of the most picturesque spots in the whole neighborhood of Boston, and one which well illustrates the fact that the evidences of human industry, such as the wharves, sheds, and schooners which here are mixed with trees and rocks, may often be very helpful to the effectiveness of scenery.

The marshes bordering our river from this point to the lower bridge are framed with woods, and especially adorned by two wooded knolls or islands. As yet there is not a single building to mar the beauty of their open levels, the best view of which is had from near the Neponset bridge, where the Oak islands, Milton Hill, and the Great Blue Hill looming in the distance, compose a quiet landscape such as is hardly to be found elsewhere within our district. Beyond, on the way to Squantum, are two striking rocky knolls covered with dark Cedars and surrounded by the marsh, and then a winding marsh road is traversed, scarcely raised above the level of the waters of the bay, which now appear on either hand.

As the ocean at Revere Beach was reached by a ten-mile drive from Winchester down the valley of Mystic River, so now the bay shore at Squaw Rock is reached by a ten-mile drive from Dedham down the lovelier valley of the Neponset. Halfway between these northern and southern riverways we find Charles River, leading, by another course of ten miles, from Waltham through the very centre of the metropolitan district to the basin just west of the State House. Nature appears to have placed these streams just where they can best serve the needs of the crowded populations gathering fast about them. Moreover, if action is taken quickly to establish an executive body charged with the duty of defending and asserting the interest of the whole community in the right treatment of these rivers, there will not be found to be any very great difficulty in acquiring in some parts that public ownership of the banks, and in other parts that simple right of way, which is all that is essential at present. The self-interest of the river land-owners and the self-interest of the separate river towns will conspire to assist such a new board in its work. A great benefit to the public would practically be assured from the start.

There remains one other kind of inland open space of more than local yet of not such general value as the rivers, — the ponds of the district, about which, as in the case of the rivers, there ought generally to be a protecting public way, even if it be no more than a footpath. Here again the intelligent interest of speculative land-owners will in time effect something, — the more quickly if such private interest can be encouraged by a board officially representing the public interest in such works. What can be done is well illustrated at Lake Quannapowitt, where a public road follows a tree-fringed shore for more than a mile, and gives access to the boating which the lake affords. Most of the ponds are, however, too small for boating; so that those who take pleasure in that sport make use of the Charles River between Waltham and Dedham, — a part of the river thus far omitted because, for the purposes of this report, it is to be regarded as one long pond. From Waltham to Newton Lower Falls the stream is still idyllic in its beauty, though threatened here and there by monstrous ugliness. Hundreds of persons from Boston and many other parts of the district are to be found here every pleasant afternoon in summer. In all this district there is no other place where quiet boating in such surroundings can be had.

Must all this beauty of the upper river, with all its valuable opportunities for recreation, be destroyed? The town of Brookline and the cities of Newton and Waltham draw their water supplies from this valley; and for the protection of those supplies they already own between Waltham and Dedham some six out of a total of twenty miles of river-bank. They ought to own much more; and as in the Fells a metropolitan commission might do the public great service by joining the domains of the various water boards, so here upon the Charles River the same body might likewise do much for the public by encouraging further purchases, by accepting the charge of gifts of lands, and by showing the landowners and the towns the many dangers both to health and to property which the continued private ownership of the banks will entail.

The Bay and the Sea. — As already seen, about one fourth of the whole area swept by a radius of fifteen miles from the State House is occupied by the bay and the open ocean. Here, accordingly, is Boston's one great "open space," whence comes her famous east wind with many another blessing in disguise. Most of the sheltered bay is shallow, yet sufficiently deep for pleasure craft of small tonnage, some eight hundred of which are owned in the metropolitan district, — many more than can be counted in any other harbor of the Atlantic coast, not excepting the grand bay of New York. In summer the channels among the islands are sometimes fairly thronged with craft, among which pass the pleasure steamers which daily carry thousands to the fine seashore of Nantasket or Nahant.

Viewing these pleasant scenes of healthful recreation, it is a delight to think that all is as it should be, that here at last is a section of the district where nature has supplied the people with the best sort of a park, — an inalienable pleasure ground such as cannot be enclosed for private use, cannot be damaged, and cannot be improved. Yet, if this is the first thought, the second is of ominous tenor. True is it that the waters cannot but remain free to all; but can the same be said of the shores? Upon inquiry it will be learned that of all the ocean shore of the metropolitan district, only Nahant Beach, which is a highway, belongs to the public. Even within the bay the public holdings are but few. To be sure, most of the islands belong either to the United States or to the City of Boston; but they are used for forts, reformatories, hospitals, and poorhouses. They might easily be clothed with foliage, to the great improvement of the scenery of the bay; but they cannot well be given over to the use of the general public. On the bay shore of the mainland only the city of Boston owns any public spaces, these being Wood Island at East Boston, the Marine Park and the Old Harbor Parkway at South Boston, and the main drainage reservations at the Cow Pasture, Squaw Rock, and Moon Island. Everybody recognizes the value of these bay-side spaces; they are more popular than any of the other great works of the Boston park commission; and they point the way by which a metropolitan park commission may at once win public favor and support.

Boston has now done nearly all that can be done upon the shore within her limits. If the public is to own any of the ocean front and any more of the bay shore, divided as both are among many towns and cities, it can only be through the encouraging and helping activity of a metropolitan park commission. And when such a commission is established, what should be its first work upon the shore? The answer is, — the acquirement of the title to the foreshore and the beach from Winthrop Great Head to the Point of Pines. Winthrop Head stands almost due east from the State House, and looks eastward and seaward halfway between the promontories of Nahant and Hull. Between it and Grover's Cliff the beach is already owned in common by the proprietors of the crowded

houses on its crest. Grover's Cliff is the property of the
United States. It is only along Revere Beach that difficulty
will be encountered in securing free public access to the
shore. The present condition of this fine beach is a disgrace.
Two railroads and a highway have been built upon it, without regard to either the safety and convenience of the public,
or the development of the highest real-estate values. The
railroads cared only for a location which would enable them
to use the beach as an attraction to draw passengers. No
account was taken of the fact that swarms of people must
induce a demand for buildings, and so the buildings have
had to find sites where best they could, generally between
the highway and the sea. A thorough reformation is called
for here in the interest, not only of the general public, but
also of the beach proprietors and the treasury of Revere.
The real interests of the railroads demand a proper arrangement of the beach. Its capabilities as a place of residence,
equipped with a broad esplanade and drive, and lined with
houses and hotels facing the southeast and the sea, are as yet
not understood ; nevertheless, the time is coming when they
will be understood, and when that public control of the shore
which can now be brought about at comparatively little cost
will be appreciated at its worth.

CONCLUSION.

The circuit of the rock-hills, the streams, and the shores of
the district has now been completed, and it only remains to
add a few words of general application.

In proposing the acquisition of the particular spaces
named, I have been influenced by nothing but my view of the
public needs, and my estimate of the district's financial powers.
That the proposed open areas lie so symmetrically within the
district, Lynn Woods mating with the Blue Hills, the Fells
with Muddy Pond, the Oaks with the Hemlock Gorge, and
the Mystic River with the Neponset, is due to nature.

As to the bounds of the proposed areas, I have not attempted to define them with precision. When the time
comes, they should in every case be so placed that the street
departments of the several towns and cities may find it easy

to construct roads immediately adjacent to the boundaries and continuous therewith. Doubtless in many places the abutting land-owners will give the lands which may be needed for such roads in view of the advantages their property will derive therefrom.

In conclusion, it may be well to point out that the cost of the maintenance of all the metropolitan open spaces need not, for many years at least, exceed the expense of guarding them from forest fires and other forms of depredation; on the other hand, if the community should wish to clean the streams, build paths or roads, or do any other proper work within the reservations, it would find in the Park Commission an instrument to do its bidding.

I desire, before closing, to express my thanks to the engineers and clerks of the towns and cities of the district for the information which many of them have kindly furnished.

The bill recommended by the temporary Metropolitan Park Commission was favorably reported by the Joint Committee on Public Reservations; but was somewhat injured in the Finance Committee in consequence of objections made without careful consideration in the supposed interests of Medford.

An arbitrary southern boundary for the Middlesex Fells, consisting of two straight lines, one running easterly from the southerly base of Pine Hill, and the other running northwesterly from the same point, was laid down in the bill. This boundary, running over hill and dale without the least regard to the lay of the land, was absurd in itself, and was distinctly injurious both to the reservation and to Medford. It was improved by a special Act of the legislature in 1895; but is still very defective from every point of view. As finally enacted, the statute created a permanent Commission of five members, serving without salary, and provided with the powers and resources needed to carry out at their discretion the general scheme which had been elaborated and published under the direction of the temporary Commission. The three members of the temporary Commission were all made members of the permanent Commission, so that a continuity of general plan and purpose was assured.

Considering Charles's agency in securing both the temporary and the permanent Metropolitan Park Commission, and the fact that millions of dollars were rapidly spent in carrying out the recommendations of his report of January 2,

1893, the charge he made for his services to the temporary
Commission is a curiosity : —

1 Feb. '93.

METROPOLITAN PARK COMMISSION.

Professional services to date : — including field studies in
the metropolitan district of Boston, a report upon the opportunities for open spaces in that district, superintendence of
the making of a map of the district, and attendance upon the
meetings and excursions of the Commission, $1000.

He also collected from the Commission $19 for carfares
and carriages, and $392 for work done by his clerk and
draughtsman. For four years (1893–1897) he further received, as a member of the Olmsted firm, a modest compensation for his assiduous Metropolitan Park work.

NOTES ON THE MAP ACCOMPANYING THE REPORT OF JANUARY 2, 1893.[1]

This map represents the neighborhood of Boston on a scale of a trifle
more than one mile to each inch, — a scale to which the people of the
United States are now accustomed, because it is used by the national
geological survey for all its maps of the populous regions of the country.
The contour lines of the map are copied from the original sheets in the
office of the State topographical survey. It should be said that they are
but roughly sketched and inaccurate in many places ; nevertheless, they
display the general form of the surface and the relative elevation of
different parts of the district in a manner not otherwise possible. The
rock-hills, the rounded drumlins, the wandering streams, the marshes,
the salt creeks, and the wave-built beaches of the coast are all clearly
brought out.

Principal highways and those traversed by street railways are shown
upon this map by double lines ; all other streets and roads by single lines.
Where streets are built upon filled flats or marshes, the black street lines
are printed over the marsh color ; the great extent of the low and filled
lands is thus indicated at a glance.

Railroads are shown by the usual convention, and the crossings of the
streets are distinguished according as they are overhead, underneath, or
at one grade.

Existing commons, squares, parks, and other open spaces reserved for
public recreation or for the protection of water supplies, and having an
area of two acres or more, are printed in green, and numbered to correspond with the key on the next page.

Open spaces suggested in the landscape architect's report are colored
buff. As stated in the report, the boundaries of these spaces have not

---

[1] The map will be found in the pocket of the left-hand cover; in the
two-volume edition, in the pocket of the right-hand cover of Vol. I.

been studied in detail ; if they had been, the small scale of the map would preclude showing them.   The scale of the map has likewise made it necessary to print the buff color along the streams and in some other parts without regard to those special parcels of real estate, such as cemeteries, churches, established mills, and the like, which a metropolitan commission would hardly think of buying, since agreements made with their owners would in most cases accomplish all that is essential.

KEY TO THE FIGURES ON THE MAP.

OPEN SPACES.	CONTROLLED BY	OPEN SPACES.	CONTROLLED BY
1. Boston Common	Boston Department of Public Grounds.	30. Washington Park	Boston Department of Public Grounds.
2. Public Garden	Boston Department of Public Grounds.	31. Fountain Square	Boston Department of Public Grounds.
3. Commonwealth Avenue	Boston Department of Public Grounds.	32. Jamaica Pond	Boston Park Comm'n.
4. Charlesbank	Boston Park Comm'n.	33. Arnold Arboretum	Boston Park Comm'n.
5. Back Bay Fens	Boston Park Comm'n.	34. Franklin Park	Boston Park Comm'n.
6. Blackstone Sq.	Boston Department of Public Grounds.	35. Franklin Field	Boston Park Comm'n.
		36. Dorchester Park	Boston Park Comm'n.
7. Franklin Sq.	Boston Department of Public Grounds.	37. Squaw Rock	Boston Improved Sewerage Department.
8. Monument Sq.	Bunker Hill Monument Association.	38. Moon Island	Boston Improved Sewerage Department.
9. Charlestown Hts.	Boston Park Comm'n.	39. Merrymount Park	Quincy Park Comm'n.
10. Playground	Boston Park Comm'n.	40. Faxon Park	Quincy Park Comm'n.
11. Wood Island Park	Boston Park Commission.	41. Quincy Water Reserve	Quincy Water Board.
12. Commonwealth Park	Boston Department of Public Grounds.	42. French's Com'n	Braintree Selectmen.
13. Telegraph Hill	Boston Department of Public Grounds.	43. Webb Park	Weymouth Park Commission.
14. Independence Square	Boston Department of Public Grounds.	44. Beals Park	Weymouth Park Commission.
15. Marine Park	Boston Park Comm'n.	45. Hull Common	Hull Park Comm'n.
16. Castle Island	Boston Park Comm'n.	46. Dedham Com'n	Dedham Selectmen.
17. Rogers Park	Boston Department of Public Grounds.	47. Boston Parental School Gr'nds	Trustees.
18. Chestnut Hill Reservoir	Boston Water Board.	48. Brookline Water Works	Brookline Water B'rd.
19. Playground	Brookline Selectmen.	49. Brookline Water Reserve	Brookline Water B'rd.
20. Playground	Brookline Selectmen.	50. Brookline Water Reserve	Brookline Water B'rd.
21. Playground	Brookline Selectmen.	51. Newton Water Reserve	Newton Water Board.
22. Muddy River Parkway	Boston and Brookline Park Commissions.	52. Needham Com'n	Needham Selectmen.
23. Old Brookline Reservoir	Boston Water Board.	53. Waban Hill Res'vr	Newton Water Board.
24. Brookline Res'vr	Brookline Water B'rd.	54. Farlow Park	Newton Department of Public Grounds.
25. Fisher Hill Res'vr	Boston Water Board.		
26. Madison Square	Boston Department of Public Grounds.	55. Playground	Newton Department of Public Grounds.
27. Orchard Park	Boston Department of Public Grounds.	56. River Park, Weston	Weston Selectmen.
28. Parker Hill Reservoir	Boston Water Board.	57. Auburndale Park	Newton Department of Public Grounds.
29. Highland Park	Boston Department of Public Grounds.	58. River Park, Auburndale	Newton Department of Public Grounds.

OPEN SPACES.	CONTROLLED BY	OPEN SPACES.	CONTROLLED BY
59. Cambridge Water Reserve	Cambridge Water B'rd.	82. Medford Water Reserve	Medford Water Board.
60. Waltham Water Works	Waltham Water B'rd.	83. Virginia Wood	Trustees of Public Reservations.
61. Waltham Common	Waltham Department of Public Grounds.	84. Playground	Stoneham Selectmen.
62. Watertown Common	Watertown Selectmen.	85. Wakefield Common	Wakefield Selectmen.
63. United States Arsenal	National Government.	86. Lake Park	Wakefield Selectmen.
64. Fresh Pond Reservoir	Cambridge Water B'rd.	87. Sewall's Wood	Melrose Park Commission.
65. Cambridge Common	Cambridge Department of Public Grounds.	88. Eastern Common	Melrose Park Commission.
66. Broadway Common	Cambridge Department of Public Grounds.	89. Waitt's Mount	Malden Water Board.
67. The Esplanade	Cambridge Department of Public Grounds.	90. Malden Water Works	Malden Water Board.
68. Central Hill Park	Somerville Department of Public Grounds.	91. Chelsea Commission	Chelsea Department of Public Grounds.
69. Broadway Park	Somerville Department of Public Grounds.	92. United States Marine and Naval Hospitals	National Government.
70. Powder House Park	Somerville Department of Public Grounds.	93. United States Battery	National Government.
71. Mystic Res'vr	Boston Water Board.	94. United States Battery	National Government.
72. Mystic Water Works	Boston Water Board.	95. Lynn Common	Lynn Park Comm'n.
73. Arlington Hts.	Arlington Selectmen.	96. Lynn Woods	Lynn Park Comm'n.
74. Arlingt'n Water Reserve	Arlington Water B'rd.	97. Lynn Water Reserve	Lynn Water Board.
75. Lexington Common	Lexington Selectmen.	98. Meadow Park	Lynn Park Comm'n.
76. Boston Water Reserve	Boston Water Board.	99. Oceanside Terrace	Lynn Park Comm'n.
77. Winchester Common	Winchester Selectmen.	100. Nahant Long Beach	Nahant Selectmen.
78. Woburn Park	Woburn Park Comm'n.	101. Nahant Short Beach	Nahant Selectmen.
79. Winchester Water Reserve	Winchester Water B'd.	102. Devereux Beach	Marblehead Selectmen.
80. Bear Hill Park	Stoneham Park Commission.	103. Marblehead Park	Marblehead Park Commission.
81. Melrose, Malden and Medford Water Reserve	Joint Water Board.	104. Crocker Rock	Marblehead Park Commission.
		105. Fort Sewall	Marblehead Selectmen.
		106. Fort Glover	Marblehead Selectmen.

CHAPTER XXII

FAMILY LIFE — JOINING THE OLMSTED FIRM

> The supreme end of Christian endeavor is not to look away to an inconceivable heaven beyond the skies, and to spend our life in preparing for it; but it is to realize that latent heaven, those possibilities of spiritual good, that undeveloped kingdom of righteousness and love and truth, which human nature and human society contain. — SERMON 1, SCOTCH SERMONS.

WHILE Charles was thus gaining strength and influence in his beloved profession, his family life was developing very happily. When he brought his wife to Massachusetts after their marriage in Colorado, it was to his father's house in Cambridge that they came; and there the first child — Ruth — was born. This event was announced to his friend Roland Thaxter (who had already named a boy for Charles) in the following terms: " Dear R.: A small daughter arrived here last evening at nine thirty, said to be perfectly lovely by those who know! At any rate she weighs eight pounds and is well formed; and both she and her mother are doing well. My respects to your young man and his mother. I hope all is serene in your life and surroundings. Affectionately, C. E."

By the spring of 1891 Charles and his wife saw their way to maintaining a modest establishment of their own; but they wanted an interesting prospect from their windows, and ready access to Boston by steam-cars; and Charles had a distinct inclination towards the neighborhood of the Blue Hills. Towards the end of April they found a house near the top of the southerly slope of Brush Hill which fulfilled in fair measure their desires, and into this house they moved on May 1st. The whole vicinity found great favor in Charles's eyes, because of the many delightful prospects it afforded at all seasons of the year. Many persons think of the New England country as beautiful in May, or in midsummer, or in October, but dreary the rest of the year; but for Charles the wintry scene was beautiful too, and he enjoyed his walks and drives through the Blue Hill region as much in winter as in summer. He especially liked walking in the country after a light fall of snow or of sleet.

In April, 1892, the family moved a few hundred feet to another house belonging to the same owner on the same hillside, but better placed as regards outlook. This second house on Brush Hill was old and low-studded, but more interesting than the first, and more appropriate for a landscape architect. A few good trees stood near it, and it commanded a prospect in which the foreground and the middle distance were as interesting as the fine background of wooded hills. Here a second daughter — Grace — was born.

The household was a simple one at first; they had no horse, and Charles walked to and from the station at Hyde Park, about a mile distant. In 1892 (October), Charles's net earnings having doubled since 1890, they felt warranted in setting up a horse and wagon and a man; and thereafter they lived in a simple but easy and comfortable fashion, exercising a pleasant hospitality, and getting the open air at all seasons by driving as well as walking. Husband and wife delighted equally in long, slow, country drives, and often enjoyed them together on Sundays and holidays. Frequently, however, Charles used his free days for walks through the country, either alone or with a friend interested in botany, ornithology, or scenery. His legs were long, and his weight was small for his height; so that he could walk for hours at a rapid rate. This power of walking fast and far was of real service to him in his profession, particularly in his Metropolitan Park work.

Charles changed his office twice before 1893. After three years in his delightful rooms at No. 9 Park Street, he moved to 50 State Street, in order to get his accumulating plans and papers into a fire-proof building, and to make himself more accessible to the well-to-do business men who might become his clients; and again after three years he moved thence across the street to 53 State Street, to get more room and a better exposure for the summer season. This last removing took place on December 1, 1892, during the greatest pressure of his work for the preliminary Metropolitan Park Commission.

Charles now had his family and his office established very much to his mind, and his prospects looked bright in all respects; but a great change was imminent, which was to affect his place of residence as well as his professional surroundings. On the 13th of January, 1893, Mr. Harry Codman, the junior partner in the firm of F. L. Olmsted & Co., suddenly died at Chicago, where he had been directing with the greatest acceptance the admirable work planned by that firm for the World's Fair. That work was well advanced, but still required a great deal of attention ; and much other important work was in the hands of the firm. Within a few days both Mr. Frederick Law Olmsted and Mr. John Charles Olmsted urged Charles to come to their assistance as a member of the firm. · This proposal pleased Charles greatly as an evidence of confidence in him on the part of one who had been his master in the landscape art; and he saw clearly the possibilities of advancement in his profession which connection with the principal landscape firm in the country presented. At the same time he much preferred to be professionally independent; and when he consulted privately a few well-informed friends, the weightiest advice was decidedly in favor of complete independence on his part. Nevertheless, before February 1st he had decided to join the Olmsted firm ; and on March 1st he actually became a partner, and began to work in the Olmsted office at Brookline, having previously devoted two weeks and a half (February 5th–23d) to visiting works in charge of the firm at Chicago, Milwaukee, Louisville, Hot Springs, Ark., St. Louis, Detroit, and Erie, Pa., and making the acquaintance of the gentlemen concerned in the several undertakings. It was Charles's strong sense of obligation to Mr. Olmsted, his high respect for Mr. Olmsted's career as a landscape artist, and his belief that he himself could be useful to the firm, which determined this important step on his part, taken against his inclination, and with a perfectly clear vision of the inevitable drawbacks to this valuable connection with an experienced firm whose methods and usages were presumably somewhat firmly fixed, and were in some respects different from his own.

The family continued to live at Brush Hill until the end of April, 1894, and were even then loath to leave their beautiful situation there, although it took Charles a full hour to go from his house to the Olmsted office, and although they had found a house in Brookline which commanded a singularly beautiful view over the Brookline reservoir towards Boston, and was also not far from the Olmsted office. This house was near the junction of Warren and Dudley streets. It was sunny and wholesome, and had several acres of sloping land to the east and south of it. Thither the family moved at the end of April, 1894 ; and soon they all became much attached to this new residence, which was handsome in itself, and was also in a desirable neighborhood. Two more little girls — Ellen Peabody and Carola — were born in this house.

The family life was now even happier than at Brush Hill; because the husband could often take luncheon at home as well as breakfast and dinner, the house being within an easy walk of the office. Moreover, income increased; so that, as the family increased in size, more service and more intelligent could be paid for. The only drawback was that Charles was obliged to be absent from home oftener and for longer periods after he became a member of the firm of Olmsted, Olmsted & Eliot than before.

A serene happiness lay at the roots of Charles's life; cares increased, but they were shared, and joys increased wonderfully, and were doubled. The wife had need of this new home. Since her marriage she had lost father and sister and a dear uncle, the father of her most intimate friend. That friend, who was a member of Mrs. Beadle's party in Europe in 1885–86, had died just before Mary was engaged to Charles. Of Mary's immediate family there remained only her younger brother Horace, who was now studying for the ministry.[1]

[1] Horace Tracy Pitkin, A. B. (Yale) 1892, studied for the ministry at Union Theological Seminary, New York (1893–1896), and at Northfield, Mass., in the summer vacations; went to China as a missionary in November, 1896, travelling thither slowly through Europe and India; sent his wife and baby home suddenly from Shanghai in April, 1900; returned himself to his post at Paoting-fu; and was murdered by the Boxers about July 1, 1900, with two American women missionaries, Miss Gould and Miss Morrill.

CHAPTER XXIII

GENERAL PRINCIPLES IN SELECTING PUBLIC RESERVATIONS AND DETERMINING THEIR BOUNDARIES

> The object of such pleasure grounds is chiefly this, — they serve the people for exercise, for enjoyment of the life-giving open air, for jovial social intercourse, and for mutual approachment of all classes, which here in the lap of fair Nature meet and refresh themselves, and in simple enjoyments learn to dispense with other less beneficial delectations of city life.
>
> The People's Garden is therefore in a double sense a very rational, beneficent, and instructive gymnastic school for mind and body; and consequently belongs among those most needed inventions of creative art which a wise and humane government should favor and protect.
> — F. L. von Sckell, 1825.

THE permanent, executive, Metropolitan Park Commission was fully organized and ready for work by the 1st of August, 1893. Messrs. Olmsted, Olmsted & Eliot were appointed its Landscape Architects, and were requested to advise the Commission at once concerning the best boundaries for five of the reservations which Charles had proposed in his report of January 2, 1893, to the preliminary Commission, namely, the Beaver Brook, Blue Hills, Middlesex Fells, Revere Beach, and Stony Brook reservations. Although the firm was hereafter the official adviser of the Commission, the whole of the Metropolitan Park work which came to the firm remained in Charles's hands; he did the preliminary study of the boundaries, gave the directions to the surveyors, wrote the reports in the firm's name, and attended the meetings of the Commission. He began his explorations in the middle of August, and started six parties of surveyors in September; but two journeys to the West, one as far as Kansas City, and the other to the World's Fair, and a short vacation at Mt. Desert prevented steady work on the boundaries until October 16th, when he began to give nearly all his time to the demarcation of the five reservations. By that time his work and that of the surveyors was much facilitated by the falling of the leaves. His method was to go on foot along the approximate boundary he was studying, having in hand the best existing

map of the neighborhood, and accompanied by the local surveyor in charge of that section, or by some resident in the
vicinity who was acquainted with the properties and the lay
of the land. On the spot he made notes and sketches which
enabled the surveyor to place the proposed boundary on the
map in a tentative way. This having been done, Charles
revisited the boundary as mapped, to revise and confirm his
first ideas, and to make notes for a written description of the
boundary, and for an oral advocacy of it before the Commission. Within sixty days he studied in this way about thirty
miles of park boundaries, brought to completion the surveys
and maps which were indispensable preliminaries to any definite action by the Commission, and wrote the first detailed
reports on the Beaver Brook, Revere Beach, Middlesex Fells,
Blue Hills, and Stony Brook or Muddy Pond Reservations.
Before the end of the year 1893, the Commission had actually
taken the Beaver Brook Reservation and nearly 1000 acres
in the Blue Hills.

It had not been possible, however, for Charles to give all
his time during the autumn to the Metropolitan work. Two
other park commissions within the district sought the advice
of the firm ; and for both of these Charles made the necessary studies and wrote the reports. The parks of Cambridge
were the first of these two subjects which engaged his attention during this busy autumn, and the parks of Winthrop
were the second. Both investigations interested him very
much, and gave him occasion to expound some of the principles of true economy in the selection of open spaces for public enjoyment. The two reports for Cambridge and Winthrop,
the report Charles made to the Park Commission of the city
of Quincy, January 2, 1893, and the first detailed letters of
advice on the Metropolitan Reservations all illustrate the general principles of park selection and demarcation. They are
therefore grouped together in this chapter, some of them
being given in full, but others being represented by only a
single sentence or by a few paragraphs. It should be borne
in mind that insuperable obstacles may prevent a commission
from carrying out immediately the accepted plans of their
landscape architects. The titles of properties involved may
be in bad condition, or owners, with whom the Commission
may prefer to avoid a contest, may ask unreasonable prices
for their lands, or serious engineering difficulties may present
themselves, or grave questions of law concerning existing
rights. The settlement with owners and the amendment of
boundaries went on for years, but the character and in the

main the outlines of the reservations spoken of above were determined by the reports which follow. All the recommended areas are now (1902) in public use except the beautiful estate called "Shady Hill," which the Cambridge Park Commission thought expensive and not indispensable, and the stretch of Quincy shore from Black's Creek to Great Hill.

A LARGE POND AS PARK.

To the President of the Cambridge Park Commission, — In the course of our recent study of the problem of selecting sites for public grounds in Cambridge, you drew our attention to the large existing reservation which surrounds Fresh Pond. The total area of this reservation is 337 acres, of which about 155 acres are water. Because of the closely-built character of the city and the narrowness of the municipal limits, this is the largest open space Cambridge can ever hope to possess. Its primary purpose is the safe storage of water, but the reservation has already been in a measure dedicated to the additional purpose of public recreation and called a "park."

As we viewed the place the other day, and perceived the beauty of the natural setting of the pond among the hills, and the incongruously stiff lines of the engineer's work about the shores, it struck us that it was time the people of Cambridge determined in what way their one large reservation might best be made to contribute to their recreation and refreshment. Does a large public reservation yield to dwellers in cities the greatest possible return when it is planned on lines as formal as those of city streets? Does it not rather return its greatest dividend of benefit only when it is made as different as possible from a town, and presents the aspect of natural scenery? It is true that the curvilinear shore line and the hills above the pond cannot be wholly destroyed, but they can be made stiff, hard, and unnatural, to the great loss of Cambridge, as we believe. It is true that roads and paths are needed even in the most natural parks, but that is no reason for their being obtruded, as if they were the essence of a park, and not the mere instruments by which scenery is made accessible. A large public reservation may include within its limits roads and paths, playgrounds, picnic grounds, and even gardens and buildings ; but if these mar or destroy its landscape, the highest possible value of the reservation, and the only advantage of a large reservation over a small one, is absolutely lost.

It is because the Fresh Pond reservation presents the outline of a singularly unified and therefore a singularly pleasing landscape, that we have ventured to address you on behalf of the preservation, restoration, and development thereof.

16 October, 1893.

PRELIMINARY REPORT ON THE LOCATION OF PARKS FOR CAMBRIDGE. — The municipality of Cambridge is four and a half miles long, and from one to two miles wide. In certain important respects the city is very favorably placed. An uncommonly large, permanent air-space is found at each end of the city. On the east is a broad basin of the salt Charles River, having an area, between Craigie and Brookline bridges and inside the Harbor Commissioners' lines, of five hundred and twenty-eight acres. On the west is Fresh Pond, with an area of one hundred and fifty-five acres. Along the whole length of the southern boundary of the city stretches another permanent open space, the channel of Charles River, with an average width, between the Harbor Commissioners' lines, of three hundred feet, and an area between Brookline bridge and Cambridge Cemetery of one hundred and eighteen acres.

Here is a total of eight hundred acres of permanently open space provided by nature without cost to Cambridge. All of this area was, until lately, unavailable for purposes of public recreation, except by boats, and most of it remains so. In late years the lands about Fresh Pond have been purchased by the city for the protection of the water supply ; and the Cambridge Embankment Company has pledged itself to provide the city with a stretch of public frontage upon the basin of Charles River. Elsewhere these priceless spaces still lie unused, like money hoarded in a stocking, yielding no return to their owners. If Cambridge is to invest money in public recreation grounds, a just economy demands that such money shall first be placed where it will bring into use for public

enjoyment these now unused and inaccessible spaces with
their ample air, light, and outlook. All Cambridge lies within
one mile of the Harbor Commissioners' lines, excepting only
that part which is north of Porter's Station and Fresh Pond.
In view of this fact, to let the river spaces go unused would
be wilful extravagance, while to make their borders accessible
will be to ensure to the city a return in public health, pleasure,
and refreshment such as can be derived from no ordinary,
contracted, inland open space. This being the state of the
case, it is our duty to recommend the purchase by the city
of every purchasable portion of the river front, from Craigie
bridge to Cambridge Cemetery. When this has been determined on, it will be time to consider what other well-
distributed spaces may, with economy, be secured.

Having thus outlined what has seemed to us to be the logic
of the situation, we submit the accompanying block plan as
the sum and substance of our report. Upon this plan are
shown only the boundaries of the city, the existing public
open spaces, and the spaces we would propose to acquire
and reserve. The drawing [not reproduced here] is only a
diagram, and we have made it a diagram in order to show
with the utmost possible clearness the relative areas, and the
symmetry and fairness of their distribution.

We have only to add a few words concerning each of the
proposed reservations, designating them by the tentative
names which, for the sake of convenience, we have put upon
the plan.

(1) " *The Front.*" — Between the two canals which pene-
trate the manufacturing district at the eastern end of the city,
it is still possible to acquire a long river frontage, and because
this place will be available for the recreation of the crowded
population of East Cambridge, we would have this reservation possess a considerable breadth, in order to make room
for children's games and other uses quite distinct from the
main purposes of the purchase, which are the preservation of
the view of the river basin and provisions for boating on its
waters. A street should be carried southward from the junction of Bridge and Prison streets, and across the canal. From
the canal Commercial Avenue is planned to run parallel with

the Harbor Commissioners' line, and two hundred and fifty feet distant therefrom. The Charlesbank Reservation on the Boston side of the river is only two hundred feet wide. Our diagram suggests a reservation of the full width of two hundred and fifty feet. Beginning at Binney Street, where the improved frontage ends, the length of the reservation may be whatever the city can afford to buy. We have shown it extended eastward to the canal, or nearly fifteen hundred feet. By building sea-walls in the form of bastions at the ends, and making the intervening stretch a beach, this reservation can eventually be made attractive and serviceable, at a reasonable expense.

(2) " *The Esplanade.*" — Along part of the next section of the Commissioners' line, that between West Boston and Brookline bridges, the Embankment Company is already making a public esplanade two hundred feet in width, which only needs to be connected with the two bridges just named to form one of the finest urban river fronts in the world. Here there will presumably be a continuous sea-wall, with a broad promenade and a broad planting space, with a roadway which will serve as a pleasure drive and also as an approach to the buildings on the abutting estates.

(3) " *Captain's Island.*" — Just above Brookline bridge an opportunity is offered by Captain's Island and the marshes about it to make a level field, available for the sports of boys, for which a provision in this neighborhood is highly desirable.

If the driveway of the Esplanade is curved as it approaches Brookline Street in such a way that it will enter upon the location of Leverett Street, and then if Leverett Street is followed across Magazine Street, an area of some twenty-five acres will be obtained between the drive and the Harbor Commissioners' line. Even if the river shore of this tract is beached instead of being walled, there will still remain a playing-ground for general use of twice the area of the well-known Jarvis Field of Harvard College. The River road will bound this playground on the north, and upon the road will front buildings, the rear yards of which will be reached from the Old Marsh lane.

(4) " *The River Road.*" — From Captain's Island to

Cambridge Hospital, along the Commissioners' line, a reservation of whatever varying widths may be found most economical should be secured.   The least width which should be considered at all is such as will provide a promenade upon the river wall twenty feet wide, and in addition at least another ten feet in which to plant trees and shrubs to hide adjacent fences and buildings.   Entrances to such a promenade would be had at every bridge, and at the end of every street which may extend to the river.   While to buy a narrow strip of flats and marsh and wharf for the purpose just described might seem to be the cheapest thing which could be done at the present time, it may well be doubted whether this would prove to be the most economical course of action in the end.   To make a promenade upon so narrow a strip, a river wall would be absolutely necessary.   Out of a total length of eleven thousand five hundred and eighty feet of Commissioners' line, only two thousand two hundred and fifty feet, or less than one fifth, is walled at the present time, and much of the existing wall is cheaply and badly built.   A good wall is costly, and after your Commission shall have made a study of land values, it will very probably appear that it would be more economical to buy a strip one hundred feet wide in which to make a gravel beach than to undertake the building of a river-side wall.   Furthermore, it may well be questioned whether, if the city is to invest any money upon the river front, it ought not to invest enough to ensure a proper financial return from the investment.   A promenade alone, whether it were made upon a river wall or at the top of a beach, would not appreciably enhance the attractiveness or value of the adjacent real estate.   On the other hand, a roadway with a sidewalk providing convenient and handsome access to abutting estates would enhance values considerably, and so would ensure the eventual reimbursement of the city treasury.

(5) " *Elmwood Way.*" — When the banks of the Charles shall have been reserved by Boston as well as by Cambridge, for the development of the scheme of improvement just described, there will arise a demand for a broad connection between the Charles River reservations and the large reservation about Fresh Pond.   A bridge will be required in the

bend of the river at Gerry's landing. From the site of this bridge, by way of Mount Auburn Street and Fresh Pond Lane, the distance to Fresh Pond is less than a mile, and there are so few buildings on this line that a reservation for a broad parkway of varying width should not, at the present time, be expensive. For Boston and the metropolitan district, the Charles River drive, with this proposed parkway, would furnish the pleasantest possible route to a series of places of interest and resort — among them the Soldier's Field and the Longfellow marshes where the athletic grounds of Harvard University are soon to be established, Harvard College itself, the Longfellow house and the Memorial garden, the Lowell house at Elmwood, Mount Auburn, and Fresh Pond — the last a broader sheet of water than either Chestnut Hill Reservoir at the terminus of Beacon boulevard, or Jamaica Pond at the end of the Muddy River parkway. We believe the present to be the time to secure an adequate breadth of way for the future making of this desirable connection, and we presume that the land-owners along the route will be quick to see the advantage which will accrue to them from an early establishment of its lines.

For Cambridge the widening of Mount Auburn Street from the angle at the Casino to a connection with the proposed parkway at Elmwood Avenue would complete a southern chain of reservations extending from the river basin at the eastern end of the city to the pond at the west end. Mount Auburn Street is to become the route of the Watertown electric car line, and needs to be widened on that account alone. We do not suggest that the river wall required to accomplish this widening should be built at this time, but only that the necessary additional twenty-five to forty feet of width from Bath Street to Elmwood Avenue should be secured before it is occupied by buildings.

Acting upon these considerations, we have represented on the diagram a strip along the river of a width and area such as would be required to provide, first, a sidewalk adjacent to the private property line; secondly, a driveway; and, thirdly, a promenade, with a river wall where one already exists or seems to be required by reason of the expensiveness of adjacent land, and a beach along all the remaining length of the reservation. We have assumed that the immediate purpose of your Commission is simply the acquisition of such lands along the river as will make it possible to develop eventually a serviceable and handsome river front. The diagram represents our view of what is requisite for this purpose. No serious obstacles to the easy acquisition of these lands present themselves except between River Street and Western Avenue. Even here, only one expensive building projects into the strip seventy-five feet wide, which we deem the least that should be acquired along the river wall. As respects the delivery of coal at the establishments between these bridges, and at the wharves of Messrs. Rugg, and Richardson & Bacon, we do not think that this should for a moment stand in the way of the accomplishment of the Commission's purpose. For passing coal from vessels to permanent establishments which use or sell it in quantities, either light iron trestles or underground runways can be devised.

(6) " *Rindge Field.*" (7) " *Shady Hill.*" (8) " *Binney Field.*"

Omitting mention of Fresh Pond, because the energy of the Water Board has already secured an ample reservation all about it, we have next to turn to the northern border of the city, where, because of the considerable distance to the river front, a few public spaces should be reserved. If the total distance from the centre of Fresh Pond to the centre of the Charles River basin opposite " The Front " be divided into fourths, the Rindge Field, Shady Hill, and the Binney Field will be found to lie almost directly abreast of the first, second, and third marks. The two spaces called fields are both well adapted to serve as playgrounds, while Shady Hill is a small oasis of idyllic rural scenery preserved in the midst of city conditions by the conservative artistic spirit of its owners in two generations. We believe that both the open fields for play and the secluded wood for rest will be worth to Cambridge vastly more than they can cost at the present time. . . .

RESERVATIONS IN A SEASHORE TOWN.

Dec. 22, 1893.

To THE CHAIRMAN OF THE WINTHROP PARK COMMISSION.
— In a letter recently addressed by us to the Metropolitan
Park Commission, we pointed out the advantages which would
accrue to the town if the shores and beaches of the township
could be made public reservations. The town's money invested in reservations on the shores will yield greater returns
in health, pleasure, and cash to be derived from increased
valuations than it could yield if sunk in the purchase of
any inland districts of the township. The broad outlooks
which the shores command over harbor, bay, and ocean are
the primary source of the attractiveness of the township.
In our opinion, Winthrop will fail to avail herself of the one
advantage she possesses over other suburbs, if she fails to
reserve her shores.

Doubtless your Commission can acquire by gift the unusa-
ble ocean foreshore along Crest Avenue. From Thornton
Station around to Pleasant Street at the mouth of Ingalls
Brook, we believe you should secure the foreshore, together
with a strip of dry land above high-water mark. As the
water along most of this shore is shallow, it will be possible
to eventually construct a drive and promenade on flats now
flooded by the tide; nevertheless, we would have you secure
all the upland you can buy with a due regard for economy,
confining your reservation to the flats only where you are
compelled to do so by the high cost of existing lands or buildings. The inland boundary of any such reservation as we
are proposing should be a continuous or flowing curve, because it will eventually become the line of a sidewalk serving
the adjacent private estates.

Ingalls Brook drains a fresh-water swamp, which you informed us might be obtained if it was desirable. The central
schoolhouse of the town stands close at hand, and the valley
will make a desirable playground for the pupils. The reservation should be bounded by Lincoln Street on the north, the
railroad on the east, and Pauline Street on the south, and by
two new streets which should be laid out to give abutters a

frontage on the reservation, one on each side of the brook as it flows westward to Pleasant Street.

If the Town desires at the present time to procure lands for other playgrounds, they can be obtained most cheaply on one or the other of the salt marshes which are found within the township. The marsh of Belle Isle Inlet and the marsh of Fishing River are still unoccupied by buildings. We would suggest that common prudence should lead the Town to establish (by special legislative authority, if that be necessary) a minimum grade for cellars and for streets, in order to prevent building upon the marshes until they have been filled to a safely habitable elevation. This safeguarding regulation, which has been enacted by several towns near Boston, will effectually forestall the baleful occupation of the marshes which you have feared was about to take place. Where this regulation is in force, the marshes are left in their natural condition until there is profit in filling them, when they command such prices as ensure their occupation by reasonably good buildings.

It is not to be supposed that the Town would care to buy and hold forever all the marshes within its limits, yet that is the only other way to prevent an unsanitary occupation of them. Winthrop has no present or prospective use for a hundred or more acres of interior open space. The open spaces of the salt waters encompass the township and supply unlimited quantities of unpolluted air. The reservation of the marshes by the Town would involve not only a large first cost, with its burden of interest, but also the sacrifice of the return fairly to be expected from the considerable taxable value which the marsh lands will possess after the increase of population shall have made it profitable to fill them to the standard elevation. In towns where open spaces are lacking, the considerations just advanced should not stand in the way of the acquirement of marshes; but in a town like Winthrop, surrounded by open spaces, such considerations may certainly be urged with reason. . . .

RESERVATIONS FOR A BAY-SHORE CITY. — In accordance with your request, I have personally inspected the shores of

Quincy Bay from Moon Island around to Nut Island, and I now beg leave to submit the following report upon the nature of this coast, together with certain recommendations as to the future development thereof.

The city of Quincy is most favorably placed. Behind her rise the rocky ridges of the Blue Hills, beside her on either hand flow the Neponset and Weymouth rivers, and at her feet is spread the Bay. [See the map in the pocket of the right-hand cover.] The peninsula of Squantum, beside the mouth of the Neponset, is matched by that of Hough's Neck, beside the mouth of Weymouth River. Hangman's Island lies nearly in the middle of the space embraced by the two peninsulas ; and Black's Creek, the only considerable break in the shore line of the Bay, again lies near the middle both of the Bay's curve and of the city. Just here, too, there appears another fortunate feature in the geography of Quincy, namely, the deep valley of Furnace Brook, a stream which seems to have been made to flow where it is on purpose to provide the inhabitants of the interior region of West Quincy and East Milton with an easy and beautiful route to the central portion of the Bay shore. The existing Adams Street follows first one side and then the other side of this valley, by a route which involves many ascents and descents ; but when the city shall have taken possession of the bottom of the valley, as it should for sanitary reasons (if for no other), it will then be possible to lay out a road which, by following the stream, will avoid all ups and downs, and by which Black's Creek and the Bay will be reached very pleasantly and easily. Streams like Furnace Brook are awkward things in cities. They cannot be done away with, because their channels are the only ways by which storm-waters can escape. They cannot safely be allowed to be walled up and arched over by private abutters ; as was proved a few years since when Stony Brook in Boston burst its bonds, and flooded a densely populated district, causing a large loss of property, and putting Boston to the expense of enlarging and rebuilding the whole length of the channel. They can be made and kept surely safe and clean only where they are owned by the public ; and, where they are so owned, a drive along one or both sides of

the stream naturally comes in time. Private enterprise, desirous of reaping high prices for building land situated on
the slopes of brook valleys, has adopted this sensible treatment in several instances, and the city of Newton is just
now carrying out a work of this kind along her Cheese-Cake
Brook. It seems to me very evident that Quincy should at
least possess herself of this valley before it becomes more
thickly inhabited.

Descending now this valley of approach, the tide is met
at the old dam of Black's Creek, about half a mile from the
open Bay. Here there is a charming view down the Creek,
comprising a distant glimpse of the Bay, with perhaps a sail
or two, the winding Creek itself and its accompanying salt
meadows, two or three boats moored in the Creek, and for
a frame a varied bank of Oaks, Pines, and Cedars on either
hand. There is no better composed landscape in all the
neighborhood of Boston; and certainly there is none prettier.

Should not the city of Quincy own and control this bit of
scenery, lying as it does on the way to the Bay? The northern and western bank of the Creek for half the distance from
Hancock Street to the Bay is, indeed, already in the possession of the city, being a part of Merrymount Park; but the
two knolls or islands of Oak woods which lie seaward from
the park and make part of its scenery are still in private
hands, as is all the southern and eastern shore of the Creek.
To defend the outlook from the existing Park, and at the
same time to preserve the beautiful picture of Black's Creek,
it will be advisable for the city to acquire by gift or purchase
the land between the stream and the entrance to the Mt.
Wollaston estate, and from this point seaward a strip along
the wooded bluff averaging three hundred feet in width.
Butler road continued to the Mt. Wollaston entrance would
thus become the boundary of the Park, and a similar road
might ultimately become the boundary along the Mt. Wollaston bluffs. Houses fronting on the reservation would naturally follow the opening of such bounding roads, and in this
way a consummation most advantageous to all concerned
would be reached. Black's Creek would be preserved to
delight the people of the future, the outlook from the knolls

of Merrymount would be saved from threatened disfigurement, and real estate along the new park border would be
greatly increased in value and attractiveness.

On the opposite or northern side of Merrymount Park
the situation is much the same. Here the northern arm of
Black's Creek, with its accompanying salt marsh, penetrates
the mainland almost up to Fenno Street. If the city does
not acquire this marsh and a strip of the upland beyond it,
the view from the northern slopes of Merrymount Park will
become in time greatly disfigured by the backs and back
yards of buildings on the upland, if not by even more objectionable structures or industries established upon the marsh
itself. Conversely, if the marsh and its border is thrown
into the reservation, disfigurement will be prevented, and the
abutting real estate will be given such a value as will ensure
its respectable occupation. Nothing need here be added as
to the Oak knolls which lie towards the mouth of the Creek.
They appear prominently in every view from either bank of
the stream, and their permanent conservation is obviously
essential to the completion of the Park. The marsh behind
the knolls would also be just as essential as the other marshes
already mentioned, did it not belong to a permanent institution, the National Sailors' Home, whose managers are not
likely to devote it to any but agreeable purposes. The burying ground of the pensioners lies on a knoll at the edge of
the marsh, and it does not seem necessary that public ownership should be carried further inland at this point.

Coming now to the flaring mouth of Black's Creek and the
shore of the open bay, the little bluff of Rufe's Hummock on
the one side and the greater Gunning-Stand bluff on the
other command the situation, and offer fine views across the
water to the rounded hills of the distant islands of Boston
Bay, with glimpses of the open sea between the islands. To
right and left are seen the extended arms of Hough's Neck
and of Squantum, embracing between them Quincy's own bay
of open water, two and a half miles wide from cape to cape,
and two miles deep. The shore in both directions is seen to
be composed of dwarf bluffs of gravel alternating with low
sea-wall beaches, behind which lie salt marshes sometimes

threaded by little creeks. This is not " a stern and rock-bound coast," neither is it in any way impressive or grand, and yet every careful student of the circumstances is quickly brought to the conclusion that for the growing city of Quincy not to possess and control this shore would be foolishness of the most flagrant sort. The members of the Commission I am addressing are fully alive to the facts of the situation, and they can undoubtedly soon bring the main body of the population to perceive, and to act for, its self-interest in this matter. This is one of those cases in which our American communities are free to work their own goodwill. " Enlightened self-interest " should very soon work here a beneficent result.

As for the owners of the shore front, they will undoubtedly be quick to see what is for their interest in the matter. Private ownership of the shore in small lots means that only the front lots will command special prices. Public ownership means that every house-lot for a mile back will possess an enhanced value. Public ownership will also tend to ensure the water front from encroachment by the sea, and from occupation by value-depressing trades.

Now when public ownership of the shore is decreed, what considerations should govern the placing of the line which shall thenceforth divide private from public property ? My answer to this question is recorded upon the accompanying map [not reproduced here. Compare the map in the pocket of the right-hand cover], but it had better perhaps be outlined in words here. Although the work will not need to be undertaken for many years, it will doubtless be ultimately desirable that the public should possess a driveway along the shore. It follows that the boundary of the public domain should be so placed as to allow of the easy construction of such a driveway, and its easy connection with the streets of the city. The map is the result of my traversing of the shore with this idea in mind. Beginning at Black's Creek and going north towards Squantum, I believe that the Park Commissioners should acquire possession of all that lies seaward from the brink of the several little bluffs of the shore. This means that the Board would generally control the slopes of the bluffs, as well as the beaches and the flats, and that the shore drive would ultimately find its place along the bases of the bluffs at the water's edge. I do not advise continuing the public reservation beyond Moswetusset on Sachem's Hummock, because the existing road from there to Moon Island affords a pleasant drive, and because there is good hope that this portion of the circuit of Quincy Bay may be obtained for the public by the proposed Metropolitan Park Commission, which will be interested in opening this route to Moon Island for the benefit of the people of Dorchester, Milton, and Hyde Park.

Beginning again at Black's Creek, and going towards the Great Hill, the bluffs are for some distance so continuous and so even that enough space for the future shore drive should here be acquired on their summits, where the reservation, and the houses which will some day front upon it, will command fine views of the bay, the islands, and the Broad Sound towards Nahant. Passing the Shell Place, Post Island, and Whale Landing, the existing Manet Avenue, widened somewhat on its inward side, should be taken into the reservation up to the point where it turns inland, and from this point to the cove at the foot of the Great Hill, I propose that only the slopes of the bank should be acquired, and that the future drive should follow the base of the bluffs. A circuit of the Great Hill itself, including the lowest of the Land Company's plotted roads, with possibly Nut Island, would then complete Quincy's shore reservation in a manner which would leave little to be desired.

Jan. 2, 1893.

TO THE METROPOLITAN PARK COMMISSION.[1]

15 December, 1893.

A Sea-beach as Reservation. — The undersigned beg to report as follows on the subject of the boundaries of the proposed Revere Beach Reservation : —

The statutory limit of ownership on the foreshore will be-

[1] The Metropolitan Park Commission has greatly facilitated the preparation of this book by furnishing copies of letters and reports from its files, and permitting the reproduction of maps and photographs originally made for its annual reports.

come the boundary on the ocean side. The boundary on the land side will be fixed so as to include whatever width of reservation above high-water mark may be deemed necessary to properly accommodate the public. If a public footway or promenade upon which hotels and houses may front be deemed a sufficient reservation for public use, a line drawn twenty-five feet from extreme high-water mark will become the boundary of the land to be taken. Streets would cross the promenade at intervals, permitting carriages to reach the beach. Buildings fronting on the promenade would be reached by carriages from the rear. The probable electric car line and the steam railroad would both be found in the rear. Both would have to be moved to accomplish even this most economical of all possible schemes of improvement.

If the railroad must be moved in any event, it may be questioned whether it would not be advisable to obtain a driveway as well as a promenade between the building land and high-water mark. A driveway here should not be less than forty feet wide. A driveway involves a sidewalk along the private land. A sidewalk should be twelve feet wide, and, if possible, a strip of eight feet in addition should be secured in which to plant one row of trees. Thus we obtain a total of eighty feet measured inland from the curve of extreme high water. If a double track electric car line should be placed between the driveway and the promenade, an additional width of twenty feet would be required, and the resulting line, one hundred feet from the curve of high water, is the line we have drawn upon the accompanying plan.

It will be noted that this line coincides with the front line of private lands abutting upon the railroad location in the settlement called Crescent Beach; also, that beyond Revere Street, Ocean Avenue is in places within and in places without the reservation.

To accomplish a handsome result, it appears to be necessary to entirely remove the beach railroad and to relocate Ocean Avenue. We have marked upon the plan the section in which it appears that a first taking may be made most easily.

14 December, 1893.

A Forest and Pond Reservation. — The undersigned beg
to report as follows upon the boundaries of the Fells Reservation : —

Spot Pond, Wright's Pond, and Winchester Reservoirs and
the banks thereof are already held for the public by various
Water Boards. The proposed reservation is designed to include all these, and to be bounded outwardly by a road which
will generally skirt the foot of the high land.

Beginning at the southern end of the Spot Pond water
reserve (at the corner of Elm and Forest streets in Medford), the boundary of the lands proposed to be taken first
follows Forest Street southward to a point just south of the
crossing of the brook which comes from west of Pine Hill.
Here a boundary road may leave Forest Street at right angles,
and lead westward on a line which will include the ice-pond
at the foot of Pine Hill, without including the first house
south thereof. The (Elizur) Wright house at the eastern
foot of Pine Hill will be included, unless it is excluded by
having an arbitrary line run behind it from Forest Street to
Forest Street again. Passing south of the ice-pond, a fine
view is had of Pine Hill over the pond, and a good frontage is
obtained for houses. Crossing the flat of the rifle range, the
boundary road must next ascend one short but steep hill in
order to reach and cross Brook's Lane at the north end of the
northernmost of the Medford pastures — in other words, at
the edge of the wild lands.

(*An Alternative Line* from Forest Street to the hill just
mentioned would leave the street at the foot of the knoll of
the Wright house and pass around the very foot of the slope
of Pine Hill and so across the flat of the rifle range. This
would leave out the little pond and the brook, and make a
bad frontage for the private lands.)

From Brook's Lane westward, the road boundary will descend a gentle valley, affording good private frontages, to the
Meeting House Brook, where connection may be made with
the brookside parkway which should eventually come up from
Medford along the stream. Crossing the stream after ascending it a short distance, the boundary ought doubtless to swing

westward and then northward, so as to include all the upper part of the wooded hill which lies south of Winchester South Reservoir.   This hill is a part of the frame of the reservoir, and must be included if the wilderness aspect of the interior of the reservation is to be permanently preserved.   For reasons known to the Commission, we have not, however, run a line around it.   The line we have run and put upon the map ascends Meeting House Brook, including the stream, until the pipe line of the Winchester Water Works is reached, and then it follows this line through a deep cut in the hill just mentioned, and onward along the pipe line to the first cultivated lands, along the edge of which it goes northward to a Pine grove, on the lane or path which is the extension of Chestnut Street, Winchester.   The route from Meeting House Brook to this point is somewhat circuitous, but it has good grades and includes no cultivated lands.

(*An Alternative Line* through Medford more closely conformed to the line described in the Act of the legislature is difficult to find.   The legislative line is arbitrary and unsuitable for a road boundary.   It makes bad frontages.   In the rear of it we find no route which can be called an improvement on the legislative line itself.   Consequently we are constrained to recommend the Commission to take up to the legislative line in the hope that lands in front thereof may hereafter be purchasable.)

From the Pine grove which is the end of the legislative line through Medford, as well as the point at which our description of the proposed boundary was left, a gentle valley which first ascends and then descends leads the boundary road to an easy connection with the extension of Mt. Vernon Street, Winchester.   Thence to Hillcrest Avenue, the boundary becomes a mere line running between a series of houses and the foot of the hills.   There is no room here for a road.   Crossing a short flat and turning around the west slope of Reservoir Hill, the boundary, which is now a road again, will reach the Water Board's Reservation at the North Dam.   Taking in the hill north of the dam, turning eastward, and leaving out a large celery farm, the Spot Pond Water Reserve is reached at the north end of Bear Hill.   The road will pass through a short section of this reserve, and emerge upon Main Street, Stoneham, opposite the end of South Street. Main Street, Stoneham, is the continuation of Forest Street, Medford, so that we have here completed the western section of the Fells. Except at the hill south of the Winchester South Dam, the boundary described lies at the outer bases of the hills which surround the Winchester Reservoirs. It is a boundary which will effectually preserve the wilderness aspect of the interior valleys, except at the one point just named. . . . [There follows a similar description of the proposed boundary of the eastern section of the Fells; but this description enunciates no new principle.]

We send herewith plans showing the boundaries described above.

15 December, 1893.

A Forest Reservation. — We beg to report as follows upon the boundaries of the Blue Hills Reservation. [Only one half of the detailed description is here given.]

In general, our endeavor has been to include only wild and steep lands, to exclude improved or farmed lands, and to draw the boundary upon lines and grades which may eventually be found practicable for a boundary road.

Beginning at the western base of Great Blue Hill, we follow Washington Street southward to Blue Hill Street, and then Blue Hill Street and Hillside Street to the bound stone which makes a corner of Quincy, where we leave the road, and carry a new boundary road southward and then eastward along the western and southern slopes of Bugbee and Bare Hills, first in Milton and then in Quincy, to the gorge of Blue Hill Stream near Randolph Avenue. This route includes the hills, and excludes Houghton's Pond, the farm lands about it and northeast of it, and the swamps along Blue Hill Stream. It is to be presumed that the swamps will eventually be taken by the Quincy Water Board. In the gorge just mentioned is an admirable site for a dam. The southern side of the gorge lies in Randolph, a town not included in the metropolitan district, so that we cannot include the whole gorge in the reservation, as we might like to do. As it is, the boundary road might find its way to Randolph Avenue through the reservation, the gorge being too narrow for it, while the boundary of the reservation must follow the stream to the avenue.

(*An Alternative Line* which would include Houghton's Pond — a charming sheet of water — can be had by leaving Hillside Street by the west boundary of the H. L. Pierce estate, and then going eastward by a line across a flat to a junction with the line at the foot of Bugbee Hill, already described. This would be a road boundary. If no regard need be had to the plans of the Quincy Water Board, the boundary might follow the Pierce line from Hillside Street to Blue Hill Stream and then along the stream to Randolph Avenue.)

Eastward from Randolph Avenue it is possible to make a road boundary along the southern line of Glover's Hill, and between it and the flat lands and swamps which the Water Board of Quincy may eventually control. Glover's Hill extends eastward in a long point, which closely approaches West Street in Braintree, near the north end of Great Pond. An old road leads across the swamp from the point of Glover's Hill to West Street, and we recommend that a strip, one hundred feet on each side of the old road, should be secured, in order to make an ample entrance to the reservation from the direction of Braintree. . . .

For a short distance Purgatory Road in Quincy follows the base of the high hills, and becomes the reservation boundary. Where a run comes down just west of the Pierce house, the boundary may leave the road, and, after ascending a little and passing a small swamp, a road boundary with good grades may be followed along the east slope of Rattlesnake Hill to the neighborhood of Babel Rock, where a connection can be made with the existing road, which leads from the east base of Babel Rock to Willard Street, Quincy. This line from Purgatory Road to Willard Street includes all the high land of Rattlesnake Hill, and excludes two houses and many acres of hollow and broken land. . . .

Babel Rock Entrance, giving access from Quincy, is the extreme eastern end of the proposed reservation. Passing westward now, a road boundary may be found in the valley of Furnace Brook, generally including the brook, passing the north slope of Rattlesnake Hill, and crossing a region of broken topography near the Quincy-Milton line. North of this valley is a range of heights, upon the further or northern side of which are many quarries. As yet the southern slope is uninjured, and for the protection of the scenery of Furnace Brook valley it seems advisable to include this slope in the reservation by drawing an angular line from summit to summit along the range.

West of a certain narrow notch which is traversable by a road, it will be best to include the whole of the round hill which terminates the range, and from this point carry the boundary down Pine Tree Brook valley, in order to make a handsome approach to the reservation from Milton and Dorchester.

From the valley of Pine Tree Brook, the road boundary must ascend to traverse the broad swelling uplands of the north slope of Chickatawbut Hill, where views of the sea are had. The line excludes farm lands, and includes the one remaining Cedar grove of the hillside. . . .

We send herewith plans, in four sheets, showing the boundaries described.

The following article on the general subject of this chapter was published in the "Engineering Magazine" for May, 1895, and was there attributed very properly to Frederick Law Olmsted; for it was only a concise restatement — with some new illustrations — of doctrines which Mr. Olmsted had been teaching all his life. It was really prepared, however, by Charles, his disciple and partner, a little more than a year after the letters of this chapter were written, Mr. Olmsted being unable at the time to write it himself.

PARKS, PARKWAYS, AND PLEASURE GROUNDS.

The aggregation of men in great cities practically necessitates the common or public ownership, or control, of streets, sewers, water-pipes, and pleasure grounds. Municipal pleasure grounds comprise all such public open spaces as are acquired and arranged for the purpose of providing favorable opportunities for healthful recreation in the open air. As there are many modes and means of open-air recreation, so there are many kinds of public pleasure grounds. The formal promenade or plaza is perhaps the simplest type. Broad gravel-ways well shaded by trees afford pleasant out-of-door halls where crowds may mingle in an easy social life, the value of which is better understood in Southern Europe and in Spanish America than in the United States. Agreeable and numerous open-air nurseries and playgrounds for small children present a more complex, but perhaps more necessary, type of public ground. Very few public open spaces suitably arranged for this special purpose are to be found in American cities, and yet it goes without saying that every crowded neighborhood ought to be provided with a place removed from the paved streets, in which mothers, babies, and small children may find opportunity to rest, and sleep, and play in the open air. Playgrounds for youths are needed, but these may be further removed from the crowded parts of towns. Public open-air gymnasia have proved valuable in Europe and in Boston. Public flower gardens are sometimes provided ; but these are luxuries, and ought to be opened at the public expense only after the more essential kinds of public grounds have been secured. Promenades, gardens, concert grounds, outdoor halls, nurseries, playgrounds, gymnasia, and gardens may, of course, be combined one with another, as opportunity offers. To properly fulfil their several functions, none of them need take out more than a small space from the income-producing area of a town.

There remains another less obvious, but very valuable, source of refreshment for townspeople, which only considerable areas of open space can supply. The well-to-do people of all large towns seek in travel the recreation which comes from change of scene and contemplation of scenery. For those who cannot travel, free admission to the best scenery of their neighborhood is desirable. It is, indeed, necessary, if life is to be more than meat. Cities are now grown so great that hours are consumed in gaining the "country," and, when the fields are reached, entrance is forbidden. Accordingly it becomes necessary to acquire, for the free use and enjoyment of all, such neighboring fields, woods, pond-sides, river-banks, valleys, or hills as may present, or may be made to present, fine scenery of one type or another. This providing of scenery calls for the separation of large bodies of land from the financially productive area of a town, county, or district; and conversely, such setting apart of large areas is justifiable only when "scenery" is secured, or made obtainable thereby.

Having thus made note of the main purposes of public pleasure grounds, we pass now to consider (1) Government; (2) Sites and Boundaries; (3) General Plans or Designs; and (4) Construction.

Park Government.

The providing and managing of reservations of scenery is the highest function and most difficult task of the commissioners or directors of park works. Public squares, gardens, playgrounds, and promenades may be well or badly constructed, but no questions are likely to arise in connection therewith which are beyond the comprehension of the ordinary man of affairs. If scenic parks, on the other hand, are to be well placed, well bounded, well arranged, and, above all, well preserved, the directors of the work need to be more than ordinary men. Real-estate dealers must necessarily be excluded from the management. Politicians, also, if the work is to run smoothly. The work is not purely executive, like the work of directing sewer-construction or street cleaning, which may best be done by single responsible chiefs. The direction of park works may probably best rest with a small body of cultivated men, public-spirited enough to serve without pay, who should regard themselves, and be regarded, as a board of trustees, and who, as such, should make it their first duty to hand down unharmed from one generation to the next the treasure of scenery which the city has placed in their care. Public libraries and public art museums are created and managed by boards of trustees. For similar reasons public parks should be similarly governed.

A landscape park requires, more than most works of men, continuity of management. Its perfecting is a slow process. Its directors must thoroughly apprehend the fact that the beauty of its landscape is all that justifies the existence of a large public open space in the midst, or even on the immediate borders, of a town; and they must see to it that each newly appointed member of the governing body shall be grounded in this truth. Holding to the supreme value of fine scenery, they will take pains to subordinate every necessary construction, and to perfect the essence of the park, which is its landscape, before elaborating details or accessories, such as sculptured gates or gilded fountains, however appropriately or beautifully they may be designed. As trustees of park scenery, they will be especially watchful to prevent injury thereto from the intrusion of incongruous or obtrusive structures, statues, gardens (whether floral, botanic, or zoölogic), speedways, or any other instruments of special modes of recreation, however desirable such may be in their proper place. If men can be found to thus serve cities as trustees of scenic or rural parks, they will assuredly be entirely competent to serve at the same time as providers and guardians of those smaller and more numerous urban spaces in which every means of recreation, excepting scenery, may best be provided.

Park Sites and Boundaries.

It is much to be desired that newly created park commissions should be provided at the beginning, by loan or otherwise, with a supply of money sufficient to meet the cost of all probably desirable lands. Purchases or seizures of land should be made as nearly contemporaneously as possible. Before making any purchases, ample time should, however, be taken for investigation, which should be directed both to the study of the scenery of the district in question and to a comparison of land values. The first problem usually is to choose from the lands sufficiently vacant or cheap to be considered (1) those reasonably accessible and moderately large tracts which are capable of presenting agreeable secluded scenery, and (2) those easily accessible or intervening small tracts which may most cheaply be adapted to serve as local playgrounds or the like. A visit and report from a professional park-designer will prove valuable, even at this earliest stage of operations. Grounds of the local playground class may safely be selected in accordance with considerations of cheapness and a reasonably equitable distribution; but the wise selection of even small landscape parks requires much careful study. It is desirable that a city's parks of this class should present scenery of differing types. It is desirable that the boundaries of each should be so placed as to include all essential elements of the local scenery, and to produce the utmost possible seclusion and sense of indefinite extent, as well as to make it possible to build boundary roads or streets upon good lines and fair grades. Public grounds of every class are best bounded by streets; otherwise, there is no means of ensuring the desirable fronting of buildings towards the public domain. In spite of a common popular prejudice to the contrary, it will generally be found that concave, rather than convex, portions of the earth's surface are to be preferred for park sites. If the courses of brooks, streams, or rivers can be included in parks, or in strips of public land connecting park with park, or park with town, several advantages will be secured at one stroke. The natural surface-drainage channels will be retained under public control where they belong; they will be surely defended from pollution; their banks will offer agreeable public promenades; while the adjacent boundary roads, one on either hand, will furnish the contiguous building land with an attractive frontage. Where such stream-including strips are broad enough to permit the opening of a distinctively pleasure drive entirely separate from the boundary roads, the ground should be classed as a park. Where the boundary roads are the only roads, the whole strip is properly called a parkway; and this name is retained even when the space between the boundary roads is reduced to lowest terms and becomes nothing more than a shaded green ribbon, devoted perhaps to the separate use of the otherwise dangerous electric cars. In other words, parkways, like parks, may be absolutely formal or strikingly picturesque, according to circumstances. Both will generally be formal when they occupy confined urban spaces bounded by dominating buildings. Both will generally become picturesque as soon as, or wherever, opportunity offers.

After adequate squares and playgrounds, two or three

local landscape parks, and the most necessary connecting parkways shall have been provided, it may next be advisable to secure one or more large parks, or even one or more reservations of remoter and wilder lands. In a city of five hundred thousand inhabitants, a park of five hundred acres is soon so much frequented as necessarily to lose much of its rurality; in other words, much of its special power to refresh and charm. The necessarily broad roads, the numerous footways, the swarms of carriages and people, all call to mind the town, and in a measure offset the good effect of the park scenery. It is then that it becomes advisable to go still further afield, in order to acquire and hold in reserve additional domains of scenery, such as Boston has lately acquired in the Blue Hills and the Middlesex Fells. In selecting such domains, however, no new principles come into play. As in selecting sites for parks, so here it is always to be borne in mind that provision and preservation of scenery is the purpose held in view, and that the demarcation of the acquired lands is to be determined accordingly.

Park Plans or Designs.

To " plan " something means to devise ways of effecting some particular purpose. It has not always been thought necessary to " plan " the various kinds of pleasure grounds. With no consistent end or purpose in mind, the members of some park commissions attempt to direct from day to day and from year to year such " improvements " as they may from time to time decide upon. That the results of this method of procedure are confused, inadequate, and unimpressive is not to be wondered at.

In order to be able to devise a consistent plan, such as may be followed during a long period of years with surety that the result will be both useful and beautiful, it is necessary, in the first place, to define as accurately as possible the ends or purposes to be achieved. As already remarked, these ends or purposes are as numerous as are the various modes of recreation in the open air. Thus a small tract of harbor-side land at the North End of Boston has been acquired by the park commission, in order to supply the inhabitants of a poor and crowded quarter with a pleasant resting-place, overlooking the water, and with opportunities for boating and bathing. Accordingly, the plan provides a formal elevated stone terrace, connected by a bridge spanning an intervening traffic-street with a double-decked pleasure pier, which in turn forms a breakwater enclosing a little port, the shore of which will be a bathing-beach. In the adjacent city of Cambridge a rectangular, level, and street-bounded open space has been ordered to be arranged to serve as a general meeting-place or promenade, a concert ground, a boys' playground, and an outdoor nursery. Accordingly, the adopted plan suggests a centrally placed building which will serve as a shelter from showers, and as a house of public convenience, in which the boys will find lockers and the babies a room of their own, from which also the head-keeper of the ground shall be able to command the whole scene. South of the house a broad, but shaded, gravel space will provide room for such crowds as may gather when the band plays on a platform attached to the veranda of the building. Beyond this concert ground is placed the ball-field, which, because of the impossibility of maintaining good turf, will be of fine gravel firmly compacted. Surrounding the ball-ground and the whole public domain is a broad, formal, and shaded mall. At one end of the central building is found room for a shrub-surrounded playground and sand-court for babies and small children. At the other end of the house is a similarly secluded outdoor gymnasium for girls. Lastly, between the administration house and the northern mall and street, there will be found an open lawn, shut off from the malls by banks of shrubbery and surrounded by a path with seats, where mothers, nurses, and the public generally may find a pleasant resting-place.

Plans for those larger public domains in which scenery is the main object of pursuit need to be devised with similarly strict attention to the loftier purpose in view. The type of scenery to be preserved or created ought to be that which is developed naturally from the local circumstances of each case. Rocky or steep slopes suggest tangled thickets or forests. Smooth hollows of good soil hint at open or "park-like" scenery. Swamps and an abundant water-supply suggest ponds, pools, or lagoons. If distant views of regions outside the park are likely to be permanently attractive, the beauty thereof may be enhanced by supplying stronger fore-grounds ; and, conversely, all ugly or town-like surroundings ought, if possible, to be " planted out." The paths and roads of landscape parks are to be regarded simply as instruments by which the scenery is made accessible and enjoyable. They may not be needed at first, but, when the people visiting a park become so numerous that the trampling of their feet de-stroys the beauty of the ground cover, it becomes necessary to confine them to the use of chosen lines and spots. These lines ought obviously to be determined with careful reference to the most advantageous exhibition of the available scenery. The scenery also should be developed with reference to the views thereof to be obtained from these lines. This point may be illustrated by assuming the simplest possible case, — namely, that of a landscape park to be created upon a paral-lelogram of level prairie. To conceal the formality of the boundaries, as well as to shut out the view of surrounding buildings, an informal " border plantation " will be required. Within this irregular frame or screen, the broader the un-broken meadow or field may be, the more restful and impres-sive will be the landscape. To obtain the broadest and finest views of this central meadow, as well as to avoid shattering its unity, roads and paths should obviously be placed near the edges of the framing woods. In the typical case a " cir-cuit road " results. It is wholly impossible to frame rules for the planning of rural parks; local circumstances ought to guide and govern the designer in every case ; but it may be remarked that there are few situations in which the principle of unity will not call for something, at least, of the " border plantation " and something of the " circuit road."

Within large rural parks economy sometimes demands that provision should be made for some of those modes of recrea-tion which small spaces are capable of supplying. Special playgrounds for children, ball or tennis grounds, even formal arrangements such as are most suitable for concert grounds and decorative gardens, may each and all find place within the rural park, provided they are so devised as not to conflict with or detract from the breadth and quietness of the general landscape. If boating can be provided, a suitable boating-house will be desirable; the same house will serve for the use of skaters in winter. In small parks, economy of adminis-tration demands that one building should serve all purposes, and supply accommodations for boating parties, skaters, ten-nis-players, ball-players, and all other visitors, as well as administrative offices. In large parks, separate buildings serving as restaurants, boat-houses, bathing-houses, and the like may be allowable. It is most important, however, to re-member that these buildings, like the roads and paths, are only subsidiary, though necessary, adjuncts to the park scen-ery, and, consequently, that they should not be placed or designed so as to be obtrusive or conspicuous. Large public buildings, such as museums, concert-halls, schools, and the like, may best find place in town streets or squares. They may wisely perhaps be placed near, or facing upon, the park, but to place them within it is simply to defeat the highest service which the park can render the community. Large and conspicuous buildings, as well as statues and other monu-ments, are completely subversive of that rural quality of land-scape the presentation and preservation of which is the one justifying purpose of the undertaking by a town of a large public park.

Park Construction.

That the man who thinks out the general plan of a park ought to have daily supervision of the working-out of that plan is undoubtedly theoretically true. It is impossible to represent in drawings all the nice details of good work in grading and planting; and yet no work is more dependent for its effect upon finishing touches.

On the other hand, however desirable the constant over-sight of the landscape architect may be, it is impracticable under modern conditions. The education of a designer of parks consumes so much time, strength, and money that no existing American park commission, unless it be that of New York, can as yet afford to engage the whole time of a com-petent man. Consequently, it is the usual practice for the landscape architect to present his design in the form of a drawing or drawings, and to supplement the drawings by occasional visits for conference with those in immediate charge, by descriptive reports, and by correspondence.

The prime requisite in the resident superintendent of park work is efficiency. Naturally enough, most of the superintendents of parks in the United States have been trained either as horticulturists or as engineers, but it is not necessary or even desirable that such should be the case. Probably the best results will be achieved by men who, possessing the organizing faculty and a realizing sense of the importance of their work, shall, with the assistance of an engineer and a plantsman, labor to execute faithfully designs which they thoroughly understand and approve.

Most men of specialized training, such as architects, engineers, and all grades of horticulturists, stand in need of an awakening before they are really competent to have to do with park work. Each has to learn that his building, his bridge or road, his tree or flower, which he has been accustomed to think of as an end in itself, is, in the park, only a means auxiliary and contributive to a larger end, — namely, the general landscape. It is hard for most gardeners to forego the use of plants which, however lovely or marvellous they may be as individuals, are only blots on the landscape. It is hard for most engineers to conform their ideas of straightforward construction to a due regard for appearance and the preservation of the charm of scenery. Neatness of finish in slopes adjacent to roads is not sufficient; such slopes must be contrived so as to avoid formality and all likeness to railroad cuts or fills. Road lines and grades which may be practicable in the ordinary world are to be avoided in the park, because the pleasure of the visitor is the one object held in view. Roads, walls, bridges, water-supply, drainage, and grading, — such of these works as may be necessary are to be executed with all technical skill, as in the outer world; but the engineer in charge should be a man who will see to it that the work is done with constant regard to the object of a park as distinguished from the object of a city street or square, or of a railroad.

Similarly, the park planter should be a man capable of holding fast to the idea that the value of a rural park consists in landscape, and not in gardening or in the exhibition of specimen plants. Guided by this idea, he will avoid such absurd traces of formality as the too common practice of planting trees in rows beside curving driveways. In devising necessary plantations he will give preference to native plants, without avoiding exotics of kinds which blend easily. Thus, where a Banana would be out of place, the equally foreign Barberry, Privet, or Buckthorn may be admissible and useful. Influenced by the same principle, he will confine flower gardening to the secluded garden, for which space may perhaps be found in some corner of the park.

If men can be found who will thus coöperate with park commissioners to the end that the lands and landscapes which the latter hold in trust shall be cared for and made available in strict accordance with that trust, excellent results can be hoped for in American parks. As before remarked, men who are capable of such work may certainly be trusted to construct and manage town spaces — squares, playgrounds, and the like — with due regard to their special purposes and to the satisfaction of all concerned.

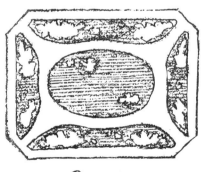

A PUBLIC SQUARE.

CHAPTER XXIV

LETTERS OF 1894 ON METROPOLITAN PARK WORK

The problem of a park . . . is mainly the reconciliation of adequate beauty of nature in scenery with adequate means in artificial constructions of protecting the conditions of such beauty, and holding it available to the use, in a convenient and orderly way, of those needing it. — F. L. OLMSTED.

AT the close of each year between 1893 and 1896 inclusive, Charles wrote a report to the Metropolitan Park Commission summarizing the work done for the Commission by the landscape architects ; but in each one of these years he wrote also a series of letters to the Commission giving current advice, or answering questions raised in meetings of the Board. The annual reports generally relate to things accomplished, the letters to things under consideration or needing to be done. The letters selected for this chapter were addressed to the chairman of the Commission with the exception of the last two, and these were on Metropolitan business. It will be noticed that they deal with a great variety of subjects, some of them apparently not strictly within the province of landscape advisers ; but it must be remembered that Charles was, at this stage of the undertaking, the one person who was familiar with all the new reservations, and at the same time knew well whatever foreign experience had to teach about the management of public domains. He also wrote in the name of the most experienced firm of landscape architects in the country.[1]

The first letter relates to subjects of prime importance, the second of which was difficult from the beginning, and has not yet (1901) been satisfactorily disposed of. In this early letter Charles evidently wishes all work on paths in the reservations to be of the simplest sort, as befits temporary provisions.

[1] It will be obvious to the reader that the letter-books of the firm have been freely used, by permission, in the preparation of this volume. The letters selected were all written or dictated by Charles himself.

Jan. 5, 1894.

We beg leave to report as follows upon the subject of work which it seems to us might with advantage be done at once upon the reservations taken, or about to be taken, by your Board.

The woodlands of all the reservations in your charge have in the past suffered much damage by fire. Upon very large areas there stands to-day nothing but fire-killed forest. Other large areas, which have lately been chopped over, are strewn with dry and inflammable brush. This condition of the woods invites fire; and another fire, with these vast quantities of lifeless material to feed upon, might easily get beyond control, and so finish the destruction of the woods and even of the soil of the hills.

Nature's method of getting rid of the dangerous lifeless material just mentioned consists in reducing it to ashes through the slow processes of decay. We respectfully advise the Commission to rid the reservations of dead wood at once by felling it, and by burning in heaps all that is not profitably salable as posts or cordwood. This work might employ from fifty to one hundred men in each of the three woodland reservations during, perhaps, fifty working days. The work should cease after March 31st. It should be superintended by careful men, who will see to it that only dead trees and bushes are cut down, that living undergrowth and especially young trees are not injured, and that fires are built and lighted only where and when they can do no harm. If this work cannot be done, we must advise the Commission to employ a large force of fire wards (a man for every hundred acres would be none too many), for the protection of the woodlands during the dangerous spring months. If, on the contrary, the dead wood can be cleared away before April, one man for every five hundred or one thousand acres would form a sufficient guard, particularly if friendly relations and connection by telephone could be established with the nearest public fire departments, or with such citizens as might be willing to hold themselves ready to respond to a call for aid. We presume that the public telephone service could be extended to several points of vantage in the reservations at no very great expense.

A second work which needs to be done at once within the reservations is the clearing of the principal existing paths so that they may be easily found and used by the public. A well-trodden path will stop an ordinary ground fire ; while a crown fire can best be fought by making back fires along paths or roads ; so that there is double reason for this work. Here and there a new path may be needed, or an old path may be required to be drained or carried over a stream. We ask that whatever work of this sort is done shall be done boldly and naturally ; particularly that no " pretty " stone-work or wood-work shall be attempted. If a ditch is needed, let it look like a ditch, and if a foot-bridge is needed, let it be as simple as possible.

It seems advisable that guide-maps of the reservations should be issued for the use of the public, and we hold ourselves in readiness to proceed to the making of the same should the Commission so direct.

A third work which will need to be done soon is the marking of the boundaries of the reservations by stone monuments, and the building of fences where private estates abut upon the boundary line.

The next letter is an example of the continuous study which had to be given to the boundaries of some of the reservations, and of the new designs which resulted from these studies as new conditions arose. The first three paragraphs of this letter resulted in an important saving of money to the district ; the next three contain the first description of a beautiful design since carried out by the coöperation of the Metropolitan Commission and the Boston Commission ; the last paragraph relates to a difficult problem not yet solved.

Feb. 23, 1894.

In order to make the record of our connection with your labors continuous, we submit the following memorandum of our doings with respect to the proposed Stony Brook Reservation.

On December 15, 1893, in accordance with previous commands of the Commission, we submitted a plan showing a boundary line which would enclose some nine hundred acres at the source of Stony Brook. We took pains to state at the

time that this boundary included much more than the central
or essential scenery of the Muddy Pond valley.   During
January the Committee on the Stony Brook Reservation inspected the line, as did the Hyde Park Commissioners, and
several new lines were placed upon the map as the result of
various conferences.   About the end of January, we understood that Surveyor Richardson received orders from Secretary Carruth to proceed to the making of definitive taking-
plans.

On February 9, 1894, Mr. F. L. Olmsted and Mr. Eliot
took occasion to state in a full meeting of the Board their
conviction that so large a reservation at the source of Stony
Brook is hardly warrantable or advisable, and their opinion
that if any land is to be taken in this section it should include the rugged glen which has Bellevue Hill at its head
and Muddy Pond in its bottom, rather than the now better
forested valley in which lies West Street.

On February 16, 1894, the Mayor of Boston being in conference with the Commission, in accordance with a suggestion
from Commissioner W. L. Chase, we submitted sketch plans
showing a reservation of four hundred and seventy-eight acres
at Muddy Pond south of Washington Street, and parkways
connecting with the Arnold Arboretum on the one hand and
the Blue Hills Reservation on the other.

To-day we submit for the consideration of the Commission
the detailed plan of the first mentioned parkway prepared by
us for the use of the Boston Park Commission.   We propose,
however, that this parkway should include the summit of
Mount Bellevue, and the city surveyor is now preparing a
map of the hill so that this connection may be studied.   As
far as the base of the hill, the parkway traverses unoccupied
and beautiful land except near the crossing of the Dedham
Railroad, where a few cheap houses stand in the way.   The
plan provides two side-roads from 200 to 650 feet apart,
affording frontage for the adjacent excellent building land,
and a pleasure drive in the middle, which latter will accompany a charming brook for about a mile.

On Washington Street, at the base of Bellevue, the pleasure drive would divide, a branch ascending Bellevue by a

spiral curve, while the main road would at once descend into
the Muddy Pond Glen. If the scenery of the glen is to be
effectually preserved, the side boundary roads should probably
be some 3000 feet apart abreast of the pond, nearing each
other as the lower ground near Hyde Park is reached, and
coming to Mother Brook through Happy Valley with a reservation 400 feet broad. The length of the reservation
between Washington Street and Mother Brook is two miles.

Beyond Mother Brook, there is no better way of reaching
the banks of the Neponset River than by opening a straight
way from the south side of Damon School to the south side
of the Hyde Park Water Company's pumping-house on the
east bank of the river. A trestle or viaduct will carry the
parkway over the two railroads and the river as directly as is
possible. The Neponset would then be included in the reservation as far as Paul's Bridge, from which point Brush
Hill Road ascends to the western entrance to the Blue Hills
Reservation.

The next four letters relate to a new function which in the
spring of 1894 was imposed on the Metropolitan Park Commission by the legislature, in spite of the unconcealed reluctance of the Commission to accept it. The winter of 1893–94
was a season of great industrial depression in Massachusetts, and an unusual number of men were out of work. The
legislature had this state of things in mind when it placed
$500,000 at the disposal of the Commission wherewith to buy
land for, and to construct, parkways which would make the
new reservations more accessible to the public. Doubtless
the legislature thought that the Commission could make the
necessary plans in a few weeks, and set some thousands of
the unemployed at work. The Act was approved April 21st,
and on May 1st Charles began the study of a first parkway,
namely, one to connect the Fells with the centre of the district. In a little over three weeks he prepared the design
described in the first of the following letters, a design which
in all its essential features has since been executed. It soon
became evident, however, that with all the delays necessitated
by the indispensable surveys, taking-plans, and negotiations
with owners, it would be quite impossible to begin actual
construction that summer; and that the Commission needed
time to consider the fair way of expending, in the interest of
the whole district, the moderate appropriation placed at their

disposal.   It was the 30th of August before Charles was prepared to suggest a preliminary plan for the Blue Hills Parkway.   This will be found in the second letter of this group.
Like the design for the Fells Parkway, it proposed a central
railway reservation with a roadway, a planting-strip, and a
sidewalk on each side of it.   From the beginning, Charles
planned for electric cars on these parkways, that by them the
populace might reach the forest reservations cheaply but in a
pleasurable manner.   The third letter of this series gives his
reasons for recommending the immediate acquisition of the
land for these two parkways, and the construction of as much
as possible of the Fells Parkway.   It is plain in these three
letters that Charles was seeking the greatest good of the
greatest number in expending the $500,000 for parkways.
The fourth and last of these parkway letters was a personal
letter to Mr. Charles Francis Adams, the chairman of the
Commission, who had great difficulty in accepting parkways
at all as work to be done under the direction of the Park
Commission.   Charles had at first sympathized very much
with Mr. Adams; but on further study and reflection, had
come to the conclusion that the laying out of parkways to
enable the people to reach agreeably their larger reservations
was appropriate work for the Metropolitan Park Commission.

May 24, 1894.

We have the honor to report as follows on the problem of
a direct and easy approach to Middlesex Fells Reservation
from the central and densely inhabited part of the metropolitan district.

The southernmost points of the Fells Reservation, as it is
at present outlined, are the two bold hills known as Pine
Hill, Medford, and Bear's Den Hill, Malden.   Between these
two points the boundary of the reservation retreats about half
a mile to the northward.   Both hills are about five and one
half miles from the State House.

What with Charles River, the railroads, the new railroad
yards in the old Asylum Grounds, the great packing-houses
and the proposed railroad shops by Mystic River, it seems
impracticable at the present time to open through the crowded
territory south of Mystic River any one broad and continuous
line of communication leading towards the Fells.

The principal existing streets leading in the desired direc-

tion from the business centre of Boston are Main Street and
Rutherford Avenue, Charlestown, and the continuation of the
same in Mystic and Middlesex Avenues, Somerville. Leading from the Back Bay District, there is Harvard Bridge,
Portland Street, Cambridge, and Cross Street, Somerville.
These two main lines of existing, but inadequate, streets converge upon Middlesex Avenue Bridge over Mystic River,
the only bridge which lies in the straight line between the
State House and the heart of the Fells.

Leaving these approaches to the bridge and the bridge
itself to be improved in the future, it is practicable at the
present time to begin the construction of a special and adequate approach to the Fells at the northern end of this bridge.
A suitable approach-road should certainly be broad enough
to include a grassed and shaded reservation for electric cars,
as well as sufficient driveways and sidewalks. A good arrangement would be the following: For the electric railway thirty-
five feet, and on each side thereof a roadway thirty feet, a
planting-strip of seven feet, and a sidewalk eight feet in
width. This gives the proposed way or boulevard a total
width of one hundred and twenty-five feet. Assuming that
this shall be the width, the question is how best to lead a
boulevard of these dimensions from Middlesex Avenue Bridge
to the Fells.

Obviously, the most direct line to Bear's Den Hill and the
eastern section of the Fells is the existing Highland Avenue,
but to widen this street to the extent desired seems impracticable because of the numerous existing buildings and the shallowness of many of the adjacent lots.

Obviously, also, a direct line to Pine Hill is equally impracticable because of the closely built streets of eastern Medford.

Fortunately there still remains halfway between Malden
and Medford a stretch of open land, through the midst of
which a boulevard may be built with little damage to existing
buildings and with great benefit to adjacent lands. By way
of this open land it is one and one half level miles from
Middlesex Avenue Bridge to the foot of the rock-hills at the
corner of Pleasant and Valley streets. At this foot of the
hills we would have the road divide, one branch leading to

Valley Street, and near Love Lane, so called, to Pine Hill and the western section of the Reservation, and the other branch leading by Fellsmere, across Highland Avenue, to Bear's Den Hill and the eastern section. Then from Pine Hill to Bear's Den Hill the proposed road on the boundary of the reservation might be arranged so as to complete the circuit and conduct the electric cars, not only to the two commanding hills and both sections of the Fells, but also completely around the especially charming, but now inaccessible, tract of building land which lies between the higher hills. The owners of this hilly tract, as well as the owners of the flat, open land before mentioned, will doubtless be glad to give land for the sake of securing the construction of the boulevard upon a route so advantageous to their interests.

If this general scheme of a Fells Boulevard should approve itself to the Commission, and if it should be thought advisable to proceed to construction as soon as possible, we would recommend the employment of three parties of surveyors, one to map the property lines and grades of the flat section, and two to map the more complicated topography of the hill sections. Presumably it would not take long to determine the most advantageous course for the boulevard across the flat land. Much work upon this section could doubtless be accomplished this summer. Meanwhile, plans for the work in the hill sections would be preparing, and much of the necessary blasting and coarser grading might be accomplished during next winter.

Aug. 30, 1894.

On May 24th last, we reported upon a preliminary plan for the middle or level section of the proposed Fells Parkway. To-day we present a similar preliminary plan of the level section of the proposed Blue Hills Parkway. This section begins at the termination of Blue Hill Avenue at the Neponset River on the boundary of Boston and Milton, and extends to Canton Avenue in Milton, following as closely as possible the line of the existing Mattapan Street. The suggestions presented in the plan may be briefly described as follows : —

[Mattapan Street straightened, 8100 feet long, 120 feet wide, with sidewalk and planting-strip on each side, two roadways, and a central railroad reservation.]

. . . Between Brook Road, Brush Hill Road, and Neponset River there are many Spruce-trees which we deem of no account, and several large Elms which the plans as drawn will preserve. . . . At Neponset River, the completion of the plan would ultimately call for a new bridge in addition to the present bridge, and the pushing eastward of the Mattapan Railroad Station of the Old Colony division. This latter work being in Boston would naturally become a part of the promised widening of the existing Blue Hill Avenue.

It will be remembered that for that section of the Blue Hills Parkway which lies south of Canton Avenue, outline plans have already been submitted by us in the form of a proposed addition to Blue Hills Reservation. Thus our scheme for this parkway, as for the Fells Parkway, is now complete.

Aug. 30, 1894.

In view of the fact that we have now completed preliminary plans of both of the parkways recommended by us to the favorable consideration of the Commission, we ask that the following brief statement of the reasoning which has influenced us may be placed on your file.

The Commission was empowered by the legislature of 1894 to expend five hundred thousand dollars in buying land for parkways and in constructing the same. The Commission having previously acquired large public reservations in the Fells and the Blue Hills, we were naturally not surprised when the problem set before us was defined to be the devising of parkways which should conveniently connect these reservations with the densely inhabited centre of the metropolitan district. Upon taking up this problem in its relations with the Blue Hills, it was found that the City of Boston was already engaged in widening Blue Hill Avenue through Dorchester to a width of one hundred and twenty feet, and that from the terminus of this broad way at Mattapan, the route to the Reservation which is at once the shortest and the least hilly is by way of Mattapan Street, Harland Street, and the valley which may be called Crossman's Valley after the solitary settler who lives there. By this route, the distance from Mattapan Bridge to Crossman's Pines at the northern corner

of Blue Hills Reservation is about three miles. The parkway
for the first half of this distance would consist of a straight
and formal avenue, but beyond Canton Avenue it seems possible and very desirable to include in the parkway both sides
of the narrow and charming gorge of Pine Tree Brook.   No
other possible route of approach to the Hills from the heart
of the city appears to us to be so worthy of adoption as this.

In its relation with the Fells, the problem set before us
proved by no means easy of solution.   Unlike the Blue Hills,
the Fells are surrounded by city-like towns whose inhabitants
are obliged to seek Boston almost daily, and yet there exists
for these communities no such direct avenue of approach to
the heart of the great city as Blue Hill Avenue affords Milton and the other comparative rural towns to the southward.

Accordingly, though only after much serious study of the
circumstances, we were forced to the conclusion that the most
valuable thing which the Commission could do in this northern
section of the district at the present time would be the opening of a broad and handsome way, beginning at each of the
two southernmost corners of the Fells Reservation, and extending thence toward the centre of Boston to some point on
the edge of the densely inhabited area at which the best possible present connection may be made with continuous streets
penetrating the crowded parts of the town, and to which it
may be hoped that a broad avenue may be opened through
the crowded area in years to come.   In searching for this
cityward terminus of the work to be done under the present
available appropriation, Broadway Park, Somerville, was
chosen because it is readily accessible from Charlestown, and
because it is reached by Cross Street, which has easy grades
by reason of passing east of Prospect Hill, as well as by Walnut Street, which climbs over the hill.   It may be noted incidentally that this advantageous point of beginning the Fells
Parkway is no farther from the State House (two and one-
half miles) than Cottage Farm bridge, Roxbury Crossing, or
the beginning of Blue Hill Avenue at Dudley Street; and
while the Blue Hills Reservation is distant from this last
named corner seven miles, the Fells Reservation is distant
from Broadway Park only three miles and a small fraction.

If the Commission desires to hear our opinion not only as to the lines upon which the present appropriation may best be expended, but also as to how it should be expended, we may frankly say that we recommend the immediate acquisition of the lands required for both these parkways, the construction of as much as possible of the Fells Parkway, and in the Blue Hills Parkway the construction of the connecting link of road which is needed to permit Crossman's Pines to be reached from Harland Street. The Fells Parkway seems to us to be sorely needed by the population which dwells around the Fells, as well as by the throngs who would be glad to visit the reservation. The construction of the Blue Hills Parkway can well be delayed in view of the two facts that there is no large body of population in its neighborhood and that visitors to the reservation will be well served by existing streets and the one link which we have just proposed should be built.

Sept. 14, 1894.

MY DEAR MR. ADAMS, — Let me try to set down a few facts for your consideration. To Mr. Richardson one day at Beaver Brook, to Mr. Philip A. Chase at various times, and to Mr. Carruth in his office, I expressed my repugnance for the "boulevard" legislation, before the enactment of the measure, as well as afterwards. The grounds of my feeling were precisely those which you expressed the other day at lunch.

To the astonishment of most of us, a "boulevard" act was passed granting $500,000, one half to come direct from the State treasury. I have supposed that this result was largely due to the fact that Malden and Medford men were leaders in the "Committee on the Unemployed;" and that these men assumed that the boulevard to be constructed would benefit their communities.

However this may have been, the Commission after some discussion asked our firm to submit schemes for "boulevards" which should connect the forest reserves with the heart of the city. These schemes are now before the Board, the Fells scheme, by vote of the Board, having already passed from us to an engineer who has staked it out, and prepared estimates of the cost of construction.

In the course of my study of the projects submitted, I reached certain conclusions, among them being : —

1st. These ways of sufficient breadth to accommodate safe, that is, separate, electric car lines, as well as roadways, are really needed. The separate car lines, affording rapid and pleasant transit to the reservations for "the masses," seem to me fully as important as the pleasure driveways.

2d. There exists no public authority other than the Metropolitan Park Commission capable of either acquiring the land or constructing these ways in the positions deemed most advantageous. Malden and Medford are incapable of the proposed Fells Parkway; Milton is even more incapable of the Mattapan and Harland Streets development. On the other hand, these places, together with the whole metropolitan district, would in my opinion greatly profit by the construction of both.

3d. The legislature having put this burden on the Metropolitan Park Commission, the proposed "boulevards" being real metropolitan improvements, and no other authority capable of making them existing, for myself, I see no way of avoiding advancing on the lines laid down — after making sure that the routes selected are the most advantageous that can be found.

4th. As the work of opening "boulevards" is absolutely distinct from the original work of the Metropolitan Commission, as the money for the work is derived from different sources, and as it is important that the public should understand that the "boulevard" work is a separate and special job put upon a commission created for other and distinct purposes, it would be well if the report on the "boulevard" work with its financial statement should be made to the legislature in a separate document, which would be separately printed and distributed. If this were done, there would be little danger that the ends originally had in view by the Commission would be lost sight of, altered, or injured by the boulevard work, or by anything which might happen to that work. If this were done, the Commission would at any time be ready to transfer the boulevard work to some other Commission or to the Greater Boston organization, should such a thing come into existence.

If I can be of any assistance at all next week, I hope you may be able to name a time when we meet on Monday afternoon, as I am already engaged for the afternoon of every day except Friday and Saturday, and those days are likely to be taken at any minute. I am writing this line in haste, after a long day and evening of work, on which account I trust you will excuse the scrawling thereof.

Yours very truly,

CHARLES ELIOT.

The next letter is a type of not infrequent letters which repeat, or urge, recommendations already made. Charles saw very clearly the improvements in detail which it was desirable to make in the boundaries of the reservations already acquired, and he was eager to have the improvements secured before land values rose much. There were also some very valuable additional reservations, or additions to acquired reservations, which the Commission hesitated to grasp, but which to Charles's mind were intensely desirable, either because they had great landscape charm, or because they would contribute to make equitable the distribution of the reservations throughout the district. The latter point was always much on his mind. The Commission, pressed with many questions of purchase, construction, and maintenance, would sometimes lose sight of measures which seemed to Charles important. In this case he was justified in feeling some anxiety; for the Hemlock Gorge — one of the "takings" urged in this letter — was not acquired by the Commission until September, 1895, although it is unquestionably the most beautiful small piece of scenery in the entire district.

26 September, 1894.

Permit us to call the attention of the Board to several recommendations made by us some time ago.

(a) Proposed additions to the Blue Hills Reservations :

1st and 2d. [Small parcels of land to improve entrances.]

3d. A body of land lying in Pine Tree Brook valley, Milton, between the present boundary of the reservation and Randolph Avenue, desirable to be obtained in order to afford a natural entrance to the eastern sections of the reservation from the direction of Dorchester and Milton Hill, while at the same time preserving some of the scenery of the course of the brook.

4th and 5th. [Very small parcels of land to make entrances.]

6th. A narrow strip across the estate of Mr. Floyd to the north side of the Western Section of the reservation, desirable to be procured in order that the boundary road may eventually be built without destroying a fine row of Chestnut-trees.

Taking-plans for none of these additions have yet been ordered.

(b) Proposed additions to Stony Brook Reservation : —

1st. The long strip of land intended to prolong the public reservation to a connection with the West Roxbury Parkway of the Boston Park Commission in the neighborhood of Weld Street, West Roxbury. It is understood that the taking-plans for this strip are in course of preparation by the engineers.

2d. A long strip to serve as a parkway connecting Stony Brook Reservation with Blue Hills Reservation by way of Neponset River and Paul's Bridge. Surveyor Richardson of Hyde Park, has, by order of the Board, prepared a map of the territory concerned. May we ask whether the Board desires us to submit sketches for a parkway to the Blue Hills by this route? . . .

(c) The proposed reservation at the Hemlock Gorge on Charles River : —

By order of the Board a map of this locality has been prepared, and we some time since suggested upon the basis of this map a boundary line for the proposed reservation. We understand that the Secretary of the Board is making himself acquainted with the assessed valuations of the lands included within the proposed boundaries. This is the most strikingly picturesque spot within the metropolitan district; the Hemlocks are annually ravaged for Christmas green, and we must hope that the Board may find some way to take prompt action.

(d) Proposed additions to the Middlesex Fells Reservation : —

1st. A narrow strip of varying width outside the present boundary of the reservation between Bear's Den Entrance and Highland Avenue, desirable to be procured in order that the boundary road may be given sufficient width without destroying certain fine trees and rocky slopes. The taking-plan of this strip has already been completed by Engineer Pierce and awaits the action of the Board.

2d. A block of land of irregular shape lying on both sides of Fulton Street between Highland Avenue and Elm Street, Medford, desirable to be obtained in order that the reservation may include the whole course of the Hemlock Pond Brook, and in order that the boundary road may find place upon the south side of said brook. The course of the boundary road near the brook has been studied and mapped by us, but the Board has not yet directed the making of a taking-plan for this addition.

3d. A strip of varying width, more than a mile in length, south of and adjacent to that boundary of the reservation in Medford which was defined by the Act of the legislature, desirable to be obtained in order that the boundary road may be built upon practicable grades, and in order that the reservation may include the several high ledges which are bisected by the uncompromising legislative lines. A desirable boundary line in this region of the Fells has been sketched by us on a map furnished by Messrs. Hodges & Harrington, but before a taking-plan is ordered by the Board we would recommend that Engineer Pierce should make a topographical survey upon which we may define with accuracy the desirable boundary lines, and the course and grades of the boundary road.

Permit us also to call the attention of the Board to the state of the work ordered by the Board under the so-called Boulevard Act.

For the Fells Parkway recommended by us, taking-plans have been prepared by order of the Board covering the course of the Parkway from Broadway Park, Somerville, to Forest Street, Medford, and the taking-plan of the eastern branch of the Parkway only awaits the decision of the Board with respect to the route to be followed in the neighborhood of Highland Rock, Malden.

With respect to the Blue Hills Parkway, we have to report

that our project for the route thereof from Mattapan to Canton Avenue, Milton, has been before the Board for several weeks, but that taking-plans have not as yet been ordered. . . .

We are able to report excellent progress in the preparation of the new general map of the metropolitan district ordered of us by the Board. We propose to show upon this map the shore lines, ponds, and streams of the district; the railroads, highways, street railroads, and common roads; the hills, woods, salt marshes, and swamps; the cemeteries and other similar open spaces; the principal or largest country-seats; the existing public grounds controlled by local authorities; and the reservations secured or proposed by the Metropolitan Park Commission.

While the parkway from Somerville to Middlesex Fells and the parkway to the Blue Hills from Mattapan were under consideration by the Commission in the fall of 1894, attractive offers were received of land for a parkway on the east shore of the two Mystic ponds, to be constructed under the so-called Boulevard Act passed in the spring of that year. A reservation including both shores of the Mystic ponds had been recommended by Charles in his report to the preliminary Metropolitan Park Commission; but when it was proposed to secure only one shore, — the eastern, — Charles felt obliged to point out that the new way had no logical beginning or end, and that it would not render the Fells more accessible from the densely populated portions of the district. Beside stating these objections to the proposed parkway he urged, November 1, 1894, that the scheme as outlined was only an incomplete sanitary measure, and "that the project is equally incomplete in respect to the preservation of landscape, in that it contemplates preserving the wild beauty of only one bank of the two Mystic ponds." A year later, when the construction of this parkway was determined on, he wrote, on the 13th of November, 1895: "If these western shores are built upon in the usual manner, the reservation on the eastern bank will obviously be greatly injured."

The danger of injurious occupation of the western bank has since been much increased by the construction of an electric road in the highway which serves the western shore of the ponds. Nevertheless, the Mystic Valley Parkway, regarded as a separate reservation, is, at present, beautiful in itself, and very useful to Winchester, Medford, Arlington,

Somerville, and Cambridge. It will be more generally useful still, when its southern end shall be connected with Fresh Pond, and with the Metropolitan reservations on the south side of Charles River. The construction of this parkway delayed the completion of the parkway to Middlesex Fells, and postponed for years the construction of the parkway to the Blue Hills. Charles always remained of the opinion that the expenditure of almost the entire appropriation under the Boulevard Act north of the Mystic River was something less than equitable. Nevertheless, as he remarked in the report of the landscape architects for 1895, "within the limits laid down, we have done what we could to secure rational boundaries."

It was the practice of the Commission to refer questions about proposed acquisitions, or abandonments, of land to the landscape architects for their advice. The following letter is a good example of the answers given ; for two general principles are illustrated, — the continuity of boundary roads, and the exclusion of buildings from the high edges of large reservations. The second paragraph mentions an addition to the Middlesex Fells which Charles thought very desirable. It has not yet (1902) been "resumed" by the public.

Nov. 9, 1894.

We beg leave to report as follows on several questions referred to us concerning Middlesex Fells Reservation : —

1st. The acquisition of the two ledges which flank the present entrance to the reservation from Summer Street is desirable, even if the land is somewhat costly.

2d. The acquisition of land in Medford south of the legislative line (as sketched on the accompanying map) is very much to be desired. It is to be hoped that Meeting-House Brook may eventually become the central feature of a parkway which will lead to the reservation from Mystic River. The alternative lines shown on the accompanying map will be found to be marked upon the ground by stakes.

3d. The proposed abandonment of lands taken from the Greeley estate in Winchester seems undesirable because the continuity of the boundary road will be broken thereby. If a boundary south of the legislative line can be secured, the boundary road of the reservation will then become a very pleasant and convenient way leading from Mt. Vernon Street,

Winchester, to Medford and Malden, and to Boston if the
Fells Parkway is opened. The way through the Greeley
valley near Mt. Vernon Street is an essential part of this
proposed through route.

4th. The proposed release of the house sites which Messrs.
—— and —— say they have planned to build upon can be
justified only by absolute necessity of economy ; because both
of these sites are upon the edge of the table-land, which abrupt
edge every one who has studied the Fells knows to be one of
the most interesting features of the scenery of the district.

5th. The abandonment of the land already released to Mr.
—— we objected to for the reason just given, and also because
houses built on the abandoned land will be unpleasantly conspicuous from the water-tower hill, and even from distant
parts of the interior of the reservation. It is to be hoped
that the Commission will not too hastily determine upon any
further abandonments.

6th. The proposed abandonment of lands near the Stoneham and Melrose township line, we are entirely prepared to
approve, supposing that the line to be adopted is that which
we originally recommended to the Commission as the most
natural boundary of the reservation in that section.

7th. The proposed road or right of way over Mr. ——'s
lane in Stoneham would make a desirable entrance to the reservation ; but we see no good reason why the Commission
should assume the fee thereof with the accompanying obligation to construct, maintain, and police a road through private
lands.

Charles sometimes tried to hasten the formal adoption of
measures on which the Commission had really determined by
sending to the chairman in advance of a meeting votes, or
orders, already drawn up in proper form. Thus on December 7, 1894, he proposed two orders relating to the demarcation of the boundaries of the acquired reservations, first on
the Engineer's maps and then by stone monuments on the
ground ; two more concerning building cheap boundary roads
" under the general supervision of the landscape architects "
in certain parts of the large reservations ; one which directed
that weekly detailed reports of work done be sent to the Secretary by the Engineer and Superintendent, and that copies

of these reports be sent to each member of the Commission
and to the landscape architects; and the two following which
related to his own work : —

"Ordered, that the Landscape Architects prepare maps indicating the main fire-guard lines from which dead wood is
first to be removed, and report to this Board."

"Ordered, that the Landscape Architects furnish the Superintendent with maps indicating in a general way the roads and
bridle-paths to be first made usable and opened to the public,
and that the Superintendent, under the general supervision
of the Landscape Architects, open and build said roads and
paths as soon as may be." . . .

It is obvious that one purpose of these proposed orders
about roads, fire-guards, and weekly reports was to give the
landscape architects better control of the work going on in
the reservations.

The year 1894 was the year for parkway studies, on account
of the Boulevard Act passed in the spring.   Beside the Fells,
Blue Hills, and Mystic Valley Parkways, Charles prescribed
the general lines of five others which had been suggested to
the legislature or to the Commission.   These were all surveyed by engineers; but the entire appropriation was applied
elsewhere, so that none of these designs were utilized.   At
the time the studies merely helped the Commission to reach
and defend negative conclusions.   The next letter tells what
the points were which these five parkways were designed to
connect.

Dec. 19, 1894.

We send herewith mounted sun-prints of the surveys
ordered by the Board some time since : —

Namely, a survey of a route for a parkway between the
Fells Reservation and Lynn by way of Lynn Woods; a survey of a route for a parkway between Everett Railroad Station and Revere Beach; a survey of a route for a parkway
between the southern end of Revere Beach and Winthrop
Great Head; a survey of a route for a parkway between the
northern end of Revere Beach and Market Street, Lynn, and
a survey of a route for a parkway between Stony Brook Reservation and the Blue Hills Reservation by way of Paul's
Bridge.   These surveys have been made along the line of
routes designated by us, but devised to connect points designated by the Commission.   These surveys, we believe, estab-

lish the feasibility of the several routes, and by laying these maps before the Commission, we understand that we have completed our duties in these matters so far as we have been instructed by the Board up to this time.

The answer which Charles gave to an inquiry from the Commission concerning a suggestion made by Mr. Edward Atkinson of Brookline states in the broadest manner his opinion about the public ownership of watercourses within populous towns or cities. The letter is as follows : —

June 1, 1894.

Concerning a suggestion from Mr. Edward Atkinson referred to us by a vote of the Commission, we beg leave to report that the high level swamps of upper Brookline, and the courses of the brooks which flow from them, ought to be owned by the public, in common with all the principal watercourses of every district destined to be densely inhabited. At the present time these valleys are almost uninhabited; so that control of the watercourses could be obtained very cheaply. On the other hand, it appears to us that the Metropolitan Park Commission should give its first attention to the acquisition of the banks of the larger streams of the district, leaving the smaller brooks to be taken care of by the local authorities. Mr. Atkinson's project is both feasible and desirable; and it is to be hoped that the Town of Brookline may see its way to carry it out.

It was Charles's desire that the Metropolitan Park Commission should collect and place on file the fullest possible information about the history of the lands selected for metropolitan reservations, and about their condition at the time of their selection. He wanted to secure for the archives of the Commission complete contour maps of the reservations, and full information about the fauna and flora of the forests ; and he hoped also to get some information about the ownership and private uses in former generations of the lands now devoted to public uses. The two letters which follow illustrate his general object, and his way of pursuing it. Messrs. Balch & Rackemann did much work for the Commission in the examination of titles.

August 22, 1894.

MESSRS. BALCH & RACKEMANN.

Dear Sirs, — In presenting a first annual report to the Metropolitan Park Commission, it is our intention and hope to summarize for each of the acquired reservations the most important of those facts of geology,[1] topography,[2] forestry,[1] and history which have had influence in creating the present scenery of the lands in question. We have already arranged for reports from our assistants in the natural history of the reservation. We should be pleased if you could suggest to us the name of one of your assistants or acquaintances who might be willing (perhaps for a small consideration) to report briefly upon the history of the land-ownership of the reservations, particularly upon the bearing thereof upon the scenery.

One of our men (Mr. Gordon H. Taylor) has made some progress in this direction, but if a man acquainted with the history of the titles should by chance once get interested in searching out the connection between that history and the present scenery, the results would be still more interesting and instructive.

We may illustrate our meaning by citing Beaver Brook Reservation. The mill privileges with the dams make the falls. How far back do they date? How came the great Oaks to have survived? Is long-continued complication of ownership to be thanked, or what? and so on.

Hoping that you may be acquainted with some one who might be led to write out for us some of this lore, we are . . .

August 22, 1894.

MR. W. O. CROSBY, Boston Society of Natural History.

Dear Sir, — Would it be possible for you to address to us on or before November 1st next brief sketch reports on the geology and topography of the Blue Hills, Fells, Stony Brook, and Beaver Brook reservations? By October 1st or earlier

[1] Published in the Appendix to the second annual report of the Metropolitan Park Commission, January, 1895.

[2] Contour maps of the reservations, 100 feet to the inch, were completed early in 1896.

you could have from us Mr. Taylor's maps of all these lands, and we should be particularly pleased if you could map the more important geology upon these sheets in time for publication in the January report.

Mr. Taylor has perhaps told you of our beginning a map of the metropolitan district on the scale of $\frac{1}{20000}$. Perhaps you would consider that the supplying without cost to you of such a sheet, together with the costless stereotyping of your geology of the reservations, would recompense you for the special trouble you would be put to.   We have at our command no appropriation for geological research as we have for guide maps, for the district map, and for research in forestry, so that we cannot offer you compensation in money.   It would doubtless be arranged so that your reports and maps could be hereafter printed separately for your use from the State's plates.   It would on all accounts be best if the reports were to be written in a manner to interest the general public as far as possible.

CHAPTER XXV

LETTERS OF 1894 CONCERNING PARKS NOT METRO-POLITAN

> It is astonishing that the art of adorning the country round our habitations should not have been discovered, the art of unfolding, preserving, or imitating beautiful nature. It may become one of the most interesting of the arts ; it is to poetry and painting what reality is to a description, what the original is to the copy. — GIRARDIN. 1777.

THE selections which make up this chapter deal with common park problems in such a way that, though the cases are particular, the principles laid down are of general application.

The first selection is a passage relating to the treatment of old commons, taken from a letter to the City Engineer of Lowell on the parks of that city.

March 29, 1894.

With respect to the old commons, we have to say that such grounds present perhaps the most difficult problem with which we have professionally to deal. The question is, What can be done to make it possible for great numbers of people to make use of such recreation grounds without destroying all beauty of appearance or effect? We are sorry to be obliged to answer, that until it is possible to spend money very liberally, but little can be done. It is evidently desirable that the surrounding streets should be curbed ; also that malls parallel with the streets should be opened and graded and provided with seats. If the commons could be fenced, thus confining the public to a few entrances, the grounds would be saved from much trampling, and the policeman in charge would have better control of his domain. If the playgrounds could be spread with a good gravel, and all other grounds and slopes kept in grass, it would be well. Low, temporary fences may be used with advantage to keep the public off of grass which is in process of recovery from abuse. Litter of all kinds ought, of course, to be promptly cleared away.

If it were possible to spend $50,000 on each common in providing suitable small buildings for the shelter and accommodation of the public (to be placed in charge of salaried care-takers), and in carrying out a complete new design calculated to meet the demands of beauty and convenience alike, excellent results could doubtless be obtained, — results such as have been reached successfully at such grounds as the Charlesbank in Boston, Union Square in New York, Washington Park in Brooklyn, and other places we might name.

In default of a large appropriation, it seems to us desirable that no works of construction should be attempted or allowed in the commons except such work as is distinctly and evidently of a temporary and makeshift character. Only in this way can these grounds be preserved in a condition to make fine results possible in the future.

A somewhat similar difficulty is dealt with in the following reply to a citizen of Cambridge who wished to have the Beaver Brook Reservation left precisely as it was before the public began to resort to it : —

28 April, 1894.

Your request that the wall across the meadow at Beaver Brook be preserved as it is has been gladly received, and will receive careful consideration.

With respect to the general tone of your letter, we must ask you to note that experience has shown the impracticability of leaving such public reservations as that at Waverley in their original condition, after the public begins to resort to them in any considerable numbers. There is no surer way of effecting the destruction of the ground cover, and so of the charm of the scenery of such places. The public soon acquires bad habits. Experience has shown that to preserve the essential attractiveness of much frequented places, some of the lesser elements of attractiveness must be sacrificed. The problem is the same in all such places, — What must be done to permit large numbers of persons to view the beauty of a given place without tending to destroy that very beauty which they seek?

In his native city of Cambridge, Charles was employed both by the Park Commission and the Water Board, — that is, his firm was employed, and Charles was designated to attend to Cambridge work. The situation was peculiar, because the only large area which Cambridge could possibly convert into a park was Fresh Pond and its shores, and this area was in charge not of the Park Commission, but of the Water Board. The following letter asks the Cambridge Water Board to determine certain questions concerning a design for Fresh Pond Park, before the firm enters on the preparation of a general plan of the park. The difficulties raised in this letter are liable to occur wherever the attempt is made to convert into a park the shores of a pond which has been previously treated as only a reservoir.

3 April, 1894.

We have received your letter of the 31st March, requesting us to call upon the City Engineer for such maps and other data as may be required, and also requesting us to hasten our plan in order that the one hundred men that you are employing may be kept at work. . . .

We shall have to ask your Board to agree to our advice in certain particulars before we definitely accept the commission to make a design for the park.

1st. The principal object of the future improvements to be made about Fresh Pond we understand to be that of creating an agreeable landscape, of which the pond shall form the chief feature, and the water shall be considered as the framing or general background, with various subordinate features appropriate to the circumstances and adapted to increasing the pleasure of visitors. Certain other means of recreation, such as playgrounds, picnic groves, and the like, may be added without material injury to the main purpose. Of course, roads and walks will have to be constructed for the convenience of visitors.

2d. It appears that with this general object in view it will be almost essential to acquire additional land in one or two places. . . .

3d. The shore of the pond south of Fresh Pond Lane is

so close to the railroad that there is not adequate room for a proper width of drive and walk. It appears to be necessary, therefore, to fill out the pond somewhat at this point. . . .

4th. The width of the space between the railroad and the point north of the pumping station is also, in our opinion, inadequate, and we should wish to have the consent of the Board to fill along the shore at this point. . . .

5th. The two headlands, one on the south shore of the pond near Woodlawn Avenue and the other at the west end of the promontory formerly occupied by the Catholic Seminary, are excessively stiff and unnatural, and the space allowed for driveway and walk at the base of these bluffs is, in our opinion, entirely inadequate. We should, therefore, wish, before proceeding with our plan, to have the consent of the Board to either diverting the driveway from the shore at these two points, or filling further into the pond, as may be thought, upon further consideration, to be most expedient.

6th. We desire the consent of the Board to reconstructing the shore wherever it is now built on straight lines. . . .

7th. . . . It will be necessary to do a certain amount of regrading of land which has already been graded and covered with top-soil. . . .

8th. We consider that it will be absolutely necessary, in order to produce an agreeable landscape, to in some way break up and disguise the monotony of the shore line. This is one of the most difficult questions with which we shall have to deal, and we are not prepared to say just what it will be necessary to do to accomplish this purpose. It seems to us that it will probably be feasible to plant in some places trees which will overhang the water and throw the present rip-rapped shore into obscurity; in other places to plant bushes between the walk and the shore; and in other places to substitute sandy or gravelly beaches of such slope that they would withstand the action of the waves, and of such construction and material as to prevent any bad effect upon the quality of the water.

As we have already suggested to you, it is possible that some of the old ponds and swamps, which it has hitherto been your intention to fill up, may well be preserved as agreeable landscape features. . . .

In regard to designating work which can be done to advantage by your present force, in advance of preparation of a preliminary study of the general plan, we are much puzzled. Our first impression is that it would be wise to stop work entirely; and we certainly think that if any work goes on within the limits of the proposed park, it will be at the risk of having to be done over again, or at any rate of being uneconomical. Nevertheless, as it may be expedient to disregard economy to some extent, we may say that a small force of men might be employed in stripping off the top-soil from [certain portions, removing fruit trees, and filling up old cellars]. . . .

It would be wise to start a nursery for such kinds of trees and shrubs and vines as will undoubtedly be necessary in the future, and if the Board desires, we will try to secure a suitable foreman to take charge of the preparation and stocking of the nursery. . . .

As we have said before, we prefer not to enter into an agreement with the Board to prepare a general plan for the improvement of Fresh Pond Park until the various questions above indicated shall have been more or less definitely determined by your Board and our conditions accepted.

In 1893 Charles made to the Park Commission a preliminary report on Parks for Cambridge, and recommended as one reservation a large level field near East Cambridge, then known as the Binney Field, which was afterwards well laid out in accordance with his designs and called Cambridge Field. One feature of his plan was a house for certain public uses in the middle of the field. This feature was unusual, and needed to be explained and advocated. The following extract from a letter to the Superintendent of Cambridge Parks describes the proposed Field House and its uses : —

20 August, 1894.

In accordance with your request, we send you herewith prints embodying suggestions for a Field House on Binney Field.

The building proposed would have a large hall for the shelter of the public in case of showers, and a broad and long covered piazza which would serve the same purpose, and also afford a place of outlook upon the playground. Right and left of the hall, in the ends of the building, would be the men's and women's rooms. On the side of the building towards the playground, commanding a view of the same, would be the policeman's room and the janitor's room. The janitor of such a building would be able to check garments, hand-bags, and the like for the public, and a closet of lockers is provided for this purpose. The janitor might also keep on sale at his counter light refreshments or fruits; and the plan provides a locked closet for the storage of such articles. The basement is arranged for storage, and affords room for piling away plank walks and the like, and also for the heating apparatus. We should be glad to give you any further explanation of our ideas respecting such a building, should you deem it desirable.

The next selection deals with one of the most vital principles of good park construction, — the one most frequently disregarded by inexperienced commissioners and superintendents, — the principle that roads and paths should first be so planned that, when built, they will surely be in the right places to exhibit the scenery, — a footpath in the right place being far better than a Telford road in the wrong one. It was addressed to a member of the Minneapolis Park Board.

18 August, 1894.

In considering what is likely to be the cost to your Board of works such as we might design, please note that after a good plan is assured, the mode of construction may be either cheap or elaborate, the point we make being that however cheaply roads and paths may be built, it is always desirable that they be placed on the best lines. There is no reason why park works in America should not proceed in the same way as have most other American public works. Most railroads, for instance, have been cheaply built, and then improved in their construction from time to time. In the same way, if park roads are placed where they ought to be, they may be cheaply made at first and improved later. Our business is the supplying of designs or ground plans; and while we of course enjoy seeing these designs carried out in a permanent and highly finished way, we are content if the lines of our designs are adhered to, even if construction is cheaply done.

The following letter describes vividly a tract already possessing great natural advantages as a park, and only needing judicious treatment as regards paths and plantings, and defence against inappropriate uses.

28 August, 1894.

When Mr. F. L. Olmsted last visited Newport, he left with you a print of a preliminary sketch plan for the paths in Morton Park. We write you at this time in order that you may understand some of the reasons which led us to place these paths in the positions assigned them on the plan.

About half of the park consists of a gentle hollow or valley enclosed upon every hand by banks upon which are growing a good variety of fine trees. The central meadow of this valley is pleasing in form and relations, and it commands a pleasing glimpse of the ocean. The other half of the park consists of a rocky hill upon which are growing a few trees. Ledges of naked rock protrude here and there, and the ground is partially covered by thickets of low-growing shrubbery. The park meadow is concealed by the trees which fringe the base of the hill, but a beautiful view of Newport Harbor is had from several of the commanding ledges. The hill also overlooks the adjacent level plain of the polo field.

The meadow is so complete in itself and as it is, that we must think the preservation of its present breadth and unity very important. Accordingly we have provided paths which, while they skirt the meadow on all sides and command good views of it, do not cross it anywhere. A path leading diagonally across the breadth of the field would, in our opinion, greatly mar its beauty. If suitable shrubbery is planted at the dangerous points, we believe that the public will be easily led to follow the path we have designed and to refrain from injurious short cutting. The meadow is so charming as a picture or landscape that we believe your Commission would be fully justified in preserving it strictly as such, and if necessary forbidding the use of it as a playground. We believe the city could better afford to buy land elsewhere for use as a playground than to permit playing to destroy the perfection of the turf of this place.

We are informed that the adjacent polo field will soon be

offered for sale, and it would seem to us that this is an opportunity of which the city ought to take advantage. The polo field does not present a unified landscape comparable to that of the meadow in the park. It is entirely separated from the meadow by the rocky hill before mentioned. It can be adapted to the uses of a playground at little expense ; and it is large enough to serve the purposes of all the usual sports, as the meadow in the park is not.

The paths which we have planned for the hill you will find to be designed simply to lead ramblers along the brink of the slopes where it is interesting to walk. Upon the ledges which command a close view of the polo field, we suggest considerable enlargement of the gravel area, so that a crowd may find room to stand or sit in view of the games in the field. To connect the hill with the meadow at the southern end of the park a series of steps will be required, something as shown on the plan, but elsewhere the grades of all the proposed paths will be such as are easily followed by the baby carriages which we suppose will frequent the park.

You did not ask us to make any special provision in our plan for the proper accommodation of crowds attending band concerts, and it is only by an error that the band-stand is made to appear upon our sketch. If band concerts are to be frequently given in the park, we would, of course, prefer to make special arrangements for the accommodation of the audiences.

The existing trees and shrubberies on the park are interesting chiefly because they are largely composed of well-developed specimens of European species. Near the foot of the hill stands a group of English Walnuts, and English Oaks, Elms, and Thorns abound. Several fine specimens of the native Liquidamber are found at the base of the rocks. We would suggest, in this connection, that it would be well if the borders of the park on Coggeshall Avenue and Brenton Street should be planted more densely with small trees and with shrubbery ; and that the fences which divide the park from private lands ought also to be more completely screened from view. On the borders of the meadow, we should like to introduce masses or scattered specimens of many native trees like the flowering Dogwood and the Sassafras, and on the rocky hill we should be glad to re-introduce the native wild Roses, Bayberry, and similar shrubs.

The sketch and this letter are intended simply to promote discussion concerning the general arrangement of Morton Park, and the purposes which the park ought to be made to fulfil, and we shall hope to hear from you before long such suggestions as the study of our sketch may bring out.

The next letter selected for this chapter was addressed to Mr. Sylvester Baxter, Charles's valued fellow-worker during the campaigns for the Trustees of Public Reservations, and for both the advisory and the permanent Metropolitan Park Commission, at the time Secretary of the Park Commission of Malden. It describes the way to get the fullest benefit from a small reservation situated in the midst of a dense population. Charles thought that it was not sufficient to provide an open, empty space, or even an area grassed and planted with trees and bushes. He thought the designer should provide all possible aids to enjoyment for children and adults, such as shelters, seats, sand piles, and room and apparatus for sports. In such grounds he wished to provide for old and young every encouragement and facility for spending hours in the open air. The problem of Hitchings Field was of a kind which particularly interested him, although it had little to do with landscape.

12 November, 1894.

The undersigned beg leave to report as follows on the problem of Hitchings Field.

This field of somewhat unsymmetrical shape is bounded by Ferry, Cross, Walnut, and Judson streets, and contains nearly four and one half acres. The question is, How may this public space be made of the greatest possible use and benefit to the considerable population which swarms about it? Without entering into the details of our study of this problem, we may answer that we have concluded (subject to correction by the Commission) that the field will best serve the community about it if it can be arranged to provide, (1st) an agreeable public promenade ; (2d) a well-arranged open-air concert ground; (3d) a playground where the minor games such as basket ball and tag may be allowed; and (4th) suitable turf spaces, sand courts, and perhaps gymnasia for the desirable open-air exercise and play of young children. Accordingly the accompanying sketch plan suggests arrangements designed to meet these assumed requirements. A mall 1800 feet long, 20 feet wide, and bordered by rows of shade trees set in planting-spaces ten feet wide, is shown as encircling the whole field. The planting-spaces may be filled with low shrubbery, or they may be grassed. Seats may be placed beside the walks here and there. This mall will fulfil the requirements of an agreeable public promenade where old and young may walk, saunter, or sit, — where babies also may be wheeled up and down.

In the middle of the ground which remains after the mall is subtracted, the plan places an open music or band stand in the form of a half circle attached to a house which ought to be built if the children are to be provided for as hereafter to be described. South of the music-stand a broad, shaded gravel space is provided for the accommodation of the audience. Chairs and settees may be set out here when concerts are to be given. If the crowd is too large for this specially reserved space, it may spread itself over the large playground next to be mentioned. Those who prefer to stroll while the band plays will make use of the malls.

The playground designed for the use of the boys occupies all the space which remains between the malls and the music court, and measures about 200 by 300 feet, or something more than an acre in area. Such a playground cannot, in our climate, be kept in neat order if it is grassed, and we, therefore, design it to be gravelled. The trees and shrubberies which are to accompany the malls will partially conceal this broad space from the surrounding streets and houses. By sloping the playground to a hollow in the middle, it will prove possible to flood it so as to provide skating in winter.

It may be that the Commission will not at this time care to attempt to make those special provisions which are necessary if any part of the field is to be arranged for the special benefit of infants and young children; and in this case only the walks of that part of the ground which lies north of the music-stand need at present be built. When, however, a children's ground is deemed desirable, a small building will need to be provided in which may be found a matron's room and the necessary closets, a check-room, perhaps a small lunch-counter, a policeman's room, and an ample hall and piazza to which retreat may be made in case of rain or showers. Such a building is placed by the plan in the middle of the field, and attached to the music-stand. Between this building and Judson Street there may be a small lawn, while to right and left of the building there may be on the one hand a fenced enclosure containing see-saws, swings, and the like apparatus, and on the other hand a similar enclosure where the babies may find a sand-box and a bit of turf to roll on.

In conclusion we may say that the accompanying plan promises to reconcile the requirements of use and beauty in a manner which cannot always be so happily expected.

A design of similar intent, though very differently situated, made about this time for the Boston Park Commission by the Olmsted firm, is described by Charles with evident satisfaction in the report of that Commission for the year ending January 31, 1895. It is the design for the North End Beach and Copps Hill Terrace, a small reservation in one of the most densely populated quarters of old Boston, but costly because made by removing buildings and wharves. Its purpose is to give a pleasant place for rest or play to men, women, and children whose fresh-air privileges are scanty.

For the small tract recently acquired by the commission at the North End, a complete plan has been prepared which may be described as follows : —

The land to be devoted to purposes of recreation lies between the ancient Copps Hill burying-ground and the sheet of water which is the confluence of the Charles and Mystic rivers. It is separated from the burying-ground by Charter Street, and it is crossed by the busy water-side thoroughfare called Commercial Street. Between the two streets the narrow public domain slopes steeply down between two ranks of tenement houses, thus opening a prospect from the already frequented Copps Hill. Between Commercial Street and the water, the original shore line has disappeared under a tangle of more or less ancient sea-walls, fillings, and pile structures.

The plan is designed to make this confined space afford opportunity for the greatest possible variety of modes of recreation. Thus, a resting-place commanding a view of the water is provided upon a broad terrace on a level with the upper street; an ample promenade adjacent to the water is provided upon a pier, the upper deck of which will be reached from the terrace by a bridge which will span Commercial Street; a good place for children to play is provided on a beach which will form the shore of the small haven to be formed by the pier; dressing-rooms will be provided for the use of bathers, floats and other conveniences for boatmen. The stone terrace and its accompanying flights of steps will be plainly but substantially constructed, while the steep earth slopes at the ends and below the high wall will be planted with low shrubbery. The foot-bridge spanning Commercial Street will be a light steel truss. The new or restored beach will terminate against sea-walled piers of solid filling, from the end of one of which the long and substantial pleasure pier will run out to and along the Harbor Commissioners' line. Between the beach and Commercial Street there is room for a little greensward and a screening background of shrubbery.

Twenty months after the above description was written, Charles touched the North End reservation again in a note written to his wife from Boston at 5 o'clock on a hot July afternoon : —

Just through with Boston Board Park Commission. A long and complicated meeting, yet hardly up to the Metropolitan article. Our plans for the North End Terrace at Copps Hill were at last approved. Last evening after dinner I talked with Mr. Gilder of the "Century" all the way to Boston. . . . I cross-examined him with reference to his slum squares in New York City, and the taking down of rear tenements, and so on. Two or three times in each year I am smitten with pity for the slum people, — pity and horror mixed. My walk from Cambridge Field (in construction) through East Cambridge to Charlesbank! Doorsteps crowded with unclean beings, children pushing everywhere, and swarming in every street and alley. What a relief when Charlesbank is reached! The quiet open of the river, the long, long row of twinkling lights on the river wall, the rows upon rows of seats all filled with people resting in the quiet air, and watching the fading of the golden light behind the Cambridge towers. The new terrace at the North End is to be another such evening resting-place. It is good to be able to do something, even a little, for this battered and soiled humanity. . . .

The statement that the land lies between Copps Hill and the confluence of the Charles and the Mystic is precise; but under it lies one of Charles's disappointments. He wanted to have in this quarter of Boston a reservation which looked down the harbor. Various considerations, into which the prospect from the reservation did not enter, determined the choice of the present site.

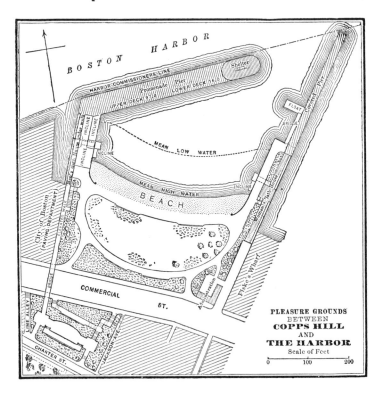

CHAPTER XXVI

FIRST SEVENTEEN MONTHS OF THE EXECUTIVE METRO-POLITAN PARK COMMISSION

Shines the last age, the next with hope is seen,
To-day slinks poorly off unmarked between:
Future or Past no richer secret folds,
O friendless Present! than thy bosom holds.

RALPH WALDO EMERSON.

THE reports for 1893 and 1894 which Charles made in the name of the firm to the Commission appointed in 1893 are especially interesting, because they contain the initial advice he gave about the boundaries of the acquired reservations, the principles on which reservation boundaries should be determined, the preparation of maps and plans, the protection of the woods from fire, the restoration of the vegetation destroyed or damaged by wood-chopping and fires, the making of paths and temporary roads in the forests, and the encouragement of seedlings and other new vegetation, and further his suggestions about the proposed reservations and parkways.

The legislature of 1894 added greatly to the responsibilities of the Commission by appropriating $500,000 for parkways, $300,000 for open spaces near the Charles River, and $500,000 for Revere Beach. Concerning these new enterprises, the Commission asked at once the advice of their landscape architects, but refused to be hurried, either by the legislature or by popular pressure, into any ill-considered expenditures on any one of these accounts. In this policy Charles sympathized entirely. He was always in favor of thorough planning before action, and of taking time for construction, while acting promptly on protective measures, and on original takings from trustworthy plans. When prompt action clearly meant the ultimate saving of money to the Commonwealth or the district, he urged promptness; but in every case he wanted to see the end from the beginning. These principles will be found to have guided him from the start in giving advice to the Metropolitan Commission. His reports on the Metropolitan Park work in 1893 (August–December) and 1894 are here given in full. They were addressed to the chairman of the Commission. These reports relate to work accomplished, or under way; they do not cover many studies and preliminary investigations made by Charles at the request of the Commission. Thus, in a letter to the Commission reporting on the work of the six months ending June 30, 1894, he remarks for the firm: " Revere Beach and Charles River Reservations. — These proposed reservations have called for the attendance of our Mr. Eliot at six legislative hearings." And again : —

" Preliminary investigations have been made with reference to parkways from Stony Brook Reservation to the Blue Hills Reservation ; from Mattapan to the Blue Hills Reservation, and from Middlesex Fells Reservation to Lynn Woods Reservation. Six parties of surveyors are now engaged under our direction in this work.

" Similar investigations will now, by order of the Board, be undertaken between Winchester and Medford, between Mystic River and Revere Beach, and between Revere Beach and Lynn.

" In the course of the work thus briefly described, and in addition to our attention to the work of the Commission in our office, our Mr. Eliot during the past six months has kept more than fifty appointments in the field, and has attended twenty-five meetings of the Commission."

LANDSCAPE ARCHITECTS' REPORT FOR 1893 TO THE METRO-
POLITAN PARK COMMISSION.

In a professional report addressed in 1892 to the preliminary or advisory Metropolitan Park Commission, Mr. Eliot (who has since become a member of our firm) reviewed the hills, streams, and coasts of the neighborhood of Boston, and sketched in colors, on a map, the areas which it seemed to him should be reserved for public use through metropolitan as distinguished from municipal action. No attempt was made to define the exact boundaries of any of the reservations proposed. At the time of writing it was not decided that an executive Metropolitan Park Commission would ever be established.

Your Commission having been created and organized, you asked us to give our attention to the definite demarcation of five of the reservations proposed in Mr. Eliot's report, namely,

the reservations at the Blue Hills, Middlesex Fells, Muddy
Pond Woods (or Stony Brook), Revere Beach, and Beaver
Brook. You directed us to prepare projects for boundaries
which would show alternative, or maximum and minimum,
limits, wherever possible, in order that a choice might be open
to your Board when the estimates of the probable costs of the
lands to be taken should be compiled by you. Six parties of
surveyors were placed at our service by your direction, and
during the months of September, October, and November we
gave much time, in conjunction with the surveyors, to the
careful study of the problem put before us. On December
15, 1893, we sent to your office the last of a series of eight
surveyors' maps, drawn to a scale of two hundred feet to
an inch, upon which we had indicated by a continuous green
line what seemed to us to be the most desirable boundary for
each of the proposed reservations. By a broken green line
we also indicated such possible alternative positions for the
several boundaries as seemed worthy of consideration. In
accompanying reports we explained the proposed boundaries
in detail.

In accordance with your request, we now submit the following memoranda of the general principles upon which we
have worked in determining the lines lately submitted to you,
as just described : —

First. The boundaries of the proposed reservations should,
if possible, be established so as to include all lands belonging
to the same topographical unit, and exhibiting the type of
scenery characteristic of each reservation. Obviously, a public domain is not well bounded if it includes only half a hill,
half a pond, or half a glen. Neither is it well bounded unless
it includes such contiguous lands as form the essential framework of the hill scenery, the pond scenery, the glen scenery,
or whatever other type of scenery it is desired to preserve.
For example, it is desirable to include in the Blue Hills Reservation all the hills of the high range down to the base of their
steep slopes. Similarly, it is desirable to include in the Stony
Brook Reservation all the uplands which enclose the glen or
valley of that stream. To city men it is most refreshing to
find themselves in what appears to be a wilderness of indefi-

nite extent. This impression cannot be enjoyed unless the boundary of a valley reservation is established beyond the summits of the enclosing hills.

Second. The boundaries of the proposed reservations should be, if possible, established upon public streets or roads, or on lines drawn where roads may ultimately be built with good grades.

The reasons for this principle are many. It is obvious that the back fences of private lands cannot make a handsome boundary for a public domain of any description. It is obvious that private lands abutting directly upon public lands will be much more liable to trespass than they would be if a public roadway separated the two. Private land in the position described is a nuisance to the public, while the public is likely to be a nuisance to its owner. Speaking generally, the policing and the general administration of a public reservation are greatly facilitated when the boundary is a road. Still more important is the consideration that, if the private lands which adjoin the reservation are provided with a road frontage looking on the public domain, they will eventually be greatly increased in attractiveness and value.

These two principles taken together explain most of the possible boundary lines submitted for your examination. Where existing streets meet the requirement of the first principle, they have been adopted as the boundary, as, for example, at Washington Street, Melrose, and Blue Hill Street, Canton. Where it has been necessary to devise new roads to serve as boundaries, this has been done, with due respect to the first principle, with due regard for grades and curves, and with care to exclude improved lands, and lands which will ultimately become especially suitable for building sites.

It remains to mention three classes of exceptions to the principles of the existing or proposed road boundary.

In some places it has proved necessary, for the sake of economy, to exclude from the reservations, by arbitrary lines, improved lands which would have been included under our first principle had they not been occupied by buildings: as, for example, at two places on Washington Street in Melrose, and again at Summit Street in Malden.

In some places the reverse operation has proved desirable, and tracts of wild land which would have been excluded under our second principle have been included in the reservation by arbitrary lines, because some subordinate yet still important element of the scenery of the reservation could by so doing be preserved : as, for example, along the north side of the valley of Furnace Brook in the Quincy section of the Blue Hills Reservation, where there has been included the face of a ridge which is in view from the whole basin of the brook, although the road must here be within the reservation in the valley of the brook. Houghton's Pond has been shown as included in the Blue Hills Reservation for the same reason. It is not an essential part of the hill scenery, but it is an exceedingly valuable addition thereto.

In some places, after a road boundary had been studied and mapped, the line was found to lie in such relations to adjacent or parallel township boundaries that rather than leave parts of townships isolated from the main body it was deemed best to adopt the township boundary as the boundary of the reservation. It was in this way, for example, that the township boundary which divides Quincy from Randolph and Braintree came to be suggested as the southern boundary of the Blue Hills Reservation. Another variety of this exceptional kind of boundary is illustrated in several places about the Fells, where arbitrary lines have been drawn so as to connect the new reservation with preëxisting watershed reservations without leaving wedges or islands of private lands between the two.

The total length of alternative lines thus studied, mapped, and described by us for your consideration is about thirty miles.

December, 1893.

LANDSCAPE ARCHITECTS' REPORT FOR 1894 TO THE METRO-
POLITAN PARK COMMISSION.

I. — ACQUIRED RESERVATIONS.

Section 1. — The Determination of the Boundaries.

At the date of this writing, the open spaces which have been
acquired for the public by the Commission are the Blue Hills,
the Middlesex Fells, the Stony Brook, and the Beaver Brook
reservations. The preliminary Metropolitan Park Commission, in its report of January, 1893, had suggested the purchase of lands at these places among others, and both the
public and the legislature had approved the suggestion ; but
the areas to be acquired and the bounds to be established had
not been determined when the executive Metropolitan Commission was created by the Act of June, 1893. Accordingly,
when we were summoned to assist the Commission in September, 1893, it was the problem of the boundaries of the lands
to be acquired which was first assigned to us.

Speaking generally, it has not been the habit of park commissions to give much attention to the boundaries of public
domains. It is generally easier to acquire the whole of a
given parcel of real estate, though half of it is not really
wanted, and then to omit the purchase of any of the next
parcel, though half of that is sadly needed, than it is to
acquire a part from this and a part from that for the sake of
obtaining what is essential, and omitting what is of less
importance, to the landscape of the domain to be preserved.
There are few public grounds which are not grossly deformed
by the imperfections of their boundaries. Almost everywhere
the immediate saving in time and trouble for the surveyor,
the conveyancer, and the commission concerned has worked
permanent injury to public interests in public scenery.

Accordingly, we took up the detailed study of the bounds
of the proposed reservations with peculiar interest. In each
case the object had in view was much the same ; namely, the
carving out from the conglomerate mass of private estates
such a body of land as in each locality seemed essential to the
achievement of the purpose of the proposed new public estate,

— that purpose being in each case the preservation of the best of the scenery of the tract in question.

At Beaver Brook, concerning the bounds of which reservation we reported on November 13, 1893, the area to be acquired was small, the boundaries of the existing estates were visible or well known, and the problem was comparatively a simple one.

At Middlesex Fells the natural boundary at the base of the wall of the plateau was found to be hopelessly beyond reach in many places, either because of the high price of open land which proximity to towns had induced, or because buildings had already been placed on the slope of the highland region. Across Medford a natural boundary was put out of the question by the legislature, which prescribed a straight line south of which no lands could be taken. Thus the boundary for the Fells which we suggested in a report dated December 15, 1893, was of necessity a compromise line, lying generally in the right position, but turned aside from its true course in many places by force of circumstances beyond our control, — in other words, by the legislative line in Medford, and by high land values such as would not have been encountered had the Metropolitan Commission begun its labors a few years earlier.

At Stony Brook and in the Blue Hills the field was freer. To preserve the desired valley at Stony Brook required a reservation two miles long, and to secure the whole range of the Blue Hills a domain five miles in length proved necessary; yet neither of these large tracts touched high-priced lands save at their ends. The method of procedure, both here and at the other reservations, was as follows: In the first place, we provided ourselves with the best obtainable maps. These were generally the ordinary lithographed township maps, and the mile-to-an-inch general map of the Boston metropolitan district. Armed with these wholly inadequate guides, one of us, with an assistant, personally explored the woods and thickets which clothe the bases of the Blue Hills and the flanks of the Stony Brook valley, and gradually determined on the general course which the particular boundary in question ought to take in order to fulfil the main purpose in mind, as well as to make it generally practicable to build a road upon the boundary in the future.

The general absence of visible property lines or other land-marks made this blind work; but the autumn weather of 1893 was favorable, and good progress was made. As soon as the general course of any considerable stretch of boundary was thus selected, a surveyor's transit line was run along it, frequent stations being numbered both on the ground and on a map drawn on tracing-cloth to the adopted scale of two hundred feet to an inch. By measurements taken from these stations and afterwards plotted on the tracing, the proposed boundary was more exactly defined; and then sun-prints taken from the tracing were submitted to the Commission and to the local authorities for approval. When approved, the surveyors defined the projected lines by accurately measured distances, radii of curves, and the like, while the legal advisers of the Board drew the papers required to accomplish the act of taking by eminent domain. Speaking generally, but very few private property lines had been either discovered or mapped at the time the takings were made. The search for these lines and for the owners of the estates acquired has proved a difficult task, which we understand is still occupying the surveyors, the conveyancers, and the secretary of the Commission.

Our work upon the problem of the boundaries of the four acquired reservations was substantially concluded when we addressed our semi-annual report to the Board on July 1, 1894. The number of miles of alternative and adopted boundary lines studied and mapped by us, with the assistance of the surveyors, in the manner thus described, exceeded thirty.

Section 2. — The Exploration of the Acquired Lands.

As one new reservation after another was secured by the Commission, many questions of management and policy at once arose, and seemed at first to call for immediate answer. It was said that numerous carriage roads ought to be opened immediately; that woodsmen ought to be put to work to save the finer specimens or sorts of trees from being strangled by the inferior; that ten thousand dollars, if so much was necessary, ought to be spent in making the old road up Great Blue Hill safely passable by pleasure carriages; and so on. We,

on the other hand, as the responsible professional advisers of
the Commission, felt it incumbent upon us to urge caution in
all these matters.   We took the ground that, the reservations
having been acquired, a sufficient number of keepers placed
on guard, and numerous fire lines cut through the worst of
the dead timber, there was no haste whatever about any further doings.   It was pointed out that the metropolitan community had caused the Commission to assume possession of
these large reservations, not for the sake of making an exhibition of fine trees, economic forestry, model roads, or any
other special thing or things, however desirable, but simply
in order to provide itself with ample preserves of fine scenery ;
and consequently that all work done within the reservations
ought to be directed solely to preserving, enhancing, or making available the charm, the beauty, or the impressiveness of
that scenery.

If this opinion were just, it would be imprudent for any
man, however adept, to undertake to determine how a road
ought to turn and climb among the Blue Hills so as to give
as much pleasure as possible, while injuring the landscape
as little as possible ; or how trees should be felled at Stony
Brook so as best to develop the hidden beauty of the glen ;
or how or whether planting should be done in the few openings in the Fells, until he had had ample time for careful
observation of the natural and artificial conditions of each
place and landscape, and the benefit of studying good contour
maps.   In accordance with these views, it was determined
that only absolutely necessary ways should be opened in the
reservations, and that only the indispensable fire-guard chopping should be done ; but that a beginning should be forthwith made in that thorough study of the historical evolution
and present state of the landscape of the reservations, upon
which alone all successful endeavors to increase the effectiveness and the accessibility of that landscape must be based.

The scenery of all the reservations thus far acquired is
essentially sylvan. . Sylvan scenery is compounded of the
shape of the ground and the vegetation.   The variously
sculptured or modelled forms of the earth's surface furnish
the solid body of landscape which man seldom finds time or

strength to mar. Vegetation, on the other hand, supplies the dress of living green which man often changes, strips away, or spoils, but which he can generally restore if he so chooses. Thus the study of the present landscape of the reservations naturally divides itself into two main branches, — the study of the forms of the surface of the reservations, and the study of the vegetation. In both of these directions we have during the past six months made diligent researches, but it is not necessary to burden this report with a detailed recital of the facts discovered. Since the forms of topography owe their origin to geological forces, we were much pleased to receive from Professor Crosby of the Institute of Technology his notes on the geology of the regions included in the reservations. These notes will be found printed in the Appendix [not reproduced in this volume].

For preliminary sketch maps of the topography of the reservations we turned to an expert topographer, Mr. Gordon H. Taylor of Brookline, who as our assistant took the field in January, 1894. By making use of sun-prints of the recorded boundary plans, by measuring compass lines along the numerous woodpaths, and by sketching the outlines of swamps, clearings, ponds, hills, and valleys, extremely serviceable maps were soon produced. The draughting of the several sheets was done in our office. Upon one sheet of tracing-cloth were drawn the boundaries, the roads and paths, and the lettering (of the Blue Hills map, for example) ; on another sheet were drawn the streams, ponds, and swamps ; and on a third the hill shading was roughly indicated by pen and pencil. Gray sun-prints obtained from the three sheets superimposed in the printing frame, when mounted on cloth, served very well for all purposes of study. Photo-lithographed in three colors, namely, black, blue, and brown, the same sheets will serve as guide maps for the use of the public and the illustration of reports.

Equipped with these maps, we have made good progress, as before remarked, in familiarizing ourselves with the "lay of the land" in the reservations. With respect to topography, the four reservations may be said to be happily distinguished by their names. Beaver Brook Reservation and

Stony Brook Reservation are both concave troughs, drained by strong streams, and bordered by more or less sharply defined ridges of ledge or gravel. Blue Hills Reservation presents a chain of bold, convex masses of rock and gravel, affording widespread panoramic prospects in all directions. Middlesex Fells Reservation, on the contrary, exhibits a plateau the surface of which is minutely broken into numerous comparatively small hills, bowls, and vales.

At Beaver Brook the charm of the place springs chiefly from what lies close at hand within the bounds, — the ponds, the cascade, the rushing brook, the open pasture, and the veteran Oaks. At Stony Brook the glen and pond and many rocks are interesting; but the eye is often drawn away to the Blue Hills, which present themselves from various surprising and delightful points of view. At the Blue Hills themselves, while several passes and defiles are very striking, and many views from hill to hill are even grand, it is the vast blue distance which tends to engross the attention, — a distance here of ocean and there of forest, and there again marked by the remote Wachusett and Monadnock, — a distance which, fortunately, is not yet disfigured by the too near approach of any town or city. Lastly, at Middlesex Fells the landscape pleases chiefly by reason of the intimate mingling of many types of scenery and objects of interest. Here is a cliff and a cascade, here a pool, pond, or stream, here a surprising glimpse of a fragment of blue ocean, or again a faint blue vision of a far distant mountain.

The same hastily prepared sketch maps have in like manner assisted us in studying the present condition of the vegetation of the reservations. To the investigation of this subject in detail we early assigned Mr. Warren H. Manning of our office, and his preliminary notes will be found following Mr. Crosby's in the Appendix [not reproduced in this volume].

However sharply distinguishable the reservations may be topographically, with respect to their vegetation they are very much alike. It is true that the summits of the higher of the Blue Hills are clothed with chaparral of dwarf Oak or with carpet of Bearberry, as are none of the other hills of the reservations. The shores of the pond at the head of Stony Brook

are decked with an incomparable thicket of swamp shrubbery.   The white Cedar and the Mountain Laurel of the
great swamp in the Blue Hills are not found elsewhere.   The
group of great Oaks at Beaver Brook has no equal in all New
England.   On the other hand, all three of the larger reservations possess the same rock-rimmed hollows filled with water
and Cat-tails, the same red Maple and Birch swamps, the same
monotonous acres of coppice Oak which for generations have
suffered cutting for firewood every thirty or forty years, the
same occasional old pastures now overgrown by red Cedar,
the same rare groves of surviving white Pine.   Speaking generally, it is an ugly fact that the woodlands of the reservations are remarkably uninteresting as woodlands.   Constant
chopping and frequent fires have thoroughly discouraged the
restorative forces of nature.   Only on inaccessible rocks or
in the depths of swamps is there any really primitive or truly
natural vegetation to be seen; for it is only these places which
have escaped the axe and the fires.   Over the larger part
of the reservations fires have almost annually destroyed the
fallen leaves, and in many places even the vegetable matter
of the soil itself is gone.   In the Blue Hills, at the time of the
taking, many hundred acres of sprout growth between five and
twenty-five feet in height were standing dead from the effects
of recent conflagrations, while several hundred other acres
were found littered with the refuse of recent fellings.

Thus these studies have made it plain that the one important element in the landscape of the reservations which men
can control, namely, the vegetation, has hitherto been grossly
abused.   On the other hand, the same studies have developed
many facts which will have important bearings upon the
course to be pursued, both by those who will direct the work
of making the scenery of the reservations accessible, and by
those who may have charge of the work of restoring the life
and enhancing the beauty of the vegetal element in that
scenery.

Section 3. — Work to be done in the Reservations.

It is, we believe, understood and agreed by all concerned
that no work shall be done in the acquired reservations except

it be directed, — first, to better safeguarding the scenery of the reservations; second, to making that scenery accessible; third, to enriching or enhancing its beauty, which is its value.

For the permanent preservation of the reservations it is desirable that stone boundary marks be firmly set at frequent intervals along the boundary lines. We are informed that the necessary stones have been contracted for, and that they will be set next spring under the supervision of the newly appointed engineer to the Commission.

Where the public reservations adjoin private lands it is desirable that fences be constructed on the dividing line, both in order to defend the woods of the reservations from spoliation by stray cattle, and in order to defend the private lands from trespass on the part of visitors to the reservations. Several miles of strong wire fence ought, in our opinion, to be built next spring, at a cost which need not exceed one dollar per rod. By order of the Commission, Beaver Brook Reservation has already been enclosed by an iron-posted and steel-barred fence. In similarly conspicuous positions, and on the borders of private house grounds, this will be a good fence to use, reserving the ordinary wooden-posted wire fence for concealed woodland frontages.

Since the principal destroyer of the beauty of woodlands is fire, it is desirable that every precaution be taken to prevent it from entering the reservations, to prevent it from starting in the reservations, and to prevent it from spreading should it start or enter. When the reservations were first acquired, in the winter of 1893–94, and large areas, particularly in the Blue Hills, were found strewn with falling or fallen sticks of dry, fire-killed wood, it was seen that the conditions were most favorable for the spreading of new conflagrations of the most destructive sort. The time available for work before the coming of dry and dangerous weather was not sufficient to permit the complete removal of the inflammable material, so that all that could be done was to clear of dead wood numerous long strips of ground selected so as to connect some of the naturally fire-proof ledges or swamps. Work of this kind needs to be continued until the intervening blocks are wholly cleared of tinder.

To prevent the entrance of fire from adjacent private lands, as well as for other reasons set forth in our report for 1893, it is advisable that public roads be built along the boundary lines as soon as may be.

To hinder the spreading of fires, it is desirable not only that inflammable matter should be removed, but that a sufficient length of makeshift, or temporary, interior roads be made passable for such fire apparatus as may be put in service ; also, that footpaths for the use of the keepers or watchmen be opened where they will be most useful ; also, that telephone connections be established between the outlying parts of each reservation and headquarters, and between headquarters and the nearest public fire stations.

For checking ground fires, cans of water and " Johnson " pumps should be always in readiness, while the men employed about the reservations should be taught to use the pumps with skill. The keepers should familiarize themselves with the places where water can surely be found even in the driest weather, and the number of these places should, if possible, be increased. If ground fires can be controlled through the exercise of untiring vigilance, crown fires, or fires running through the tops of trees in the manner which has done such great damage in the past, will no more sweep the reservations, for they will have no chance to start unless they come from outside.

Besides fire, there are other destroyers of trees and woodlands for which the keepers of the reservations must be constantly on the watch. Such are the injurious insects, the most dangerous of which at the present time is the imported gypsy moth. Much of the woodland of the Fells has already been attacked by this voracious creature, which must be fought as zealously as fire, if the trees are to be saved alive. Lastly, the keepers must be watchful lest human visitors to the reservations, tempted in summer by fine sprays of bloom, and in winter by evergreen leaves and bright berries, do not soon damage the beauty of some of the most charming spots.

Two special pieces of safeguarding work remain to be mentioned. When Beaver Brook Reservation was acquired, the famous Oaks were found to be much burdened with wounded and decaying limbs. So important are these trees, both as remarkably large specimens, and as the most striking element in the scenery of their neighborhood, that we at once advised that they be surgically treated. The work of removing dead and decaying boughs, tarring the cut surfaces, and cementing the worst cavities occupied six men six weeks. This unusual undertaking was well conducted by Mr. George A. Parker, under the supervision of Mr. Manning of our office. These operations naturally robbed the trees of much of the picturesqueness of old age, but the expected prolongation of the life of the grove certainly justifies this loss of pictorial interest.

In the upper part of the same reservation there lie two small mill-ponds, beside one of which stood the flour mill celebrated by James Russell Lowell in the verses called " Beaver Brook." Both ponds are charming features of the local scenery. The old dams were found to be much in need of the repairs which have lately been completed. This was the second of the two special preservative works just referred to.

Coming now to the discussion of work to be done towards making the landscape of the reservations more accessible, and towards enriching or enhancing its value, we have first to point out that it seems to us most advisable that these two objects should be pursued simultaneously and under one direction. Certain of the old woodpaths of the Blue Hills and the Fells have during the past season, and under instructions from our office, been linked together and improved, in order to make it possible to reach the remoter quarters of the reservations without being compelled to walk miles. These roads will well serve those administrative purposes for which they have been built, they will make valuable fire-guards, and the public will make use of them and will enjoy them.[1] It is true, also, that much may be done to lead many people to avail them-

[1] To enable persons who do not own horses to enjoy the new roads, we suggest that a buckboard service be established to traverse Blue Hills Reservation twice daily between Readville and West Quincy during the pleasant months, passengers to be allowed to stop off at any of the different points of interest ; also, that a similar service be established between Winchester and Wyoming or Malden, by way of the south end of Bear Hill and the south side of Spot Pond in the Fells Reservation.

selves of the beauty of the present scenery of the reservations by providing hitching-places for horses, stands for bicycles, numerous bridle and foot paths, and plenty of sign-boards to mark the way to points of interest or special vantage. The superintendents of the reservations should see to it that the work of providing these helps to visitors be done before next summer. The sketch maps already described will enable them to do this with satisfaction and despatch.

On the other hand, — and on this point we desire to speak emphatically, — such roads as have thus far been opened in the reservations are not to be considered as other than temporary affairs. Built to serve pressing administrative necessities, and generally following closely the courses of ancient woodpaths, these roads do not, and cannot be made to, exhibit the scenery of the reservation as it ought to be and may be exhibited. One may easily drive through the whole length of the Blue Hills range by the present service road, and come away disappointed. Contrariwise, it is easily possible to imagine a road along the range which, presenting one quiet or surprising picture after another, could not fail to awaken admiration of the scenery in every observer. The reservations will not return to the community that dividend of refreshment which is rightly expected of them, until roads and paths shall have been built with special reference to the exhibition of the scenery. Such roads and paths, however, cannot possibly be devised hastily or without prolonged study, not only of the ground, but of complete topographical maps. Even with map in hand, it is extremely easy to make the most unfortunate mistakes in work of this kind, as it is equally easy to go wrong in attempting to open or close vistas, or to modify vegetation for the sake of scenery.

Much work of this latter sort greatly needs to be done in the woodlands of the reservations. Excepting work directed to ponding or turning water, the selection of high or low, evergreen or deciduous, crowded or separated types of vegetation is practically the only work which can be done for the enhancement of the beauty of the landscape of the reservations. In these woodlands which have been so badly damaged, work of this kind, well handled, will be productive of remarkable and important results. In general, this work ought to be directed to the selection and encouragement of those forms of vegetation which are characteristic of each type of topography. Sameness of treatment, regardless of site and exposure, is to be scrupulously avoided. On the windy summits of the Blue Hills the dwarf growths native to such hill-tops ought to be preserved, or induced to take possession. On sunny crags and ledges, Pitch Pine, Cedar, and Juniper should be led to find place, while the Hemlock should appear among shady rocks. At the bases of bold ledges now concealed by dull curtains of stump growth, large areas may profitably be cleared and even pastured for the sake of exhibiting the forms of the rocks, and the grand distant prospects discernible between them. In other places, where only short-lived sprout-growth now exists, seedlings of long-lived trees should be encouraged to start. On slopes of poor soil permanent thickets may be advisable, while some rich glade or valley may be devoted to the development of soft turf and broad-spreading trees. There is thus no limit to the variety of sylvan types of scenery which may gradually be developed within these broad reservations.

We are prepared to immediately advise the superintendents of the reservations in certain departments of this work, should the Commission decide to begin labor in this field this season. The more delicate and difficult operations of this art of enhancing the beauty of the vegetal element in landscape must, however, wait upon the building, or at least the planning, of the permanent roads and paths.[1] These roads must be made to exhibit the scenery, and the vegetal scenery must be im-

---

[1] "The mere act of removing certain trees from a natural forest and leaving others standing is a fine art, if done with a view to beauty, although human interference, in this instance, adds nothing whatever that is tangible or material. It only adds beauty, or reveals beauty, by taking away the impediments that prevented it from being seen. Among the recognized fine arts there are two that consist *entirely* in removal. In sculpture and mezzotint no grain of marble dust or copper powder is added to the work ; the artist does nothing but take away matter, at first in large quantities, and then in smaller and smaller quantities as his work approaches completion. The work of clearing in a wood is analogous to these arts, when carried out with an artistic intention only." — PHILIP GILBERT HAMERTON.

proved with reference to the roads. Thus we have double reason to regret that topographical surveys sufficiently detailed to serve as the basis for the planning of permanent roads have only lately been ordered by the Commission, and that the contour maps cannot be finished before March, 1896. Not until these maps are completed will it be possible to devise plans for the ultimate development of the scenery of the reservations, and for making that scenery accessible in the most advantageous ways. Meanwhile, we recommend that the Commission and the public rest content with careful guarding of the reservations from injury, a cautious beginning of the work of modifying the vegetation as instanced above, and the opening of a few temporary or makeshift roads and paths.

II. — PROPOSED RESERVATIONS.

The report of the landscape architect to the preliminary or inquiring Metropolitan Park Commission suggested the acquisition of reservations of three principal types ; namely, forest, river-side, and sea-coast. For reasons stated in its first report, the permanent or executive Commission determined that the first appropriation of one million dollars should be spent in buying public forests. Not content with this programme, representatives of various sections of the metropolitan district obtained from the legislature of 1894 several acts commanding the expenditure of further sums of money for the acqui sition of river-side and sea-coast reservations. Accordingly, we have during the past season studied, prepared, and presented plans suggesting boundaries for lands proposed to be acquired at Revere Beach, and on the banks of the Charles and upper Mystic rivers.

Concerning Revere Beach it need now only be said that the plan, as thus far outlined, contemplates the eventual abolishment of private ownership on the shore between the existing railroad and the water, the removal of the railroad to a new location, and ultimately the construction of a proper sidewalk, driveway, and promenade, upon a long, sweeping curve extending the length of the beach.

Free gifts of land on the eastern shores of the Mystic

ponds and on the banks of the upper Mystic or Abbajona
River in Winchester naturally led the Commission to consider
the acquiring of intervening and adjacent properties. The
plans, as outlined, will give to the public the possession of
both banks of that short reach of tidal river which lies
between High Street, Medford, and the lower Mystic Pond,
the eastern shore of both ponds from the water's edge to the
top of the bluff, both banks of Abbajona River from the
upper pond as far upstream as Walnut Street, and the eastern bank from Walnut Street to the Winchester town hall on
Pleasant Street at the foot of Mt. Vernon Street. Within
or upon the borders of this long strip of public land a pleasant driveway can easily be built. The Abbajona River will
need to be bridged once only. The Lowell Railroad will be
crossed by the existing Bacon Street bridge.

The banks of the tidal portion of Charles River, the central waterway of the metropolitan district, were long supposed to be about to become pecuniarily valuable for industrial or commercial purposes; but as the population of the
river-side lands has multiplied, and as this population has
come to feel the need of agreeable open spaces, a new idea of
the value of the river and the river-bank has developed in
the public mind with great rapidity. It was only in 1885
that the Boston Park Commission removed a row of industrial establishments for the purpose of making a public
promenade on the edge of the river between Craigie and
West Boston bridges. Few citizens realize in what degree
the new idea of the value of the river has crystallized itself
in effective action during the few years which have passed
since "Charlesbank" was opened. From Craigie bridge to
Watertown bridge by the course of the stream is eight miles.
Out of the sixteen miles of bank bordering this tidal portion
of the river the surprising length of seven miles has already
been acquired by public or semi-public agencies;[1] while an

[1] Below Cottage Farm the existing public banks measure approximately
as follows : —

		Feet.
Charlesbank (Boston Park Commission)	. . . .	2,000
The Front (Cambridge Park Commission)	. . .	1,300
The Esplanade (Cambridge Park Commission)	. .	7,000 [over]

additional two and one half miles, namely, the Boston bank
from West Boston bridge to Cottage Farm, is dedicated in
the public mind, if not in fact, to the custody of the Boston
Park Commission. Only two miles of bank are occupied by
practically irremovable industrial establishments.[1] Thus it
appears that there remain only about five miles of shore,
concerning which it may still be asked, Shall this river-bank
become public or remain private property?

The argument for public ownership has been so often repeated of late, and is now so generally understood and applauded, that it need not be repeated here. As at Middlesex
Fells the Metropolitan Commission has made a great public
forest by joining together the fragmentary public holdings
previously acquired by various water boards and local park
commissions, so now the same commission has been commanded to connect the arsenal reservation with the public
landings and river-banks of Watertown on the one hand, and
with the Longfellow meadow and the Charles River drive of
Cambridge on the other hand, to the end that the public
river-side domain may acquire that great increase in value
which arises from unity, continuity, and completeness.

By direction of the Commission, we have accordingly given
our best attention to the five miles of remaining river-bank
just mentioned, and have devised plans suggesting boundaries for the proposed additions to the public domain. Like
the plan adopted for the Charles River road of the Cambridge Park Commission and the plan suggested for the pro-

---

Above Cottage Farm the present public and semi-public banks measure
approximately as follows : —

	Feet.
Charles River drive (Cambridge Park Commission) . .	13,000
Cambridge Hospital	500
Cambridge Cemetery	2,500
Longfellow Meadow and Soldier's Field	6,000
United States Arsenal	4,000

[1] These commercial holdings measure as follows : —

	Feet.
Boston & Albany Railroad	3,000
Brookline Gas Company	1,000
Abattoir	3,000
Other establishments	3,000

posed beach road at Revere, these plans of boundaries for a
metropolitan reservation at Charles River are based upon the
idea that a public sidewalk and roadway will eventually be
built adjacent to the abutting private land.   Between this
roadway and the water will be a strip of land or marsh of a
width which will necessarily vary in more or less exact proportion to the probable cost of the area in question.   At a
few points the plans are so devised as to make it possible for
established coal-dealers to use wharves outside the driveway.
Whether the remaining open portions of the area between the
driveway and the stream will remain marsh subject to tidal
flooding, or become fresh-water grass-land usable by the public, is yet to be seen.   In either event, the proposed public
open space will be well worth having ; but if the tide can be
dammed out of the river, as the late joint Commission suggested, not only can the marshes of the public reservation be
made usable at no great expense, but the river itself, freed
from its unsightly flats and mud shores, will (also at no great
cost) become a valuable and even beautiful water park.   On
the other hand, if the tide must continue to flow up to Watertown, flooding the marshes on its way and damming back the
fresh waters, the public river-banks can be made usable only
by means of expensive filling, beaching, or walling operations ;
while the resulting public domain, consisting of the river and
its banks, will be decidedly less serviceable, as well as much
less beautiful.   Thus it may well be true that the negative saving in the cost of treating these miles of public river-bank,
plus the positive benefit to adjacent estates and the district as
a whole, would pecuniarily justify the district in building the
dam, even though the dam (as is quite unlikely) should make
it necessary to employ continually a dredge and an ice-boat
in the harbor, as is done at Philadelphia and at Baltimore.

In addition to general recommendations as to the acquirement of forest, river-side, and sea-coast reservations, the
landscape architect to the preliminary Commission called
particular attention to two small but remarkable spots, the
destruction of which would work great loss to the higher
interests of the metropolitan district.   The executive Commission visited both of these places, and found both of them to be

as described, but nevertheless determined to spend the available metropolitan loan in rounding out the bounds of the large forest domains, and to take action towards the preservation of the Beaver Brook Glen and Oaks, and the Hemlock Gorge of Charles River, only in case local or private enterprise should supply at least a large part of the price of the desired lands. Fortunately for the metropolitan district and its future generations, Mr. Edwin F. Atkins of Belmont and his mother, Mrs. Elisha Atkins, came promptly forward with a gift of $10,500 towards the cost of the acquisition of the ponds, the glen, and the cascade at Beaver Brook ; and this gift sufficed to cause the Commission to exercise its right of eminent domain, to appropriate the additional sum required, and to assume for the public the custody of this charming spot.

As a part of our professional duty towards the Commission and the public, it is incumbent upon us to again call attention to the Hemlock Gorge of Charles River. Whether it be viewed from the high summit of the aqueduct arch, from the low level of Boylston Street bridge, or from the points of ledge near the Newton mills, this passage of the river through the rocks and Hemlocks presents a scene such as cannot be matched in the whole metropolitan district. Will not a few of those generous persons who are continually enriching the Boston Art Museum unite now in securing the permanent preservation of this so beautiful natural picture ? With the Metropolitan Commission standing ready to assume the custody of the place, it will be worse than regrettable if another Hemlock is permitted to be removed, or another obtrusive building to be inserted.

III. — METROPOLITAN PARKWAYS.

In addition to commanding the acquisition of reservations at Revere Beach and Charles River, the legislature of 1894 directed the Metropolitan Park Commission to invest $500,000 in so-called " boulevards."

Immediately upon the passage of this act, a variety of widely different schemes were proposed. It was argued that the Commission should assume charge of the maintenance, watering, and policing of certain selected and more or less

THE HEMLOCK GORGE AT NEWTON UPPER FALLS, CHARLES RIVER

direct or continuous existing highways, and thus preserve them as pleasure driveways exempt from the dangerous intrusion of electric cars. In other quarters it was held that the legislature intended the appropriation to be spent for the relief of "the unemployed," and that if only work were furnished, it did not much matter what existing highways were improved, or how remote from the centre of population they might be.

In May, 1894, we were first asked to give attention to the problem presented by this new act of the legislature. As to the place where the appropriation should be expended, it seemed to us, after due reflection, that wise economy demanded, first, that only the interior parts of the metropolitan district should be considered, because the permanent results of work done therein would benefit many persons for every single person who would enjoy the results of labor expended in remoter regions; and, secondly, that the particular part of the interior to be selected should be determined by the generally acknowledged desirability of improved means of access to the recently acquired public forests of the Fells and the Blue Hills. Again, as to the sort of improved highway to be opened or built, it appeared to us that the public advantage would be best served, not by opening merely driveways to be enjoyed only by bicyclers and carriage-owners, but by providing, in addition to roadways and sidewalks, separate passageways for the cheap, agreeable, and rapid transportation of the multitude by electric cars.

Guided by these considerations, which to us seemed fundamental and governing, we studied to determine the most convenient, and at the same time practicable, routes for two such car and carriage highways, one of which should lead from the Fells and the other from the Blue Hills, towards the densely built centre of population of the district. The product of these studies may now be briefly described.

Pine Hill, Medford, and Bear's Den Hill, Malden, form the two southernmost corners of Middlesex Fells Reservation. Between the two hills lies a section of Medford about a mile square, not yet much occupied by buildings because of its distance from steam and street railways. Both hills are less than five and a half miles distant from the State House.

Starting from the reservation at the bases of these hills, how far towards the heart of the metropolitan area can a convenient way for cars and carriages be opened without incurring an expense unwarrantable at the present time? The answer made by our plans is three miles, and the cityward terminus of the proposed Fells Parkway is placed by these plans at Broadway Park, Somerville. The proposed parkway may best be likened to a great tree. Its tangled roots are the main streets of Charlestown, East Cambridge, Cambridge, and Somerville. Its trunk bridges Mystic River and extends nearly to Pleasant Street, Malden. Its main branches touch Malden and Medford, reach the Fells Reservation at Bear's Den Hill and Pine Hill, and stretch along the boundary of the Fells to Winchester and through the Fells to Stoneham and Melrose. Upon reaching Broadway Park, after threading the maze of city streets, cars and carriages will find relief and opportunity to speed away to the Fells or the northern suburbs. Incidentally, the square mile of Medford territory already mentioned will be made agreeably accessible, particularly if the electric cars should complete a circuit by following the boundary road of the Fells from Bear's Den around to Pine Hill.

Crossman's Pines, the northernmost corner of the western section of the Blue Hills Reservation, is distant more than nine miles in an air line from the State House; but owing to the fact that the municipality of Boston extends four times as far south of the State House as it does north, and because Boston has undertaken the construction of a broad highway out to her uttermost boundary at Mattapan, the length of the Blue Hills Parkway proposed to be acquired by the Metropolitan Commission is no greater than the length of the proposed Fells Parkway already described. From Crossman's Pines to Harland Street, Milton, is about three fourths of a mile; and by Harland Street to Canton Avenue is three fourths of a mile; from Canton Avenue by Mattapan Street to Mattapan Square, which is the terminus of the widened Blue Hill Avenue and the proposed cityward terminus of the Blue Hills Parkway, is another mile and a half. Except in equality of length, this parkway, however, bears little resemblance to the Fells

Parkway.   The tree to which it may be likened has one root of great length and importance, — Blue Hill Avenue ; but beyond the region covered by its trunk and branches there are found no such considerable bodies of population as lie around and beyond the Fells.   For the present, therefore, this southern parkway will serve only as a means of approach to the great public domain at the Blue Hills.   Its electric railroad will, however, tend to populate a large region which has hitherto been inaccessible from the city.

The accompanying skeleton map [1] illustrates the relation of the two proposed parkways to the central parts of the metropolitan district and the regions about the two great reservations.   It appears that the beginning of the widened Blue Hill Avenue at Grove Hall is a mile farther from the State House than the beginning of the proposed Fells Parkway at Broadway Park, and that Broadway Park is no farther from the centre of the metropolis than Cottage Farm bridge or Roxbury Crossing.   On the other hand, either of these latter places can at the present time be reached with ease by car or carriage, while Broadway Park can be attained from inner Boston only with toil and difficulty.   Somerville and Arlington, Winchester, Medford, and Malden undoubtedly stand in great need of a direct and adequate avenue of approach to Boston.   Charlestown is so densely built as to make the opening of a new and sufficient way impracticable.   The broad territory occupied by the northern railroad companies, which now extends from Rutherford Avenue almost to Somerville Avenue (a distance of three fourths of a mile), blocks all other possible routes ; while the great packing-houses in the Miller's River valley, the grade crossings of the Fitchburg Railroad, and the high prices of East Cambridge lands stand in the way after the railroad yards are passed.

Without giving to the study of this difficult matter more time than we can afford to give to a problem not specifically set before us, we may say that at present we believe a practicable, and sufficiently suitable and well-placed, passage through the difficult region would be obtained, if the present location of the Lowell Railroad, between Cambridge Street, Somer-

[1] See, instead, the map in the pocket of the right-hand cover.

ville, and Charles River at Craigie bridge, could be acquired and devoted, with adjacent lands, to the purpose in view. Now that the railroads use one station and own the old McLean Asylum grounds, there seems to be no good reason why the Lowell tracks should not join the Fitchburg tracks on the northern side of the ditch called Miller's River, where an East Cambridge station might still be maintained, if necessary. Such a concentration of the tracks would clear the way for an electric car and carriage avenue, which, crossing the Fitchburg Railroad above grade, would link the Charles River Basin and its public banks with one after another of the main highways of East Cambridge and Somerville, and afford the outlying cities and towns the inlet to the great city which they sorely need. From Charles River to the crossing of the Fitchburg Railroad is half a mile, from the Fitchburg Railroad to Cambridge Street, Somerville, is half a mile, and from Cambridge Street to Central Hill Park, by a line adjacent to the railroad, but well above it, another half mile. At Central Hill Park the last of the great radial highways would be tapped and the new trunk-line avenue might end. From Central Hill Park to Broadway Park and the beginning of the proposed Fells Parkway is only a third of a mile. Thus it appears that the relief of the northwestern suburbs in this particular is perhaps not quite as desperate an undertaking as it has commonly been supposed to be.

General plans of the proposed Fells and Blue Hills parkways, filed in the office of the Commission, illustrate their relations to existing streets and the various subdivisions of both. The standard width proposed (one hundred and twenty feet) is simply the narrowest width within which it is safely practicable to make a separate reservation for electric cars. The roadways accompanying the car-track reservation may, of course, be increased in width, but not without a disproportionate increase in the cost of the necessary land. The use of the wider of the two roadways is proposed by us to be restricted to pleasure carriages, except for the necessary service of the houses fronting upon it.

December 31, 1894.

CHAPTER XXVII

LETTERS OF 1895 ON PARKS METROPOLITAN AND OTHER

We live in deeds, not years; in thoughts, not breaths;
In feelings, not in figures on a dial.
We should count time by heart-throbs. He most lives
Who thinks most, feels the noblest, acts the best.

PHILIP JAMES BAILEY.

BESIDE the large problems of areas, boundaries, roads, and paths for the metropolitan reservations, many smaller but urgent questions were answered by Charles. Thus, he wanted plenty of sign-boards put up to direct the public to the various objects of interest in the somewhat labyrinthine forests; but where? and what should the sign-boards say? and what colors would be best? On March 20, 1895, Charles wrote to the Secretary of the Commission: "We will, as you suggest, prepare a schedule of the most necessary sign-boards for the Blue Hills and Stony Brook Reservations." After much consideration, and some experiments as to the least obtrusive but sufficiently distinct colors, he chose black lettering on brown boards as preferable to any other combination for park purposes winter and summer.

In the middle of the same year, Charles wrote thus to the chairman of the Commission : —

July 16, 1895.

Attention has been given to the naming of the principal hills, valleys, and streams of the reservations, much study having been directed to discovering the oldest or most generally accepted designations for such places as have been named in times past, as well as to searching for suitable designations for unnamed points of interest. Many names of Indian chieftains have been applied to hills especially.

Points have been selected to be marked by sign-boards giving the directions and distance of frequented places, and the superintendent has already put up a certain number of these signs. It might be well to place " label signs " at each newly

named spot in order to familiarize the public with the nomen-
clature of the reservations.

The topographical surveys of the Hills and the Fells Reservations have been actively prosecuted during the past six
months by Messrs. French, Bryant & Taylor, and we have
several times advised with them concerning the draughting of
the sheets of the maps and the quality of the work in the field.
It is advisable that the accurately determined triangulation
points of these surveys should now be permanently marked
on the ground by means of stones and iron bolts; and we
recommend that the Commission authorize the Superintendent to procure the stones and bolts, and set them at once
under the guidance of French, Bryant & Taylor. It is also
advisable that the boundaries of all the acquired reservations
should be permanently marked by stones and bolts, before
another winter shall further displace the stakes of the first
surveyors. We therefore recommend that the Commission
authorize the Superintendent to complete this work under the
guidance of Engineer Pierce.

The study of the distribution of botanical species in the
reservations was resumed with the spring, and continuous
progress is making. The many botanists engaged seem to
take a lively interest, and they have enjoyed several excursions to the woods in company. Professors Shaler, Storer,
and Sargent of Harvard University have all visited the Blue
Hills at different times in company with Mr. Eliot; while
Professor Crosby of the Institute of Technology has continued his detailed geological explorations. By the time the
topographical surveys are delivered to us completed, probably
by the 1st of December next, we now expect to be prepared
to describe and to delineate upon the maps a comprehensive
scheme of treatment of the woodlands of the reservations
such as will ensure their slow, but ultimate restoration to
something like their primitive character and beauty.

The way in which Charles did his studying in the field is
well described in the following note written to his wife in
midsummer, 1895. He would spend many consecutive hours
on foot in the area to be studied, observing the contours, the
vegetation, the routes for roads and paths, and the accessible

prospects, and making notes for future use. Sometimes he took an assistant with him, but oftener he went alone. When bound on these explorations, it was a matter of quite secondary consideration where he slept, or where he took his meals. All summer his life was a wandering one, his wife and children being either at New Hartford or Mt. Desert.

THE LANGWOOD, MIDDLESEX FELLS,
MELROSE, MASS., Sunday, July 20, '95.

. . . You see I am a wanderer. Friday night at 17 Quincy Street, with a supper at Oak Grove Café, so as to be on hand for a review of Fresh Pond plans, which lasted from 8.30 to 2 P. M. This was a private view with Kellaway of the office, and I begin to have hopes that the place may look well ten years hence.

Saturday night here, after visiting the Field in East Cambridge and supping at Union Station, so as to be on hand for certain solitary explorations, which consumed a long morning to-day, and soaked my clothes with interior moisture to that degree that I had to change all, and wring them for fear of mildew in my bag! It has been a damp, still, densely hazy, hot day: so hazy that even the near-by islands of Spot Pond have retreated into soft smoky blue distance, and the Fells seen from the high points have seemed of infinite extent. First I met two great brown herons, or cranes, who turned to look at me from a charming bog-hole, and then rose and flew slowly across my path. Next came two completely lost but happy young bicyclers pushing their machines up a very stony trail in search of Wirepoykin Hill, which I assisted them to find. Then in a hollow I came suddenly upon a workingman papa, with his nine-year-old boy, and the man moved suddenly to close a hand-bag which he carried, and then saw he was too late and looked guilty ; but I told him picking berries was allowed, and that he had better use a tin pail! Lastly, about noon, I found two carriage loads of young and old folks, who were preparing to picnic in a little grove they had discovered near where their wood-road had become impassable. I could n't see any way to turn the carriages, and I guess they had to back a long way when they got ready to go home, — but they doubtless thought that part of the fun.

When one reflects that this innocent pleasuring is now likely to go on here for many generations, one begins to see that something worth while has been accomplished.

Although the central interest of Charles's professional life after 1893 was the Metropolitan Parks, he had many other interests and assigned duties as a member of the Olmsted firm. Thus, proposed parks in municipalities within the metropolitan district were always assigned to him to study and report on. As samples of his work on such parks in 1895, four letters are here grouped, one about parks for Waltham, a suburban city nine miles west of Boston, one about a park and a parkway for Chelsea, a suburb of small area northeast of Boston, and two about open spaces in Cambridge, a city of large area. The letters are given in full. They set forth a large variety of the considerations which affect the selection and management of public grounds : —

Feb. 15, 1895.

To the Park Commissioners of the City of Waltham, — In obedience to your request for such suggestions as we may advisedly offer you at this time, we beg leave to reply as follows : —

In the first place we congratulate you and your fellow-citizens on the possession of so noble a hill and so charming a river. That town is fortunate which finds within its borders scenery of two such beautiful contrasting types.

It goes without saying that your Commission has done well in securing the summit of Prospect Hill for the enjoyment of the public. Park Commissions ought everywhere to regard themselves and be regarded as, primarily, trustees of scenery; because the refreshment which townspeople find in scenery is the most recreative mode of enjoyment which a park commission can possibly supply. Sewers, water-pipes, well-paved streets, playgrounds for youth, concert grounds, public gardens, open-air nurseries, — all these and the like are good and more or less necessary, and yet the city which, while gaining these things has permitted its scenic opportunities to be destroyed, may rightly be said to have gained the world, but lost its soul.

We speak in this way because it is our opinion, formed

after careful study of the situation, that the duty of your Commission as trustees of scenery for the people of Waltham has not been completed by the acquisition of Prospect Hill. The banks of Charles River ought, undoubtedly, so far as may be possible, to be acquired and held in trust by your Board. The Water Board already owns a long stretch of the river-bank. Whatever private rights exist in the land between the pumping station and the bridge, and between Mount Feake Cemetery and the river, ought, in our opinion, to be resumed by the public; together with whatever other portions of the river-bank may be obtainable. The public domain ought to be continuous, save in the crowded business centre of the town. Every endeavor should also be made to cause Newton to take similar action upon her side of the stream. Boat clubs and even private citizens might well be allotted sites for landings; but the fee of the banks should belong to the two cities whose people already enjoy the right of boating upon the stream itself. In view of the fact that this river scenery is still in jeopardy, while Prospect Hill is at least safely secured, it is our opinion that whatever moneys are next available for park purposes should be devoted to purchases on the river-bank rather than to constructions on the hill.

It is true, indeed, that a shelter and prospect-commanding terrace on the hill-top will greatly enhance the usefulness of the hill park, and that roads are needed to make the hill comfortably accessible.

On the other hand, the wisdom and far-sighted economy of a Commission, as of an individual, are evidenced by the way in which work is mapped out, and the essentially first duties separated from the secondary. After traversing Prospect Hill and inspecting the present boundaries of the public domain, we cannot but think it most advisable that the boundaries should be considerably enlarged as well as rectified. Just where the boundaries of the reservation ought to be placed, and just how the reservation may best be reached from Waltham, it is impossible to say until a topographical survey shall have been made. We recommend that the work of making this survey be begun as soon as the snow disappears, in order that the field work may be completed before the leaves come out. It seems clear to us that the Commission will do Waltham better service by improving the boundaries, than by constructing anything upon the hill at this time. The survey which we deem essential as a guide in the study of proper boundaries will hereafter prove useful in devising interior roads and other constructions.

It only remains for us to point out that with Beaver Brook Reservation at the eastern end of the city, Mead's Pond in the north, the new Cambridge water reservoirs in the northwest, the banks of Charles River in the southwest, and Prospect Hill in the middle west, Waltham will be well provided with public open spaces possessing scenery. If public playgrounds are required, they may be obtained regardless of scenery in the near neighborhood of crowded districts. The only other public grounds which the city need consider are those strips upon the banks of natural streams, the universal desirability of which has been pointed out by City Engineer Johnson. Several cities of the neighborhood — notably Newton and Medford — have already acquired stream reservations. It would doubtless profit Waltham to do the same.

December 21st, 1895.

To the Secretary of the Chelsea Park Commission, — In obedience to instructions received from the Metropolitan Park Commission we have visited Chelsea, and now beg leave to submit the following suggestions concerning the choice of sites for public pleasure grounds.

The city of Chelsea, omitting the grounds of the Naval Hospital, measures only about one and one half miles square. It is a closely built city, its streets occupying an upland of irregular form which is two thirds surrounded by the salt waters and marshes of Island End Creek, Mystic River, Chelsea Creek, and Snake Creek. Between Island End Creek and the head of Snake Creek Chelsea adjoins the city of Everett. Snake Creek is itself the boundary between Chelsea and the town of Revere. The city is divided into two almost equal parts by the railroad known as the Eastern Division of the Boston and Maine system. Almost exactly in the middle of the northern half of the city there is found a high and narrow ridge of clay and stones, known as Powderhorn Hill, and already occupied in part by the Massachusetts Soldiers' Home. This still open ridge commands a panoramic view of the whole circle of the surroundings of Chelsea, from the sea in the east to Prospect Hill in the west. The hill is capable of development as a public promenade or terrace of a very striking and unusual sort, and we must earnestly recommend its acquirement by the Chelsea Park Commission.

The southern half of Chelsea is so closely built that it seems impossible to find any room for even playgrounds until the eastern and western limits of the dense town are reached. On the low lands near Island End Creek and Chelsea Creek several opportunities present themselves for the purchase of level spaces entirely suitable for playgrounds. Such grounds, we think, ought to be large enough to be capable of subdivision into, at least, two principal sections, — the end nearest the population had best be arranged for the recreation of quiet people, small children, nurses and babies, while the remoter section may be devoted to the boys. If the extreme ends of these grounds could be extended to the shores of the creeks, public boating stations might eventually be established. The views which would thus be obtained over and up and down the creeks would add considerably to the enjoyment of the public. Accordingly, we would recommend that an eastern playground be obtained east of the railroads and adjacent to Chelsea Creek, and a western playground north of the Naval Hospital and adjacent to Island End Creek. The last named ground might advantageously adjoin the Hospital grounds as well as the Creek, since it would then possess two sides upon which it could not be seriously shut in. The eastern ground might perhaps be divided between the two sides of Eastern Avenue, the women's and children's pleasure ground being placed on the western side of the street, and the boys' playground between the street and the water.

It remains only to point out that the valley of Snake Creek, which bounds Chelsea on the northeast, affords an opportunity for a useful and beautiful parkway similar to that which has already been constructed in the valley of Muddy

River on the boundary between Boston and Brookline. A park or parkway in this valley would be a benefit to Chelsea, but Revere would also profit from it, while Everett, Somerville, Malden, and the remoter towns would find this valley the pleasantest route to the sea at Revere Beach.[1] From the head of the Creek to the bridge of the Boston and Maine railroad is a little more than a mile, and it is only a mile farther to the circle which is the southern terminus of the Revere Beach Reservation of the Metropolitan Commission.

THE BUILDING IN CAMBRIDGE FIELD.

23rd February, 1895.

To THE SUPERINTENDENT OF PARKS, CAMBRIDGE, MASS., — In reply to your request for a few suggestions concerning the maintenance of Cambridge Field, we beg leave to submit the following memoranda : —

The field is to be used by crowds — there can be no doubt of that. Water-closets for both sexes will certainly need to be provided. The women's closets should have a vestibule in which a woman should be in constant attendance, as in all well-managed public grounds the world over. With such closets and a band-stand, we suppose that every absolute need in the way of buildings would be met. There would remain to be attended to only the care of the grass and gravel spaces, and the necessary service of police.

The general plan submitted by us calls for a much larger building than is required to meet the primary needs just mentioned, and we distinctly recommend the construction of this larger building for the following reasons : —

It is important that when the field is opened to the public, it should at once become a success such as will induce respect and greatly help the formation of good habits in the people who will frequent the place. Experience proves that when such a ground is finished in a poor or makeshift manner, the public is very apt to abuse it, while if the finish is good and the arrangements ample and attractive, improved behavior follows. The recent World's Fair illustrated this happy result very forcibly.

[1] See the map in the pocket of the right-hand cover.

The building proposed by our plan is the keystone of our design for Cambridge Field, and ought to be well devised by a good architect with special reference to producing a pleasing result. It should be planned to serve as a central hall, or meeting-place, or shelter from showers; to it should be attached the band-stand; within it should be found a check-room for the deposit of clothing, bats and balls, skates, or other articles; also, a counter for the sale of milk, beef tea, coffee, soda, or light refreshments; also, the necessary closets and wash-rooms, and a special room for the use of the attendants upon small babies.

Strange as it may appear at first sight, we believe that after such a building is once built, the annual cost of maintaining the whole field, building and all, will be no greater than it would be were no such building erected. The granting of a privilege to sell refreshments (soda in summer and hot coffee in the skating season), to maintain a stand for sharpening skates, and to sell skates and other instruments of games, would probably induce some worthy person to take the position of care-taker without other pay, or for very small pay. A man and woman, with a boy or girl, would be a sufficient staff. The man would have general charge of the field, and would work about the place much of the time. The woman assisted by a child would attend the check and refreshment counters meanwhile.

At the Overlook Shelter in Franklin Park the man who has the privilege of selling refreshments supplies all the janitor service required, including supplies of soap and towels. The Commission receives no rent from him, but, on the other hand, the Commission is at no expense whatever for maintaining a very important and successful adjunct of the park.

We believe the Cambridge Park Commission would do well to make a similarly well-managed building the central feature of Cambridge Field. With the building, and a good man in charge, the enterprise can almost certainly be made successful from the start. Without the building and its care-taker, the field will necessarily seem a somewhat unprotected and uncared-for place, to which gentle people will hardly care to resort, and in which the ruder element will see opportunity to display its rudeness. We believe that ten thousand dollars sunk in this building will be as good an investment for the city as the Park Commission can make.

June 20th, 1895.

To the Chairman of the Park Commission, Cambridge, Mass., — We beg leave to report as follows, concerning the proposed preservation of the existing gate in the middle of the length of Broadway Square.

The experience of cities has long since proved that it is necessary to fence public grounds of small area in order to prevent the trampling of " short-cut " paths across the grounds in all directions. A fence having been provided in order to preserve some untrodden breadths of greensward within a square, gates are to be opened only at such points as may accommodate the majority of people desiring to take pleasure in the square, or to cross it on their way to distant points. Every gate or opening in the boundary fence almost necessarily involves a path to every other gate or opening. The greater the number of gates, the more a square must tend to resemble the trodden desert, which is the normal condition of grounds in crowded neighborhoods, when unprotected by fencing.

The plan for Broadway Square submitted by us will preserve considerable areas of lawn free from cross walks. It will also preserve a section of the grounds near Broadway where the children of the neighborhood may find a place to play in an arbor out of the line of march of persons who may use the square for short cuts. The scheme presented will in this way make a particularly useful as well as attractive piece of public ground. This special usefulness and attractiveness will be chiefly due to the simple expedient of closing the middle gate on Broadway. If the gate must be kept open, no such plan as we have laid before you ought to be followed. The opening of the middle gate would make a wholly different plan of treatment advisable ; and this new plan would not develop for the neighborhood the usefulness and the attractiveness which the present plan will produce. We are distinctly of the opinion that the neighborhood can well afford to forego the use of the middle gate and its accompanying diagonal and straight cross-walks, for the sake of the far greater pleasantness, beauty, and usefulness which the plan you have before you will secure.

Two other interesting designs are included in this chapter, one for a park at New Bedford, which has a pond as its main feature, and another for a new suburb of Detroit arranged around a long, central common. For lack of money, Button-wood Park at New Bedford has not yet been finished ; but Charles's design was accepted as the ultimate plan of the park, and all work thus far done has followed closely the recommendations of the following letter. The Detroit design was not utilized.

February 26, 1895.

To the Chairman of the Park Commission, New Bed-ford, Mass.

Sir, — We beg leave to submit the following preliminary report concerning the proposed park at Buttonwood Brook.

The boundaries of the land at present owned by the city, as they are shown upon the map sent us by your engineer, are obviously too contracted and irregular. For instance, the boundary as it now lies runs through a part of the exist-ing ice pond. In order to enable the city to derive the de-sired benefit from a park to be situated in this valley, it seems to us necessary that the boundary of the tract to be devoted to park purposes should be extended so as to touch Hawthorn Street on the south, and Kempton Street on the north. On the west also the proposed location of Brownell Avenue lies so near the pond that we must urge the reloca-tion of this street, and the extension of the park accordingly. The accompanying sketch plan is, therefore, based upon the assumption that the new park may be bounded by the four streets called Rockdale, Brownell, Kempton, and Hawthorn.

We have, from the first, been informed that the principal object in view in securing this particular tract of land for a park was the provision of boating and skating on a pond to be formed in the valley. We believe that we warned the Commission, at the time of our first visit, that the brook, in our opinion, was incapable of furnishing a supply of water sufficient to warrant any attempt to make a pond. The water-shed of the brook above the park is too small to furnish a sufficient supply. Assuming, however, that it is still the wish of the Commission to create a pond, we have drawn our preliminary plan accordingly, taking it for granted that the Commission will obtain a supply of water from some source. It occurs to us that it might be possible to make an arrangement with one of the mills in Dartmouth, on the course of the stream next west of Buttonwood Brook, by which the water could be pumped from this stream to the summit of the ridge between the valleys, from which point it would flow down to Buttonwood Brook and so feed the pond. It might even be possible for the Commissioners to set up a pump of their own, say at the point where the railroad to Fall River crosses the stream just mentioned.

Thus for present purposes we have assumed that an ample water supply can be had, and we have accordingly shown upon the plan a pond some twenty acres in area, the surface of which would be at an elevation slightly above that of the present ice pond, namely at grade 93. This pond has been made the central feature of our design. Its shores will be irregular, in places consisting of gentle beaches, and in other parts of banks of trees and shrubbery. An encircling foot-path will pass from beach to beach behind and among the trees. At the southern end of the pond this footpath will pass over the concealed dam by which the water will be retained in the pond. For the sake of certain picturesque effect, the inlet and outlet will both be made somewhat tortuous. Beside a cove on the east shore of the pond, it is designed to place a substantial building, which will serve as the central rendezvous for all who visit the park. In winter this will be the skating-house, where skates can be kept in lockers, and hot drinks may perhaps be obtainable. In summer the same building will be the boating-house, the boats being drawn up upon beaches or landings extending from the house to right and left. The southern quarter of the park, lying south of the house, can be easily transformed into a fairly level ball-field, and those who use the field may also use this house for the storage of their bats and balls. East of the house the broad field-like land, which is easily attainable, may well serve as tennis lawns. Close to the house, upon this side, a playground for smaller children may be provided, if it is deemed advisable; here might be placed swings and other apparatus. This ground should, of course, be separated by planting from the broader open fields.

Turning now to the outer portions of the park, the plan suggests that one principal entrance should be placed near the top of the slight hill in Kempton Street. Here will be the electric cars, and here a driveway and two walks can be opened into the park in such a way as to present to visitors, as soon as they have entered, a particularly fine view of the whole park. By careful planting of trees in the great field and by the shores of the pond, several pleasing vistas can be arranged and preserved. One view from this hill will extend the whole length of the open lawn down to the end of the ball-field. Another pleasing vista will be laid along a line passing just west of the boating-house, and extending to the little bridge by which a path will cross the outlet of the pond.

From the top of this hill the one circuit driveway of the park will descend to right and left. Passing along the outer edges of the open fields it will skirt the western bank of the pond, where it will be bordered generally by woods. This circuit drive has, of course, been arranged to afford the most extended and the most agreeable views which it is possible to obtain within the proposed limits of the park. It is important that those who will use this drive, as well as the footpaths of the park, should, so far as may be possible, be removed from the noise and sights of the town, and accordingly the plan proposes a somewhat dense mass of trees and shrubbery between the circuit road and the bordering streets. The great fields or meadows which lie within this frame of verdure, as well as within the circuit of the pleasure drive, will be most pleasing and most impressive, if they can be kept open and uncut by numerous paths. Upon the plan the number of cross paths has, therefore, been reduced as much as seems possible, those that are shown being such as seem to be absolutely necessary in order to afford access to the boating and skating house from the entrances of the park.

It is to be hoped that the broad, open fields may be well prepared to produce a close turf, and it will probably be advisable to rely upon pasturing by sheep for keeping this turf in good condition. Sheep are used for this purpose in Central Park, New York, Franklin Park, Boston, and in all English parks. In the extreme northwest corner of the public domain the plan, accordingly, provides a place for a sheep-fold and sheds, as well as for a yard and stable in which the carts, watering-carts, and the other tools required for the maintenance of the park may be stored. Here also may eventually be built a house for the use of the head keeper.

You will notice that the plan suggests the widening of Kempton Street and the construction all about the park of sidewalks, having rows of trees planted in a grass strip of reasonable width. Many other details of the plan might be mentioned, but enough has probably been said for present purposes.

It may be well for us to point out again that this preliminary sketch is based upon three assumptions. First, that the boundary of the park may be extended to Kempton and Hawthorn streets. Secondly, that the location of Brownell Avenue may be shifted to a line parallel with the city boundary and one hundred and fifty feet distant therefrom. Thirdly, that an ample supply of water can be obtained. We shall hope to hear from the Commission that all these assumptions may become realized as facts. We shall wait to hear from you before we proceed further in the study of the park.

June 4, 1895.

Mr. —— ——, Detroit, Mich. — We are sending Mr. —— two new sun-prints of our design for the subdivision of Log Cabin Farm into roads and building-lots. In obedience to a request made by Mr. ——, we now write you in order to call your attention to a few of the more conspicuous features of our design or general plan.

In the first place we deemed it especially desirable that this new suburb should possess some central feature of interest and beauty, which would distinguish it very decidedly from all the other suburbs of your city. Accordingly, we conceived the idea of a very long central common or park of greensward extending along the axis of Hamilton Boulevard, and terminating at its farther end in a symmetrical sweep of roadway, which would enclose within the common a certain wooded knoll which is found in that part of the estate. This green, central common we next suggested should be surrounded by a suitably broad public road, which would, in turn, be accompanied by an electric car line on one side, and on the other side by a shaded sidewalk giving access to the long adjacent frontages of building land. This great common and these boundary roads, we understand, have already been provided for by an agreement made between your company and the city of Detroit.

In order that the car line, which we propose should make a loop around the common, might be of advantage to all the adjacent parts of your estate, it next seemed necessary that numerous branch roads should be led toward the common and the car line from all sides. Agreeable to suggestions received from several of your company at the time when Mr. Eliot made his first visit to the lands, these side roads (like the boundary roads of the common) have all been planned to follow curvilinear lines, thus again differentiating your new suburb from all others near Detroit.

The distance from the common to the outer boundaries of the company's land being very considerable, it next seemed desirable to introduce one other circuit road connecting the outer ends of all the branch roads just mentioned, and thus unifying the whole estate. This broad circuit road has been planned in accordance with a suggestion made by Mr. —— to have a special reservation for the use of persons on horseback placed in the middle of the highway.

With the Common or Plaisance and the Wetherell Woods, the loop car line, the curving branch roads, and the encircling parkway, your estate will, we feel sure, possess no rival in Michigan, so far as beauty and general attractiveness are concerned.

Before we proceed further in our more detailed studies, we ask that you communicate to us all criticisms and suggestions which you may be able to collect.

CHAPTER XXVIII

REPORTS OF THE LANDSCAPE ARCHITECTS FOR 1895 TO THE METROPOLITAN AND BOSTON PARK COMMISSIONS

> The perpetual admonition of Nature to us is, "The world is new — untried. Do not believe the past. I give you the Universe a virgin to-day." — RALPH WALDO EMERSON.

TO THE METROPOLITAN PARK COMMISSION.

WE have the honor to submit the following report, covering the first eleven months of the year 1895, together with some suggestions and recommendations as to several of the more important problems which call for attention. . . .

The Rock-hill or Forest Reservations.

The reservations of this class acquired and opened by the Commission are, strictly speaking, only two, — the Blue Hills and the Middlesex Fells; nevertheless, the Stony Brook Reservation will here be included in the same class, because of its similar rocky and wooded character.

The boundaries of the Blue Hills Reservation, originally studied with care, as described in previous reports, have recently been amended as follows : [by a short strip to save a row of fine trees; by a narrow, winding tongue, a small triangle, a sliver of land, a small triangle, a small sliver, a large triangle mostly swamp land, all to improve entrances or boundary roads ; and by the extension of the lines from Cedar Rock and Little Dome to Randolph Avenue in a manner which embraces between the future boundary roads the charming valley of Pine Tree Brook, while also providing a convenient entrance from the direction of Milton and Dorchester.]

The reservation is now bounded on the south by Monatiquot Stream and a short stretch of Hillside Street, Milton ; and on the northern or cityward side by lines which, save at

Hillside Dell, and the Quincy Quarry Ridge, and between Randolph Avenue and Forest Street, are generally practicable for roads. It is obviously desirable that a road boundary be secured between Forest Street and Randolph Avenue, so that the divided ends of the boundary roads already arranged for may be connected.

Middlesex Fells Reservation has had its original boundary lines similarly amended by the following changes: (1) The addition of a strip of land in Medford, extending from Forest Street to the Winchester-Medford line, and so shaped as to permit the eventual construction of a boundary road in direct continuation of the western branch of the Fells Parkway. The boundary thus secured is the best which can be had within the limiting line across Medford so peculiarly prescribed by the General Court, and is a great improvement upon the straight, and, so far as a road was concerned, the impracticable, line which it supplants. (2) The abandonment to the former owners of an irregular tract of land in Winchester, much of it lying on the western slope of Grinding Rock Hill. The new line has been devised so as to be practicable for a boundary road, but in so far as it releases to private possession some of the water-shed and some of the framing landscape of the Middle Reservoir, it is open to serious objection. (3) The abandonment to the former owners of an irregular tract of land lying in Melrose and Stoneham, east of Washington Street and a line drawn from the "red mills" to Emerson Street. There is thus surrendered to private ownership a considerable body of nearly level land, already divided into three parts by two highways (Ravine Road and Wyoming Avenue), while the reservation properly retains within its limits the important high plateau and the slopes thereof. (4) The abandonment to the former owners of a small parcel of land in the rear of houses on Loanda Street, Melrose. (5) The addition of two small triangles comprising rocky outcrops which will permanently ornament the entrance to the south boundary road from Summer Street, Malden.

The Fells Reservation consists essentially of a broad plateau thrust southward from Stoneham between the valleys of

the Abbajona and Malden rivers. At the time of the taking
by the Metropolitan Commission, these valleys were rapidly
filling with buildings ; but it so happened that only two modern suburban houses had as yet been built upon the brink or
sloping edge of the plateau where the finest distant views are
naturally obtained. Several gentlemen had dreamed of building upon the edge of the tableland in different places, and
for these interrupted dreams they now ask to be pecuniarily
compensated. However reasonable or extravagant their claims
may be, it is to be hoped that further surrender of the brink
to buildings may be averted, not only because of the importance of free access to the view-commanding edge of the plateau, but also because buildings in this position will necessarily
be conspicuous from the interior of the reservation, where it
is important to secure the appearance of indefinite extent.

At Stony Brook Reservation the original or preliminary
boundary lines remain unchanged.

With respect to the preparation of general plans for
making the scenery of these reservations agreeably accessible,
and for restoring and enhancing the beauty of their much
injured woods, comparatively little progress has been made
during the past year. The delay has been partly due to the
pressure of other work demanded of us by the Commission ;
but the weightier of the problems involved have been postponed intentionally. Various reasons for thus postponing
consideration of these questions were detailed in our last
annual report (see chap. xxvi., pp. 495 and 501–504). The
evolution of plans for the fitting treatment of the woods, as
the mutable element in the scenery, must go hand in hand
with the devising of the permanent roads and footways which
shall make the scenery accessible, while injuring it least and
showing it best. To lay wise plans for these delicate and
important works will require considerable time, even after
the topographical maps ordered near the end of last year are
received.

Meanwhile, under the careful guardianship of the Commission, the existing woods have been successfully defended
against fires ; while large, inflammable areas of previously

burnt and killed trees have been cleared away. In addition to these important conserving works, the Commission has directed the opening of a carriage road through the length of Blue Hills Reservation, and several similar roads in the Fells. This road-building has been done under the direction of the general and local superintendents of the reservations, with merely occasional suggestions from our office as to the choice of the woodpaths to be followed. The resulting roads are doubtless enjoyed by the driving public, but they possess bad grades and bad lines, and they certainly do not exhibit the scenery of the reservations as advantageously as it ought to be and may be exhibited. In view of these facts, and of the hitherto unavoidable uncertainty as to what parts of the wood roads may desirably become sections of the comprehensive scheme of permanent roads, we have consistently recommended the avoidance of all expensive construction. Until complete general plans can be prepared from data furnished by the topographical surveys, it seems advisable that the building of stone-filled and finely gravelled carriage roads should be avoided, and that such moneys as are available should be devoted to clearing a greater number of by-paths and bridle roads, and marking them systematically by guide-boards.

Similar and additional reasons obliged us, during the past summer, to advise the barring out of carriages from all the too narrow and rough by-paths of the reservations, including the path which leads to the summit of the much-frequented Great Blue Hill. This path possesses neither lines nor grades such as might fit it to become the permanent road to the hill-top. No money should, therefore, be thrown away in either widening or "stoning" it for carriage travel. It may properly be made a smooth footpath, and this has been done; but carriages should be excluded, because of its narrowness, crookedness, and steepness, as well as because of the danger and inconvenience to which foot passengers would be subjected by them.

In view of the unfortunately prolonged postponement of the making of general plans in accordance with which work may go on with surety, it is pleasant to report that the topographical surveyors, Messrs. French, Bryant & Taylor, have just at this writing completed their work; so that photo-lithographs of the maps of the Blue Hills and Fells reservations may soon be obtained. The scale of the original sheets of these maps is one hundred feet to an inch, and the contour interval five feet. The positions on the ground of the corners of the several sheets of the maps are marked by stone monuments or iron bolts, as are also the positions of the primary triangulation points and the bench marks of the surveys. The corresponding topographical survey of Stony Brook Reservation is now progressing under the direction of the engineer to the Commission, Mr. W. T. Pierce, whose appointment early in this year was noted at our office with particular satisfaction, which will be understood when it is remembered that all surveying up to that date had been distributed among several engineers whose offices were in different places.

The Lake, Brook, and River Reservations.

The public domains of this class opened and controlled by the Commission are five in number; namely, Stony Brook (already mentioned under Forests), Beaver Brook, Hemlock Gorge, Mystic River, and Charles River reservations.

At Beaver Brook Reservation the boundaries originally secured will protect reasonably well the delightful scenery of the place, although the lines are not generally such as will ever be suitable for streets. A part of the eastern boundary is formed by the existing highway called Mill Street, and we have made several plans and had several conferences with the engineer to the Middlesex County Commissioners with reference to securing a demanded widening of the " travelled way " without injury to the trees which line the eastern edge of the reservation. It seems important that binding agreements concerning widenings and maintenance should be entered into with all local or county authorities controlling such existing streets as border the reservations, or else that the control of such streets should be lodged in the Metropolitan Commission itself, just as the control of new boundary roads hereafter to be built on the now roadless edges of the reservations will be.

The boundaries of the new Hemlock Gorge Reservation
have been contrived so as to preserve the peculiarly interesting scenery of Charles River at this point, so far as this can
be accomplished without unreasonable expenditure.   The existing Boylston Street (or Worcester turnpike) forms the
northern boundary, and Ellis Street the eastern boundary,
save that the estates of a church and of the Newton Mills
have been omitted from the "taking."   Central Avenue
bridge makes the southern end of the public river-bank, while
the western border of the reservation is fixed upon a new
street to be eventually opened on a long curve extending from
Central Avenue to Reservoir Street.   It will be observed that
the banks of the storage reservoir adjacent to Worcester
Street have been included in the reservation in addition to
the Hemlock Gorge.   This pond or "back-water" will doubtless make a useful boating and skating place.   A topographical survey of this beautiful reservation is yet to be obtained.

Early in 1895 the Commission determined to acquire a continuous strip of ground in Medford and Winchester (see
accompanying map), forming a part of the possible Mystic
River Reservation, which had been suggested in the report
addressed by Mr. Eliot to the inquiring Commission of 1892–
93.   At the time when this partial project (called the Mystic
Valley Parkway) was under discussion, we felt obliged to
point out that the proposed public strip began and ended
illogically; that, instead of leading to the Fells, it paralleled
that reservation; and that, if it were to be regarded as an
independent reservation, it was badly bounded, in that none
of the western shore of the Mystic ponds was included.

Within the limits laid down, we have, however, done what
we could to secure rational boundaries.   From Main Street,
Winchester, southward to the Upper Mystic Pond, both banks
of the little Abbajona River will hereafter be preserved from
building operations.   Along the eastern shore of the Upper
Pond all the land which lies between the pond and the Lowell
Railroad has been acquired, and along the Lower Pond all
which lies between the water and the top of the adjacent and
almost continuous bluff.   In addition to these studies for
boundaries, complete designs for a continuous pleasure drive-

way, extending the whole length of the reservation, have been prepared and handed to the engineering department, where they have served as guides in the preparation of working-plans and profiles. Several conferences have been had with the engineer of the Middlesex County Commissioners respecting a widening of Bacon Street, Winchester, intended to accommodate the pleasure driving which must use that street to cross the Lowell Railroad and the Abbajona River. Other conferences have been held with representatives of the Brooks estates, concerning the connection of proposed new streets with the public pleasure-drive. It seems desirable that this precedent should be followed hereafter in all cases, and no street be permitted to obtain entrance to the boundary roads of the reservations unless the plans thereof are first approved as to both lines and grades.

When the legislature commanded the creation of a Charles River Reservation, it became our duty to review once more the peculiar conditions presented by this central stream of the metropolitan district, as well as to point out those parts of the river-bank which might be deemed to be of first importance to the public. The Park Commission of Cambridge was found to be already in possession of the north bank of the river from West Boston bridge to the Cambridge Hospital. The Park Commission of Boston we knew to be still intending to ultimately control an embankment from West Boston bridge to Cottage Farm. Immediately above Cottage Farm the south bank was found to be owned by the Boston and Albany Railroad and the Brookline Gas Light Company. Harvard University proved to be the owner of a long stretch just above North Harvard Street, while above Western Avenue the Abattoir possessed the bank. On the north side, the Cambridge Hospital, the Cambridge Cemetery, and the United States Arsenal were similarly found to own considerable river frontages. Accordingly plans were prepared for acquiring all frontages lying between the above-named tracts, as well as between the Abattoir and Maple Street, Newton, and between the Arsenal and the public landing in Watertown; and in submitting these plans to the Commission it was recommended that the designated tracts be acquired in

CHARLES RIVER RESERVATION

The Longfellow marshes with the water at Grade 8

CHARLES RIVER RESERVATION

The Longfellow marshes flooded by the tide

CHARLES RIVER RESERVATION

The river at Lemon Brook, with the water at Grade 8

CHARLES RIVER RESERVATION

The river at Lemon Brook, the tide having partly ebbed

sequence, beginning with the tract next above the Brookline gas works, and continuing upstream, along both banks, as far as the appropriation might allow.

The inland boundary of the lands which have since been " taken " is generally intended, as in the other reservations, to ultimately become the sidewalk line of a boundary street. Of the varying space between the north and south boundary roads, about half is salt water and flats, and the other half salt marsh; the former being easily convertible into fresh water of a permanent level, and the latter into fresh green meadow, by the building of a dam which shall exclude the tides. That it is clearly desirable to shut out the high tides is shown by the two contrasting pictures printed herewith. That it is even more advisable to hold the river water at a fairly constant elevation is shown by the second pair of pictures. The marshy plains can be saved from flooding, the marshy river-banks can be made usable and beautiful, the water area can be made navigable for boats and safe for skating, while its surface can be kept at or near one level, by the building of a dam, as was recommended to the General Court by the State Board of Health and the Metropolitan Park Commission in 1894.

The Bay and Seashore Reservations.

The public seashore already acquired through the agency of the Commission consists of the so-called Revere Beach.

For the " taking " of King's Beach, Swampscott, we were asked to suggest boundaries; but we understand that this reservation is hereafter to be controlled and managed by the local Park Commission of the town of Swampscott.[1]

The problem of the inland boundary line of Revere Beach Reservation required much study and many preliminary trials before it was satisfactorily solved. The natural curve of the beach is very fine, and it was our desire that the row of buildings which must eventually face the public beach throughout its whole length should be compelled to conform with exactness to this long and grand sweep. It was found, however, that the private lot lines on the beach conformed, for the

[1] Later assumed by the Metropolitan Park Commission.

most part, to the lines of the "location" of the Revere Beach
Railroad; and that these lines, instead of paralleling the natural lines of the beach, proceeded eastward by a succession
of alternating straight lines and curves. It was not advisable
to leave any sliver of the railroad location, or of any public
or semi-public streets or passageways, outside or west of the
reservation; neither was it advisable to place the boundary
line so near the water that the cost of future works of construction would be greater than the present cost of more land.
On the other hand, to push the boundary line far into the
private lands west of the railroad seemed likely to prove
expensive. The boundary finally fixed upon is, therefore, a
compromise line, which we believe will preserve the desirable
natural curve, while saving future outlays for construction,
so far as is possible without involving too great immediate
expense. For the slivers here and there taken from private
lands west of the railroad ample compensation is offered by
the total removal of the railroad and of all the view-blockad-
ing buildings between the railroad and the sea.

The circle at the southern end of the beach is intended to
form the common terminus of the present highways which
lead from Winthrop and from East Boston, and of the prospective highway which, it must be hoped, may some day
bring thousands to the beach from the direction of Chelsea,
Everett, Somerville, and Malden. The shore of Saugus River
is included in the reservation up to the point which a bridge
from Lynn may be expected to reach before many years. No
detailed plan for the development of the reservation has as
yet been prepared, but undoubtedly it may be expected to
include an ample sidewalk adjacent to the abutting private
land and a suitably wide accompanying driveway.

In addition to the Revere Beach studies, plans have been
prepared for a possible extension of the seashore reservation
along the coast of Revere and Winthrop to Great Head,
where a view of Boston harbor, as well as of the ocean, is
obtained. These plans, however, were ordered by the Commission in response to the request of the local Winthrop Park
Commission, and solely for the purpose of enabling the two
boards to jointly consider the advisability and the probable
expense of the proposed extension.

Metropolitan Parkways.

It will be remembered that a so-called "boulevard act," passed by the General Court of 1893–94, placed burdens upon the Commission which were entirely beyond and outside of all suggestions as to public reservations offered by the inquiring Commission of 1892–93. Realizing the gravity of the problems likely to arise if such enabling legislation should be duplicated, we suggested to the Commission the desirability of procuring a map of the metropolitan district, such as would enable the Commission to study the coming questions intelligently. A new map was ordered; and, after the lines of latitude and longitude had been plotted, the corners of the township boundary lines, as recently ascertained by the Massachusetts town boundary survey, were placed on the drawing, where they served as the framework into which all the more detailed information concerning the streets, etc., of each township was afterwards fitted as accurately as was possible. Much of the obtainable detailed information is well known to be erroneous; but the skeleton being now fixed by the work of the State survey, the details can be corrected from time to time, as better information is received. The sketched contours of the United States geological survey and the data concerning wooded areas gathered by the same survey have also been placed upon the map, together with some new information as to the courses of streams specially obtained by sending men into the field in certain districts. Under an arrangement made by the Commission with the governing committee of the Appalachian Mountain Club, this new map is to be published by the club at a greatly reduced scale, namely, 1–62,500.

With respect to the improvement of main avenues leading southward and westward from Boston, the present year has seen a remarkable advance. Dorchester Avenue is now a fairly finished city street all the way to Neponset River, — six miles from the State House. Blue Hill Avenue is in process of widening from Grove Hall and Franklin Park to Neponset River at Mattapan, — six and one half miles from the State House. Washington Street is fast building up all the way to Forest Hills. Columbus Avenue is in process of extension to Franklin Park. Huntington Avenue is being widened to Brookline. Beacon Street has been widened to Chestnut Hill Reservoir. Commonwealth Avenue has been widened to the Reservoir and onward through Newton to Charles River at Auburndale, — ten miles from the State House. Moreover, in the widened Blue Hill Avenue, Huntington Avenue, Beacon Street, and Commonwealth Avenue special central reservations have been secured for electric cars.

Turning to the region north of Charles River, which so nearly bisects the metropolitan district, we find numerous principal radial streets, such as Massachusetts Avenue, Mystic Avenue, Highland Avenue, Broadway (Everett), and the Lynn and Salem turnpike; but none of these have yet been widened or arranged with separate tracks for electrics. The northern suburbs are apparently hampered in their development by their complex subdivision into separate townships, as well as by the natural obstacles to convenient access presented by the Mystic River, its branching creeks, and the accompanying salt marshes.

However this may be, it presently became clear that, in taking up the work of opening " parkways " under the special command of the legislature, no regard could be paid by the Metropolitan Park Commission to the relative lack or abundance of existing avenues on one side or the other of the central city, but that the available appropriation could most suitably be devoted to the acquirement and construction of such car and carriage highways as might best connect the centre of population of the metropolitan district with the newly opened public forests at the Middlesex Fells and the Blue Hills. General plans for the Fells and Blue Hills Parkways, devised in accordance with this theory, are submitted herewith.

The general course of the proposed Middlesex Fells Parkway was described in our last annual report. [See p. 510.]

Early in the present year the Commission obtained possession of the land required for the realization of those parts of the general design which lie between the Fells Reservation and the east and west highway which in Malden is called Pleasant Street and in Medford Salem Street. These were the first "takings" of land made in this neighborhood for highways to be built and governed by metropolitan as distinguished from local authority, and the details of the plans and taking lines were studied with great care. Before the lines were finally determined, many topographical surveys had been made by the engineer, and many alternative courses had been sketched by us. For these two branches of the proposed parkway grading-plans have also been prepared and handed to the engineer, who in turn has drawn working-plans and specifications for the guidance of the work of construction which is in progress at this writing. Each branch of the parkway possesses two roadways, one of which is thirty-six and the other twenty-six feet wide. Between the roadways is a grassed space for the exclusive use of electric cars, and outside of the roadways are the necessary sidewalks. The total normal width is only one hundred and twenty feet, but it is understood that all buildings fronting on the parkway will be set back at least twenty feet, so that the total width between buildings will be one hundred and sixty feet.

Where the western arm of the parkway diverges from Forest Street, Medford, the broader of the two roadways continues, towards the city, the Winchester-Medford boundary road of the Fells Reservation. As far as Valley Street, Medford, the parkway possesses an abnormal width for the sake of including between the two roads the course of a brook, as well as space for electric cars. Near Valley Street it is to be hoped that the improvements now making by the city of Medford along Gravelly Creek may be extended to connect with the parkway. Thence to Salem Street the new parkway is an improved substitute for Valley Street, the course of which it closely follows.

The eastern arm of the parkway, now under construction, leaves the reservation at the foot of Bear's Den Hill, the broader road being the easternmost. As far as Highland Avenue, Malden, its course is through rough lands, not yet subdivided by streets. Between the avenue and the Malden park, called Fellsmere, the parkway is obtained by widening

Auburn Street on its eastern side, where several houses have been necessarily disturbed. Along the eastern side of Fellsmere the broader road of the parkway makes the boundary road of the park, while it is hoped that the Malden Park Commission may eventually carry the narrower roadway around the western side of the Mere to a connection with Murray Street, which becomes a part of the parkway between Fellsmere and Pleasant Street. From this last mentioned section three houses had to be removed. Deep cutting was also required here, in order to obtain a practicable grade.

South of Salem and Pleasant streets, where no land has been acquired and no construction begun, the general plan calls for a union of the two branches of the parkway in a circle, and its continuation thence to Mystic River by a line which curves in order to avoid a factory, in order to cross the Medford Branch Railway at right angles, and in order to skirt closely along the edge of the fine building land which lies just west of the modern suburb of Wellington. For effectiveness, a straight avenue across such level land is preferable ; but a straight line would in this case secure none of the economies and advantages just mentioned. South of Wellington the proposed parkway is planned to join the existing Highland Avenue, from which avenue it parts again at the southern end of the bridge over Mystic River, in order to strike a straight course for Broadway Park, the widened boundary roads of which will carry pleasure driving comfortably to Broadway. From Wellington to Broadway the two parallel roads should be of even and ample width, in order to accommodate heavy traffic as well as pleasure driving. Here, as elsewhere, it is expected that traffic will be excluded from one of the roadways of the parkway.

Concerning the general course of the corresponding Blue Hills Parkway, we wrote a year ago. [See p. 510.] Since that date, Blue Hill Reservation has been extended from Crossman's Pines to Harland Street, Milton, in the form of a narrow strip, the western edge of which is the foot of a range of hills, while the eastern edge is a straight line drawn arbitrarily through the midst of a swamp. A boundary road giving access to adjacent building lands will eventually be called for on the western edge of this strip, and the possible electric car tracks may then find place alongside. For the accommodation of pleasure driving to and from the reservation, and particularly from Hoosic-Whisick by way of Ponkapog Pass, the general plan suggests an entirely separate roadway leading from Crossman's Pines to Canton Avenue opposite Mattapan Street, by way of the centre of the strip just mentioned and the bottom of the charming valley of Pine Tree Brook. In order to obtain this desirable separate pleasure driveway, to preserve the scenery commanded by it, and at the same time accommodate ordinary traffic, it is suggested that Harland Street be discontinued so far as it now lies within the valley, and that two boundary roads, one on each side of the valley, be substituted for it. These roads will include between them the best of the local scenery. They will also develop adjacent building land, while supplying the desired route for traffic.

At Canton Avenue it seems necessary that the separate pleasure drive should end ; but a parkway like the Fells Parkway, one hundred and twenty feet wide, is planned to follow the course of Mattapan Street all the way to the Neponset River at Mattapan, where the Blue Hill Avenue of Boston will be joined. Again, we should prefer a straight line for this section of the parkway, but economy seems to command the crook which the plan shows near Mattapan. The present Mattapan Street is not quite, though nearly, straight, and the contemplated widening consequently cuts peculiar slices from many estates. It also involves the moving of several houses. By careful adjustment of the lines, the large trees near Mattapan can, however, be preserved, either in the central or the sidewalk planting-strips. A new and more capacious bridge over Neponset River will naturally be needed whenever the parkway is built. Thus far, no land having been acquired, construction has not begun ; but the general plan having been approved by the Commission, it is herewith submitted for publication.

In conclusion, we may perhaps point out that the various public open spaces now or soon to be controlled by the Me-

tropolitan Park Commission include more numerous large
public pleasure grounds than are governed by any other
public authority in northern America, excepting the govern-
ments of the United States and Canada.   Blue Hills Reservation is five miles long ; Middlesex Fells Reservation, two
miles square ; Stony Brook Reservation, two miles long ;
Charles River Reservation (including semi-public river-
banks), five miles long ; Mystic Valley Parkway, two miles
long ; the Fells and Blue Hills Parkways each three miles
long, and Revere Beach Reservation three miles long.   The
legislation of 1893, by which the cities and towns surrounding Boston were enabled to coöperate with Boston in obtaining suitable public open spaces, has certainly proved effective.

November 30, 1895.

A few weeks after the foregoing report was sent in, Charles
had occasion to deal, in the annual report of the firm to the
Boston Park Commissioners, with the evil of huge hoardings
set up beside highways, parkways, and railroads.

Upon private lands adjacent to several of the boundary
roads and parkways, huge advertising boards or " hoardings "
have been set up during the past year, to the disgust of all
sensible persons.   Throughout the State, similar advertising
has greatly increased of late, " hoardings " being placed on
private lands within view of all the principal railroads and
highways.   It seems that the Public Statutes permit the
painting or posting of advertisements on natural or artificial
objects, wherever the consent of the owner can be obtained by
the advertiser.   Moreover, the penalty attached to such painting or posting without consent is very small, while the difficulties in the way of catching offending persons are great.   It
is obvious that the conditions are favorable for a rapid increase of the advertising plague throughout the country, until
the vacant lands adjacent to every much-frequented spot shall
all be adorned by reminders of soaps, pills, and tonics.

That such advertising is in many places damaging to public
interests, and even to private property, cannot be doubted.   It
should be allowed only as the keeping of dogs, the building
of stables, the opening of drinking-saloons, and the giving of

public entertainments are allowed in civilized communities; namely, upon permit granted by police commissioners or selectmen. Public opinion undoubtedly condemns such advertising along the Boston parkways, and it is lamentable that the statutes are so far behind the times as to prevent the execution of the public will in this matter.

In the same report he replied with patient moderation to ill-considered criticisms on the Boston parks which about that time appeared frequently in Boston newspapers. Most of the critics complained that "nature" was too much interfered with in the parks which Mr. Frederick Law Olmsted had designed for the city during the twenty years preceding; and their notion of "nature" seemed to be the desirable surroundings of a family country-seat, or the aspect of a lonely New England farm with its brook, lanes, fields, and wood-paths.

The Boston parks, after nearly twenty years of effort, have only lately reached that stage of development which enables the general public to begin to understand what parks really are, and what the designing of them means. Crowded populations need space for exercise, for air, and for obtaining the refreshing sense of openness, and the sight of sky, distance, and landscape, of which they are so completely deprived in the streets. The Adirondacks, the White Mountains, and the Maine woods supply for many persons who can afford to travel to them the needed antidote to city life. The nearer, more thoroughly humanized, and yet unsophisticated landscape of rural townships affords annual refreshment to thousands of others. For the recreation of those who must remain in town, why is it not possible to purchase an attractive and acceptable rural area, comprising woods, fields, streams, and ponds, and preserve it forever in that charming condition which is the product of the natural partnership of man and nature? No gravel paths are half so charming as the turfed wood-roads of New England farms, no shrubbery so pleasing as those which nature rears along the farmer's walls, no pools so lovely as those which, fringed with natural growths, fill and drain away according to the season and the supply of rain. Possibly it is a pity that such preservation of rural conditions in public parks is impossible, but that it is impossible is

certain. The woodland and the farming land, the embowered
pond, the river-banks, which possessed such fresh beauty and
such virgin charm so long as they were frequented merely
by the farmer and his boys, occasional sportsmen, or the
owners of the country-seat, will inevitably be despoiled of
much of their attractiveness when they are invaded by thousands of persons every week or afternoon. The undergrowth
of the woods is soon broken and trampled, the beautiful
fringe of the little pool is reduced to mire, the old trail along
the river-bank is soon worn so wide and deep that the roots
are exposed and the trees slowly killed. But because it is
thus impossible to preserve the charms belonging to the quiet
country-side, is it necessary to abandon the attempt to secure
for city people some measure, at least, of that refreshment
which they so sorely need? The Boston parks, incomplete as
they still are, already answer this question in the negative.
Formed slowly, in accordance with well-studied plans, it is
now evident that Charlesbank and Charlestown Heights, the
Fens and the Parkway, Leverett, Jamaica, and Franklin
Parks supply, each in its own way, kinds and means of recreation both helpful and valuable. Fresh air and exercise in
pleasant surroundings are obtained at the two first-named
places. The Fens and Parkway will furnish miles of agreeable roads which, with all the adjacent houses of the future,
will command views of stream-side scenery very unusual in
the midst of a city. Lastly, in Franklin Park there is found
a leafy screen which hides the town, a breadth of view, an
openness, a peculiar kind of scenery, which, in spite of necessarily broad roads and gravel walks is refreshing, interesting, and beautiful in a high degree. Such park scenery bears
little resemblance to either the ideal landscape of painters,
or the so-called natural landscape of farms, orchards, and
wood-lots. No designer of parks has ever pretended to imitate these kinds of landscape; and no sensible person will
criticise a park for their absence or presence. It is the calling and duty of the conscientious landscape architect to devise
ways of arranging land and its accompanying landscape so
that, whatever the particular purpose in view may be, the
result shall be as thoroughly convenient, and at the same time

as thoroughly beautiful, as possible. This is the problem which presents itself in countless forms — in the smallest suburban lot and the finest country-seat, the new seaside pleasure resort and the new factory town, the public school-boys' playground and the ornate city square. The country park of a great city presents this universal problem in one of its most difficult phases. Such a park is a tract of land dedicated to a particular purpose, namely, the refreshment of the bodies and souls of great numbers of people. In arranging land and landscape with this purpose in view, it is undoubtedly desirable to follow as far as possible the dictates of poetic and artistic feeling for breadth of composition and picturesqueness of detail. On the other hand, it is a law of nature which must not be forgotten, that satisfying beauty springs from fitness, or adaptation to purpose, much more surely and directly than from added ornament, or the most careful imitation. At all events, it is in this faith that the undersigned have worked for years upon the plans and designs of the Boston parks, with what measure of success only time can determine.

January 27, 1896.

CHAPTER XXIX

WHAT WOULD BE FAIR MUST FIRST BE FIT

Wilt thou not ope thy heart to know
What rainbows teach and sunsets show ?

RALPH WALDO EMERSON.

THE two book reviews and two newspaper articles which are united in this chapter all teach the same doctrine, namely, — that the landscape of civilization is an artificial landscape, which may be either beautiful or ugly, and that the root of landscape beauty is adaptation to the delight and service of men.

Art Out of Doors. By Mrs. Schuyler Van Rensselaer.

Before attempting to note the conspicuous merits and deficiencies of this charmingly made book, it may be well to sketch the outlines of that exceedingly broad field of human labor in which Mrs. Van Rensselaer would have us work " artistically." Ever since man became man he has been remodelling the face of the earth. His blind trails through the forests have become highways and railroads. His wigwams and pueblos are now farmsteads and great cities. The prairies are become his grain-fields and the forests his lumber yards. Purely natural scenery is already a distant rarity, what is called such being generally the distinctly humanized landscape of coppice, pasture, and farm. That all this labor of men is vandalism is the cry of sentimentalists; but men of sense remain of the opinion that the world would be a dull place without its fields and roads, its cottages and mansions, its villages and cities, its rails of shining steel, and all its other grand, lovely, or pathetic evidences of man's toiling and aspiring life. The transformers of the earth have seldom aimed to produce beauty, yet beauty has time and again sprung up under their hands — witness the English churchyard, the Swedish farmstead, the New England pasture or village. There is no mystery about this. Human happiness is not won by giving one's thoughts to the direct pursuit of it ; neither is beauty in the surroundings of life. Although man is conscious and Nature is unconscious, the man who hopes for beauty must work as Nature works, and must trustfully obey her laws of purpose, utility, and adaptation to circumstance. Beauty is not to be won as an immediate aim. It is a result, a development, a flower.

It is to be regretted that no general account of either the breadth or the depth of the subject described by its title is to be found in the book before us. Its various chapters deal lightly and pleasantly with such special problems as the groupings of trees and shrubs, the attachment of houses to their sites, roads and paths, formal gardens, piazzas, and so on ; the plea of the book being that all such problems should be solved in an " artistic spirit." The advice offered is well put, and the book should have a multitude of readers. Our only fear is lest the author has inadequately warned these readers of the main facts, that good " art out of doors " must be founded in rationality, purpose, fitness ; and that its field is not only the garden, the shrubbery, and the park, but also the village, the factory, and the railroad yard. According to this book, landscape architecture is much like house-furnishing : a selecting of agreeably harmonizing elements in the shape of buildings, rocks, trees, climbing-plants, and so on. The essentially virile and practical nature of the art and profession is ignored, together with most of its greater and more democratic problems. But when this has been said and allowance made, the book remains the best book in its field that we have had in many a day. Its style is exceedingly good, and its tone puts it above comparison with the books of the horticulturists which are its only contemporary rivals for the public ear.

Italian Gardens. By C. A. Platt.

The scenery of the earth was made for man, not man for scenery. Civilized man enjoys natural scenery as the savage cannot, and he permanently preserves what he may of it in parks and public forests. Elsewhere he is necessarily a transformer and destroyer of nature. The landscape of civilization is an artificial landscape, and as such it may be either beautiful or ugly — beautiful when it is the blossom of use, convenience, or necessity; ugly when it is the fruit of pompous pride or common carelessness. The gardens of the Renaissance in Italy, France, and England have been thoughtlessly ridiculed in modern days because of their unlikeness to wild nature. As well revile a palace for its unlikeness to a wigwam. The vast extent and the tiresome repetitions of some of the gardens in question may convict them of the sin of vainglorious display; but if they fitly served any human need or pleasure, their unnaturalness was no sin. Likeness or unlikeness to wild nature is no criterion of merit. Farmsteads, country roads, villages, city streets, and world's fairs are all more or less removed from nature and naturalness, yet even the last-named may be beautiful, as we have lately seen. Fitness for purpose is the safe foundation of the art of arranging land and landscape for the use and enjoyment of men.

That the gardens of the classic world and the Italian Renaissance fitly served a worthy purpose, there can be no doubt. In the Italian climate, halls and drawing-rooms out of doors were even more to be desired than parlors indoors. Groves, parterres, terraces, and approaches were designed conjointly with the house or palace to form one composition — the so-called "villa." The boundary of the villa was a sharp line separating it from the hills of Tivoli or the plains of the Campagna. Inside, the boundary was the formality which befits stately living; outside, yet in view from the terraces, was the informality and picturesqueness of the natural world.

Rightly thinking that these villas of Italy may teach lessons of value to the America of to-day, Mr. Platt has published in the book before us forty full-page pictures of their buildings, pavilions, terraces, water-basins, and gardens, with many smaller drawings and photographs of architectural details. He has made an uncommonly charming yet truthful picture-book. We are compelled to wish he had done more. The text of the book is very handsomely printed with wide margins, but it consists of the briefest of notes. Even if it be "taken purely as supplementary to the illustrations," as we are asked to take it, it is very unsatisfying. For the fairly-to-be-expected elucidation of the plates, plans (as well as fuller notes) are sadly needed, yet only one is provided. On the first page mention is made of the great book of Percier and Fontaine, and it is stated that there exists no other work " of any great latitude " treating of Italian gardens. Evidently our author is not acquainted with W. P. Tuckermann's " Die Gartenkunst der Italienischen Renaissance-Zeit," published in Berlin in 1884, and containing, besides twenty-one plates and numerous other cuts, some twenty ground plans and cross-sections of Renaissance villas.

In the grassless regions of our South and Southwest, in the necessarily rectilinear public squares of our cities, in connection with stately buildings in all parts of our country, be they public offices in Washington or hotels by Lake George, the formal lines of the Italian villa will always be acceptable because they will always be fitting. Our public has still to learn that only by designing buildings and their surroundings as one harmonious composition can a happy result be secured in either the formal or the picturesque style. The recent World's Fair taught this lesson very clearly. Mr. Platt's delightful pictures teach it also. If those whom these pictures interest will turn from them to the works of Tuckermann, Repton, and the other professional writers on landscape architecture, and then will practice what they learn therefrom, Mr. Platt will have accomplished a good work for America.

January 3, '94.

WHAT WOULD BE FAIR MUST FIRST BE FIT.

A constantly increasing number of Americans are desirous of securing some measure of beauty in the surroundings of their every-day lives. These people are not content with things as they are. They want more and more of pleasantness in and around their own houses and about their village, town, or city as well.

To these earnest and inquiring people come a numerous company of writers and would-be missionaries, who, however, preach strangely differing gospels. First to appear are the gentlemanly agents of the commercial nurserymen. These bring many books of pictures of more or less lovely and rare plants, shrubs, and trees, and say, " Look, you can make your surroundings beautiful if you will plant some of these interesting and lovely things. You ought to screen that ugly fence with Roses, scatter ' specimen ornamentals' about your grounds, and put a bed of Cannas before your door." Next come the more pretentious landscape gardeners, who prescribe curves for paths .and other approaches as being more " natural" than straight lines, and then propose plantations to fit or account for the curves. These gentry talk much about Nature, and affect to consider formal treatment of ground and planting a sort of profanation. They are of many schools, for some will urge the planting of purple Beeches, blue Spruces, and all manner of exotics, while others say, " You will do well to use few but wild native shrubs. What can be lovelier than this wayside group of red Cedar, Bayberry, and wild Rose?" Thirdly come the modern American architects, whose technical training has been acquired at the Parisian Ecole des Beaux Arts. These hold up their hands in holy horror at the landscape gardeners of all schools, and say to the inquiring public, " Let us show you how wrong these men are! What you really need to make your surroundings beautiful are straight avenues, terraces and balustrades, a ' rampe douce' at your door and a sun-dial in an old-fashioned garden."

This is no fanciful picture of the strange conflict of modern doctrine concerning beauty in the surroundings of daily life. It is no wonder that the inquiring public is bewildered. Controversial papers and books are continually appearing. Bad language is employed by all parties; but the modern architects appear to be decidedly the most skilled in its use. Such adjectives as asinine, silly, and ridiculous are not uncommon in the writings of Messrs. Blomfield, Thomas, and Seddings, who, however, are English and not American controversialists.

How absurd all this quarrelling seems when once a moment can be obtained for sober reflection. Is beauty, as a matter of fact, often won by following shifting fads or fashions, by

heaping up decorations, by gathering architectural or botanical specimens, however remarkable or even lovely? On the
contrary, it is by wrong-headed attempts to win beauty in
these impossible ways that the ignorant rich and their imitators so often succeed in putting pretentious ugliness in place
of simple loveliness and charm; witness the greater part of
Newport, and many another once pleasing region now sophisticated and destroyed.

Little or no thought being given to the fundamental arrangement of lands and buildings for convenience and beauty,
an attempt is often made to retrieve the situation by adding
decorations, such as statues, fountains, and bridges, or, more
generally, a selection from the marvellous products of modern
nursery gardens. In those rarer cases where some real attention is devoted to the all-important fundamental arrangement, the design is apt to be strictly limited by the supposed
requirements of the particular style of treatment which may
be selected. The picturesque, the gardenesque, and the formal styles are soberly discussed; but selection is apt to be
made according to fancy merely, and the results, as in the
first-mentioned class of cases, are generally amusing or striking rather than beautiful. A house scene filled with irrationally curved paths is seldom lovelier than one which is
decked with a collection of contrasting specimens. A private
country house approached by an unnecessary triple avenue,
and fitted with steps and terraces broad enough for a state
capitol, is equally amusing in its way.

The cause of the failure to attain to beauty in these and all
similar cases is doubtless the same; it is (is it not?) the common lack of rationality at the foundation.

How is it that so much of the natural scenery of the world
is beautiful, and that so many myriad kinds of living things
are lovely? The fact may not be explicable, but " it is one
of the commonplaces of science that the form which every
vital product takes has been shaped for it by natural selection through a million ages, with a view to its use, advantage, or convenience, and that beauty has resulted from that
evolution."

How is it that so much of the humanized landscape of the

world is lovely? Is not the same natural law at work here
also? The generations who by their arduous labor made the
scenery of Italy, England, and the valleys of New England
what each is to-day —

> " wrought with a sad sincerity.
> Themselves from God they could not free,
> They builded better than they knew,
> The conscious (earth) to beauty grew. "

In New England, for example, the hard-worked men of
the last century cleared and smoothed the intervales, left
fringes of trees along the streams and hanging woods on the
steep hillsides, gathered their simple houses into villages and
planted Elms beside them, for " use, advantage, and convenience " merely, and yet beauty is the result. Truly, —

> " this is an art
> Which does mend nature, change it rather ;
> But the art itself is nature."

The moral to be taken to heart by the sophisticated and
self-conscious seekers after beauty in our present day is obvious. Success in achieving the beautiful is to be hoped for
only when we bow to the law of nature, and follow in the
appointed way. Special purpose is the root, and fitness for
purpose the main stem, of the plant of which beauty is the
flower. As William Wyndham wrote to Humphrey Repton,
" Lands should be laid out solely with a view to their uses
and enjoyment in real life. Conformity to these purposes
is the one foundation of their true beauty."

Thus, the right planning of the arrangement of lands for
private country-seats or suburban houses, for public squares,
playgrounds, or parks, for villages, or for cities, is not a
question of " the gardenesque " or " the picturesque," " the
artificial " or " the natural," " the symmetrical " or " the
unsymmetrical." Whoever, regardless of circumstances, insists upon any particular style or mode of arranging land
and its accompanying landscape, is most certainly a quack.
He has overlooked the important basal fact, that although
beauty does not consist in fitness, nevertheless all that would
be fair must first be fit. True art is expressive before it

is beautiful; at its highest it is still the adornment of a service.

The modern practitioners of Renaissance architecture need especially to be reminded that they have not a monopoly of the lovely. " Symmetry is beautiful, but so, also, is the unsymmetrical relation of the parts to a whole in Nature." Since all natural landscape, save that of the plains and the oceans, is unsymmetrical, it follows that humanized landscape is also generally and fittingly informal. Such landscape properly becomes symmetrical or formal only occasionally and for good reasons. The roads of a hilly park rightly curve to avoid obstacles or to secure easy grades; but a particular spot within that park, intended for the gathering-place of crowded audiences at band concerts, is rightly graded evenly and symmetrically and shaded by trees set in rows. Again, the fields and woods of a country-seat are rightly disposed picturesquely, while those outdoor halls and rooms of the mansion called the terrace and the flower garden are just as rightly treated formally and decoratively. The naturalists are justified in thinking formal work often impertinent and out of place. The formalists and the decorators are justified so long as their work is rooted in usefulness and adaptation to purpose. " Each has its proper situation ; and good taste will make fashion subservient to good sense," wrote Humphrey Repton. It is to be hoped that our quarrelling faddists may take to heart this saying, and may turn themselves to the advancement of Repton's real and much-needed art of arranging land, vegetation, buildings, and the resultant landscape for the use and delight of men.

April 1, 1896.

Of the above article the late W. A. Stiles, Editor of " Garden and Forest," wrote to Charles, March 31, 1896 : —
" If it teaches all our readers as much as it has taught me, you ought to feel gratified as an educator."
He had previously (March 28th) said of it : " I consider [it] one of the most discriminating and useful articles that has ever been published in ' Garden and Forest,' that is, it states principles which have never before been stated, or, at least, which have not been defined and separated from other matters so cleanly and clearly."

" THE GENTLE ART OF DEFEATING NATURE."

To the Editor of the "Transcript," — Your readers may well be weary of the subject of your recent editorial with the above title, since you have published substantially the same lamentation annually during several years. The following jottings contain, however, only cheerful words, and you may therefore be ready to give space to them.

That the red men have disappeared from the neighborhood of Boston may or may not be cause for tears ; but when the departure of the " Indian maiden " is lamented, it seems as if it might be well to mention that she fled, not last year, but generations ago. Nature long since and gladly surrendered to man the spaces now known as Jamaica and Franklin parks. The shore of Jamaica Pond was, until lately, occupied by two vast icehouses, and by the generally stone-walled and more or less well-kept back yards and pleasure grounds of suburban houses. A water company was, also, continually busy drawing off the water, with the result that a broad beach and even several shoals were laid bare every summer. Similarly, Franklin Park was, until lately, a conglomeration of the woodlots, pastures, fields, lawns, gardens, and avenues appurtenant to many suburban mansions and estates. Your headline printed above seems therefore to indicate serious self-deception. " Nature " was " defeated " long before the Park Commission was created.

To suggest that the Commission ought to have restored the primitive forests (which was Nature in these parts) would be too absurd. To suggest that the Commissioners should have preserved the man-made groves, fields, gardens, and pond shores precisely as they found them when they took possession for the city would be equally, though perhaps not so obviously, irrational. The areas in question had been laboriously worked over in times past by numerous owners guided solely by regard for their individual profit and pleasure ; and let it be noted that much beauty resulted. Common sense has similarly directed the Park Commissioners, representing the present single owner, the city, to straightforwardly adapt the new public estates to the common use and benefit of the people. The acquisition of land for a particular purpose necessarily involves the adaptation of the land in question to its designated purpose, else the price of the land is thrown away. And this necessity will alarm no one who is unde-ceived concerning "nature." The work of man and his do-mestic animals on the land and vegetation of rural New Eng-land has greatly increased the variety, interest, and beauty of the primitive landscape, and if the Park Commission will ad-just the park lands to their peculiar modern uses with equal frankness and directness, experience teaches that the happiest results may be expected. It is, indeed, a law of God that interesting and even beautiful appearance shall be the blossom of adaptation to purpose, and in this law we all of us need to have stronger faith.

With respect to changes and adaptations already made or planned, the Park Commission and the park architects wel-come honest criticism; but the questions of design which are involved are fully as technical and professional as those which confront the architects of buildings, and almost too compli-cated to be helpfully debated in print. Some preliminary account of them may be found in Mr. Olmsted's "Notes on the Plan of Franklin Park," and in the successive reports of the landscape architects. It is, moreover, to be remembered that the adopted plans in accordance with which the parks are slowly forming were devised to meet the requirements and purposes of the future as well as the present; and that for true economy's sake the Commission has from the first chosen to build whatever is built as for the future, regardless of whether this particular path is strictly necessary to-day, whether this road might be narrower for the present, or this bridge less strong, until the day comes when it may be crowded. This question of the advisability of immediate or permanent, as opposed to postponed or temporary construc-tion is, of course, debatable; but it should always be argued apart from questions of design. It should be remembered, also, that in the course of thus adapting means to ends, tem-porary ugliness is something only to be expected. Raw stones, gravel, and loam, and newly planted and small trees make ugly landscape, particularly when they surround half empty ponds, like those which have been so often cited in the " Transcript." On the other hand, we of the present ought to be ready to bear some trials and burdens of this sort if the people of the future may thereby secure recreation grounds well fitted to their needs. The banks of the long waterway of the Fens and Muddy River were lately completely changed from their " natural " state, and for a time left very raw, but they already plainly indicate to those who thread the stream that adaptation to new purposes does not necessarily involve any final, or even long, banishment of beauty.

CHAPTER XXX

CHARLES RIVER — 1891-96

'T is we ourselves, each one of us, who must keep watch and ward
over the fairness of the earth, and each with his own soul and hand do
his due share therein, lest we deliver to our sons a lesser treasure than
our fathers left to us. — MORRIS.

THE treatment of the tidal estuary called Charles River
was the most important park problem which the new Metropolitan District had to solve; and after nine years of the
extraordinarily successful operations of the Metropolitan Park
Commission, it still remains the one supremely important
æsthetic and financial problem on which final action has not
been taken by the Commonwealth, although successive approaches have been made towards a fortunate issue of the
long-drawn discussions.[1] The wise solution is sure ultimately
to give the District a central water-park of surpassing beauty
and usefulness, and to make Boston the best parked city in
the world, because of the extent and variety of its easily accessible public reservations.

Charles's writings on this subject from 1892 to 1896 inclusive enable one to follow the course of discussion, and
the progress of executive action, on this vital subject; and in
them one may also trace the change his own mind underwent
between 1891 and 1894. His early studies of the estuary
were all made under the influence of the long-accepted doctrine that Boston Harbor is kept from filling up by the "scouring" effect of the ebbing waters of the numerous creeks and
inlets above the Navy Yard; and it was not until the spring
of 1894 that his mind was free to entertain the thought of
excluding the tide altogether from the Charles River Basin.
When, however, eminent engineers like Hiram F. Mills and
Frederic P. Stearns declared in the Report of the joint Board
on the Improvement of Charles River (House Doc. 775,
April, 1894) that in their judgment a dam near Craigie's

[1] For early projects concerning the river and its basin, see the plan
facing p. 34 in the Memorial History of Boston, volume iv., A. "Dam
to form a pond of this river." 1814; a pamphlet by Uriel H. Crocker of
Boston, published in 1870, with a map; and lithographs published from
1873 to 1885, by Charles Davenport of Cambridge.

Bridge, high enough to exclude the highest tides, would do no harm whatever to the harbor, and supported their opinion with convincing arguments drawn from new investigations, and from the altered conditions of the harbor as regards the discharge into it of sewerage, silt, and material from its shores, Charles welcomed this well-grounded opinion, and thereafter felt free to advocate the complete exclusion of the tide from Charles River in the interest, pecuniary, sanitary, and æsthetic, of all the municipalities which touch the river, but particularly of Boston, Cambridge, and Watertown. So long as the thorough method of reforming the river — namely, the construction of a high dam to exclude the tides, which twice daily dammed the river and soaked its lowlands — seemed to Charles impracticable, however desirable, he advocated inferior but useful expedients, such as sea walls, ripraps, and low dams at Cottage Farm, or higher up the stream, to hold back the descending water ; but as soon as the most effectual method appeared to be both safe and practicable he advocated that and no other.

In recent years it has become the universally accepted view that Boston Harbor and its approaches must be made, and kept, deep enough for modern vessels by dredging and blasting. The theoretical " scour " action — never of proved effectiveness — has given way to the sure-working dredge and drill.

The legislature of 1891 created a commission on the Improvement of Charles River, consisting of the Mayors of Boston, Cambridge, and Newton, the chairman of the Selectmen of Watertown, and three citizens to be appointed by the Governor, the commission to serve without pay, and for two years as their term of office. Charles was appointed by Governor Russell a member of this body. The commissioners personally examined the state of the river and of its banks, held a long series of public hearings, at which many interested citizens of Boston, Cambridge, Watertown, and Newton appeared, and in two reports, one presented in March, 1892, and the other in April, 1893, summarized the evidence before them, and stated their own conclusions. Both these reports were written by Charles as the scribe of the commission — he was not officially its Secretary. The reports prepared by him were intended to express the mind of the commission, and were accepted by them at a second reading. The opportunity to investigate thoroughly this central problem of " greater Boston " was of value to Charles ; and this value was heightened when the task of draughting the reports was assigned to him. The two reports of the commission follow : —

FIRST REPORT OF THE CHARLES RIVER IMPROVEMENT
COMMISSION.

THE undersigned commissioners, appointed under chapter 390 of the Acts of 1891 for the purpose of considering what improvement can be made in the Charles River Basin between the dam at Watertown and the Charles River Bridge in Boston, and for other related purposes which are stated in the Act, a copy of which is hereunto appended, respectfully submit the following report, covering their investigations to February 1, 1892.

The commissioners first met and organized July 23, 1891, and immediately set themselves to study in person the complicated problem they found before them. The ragged banks of the Charles were familiar enough to all the commissioners, and yet a journey up and down the stream in a tow-boat proved instructive. It not only afforded the commissioners present a new and comprehensive view of the condition of the river and its banks, but it also gave them a vivid impression of the serious obstruction to navigation presented even to a tow-boat by the numerous bridges, and by the railroad bridges in particular.

In pursuance of the policy of gathering all the important facts of the case before drawing conclusions or making recommendations, the commissioners next instituted a prolonged series of public hearings, at which full opportunity was given the citizens of Boston, Cambridge, Newton, and Watertown to present facts, and to state their views as to the future of the river and its banks. The views, desires, and ideas set forth at these hearings were diverse and conflicting, but many solid and pertinent facts were incidentally brought out. It is upon these facts of nature, of past history, and of the present time, that any and every intelligent solution of the problem presented by Charles River must be based, and therefore the commission offers no apology for submitting the following summary of these fundamental facts as the principal part of this preliminary report.

The natural or physical character of Charles River is and always was peculiar. In the first place, the so-called " river "

is not a river. It is a tidal estuary, a shallow and muddy
trough, broad in its seaward part, narrow and tortuous in its
inward extension, and filled and almost emptied by the tide
twice every day. At high tide the original Back Bay was
about three miles long and two miles wide, and the original
" river " wound its way inland five crooked miles to the natural head of the tide in Watertown. When the tide is out,
the upper mile of the trough in Watertown is drained practically dry; the four succeeding miles of narrow channel
retain only from one to ten feet of water, and the bottom of the
lower basin is exposed over at least half its area. The rise and
fall of the tide averages about ten feet, and the consequent
rapid seaward rush of the ebb out of the river is an important factor in producing that scouring of the ship channel
of Boston Bay which is necessary for the preservation of its
depth. Except at the extreme inland part of its course, the
natural rim of this tidal trough is the ragged edge of a salt
marsh. These marshes are plains of mud, overlying gravel
or clay, covered with salt grasses, and penetrated by numerous
crooked and narrow creeks. The mud of which the marsh
consists is in some places only one or two feet deep, but in
other parts its depth is twenty or even fifty feet. The level of
the surface is everywhere approximately that of mean high
water. Spring tides overflow the marshes, and then the river
assumes a deceptive appearance of great breadth; for the area
of marsh land bordering upon the channel greatly exceeds the
total area of the trough or waterway. In the neighborhood
of many of the principal creeks, such as Miller's River and
Muddy River, and in parts of Somerville, Cambridge, and
Brighton, distant as much as a mile or more from salt water, are
other large areas, elevated little, if any, above the level of the
salt marsh. If it were not for the fact that the daily periods
of low tide in the river afford natural drainage for these last-
named districts, they would be permanent fresh-water swamps.
Even as things are, these low lands and the mud marshes
afford only unwholesome and unstable sites for the buildings
and streets of cities.

The course of the historical development of Charles River
and its banks has been perhaps equally distinctive and pecul-

iar. In the early years of the Massachusetts Bay Colony
the river was the principal highway of the district. For years
a boat was the only means of conveyance to Newtown (later
Cambridge), Gerry's Landing, and Watertown. Ferries to
Charlestown and to Lechmere's Point (East Cambridge) sufficed for almost two hundred years. As population increased,
the use of the river as a commercial highway increased also;
but the use of it as a highway for travel was abandoned when
bridges and causeways across the marshes furnished more
direct routes. On the Boston side, and on the Cambridge
side after the building of the modern Craigie and West Boston bridges, dealers in lumber, building-stone, and other bulky
and heavy articles gradually took possession of the shores
near the bridges and causeways, and built wharves. Further
up stream an occasional wharf appeared. At one time the
commercial future of the river looked so bright that certain
capitalists invested considerable sums in digging a so-called
Broad Canal through the flats and marshes on the Cambridge
side, for the purpose of furnishing wharfage to the foreign
and domestic commerce of ambitious Cambridgeport and the
short-lived Middlesex Canal.

Meanwhile, the same increasing population which called
for lumber, stone, and coal "at wharf prices" came also to
require direct and swift communication with the centre of
population in Boston. Numerous bridges, carrying omnibuses, horse-cars, and steam-railroad trains were accordingly
provided, and all were equipped with draws for the passage
of vessels.

Again, the pressure for building room within the naturally
narrow limits of the original peninsula of Boston necessitated
the making of more land by filling the shallow coves which
bounded the original town. The Town Dock became Dock
Square, the North Cove was filled to Causeway Street, and
the South Cove and the Back Bay disappeared in like manner. As this filling went on it was accompanied by the building of retaining walls on the lines of the new water fronts,
and, where commerce demanded it and the harbor commissioners permitted it, by the construction of wharves outside
the walls. The mouth of Charles River was considerably

contracted by wharf-building, and the Back Bay was narrowed on the Boston side by as much as a mile, but there no wharves have been built outside the wall line. Many hundreds of acres of flats and marshes were thus reclaimed, the largest area filled by any one owner having been the Back Bay, which was filled by the Commonwealth, and afterwards sold in building lots at a large profit.

Buildings set upon these filled lands are founded on piles, as are all heavy structures, such as the abutments of bridges, the retaining sea walls, and even the sewers under the streets; but farther from town, in districts where the price obtainable for building land has not warranted expenditure for filling, piling, and proper sewers, the marshes have been built upon in many places without previous filling, or after only so much as suffices to keep the doorsteps of the houses out of water. The marshes are the cheapest lands near Boston, and they naturally tend to become the site of the cheapest tenements and the obnoxious trades. Years ago the crowded settlement of some parts of the Charles River lowlands bred conditions which proved unbearable; as in the lower part of Cambridgeport, where in 1872 several acres of buildings were lifted by the city of Cambridge at a great expense, in order that gravel might be thrown under them and the cellar grade raised twelve and thirteen feet above mean low water.

One still more dangerous result of the increase of population in the neighborhood of Charles River remains to be noticed; namely, the pollution of the bed of the river by the sewage which has for many years been discharged into the stream in ever-increasing quantity. The fresh-water river comes over the dam at Watertown polluted to a considerable degree; but the salt-water estuary below the dam has been the receptacle of the filth of the population on its banks from before the days of the first sewer until now.

The present condition of Charles River is the natural product of the peculiar character of the river and of the unintelligent treatment it has received. This present condition must now be summarized, in connection with the conclusions which the commission draws from its study of the natural, the historical, and the present facts.

First. The river is to-day a much less efficient source of
" scour " than it used to be. In the first place, the filling of
the shallow coves and the Back Bay has done away with a
great part of that high-level water, the rapid ebbing of which
causes " scour ; " and, in the second place, the choking of the
mouth of the river by the countless piles of the railroad
bridges has checked the force of both the inward and the
outward currents to a considerable degree. In this way the
pile bridges tend to cause a more rapid sedimentary shoaling
of the river itself, as well as a diminution of " scour " in the
harbor channels. The community cannot afford to interfere
with Nature's method of preserving the channels of Boston
Bay. It is obvious that the pile bridges should be removed,
and span bridges carried upon piers substituted.

Secondly. Whatever may have been the commercial importance of Charles River in the past, the river to-day is relatively unimportant as a highway. The commerce of the
river has not kept pace with the growth of population in the
neighborhood of the stream. Since the opening of the railroads, and particularly in recent years, the coasting trade
(especially the coal trade) has for reasons of economy begun
to employ large vessels, many of which draw too much water
to venture within Charles River. Other causes have doubtless operated to check the development of the commerce of
the stream ; but, without naming others, it is sufficient to
point out that there is now only one wharf used for commercial purposes in the three miles of Boston's frontage on the
river, while on the Cambridge side and further up stream
several old wharves have been either abandoned or converted
to uses not connected with navigation. A leading lumber
dealer, who formerly did business on Broad Canal and is now
established beside a railroad track, informed the commission
that he would not go back to the water-side if he could go
rent free ; and a coal merchant of Newton gave somewhat
similar testimony. It is evident that the experience of the
world in general is being repeated here. The railroad is
gradually becoming the universal domestic carrier. And yet,
in spite of the obviously decreased relative importance of the
carrying trade upon the river, to close the river absolutely

would certainly be folly. Even if the railroad should in time monopolize the coal trade of the valley, the fact that coal might be obtained by water would tend in a most effective way to reduce railroad rates and charges. For this reason, among others, the commission finds itself compelled to disagree both with those who advocate costly works of river improvement for the sake of admitting large vessels, and with those who desire to see the river absolutely closed. On this head the commission holds to one simple conclusion, — that the possibility of navigation should be maintained.

Thirdly. It may be set down as certain, that, to the great majority of the inhabitants of the metropolitan district, Charles River to-day presents itself in one aspect only, — that of an obstruction to travel. The stream which was once the only highway of the district is become the principal obstacle in many highways. The bridges have been multiplied until there are now twelve ordinary bridges and five railroad structures crossing the river, and still there are not enough. Moreover, travel on the bridges is liable to delays arising from opening the draws for the passage of schooners, scows, and tugs. Long lines of street cars, carriages, and wagons are thus delayed on all the lower bridges daily during the open months. It is true that the steam-railroad trains are delayed by open draws comparatively seldom; but this is because the daylight traffic on the railroad bridges is so constant that the companies generally compel vessels to wait until night, or as long as the law allows. The bridges carry not only the four hundred regular trains which leave the northern stations of Boston every day, with the corresponding number of incoming trains, but they also serve the companies as rent-free switching yards, where engines engaged in making up trains cross and recross continually. To accommodate the business, the railroad bridges have been widened of late years until they now fairly roof the river, while they choke it with their supporting piles, as already described. The Maine and Fitchburg railroads appeared before the commission by counsel, and, after citing figures showing the thousands of persons carried by them over Charles River every day, they expressed their very natural desire that the draws might be permanently closed. It appears, however, to this commission, that the concentration of the railroad tracks upon one broad bridge, elevated sufficiently to permit the passage under it of tow-boats and large barges, would solve the railroads' difficulty in a manner much more conducive to the public welfare. Such an elevated bridge would at once accomplish three important reforms : it would permit trains to enter Boston without delay attributable to the crossing of Charles River ; it would at the same time allow of the navigation of the river by all mastless vessels not too deep for the channel ; and, if it were built upon piers, it would restore its ancient force to the scouring current of the ebb tide. Such high-level approaches to terminal stations have proved entirely practicable in Philadelphia, in London, and elsewhere ; all the passenger tracks here concerned can gain the necessary elevation without difficulty ; the dangerous and wasteful grade crossings of these passenger tracks can at the same time be disentangled ; and the commission hopes to see this most desirable improvement carried out very shortly, if not voluntarily by the companies concerned, then under mandatory legislation to be framed by the railroad commission or by the General Court.

As to the highway bridges, the commission concludes that, as the present pile structures decay, they should be replaced by permanent span bridges founded upon piers, and elevated at the channel to permit navigation.[1]

Fourthly. If the river of to-day forces itself upon the attention of most people as an obstacle, it presents itself to many others in the aspect of a dangerous nuisance. People who live near it are well acquainted with the peculiar odor which rises from the flats and muddy banks when exposed. The fact is that the upper layer of the bottom of the river is thoroughly polluted with sewage.

In view of this fact, it is a fortunate circumstance that clean gravel underlies this sludge and mud in so many parts of the river bottom. When the completion of the Metropolitan intercepting sewers shall have ended the direct discharge

[1] The new West Boston Bridge now (1902) under construction is of this nature ; it is also drawless.

of sewage into the stream, it will not be very difficult to clean the river bed by means of the powerful pump-dredges which are now available;[1] for experience seems to prove that this foul material is harmless when it is thrown out on the landward side of a sea wall, and buried under several feet of clean gravel.

It is evident that the retaining sea-wall is the first step in the necessary sanitation of Charles River. Such walls already edge the water on the Boston side, from the river's mouth to the Cottage Farm Bridge. Elsewhere, only a few thousand feet of wall are as yet constructed. The walls are built upon lines laid down by the United States engineers and the State harbor commission. They make the cleanest possible river bank, and, though they become slimy between high and low water marks, they are undoubtedly the most sightly form of bank possible under the circumstances.

After the building of the sea wall, the pump dredge should complete the process of sanitation by transferring material from the water side to the land side of the wall, thus effecting by one process two desirable results: the raising of the marsh to a safe level, and the excavation of the river to such a depth that its bottom between the sea walls shall not be exposed at low water. It is true that the unhealthful exposure of the river bottom to the air might be prevented by simply holding the water in the river trough at a high level by means of a dam; and it may possibly be advisable to resort to this method in the upper portion of the river's course, where dredging to the depth required to retain water at low tide would be excessively expensive.

But from the United States Arsenal to the river's mouth this makeshift method of suppressing the nuisance arising from the flats would in all probability entail more serious dangers than it would cure. In the first place, it would destroy the scouring force of the ebb tide. In the second place, it would convert the basin behind the dam into a genuine settling basin, in which sedimentary shoaling and the making of new flats would go on rapidly. In the third place, it would result in a deleterious rise of the ground

[1] This has been in large measure accomplished.

waters of all districts near the river.   In the fourth place,
it would deprive the large low-lying areas of the district of
their only means of getting rid of storm and surface waters.
The sewers which now drain these districts fall towards the
river with the least possible grades, and yet the tide in the
river dams up their outlets except at the periods of low water.
During rainstorms or thaws these sewers simply fill up until
a low tide in the river relieves them.   Moreover, the Metropolitan sewers now in course of construction will not be
able to relieve this situation, — no sewers and no pumps big
enough to afford relief could well be· built.   By means of
automatic gates, placed at the intersections of the present
sewers with the new trunk sewers, the storm waters of the
valley must continue to be discharged into their natural outlet, — the trough of Charles River.   Extremely dilute sewage
will be carried into the river with the storm waters on these
exceptional occasions, which may occur on the average perhaps
twice in every month ; but, if the river bottom is lowered so
that it shall remain covered, if the river banks are cleanly
walled, and if the natural swiftness of the tidal currents is
restored, no appreciable nuisance will result from this source.

It appears from the foregoing statement that Charles River,
which was formerly a convenient artery of trade, has now
become chiefly an obstacle and a nuisance.   On the other
hand, it appears that, if ways and means can be found to
accomplish the reconstruction and elevation of the bridges,
to excavate the filthy river bed, to build the sea walls and to
fill the marshes, the river's present evil character will be
reformed, and it may again exercise a wholly favorable influence upon the life of this community.

What will be the most profitable use to which the community can then put the reformed river?   As already detailed,
the stream will be of use as a source of scour, as an outlet for
storm waters, and as a navigable channel by which coal and
other heavy commodities can be delivered cheaply if necessary ; but, when a densely populated city shall extend five or
ten miles from the State House, the greatest benefit derivable
by the community from the river will arise from the large
open space which the stream provides.   Many a crowded city

would give much for such an air space ; and there can be no
doubt but that our community will come to value it at its full
worth.   When that day comes, it will be evident to all that
the full benefit of the open space cannot be reaped unless
the public shall have access to the river bank.   Indeed, this
truth is now partially recognized.   Boston, through her park
commission, has already opened to the public almost half a
mile of river embankment, which takes the place of a row of
lumber, stone, and coal yards.   The Park Commission has,
furthermore, obtained permission from the General Court to
extend this embankment another third of a mile to the angle
in the Basin at the foot of Chestnut Street; and this Commission hopes to see this improvement accomplished at an early
date.   Boston has also laid out a river-side street, extending
about a third of a mile along the river wall, near Cottage
Farm railroad station.   Cambridge is contemplating the purchase of the so-called Captain's Island and the adjacent
marshes ; [1] and the Charles River Embankment Company is
under contract with Cambridge to build half a mile of river-
side boulevard two hundred feet in width.[1]   On the upper
river, though there are as yet no reservations for public purposes, there are several considerable stretches of shore which
are held for semi-public and wholly harmless purposes; such
as the frontages owned by the United States at the Arsenal,
by Harvard University for athletic and park purposes, by the
Cambridge Hospital, and by the Longfellow Memorial Association.

Where the river is broad, combinations of marsh owners,
such as the Charles River Embankment Company and the
Roxbury Mill Corporation, embark upon the work of improving their properties for residential purposes with no apparent
hesitation ; but it is only natural that the riparian owners of
the narrow parts of the river should be fearful of the evil effect
on their properties which an unsightly occupation of the opposite bank would cause.   These owners of opposite banks are certainly in an unenviable position to-day, and it would be to their
advantage if they could agree among themselves upon a general plan of development, in accordance with which certain

[1] Done.

parts of the river banks might be devoted to industry and commerce, while other parts might be allotted to residences fronting upon public embankments. If such a plan were once adopted and made rigidly binding upon all concerned, individual owners might then develop their particular portions as fast or as slowly as they pleased, without fear of any sudden revolution in values. Moreover, the adoption of such a definitive plan would undoubtedly encourage the development of the river lands to the benefit of the community as well as to the profit of the owners.

On the other hand, if the local owners fail (through their own short-sightedness or quarrelsomeness) to agree upon any such general plan, they must expect to see their shore lands taken from them by right of eminent domain, the work of reformation done by public authority, and much of the cost thereof assessed in betterments upon the marshes in the rear of the improved strip. For so important to the community is the reformation of the river and the prevention of the unsanitary occupation of the banks, that, if the owners of the banks fail to act effectively for their own advantage and the public weal, the cities and towns which abut upon the river, or, if they cannot agree, then the Commonwealth itself, must take the banks, do the work, and collect the cost from the municipalities and the individuals concerned.[1]

Postponing all further discussion of the ways and means of effecting the reservation and eventual reformation of the river banks, the commission suggests the desirability of legislation enabling towns and cities to coöperate in securing and eventually improving public open spaces lying in more than one town or city.[2]

The commission also recommends the passage of the following joint resolution : —

Resolved, That the Senators and Representatives of Massachusetts in Congress be requested to advocate an additional appropriation for the dredging of Charles River.

[1] Done through the Metropolitan Park Commission with an appropriation of $300,000 made in 1894.

[2] Done for the Metropolitan District by the creation of the Metropolitan Park Commission in 1893.

The commission believes that the amount appropriated for the work of the commission will be sufficient for the completion of its investigations, provided that the General Court will assign quarters for its occupancy.

SECOND REPORT OF THE CHARLES RIVER IMPROVEMENT COMMISSION.

THE undersigned commissioners, appointed under chapter 390 of the Acts of 1391, for the purpose of considering what improvement can be made in the Charles River between the dam at Watertown and Charles River Bridge in Boston, and other related purposes stated in the Act, respectfully submit the following report, which, with the report already submitted, covers their investigation to date :

The commission, believing that the testimony at the many hearings shows conclusively that the desire of the people is that the river shall be improved, particularly from a sanitary point of view, and that this improvement may be best made by making the banks of the river desirable for residential purposes, submit with this report an Act creating a commission, to be known as the Charles River Improvement Commission, and recommend the passage of the Act.

The evidence before the commission showed that the navigation of the Charles River will, in the near future,[1] be limited to barges and mastless vessels. The commission therefore recommends that the railroad bridges now crossing Charles River be discontinued, and the different railroads required to build a single structure capable of accommodating all railroad travel.

The commission recommends that action be taken by the legislature by which authority will be given to the city of Boston to continue the Charles River embankment along the whole of the city's frontage on the river.

The commission recommends the immediate construction of the embankment from West Boston Bridge to the Union Boat Club building.

[1] Permission to rebuild West Boston Bridge without a draw was obtained by the Act of March 23, 1899.

The commission also recommends that such authority as may be necessary shall be given to the city of Cambridge, enabling it to construct an embankment along the whole or any part of the Cambridge side of the river.

20 April, 1893.

The legislature of 1893, instead of adopting the act recommended by the commission of 1891–93, appointed a Joint Board on the Improvement of Charles River, consisting of the Metropolitan Park Commission which had just been created, and the State Board of Health, with instructions " to prepare plans for the improvement of the bed, shores, and waters of the Charles River between Charles River Bridge and the Waltham line Charles River, and for the removal of any nuisances therefrom, and to report to the next General Court." The Joint Board was authorized to employ engineers and experts and to spend $5000. They employed Frederic T. Stearns as engineer, and Olmsted, Olmsted and Eliot as landscape architects.

The proposals made to the Board by their engineer covered the following points: (1) The preservation of the traffic on the river; (2) the sanitation of the stream and its banks; (3) the prevention of the periodic flooding of the marshes and low lands near the river; (4) an improvement in the discharge of the existing sewers on the Back Bay; (5) the preservation of the present level of the ground-water in filled lands; (6) the prevention of the soaking of the marshes near the river with salt water twice a day by the ordinary high tide; (7) the draining of the marshes. Assuming that these immense gains might be attained by means of a dam high enough to exclude the tide, as proposed by the engineer, Charles wrote the following report to the Joint Board to show what great landscape and park advantages would result from the adoption of the Board's plans.

H. P. WALCOTT, M. D., *Chairman of Joint Board on the Improvement of Charles River.*

SIR : — We have the honor to report as follows upon the improvement and best utilization of Charles River and its borders between Waltham line and Craigie Bridge. Wherever the words " Charles River " or " the river " are used in this paper, they are to be understood to refer only to this portion of the total length of the stream.

The problem presented by the existence of the channel, flats, and marshes of Charles River in the heart of the metropolitan district of Boston has long been the subject of public discussion ; and, although this discussion has been thus far almost barren of results, it has at least served to familiarize the metropolitan community with the nature of the river and the history of its pollution and defacement. This discussion has also developed the fact that public authority over the river and its borders is unfortunately divided between the United States, the State, three cities, and one town. If absolute deference were to be paid to each and every public authority and private interest concerned, no satisfactory solution of the problem of the river could ever be reached, because these authorities and interests are conflicting ; therefore, in our discussion of the subject we make no attempt to reconcile conflicting interests or to conform to the supposed or alleged desires of any governing body or interested person. We first inquire, What is the most important service which Charles River renders, or may be made to render, to the welfare of the dense population of its valley? and after this mode of usefulness has been explained, it will be our endeavor to set forth a logical scheme of improvement such as will develop the natural usefulness of the river in the highest possible degree.

It is not for us to attempt to suggest the proper way of executing the improvement to be proposed. We are warranted in assuming that a way can be found to carry out any scheme which can be shown to be conducive to the greatest good of the greatest number.

The principal function of every river is the discharge of surface waters. The channel of the Charles conveys to the ocean the surface drainage of two hundred square miles. The estuary of the river is navigable by coasting vessels, and the considerable volume of the fresh-water river has led to the use of the stream as a convenient conduit of factory wastes and sewage. These modes of usefulness, however, are evidently subsidiary to the primary or fundamental usefulness of the stream as a common drain. The use of the stream as a sewer may be discontinued, as, in fact, it soon will be,[1] and the use of the stream by commerce may be abandoned when that use shall be found to conflict with more profitable uses. On the other hand, the service of the channel as a drain will inevitably become of ever-increasing importance as population thickens in the river valley. Every additional roof and street built within the watershed enhances the rapidity of the flow of rain-water towards the watercourses and adds to the volume of the floods in the river. A due regard for public economy demands that the channel of every brook flowing through a closely settled district should not only be kept free from obstruction but be made capable of enlargement. It is vastly cheaper to acquire early, through public authority, ample space for the safe conveyance of the increasing floods of such streams, than it is to clear away obstructions and remove buildings after damaging overflows have demonstrated the necessity of so doing. The costly case of Stony Brook in Roxbury teaches the need of prompt action in this important matter. Meanwhile, it is satisfactory to be assured that, however inadequate the channels of the tributary brooks of Charles River may be, or may become, the open channel of the river itself will doubtless be sufficiently capacious for all time. This channel has a width of one hundred feet at the Waltham line, two hundred feet at the head of the tide in Watertown, and five hundred feet at Cottage Farm, where the river expands into the so-called basin. The length of the channel from Waltham line to Cottage Farm is eight miles, and the total area of the open water-way between these points is about three hundred acres. This is the considerable space which must permanently be kept open in order to provide a safe way of escape for the floods of the Charles River watershed.

It is next to be noted that well-distributed open-air space is just what every crowded district must possess, if the public health is to be preserved, and that many cities have been compelled to pay large sums of money in order to secure public

[1] The Metropolitan Sewerage System was put into operation 1892–1897. Extensions and improvements are continuous.

open spaces no larger than that which nature has freely given to the cities of the lower valley of the Charles. If the crowded districts of the valley care to reap the advantage of this free gift of nature, they have only to take possession of the banks of the river. Money spent in making the existing natural open spaces accessible and enjoyable will surely yield a greater return, both in public health and pleasure, and in profits from the increased assessable values of adjoining lands, than it could yield if it were spent in buying detached inland tracts. This is an obvious truth, and already the municipalities of Boston and Cambridge have taken action accordingly. Boston has secured and constructed the very popular public ground called the Charlesbank, and proposes to construct, eventually, a public promenade along the whole shore of the basin. In this part of the river the use of the banks for commercial purposes has already been abandoned in favor of the more profitable use thereof for purposes of residence and recreation. Cambridge is engaged in acquiring the larger part of her long frontage on the narrow river [1] as well as the border of the basin.

It appears, then, that the acquisition for the public of the remaining portions of the river bank ought to be accomplished at once, either by the separate towns and cities concerned, or by some central authority empowered to act for all. This is not an extravagant proposition; it is dictated by considerations of real economy. Open space is needed. Nowhere west of the State House can so much well-distributed space be had for so little money as on the banks of Charles River. Furthermore, there is every reason to believe that, if the proposed reservation were to be bounded by roads affording building frontages, the private owners of the adjoining lands and the public treasury would alike be financially benefited.

In this connection it should be noted that private capital begins to perceive that the highest possible value will be obtained for the river lands only when they are made attractive to the builders of dwellings and apartment houses. The Charles River Embankment Company is laying out nearly a mile of the Cambridge shore of the basin in a style [2] which is

---

[1] Accomplished in 1899.   [2] Accomplished in 1900.

calculated to induce the building of fine residences; and, in order to establish values beyond a doubt, the company has presented to the city of Cambridge an esplanade upon the river front, extending the whole length of its domain and measuring two hundred feet in depth. The owners of large tracts of land lying further up the stream would doubtless give their river banks in a similar spirit, if by so doing they might secure the advantage of a frontage upon a continuous river-road and reservation. Not that it is to be expected or desired that all the banks of the river should become new "Back Bay" districts. Obnoxious industries would doubtless be banished from the valley by the enhanced land values which may be expected to result from making the river bank a reservation, but manufactories of the higher sort would probably remain and be established on lands not remote from the reservation; and if the low lands of the valley should eventually become the seat of a population of well-housed working people, who would find refreshment on the public river-bank at the noon hour and in summer evenings, a most desirable result would be secured. Playgrounds for children would naturally be provided at intervals along the banks.

The advantage which would be reaped by the towns and cities of the river valley from the joint possession of a thoroughly pleasant route of travel to and from Boston is so obvious that it need only be mentioned. Roads built upon the boundaries of the proposed reservation would provide a continuous parkway from Waltham to the heart of Boston.

Upon the accompanying plan the heavy line indicates the outer boundary of the lands proposed to be acquired for the public domain, and adjacent lines indicate the existing and proposed boundary roads. It is professionally incumbent upon us to urge the prompt acquisition by public authority of all the land within the heavy lines.[1] The few commercial and industrial establishments which now stand within these lines would not necessarily be required to move away at once. Whatever public authority shall undertake, the acquiring of the proposed reservation may well permit these concerns to

[1] Compare the acquisitions of public lands on Charles River indicated on the map in the pocket of the right cover of this volume.

occupy their present sites perhaps for years, at all events until money shall be forthcoming wherewith to begin the necessary work of construction. This work may be long postponed, but it can never be even begun unless the land is acquired, and the land can never be obtained so cheaply as it may be to-day.

It is now desirable to return to the consideration of the river as a drain, — a topic which was temporarily abandoned in order to point out that because it is a drain it is also an open space, and an open space of which advantage should be taken for the benefit of both the public and the land-owners most concerned.

For a large part of the district under consideration, namely, for all the low lands along the river east of the United States Arsenal, the river as it exists to-day is a very inefficient drain. Between the arsenal and Cottage Farm there border upon the river as many as five hundred acres of unfilled or only slightly filled salt marsh, while back of the salt marshes in Brighton and Cambridge there lie about as many more acres only very slightly raised above the level of average high water. When the tide is out there is ready drainage for this land ; when the tide is in there is no drainage and the lands are drowned.

Engineers know but two ways of remedying poor drainage. Either the badly drained lands must be raised, or the level of the water in the drainage channels must be lowered. To raise the drowned lands in question to a drainable elevation with filling material costing fifty cents per cubic yard would cost two million dollars. To build a dam and a lock by which the high tide would be kept out, and the water in the river maintained at a constant level sufficiently low to make all the marshes drainable, would cost perhaps half a million. The important sanitary and financial advantages to be derived from the construction of such a dam and lock are detailed in the accompanying report of the engineer, and need not be repeated here.

We have already urged, and shall continue to urge, the acquisition of a continuous river-bank reservation, whether the river is to remain a tidal estuary or not ; but it is evident that if the tide could be excluded, and the resulting fresh-water stream maintained at a fairly constant level, the problem presented by the shores of the stream would be greatly simplified. Thus, if the surface of the water were to be maintained at Grade 8, as is proposed by the engineer, not only would the marshes within the reservation become drainable at once, and without filling, but the low mud banks would, with a little assistance, become quickly clothed with trees and bushes. The cost of sea walls and ripraps would be avoided, and the appearance of the stream would be greatly improved.

It would be well to make sure that eight feet should be the minimum depth of water in the fresh-water channel, because a less depth would encourage an undesirable growth of water plants. It would also be advisable to exclude salt water as completely as possible, if only because it would injure fresh-water plants growing upon the banks. If proper precautions were taken, the effect of the proposed dam upon the projected public reservation would evidently be wholly favorable. Accordingly, while the accompanying plan has been drawn to represent the boundaries of a reservation such as must be recommended whether the stream be salt or fresh, the banks of the stream are shown as they might be if the surface of the stream were to be maintained at Grade 8 by a dam situated as recommended by the engineer. Shore lines, landings, bridges, paths, sidewalks, and roads within the reservation are not accurately defined upon the plan, both because the scale of the drawing is too small, and because these details may more properly be devised by whatever executive authorities shall have charge of the work in the future.

In briefest form we have outlined a scheme of improvement such as will develop in the highest possible degree the natural usefulness of the river as an open space and as a drain. It only remains to describe the accompanying plan in greater detail, for which purpose we divide the river into three sections, as follows: first, the fresh-water section; second, the marsh section; third, the basin section.

THE FRESH-WATER SECTION — WALTHAM LINE TO WATER-TOWN BRIDGE.

This is the only fresh-water section of Charles River with which the present inquiry is concerned. The stream here meanders tranquilly through a chain of open meadows generally bordered by low bluffs. Dams at Bemis and Watertown detain the natural current and spread the water surface in an agreeable manner. Neither the meadows nor the bluffs are as yet much occupied by buildings except in the near neighborhood of the two dams.

The public reservation outlined upon the accompanying plan begins arbitrarily at the Waltham line, in accordance with the terms of the act of the legislature creating your commission, and extends eastward between boundaries which it is proposed shall be formed by existing or prospective public roads, affording frontage for the adjacent private building land. [Here follow details concerning the boundary roads on both banks of the river.]

It should be noted in passing that Cheesecake Brook has already been included in a public reservation bounded by a road upon each bank, and that both the adjacent land-owners and the public of Newton are well pleased therewith.

The mills at Bemis cannot be included in the reservation, for obvious reasons; but they are easily passed by River Street and California Street, and the existing buildings are not a serious blot upon the landscape of the river valley.

[Here follow more details about boundary roads.]

Abreast of Watertown dam connection can easily be made with the public reservation which the city of Newton proposes to create along the course of Laundry Brook.

THE MARSH SECTION — WATERTOWN BRIDGE TO COTTAGE FARM.

This middle section of the river is characterized by extensive areas of salt marsh which border the wandering channel. Here and there the marsh has been filled and a bit of sea wall built, but more than nine tenths of the total length of the river bank is still in its natural state. The marshes are generally unoccupied.

The plan suggests that a bridge should eventually be built in continuation of California Street, and that the public reservation should include the narrow strip of land which lies between Wheeler Street and the river, so that the continuity of the river drive may be unbroken. . . . [Details of boundaries.]

On the south side of this section of the river the Boston & Albany Railroad is built on an embankment not far from the river's edge, while several commercial establishments occupy the river bank in the neighborhood of the village of Watertown. It is desirable that the land which lies between the Boston & Albany Railroad and the stream should be made part of the public reservation, but more than this seems impracticable.

Continuing eastward, the plan suggests on the north bank a drive through the grounds of the United States Arsenal, passing in rear of the wharf, and a street connection on the south side of the river, by which travel may pass in rear of the great buildings of the abattoir. East of the abattoir it is again possible to secure a river drive on the south bank as well as on the north. The plan proposes that this drive should follow a long curve from Western Avenue at the foot of Market Street to the northwest corner of the Soldier's Field of Harvard College. On the broad and level marshes which will adjoin this section of the river drive it will be possible to obtain a mile-long course for driving, unbroken by any cross roads. We know of no other so favorable an opportunity for the making of a " speedway." [1]

From Soldier's Field to the works of the Brookline Gas Company, at River Street Bridge, the plan shows the boundary of the reservation established upon a curved road, a branch of which may in the future follow the edge of the river past the Longfellow Meadow, and so over a new bridge to Mount Auburn and Fresh Pond.[2] Beyond the Brookline Gas Company's works the Boston & Albany Railroad controls the river bank as far as Cottage Farm, so that no new

---

[1] This speedway was finished in 1900.

[2] Accomplished in 1900 except the new bridge. The parkway passes through " Elmwood."

frontage can be developed by the construction of a road. Moreover, people driving on the river roads will find their shortest way to Boston by crossing the river at Western Avenue bridge and recrossing it at Cottage Farm.

It is proposed that the north side road on the boundary of this section of the reservation should be placed about half way between the river and the existing Coolidge Street, and that after passing Cambridge Cemetery and the Cambridge Hospital it should connect at Mt. Auburn Street with the river road, the site of which has already been acquired by the Park Commission of the city of Cambridge. This road must find its way between the water and the buildings of the river-side wards of Cambridge as best it may. At certain points, as, for instance, at the Riverside Press, space for the broad driveway and promenade is all that can be had. At other places, as, for instance, at Captain's Island, space valuable for playgrounds has been secured between the drive and the stream. It is understood that the Cambridge Park Commission proposes to remove, in time, the few commercial establishments which at present stand in the way of the construction of this drive and park.[1]

THE BASIN SECTION — COTTAGE FARM TO CRAIGIE BRIDGE.

The existing bridge at Cottage Farm is crossed at grade by the tracks of the freight branch of the Boston & Albany Railroad. There is no need that both this bridge and the river road should be carried over these tracks. Moreover, the present bridge does not connect with any highway leading to the south. For these reasons and others we have deemed it best to suggest the discontinuance of the existing bridge and the building of a new structure a short distance further east. In the suggested position the bridge would not only connect Cambridge and the river roads more conveniently with Boston, but it would also make good connection by way of Audubon Road with the new parkway along Muddy River, and so with all the Boston parks and all the southern suburbs. This new bridge would also mark the point of entrance of Charles River into the Basin, while the view from the bridge

[1] Done.

down the whole length of the Basin to the State House would be very fine.

Above this bridge the shores of the reservations proposed by the plan would be irregular and clothed with trees and bushes, except where it might be desirable that the public should reach the water's edge at beaches or boat-landings. Below this bridge the shores of the Basin would be treated formally with low walls or curbs of stone, broken by bastions affording views over the water, landings for use of steam or electric passenger boats, docks for row-boats and the like.

The Cambridge side of the Basin is already provided with a broad public reservation which is now almost continuous. On the other hand, the Boston side of the Basin, except between Craigie Bridge and West Boston Bridge, is bordered either by the back yards of private buildings or by a narrow alley which gives access to back yards and stables. It has seemed to us that the open Basin is quite broad enough to permit of the insertion of one additional row of buildings adjacent to the existing water-side alley, and the construction of a driveway and promenade on the water-side of this new row. On this plan it may be expected that buildings of an agreeable aspect will gradually be constructed fronting on the Basin, while the money which will be obtained from the sale of this building land will certainly pay the whole cost of filling and finishing the drive and promenade.

The dam which is shown upon the plan as connecting the completed Charlesbank with the newly acquired reservation on the Cambridge side called The Front is fully described in the engineer's report. It is proposed that a lock should be built in this dam, primarily for the accommodation of the United States Arsenal, and secondarily to serve the purposes of such industrial establishments as may linger on the river bank or be built near it. Coal is now practically the only freight carried up the stream, and the delivery of coal is not incompatible with the enjoyment of the river bank by the general public. It is significant, however, that "all-rail" coal is now offered for sale in Brighton and Newton near the river. The case of the Charles is wholly different from that of Chicago River, for example, — a stream which is the only

harbor of a great commercial city. Boston, with Charlestown, East Boston, and South Boston, possesses ample harbor
frontages below the mouths of all her rivers.

Charles River, freed from sewage, from defiling industries,
from mud flats and from mud banks, and dedicated with its
borders to the use and enjoyment of the public as a drainage
channel, an open space, a parkway, a chain of playgrounds
and a boating course, will perform its highest possible service
to the metropolitan community, and will return to the community profits both tangible and intangible, which will annually increase.

April 16, 1894.

On the presentation of their report in April, 1894, the joint
Board on the Improvement of Charles River went out of existence. The legislature, being properly careful about any possible injury to Boston Harbor, directed the Board of Harbor
and Land Commissioners " to inquire into the construction
of a dam and lock in the tidal Basin of Charles River with
special reference to interference with tide-water and its effect
on the harbor of Boston." That Board proceeded in the
following autumn to hold a series of hearings at the State
House, at which eminent legal counsel, employed by certain
citizens of Boston, appeared in opposition to the high dam proposed by the joint Board, the opposition being based chiefly
on sanitary grounds.

The hearings gave Charles occasion to publish his views
about the dam in the following letter to the " Transcript."

THE PROPOSED IMPROVEMENT OF CHARLES RIVER.

The State Board of Harbor and Land Commissioners gives
a hearing on the proposed question of the Charles River Dam
on Thursday, Oct. 18, at 10 A. M., and citizens of Boston who
desire to see a stream, which is now a health-threatening nuisance and a value-depressing mud-hole, converted into the
chief ornament and the best lung of the metropolis ought to
attend and give expression to their wish.

The argument for the construction of the proposed dam
can be put into a nutshell. In the first place the dam, by
shutting out the high tide, will improve the drainage of all
the lowlands near the river. The sewage of the Back Bay

district will cease to "set back" during storms. Moreover, the marshes of the river will be freed from daily flooding. These results will be accomplished without changing the level of the underlying ground water, so that all the river lands will at once become much more habitable, healthy, and valuable than they have ever been.

In the second place the dam, by maintaining a permanent instead of a fluctuating water level in the river will add much to the usefulness, the healthfulness, and the beauty of the stream itself. The channel will become navigable at all times, and vessels will not have to lie aground at wharves and landings. Boating for pleasure will become possible at all hours. The flats and the slimy walls will be covered forever.

In the third place, the dam will save much money in one direction, and increase wealth in another. Six hundred and sixty thousand dollars' worth of dam will make the expenditure of several millions for sea walls and filling unnecessary. Compared with a tidal and walled river, a fresh-water stream secured by a dam will be a far better thing at less cost. Moreover, the fresh-water stream flowing at a constant level, bordered by public roads and reservations already secured or projected, and edged by low walls about the basin and by low bushy banks above Cottage Farm, will certainly enhance the value of all adjacent lands, and soon return to the public treasury the whole cost of the dam.

Boston citizens ought to be aware that the question which troubles the residents of Beacon Street — namely, the question, whether, for the sake of the architectural uniformity of the Basin, a row of buildings ought eventually to be built facing the water in the rear of the present houses — is a question which is entirely separable from the question of the dam. The killing of the dam project will not kill the other notion. Architectural completeness will seem desirable to some people whether the water of the basin remain salt or become fresh. Meanwhile Boston possesses above the site of the proposed dam seven miles of frontage on the tidal estuary of Charles River with hundreds of acres of lowlands (including the Back Bay itself) which would be greatly benefited by the work the State Board of Health and its engineer have recommended.

The only considerable obstacle to the immediate procurement
of this benefit is the fact that engineers are divided in
opinion as to whether the diminution of current caused by
building the dam will or will not result in shoaling Boston
Harbor. The latest thoroughly competent and well-studied
opinion on this subject, that of Engineer F. P. Stearns, is
favorable to the view that the dam can have no ill effects in
this direction. Supposing, however, that some shoaling should
take place, it would obviously be cheaper for the metropolitan district to keep a dredging machine at work continually
than to forego the sanitary, recreative, and financial benefits
which will accrue from the construction of the proposed dam.

October 17, 1894.

The Board of Harbor and Land Commissioners made no
inquiry of their own on the subject referred to them — indeed
they had not been provided with the means of making any
useful inquiry — and contented themselves with reporting to
the next legislature that " This Board is powerless to say, on
the imperfect information it has, what effect a dam as proposed would have on shoaling in the upper harbor. We
must, however, record the opinion that nobody knows what
the effect would be . . . we are unable to find the consequences of building the proposed dam as at all certain of
being foreseen ; and . . . we are unable to report in favor
of the recommendations of the joint Board." This report
arrested the project for a high dam near Craigie's Bridge.

The Metropolitan Park Commission and the Cambridge
Park Commission, to both of which Charles was giving landscape advice, were ready to improve the banks of Charles
River in 1895 and 1896, and wished to do so ; but all work
of construction had to be postponed, or injuriously modified,
because the question of excluding the tide had not been settled. Charles, therefore, had the defeat of the dam very much
on his mind ; and in August, 1896, he wrote the following
paper and had it put into type, but refrained from publishing
it, because some of the Metropolitan Commissioners thought
its publication at that time inexpedient.

MUDDY RIVER AND CHARLES RIVER.

WHAT THE DAMMING OF CHARLES RIVER WOULD ACCOM-
PLISH. — Only a few years ago the tide from the sea ebbed

and flowed in a narrow channel which wound through broad
or narrow salt marshes from the Back Bay to Brookline.
At low water twice each day the muddy bed of this tidal
creek was exposed to the air and to view, while at extreme
high water the marshes were flooded so that the salt tide
lapped the bases of the bluffs on either hand. Before the
Brookline branch of the Albany Railroad was built along the
foot of the western bluff, the sinuous creek, the sunny
marshes, and the framing woods composed a pretty picture
of a type characteristic of the Massachusetts seacoast. But
with the coming of the railroad and the accompanying great
increase in the adjacent population, an ominous change took
place. The bluffs became the back yards of suburban houses,
the edges of the marshes were made places for dumping rubbish, the marshes themselves began to be occupied by shabby
buildings, which rented cheaply just because they were set
too low. The situation, indeed, seemed hopeless. The valley
of Muddy River was obviously destined to become one of
those all too numerous plague spots of the neighborhood of
Boston, which are not only ugly and dangerous in themselves,
but also extremely damaging to all surrounding life and
property.

But how " destiny " is sometimes cheated of its prey in
Massachusetts ! At this moment hundreds of bicycles are
flying along a smooth winding road which follows the brink
of the eastern bluff, and commands through the trees charming
glimpses of a tideless stream winding between bushy banks
and forming pond-like " broads " and basins. This afternoon
many boats and canoes have carried many boys and girls
down between luxuriant Elder bushes, Button bushes, and Willows all the way from Brookline to and through the Back
Bay Fens. Still other children have been rambling along
the streamside paths, resting under the trees of the eastern
bluff, or gleefully watching the passage of the boats under
the bridges. Even the noisy railroad tracks have disappeared
behind a bank of Sumac.

What has happened ? Simply this : Common sense, right
reason, and foresight, well known to be profitable when applied in the affairs of individuals, have here been exercised

by the whole community for the benefit of the whole community. The City of Boston and the Town of Brookline
have thwarted " destiny " through the coöperative action of
their park commissions. The private owners of the back
yards, bluffs, and marshes have been bought out. The River-
way has been built, affording not only an agreeable pleasure
drive, but also a desirable frontage for private and apartment houses. By means of a dam the tide has been completely shut out, and prevented from alternately drowning
and exposing the lowlands. By means of a gate at Brookline Avenue, the fresh water, which now fills the channel, is
kept permanently at about the level of high water in Boston
Bay. By means of suitable paths and bridges the completely
changed but pleasing scenery of the transformed valley has
been made accessible and enjoyable.

Most of the readers of the " Transcript " have noticed the
flats and marshes of Charles River when occasionally crossing the several bridges which connect Brighton and Newton
with Cambridge and Watertown ; but very few persons have
seriously studied the problem of the river as it presents itself
along the six discouraging miles between the head of the
great Basin at Cottage Farm and the " head of the tide " in
Watertown.

The tidal Basin below Cottage Farm is surrounded by high-
priced filled lands and is already walled about. A broad
parkway and promenade have been provided for on the Cambridge side, and the Boston Park Commission will undoubtedly arrange for a handsome treatment of the Boston shore
whenever its other great works are fairly complete. Thus,
so far as the Basin is concerned, things might remain as they
are for years without serious detriment to any public or private interest. On the other hand, all who are well acquainted
with the narrow, wall-less, and marsh-bordered river above
Cottage Farm are united in believing that prompt and vigorous action is required for the mere preservation, not to speak
of the enhancement, of the value of much private, as well as
common, property. The river as it exists to-day is simply an
unbearable nuisance. The ebb tide exposes 130 acres of mud
flats above Cottage Farm, while the flood tide occasionally

overflows and drowns more than 400 acres of land. Because
the river is such an ungainly neighbor, these marsh acres,
although they lie at the centre of the metropolitan district,
command to-day only very low prices ; moreover, where they
are occupied at all, the streets and buildings are invariably
of that cheap and shabby sort which inevitably reflects injury
upon the value of even the best adjacent uplands.

It is already several years since the need of action was first
clearly perceived ; and at least two State Commissions have
made reports upon the problem. In 1894 no less an authority than the State Board of Health emphatically condemned
the river, and joined with the Metropolitan Park Commission
in suggesting the construction of a dam which should wholly
exclude the tides, and permit the maintenance of a fresh-
water stream at a constant level. Unfortunately this Joint
Commission went out of existence on filing its report ; and
so took no part in the defense or advocacy of its scheme.
An Act was, however, passed by the legislature, empowering
the Metropolitan Park Commission to acquire lands on the
banks of the river ; while the question of the possible effect
of a dam upon Boston Harbor was referred for investigation
to the Harbor Commissioners. The Park Commission has
now secured the lands in question, and the Harbor Commission has reported. The latter Commission took it upon itself
to consider, not only the question specifically referred to it,
but, also, the whole question previously reported on by the
defunct Joint Board. So far as the harbor was concerned,
the report amounted to this ; that inasmuch as nobody could
foresee what the effect of a dam might be, it had better not
be built. In other words, the Commission did not investigate the one subject which was especially referred to it. Beyond this, the many and long public hearings given by the
Harbor Board were chiefly useful in bringing out the fact
that, while Cambridge, Watertown, and Newton, the places
most in need of immediate relief, were strongly in favor of
building the suggested dam, the only opposition came from
one short section of the bank of the lower Basin ; in other
words, from a district which is, fortunately for itself, so
placed (on land already filled by the State) as to escape

entirely all the loss, damage, and danger which the postponement of action inevitably inflicts upon the districts adjacent
to the river above Cottage Farm. The residents on the water
side of Beacon Street certainly would not have their own very
natural contentment with the Basin as it exists stand in the
way of the safeguarding of health and property along six
miles of the central river of the metropolitan district; and
yet this is exactly the position in which they have been placed
before the public of the district. It is plainly only charitable
to assume that the men of Beacon Street were stampeded
into a " strike," as other men often are, by the cry that their
private interests were assailed, when the fact was that the
whole programme of the Joint Board was put forth tentatively (no draft of an act was submitted with the report);
and the particular suggestion that the cost of the dam might
be secured from the sale of new filled lands was equally evidently an entirely unessential part of the project, for which
an increased bond issue or some other method of raising
money might readily have been substituted.

Meanwhile, as a matter of fact, the application of the suggested remedy is delayed. If, however, the people of Boston
and Cambridge and their neighbors will look upon Muddy
River and review its history, and then consider what the much
larger Charles River would be like, if similarly transformed
by damming out the tide, the waiting period will not be long.
The flats put permanently out of sight under water, and the
drowned marshes rescued from the recurrent floods; navigation freed entirely from dependence on the tides, public landings being provided, if needed, for the discharge of stone,
brick, lime, and other heavy water-borne freight; a water
parkway in the centre of the metropolis six or eight miles in
length, according to the position which may be chosen for the
dam; the ugly and muddy, but now public, shores of the
stream converted into green slopes, and bushy or tree-clad
banks; new driveways and footpaths along or near these
banks, leading pleasantly to Boston from all the western
suburbs; abundant opportunity for pleasure-boating in summer and for skating and ice-boating in winter; electric
launches running regularly and calling at many landings

THE CHARLES RIVER BASIN — THE BACK OF BEACON STREET, AT LOW TIDE

ONE OF THE ALSTER BASINS AT HAMBURG

along the transformed river between Watertown and the dam — such are some of the good things which may be substituted for the existing offensiveness, emptiness, uselessness, and squalor, by the exclusion of the tide.

Shall, then, the proposed dam, so urgently needed for the river above Cottage Farm, be built at Cottage Farm; or shall it be built near Craigie's Bridge, to the end that the central business district, the West End, and the Back Bay may all alike have access to the benefits which a dam will secure in Charles River, precisely as a dam has already secured the same benefits, on a smaller scale, in Muddy River? The districts above Cottage Farm cannot be expected to wait long; so this is a question which the people of Boston generally, and not the water-side of Beacon Street only, ought to discuss and consider with care and at once.

August, 1896.

If this paper betrays some impatience at the delay of a measure which had been convincingly advocated by the strongest commission that had ever studied the problem of Charles River, it should be remembered that the proposals of the Joint Board brought great relief to Charles's own mind, freed him from what had previously been a conflict of interests and duties, and seemed to him just, economical, effective, and wholly beneficent. The delay of two years, which had already taken place, was injurious to the work of all three of the park commissions (Metropolitan, Boston, and Cambridge) for which the Olmsted firm was furnishing designs; and this public injury was almost daily brought home to Charles in the natural course of his professional labors. The following letter to the Chairman of the Cambridge Park Commission well illustrates the difficulties of the situation : —

26th March, 1896.

. . . In our letter dated March 13th, 1896, we suggested the immediate completion of the sidewalk and first planting strip of the parkway from Boylston Street to Mt. Auburn Street, and the postponement of further construction for the present. The building of this broad sidewalk would make the river bank accessible in a way which would be much enjoyed. The views up stream from this shore when the tide is fairly high are often lovely, particularly towards evening. It seems to us that the public would be sufficiently well served by this treatment of the problem for the present.

Our reason for making this suggestion is, of course, our extreme reluctance to see walls built where they would not be necessary if the river should be ponded by a dam. When the people of a crowded city visit a recreation ground, they go to escape from the straight and hard lines of brick and stone and to find refreshment in green and picturesque surroundings. Stone walls will not make such agreeable banks to look at from the promenades as green banks, while from boats on the water the green banks would be vastly preferable. One would about as soon row a boat for pleasure down Washington Street as row between stone walls on the Charles above Cottage Farm. . . . Some riverbank walls will be needed, even should the river be ponded, but we must hope they may be few.

Suppose, for a moment, that only the sidewalk and planting strip should be built at present, as above suggested. For the first time a bit of the shore of the Charles would be made accessible for recreation. It would be evident, however, to every visitor that the work was unfinished, and the question would be, why? It seems to us that one object-lesson of this kind would help towards the desired dam more than anything else which can be done at this time. On the other hand, if Cambridge abandons the projects of the dam and builds sea walls on the plea that she cannot wait, every foot of wall that is built will make the winning of the dam all the harder. The dam will save the Cambridge Park Commission and the Metropolitan Park Commission the cost of many hundred feet of wall, and it will give the metropolitan district a far more valuable, because more beautiful, river park than can be had if the river is walled and the dam abandoned. We trust that your Commission will give these facts and suggestions very serious consideration before ordering the construction of the wall shown on the plan to which this letter refers.

We sincerely believe that as soon as the Boston Park Commission can find time and opportunity to take up the treat-

ment of the Boston side of the Basin below Cottage Farm,
there will be little difficulty in their satisfying the residents
of Beacon Street; and when these people are quieted by the
removal of their fears through the defining of a scheme, there
will be still less difficulty in uniting the Boston, Cambridge,
and Metropolitan Park Commissions in a demand for a dam
which will overcome all remaining opposition. Just when
the Boston Commission may have so far completed its other
works as to be able to take up consideration of the Basin, we
cannot predict. It may undoubtedly be several years; but,
even so, it seems to us that in view of the sanitary, financial,
and æsthetic arguments for ponding the river, Cambridge can
hardly afford to build any sea walls.

It may now be observed that the preliminary measures
which the Charles River Commission of 1891–93 recommended in its first report have all been taken. The banks of
the river have become public property; the bridges above
Craigie's Bridge are to be drawless, so that the traffic within
the basin and river must be carried on by barges and tow-
boats; the sewage has been diverted, with insignificant exceptions; a high bridge on piers has been substituted for the
former pile bridge to Charlestown, called Charles River Bridge,
and another high bridge on piers is now replacing the pile
bridge to Cambridge, called West Boston Bridge.

It but remains (1902) for the legislature to consummate
all this good work of preparation by ordering the construction
of a dam near Craigie's Bridge, high enough to keep out the
highest tides, and with a lock for mastless vessels.

During his long studies of Charles River, Charles had repeated occasion to consider the choking of its mouth by the
railroad switching yards supported on thousands of piles, and
he found the existing condition of the river in that respect so
bad, that he could not believe it would be permanent. The
reports of the Commission of 1891–93 had dwelt upon this
evil, and suggested some remedies or ameliorations. While
Charles was studying the subject a second time for the Joint
Board of 1893–94, he made in February, 1894, a plan for a
northern railroad station, on the north bank of the Charles,
with what he thought suitable approaches, and described his
plan in the following passage from an unpublished letter: —

At the northern end of the Basin, that part of the river
which lies between East Cambridge, Charlestown, and Bos-

ton is choked by innumerable piles supporting railroad
bridges. The cost of space for a suitable union station on
the mainland of Boston being very great, the railroads have
contrived to obtain permission to cover the river with a timber platform which they use as a rent-free switching yard and
terminal. It is well known that, in the view of national and
state legislation, this virtual obliteration of the river by the
railroads is only temporarily permitted. When the renewal
of this permission shall be at last refused, the railroads will
be compelled to place their terminal station on the north
bank of the Charles River, presumably about in the position
indicated upon the plan. By this arrangement the breadth
of the stream will be restored and its banks and bridges will
become susceptible of fine architectural treatment.

As compared with the present stand, this new station will
be distant from the corner of Washington and Summer streets
about half as far again; from Copley Square it will be no
farther distant than the present station, and the route to it
by way of Dartmouth Street and the banks of Charles River
will be much more agreeable than the route through the city
which is followed to-day. In this connection the plan suggests an improved position for the future bridge to Charlestown and a way of entrance into the city, for a boulevard
leading from the northern suburbs by way of Sullivan Square,
Charlestown, to both Lafayette Square, Cambridge, and the
Back Bay.

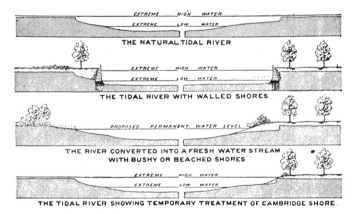

A NEW NORTH STATION NORTH OF CHARLES RIVER

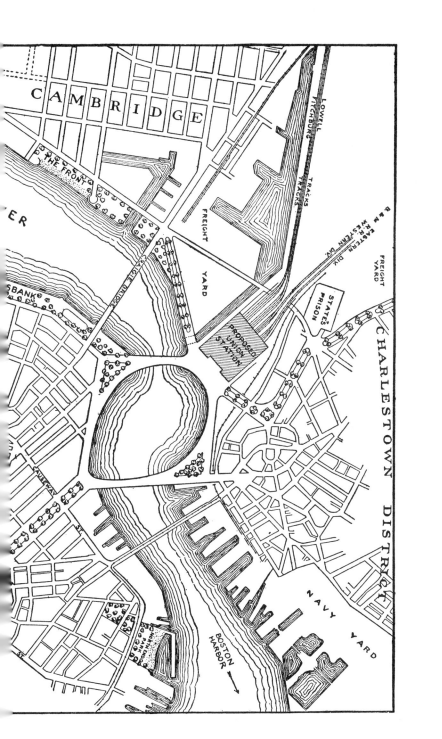

CAMBRIDGE

THE FRONT

FREIGHT YARD

LOWELL
FITCHBURG
TRACKS
TRACKS

B & M
EASTERN DIV.
EASTERN DIV.

FREIGHT YARD

STATE'S PRISON

PROPOSED UNION STATION

CHARLESTOWN DISTRICT

ER

S BANK

WAY

CHARLES
PARK

NAVY YARD

BOSTON HARBOR

CHAPTER XXXI

POLICY AND METHODS OF THE METROPOLITAN PARK COMMISSION, 1896

The only failure a man ought to fear, is failure in clinging to the purpose he knows to be best. — GEORGE ELIOT.

A LARGE number of bills calling for various park or parkway appropriations were presented to the legislature of 1896. The presentation of these bills and the reception accorded to them seemed to Charles to prove that the principles on which metropolitan money could alone be equitably expended for park and parkway purposes were but imperfectly understood by the legislature and the public. He thereupon addressed to the Metropolitan Park Commission, in February, the two letters with which this chapter opens; and later (April 1st) he read before a meeting of the Commission with the Committee of the legislature on Metropolitan Affairs the convincing paper which follows the letters. Having thus defined anew what he believed to be the true principles in selecting parks and parkways for the metropolitan population, Charles published in the "New England Magazine" for September, 1896, a description of the achievements of the Commission during its first three years (1893, 1894, and 1895), and of the financial arrangements and executive machinery which had enabled it to achieve such remarkable results in so short a time. Extracts from this concise statement conclude this chapter. It appears in this article that Charles thought that the work done by the Massachusetts Metropolitan Park Commission, and the methods of the Commission, offered an example which other American communities might follow to their advantage.

February 25, 1896.

In view of the numerous special bills for special park works lately presented to the General Court, and of our professional relation to the general work of the Metropolitan Park Commission, it seems to us that we are in duty bound to acquaint the Commission with our impressions and opinions concerning the questions at issue.

If the metropolitan district is viewed broadly, the distribution of the existing large public reservations is found to be remarkably equitable. (1st) The Charles River Reservation already secured ensures the eventual completion of a water park seven miles long, extending westward from the very centre of the metropolitan district. (2d) The Middlesex Fells and Stony Brook Reservations both lie just within the sweep of the eight mile radius from the State House, and while the first-named reservation lies north-northwest from this central point, the second lies correspondingly south-south-west. (3d) Of the smaller Beaver Brook and Hemlock Gorge Reservations, the first lies five miles southwest of the Fells and the second the same number of miles northwest of Stony Brook. It is also five miles from the one to the other. (4th) Again, the Blue Hills and the Lynn Woods mate closely one with the other, both lying between the circles swept by the eight mile and eleven mile radii from the State House. The Blue Hills Reservation is now topographically complete; but this is not the case with the Lynn Woods. Certain lands and hills in Saugus ought to be added to the last-named domain. (5th) Lastly, Revere Beach Reservation lies northeast from the State House, and it is not balanced by any similar reservation on the shore southeast of the centre of the district. On the other hand, Revere Beach fronts the open sea, and is on that account more valuable and more worthy of first attention than any part of the near southeast coast, since all the latter possesses frontage on the Bay only.

Such being the present distribution of the principal reservations, where, if at all, ought new reservations to be acquired? In the first place, it seems to us that Lynn Woods Reservation ought to be rounded out at the expense of the metropolitan district, and the completed domain made one of the metropolitan reservations. Population is yet sparse about the outer borders of this reservation; but so it is about the Blue Hills. If the Blue Hills are justly an object of metropolitan expenditure, so also are the Lynn Woods. It may be supposed that the city of Lynn would sell its Park Commission's holdings in the Woods for what they originally cost

the city treasury, just as the town of Stoneham sold its Bear
Hill Park; while the Lynn Water Board would presumably
transfer the care and maintenance of its land, just as the
Winchester Board has done.

In the second place, it seems to us that when money is
available or gifts can be obtained, the seashore reservations
of the Metropolitan Commission ought to be greatly extended.
If three miles should be added to Revere Beach Reservation so as to extend its limits to Winthrop Great Head, this
northern seashore reservation would then be six miles long.
If then a search be made for a fairly equivalent and equally
accessible stretch of southern shore, it can be found only at
Quincy Bay. Winthrop Great Head is five miles from the
State House; so also is Squaw Rock, Squantum. The Point
of Pines at the end of the six miles of Revere Beach is eight
miles from the State House; so also is Nut Island at the far
end of the six mile curve of Quincy Bay. Revere Beach is
appropriately made a public reservation because its exposure
to the sea prevents its occupation for commercial purposes.
The shores of Quincy Bay may as appropriately be dedicated
to public enjoyment, because the shallowness of its waters
similarly precludes commerce. Deep-water frontages of
ample length are found in the adjacent estuaries of the Neponset and Weymouth Rivers.

In the third place, it seems to us that metropolitan money
may very advisably be spent in acquiring water rights and
river-bank lands along the boating course of Charles River
between Waltham and Newton Lower Falls. This section of
Charles River, three miles in length, with the adjacent Water
Reserve of the Cambridge Water Board, lies, like Lynn
Woods and the Blue Hills, just within the sweep of the
eleven mile radius from the State House, and almost exactly
west of the centre of the metropolitan district. We have
lately reported on this subject to the Joint Commission, and
need not repeat ourselves here.

Summarizing the foregoing recommendations, we may say
that we believe the most important and the most equitable of
all possible additions to the present series of metropolitan
reservations to be the following: (1) the balancing of the

Blue Hills Reservation by the acquisition of the Lynn Woods; (2) the balancing of Revere Beach Reservation extended to Winthrop Great Head by the acquisition of the shores of Quincy Bay; (3) the acquisition in the far western section of the district of the banks of Charles River between Waltham and Newton Lower Falls. [Compare the map of December 1, 1901, in the pocket of the right-hand cover.]

February 28, 1896.

We would respectfully call the attention of the Commission to the unfortunate confusion of " boulevards " with " reservations " exhibited in the draughts of bills lately referred to the Legislative Committee on Metropolitan Affairs. It seems important that the distinction should be clearly made, and firmly held to.

Reservations are lands acquired to preserve scenery or landscape, free from buildings, for the enjoyment and refreshment of the people. Middlesex Fells Reservation preserves the scenery of certain ponds lying upon a rocky plateau. Revere Beach Reservation preserves the long curve of a beautiful beach and its accompanying outlook over the sea. Parkways or boulevards, on the other hand, are generally merely improved highways designed to conduct travel in one direction or another as agreeably as may be possible. Beacon Street, Brookline, is such an improved highway ; and the so-called Arbor-way of the Boston Park System is another.

In a letter addressed to the Commission on February 25th, we expressed certain views respecting metropolitan reservations, and we now beg leave to add a few words concerning metropolitan parkways. It is obviously impossible that every city and town in the district should be connected with the reservations by agreeable parkways, just as it is impossible that every ward in each separate city should be similarly connected with the local parks or squares. Plans might, indeed, be drawn for such universal parkways, but it would, at present, be impracticable to raise money enough to build them. Accordingly, if only a few parkways are to be constructed out of the metropolitan money, it is but just that they be placed, without regard to local pressure, solely with a view to securing the greatest good of the greatest number. Now we find that, upon setting out to plan the distribution of two, four, or six metropolitan parkways, having these ideas of equity and symmetry in mind, we are at once confronted by the fact that the south side of the metropolitan district has already provided itself with numerous modern, broad highways and parkways, while the north side of the district has as yet provided itself with none. The result is that expenditures made in the southern section of the district naturally produce more striking results than can be hoped for in the northern section. For example, the expenditure already made by the Metropolitan Commission for the West Roxbury Parkway has resulted in the connection of Stony Brook Reservation with the Boston and Brookline park system, and so with the Charles River Basin in the centre of the metropolitan area. On the other hand, no similar expenditure would accomplish the connection of the corresponding Middlesex Fells Reservation with the Charles River Basin. Again, the appropriation already made for the Blue Hills Parkway will connect the Blue Hills with the centre of population of the metropolitan district, while no similar expenditure would give the no more distant Lynn Woods any such direct and valuable approach to that centre.

It will be perceived that the problem, which in theory is simple, is in fact extremely complex; and further, that while the expenditures already made by the Commission on the south side of the city are obviously justifiable on the ground that they do secure the greatest good of the greatest number, the expenditures for north-side parkways are by no means as clearly equitable. It was just now noted that Blue Hills Reservation has been connected with Boston. Not even a beginning has been made towards connecting Lynn Woods with Boston. It was just now noted that Stony Brook has been connected with Charles River Basin. Not even a beginning has been made towards such a connection for the Fells; except that Cambridge has secured the banks of the Charles River and Fresh Pond, which are links in the desirable chain. The metropolitan appropriations thus far spent for parkways in the northern half of the district have secured (1) the eastern shores of Mystic lakes, which, however lovely in themselves, in no way assist in connecting the Fells with the Basin as Stony Brook is connected ; and (2) two sections of narrow parkway which unite the two southern extremities of Middlesex Fells Reservation with the main east and west highway of the region north of Mystic River. These two sections of parkway enable Malden and the towns east thereof to approach the western Fells, and Medford and the towns west thereof to approach the eastern Fells more easily and pleasantly than hitherto ; but as they do not help the central body of metropolitan population to reach the woods, they do not (by themselves) seem to us to be worthy objects of metropolitan expenditure.

In view of this unfortunate condition of affairs, it seems desirable to make sure of some one more truly metropolitan way for the north side, before undertaking or even discussing any parkways for the other parts of the district. The most obvious remedy for the present situation is the extension of the Fells Parkway to Broadway Park, Somerville.[1] The Fells would thus be provided with an approach corresponding to the Blue Hill Avenue approach to the Blue Hills, — not a beautiful driveway, but still a valuable means of access from the heart of the district. If the Commission is inclined, however, to secure a more picturesque parkway, corresponding to the approach to Stony Brook Reservation through West Roxbury, we would suggest the acquisition of the course of Meeting-House Brook, and the banks of the Mystic River as far as the Somerville Pumping Station of the Boston Water Works, where Alewife Brook joins Mystic River. By way of this route, Alewife Brook, Fresh Pond, and Charles River, the Fells Reservation would be seven miles distant from the head of the Charles River Basin. By way of Muddy River and the West Roxbury Parkway, Stony Brook Reservation is six miles distant from the same point. The acquisition of one or other of these ways of approach to the Fells from the central part of the district seems to us of much greater and more immediate importance than the acquisition of a Woburn Parkway, a Dedham Parkway, or any other special connection.

[1] This parkway was completed in 1898.

Indeed, the immediate acquisition of one or other of the suggested approaches to the Fells seems necessary to the maintenance of the balance of benefit upon which metropolitan, as distinguished from local, expenditures ought to be based.

Lastly, if, after securing at least one good north-side parkway, any additional money should be available for parkways, we have in mind two well-balanced routes which would lead street-cars and carriages to the seashore reservations, just as the Fells and Blue Hills Parkways will lead them to the forests; but these need not be described at this time.

GENERAL PLAN OF THE METROPOLITAN PRESERVATIONS.

1 April, 1896.

The Metropolitan Park Commission, created by Chapter 407 of the Acts of the General Court of 1893, has now been at work during two years and a half. The third annual report lately submitted to the legislature details the remarkable results which have been accomplished, and I shall not attempt to recite the contents of that volume. Let me rather endeavor to picture for you the beneficent achievements of this Commission as they appear to a professional practitioner of the art of arranging land and landscape for human use and delight, and then let me add a few suggestions and recommendations such as professional men, from physicians to artists, are in duty bound to offer, regardless of the probability or improbability of their being accepted and followed.

In thus reviewing the work already accomplished by the Metropolitan Park Commission, it is necessary at the outset to remind ourselves that the Commission was originally created not for the purpose of constructing inter-urban highways, boulevards, or parkways, but in order that some of the more striking scenery of the district surrounding Boston might be preserved for the enjoyment of existing and coming generations. The numerous and influential petitions which were addressed to the General Court of 1892 called attention to the fact " that the seashore, the river-banks, the hill-tops, and the other finest portions of the scenery of the district surrounding Boston, to which the people have long been accustomed to resort for healthful pleasure, are now being converted to the private purposes of their owners, to the great detriment of the present population and the irreparable loss of succeeding generations."

The bill which was enacted sought to remedy the unfortunate condition thus described by creating a commission endowed with power to "acquire, maintain, and make available to the inhabitants of said district open spaces for exercise and recreation." Let us, therefore, first consider the "open spaces" which have been, or may most advisably be, acquired by the Commission for the benefit of the metropolitan district, and then, if time permits, let us take up the subject of parkways or boulevards, to which the attention of the Commission was directed, as will be remembered, by subsequent legislation (1894) which had its origin, not in any general demand for parkways, but in a widespread desire to assist the unemployed.

The selection of lands for the public open spaces of American towns and cities has too generally, as it seems to me, been governed by a certain inherited preconception of what "parks" ought to be like. In old England the word "park" means a stretch of grassy land dotted with great trees, the home of the deer and other animals of the chase. Hyde Park and all the older parks of London were originally deer-parks, and it has come about that the type of scenery which is created by the pasturing of smooth land with deer has become the scenery which is associated with the words "park" and "park-like" even here in America, where we do not care to preserve deer for hunting, because we have them so near at hand in the wild woods. The large public open spaces of American cities ought, it seems to me, to be selected on common-sense principles and without regard to inherited predilections. What are some of these common-sense principles? First, the lands selected should possess, or afford opportunity for the creation of, interesting or beautiful scenery of one type or another; but this scenery need not necessarily be "park-like." Secondly, the lands selected should generally, though not always, be such as are least well adapted for streets and buildings. Thirdly, the lands selected should be related to the body of the district, which is taxed to buy them and to maintain them, as symmetrically as due attention to the foregoing requirements will permit.

The central reservation acquired by the Metropolitan Park Commission certainly fulfills all these demands. By buying those almost unused marsh banks of Charles River which had not already been acquired by local park commissions or semi-public institutions, the Metropolitan Park Commission has made it possible for the district to create for itself, at any time it may desire, a river park extending more than six miles westward from the State House, — the geographical centre of the whole metropolitan area. It is true that this stream is not at present attractive in appearance; but by damming out the salt tides, the pleasing scenery of the fresh-water Charles, with its delightful opportunities for boating and skating, can be extended all the way down the river to the central basin itself.

Next to be noted are a series of reservations of a very different character. Lying north-northeast of the State House and between eight and eleven miles distant, the Lynn Woods Reservation of some 2000 acres had been acquired by the city of Lynn some years before the establishment of the Metropolitan Park Commission. Lying in the corresponding southerly direction from the State House and exactly the same number of miles distant are the highest hills of the whole neighborhood of Boston, — hills whose broken sky-line is the chief ornament of every prospect from the towers of the great city, from the other hills about it, and from the bay and the sea. Among these loftiest hills of the district there is extremely little land adapted to development as house-lots, but there is abundant interesting scenery, and opportunity for the slow development of even greater impressiveness and beauty. Thus the Blue Hills Reservation conforms to the requirements first laid down.

The Lynn Woods and the Blue Hills, these two large areas of wild land, preserved until this day, apparently expressly in order that they may serve the people of the cities as forest recreation grounds, lie on the extreme edge of the metropolitan district, and between them and the central reservation on Charles River lie many square miles of more or less densely

settled, but now rapidly growing, suburbs. When the Metropolitan Commission was established, the southern section of
these suburbs already possessed many hundred acres of public
open space in the Brookline and Boston Parkway, Jamaica
Park, the Arboretum, and Franklin Park, while the corresponding northern suburbs had few public grounds, — indeed
almost none. Accordingly, the Metropolitan Commission has
acquired in the southern region only the comparatively small
but costly Stony Brook Reservation, while in the northern region there has been secured the broad domain of the
Middlesex Fells. Bellevue Hill and the narrow valley of
Stony Brook unquestionably present the most strikingly picturesque landscapes to be found in the region between Dedham and Boston, and the new reservation will make a pleasing
addition to the long chain of the Boston and Brookline parks.
The Fells, on the other hand, include the most interesting
scenery to be found between Woburn, Wakefield, and Boston, scenery well worthy of being preserved in a single reservation to answer for the northern suburbs the purposes of
Jamaica Park, Franklin Park, the Arboretum, and Bellevue
Hill combined into one area.

Westward again two small reservations yet remain to be
mentioned, each of which preserves scenery of remarkable
beauty.

Beaver Brook is just five miles distant from the nearest
corner of the Fells, and Hemlock Gorge is the same number
of miles distant from Stony Brook. The distribution of
these inland reservations is, I submit, most remarkably symmetrical. Indeed, the only reservation yet acquired by the
Commission which is not symmetrically placed is the ocean
beach at Revere; and no one who has seen the crowds which
resort to that beach in warm weather will ever question for a
moment the wisdom of buying it for the use, and at the cost,
of the metropolitan population.

Let us see now if there are any other lands or places, the
acquirement of which, without too great expenditure, would
enrich the life of the metropolitan district, and, at the same
time, make the distribution of the reservations even more
equitable and symmetrical than it is to-day. You will already

have anticipated my first remark under this head. If the Blue Hills are properly an object of metropolitan expenditure, so also are the no-more distant Lynn Woods. The two reservations are similarly related to the central body of the metropolitan region, while one is related to Lynn exactly as the other is to Quincy. The burden of the maintenance of Lynn Woods, and the cost of extending the new arbitrary boundaries to suitable topographical lines, ought, in some way, to be transferred to the broad shoulders of the metropolitan district.

It cannot be questioned that the seashore of Boston Bay presents fresh air and novel scenery especially attractive to the populations which now crowd around it. In this seashore Boston possesses something which every inland city envies her. Accordingly, I believe that, wherever the shore is purchasable at reasonable prices, and is ill-adapted for commercial uses, it ought to be bought, and put to use as a place of public recreation.

The present Revere Beach Reservation is three miles long. It fronts the open sea where there is no harborage for vessels. If it is extended southward to Winthrop Great Head, it will then be six miles long, though it will still lie between the lines swept by the five mile and the eight mile circles from the State House. It seems to me that both the local residents and the general public would be greatly benefited by such an extension. On the other hand, I would not advocate it without at the same time recommending a seashore reservation on the other side of Boston. Revere Beach is too remote from the suburbs which lie south of the Charles. It so happens that the same five mile and eight mile circles from the State House mark the beginning and the ending of six miles of southern shore which, because it borders upon the extremely shallow Quincy Bay, is unavailable for commerce. Ample wharfage upon deep channels is found in the adjacent estuaries of the Neponset and Weymouth rivers. I, therefore, believe that the metropolitan district would do well to secure the shore of Quincy Bay from the already public Moon Island all the way round to Nut Island. If twelve miles of public seashore seems to any one too much, let him remember that these narrow strips of coast require no garden decorations, and no large expenditure for maintenance, and also that they provide for townspeople recreation and refreshment very different from that which parks or gardens, however lovely, can supply.

Supposing now that Lynn Woods Reservation is made a metropolitan domain, and that these northern and southern seashores are secured for public enjoyment, what large part of the metropolitan area will then remain unfurnished with any reasonably accessible scenic recreation ground? A mere glance at the map suffices to make it plain that the far western part alone will then be unprovided for. It so happens that in this very region, and no more distant from the State House than are the Lynn Woods and the Blue Hills, there lies a reach of Charles River about four miles long, which, with its varied and often beautifully wooded banks, presents the opportunity for the making of a reservation as different from the Blue Hills in its character and in its modes of use, as the Blue Hills are different from the shores of Revere or Quincy. Charles River between Waltham and Newton Lower Falls is already much resorted to for pleasure boating. It is certainly more sensible to take advantage of natural opportunities like these presented by this river, by the Blue Hills, and by Revere Beach, than it is to make all recreation grounds of one pattern, and that the typical " park " pattern, as so many American cities are doing. I believe that this section of the Charles ought to be added to the existing series of metropolitan open spaces.

Before speaking of parkways opened, or to be opened, at the cost of the metropolitan district, it seems necessary to point out once more the difference between parkways and reservations, a distinction which has been lost sight of in some quarters of late. A reservation is a tract of land kept free from streets and houses for the sake of its scenery. A parkway is simply a highway made as agreeable as may be possible.

As we have seen, the Metropolitan Commission has executed the will of the people so far as reservations are concerned, and in so doing has followed a comprehensive and symmetrical scheme. For parkways, as distinguished from reservations, no such comprehensive scheme has ever been made. A swarm of special bills calling for parkways here, there, and elsewhere, has been pressed upon the legislature; but whether the general public really desires that parkways should be opened at the cost of the common purse is by no means clear. If the people do demand such parkways, as they certainly did demand reservations, let them express their wish in the same forcible way, and then let the legislature direct some commission to work out a comprehensive and fair scheme. Complaint is sometimes made that the Metropolitan Park Commission (which ought to be called the Metropolitan Reservations Commission) has refused to divulge its plans for parkways; but the fact is that neither this Commission nor any other has ever been asked to make a general scheme for such ways. The only parkways attempted by the Metropolitan Commission have been those, the expenditure for which was authorized by an act of 1894, passed, as before remarked, on the recommendation of the Committee on the Unemployed. This act appropriated a sum of money obviously not large enough to provide boulevards in all parts of the district; and so the firm of which I am a member was asked by the Commission to devise two special parkways such as might fairly be deemed to be of first importance. Accordingly, we brought in plans for ways intended to facilitate access to the Fells on the one hand, and the Blue Hills on the other, by means of street-cars, as well as carriages and bicycles. These plans were outlined in the annual report for 1895 and published in detail in the report for 1896, to which reports I beg leave to refer you. If the cost of only two parkways is to be borne by the metropolitan district, I believe that the construction of the two which were thus suggested will distribute the benefit as broadly and as equitably as is practicable. One of these suggested parkways will make it possible for bicycles, carriages, and electric cars to move rapidly and pleasantly from the crowded interior of the district to the Blue Hills, while the other will make it possible to reach similarly the Fells. The value of both these reservations will be much increased by the construction of these agreeable approaches. That both parkways will develop building lands at present remote from all means of rapid transit is not to be counted against them ; since it is from the increasing taxable value of these very lands that a large share of the cost of constructing the new ways may be derived.

The annual report of the Commission tells how it happened that only the two northern sections of the proposed Fells parkway were acquired, while the money which might have secured the route of the important southern section was spent in ensuring certain gifts of money and of lands in Winchester and West Medford. Now the Mystic Lakes are beautiful. Public spirit is admirable. I know, also, that it is wrong to look a gift horse in the mouth. Nevertheless, I cannot think that the West Medford and Winchester parkway possesses for the metropolitan district, considered as a whole, one half the present value that would attach to the comparatively dull and ugly Fells parkway the moment it and its electric railway should be opened. The Winchester parkway will make a pleasant drive ; but it will not help the great body of the people to reach the Fells, a reservation which, though it lies no farther from the State House than the Arnold Arboretum, must remain comparatively unused until some direct and fairly agreeable means of approach is provided.

No broadly comprehensive scheme of parkways having been devised or even studied, there is nothing more to be said, save to point out that the devising of such a scheme is a much more complex and difficult matter than was the devising of a scheme of reservations. Upon what basis ought the cost of a system of metropolitan parkways to be apportioned ? Ought the present lack of parkways in the region north of the Charles, and the abundance of them in the region south of that stream, to affect the apportionment? and so on. Until some one can find time and strength to solve some of these hard problems, it seems obvious that the community had better go slowly. I can testify that no landscape architect cares to tackle a problem, the fundamental data of which cannot be supplied to him. It is easy enough to draw lines on a map; but it is impossible to make such lines mean a practicable, purposeful, and equitable scheme, unless definite facts to go upon are furnished the designer.

Meanwhile, it would certainly be wrong to tax the metropolitan district for any one, two, or three of the scattered and unrelated parkways which have been proposed, most of which have, strangely enough, been placed on the remote outer edge of the district, — for instance, at Lynn, Woburn, Dedham, and Quincy. It is probable that tempting gifts will be forthcoming from time to time. But it is to be hoped that the Commission in charge may have strength to decline them; for it would obviously be just as wrong to tax the district for the maintenance of ill-balanced parkways, as for their right-of-way, or their construction.

From the New England Magazine.

THE BOSTON METROPOLITAN RESERVATIONS.

September, '96.

A great work has been quietly accomplished in the neighborhood of Boston during the last two years, and a sketch of it may perhaps encourage the people of other American neighborhoods to go and do likewise.

Surrounding Boston and forming with Boston the so-called metropolitan district lie thirty-seven separate and independent municipalities, comprising twelve "cities" and twenty-five "towns," all of which lie either wholly or partly within the sweep of a radius of eleven miles from the State House. The population of this group of towns and cities is about one million of people, and the total of taxed property about one thousand millions of dollars.

In 1892 the central city of Boston already possessed and had in part developed a costly series of public squares and parks within her own boundaries, sixteen of the surrounding municipalities had secured one or more local recreation grounds, and some of these communities had acquired still other lands for the sake of preserving the purity of public water supplies. Nevertheless, it was evident to all observing citizens that a great body of new population was spreading throughout the district much more rapidly than the local park commissions and water commissions were acquiring public open spaces, and that if any considerable islands of green country, or fringes of sea or river shore, were to be saved from the flood of buildings, and made accessible to the people, it could only be by means of some new and central authority raised above the need of regarding local municipal boundaries, and endowed by the people with the necessary powers and money. Accordingly, the whole problem was laid before the legislature of 1891 by a committee appointed at a meeting of the local park commissions, aided by representatives from the Trustees of Public Reservations, the Appalachian Mountain Club, and other organizations, and by numerous and influential petitions from all parts of the district. A preliminary or inquiring Commission was the result. This Commission, headed by Charles Francis Adams as chairman, examined the district in detail, discussed the problem with the local authorities, became thoroughly convinced of the need of prompt coöperative action, and so reported to the succeeding legislature; whereupon an act was passed establishing a permanent Metropolitan Park Commission, which act was signed by the governor June 3, 1893.

[Here follows a description of the reservations and of their distribution through the District. The description has been anticipated in this chapter.]

What is the nature of the executive and financial machinery by which these remarkable results have been achieved in so short a time? The Commission consists of five gentlemen who serve the community without pay. The Governor of the Commonwealth, acting for the metropolitan district, appoints one new member every year, the term of service being five years. The General Court of the Commonwealth, acting for the metropolitan district, authorizes from time to time the sale of bonds by the State Treasurer, who is directed to collect annually the amount of the interest and the sinking fund charges from the towns and cities of the metropolitan district in accordance with an apportionment newly made every five years by a special commission appointed by the Supreme Court. Bonds running forty years and bearing interest at the rate of $3\frac{1}{2}$ per cent. have thus far been authorized to the amount of $2,300,000, and the total sum to be collected from the district annually is found to be $111,253.99. The first quinquennial apportionment requires Boston to pay 50 per cent. of this annual requirement, or $55,627 per year, while the other thirty-six cities and towns are called upon for varying amounts ranging from Cambridge's $6\frac{8}{10}$ per cent. ($7,600.50 per year) to Dover's four thousandths of 1 per cent. ($48.92 per year). The validity and constitutionality of this ingenious financial system has recently been affirmed by the Supreme Court on appeal. It should be added that the law provides for the annual collection from the coöperating towns and cities of the cost of maintenance of the several reservations, and it is probable that the total sum required for this purpose will soon equal that required to meet the charges on the bonds. Whatever the total amount may be, it is to be assessed in accordance with the quinquennial apportionment; but down to the present time the Commonwealth has itself paid the general and maintenance expenses of the Commission, the legislature having appropriated $10,000, $20,000, and $38,943 in the years 1893, 1894, and 1895 respectively.

The following condensed statements concerning the work of the Commission have been compiled from the three successive annual reports of the Board : —

The Commission was originally composed as follows : —

Charles Francis Adams, Chairman, Quincy; William B. de las Casas, Malden ; Philip A. Chase, Lynn ; Abraham L. Richards, Watertown ; James Jeffery Roche, Boston. William L. Chase of Brookline succeeded James Jeffery Roche resigned, but died in July, 1895, and was succeeded by Edwin B. Haskell of Newton. Augustus Hemenway of Canton has also been appointed in place of Charles Francis Adams resigned. William B. de las Casas is Chairman of the present Board. The Commission meets every week and sits from two until six o'clock ; its members also make frequent excursions to the scenes of their labors.

Executive Department. — Secretary, H. S. Carruth, July, 1893, to January 1, 1896. John Woodbury, January 1, 1896, to date. — The secretary is the salaried executive officer of the Commission, and all departments report through him. He is the general manager of the work of the Commission, and arranges for the financial settlements with the owners of the lands acquired. The total number of acres thus far taken for reservations is 6822, embracing lands belonging to 603 claimants for damages. At the date of the last report 367 of these claims, representing 5156 acres, had been adjusted at prices ranging all the way from forty dollars an acre to one dollar per square foot. So far there have been very few cases of litigation. It is pleasant to note that six persons have presented lands to the Commission. The sum of the three annual appropriations of the General Court ($68,943) has been expended by the executive department for office rent, salaries, travelling, repairs, tools, etc., and for the pay of the keepers or police of the reservations (about $20,000 to date).

Law Department. — Messrs. Balch & Rackemann, attorneys and conveyancers, have from the first draughted the legal papers required for the taking of lands by eminent domain and for other purposes. They have represented the Commission in such suits as have been brought by land-owners who have been unable to come to terms with the secretary or the Commission. They have also prosecuted a few violators of the ordinances governing the reservations. The principal work of this department has, however, been the searching of the titles to the lands of the reservations in order to make sure that only rightful claims are paid. This tedious task has been accomplished by employing a large force of skilled assistants.

Landscape Architects' Department. — Messrs. Olmsted, Olmsted & Eliot have from the first advised the Commission as to the choice of lands for the reservations, as to the boundaries of each reservation, and as to all questions relating to the appearance or scenery of the lands acquired. More than thirty miles of boundaries have been studied and re-studied in detail.

Engineering Department. — Engineer, William T. Pierce. — With a varying number of assistants the engineer prepares the plans of "takings," land maps to accompany filed deeds,

projects for necessary works here and there in the reservations, and so on.   During the first year or two different engineers were engaged in different places for special works.
Topographical surveys of the Fells and Blue Hills Reservations have been executed for the Commission by surveyors
employed under a contract.   The engineering department is
at present principally occupied in supervising the construction
of certain "parkways" not previously mentioned, money for
which to the amount of $500,000 was placed at the disposal
of the Metropolitan Park Commission by an Act of 1894,
which in this case divided the financial burden evenly between
the Commonwealth and the metropolitan district.

Construction Department. — Wilfred Rackemann, General
Superintendent. — About twenty miles of old wood-roads in
the forest reservations have been made usable by pleasure
carriages, and many additional miles have been made practicable for horseback riders.   The whole area of the inland
reservations has been cleared of the wood-choppers' slashings,
the fire-killed trees, and all the dangerous, because dead and
dry, tinder with which the lands were found heaped.   About
one hundred men have been employed during three winters in
this last-mentioned safeguarding work.   Several buildings
have also been torn down, fences built, and odd jobs of all
sorts done.

The draughts on the sum of the loans ($2,300,000) may,
accordingly, be classified thus : —

Payments for lands (to date of last report) . .	$940,739.77
Counsel and conveyancers' fees and expenses . .	52,199.79
Landscape architects' fees and expenses . . .	7,147.78
Engineering expenses (including cost of topo- .	
graphical surveys, $17,012.90)	31,857.57
Labor and supervision thereof	146,402.60
Miscellaneous expenditures	16,303.90
Total	$1,194,651.41

It is estimated that the whole of the balance of the loans
($1,105,348.59), and possibly more, will be required to meet
the remaining claims of land-owners, the cost of removing
the Revere Beach Railroad, and a few other minor but necessary works.

Every rural, as well as every crowded, district of the United States possesses at least a few exceptionally interesting scenes, the enclosure or destruction of which for private pleasure or gain would impoverish the life of the people. Very often these strongly characterized scenes are framed by lands or strips of land which, like the Blue Hills, or the banks of the Charles, and Revere Beach, are either almost unproductive, or else are put by their private owners to by no means their highest use. In many districts now is the time when these financially profitless summits, cañons, crags, ravines, and strips of ground along the seashores, lake shores, rivers, and brooks ought to be preserved as natural pictures, and put to use as public recreation grounds. To enable benevolent citizens or bodies of voluntary subscribers to achieve the permanent preservation of such scenes, Massachusetts has created a board of trustees, known as the Trustees of Public Reservations, who are empowered to hold free of all taxes such lands and money as may be given into their keeping — an institution which ought to be found in every State. In special regions, however, where the establishment of such a board of trustees would be ineffectual, either because large sums of money are required promptly, or because the power of eminent domain must be invoked, the methods of the Massachusetts Metropolitan Park Commission may be profitably followed on either a humbler or a grander scale. The establishment and the successful working of this Commission proves that at least one great and complex American democracy is alive to the usefulness of the beautiful, and the value of public open space; also that this democracy is capable of coöperation and of foresight, ready to tax itself severely for an end which it believes in, and able to secure as executors of its expressed but undefined desires commissioners capable of realizing these desires in a remarkably comprehensive and equitable manner.

CHAPTER XXXII

SELECTED LETTERS OF 1896

Art when really cultivated, and not practised empirically, maintains, what it first gave the conception of, an ideal beauty to be eternally aimed at, though surpassing what can be actually attained ; and by this idea it trains us never to be completely satisfied with imperfection in what we ourselves do and are ; to idealize as much as possible every work we do, and most of all our own characters and lives. — JOHN STUART MILL.

THE letters selected for this chapter are all of the year 1896, and they relate not to routine business, but to special subjects which were brought to Charles's notice either by the public bodies which he was advising, or by private persons. Some of them were written to resist, or to help the Commission to resist, injuries to the reservations ; one to suggest a handsome framing for the western end of Charles River Basin, and to advocate forethought and coöperation on the part of all the parties interested, to the end of securing a well-considered plan for this æsthetically important locality ; one to urge the importance of providing a body of good keepers, and to describe the quality and functions of good keepers ; one to propose an appropriate monument to Elizur Wright in Middlesex Fells ; and one to define the natural associations of instruction in Landscape Architecture in a university.

Throughout the year Charles attended the numerous meetings of the Metropolitan Park Commission, kept many appointments in the field with its members, officers, and agents, and made for it many designs ; but he also studied on the spot playgrounds, parks, or parkways for Cambridge, Fall River, Westport, Brookline, Reading, and Quincy in Massachusetts, for Providence and Newport in Rhode Island, for Portland in Maine, for Hartford, Conn., for Brooklyn, and Louisville, and made designs for the grounds of the American University at Washington, the Rhode Island College of Agriculture at Kingston, the Missouri Botanic Garden at St. Louis, and the Victoria Hospital at Montreal, and for more than a dozen private places besides. Occasionally he felt overburdened, but generally he rejoiced in his work. How he felt in busy midsummer days may be inferred from these three hasty notes to his wife at New Hartford. Peach's Point is at Marblehead, where his uncle Robert S. Peabody had a summer place. The plans referred to in the first note were general designs covering the whole of the large reservations.

July 16, '96. Thursday Morning.

. . . Some days this world seems almost terribly interesting, and my own part in its drama most strangely important! Yesterday a new plan for the Fells Parkway went through the Board with a rush. Next Wednesday the Metropolitan, Boston, and Cambridge Boards visit Charles River together, and big things will follow for the district! Revere Beach was visited by 45,000 people last Sunday! and the Commission has ordered construction plans, so that the crowd can be taken care of next summer.

Aug. 6, '96. OFFICE, Thursday A. M.

Tuesday I lunched with Miss O. and F. L. O., Jr., and dined at the park restaurant, Dan driving me over. Wednesday, lunch in Boston and dinner at Peach's Point, going down with R. S. P. after Metropolitan meeting. Chairman now says our engagement for plans is in "abeyance"! To-day I am to lunch at park with commissioners, and spend the afternoon with them. I mean to spend this night also at Marblehead! and to-morrow night in Hartford; so as to go out to you some time on Saturday. Probably I shall have to go to Bridgeman's at Norfolk, and so reach New Hartford from there at 5.11 P. M. . . .

'96, BROOKLINE, Wednes. A. M.

. . . I am O. K. and very busy, J. C. O. having fled to Deer Isle last Sunday and not having returned as yet. Positively I am swamped.

The first letter given below mentions, in answer to an inquiry, some of the beauties which Boston has missed through lack of foresight and of careful planning in laying out thoroughfares and preserving vistas. The worst of these misfortunes is the last mentioned. For all most Bostonians see of their beautiful harbor during their daily pursuits, the city might as well be ten miles inland. The sight of blue water is cut off from State Street by the elevated railroad and some insignificant buildings across the lower end of the street.

January 16, 1896.

DEAR MADAM, — I am sorry to say that I cannot tell you where to find the old Back Bay and Commonwealth Avenue plans. I thought I had a note of them somewhere; but I do not find it.

Of the fine chances which have been missed, a few may be noted as follows: A noble terminus at Massachusetts Avenue for the long straight of Commonwealth Avenue. A dignified plaza such as might have been secured at the parting of the old Brookline, Newton, and Brighton roads. A vista avenue across the Back Bay, so placed as to have a monument on Parker Hill at the far end of it. A glimpse of the Harbor from the heart of the town — say from the Old State House — such as might have been secured after the Great Fire. At present it is noticeable that the seaport is invisible save from the wharves themselves.

As to the Common, our plans were by no means radical, and the present plan seems to me not bad — only colorless.

The next seven letters were all addressed to the Chairman of the Metropolitan Park Commission.

January 31, 1896.

With respect to the proposed abandonment of lands to Mr. —— of Malden and to the Boston Rubber Shoe Company, we beg leave to report that we had supposed that the omission from the original taking of one of Mr. ——'s conspicuous " summer houses " and all the used portions of his estate had secured Mr. ——'s friendly consent to this " taking line." We regretted the original omission of the western summer-house rock extremely, because of the danger of some very ugly thing being set up there eventually, to the injury of many important and fine prospects. We now regret extremely the return to Mr. —— of his southernmost rocks and cliff. . . . Our reasons for regretting the abandonment of the cliff are (1) the loss of a fine view-point on the edge of the settled area; (2) the loss of a fine foreground which the Pines on the cliff supply to many views from rocks in

the interior of the reservation; (3) the danger that ugly
buildings may hereafter be substituted for the Pines; (4)
the loss of the fine appearance of the edge of the reservation
from outside points in Malden.

The abandonment to the Shoe Company which is involved
in this abandonment to Mr. —— throws out many ledges,
but they are not to be compared in public value to the rocks
surrendered to Mr. ——.

February 1, 1896.

With respect to a proposed abandonment of a part of the
—— property, Middlesex Fells Reservation, we beg leave to
report as follows : —

This estate lies between Washington Street and the famous
Cascade on the eastern verge of the Fells. The half circle of
high bluffs is very fine, and it will be lamentable if all the
buildings between the street and the bluff cannot be removed.
This cove in the wall of ledges is one of the most attractive
spots on the Reservation.

If financial considerations compel an abandonment, we
would suggest that such abandonment be limited to the northeast part of the estate in question, the site of the southernmost of the —— buildings being retained within the reservation. Both banks of the Cascade Brook will thus be
preserved to the public, as well as a fair chance to approach
and view the cascade itself. We would draw the new line as
close to the remaining buildings as may be possible, so that
space may be obtained for " planting out " their objectionable
back yards and out-buildings.

It should be noted that this proposed abandonment seems
dangerous in much the same way as the proposed abandonment of the — —— property on Forest Street, though by
no means in the same degree. Both estates, if abandoned,
will offer, in time, very favorable situations for road-houses
or beer-gardens, which places will appear to lie within the
reservation. Such places may indeed be established on the
private or opposite side of any of the boundary roads, but in
this position drinking-houses will be found to be far less
objectionable than when placed so that their rear fences project into the reservation itself.

February 3, 1896.

We beg leave to report with respect to the proposed abandonment to the Langwood Hotel Park and Trust Company.

This company owns a large island of private land in the midst of the eastern Fells. If this land should be occupied by large or numerous buildings, it would, of course, be an eyesore ; but the high price of the property compelled the Commission to refrain from taking it. Since this private island already exists, there is no objection to increasing its area for the sake of economizing, provided that such abandonments as may be made do not surrender any particularly charming spots, and do not extend so far as to bring future buildings into view from parts of the Fells which are now safe from such intrusion. . . .

February 7, 1896.

In obedience to the request of the Commission, we herewith submit alternative plans suggesting possible approaches to a bridge over Charles River at the western end of the so-called Basin. The Commission is aware that the outline of the Basin has been from time to time determined by the State Board of Harbor Commissioners with little regard to public convenience, and with no regard for appearance, or the making of a handsomely framed urban sheet of water. Between Craigie and West Boston bridges the cities of Boston and Cambridge have each secured straight-walled public banks. On the northern side west of West Boston bridge, the so-called Embankment Company has built and deeded to the city of Cambridge another long section of straight roadway and promenade, and the Cambridge Park Commission owns the remainder of this shore.

Unfortunately, the Boston shore of the Basin west of West Boston bridge possesses two awkward angles, and it has moreover been so laid out as to compel the backing of buildings towards the water. If parks on land need boundary roads and fronting buildings, water parks, the edges of which cannot be planted out, need them much more. The first Boston Park Commission suggested a public driveway and promenade along the Boston shore, and it may be assumed that this work will be accomplished some day.

The accompanying plans are based on alternative suggestions for eventually securing a fine frontage on the Boston
shore of the Basin ; and they demonstrate the fact that a
handsome terminus is still obtainable at the western end of
the Basin, if forethought can be exercised, and coöperation
secured. Such forethought and coöperation have hitherto
been lacking in all matters connected with the development
of the great Basin. If the city authorities of Boston and
Cambridge, the Harbor Commissioners, and the owners of
the flats and filled lands can now be induced to agree upon
some harmonious plan, the work of construction may be postponed for years without danger to the ultimate fine result.
It is in the hope that such coöperation can be brought about
that the accompanying plans are submitted.

The plans referred to in this letter, with full descriptive
notes accompanying them, are in possession of the Metropolitan Park Commission ; but thus far (1902) no attempt has
been made to bring about the execution of this important
improvement. Meantime the ultimate carrying out of any
handsome design for the head of the basin has been made
much more difficult and expensive than it was in 1896 by
the rapid erection of many buildings on the Boston side of the
basin.

February 25, 1896.

We beg leave to report that Mr. Eliot attended the conference called by the Commission for February 20th, on the
subject of the proposed Charlesmouth Bridge. The suggestion seemed to meet with general approval. It was noted
that the only obstacle to the eventual selection of the proposed site for a bridge is the inadequate width of St. Mary's
Street and the other approaches on the Boston side. If suitably broad approaches can be secured, the bridge will doubtless be eventually built. The Boston Street Commissioners
and the City Government of Boston have it in their power to
make the desired widenings, and in order to induce them to
take action, we would suggest that the Park Commissions
concerned address a joint petition to the proper Boston
authorities. We have furnished the several Boards with
sun-prints of the general plan for the bridge, and we would

suggest that the Metropolitan Park Commission head a suitable petition and circulate it at an early date.

Some discussion was had at the aforesaid conference as to the advisability of a dam instead of a bridge at Charlesmouth, and the opinion of the majority of those present seemed to be that while a dam at the proposed bridge site would effect the desired economy in river-bank park construction, it would interrupt pleasure boating, and would not benefit the Back Bay and Cambridgeport filled lands as a dam at Charles-bank would. We have written Dr. Walcott since the conference, urging a public restatement of the sanitary benefits to be derived from a dam at Charlesbank as distinguished from a dam at Charlesmouth, feeling that unless the residents of the Back Bay can be led to see clearly these benefits, there can be but small hope of obtaining the favorable action of the National and State authorities. We indulge the hope that Dr. Walcott, Mr. Mills, or Engineer Stearns may yet make this clearer statement which is so much needed.

April 29, 1896.

It is perhaps unfashionable " to go on record " in these days ; nevertheless, we shall ask leave to file with the Secretary the following expression of opinion on two points which seem to us of grave importance.

The first work of a new park commission is the acquisition of lands possessing interesting scenery or adaptability to some special public purpose ; but a much more difficult work is the development and management of the lands so acquired. In our annual reports and in special letters we have set forth the need of planning in advance the work which must be gradually done, if the new open spaces are to benefit the community in a degree which will justify their removal from the tax lists. When topographical maps have once been provided, expenditure for planless road or forest work in public lands cannot be justified. We submit this simply as a fact which is generally recognized.

In addition to the work of acquiring and the work of developing public open spaces, every park commission is further charged with the duty of caring for the lands acquired, and

of regulating their use by the public. Public reservations
are worse than useless, if they are not as carefully controlled
as they are wisely developed. It is very easy for a public
forest to acquire an evil reputation, in which event it becomes
an injury instead of a benefit to adjacent property. Thus
the right keeping of a public open space is a matter of primary importance.

For the prevention of crime in a public domain, it is important that the keepers should be active men, both in fact
and in appearance. Since it is impossible to really patrol
every acre, it is necessary that the patrolmen should exercise
a moral influence by their bright, wide-awake, and active appearance. They must at all times avoid even the appearance
of loafing. They should change their routes every day, and
the time of their appearance at any one place should vary.
They should give little of their time to the main roads;
for people in carriages are neither likely to commit crime
nor to misuse the reservations. They should be careful to
avoid the bullying tone which is so common among ordinary
policemen; and they should continually bear themselves as the
courteous guides and helpers of the public, whose servants
they are, cautioning rather than threatening those who may
seem inclined to break the necessary regulations, and explaining to the children and the ignorant the reasonable grounds
of such rules as may seem hard to them. To induce both the
public and the officers themselves to take this view of the
keeping of the reservations, it seems to us very necessary that
the difference between a keeper and a police officer should be
plainly marked by a difference in uniform. If the regulation
police uniform, or anything like it, is adopted for the reservations patrol, the patrolmen will soon be aping the manners
of the city police, while the mischievous or vicious persons
who may resort to the public forests will take to outwitting
and circumventing the "cop" as they do in town.

It is customary to divide a force of keepers into three
classes; and we would recommend that this practice be adopted
by your Board. "Patrol-keepers" receive the highest pay
and are on duty daily. "Post-keepers" receive less pay, and
are stationed either daily, or when occasion may require, at

special points — as at entrances, ponds, or hill-tops. " Extra keepers " are usually selected laborers, who may be called upon to serve as keepers on special occasions. [See Appendix IV, for papers accompanying this letter.]

We would respectfully suggest that the whole system of keeping the new reservations be reorganized at the earliest convenient opportunity.

November 4, 1896.

As requested by the Commission, we hand you herewith a preliminary sketch for a lookout bastion or terrace on Pine Hill, such as might, we think, carry an inscription phrased to suitably commemorate the work of Mr. Elizur Wright in starting the public movement for the preservation of the Fells.

The ridge of Pine Hill is a long and narrow ridge ; and it is so wooded that views from it are obtained only by stepping out upon such ledges as here and there project a little outward from the main body of the hill. We find that Miss Wright has had in mind as the most appropriate memorial to her father a stone tower, to be placed on the southernmost of the projecting ledges of the hill. This is the ledge which is in view from a large part of Medford, and, indeed, all the country to the southward. While a tower on this ledge would certainly be a conspicuous monument, it is quite unnecessary so far as obtaining the view is concerned, because the ledge is so abrupt that the southern view is obtained in all its fulness from the rock itself. It seems to us that a narrow and somewhat lofty tower at this point would, in a measure, dwarf the apparent height of the hill, and would disfigure it.

A tower built in the rear of the ledge above mentioned, and upon a point near the highest of all the ledges on the hill, would be free from these objections, because the trees around it would conceal it, though the summit of it might rise above the trees so as to command a view in all directions. On the other hand, we suppose such a tower would hardly be conspicuous enough to fulfil the idea of a memorial; and then again, we think that hollow, stone towers are very objectionable in public grounds, unless a guardian can give his whole time to the care of the place, and that, we suppose, would not be possible in this instance.

It so happens that there is found adjacent to the ledge which .Miss Wright has had in mind another, and even bolder ledge, separated from the first ledge by a narrow hollow, by way of which the shortest path from the direction of Medford finds its way to the summit. After climbing up this hollow, we find it will be possible to turn the path out on to the western ledge, where a wall of stones may be built up in such a way as to provide a level standing-place or terrace, from which to look over to the westward ; and then, if a stone arch can be thrown across the gully, the eastern ledge, which Miss Wright has had in mind, can be easily reached; and here the walls of stones may be raised to the same grade as that of the western terrace, in which case this eastern terrace will be from twelve to fifteen feet above the present surface of the rock. Thus from this eastern terrace the view to the southward will be obtained in all its breadth, while in looking at the hill from the south, a horizontal line of stones rather than a vertical line will attract attention. The proposed stone walls will be, in effect, backed by the trees on the hill-top. An inscription dedicating the hill, or this stone structure, to the memory of Mr. Wright can, of course, be placed either on the arch over the hollow, or on any part of the parapet of the terraces. The old stone walls which still are found on Pine Hill may be used to supply the stone for the proposed work, and we would suggest that the work be done under the direction of some foreman especially skilled and experienced in such rough stone construction.

The next three letters were written to the chairman of the Boston Park Commission. All three dealt with important matters concerning which discussion was rife at the time, and all three opposed the action desired and warmly advocated in each case by a section of the public. In each case Charles's argument prevailed.

May 19, 1896.

LOOKING INTO OR OVER A PARK, AND LOOKING OUT OF IT. — We beg leave to submit the following considerations respecting the bank now building along Blue Hill Avenue.

The mound in question is on the border of that part of Franklin Park designated the Country Park, to distinguish it from the more open areas known as the Playstead, the Greeting, etc. The Country Park is a tract of land acquired and arranged at large expense for a particular purpose, a purpose distinct from that which the Common, the Fens, the Parkway, and the Greeting are designed to serve. The Country Park is intended to provide the people of Boston with a broad (or seemingly broad) stretch of rural landscape well screened from city sights and sounds. Experience has proved that the enjoyment of scenery thus separated from and strikingly contrasting with brick walls and stony pavements is extremely refreshing to dwellers in cities. It was in order to provide opportunity for securing such completely green scenery that the large area of Franklin Park was bought; while one of the principal reasons for preferring the present site of the park to other sites which were suggested was the fact that much of the chosen site was already bordered or framed by rocks, hills, and woods which shut out the city. Beginning at Glen Road, Jamaica Plain, the rocks and woods of the Wilderness, Juniper Hill, Waitt-Wood, Rock Milton, and Rock Morton effectually enclose three fifths of the street frontage of the Country Park. It is only from Canterbury Hill to Refectory Hill that nature has provided no bordering screen, and here the published plans have always indicated that the border was to be thickly planted with an impenetrable plantation of trees.

As a matter of fact, these boundary plantations were actually formed a few years ago of small trees and without much previous filling of the border lands, simply because of the difficulty and cost of obtaining either large trees or filling material. When the Street Commission notified the Park Commission of its desire to widen Blue Hill Avenue on the park land, we were constrained to object strenuously on the ground that this already too low and too narrow border plantation would be practically destroyed, to the great injury of the whole interior of the park. It then appeared that the Street Commission desired not only to widen, but also to lower, the grade of the avenue, and that considerable filling material would be obtained from the necessary excavations. A means of compromising the difficulty was thus presented;

and the Park Commission finally permitted the Street Commission to use park land for widening the avenue, on condition that the damage to the border plantation, and the diminished distance between the avenue and the park drive, should be counterbalanced by the raising of a bank between the drive and the avenue, upon which a new and effective border plantation might be grown.

The finished bank at its highest point, south of Refectory Hill and the entrance to the yard of the refectory, will rise only seven feet above the grade of the sidewalk of the avenue ; and in view of the fact that the important circuit drive of the park is only 160 feet distant from the avenue, we cannot recommend that the bank be lowered. Whoever will look towards this weak spot in the border from distant points within the park will certainly wish that the bank might be higher rather than lower. Without it and its future crown of trees, a whole district of houses and streets will rise into full view from the very heart of the park, where it ought to be possible to completely forget the town in the feeling that the park has undiscoverable limits. On the other hand, the Commission may rest assured that the appearance of the edge of the avenue will be fully as agreeable as the edges of the other streets which bound the country park.

It should be noted in passing that the abutters upon a rural or country park are not assessed betterments because of views over the park, but chiefly because of their proximity to that which other people are remote from. Such adjacent landowners cannot be granted special favors in the way of view-commanding openings without injury to that which chiefly makes the park valuable. It is impossible to have one's cake, and eat it too. To ask to have the bordering screens torn down is to ask for the destruction of that which the abutters' and all other tax-payers' money has been expended to secure and preserve.

Lastly, will the bordering wood on the new bank be really or permanently damaging to adjacent private property? Probably no more so than the natural woods along the previously wooded borders of the park — certainly not if the experience of other cities is in the least indicative. Central

Park, New York, and Prospect Park, Brooklyn, both have thick border woods, which in many places are growing on artificially built ridges. The adjacent buildings in both cases are generally of the highest class. Only lately the Commissioners in charge of Jackson Park, Chicago, have felt compelled, owing to the flatness of the ground, to raise screening mounds along the whole inland border of that park, some two and three quarter miles long, and on these mounds they have planted shrubbery and trees of large size : so important have they thought it to shut out the view of the city, from the streets of which the people fly for refreshment to the park.

We beg leave to call your attention to Mr. F. L. Olmsted's original Notes on the Plan of Franklin Park, which were submitted to the Park Commission with the plan ten years ago — particularly to pages 61 and 62.

Concerning entrances to the park from Blue Hill Avenue south of the footpath to the refectory, we desire to point out that it is extremely easy to multiply entrances to the great injury of the scenery of the parks. Moreover, additional entrances involve additional policing, additional branching paths, and additional difficulties at points where carriage-traffic crosses on crowded days. We are, however, already engaged on plans for one or two new footpath entrances, and we shall give the question of the advisability of a road entrance at the corner of the avenue and Canterbury Street very careful consideration.

May 21, 1896.

BICYCLE PATHS IN PARKS. — We ask that the following account of our views respecting bicycling in the parks and parkways be placed on file : —

First. A rural or country park is, of course, designed to serve the greatest good of the greatest number. Such a park is, however, designed to benefit this greatest number not in all possible ways, but especially in one particular way, — namely, by providing scenery in striking contrast to the ordinary scenery of city streets. The removal of large spaces from the taxable area of a city is not justifiable, if the lands so removed are used for purposes which smaller or less costly spaces would serve as well or better. Large parks are not created in order to provide flower gardens, zoölogical gardens, eating-houses, race-courses, football fields, or any other such things or conveniences ; but primarily in order that the public may have access to interesting scenery. The general landscape is of first importance. No structures, games, or practices tending to injure the landscape, or incommode the public in its enjoyment of the landscape, ought to be permitted. To allow any such things or practices to grow up in a country park is to defeat its primary and only justifying purpose.

Secondly. Of all the people who resort to the landscape of a park, much the largest number enter on foot. This, indeed, is as it should be ; since it is really impossible to thoroughly enjoy scenery except when moving slowly, as in walking. Moreover, the most charming scenes are accessible only to walkers. It is proper, therefore, that parks should be planned with special reference to the convenience and enjoyment of foot passengers. So many people desire to drive through parks that roads are necessarily opened ; but thronged roads injure parks from the point of view of the people on foot, and crossings of footpaths at grade are, therefore, made as few as possible, or else the grades are separated, as at Ellicott Arch in Franklin Park, and throughout Central Park, New York. For the use of the comparatively few people who wish to visit parks on horseback, bridle-paths are sometimes constructed, but such paths in parks are even more objectionable than carriage roads, unless grade crossings can be avoided entirely, as in Central Park. It is on this account that only one short stretch of bridle-path has been built in Franklin Park. The bridle-path from the Fens to the Park, along the parkway, involves comparatively few crossings not otherwise occasioned ; it injures comparatively little scenery ; and it is justifiable on the ground that without this one soft path from town to country horseback riding out of the heart of Boston would be practically impossible, owing to the extreme hardness of the modern carriage roads.

Thirdly. If, as seems obvious, both carriage roads and bridle-paths are objectionable in parks, it is plain that special bicycle paths would be still more so. The bicycle is a silent steed, and one which moves with much more dangerous rapidity than either the driving or the saddle horse. For bicycle paths a separation of grades would be even more necessary than for bridle-paths. A separate path would enable bicycles to traverse the park much more swiftly than is possible while they must keep to the road used by slower vehicles ; but these slower carriages are already moving quite as fast as it is possible for their occupants to move and still enjoy the scenery, so that if their motion is accelerated, park ground will be put to a use quite inconsistent with its main purpose. In other words, a park is a preserve of scenery ; and as such it is no place for the driver's speedway, the rider's race-course, or the bicycler's scorching-track. Just at present the new Boston and Brookline Parkway is thronged on Sunday with carriages and bicycles ; and while the fever to be seen on this particular road lasts, some difficulty will doubtless be encountered in regulating the traffic. That the use of the way ought to be better regulated than it is seems plain. Large bodies of boys running with close ranks through the midst of the strollers and the baby carriages of a footpath would not be tolerated. Speeding horses on the park roads would not be allowed. The so-called Club-runs of bicyclers at high speed along the parkway ought to be likewise forbidden for similar reasons. If the bicyclers are not content to limit themselves to a reasonable speed, and to observe the rules of the road, they may properly be asked to ride elsewhere than on the parkway. To deprive the horseback riders of the bridle-path would inflict a death-blow upon riding ; but the mileage of roads near Boston fit for bicycling is enormous, and however it may be in other cities, no hardship will be worked either by denying the petitions for separate bicycle paths, or by regulating the use of the existing road of the Boston parkway.

November 12, 1896.

A PLAYGROUND SELECTED BY THE COMMON COUNCIL. — Concerning the proposed playground at Neponset, we will ask you to glance, for a moment, at the accompanying small scale diagrams, which will serve to explain why we think it bad policy to acquire the playground in question without improving the boundaries suggested by the vote of the Common

Council. . . . Certainly it seems to us very plain that the jagged boundaries which the playground will possess if the land is acquired in accordance with the Council's vote will bring the Park Commission into ridicule, while they will also involve expensive additional purchases and readjustments. It may, of course, be possible to obtain legal permission to sell portions not essential to a well-shaped playground, but the prices obtainable from such sales will not be worth while, and there will be danger of trouble with such persons as own lands adjacent to those parts which may be sold. They will be able to say: "By act of the Park Commission we had a park adjacent to our land and we benefitted thereby; now we find that the backs of lots and houses are to come against our land, and we certainly are entitled to damages." From every point of view that we can think of, the taking of this playground in exact accordance with the Council's vote seems to us unwise, and full of danger, both with respect to the unnecessary expense which will be involved, and with respect to the establishment of the precedent.

Questions having arisen as to the uses to which Cambridge Field, a playground in which Charles had a strong interest, might best be put, Charles wrote as follows to the Superintendent of Cambridge parks.

October 13, 1896.

The Best Use of a City Playground. — We are glad to hear that the proposed track on Cambridge Field will not be used for cycling, though we fear that if you provide a track, it will be difficult to maintain in force such prohibitive regulations. We regard the proposed diamond, also, in exactly the same way. It will be difficult, if not impossible, to prevent its use for daily ball-matches arranged beforehand. If such matches are thus encouraged, it will mean that the field will be monopolized by semi-professional players, while the boys who should be using it will become merely spectators. The field ought to be so managed as to provide games and exercise for hundreds of boys rather than for eighteen boys or men.

How can these dangers of misuse attending the provision of tracks, diamond, and the like be avoided? Can they not be most easily avoided by omitting the construction of all such special arrangements? Tracks for running races can be improvised any afternoon in various parts of the field by clubs or groups of boys or men. Diamonds for boys' games of ball can also be improvised, the bags to mark the bases being issued from the field office, but only in safe numbers; and so with many other games and exercises, the pursuit of which ought to be encouraged by employing, if necessary, a teacher, as was suggested in our last note. Competition makes the zest of all games, of course; and, with a little direction, it can be counted on to fill the field with boys engaged in a great variety of exercises, from running, jumping, leap-frog, and the like, to putting the shot and parallel bars. Baseball is one of the least desirable games for such a field, because so few persons monopolize so much space. Every effort should be made to introduce other desirable sports. If competitive baseball is to possess the ground, the field will not be as useful as it ought to be. You surely do not want to do anything that will tend to make it a Coliseum or a Madison Square Garden, — a place for exciting shows. Of course, if the city really wants to provide such a place, the present plan of the field is radically wrong. The present design does not contemplate exhibition games of any kind.

The following letter, addressed to Mr. Charles Francis Adams, a member of the Harvard Board of Overseers, foretells the policy which Harvard University adopted three years later. In 1899–1900, a four years' course in Landscape Architecture was announced in the Lawrence Scientific School in close association with the course in Architecture which had only recently been fully developed in that school. The instructors in landscape design are (1902) Frederick Law Olmsted, Jr., and Arthur Asahel Shurtleff, both of whom were employed in the Olmsted office while Charles was a member of the firm. The distinction made in the letter between landscape architecture on the one hand, and forestry, gardening, and engineering on the other, is fundamental, and must be established and recognized before the profession can obtain a firm footing. It is a distinction which Frederick Law Olmsted has taught all his life by precept and example, and by the quality of his professional work. Incidentally, another useful distinction is clearly brought out in the letter by the use of the word "crop-growing" — the distinction between economic forestry and arboriculture. Now that forestry has begun to interest intelligent Americans, this distinction needs to be observed.

December 12, 1896.

Economic forestry might well be taught at the Bussey: it is a kind of crop-growing. But the present Arnold Professor has, so far as I know, never taught even his own subject — Arboriculture — and I don't suppose he could be induced to offer a course in Forestry.

As to Landscape Architecture, I believe that such instruction as might be formally offered by the University ought by rights to be associated with the courses in Architecture given at the Lawrence School, rather than with the courses in Agriculture, Horticulture (and Forestry) given at the Bussey. The popular notion that my profession is chiefly concerned with gardens and gardening is utterly mistaken. Landscape Architecture is an art of design, and in a very true sense covers agriculture, forestry, gardening, engineering, and even architecture (as ordinarily defined) itself. Hear William Morris on this subject: "Architecture, a great subject truly, for it embraces the consideration of the whole of the external surroundings of the life of men; we cannot escape from it if we would, for it means the moulding and altering to human needs of the very face of the earth itself."

Since the word "architecture," as commonly used, does not convey this broad meaning, we have to put "landscape" before it to designate the broad architecture which we practise, meaning by landscape "the visible material world; all that can be seen on the surface of the earth by a man who is himself upon that surface." (Hamerton.) If you will recall our metropolitan park reports (to mention none of Mr. Olmsted's), I think you will perceive how far my profession has advanced beyond landscape gardening; and why I think it would be best to give the proposed instruction in a School of Design rather than in a School of Horticulture.

In the following February Charles wrote to the same effect in reply to some questions about improving and strengthening the Bussey Institution (a department of Harvard University) from Mr. Ernest W. Bowditch, who was a member of the Overseers' committee to visit the Institution : —

. . . As for myself, I had a year at the Bussey, and I set a high value on the instruction given there by Mr. Watson, with respect to plants and planting. If there is now a greater demand for instruction in Watson's important subject, I have no doubt we can meet it satisfactorily.

For the equally important instruction in surveying, grading, and road engineering, students of the Bussey who want to become "landscape architects" have to go to the Lawrence Scientific School. I myself lived in Boston, and went out to the Lawrence and the Bussey alternately. I see no great loss in this arrangement. There is hardly a sufficient demand to warrant the University in duplicating the Lawrence School's engineering instruction at the Bussey, or the Bussey's plant instruction at the Lawrence.

It is true that neither school offers instruction in the art of landscape design — the art which Mr. F. L. Olmsted called "landscape architecture" away back in 1856 — the art which guides and coördinates the work of (landscape) gardeners, foresters, and engineers. If it is time that the University should formally offer instruction in this art, I, for one, think it ought to be offered in close connection with instruction in the other arts, and particularly in connection with Architecture, of which great subject our art, as I look at it, is an important part. It is in Cambridge, rather than at the Bussey, that I think landscape architecture should be taught. . . .

CHAPTER XXXIII

MAKING GOOD USE OF THE SKILL AND EXPERIENCE OF A LANDSCAPE ARCHITECT

> Having already expressed my opinion that it is essential that a professor should explain the principles upon which he suggests any improvement, I would now warn the proprietor not hastily to adopt any plan which cannot be thus explained. A professor destitute of true principles will overlook those little circumstances upon which real improvement frequently rests, and will proceed to a total subversion of the scene which he knows not how to adorn. — GILPIN.

January 16, 1896.

ADVICE CONCERNING THE HOUSE SITE ON A LARGE ESTATE. — We send you under separate cover three sun-prints embodying the results of studies made of your place near ——. Many other studies have been made during the past weeks, but the two which we send you to-day (Nos. 1 and 5) we think are decidedly the most promising. The largest of the three sheets is a sun-print of the general topographical map of your estate, upon which schemes Nos. 1 and 5 have been sketched — the first by green lines and the second by red. The scale of this largest sheet is 200 feet to the inch. The two small sheets represent the same schemes at the larger scale of 60 feet to the inch.

The two schemes may be distinguished by calling No. 1 the Notch Scheme and No. 5 the Hill-top Scheme. The Notch Scheme places the house in a position straddling a certain hollow of the land which lies next west of the highest summit of the estate. The floor of the house, in this case, would be at or about grade 312; in other words, amply high enough to command a great prospect to the southward, while a beautiful glimpse of the northern view will, by this scheme, be obtained down a straight vista to be cut through the woods to the brink of a certain deep hole in the ground, which you will discover both on the general map and on the cross section.

In scheme No. 1 the south front of the house would naturally become the living front, where a terrace will offer fine views toward the south. The western end of the house would naturally become the garden front, and the ground lies in such a form that a circular garden, such as is shown on the sketch, would fit most perfectly. The eastern end of the house would then become the service wing, where would be found the necessary service yards and other appurtenances. Lastly, the northern side of the building would make the entrance front, and here a peculiarly fine effect might be produced by taking advantage of the peculiar formation of the ground, whereby a green lawn may slope gently away from the house, bordered by the two lines of approach-road, and flanked on either hand by the existing woods, banked down with Rhododendrons or other suitable fringing growths. At the end of this formal entrance court and on the brink of the deep hole in the ground previously mentioned, a little architectural work in the form of walls, and possibly columns, would doubtless enhance the beauty of the view of the blue distance, which will be had down and over the entrance court from the doorway and hall of the house itself.

As a whole this scheme is distinguished from the alternative, or Hill-top, scheme by the possession of better shelter from winds and the more comfortable appearance of the building, placed (as it would be) in close relation to the existing levels of the land to the right and left of the hollow which the house will bridge over. We are convinced that ample views will be obtained from this site, while there will be no sense and no appearance of being perched up in the air. The highest hill-top of the estate will be found at but a short distance, and on this hill-top may be placed the necessary water tower to which it will be pleasant to resort from time to time for the sake of obtaining the complete panoramic view of the whole horizon. East of the house and south of the water tower, there lies a very agreeable natural terrace or approximate level where a ramble or shrub garden can easily be made, at the further end of which views slightly different from those obtained at the house will be had in agreeable ways. This pleasure ground (as the English would call it)

is not sketched upon our drawing, but you can doubtless discover its situation upon the ground. The southern views
from the terrace of the house would be obtained by clearing
away the forest from its present edges back to the position of
the terrace, so that when one looks from the house, the view
will be over a descending lawn, which, in turn, will be framed
on either hand by woods to be faced by flowering Dogwoods,
Sassafras, and others of the smaller trees. For ourselves we
are quite clear that such a view is preferable as a daily and
hourly companion to any view of the panoramic order.

Scheme No. 5 is sketched to represent a house of somewhat
larger proportions than is sketched in scheme No. 1, but no
account should be taken of this, as the shape of the house is
in both cases merely a preliminary assumption. The house
floor in this scheme is placed at grade 334, or almost as high
as the very highest point of the existing hill. It is difficult,
of course, to reach this grade by a road suitable for pleasure
driving; but it can be done on the lines shown, though at
considerably greater expense than would be called for by the
lines of roads shown on sketch No. 1. The northern side of
this No. 5 house would serve as the entrance front, where
would be found a walled court, approached by a climbing
road, as is indicated by the grades marked thereon. The
western end of the building becomes the service department
in this case, a yard being provided for the wagons of the
butcher and baker, and a laundry yard outside thereof. The
eastern end of the house may, in this scheme, be considered
either the children's or the bachelors' wing, and a terrace or
piazza might be attached thereto at grade 332, as indicated
on the sketch. The southern front would here again present
terraces from which stairways would descend into a flower
garden built about 10 feet below the level of the terrace. To
right and left of this central flower garden level grass terraces
might well be provided for tennis courts or children's playgrounds, as is also indicated. These various lawns on the
south side would necessarily be supported by retaining-walls,
which would, however, at no point exceed 10 feet in height,
and for much of their length would not exceed 5 feet.

In all directions from a house situated as is suggested by

this scheme (No. 5), the surface of the ground would fall away quite rapidly, so that the building would necessarily appear to crown the hill in a manner which seldom appears well to our eyes.   It is, at all events, extremely difficult for architects to succeed in adapting structures to such positions.   To obtain views from this summit it will be necessary to cut away the trees for considerable distances down the slopes; and there are no natural hollows here such as suggest the outlines of the north and south lawns or clearings of scheme No. 1. We should imagine that if the site suggested by scheme No. 1 were to be chosen, the house ought to be designed in, at least, a semi-formal or classic style of architecture, while the house which might be designed to fit the site suggested by scheme No. 5 ought, we suppose, to take on a broader or more picturesque and broken form and mass.

Of course, we submit both these schemes as tentative efforts at a solution of your problem, and intended rather to provoke discussion than anything else. We have asked Mr. —— to have a skeleton tower built on the axial line of each of these schemes ; by carrying the general map up each of these towers, and noting where the red and green vista lines cut across the fields to the south of the wooded ridge, you may be able to get a fair idea of the views which will be had from the two sites. We have found the problem much more difficult and complicated than we had imagined it would be, chiefly because of the complications arising from the steep grades of the ground, — grades which must be overcome by the approach-roads leading to whatever site may be chosen. . . .

February 6, 1896.

ADVICE ON IMPROVING THE GROUNDS OF AN INSTITUTION.

To the President of the Board of Governors, Royal Victoria
    Hospital, Montreal.

The problem which is presented to us is a most difficult one, since from our standpoint the present arrangement is about as unsatisfactory as it well could be. The steep formal banks and certain roads and plantings destroy all opportunity for breadth in the grounds. The banks bear no relation to the lines of the buildings, and are so steep that it is very

difficult and expensive to maintain them in good condition.
Such banks tend to give the buildings which they surround a
perched-up appearance, which in this particular case is exceedingly undesirable. The buildings are so very tall and narrow
that the grading should be so arranged as to make them
appear to sit lower rather than higher than they do. This
can be accomplished by making long, gradual slopes, rather
than a series of sharp, steep banks, and such slopes can be
kept in order much more easily than the steeper ones. With
a view to securing such slopes, we have prepared and show in
our study two cross sections on which is indicated the present
surface and the surface that we would propose. You will
observe that what we propose will require the removal of the
edges of the sharp banks and a filling at the base, and that
little additional soil will be required. Probably this will
necessitate some blasting at certain points to secure a sufficient depth of surface soil, but we do not think it will be a
very difficult operation to carry out such a plan. Before a
final plan is made, it will be desirable to determine by sound-
ings (with a bar) the depth of rock at the places where the
changes are to be made. It would also be desirable to have
a much more complete topographical map. With such information, we should be able to prepare a contoured grading
plan and an estimate of the cost of carrying it out, and thus
place the matter before you in such a way that your Board
could come to an intelligent decision as to the changes recommended.

    You will observe that we have changed the upper and
lower front entrance roads to paths. It was noticed, when
our representative was last on the ground, that the ambulance
service passed in at the front gate to a back door, thus passing by the windows of the wards and the point where visitors
enter. It seems as though this service could be better performed by having the ambulance pass through University
Street and up the back road to the entrance to the accident
room. This entrance would also be used by all tradesmen
and for other transportation connected with the hospital
service, thus shutting off these unpleasant features from the
view of patients in the wards and visitors in the main office.

Another important advantage in reducing these roads to walks is that room will be provided for the more gradual slopes that we propose. The roads as now located at the back of the building will have to be modified ultimately to carry out the proposed addition. We have arranged the road to provide for such an addition. You will observe that by the use of retaining-walls we have provided more room, which is much needed, both in the upper and lower levels, at the points back of the buildings where teams take away ashes and other refuse. We have also reduced a part of the road on the west side of the buildings to a path and struck out the balance of it. We believe this also to be a very important improvement. At present, the only opportunity which you have on the ground for a broad stretch of lawn is on the tract of land between Pine Avenue and the base of the bluffs to the west of the buildings. That part of the road which we have stricken out cuts across this stretch of lawn in a disagreeable manner, and it does not seem to be essential.

There is also a plantation of fruit trees on this tract which we advise you to have removed to the back part of the grounds where there are already trees of this kind. We should also advise you to have the flower beds and pools which are spotted about over this surface removed, as we are satisfied that you do not gain enough from this style of gardening to warrant its continuance. If you desire flower gardening of this kind, space should be provided for it outside this broad stretch of lawn in a formal or show garden, where special provision could be made for such features as aquatic pools, formal flower beds, rose gardens, etc. This would be a special place to which all this class of gardening would be restricted, and in which it might be maintained more economically, and with much more satisfactory results than appear possible at present. Such a garden would be a place to be visited by the patients, employees, and friends of the institution. It would not be a place where many flowers could be cut for the hospital. The best way to secure flowers for the wards is the way they are already provided : they come, we understand, from a garden where the flowering plants are grown in rows as you would grow vegetables,

simply for the sake of cut flowers. We are not prepared to
recommend the formal garden that we are suggesting, because we do not believe the result would justify the necessary
cost of maintenance. In place of this we would recommend
the liberal use of hardy perennial flowering plants (especially
the finer natives) in the borders of the existing and proposed
plantations.

Our purpose in the proposed planting is to give more
seclusion to the grounds by providing a border plantation
along the fence to hide the steep bank and cover the thin soil
along Pine Avenue above Carleton Road, and to cover steep
banks where the soil is so thin that grass will not do well.
We should expect that the nicely kept ground would be
limited to the front of the buildings. The steep banks back
of the house will be covered in such a way that they will
ultimately take care of themselves. We have prepared a
preliminary estimate of the cost of plants to carry out the
proposed planting, and find that they would cost not over
three hundred dollars. A part of these plants would be
secured abroad and a part in American nurseries. We have
made careful inquiries of Canadian nurseries and have visited
a number of them, and we find that better plants can be
secured at less cost from American nurseries, with duty and
freight added. We should recommend considerable planting
in any event, and would advise you to give us authority to
place orders for plants to the amount stated, so that they can
be delivered on the ground in time for spring planting. In
some parts of the grounds they can be planted at once.
Where it is advisable to make changes in the present surfaces, the planting can be omitted and the plants placed in
nursery rows, where they can stay for a year or two and then
be in the best condition for transplanting when the ground is
finally prepared.

It was observed to be the practice to mow off the undergrowth on the steep, wild, rocky banks back of the building.
This practice should be absolutely prohibited ; for it not only
results in the destruction of great numbers of very attractive
native flowering plants and herbs, but it will ultimately result in the banks being denuded of all attractive vegetation
and becoming raw and unsightly.

You will observe that we have also suggested a line of road leading with a reasonable grade to the back part of the grounds. To locate such a road accurately a contoured survey would be necessary.

March 5, 1896.

ADVICE CONCERNING THE HOUSE SITE ON A SEA-SIDE ESTATE.

To MESSRS. SHEPLEY, RUTAN & COOLIDGE, Chicago, Ill.

We send you to-night a sun-print of two preliminary sketches for the placing of the house on Mr. ——'s hill at ——. If the house is to be placed on the ledge where the wooden tower now stands, we find that it must almost necessarily take a picturesque and irregular form. We would suggest that a house on this site be built, so far as possible, to fit the ledges, that the ledges be used as the visible base of stone walls, and that the style of architecture above these walls be made correspondingly picturesque. The sketch which we submit for the general shape of such a house and the approaches to it is tentative, of course, but the limitations of the site with respect to steep grades, knobs of rock, and the like are so very sharply marked, that no great variation can be made from the suggested outlines without greatly increasing the cost for retaining-walls, for blasting, and the like. You will notice that the dining-room is placed by this plan so that it will receive the morning sun, and obtain the view which is now obtained from the ledge on which the wooden tower stands.

The alternative sketch which we submit is an attempt to find a site for a house of symmetrical and formal style. Such a site we find immediately adjacent to the western side of the ledge on which the wooden tower stands, which ledge will become in fact an eastern prolongation of the south terrace of the house. Like the house suggested by the first sketch, this second house calls for terrace walls of varying height up to a maximum of 12 feet. The axis of the symmetrical building is placed by this sketch on a line which, if extended northward, will be also the axis of the approach-road; and this road will lie in a hollow of the land, which is capable of being smoothed so as to become a grassy glade bordered by woods and ledges, and by occasional thickets of shrubbery. Such an approach would, we think, be decidedly effective. For the picturesque house such an approach would be unsuitable, but for a house in the formal style, it is very much to be desired.

We will ask you to notice the grade figures suggested for the floors and for the ground adjacent to the base of the walls of the building, as they vary considerably ; for instance, the forecourt of the formal plan would require to be filled, and other parts of both designs would require to be excavated, all as indicated by the figures and the contours of the sun-prints.

We will ask you to explain and discuss these preliminary studies with Mr. —— at your earliest convenience, and we suppose you will be able to bring him to a decision as to which style of house and which site he would, on the whole, prefer. You will notice that the dining-room in the formal house is again placed at the southeast corner, and that the floor grade is such as to give the room much the same view as will be obtained by the dining-room of the picturesque house, although the view will be cut off a little by the profile of the upper ledge which rises just north of the ledge on which the tower stands.

We shall be obliged to you if you will kindly say to Mr. —— that we shall, of course, be glad to revise and change the plans, as may be best; that the drawings which we send are intended only to promote discussion, and help to a decision of a problem which we must say we find extremely complicated.

December 24, 1896.

ADVICE CONCERNING THE ARRANGEMENT OF THE BUILDINGS ON THE LANDS OF A COLLEGE.

To the President of the R. I. Agricultural College, Kingston, R. I.

Mr. Eliot of our firm having made another visit to the College, at your request, the following suggestions are respectfully submitted : —

Viewed broadly, the college lands fall into three divisions — the cultivated plain, the steep hillside, and the plateau. The college buildings occupy the plateau. They are conspicuous from a distance and conversely they command broad views. A plan has been considered for placing subsequent

buildings on the plateau in a manner to ultimately form a
rectangular enclosure. The slope of the surface is unsymmetrical and a little steep, but we nevertheless think well of the
proposed arrangement, which, indeed, we suggested some years
ago. The building next to be erected will, we understand,
occupy the middle of the northern end of the proposed quadrangle. Just north of it will be the public way leading from
the plain to Kingston village. Here also is a roughish hollow
which divides the plateau. North of this hollow there is to-day
an orchard and an experimental garden, and then more open
plateau land entirely suitable for the dairy, barns, and other
farm buildings of the College which are still to be built. It
is true that an existing building in this part of the plateau is
at present used in part by students of art, but we presume
they can be even better provided for in the future in some
part of the main quadrangle, near the library and the other
departments with which they are naturally allied. The agricultural department buildings can doubtless be arranged on
this northern part of the plateau in a manner which will make
them pleasing objects from all points of view. One building,
it will, however, be difficult to make agreeable ; namely, the
central boiler or heating house, which will most conveniently
find place between the college buildings and the farm buildings in the hollow above mentioned. It ought, if possible, to
be kept so low as to be inconspicuous.

Along the length of the western front of the range of buildings the view over the plain is strikingly broad and fine. A
few high-branched trees planted not far from the buildings
will not obstruct the view, but trees a little further down the
slope would do so seriously. Much of this slope has, accordingly, been converted into grass-land or lawn, and we would
recommend that the process be continued as opportunity offers,
the remaining hollows and rocky places being gradually filled
or graded down to an irregular or waving line which may be approximately defined as the upper limit of the rough, untamed,
or steep slope of the hill. On the upper parts of this slope
care should be taken to encourage or plant small-growing
trees only, such as Sassafras, flowering Dogwood, and the
various Cornels, while the lower part of the slope should be a

continuous wood of forest trees, like those which grow now on the slope in some places. They should eventually occupy the whole breadth of the college property. The most pleasing species of the existing undergrowth should be carefully preserved and encouraged throughout this belt, and no attempt should here be made to smooth the surface. Not only will the view from the buildings be greatly helped by a continuous belt of foliage in what a painter would call the middle distance, but the view of the college buildings from the public roads on the plain will be greatly improved by such encouragement or planting of trees near the foot of the slope. To carry out this plan the straight rows of evergreens in the neighborhood of the chicken farm, as well as the chicken farm itself, will need to be eventually removed. It will doubtless be quite possible to find fully as good a place for the hens and turkeys; and the removal of their inexpensive quarters will make it possible to begin upon the work of continuing the now broken belt of forest.

Other questions, such as the form and position of the road to be built just east of the main building, the position to be chosen for a house for pot experiments, etc., were discussed with you by Mr. Eliot; but if we have omitted to remind you of any of the more important matters touched upon, we trust that you will call them to our attention.

January 7, 1897.

ADVICE ON THE COMPARATIVE VALUE OF TWO TRACTS OF LAND FOR A TOWN PARK.

To MESSRS. PARKER, HUNT & TEMPLE, Committee, Reading, Mass.

You have asked for our professional judgment as to the comparative availability and value for " park purposes " of two tracts of land in Reading. Having, accordingly, visited the town, and examined the lands in question, we beg to report as follows : —

Location. — The northern tract lies northwest from the old Meeting-house Green. The nearest point of this tract — the Water Tower Hill — is half a mile from the green, while the further edge is something more than a mile distant. The southern tract lies southwest from the green and between half and three quarters of a mile distant. It seems to us that both tracts are sufficiently close to the body of population.

Surface. — The northern tract consists essentially of the valley of a brook which flows southwestward through level meadows of irregular outline, bordered by uplands neither high nor steep, excepting where, in the southeast corner, they rise perhaps a hundred feet above the meadows to form the Water Tower Hill. So level are the meadows that the closing of a gate in a low dam floods them for half a mile or more, while the lowering of the gate drains them, or might drain them.

The southern tract, also, consists of the valley of a small brook which, in this case, flows southeastward towards Quannapomitt Lake. The land bordering the brook is generally soggy; but it is not meadow land. We were informed that this land, though so far from the lake, is so nearly at its level that it might prove impossible to thoroughly drain it; a fact which ought to prevent the occupation of the land by buildings. Adjacent to the wet land is a considerable area of remarkably level and smooth land, and beyond this a little rough and steeper pasture ground, but no continuous border of high land and no high hill at all.

Vegetation. — Excepting for the meadows, which are clothed with meadow grass, Cranberry, and numerous sorts of low-growing meadow plants, the northern tract is almost entirely wooded. These woods consist of high Pines, high mixed woods, pasture growths of Cedar and Birch, old sprout growth, and sprout growth following recent clearings, according as the owners have treated their several wood-lots. Considering the proximity of the town and of great cities, a remarkably large part of the total area of woodland is clothed with high timber, or with the even more beautiful growths which in our land and climate spontaneously appear in abandoned or partly disused pastures.

The southern tract possesses no vegetation comparable in interest or beauty with that just described. There are thickets of shrubs in the wet land, smooth fields on the plains, several groves of mixed trees or Pines, and a few fine single trees on the higher pastured slopes. It would, however, require fifty years or more to give this tract the wooded borders which so effectively seclude the northern tract.

Scenery. — If in purchasing a public domain Reading desires to possess herself of an interesting and beautiful landscape or piece of scenery, we believe the foregoing account is sufficient to make it evident that the northern tract is to be preferred to the southern. The peculiar forms of the surface of the ground, the central meadow, the framing slopes of woods, the crowning hill-top, with the water tower, all combine to make a piece of scenery of quite remarkable interest and charm. It is, moreover, a landscape, the quiet loveliness of which cannot be marred, as park landscapes too often are, by the erection of buildings on the borders. Existing woods make this particular landscape practically complete in itself. The town may be built solidly up to the border, but the seclusion of the meadow scenery will remain perfect. As public reservations are desired for the express purpose of affording relief from the scenery of the town, this point is an important one.

Availability. — It is to be noted that while the northern tract excels the southern as respects its scenery, it is not, therefore, any the less available for the ordinary purposes of public grounds. The southern tract affords excellent fields for baseball and other sports, but when the northern tract is fully explored, areas suited to these purposes can doubtless be selected. The southern tract can be flooded for skating, but so can the meadow of the northern tract, while the intricate and wooded shore lines of the resulting pond will furnish a feast of landscape beauty which the southern tract cannot supply. And so on throughout the list of pastimes for the enjoyment of which it is desirable that public grounds should furnish opportunities. We are convinced that the northern tract can be so arranged as to meet all these requirements and to furnish uncommonly enjoyable scenery in addition.

Cost. — Respecting the probable comparative cost of the two tracts, we are not informed ; but we do not believe that the cost of both would exceed what would be a reasonable expenditure for the town of Reading, particularly if the future can be called upon to share the first cost with the present. It is not probable that either tract will ever be any cheaper.

Management. — Supposing the northern tract to be acquired, it would be desirable to adopt as soon as possible a plan or programme of procedure for its gradual development, and this plan should then be followed steadily, systematically, and continuously during many years, even if only two men are employed as keepers, police, and fire-guards. Two men working to a well-studied plan will accomplish much for the scenery in the course of five or ten years, while a large gang, working without well-considered direction, may easily greatly harm the landscape in one season. That such domains can be properly cared for economically has been proved by the experience of Lynn and other cities possessing wild or naturalistic parks.

Lastly, we may be permitted to remind you that we have not reviewed the whole township of Reading, but only the two tracts specially called to our attention; and respecting these, it is our conclusion that the northern tract is by far the better worth purchasing.

CHAPTER XXXIV

GENERAL PLANS. 1894–97

A mountain range should be viewed in sections, and only once in its entirety: a city should be divided in like manner, and we should avoid getting the same view repeatedly. To break up a wide prospect effectively is, however, a much more difficult matter than to expose it completely.

When you come upon a particularly fine prospect, and remark on it: "What a pity that great tree is there, — how much finer this would be if it could be removed!" you would be very much surprised to find, upon the tree being cut down, that you no longer had a picture before you. The highest type of garden is like a picture gallery; and pictures require frames. — PÜCKLER-MUSKAU.

THE Metropolitan Park Commission had hardly been at work a year when Charles felt bound to protest against the amount of labor expended on paths and roads, in advance of the preparation of any general plans for the development of the scenery of the forest reservations, and indeed before accurate topographical surveys had been ordered. This chapter contains a series of letters arguing against premature and planless work on roads and paths, urging the early preparation of landscape and road designs based on accurate topographical maps, and explaining the wastefulness of both inaction and planless action. Through two years and a half Charles never lost a fair opportunity of pressing these views on the Commission, sometimes orally and sometimes in writing, in the Board meetings, or in conversation with individual members of the Board; but so far as the Blue Hills, Middlesex Fells, and Stony Brook Reservations were concerned, all his efforts were in vain. Unless it is otherwise stated, the letters of this chapter were addressed to the chairman of the Commission; and with the single exception which will be observed, they were signed Olmsted, Olmsted & Eliot. An extract from a paper Charles read before the American Forestry Association in September, 1895, and two letters he sent to "Garden and Forest" on the same general subject are placed in chronological order with the letters to the Commission. All the time that this discussion was going on, Charles was making numerous investigations and designs for the Commission in other regions.

Aug. 30, 1894.

In order that the Commission may thoroughly understand the work now being done within the new forest reservations, we beg leave to make the following statement : —

It will be remembered that in accordance with our recommendation considerable labor was devoted last winter to clearing dead wood from certain strips of the forest, selected as presenting the most advantageous preliminary fire lines. This work was carried on in accordance with the following memorandum of an understanding arrived at by Mr. Eliot in consultation with Secretary Carruth and Overseer Rackemann : —

Memorandum of understanding between Messrs. Carruth and Rackemann with respect to forest fire lines in Blue Hills Reservation, 8th January, 1894.

Lines to be worked along designated wood-roads.

Roadway to be cleared of worst rocks and stumps, and trees and boughs to be cut away sufficiently to make road traversable by two horsemen riding abreast.

Fifteen feet each side of road to be cleared of high shrubbery, and these two strips, together with the road, to be cleared of dry leaves, except where swamp or rock is reached short of fifteen feet.

One hundred feet each side of road to be cleared of all dead trees and bushes, fallen or standing.

Although a good deal of live wood was unnecessarily cut in several places, this work, we believe, was in general well and cheaply done.

When the coming of dry spring weather prevented a further prosecution of the work of clearing away and burning the dangerous dead material, the foremen employed by Overseer Rackemann were turned by him to the work of improving the old wood-roads, and particularly the entrances of the reservations. In the western section of the Fells Reservation, the entrances from Mt. Vernon Street, Winchester, from Mr. Dyke's lane, Stoneham, and from Main Street, Stoneham, were soon made usable. In the eastern section of the Fells, similar work was done at Woodland Road, Stoneham, Mountain Road, Melrose, and Bear's Den Path, Malden. In the Blue Hills Reservation, Babel Rock entrance at the eastern end was the first to be opened, and Blue Hill entrance at the west end was the last. Generally Mr. Rackemann has sought our advice as to the paths to be selected for improvement, but on Bear Hill in the Fells and in the west middle section of the Blue Hills considerable labor has been spent upon lines which were not designated by us, in the one case on account of the expressed desires of the local Stoneham Park Commission, and in the other case presumably by reason of some misunderstanding. Speaking generally, we believe this work upon the paths has been done upon lines well chosen to afford temporary but easy access to the reservations.

With respect to the amount of labor to be expended on the improved paths, and the degree in which they ought at this time to be made permanent or finished, we must confess that our ideas have from the first been quite different from those of your executive officers, Messrs. Carruth and Rackemann. Mr. Eliot, when visiting the Reservations, has always spoken for simplicity and cheapness of construction. To make many paths accessible to walkers or to " two horsemen riding abreast " (we quote our memorandum previously cited) has from the first seemed to us to be more desirable at the present time than to open any carriage drives. It has been our frequently expressed desire that no work should be done upon the old paths which might not be readily abandoned after the making of a complete topographical survey should provide us with the means of determining the best locations for permanent and finished roads. We admire the zeal of your executive officers; but we must say that we fear they have too frequently forgotten these primary considerations when engaged in the prosecution of their work. It seems to us that it would be advisable to place some limit upon the expenditure to be incurred in this work of improving paths, either in the form of a maximum average cost per rod or per mile, or else in the form of an appropriation which should not be exceeded in the course of a season. In fact, we have seldom or never heard of work of this kind being done under no limitations as regards expense, excepting the one limitation on the number of men to be employed.

In conclusion, permit us to remind the Commission that in our view of the case the work of relieving the forests of the vast accumulations of dead and inflammable wood is of much greater present importance than the opening of either foot-paths or carriage roads. Until this material is removed, the forests are in danger of destruction by fire. Fires which run over the surface of the ground in woodlands containing no material to feed a fierce flame do little damage; but fires which are fed by dead, dry, and fallen trees are capable of working great, and on steep slopes, irreparable injury. We are therefore impelled to suggest that if economy is to be regarded at all, it be exercised with respect to this summer's work on the paths rather than in next winter's work in the woods.

In case the Commission should conclude to proceed to obtaining detailed topographical maps of the reservations, we append to this letter revised specifications for surveys such as we deem necessary, suggesting that the Secretary be author-ized to obtain bids from engineers for work to be done accord-ingly.

October 25, 1894.

We are informed that the Board has voted to build several miles of road within, or on the borders of, the several forest reservations, the cost of the same to be charged to the " bou-levard fund," so called. We ask to be permitted to suggest that this work ought not to be begun until after topographical surveys have been made and the maps have been duly studied.

It is true that for the sake of making the Fells and Blue Hills Reservations accessible to your employees, your fire patrol, and your police, we have, during the past summer, assisted Overseer Rackemann in determining how a few of the old pathways should be made usable by wagons and car-riages; but we have done this only because circumstances have compelled us to this course. We think it desirable that many of the remaining wood-roads should be made more easily traversable than they are to-day; but we must hope that no more sixteen-foot roads, such as Mr. Rackemann has built in Blue Hills Reservation, may be opened until after we have opportunity to determine from study of a topographical survey the best routes, lines, and grades. We feel similarly with respect to the proposed marginal roads. Mr. Rackemann can build roads of fair grades " by the eye " along or near most of the boundaries of the reservations; and perhaps it is advisable that temporary roads of this sort should be built and opened soon. If this course is to be adopted, we hope the Board will instruct both Mr. Rackemann and ourselves as to the proper division of responsibility for the work to be done. If, however, permanent boundary roads are to be built, topographical surveys and definitive plans should be obtained before work is begun.

At a meeting of the American Forestry Association held at Springfield, Mass., in September, 1895, Charles read a paper on the new public forests near Boston, in which he gave an account of their origin and character, and described the precautions taken against fire, and the topographical, botanical, and forestal surveys which were in progress. He then took up the subject of general plans, and dealt with it in three paragraphs, as follows : —

That the new reservations may return to the metropolitan community such dividends of refreshing enjoyment as will justify their cost, it has been understood from the first that the beauty of the forest scenery must be not only safeguarded, but also restored, developed, and enhanced, and at the same time made accessible by roads which shall not be grossly disfiguring. In order to make the most of every scenic opportunity, ensure harmonious results, and secure the attainment of the ends in view with all possible economy, it was obvious from the start that well-considered and comprehensive general plans would need to be prepared, adopted, and adhered to. Such plans should be in hand before the living growth is touched, or the building of permanent roads begun. On the other hand, such plans cannot be well devised without thorough preliminary study of both the forestal and the topographical conditions, and the Commission has, accordingly, made liberal provision for the collection of the present facts in both departments.

The general plans to be thus devised upon the basis of the present facts will doubtless be drawn with reference to that more or less distant time when thousands of people will resort to the public domain every day or week. On the other hand, the progress to be made in the execution of the plans from year to year may be as slow or rapid as seems best. The plans will place the roads so as to exhibit the scenery of the réservations to the best advantage, and the forest scenery will, in time, need to be planned in detail, with special reference to the roads as points of view. The nice work of opening vistas, inducing screens or thickets, strengthening the planting of foregrounds and the like, will necessarily be postponed until the permanent roads are built, or, at least, roughed out. In the forester's department only general work will be in order at first. The purpose of the plans for this general work will be to restore destroyed beauty, rescue jeopardized beauty, ensure more lasting beauty, increase the variety of beauty, and emphasize the more remarkable types of beauty exhibited by the various sections of the woods. Thus, for some rocky summit the plans may suggest the encouragement of the characteristic pitch Pine, scrub Oak, and Bearberry, and the removal of incongruous Maples and the like. For the sake of variety, it may be planned that some of the existing openings should be preserved by pasturing with sheep, or that from other fields hay should be taken annually for feeding the sheep in winter. Where on smooth land, which once was pasture, seedling trees are now jostling each other too closely, the plan may read: "Sell standing the trees which are crowding the spreading Oaks, leaving enough of the younger trees to take the place of the veterans fifty odd years hence." Again, in those many places where scenery is now smothered by monotonous thickets of sprouts from chopped or burnt stumps, the general plan may perhaps read thus: "When first marketable, sell standing two thirds of these sprouts, killing the stumps. Sell the remaining sprouts after seedling trees shall have become well established." Further illustration of the nature of the general plan is unnecessary. With such a plan guiding both the woodland work and the construction work, effective coöperative and harmonious results can be economically secured. Without a plan, both kinds of work will become mere temporizing, and no consistent and effective final result can be expected.

For the effective execution of the work to be done in the reservations in accordance with the general plans, it is to be expected that the Commission will secure as head keeper of each public forest a man acquainted with the flora and fauna of the woods, a good manager, competent to devise economies and to discover sources of income, skilled to direct road repairs, as well as woodland work, fitted also to serve as the captain of the necessary patrol, and as paymaster of the patrolmen, the road laborers, and the woodsmen. Under each head keeper there will naturally be needed a foreman or foremen in charge of road maintenance, and a foreman or foremen of woodcraft. The keepers and some of their assistants will presumably be provided with houses situated within the reservations, and to these forest lodges the public will be invited to resort when in need of shelter or supplies for picnicking. Over the head keepers, and in general command during the period of active work, there will naturally be placed two executive officers, reporting directly to the Commission, a forester, and an engineer, each of whom should be willing and eager to coöperate with the other and with the devisers of the general plans, to the end that the scenery planned to be preserved, restored, or created, may be eventually and surely secured. If consistent and fine results are to be attained, the engineer must be ever ready to subordinate his special works for the sake of the general effect or "landscape," and the forester must likewise be willing to work in the same spirit. Administered in these ways by sufficiently active men, the forest scenery may, in a few years, be restored to that fortunate state the beauty of which, barring fires and other accidents, is inevitably increased by the passage of time.

February 4, 1896.

A committee having been appointed by the Commission to consider possible changes in the organization of the working forces employed by the Board, we ask leave to take this opportunity to speak of our own relations to the work the Commission has in hand. Up to the present time we have been engaged, without mentioning particulars, in advising concerning the choice of sites for the reservations, concerning the

boundaries of the lands to be acquired, concerning the preliminary botanical, forestal, and topographical surveys, and
the preliminary works of wood-road improvement and dead-
wood burning.

We have also reported and advised concerning the choice
of routes and the general plans for the proposed metropolitan
parkways. With respect to these parkways, we suppose it
will be advisable that we should oversee the making of the construction drawings and specifications as they may be ordered
from time to time, so as to make sure that our carefully made
designs are not botched in execution. Such supervision is
not likely to cost the Commission more than five hundred
dollars in any one year. As to possible new parkways or
new reservations, we may say that we shall always be glad to
furnish the Commission with an estimate of the amount of
our probable charges upon request.

With respect to the seven existing reservations at Revere
Beach, Charles River, Middlesex Fells, Blue Hills, Stony
Brook, Beaver Brook, and Hemlock Gorge, we desire to be
instructed as to what our course shall be. The boundaries of
these reserves are now generally fixed, their temporary roads
and paths are practically complete, the necessary clearing
away of dead wood is almost finished. In other words, the
several purposes heretofore in view have been accomplished.
The question, therefore, rises, What, if anything, is next to
be done? and What service, if any, does the Commission
desire of us?

The service which is usually asked of us by park commissions is the devising of so-called "general plans." Such
plans are based on topographical surveys, and on close study
of the local scenery and of the prospective uses of the land.
Basing our planning on such surveys, we are accustomed to
charge for the ultimate plan an agreed lump sum, the payment of which is commonly distributed over a term of years
varying from three to five, during which period we are open
to consultation on all related questions.

That your Commission has had in view the preparation of
general plans at an early day is evidenced by the fact that
topographical, botanical, and forestal surveys have been or-

dered and obtained. . . . The expenditure for these surveys can hardly be justified, unless they are promptly put to use in the making of plans which shall guide all work to be done in the reservations for many years to come. Our studies of park work, and our experience in it as well, have taught us that such guiding plans cannot be made too soon after public reservations are acquired. If, however, the Commission is of the opinion that the time is not yet ripe for the beginning of devising of plans, we shall want to ask to be allowed to disclaim responsibility for the work which may be done in the reservations. On the other hand, should the Commission desire to secure plans, we shall be happy to confer with your Committee as to the terms of a contract or agreement.

In explanation of the purpose and the nature of general plans and of the usual organization for the execution of such plans, we append to this letter (1) an article in the " Engineering Magazine " of November last, written by Mr. Eliot, but based on teaching of Mr. F. L. Olmsted, (2) an address before the American Forestry Association made by Mr. Eliot in August last, and (3) a specimen copy of an agreement between a park commission [1] and our firm. (See Appendix V.)

June 22, 1896.

In view of the fact that a majority of the members of the Commission are now comparatively new to the work of the Board, we beg leave to submit the following fresh and, we hope, clear expression of opinion that all work in the reservations should be guided by well-considered, comprehensive, and officially adopted plans.

Whenever a piece of ground, public or private, has been set apart for a defined purpose, careful planning for the economical and thorough accomplishment of that purpose becomes logically necessary. If the purpose of the metropolitan reservations was the production of crops of fruit or vegetables for profit, it is certain that skilled market gardeners would be called upon to make careful plans for securing the largest possible return from the various soils and exposures. But because the dividend which is looked for from the new reser-

[1] The Keney Park Trustees of Hartford, Conn.

vations is intangible, consisting in refreshment to be derived
from variety and beauty of scenery, careful planning for
securing a good dividend, and for increasing it, is not one whit
less necessary. Indeed, it is more necessary by so much as
the purpose in view is loftier. If even mean or ordinary purposes are to be successfully accomplished only through foresight and good planning, is it likely that higher purposes can
be achieved without taking thought? Reservations of scenery
are the cathedrals of the modern world. The comparatively
rural people of the middle ages found spiritual help in architectural beauty and grandeur. The more and more crowded
populations of to-day seek similar inspiration from the open
world of hills and valleys, streams and lakes. Thus the
responsibility which rests upon the trustees of our open-air
cathedrals is as grave as it is new. Successive generations
of tax-payers will be deprived of benefits rightfully theirs,
if the reservations are not cared for, and comprehensively
developed in ways wisely devised to produce the most interesting, the most varied, and the most delightful scenery the
open spaces in question are capable of presenting.

A scheme for working towards these ends is what we mean
by a " general plan." The word " plan " need not alarm any
one. It means simply a consistent programme of work, or
plan of campaign, to be directed to the attainment of well-
defined purposes, and the word is therefore just as applicable,
and the thing itself just as necessary in the case of reservations of scenery, as it is in the case of public squares or buildings. Desultory, makeshift, or fragmentary management is
as uneconomical and ineffective, and therefore as inexcusable,
in the one case as in the other. All uncalled-for artificiality
is of course to be avoided ; but the way to ensure this is not
by making no plans, but by officially adopting plans con-
scientiously devised to achieve the high purpose of the reservations. The means and methods to be suggested in plans
for securing landscape are as different from those of building-
plans as the purpose in view is different. Unlike the architect, the landscape architect starts in the new reservations,
for example, with broad stretches of existing scenery. It will
be his calling and duty to discover, and then to evolve and

make available, the most characteristic, interesting, and effective scenery. Practically, his work will be confined to planning such control or modification of vegetation as may be necessary for the sake of scenery, and to devising the most advantageous courses for the roads and paths from which the scenery will be viewed. The two departments of this planning should obviously go forward together. "Roads must be placed, not alone with reference to economy of construction in respect to passage from place to place, but with reference to economy in the ultimate development of resources of scenery." — F. L. Olmsted. Many of the roads already opened in the reservations do not fulfil this no more than reasonable requirement of true economy and common sense. These roads follow lines selected without reference to scenery by the wood-choppers of the past for their commercial purposes. The new roads were hurriedly built on these old lines, contrary to our recommendation, because it was deemed advisable to admit the public to the reservations without waiting for the completion of plans. The essential topographical maps were at the time not even ordered. Since the first day of this year, however, the maps have been at hand, and their absence can no longer be pleaded as an excuse for hodgepodge or happy-go-lucky work in either the road-maker's or the woodsman's department. There is indeed a certain amount of work in the latter department which, even in the absence of general plans, may be safely and advantageously prosecuted. On the other hand, the greater part of the woods ought not to be touched before general plans are satisfactorily made up. To permit road-makers or woodsmen to work here and there without plans would be much like allowing masons and carpenters to start a public building before the architect had thought it out. The topographical, forestal, and botanical surveys ordered by the Commission to provide data for planning are now completed, and we have become, in the course of the past three years, thoroughly familiar with the wooded as well as with the other reservations. We believe the framing and the official adoption of general plans to be very important; in fact, by all odds the most important work to which any and every public Executive Board can give its attention during its early years. The Metropolitan Sewer and Water Commissions have planned their comparatively prosaic and mechanical undertakings far-seeingly and comprehensively. Shall the Metropolitan Park Commission fail to take equal pains with the more delicate and difficult work which the tax-payers have confided to it?

The foregoing general statement contains, we believe, the whole truth of the matter, and we append the following memorandum only to bring out one point a little more sharply.

It is sometimes said that even if general plans for conserving and availing of scenery were practicable, they would not be desirable where the domain in question is " wild land " intended to be kept " natural " for the enjoyment of city people. It is admitted that thoroughly thought-out schemes are necessary and desirable for houses, public buildings, streets, squares, and urban parks, but " let Nature alone " in the hills and woods, and she, it is said, will frame lovelier landscapes than any which can be evolved or developed by intention.

Now, whatever may be the case in other lands and climates, so far as New England is concerned our answer is a " general denial," and our appeal is to the facts. Why, for example, are the Middlesex Fells more interesting than the Lynn Woods? Largely because the vegetation is more varied. And why is it more varied? Because of Man and not Nature. In the Fells are more pastures, more grassy glades and fields, and there is also more variety in the height and density of the forest trees. Nature, indeed, is constantly striving to abolish even the meagre existing variety, and to shut in all the paths and roads between walls of close-standing tree-trunks. Thus, if the reservations are left to Nature, monotony will follow; and not only will the existing scenery be soon obliterated (as one visit to the woods makes plain), but the existing economical opportunity for securing additional interest and beauty will be lost never to return, unless after a sweeping forest fire.

Permit us, lastly, to illustrate the nature of what we mean by comprehensive planning by citing just one instance.

Here is a fairly smooth valley between two rocky hills which rise at the end of a long pond or reservoir. The hills

are well wooded, but the valley contains only a low and mixed
growth of seedling trees and shrubs.   It appears to offer a
very favorable opportunity for developing great trees from
the most promising specimens of the young growth.   There
is all too little woodland of this type in the reservations,
and so, for variety's sake, we tentatively plan to eventually
remove the poorer trees for the encouragement of the better.
In so proposing, we have probably suggested the highest possible development of this particular part of the public domain,
if it is to be considered in and for itself alone.   But we know
from experience that this is not the way to go to work.   Our
planning must be comprehensive and not fragmentary, and
accordingly we avoid all hasty conclusions.   In the end, we
reverse our first decision, and plan to remove all the young
trees of the valley, thus encouraging the shrubbery only.
And why?   Because it turns out that it is through this valley that a striking distant view of the Great Blue Hill is
obtainable from a crag a mile away at the other end of the
chain of ponds.[1]   Large trees in the valley would completely
obliterate this remarkable picture.   When it is remembered
that the metropolitan district has borrowed and spent a million dollars expressly in order to secure the enjoyment of this
picture, with others like it, the wastefulness, and therefore
the wrongfulness, of both inaction and planless action becomes evident.

July 10, 1896.

Enclosed please find our semi-annual bill for professional
services during the half year lately ended.

In handing you this bill, we would respectfully call your
attention to the fact that we have not as yet received any
reply to our letter of February 4th, last.   We asked that we
might be definitely and publicly freed from all responsibility
for work done in the new reservations, or else that we might
be definitely engaged to draw up for the consideration of the
Commission those comprehensive schemes or programmes of
work which are commonly called " general plans."   You will
readily understand that we cannot professionally afford to
have our names associated with work done regardless of com-

---

[1] Charles's favorite prospect in the Fells.

prehensive studies. We, accordingly, beg leave to repeat the request of our letter of February 4th, that our position respecting the work to be done in the new reservations may be publicly defined. A copy of our letter of February 4th is enclosed herewith.

July 30, 1896.

W. B. DE LAS CASAS, ESQ.

Dear Sir, — It will be entirely agreeable to us to amend the clause which follows " November 30th, 1899," on page 1, so that it will read thus : " and shall also, from time to time during the continuance of this agreement, give such advice on the ground or in their office and in writing or verbally, and shall supervise the preparation in their office," etc., etc. I should be glad to meet Mr. Haskell with yourself in order that the whole question may be mutually understood.

As to dropping plan-making entirely, you doubtless see as plainly as I do what the results are sure to be. The consequences are visible all over the Union, and alas! in almost all the work that my firm has been connected with. There is always and everywhere a reluctance to spend money for consistent schemes of work, and plans are consequently put off. By and by there comes a demand for some work of construction, as at Revere Beach and Stony Brook to-day ; and then there is a sudden call addressed to us, with notice that a hundred men are to be put to work next week and what shall they do? We have just such a letter this morning from Brooklyn, N. Y. Not only are we in such cases greatly troubled by the haste demanded, but we are generally hampered by the necessity of regrading such roads or other constructions as are almost invariably introduced during the planless period. It is because I have studied these matters, and know the extremely uneconomical results of postponing plans, the waste of resources of scenery, as well as the waste of money spent in planless or non-comprehensive work, — it is because as a reasoning being I feel the shame and pity of such postponements so keenly, that I have all along hoped that your Commission would avoid the common pitfall.

In the ordinary affairs of life, planning for the accomplishment of purposes is found necessary to success of any

kind. In the extraordinary work, the same thing is true:
painters and poets have to "lay out" their work. The Metropolitan Commission itself has wisely planned the selection,
the boundaries, and the distribution of the acquired reservations, having certain purposes in view. The next most important thing for the Commission to undertake is, logically,
the careful planning of the interior of the reservations.
When I reflect that the money expended for labor since
January 1st has been sufficient to pay the cost of giving that
labor something worth while to work for, I am again, as a
reasoning mortal, shocked and saddened.

Yours truly,

CHARLES ELIOT.

Aug. 11, 1896.

By vote of the Commission, we were directed on July 2d
to make plans for a road through the length of Stony Brook
Reservation. We have studied the problem both on the
ground and on the map, and a preliminary line is now being
staked for inspection and adjustment. We find, however,
that we can by no means recommend the Commission to build
a road on the lines thus sketched, or, indeed, on any lines
which it might be possible to devise independently of the
consideration of a general plan for the whole reservation.
The line which we have studied possesses good lines and
grades, and it would have our approval if it were possible for
us to think it right to plan roads in public reservations as
roads and railroads are planned in the world at large. It
seems to us that since the purpose of such reservations is the
conservation and presentation of scenery, it is fundamentally
illogical to begin with the planning of roads. The scenery
itself should first be studied, and plans should first be laid
for faithfully preserving the best of the available landscape,
for restoring the beauty of damaged scenes, and for enhancing the attractiveness of the less interesting parts. Roads
should be planned, or begun upon, only when it has been
determined what will be the most interesting scenery which
they can reach and make enjoyable. For example, the
through road should pass on this side or the other of Turtle

Pond, according as this side or that can be made to present the most pleasing prospects; and so on. Regard should also be had to placing the roads so that they will injure the finest prospects either not at all, or as little as possible. It is only by painstaking in these ways that the resources of scenery can be economized and the purpose of the reservation successfully fulfilled.

We need hardly add that, since cross connections and connections with the boundary roads will certainly be required, they ought to be considered and planned at one and the same time; otherwise the lines and grades at junctions will surely be either awkward and inconvenient, or else uneconomical.

Holding these views as we do, we respectfully ask to be either commissioned to prepare a general plan, or else definitely excused from responsibility in the premises.

[*From Garden and Forest of August 26, 1896.*]

THE NECESSITY OF PLANNING.

The daily work of the architect and the landscape architect is popularly supposed to consist in ornamenting lands and buildings so as to make them appear beautiful. Rooms may be inconveniently and awkwardly shaped, but they can be "beautified" by rich furniture and upholstery. Whole buildings may be irrationally planned, but they may still be made "artistic" by means of mouldings, carvings, and mosaic. House grounds and college grounds, private gardens and public parks, may be senselessly, as well as ineffectively, arranged, but they may still be glorified by yellow and purple leafage. In short, "The world is still deceived with ornament."

On the other hand, although all seekers for the truth concerning beauty have discerned elements which defy analysis, such special students have nevertheless deduced from the visible and historical facts a whole series of fixed principles, which are quite as surely established as any of the other so-called laws of nature. Among these, perhaps, the most important is this, that, "in all the arts which serve the use, convenience, or comfort of man, from gardening and building down to the designing of the humblest utensil which it is desired to make beautiful, utility and fitness for intended purpose must be first considered." It is to be remembered that this is not theory but law. As a matter of fact and experience, satisfying beauty is not won unless the law of nature is obeyed.

That faithful and well-reasoned planning for the accomplishment of purpose is necessary to the success of the work of architects of buildings is now generally understood. "A plan" is a skilful combination of convenience with effectiveness of arrangement. "A design" is made up of plan, construction, and outward appearance, and by no means consists of the latter only. Indeed, the external aspect of a structure depends directly on the mode of construction, the construction depends, in turn, on the plan, and the plan on the purpose in view, with the result that the whole appearance of the building inevitably and naturally expresses this purpose.

If it be true that expression, character, and even beauty are thus most surely won, in the case of buildings, by keeping decoration subsidiary, and designing with a purpose in view from the start, it is equally true of all the wide field of architecture, using the word in its broadest imaginable sense. "Architecture, a great subject, truly," says William Morris, "for it embraces the consideration of the whole of the external surroundings of the life of man; we cannot escape from it if we would, for it means the moulding and altering to human needs of the very face of the earth itself." A bushy pasture, or a smooth green field, in forest-clad New England is as truly a product of human handiwork as a green meadow in treeless and dusty Utah; yet each is beautiful, and neither owes a particle of its beauty to decoration. The English deer-park with its broad-spreading trees, or the church-yard with its ancient stones and Yews, the typical Yankee farm with its low buildings and great Elms, or the live Oaks and quaint structures of the plantations of Louisiana, these and all similarly interesting landscapes are interesting, not because they have been decorated, but because they are strongly characterized and highly expressive. Their moving beauty is the natural product of straightforward work for the adaptation of land and landscape to human needs and uses.

Believing these things, it will be impossible for us, when a
tract of land is newly dedicated to some special purpose, be
it that of a suburban lot, a railroad station yard, a new village, a country-seat, or a public park, to stand by and see it
thoughtlessly laid out and then, perhaps, turned over to the
decorators.   We shall insist on premeditation and careful
fundamental planning, knowing that therein lies the best, if
not the only, hope of happy results.   Once possessed of faith
in that law of nature in accordance with which beauty springs
from fitness, we shall be ready to agree that, when purpose
is served, formal gardens, rectilinear avenues, and courts of
honor are not only permitted, but commanded.   On the other
hand, we shall be equally strenuous in demanding studied
planning, and adaptation to environment and purpose, in the
laying out of whatever work may need to be done to make
the wildest place of private or public resort accessible and
enjoyable.   Positive injury to the landscape of such places
can be avoided only by painstaking, while the available resources of scenery can be economized only by careful devising.   So with the whole range of problems which lie between
these extremes.   No work of man is ever successfully accomplished without taking thought beforehand ; in other words,
without planning.

Strange as it may appear, opposition to such planning
for effective results will not, in practice, be found to come
from those who attempt decoration only because they know not
how else to attain to the beautiful.   Just as the literary class
in China ruinously opposes change of any kind, so there is
with us a comparatively small, but influential, body of refined
persons, far too well educated to be " deceived by ornament,"
who most unfortunately, though unintentionally, assist in the
triumphs of ugliness by blindly opposing all attempts to adapt
land and landscape to changed or new requirements.   Enjoying the pleasanter scenery of their surroundings as it exists,
— certain shady roads, or some lingering fields or farm lands,
— these estimable people talk of " letting Nature alone " or
" keeping Nature natural," as if such a thing were possible in
a world which was made for man.   No, the " moulding and
altering " of the earth goes forward of necessity, and if those

who ought to be leaders will not help to guide the work aright, the work will surely be done badly ; as it is, in fact, done badly in the neighborhood of all our great towns. To refuse to exercise foresight, and to adapt to purpose in due season, is simply to court disaster. Instead of hanging back, it ought to be the pride and pleasure of these very people to see to it that proper plans are seasonably laid fcr the widening of roads so that fine trees shall not be sacrificed, to see to it that electric-car tracks shall be placed only in suitably selected and specially arranged streets, that public reservations of one type or another shall be provided in accordance with some consistent general scheme, and that such reservations shall be saved from both decorative and haphazard development by the early adoption of rational and comprehensive plans. There is needed a little less selfish contentment in the doomed landscape of the present, a sharper sense of responsibility to the future, and a living faith in that law of God, in obedience to which everything which is well adapted to use and purpose is sure to be interesting and expressive, and if not beautiful, at least on the way to be.

Jan. 27, 1897.

TREES IN PUBLIC PARKS.

To the Editor of Garden and Forest.

It is with sorrow that I am obliged to confess that I never read your editorial of December 23, 1896, until January 2, 1897, — but perhaps it is even now not too late to express appreciation of your vigorous words respecting the all too prevalent feeling that nothing can justify the felling of a tree. Unless this superstition can be put to rout, we may as well attempt no parks or reservations ; for if the axe cannot be kept going, Nature will soon reduce the scenery of such domains to a monotony of closely crowded, spindling tree-trunks. Among men versed in such matters there is no question about this. Mr. Olmsted and Mr. J. B. Harrison once compiled a pamphlet, entitled " Observations on the Treatment of Public Plantations," in which they printed some forty quotations from the writings of all the highest authorities from Loudon to Douglass, and all substantially agree with you in saying that in such places " the axe should never be allowed to rest."

But how shall the use of the axe be guided? This is the practical question for park commissioners ; and it seems to me that your editorial gives only half an answer. You recommend the employment of " experts in the care of ornamental trees," and experts must indeed be engaged, at least as teachers of technical methods. But how shall the experts themselves be guided ? Shall they be permitted to reduce the groves and woods of our public domains to collections of specimen trees, or to the monotony of the German forests, as, by the way, they surely will do if they are not controlled? In the landscape of a park your arboriculturist, with his zeal for " good " or " ornamental" trees, is almost as dangerous a person as your horticulturist, with his passion for curious, decorative, or novel plants. A good park plan is fundamentally a scheme for the creation of more and more pleasing scenery through modifications to be made in the preëxistent vegetation, by clearings, thinnings, plantings, and the like, and only secondarily a scheme for making the resulting scenery agreeably accessible by roads and walks. Engineers who direct the building of park roads are expected to conform their work to the requirements of the adopted general plan. Woodmen, foresters, and planters should be similarly controlled by the requirements of the same plan, — but you do not say so.

Permit me to add that your incidental remarks about the Boston parks (with which I am familiar) strike me as exaggerated. It is true, indeed, that road construction has proceeded more rapidly than planting and woodmen's work, and that some of the older plantations are suffering for lack of thinning. On the other hand, none of the wooded or planted areas of the Boston parks are yet in the deplorable condition of the border plantations of Brooklyn's Prospect Park, which you mention ; nor are they likely to reach that condition yet awhile. The Boston Park Commission, influenced largely by a recent mayor, has simply chosen to spend its money in building roads rather than in tree-cutting, pruning, and planting; but it has not been forgotten that woodmen's and planters' work is at least as essential to the realization of the general plans as the work of the engineer, and there is good reason to suppose that this work, the postponement of which has as yet wrought no great harm, will soon be entered on with vigor.

January 22, 1897.

MY DEAR MR. SARGENT, —

I am sending you the new "metropolitan" park report by this mail, and I beg leave to ask your attention to the argument concerning "general plans," which begins in the middle of page 39 and ends on page 41. It is the same argument which "Garden and Forest" has presented over and over again ; and that you should take ground in opposition has naturally surprised me.

The Metropolitan Commission has followed designed lines in all that it has done up to this time, — in selecting the sites of the reservations and parkways (see the circular diagram and the accompanying text), in making choice of the exact boundaries, and so on ; but now that their work is narrowed to the interiors of the lands acquired, the Commission abandons all attempt to secure comprehensive results, and proceeds to open miles of roads on the lines of the old paths, and to make clearings, and then open groves, as I mentioned this morning, without a thought for design, or for any comprehensive results. You know for a certainty that the full scenic value of the reservations (or anything approaching it) can never be won by such methods. Such methods, if continued in, will simply make it impossible for the community to ever get what they ought to get out of the reservations. If any public Board other than a park board followed such irresponsible, hap-hazard, and plan-less methods, — say, the trustees of a church-building fund, or a sewer commission, — you would agree that they would be blameworthy. As a matter of fact, they would, I suppose, be indicted !

Yours sincerely,
CHARLES ELIOT.

By 1902 the Commission had ordered from their landscape architects general plans for the Blue Hills, Middlesex Fells, Stony Brook, and Beaver Brook Reservations, successive votes having been passed at various times which ultimately covered the whole of these reservations.

The following letter illustrates the difficulties which arose from the use of the unplanned, smoothed wood-roads : —

March 12, 1897.

Superintendent Price told me yesterday of the great difficulty which the people who use the Fellsway experience in traversing the Hemlock Pool road. This, of course, is a good specimen of the kind of difficulty which always arises when temporary or makeshift roads are opened. The road in question ought not — so it seems to me — to be widened, with the necessarily considerable expense for cutting and filling; at least, not until some one can, after thorough study, make sure that the road is in the best possible location. I have no idea that it is in the best possible location at every point. It certainly does not exhibit the scenery of that part of the Fells through which it runs as effectively as it might be exhibited. Accordingly, I told the Superintendent that the only thing I could recommend him to do to relieve the present difficulty was to fell such trees as stand immediately adjacent to the present narrow roadway, — such trees as look as if the hubs of wheels might easily strike them. The road will look much wider if all these trees are removed, and it will also be possible to turn out at many places in case of need. There are so many other trees in the rear of those I am speaking of, that I see no harm in relieving the situation by the means suggested.

CHAPTER XXXV

REVERE BEACH. 1896

Society everywhere is in conspiracy against the manhood of every
one of its members. The virtue in most request is conformity. It
loves not realities and creators, but names and customs. Whoso would
be a man must be a non-conformist. — RALPH WALDO EMERSON.

THE first letter from the landscape architects to the Metropolitan Park Commission about Revere Beach (December
15, 1893) is printed in the previous chapter on General
Principles in selecting Public Reservations, p. 435. It describes the minimum public investment on a sea-beach; and
also a more liberal and advantageous plan. At the end of
1894, the plans for Revere Beach contemplated the removal
of the railroad from the top of the beach, and the construction of a sidewalk, driveway, and promenade the length of
the beach, and on its long, sweeping curve. In their report
dated January, 1895, the Commission say that although the
legislature of 1894 had placed $500,000 at their disposal for
acquiring Revere Beach, they had not seen their way to take
any active measures to that end. Study of the problem had
convinced them that $1,000,000 would be needed to complete
the undertaking in a satisfactory manner. Thereupon, the
legislature of 1895 appropriated $500,000 more for Revere
Beach. Before the end of that year the beach had been
"taken" by the Commission for a distance of three miles,
and the settlement with owners had been well begun. Information to this effect having reached the public, multitudes
began to resort to the beach as soon as warm weather set in;
although the Commission had not even decided on the constructions which would be desirable for the security and convenience of the public. On July 12th — a warm Sunday —
45,000 people visited the beach; and the spectacle gave the
Commissioners and all their agents a strong impression that
constructions on a large scale were imperatively needed.
Charles was directed to prepare designs for the best use of
the reservation by the public; but this best use had to be
imagined or prophesied, since the situation was both novel
and intricate. From the middle of July till the end of De-

cember, Charles gave a large portion of his time to the problem of the beach. His views of what was most desirable underwent some changes and enlargements; and he was obliged to study undesirable alternatives and arrangements obviously not the best possible, because the resources of the Commission were limited, and the best might not be attainable. To make provision for orderly sea-bathing was imperative; yet the buildings for bathers threatened to impair very seriously the chief beauty of the reservation, namely, the long, unbroken sweep of the curving beach.

The ultimate plans adopted by the Commission — the execution of which is as yet (1902) only partial — illustrate Charles's foresight and faculty for imagining future conditions and needs, and also his gift of persuasive exposition. When he first broached some of his ideas, they were not received very sympathetically by the members of the Commission. Thus, on August 26th, Charles made the following concise entry in his pocket diary concerning a meeting of the Commission: "Discussion of Revere Beach problems. Suggested putting dressing-rooms back of driveway. Met with Howls! Talked of traffic road east of Revere Street as continuation of Ocean Avenue. More Howls!" These initial differences of view, however, did not prevent a patient discussion of the subject, and only made the policy adopted more assuredly wise.

The first of the letters which constitute this chapter mentions in the opening sentence the abandonment of the large hotel property at the Point of Pines, a costly property, which the Commission, much to its regret, could not pay for; and proceeds to discuss the proper lay-out for the remaining reservation. Two fifths of the entire length of the beach lies east and south of Revere Street. The questions of roadway or no roadway, of the minimum elevation of the promenade, of the avoidance of sea-walls, and of the position of the traffic road behind the reservation were all fundamental. The other letters deal mainly with the disposition of the various buildings and shelters which seemed necessary. It was in regard to these arrangements that Charles's ideas underwent a decided evolution in the course of the five months of study and discussion. The letters of this chapter were all addressed to the chairman of the Commission.

August 19, 1896.

At the meeting of the Commission held August 12, 1896, we submitted a plan for abandoning the sea front of the Point of Pines hotel property, and acquiring a strip for a parkway which should lead in the rear of the hotels towards Lynn.

To-day we submit the same plan slightly modified, as directed by the Commission, together with a plan for the development of the reservation between the Point of Pines and Revere Street. This plan, in common with that for the remainder of the reservation south of Revere Street, is based on the following reasoning, which we ask leave to place on file.

Most of the people who resort to the reservation naturally desire to walk on the beach itself ; but at high water they are driven back upon the dry shingle, where walking is diffi-cult. A paved promenade at the top of the beach seems, therefore, necessary.

Those who resort to the reservation in carriages have been accustomed to drive up and down the beach; but when the place is at all crowded, this practice is dangerous, and we presume it will be forbidden. If it is desired to give people a view of the sea from carriages and cycles, a roadway adja-cent to the promenade will be required.

The private lands adjacent to the reservation are presum-ably destined to be occupied by hotels, restaurants, shops, apartment houses, and private dwellings (though we hope it may be possible to impose some restrictions) ; and since large numbers of people will often want to resort to these build-ings, a broad sidewalk seems necessary.

It is, in many respects, inconvenient to insert a carriage road between this sidewalk and the beach promenade. If the whole available space were to be devoted to the use of persons on foot, it would not be more than sufficient to accommodate such crowds as may be expected in the future. On the other hand, we believe a carriage road will not work any very great inconvenience for some years to come, and we have, accord-ingly, placed a driveway on the submitted plan.

It appears from the topographical survey that the elevation of the top of the beach varies from grade 15 to grade 20, the elevation of mean high water being grade 10. Extreme high water rises to grade 14, and in this exposed situation some allowance must be made for great waves. For the sake of

REVERE BEACH IN 1892

Showing how shabby structures intruded on the beach

REVERE BE[...]

The sidewalk, driveway,

ERVATION IN 1900

nenade on the crown of the beach

the adjacent private lands, as well as for the sake of economy in filling-material, it is, on the other hand, desirable to keep the elevation of the new walks and roadway as low as possible. The usual minimum elevation of streets and sea-walls adjacent to tidal waters about Boston is grade 16. In this case, we can, however, recommend no grade short of 18, and even then it is probable that the waves during great storms may reach the roadway.

It is desired, for convenience and economy as well as appearance, to avoid the building of bulkheads or sea-walls. The new line of grade 18 must, then, be kept far enough back from the line of mean high water at grade 10 to permit of waves running up the beach and wasting their strength before reaching the promenade. To secure this result, so far as is possible in the circumstances, the promenade ought to be kept some 70 feet back from the line of high water. For the promenade itself, the plan suggests a width of 25 feet, for the roadway 40 feet, and for the sidewalk 20 feet, making a total of 155 feet required between the curve of the high-water line and the curve of the taking line. This breadth is already in the possession of the Commission, throughout the length of the beach, excepting at the one place above mentioned, where it cannot be obtained without acquiring additional land, and diminishing the already shallow depth of the private lots between the taking line and the new location of the Boston, Revere Beach & Lynn Railroad. South of Revere Street there is generally but little space to spare; in other words, if a wider sidewalk, road, or promenade were demanded, it could be obtained only by building a sea-wall. For some distance north of Revere Street, rather more than the necessary breadth is owned by the Commission, because of the acquisition of the location of Ocean Avenue. Here we recommend that the regular curve of the road and sidewalk be continued, regardless of the lines of Ocean Avenue, and that such land as is not required be hereafter disposed of, or else utilized as part of a traffic road and electric car reservation, to be laid out parallel with the pleasure driveway, for the sake of permitting traffic between Revere, Chelsea, and Lynn to pass along the reservation without entering it. Ocean Avenue north of Revere Street is practically discontinued for traffic purposes by the laying out of the reservation. A certain amount of wagon and electric car traffic will, in the future, desire to pass to and fro between Chelsea, Revere, and Lynn; and we fear it will force itself upon the reservation and the pleasure drive (where there is not room for it) unless a separate way is provided now, while the land is cheap. We have, accordingly, indicated on the accompanying plan a traffic way, placed adjacent to the pleasure road of the reservation, and subdivided as follows: 1st, an electric car reservation 30 feet wide; 2d, a roadway 25 feet wide; and, 3d, a sidewalk adjacent to the private land 15 feet wide.

At Revere Street the plan suggests the acquisition of the estate at the corner of Ocean Avenue, in order to enable Revere Street to be divided, so as to lead into the reservation as easily one way as the other, and, at the same time, provide a street-car terminus between the branches. Such an enlargement at this point will, also, enable the passengers by the steam railroad to reach the reservation more comfortably.

By the first meeting in September we hope to be able to report concerning buildings and other structures, several of which are evidently called for in this reservation.

September 9, 1896.

On August 19th we submitted a preliminary plan and report descriptive of the grades, lines, and subdivisions proposed for the roads and footways of Revere Beach Reservation. To-day we submit a preliminary report on the various structures which will be required sooner or later.

For the comfort and convenience of the great body of visitors, a few level terraces and roofed pavilions or shelters are much needed. It is obvious that those should be placed near the railroad stations and the termini of the electric car lines: in other words, near Beach Street and near Revere Street.

Unfortunately, the available space between the proposed driveway and the sea is no more than sufficient for the running up of storm waves (see letter of August 19th), and the suggested platforms must, therefore, be constructed either on piling or on filling held in place by massive sea-walls. Piling is objectionably ugly, and it is hardly a safe mode of construction in so exposed a situation. Pile wharves, or even sea-walls, extending any considerable distance seaward from the top of the beach, would also greatly mar the appearance of the beach as a whole and as seen from the driveway, depending as this does on the grand simplicity of the long and continuous concave curve. Accordingly, we have rejected entirely the idea of piling and the idea of protruding any sea-walls further than sixty feet seaward from the edge of the proposed promenade. If the desired terraces are confined to this narrow width, they must, of course, be made long, but rather than make them excessively so, a second floor or upper deck may eventually be superposed. In addition to the two large terraces at Beach Street and Revere Street, smaller structures of the same kind should eventually be built adjacent to the two circles at the extreme ends of the reservation.

Facilities for orderly sea-bathing are also urgently needed. At least one thousand dressing-rooms should apparently be provided at once, and another thousand will be needed before many years. One dressing-room occupies from twenty to thirty square feet, and a thousand of them would extend four thousand feet along the beach. Arranged in this primitive way, there would be no suitable means of controlling their use. If, however, a more compact arrangement is attempted, a piled or sea-walled foundation becomes necessary, precisely as in the case of the terraces. An accompanying diagram represents the block plan of a terrace combined with a bathing establishment. The latter is shown occupying the Strathmore site, and the terraces extend north and south thereof. The terraces are merely enlargements of the beach promenades, and until provided with upper decks, they may, like the promenades, be planted with one or two rows of poplars, and provided with numerous seats. The bathing establishment is designed to be entered half-way between the ends of Beach Street and Shirley Avenue, and if this plan is adopted, it will be advisable to secure a broad passageway leading through the middle of the block to Ocean Avenue and the railroad station. Upon entering the building, men and women will pass the office through turnstiles to the right and left respectively, and after bathing they will go out at the same place. There should be only one way for men in bathing-suits to go and come from the beach and one for women, and both should be watched to prevent the passage of persons not in bathing costume. By building two floors of dressing-rooms, and carrying the second floor over the promenade (thus arcading the latter), about 850 dressing-rooms can be obtained in the space bounded by the ends of Beach Street and Shirley Avenue, and by a sea-wall built sixty feet from the promenade. A larger number cannot be obtained here without sacrifice of light, or air, or both. As sketched, every dressing-room will open upon a roofless alley. To avoid the objectionable arcading of the promenade, the rooms so secured may be arranged on a third tier or floor without appreciable sacrifice of light or air ; and, in any case, the proposed upper decks of the terraces may be joined by a gallery twenty feet wide, built above the water-side dressing-rooms, where the best view of the bathing will be had.

Another diagram presents an alternative scheme for taking the bathing establishment out from between the two terraces already described and placing it directly behind one unified terrace and on the land side of the beach driveway. In this case all the dressing-rooms would be over a hundred feet farther from the water, and bathers would have to cross the driveway by fenced bridges ; nevertheless, this scheme presents advantages which make it well worthy of consideration. At the cost of additional land this plan would save the cost of the sea-walls and filling required for the bathing establishment already described, and, what is more important, it would better preserve the continuity of the beach, and the view from the drive and the adjacent private buildings. This alternative diagram places the bathing establishment just south of Shirley Avenue and between the beach road and Ocean Avenue. As the bridges over the driveway must be fifteen feet above grade, the dressing-rooms may as well be elevated also. In the centre of the ground floor may then be placed the office, the entrances and exits of the bathing establishment, and the necessary checking-stands and lavatories, for which it is hard to find room on the ocean side of the driveway. The remainder of the ground floor, it is proposed, should be used for the termini of electric car lines, where the arriving and departing crowds can be suitably controlled by fences built on spacious platforms. At present the crowding about the cars in the narrow streets is so unpleasant and so dangerous as to keep many people from attempting to go to the beach at all. The alternative scheme herewith submitted would correct this evil in addition to providing a terrace and a bathing establishment.

The advantages and disadvantages of the two schemes may be summarized as follows : —

SCHEME A.

Advantages.	*Disadvantages.*
Site already secured.	Site very narrow and somewhat
Dressing-rooms brought as near as possible to the water.	dangerously exposed to storm waves.
	Terrace divided.
	Beach, as a whole, marred in appearance.
	Beach-drive and adjacent buildings cut off from view of the sea.

SCHEME B.

Advantages.	*Disadvantages.*
Beach marred by terrace only and this terrace in one block.	Site for bathing establishment still to be secured.
View from beach-drive less obstructed.	Dressing-rooms removed from the water, and approachable only by stairs.
Site a safe one.	
A car-station secured in addition to terrace and bathing establishment.	

Whichever of these alternative schemes is adopted for the Shirley Avenue location, it should be duplicated at Revere Street, so that the great crowds of summer holidays may be divided.

The stacks of dressing-rooms can be framed of iron and carried on iron beams. The surrounding fences can be topped with flagpoles; and there is no reason why both the terraces

and the bathing establishments, when fitted with the necessary railings, electric light poles, and flagstaffs, should not
present a pleasingly festive appearance. We would respectfully suggest the employment of some well-known and successful architect to act coöperatively with us in the preparation of detailed designs.

November 21, 1896.

Permit us to summarize for the special meeting on Monday
the evolution of our schemes for the bathing pavilions at
Revere Beach.

Since the Strathmore Hotel was burned, its site has been
much used as a plaza. The scheme which first and naturally
suggested itself was, therefore, to construct a permanent plaza
or terrace at this point, place the entrances to the bathing
pavilions at the ends of this plaza, and stretch the dressing-
rooms beyond the offices to the north and south. This scheme
was submitted as No. 28 in our office series of Revere Beach
plans.

Upon reflection it was found, however, that this obvious
solution of the problem was open to grave objections. (1)
It divided the administration offices, which, for economy's
sake, ought to be concentrated. (2) It placed offices and
dressing-rooms just where they would conceal from visitors
arriving at the plaza the long sweep of the open beach, which
is the finest thing about the reservation. (3) It placed the
necessarily ugly yards of dressing-rooms where they would be
most conspicuous in all views from the further parts of the
beach, and from the driveway at the top of the beach.

To correct these imperfections of the first scheme, another
plan was devised. In this plan the administration offices
were brought together in the middle, the yards of dressing-
rooms were attached on either hand, and terraces for the use
of the general public were added at the ends. Thus the
administration was concentrated, the general public was provided with good view points, and the dressing-rooms were
concealed behind the partly double-decked terraces.

The second plan was a great improvement on the first, but
again we found it subject to grave fundamental objections.
What was it that the metropolitan district sought to secure

REVERE BE
Terrace and shelters in front of the Bath-H

ERVATION

ng on the dry sand; bathers, raft in deep water

when it purchased this costly sea-coast reservation ?   It was the grand and refreshing sight of the natural sea-beach, with its long, simple curve, and its open view of the ocean.   Nothing in the world presents a more striking contrast to the jumbled, noisy scenery of a great town ; and this being the case, it seems to us that to place buildings on the beach is consciously to sacrifice the most refreshing characteristic of a sea-beach, and the most valuable element in the people's property therein.   Accordingly, a third plan was next prepared, putting the bathers' dressing-rooms and the necessary administrative offices on the landward side of the beach roadway, where they will be off the beach and yet within sufficiently easy reach thereof.   For the bathers this plan has some disadvantages, but the general public consists of the bathers plus a far greater number of other persons, and this third plan is the only plan which secures for the general public a full, continuous, and unshattered view of the beach and the sea.

Charles finally concentrated his matured opinions into the following letter, which was signed by the Commission's landscape architects and engineer, and by the architects who had been selected to design the buildings for this reservation : —

BROOKLINE, MASS., December 3, 1896.

The undersigned, having studied and reported, as requested, certain designs for plazas and bathing establishments at Revere Beach, beg leave to place on file their unanimous opinion that it is undesirable to place any large constructions seaward of the proposed promenade, — an opinion which is based on the following reasons among others : —

(1) Construction outward from the promenade flies in the face of nature, which demands all the available space for the harmless running up of storm waves.   Retaining and foundation walls built seaward will receive the blows of the waves, buildings reared upon them will often be soused with spray, plazas thus constructed will be drenched when the waves are high.   Structures of any kind in such a position will be a source of anxiety, if not of expense for repairs and reinforcements.

(2) Buildings placed between the promenade and the ocean will be so jammed against the promenade, on the one hand, and so set up on the sea-wall, on the other, as to appear cramped and awkward architecturally.

(3) Sea-walls, plazas, and buildings so placed will unavoidably appear as conspicuously obtrusive objects in all raking or alongshore views, both from the drive and promenade, and from the beach.

(4) A plaza will inevitably induce the congestion of crowds upon it, particularly if it appears to be cut off from the promenades by bathing establishments placed at its two ends. A continuous promenade without any plaza, built on the natural curve, commanding uninterrupted views, provided with occasional shelters, and marked by flagstaffs and lamp-posts, will, on the other hand, lead to the dispersion of the public, while it will, in our opinion, make the reservation a far finer possession than it can be made in any other way.

Respectfully submitted by

OLMSTED, OLMSTED & ELIOT,
Landscape Architects.
STICKNEY & AUSTIN,
Architects.
WM. T. PIERCE,
Engineer.

On the 24th of December, Charles had the satisfaction of writing in his diary : " Board adopted new scheme for house in rear of driveway." This " house " was the large administration building and bath-house with tunnels under the driveway for the passage of bathers. The Commission had been gradually convinced that the curve of the crest of the beach should not be interrupted by buildings projecting on to the beach; and they finally came unanimously to Charles's opinion on this vital point.

In the whole course of Metropolitan Park business no event gave Charles more satisfaction than this ultimate agreement to preserve the crest of Revere Beach from the intrusion of buildings; and, it may be added, no determination of the Commission has ever been more promptly or more completely justified. In writing to his friend and coadjutor, Mr. Sylvester Baxter, on January 23, 1897, about the report of the

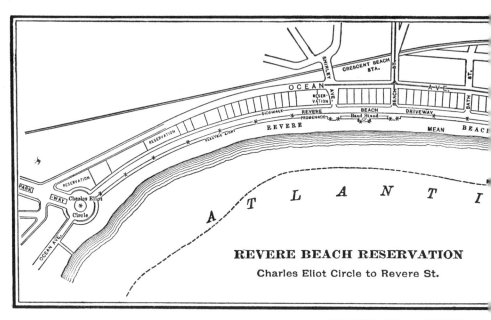

REVERE BEACH RESERVATION

Charles Eliot Circle to Revere St.

ONE MILE AND A QUARTER OF

Showing the beach, the approaches, the driveway and

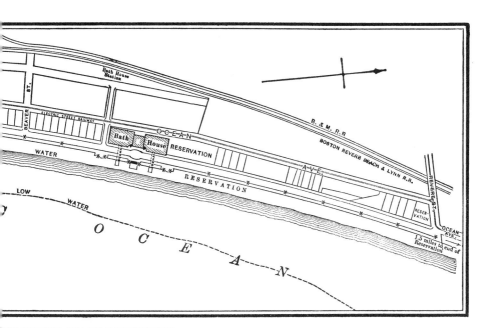

THE REVERE BEACH RESERVATION

romenade, the bath-house with its subways and the terraces

Metropolitan Park Commission for the year 1896, Charles said of the landscape architects' discussion of the problem of Revere Beach in that report: "This is a difficult and novel question, the beach being the first that I know of to be set aside and governed by a public body for the enjoyment of the common people."

CHAPTER XXXVl

REPORT TO THE METROPOLITAN PARK COMMISSION FOR 1896

Roads and walks should never be turned from their obviously direct course without a sufficient reason. A change of level of ground surface, a tree, or a group of plants, will induce and seemingly demand a change of line. . . . When roads and walks are carried over irregular surfaces, the natural turnings and windings necessary to follow an easy grade and keep as closely to the original surface of the ground as possible, will usually develop pleasing curves. — THE GARDEN.

PART I. ACQUIRED RESERVATIONS.

The Rock-hill or Forest Reservations.

. . . (1) THE eastern and western boundaries of Stony Brook Reservation have been relocated through exceedingly rough country in such a way as to make the lines and grades and the work of constructing the boundary roads much easier, though still difficult. It was the completion of the topographical map which enabled this needed readjustment to be studied and accomplished intelligently. . . . A comprehensive scheme for guide-boards for the preliminary roads of the reservations has been devised and submitted. A botanical list of the plants of the reservations, edited by Mr. Walter Deane of Cambridge from the collections of many cordially coöperating botanists, was made up and published in the spring. It will interest all botanists to watch for the possible return of many long since evicted plants. The wild birds and animals of the reserved and protected woodlands have already greatly increased in number.

A preliminary report with respect to such work as might first be attempted in the living woods of the reservations was submitted early in the year, but no active work has yet been ordered. For reasons summarized below it is indeed our opinion that, except for certain rescuing work, it will be wiser to leave the woods alone, rather than to labor in them without regard to carefully considered general plans. . . .

While little important work has been accomplished in the reservations during the year, the gathering of information on which to base comprehensive plans for guiding work in the future has gone on steadily.   As the publication in 1891 of a general topographical map of the whole Boston district first made possible the devising of a comprehensive scheme for a Metropolitan Park System, so the completion of the topographical maps of the separate forest reservations has now first made it possible to study intelligently schemes for their gradual development as treasuries of accessible and beautiful landscape.   The contracting surveyors, Messrs. French, Bryant & Taylor, finished the maps of the Fells and Blue Hills Reservations early in the year; and the map of Stony Brook Reservation was completed by the Commission's engineering department a few months later. . . .

By means of sun-prints from the full scale tracings [of these maps], as well as copies of the lithographed maps, the further mapping and study of the existing condition of the woods and ground-cover of the reservations have gone forward, until they are now so far advanced that a detailed report on the present state of the woods, illustrated by maps and photographs, will soon be completed. . . .

But it may be asked, Why all this preparation ?   Is it clear that it is necessary, or even advisable, to attempt to plan in advance how vegetation ought to be controlled and directed, and where roads ought eventually to be built?   Why not swing the axe and build roads from time to time, as circumstances may seem to dictate or occasion require ?

To us it seems that a due regard for the high purpose of public reservations, as well as a due regard for the economical fulfilment of that purpose, prohibits piecemeal, unrelated, and hand-to-mouth work in such domains. . . . Park commissions are the trustees of the people's treasure of scenery; they are responsible for the safe-guarding and the increase of this treasure, and they are charged with the duty of making it most effectively accessible.   Being trustees, they cannot safely proceed planlessly, any more than can those who are charged

with guarding and making accessible the people's treasure of
books and pictures, or with providing the people's drinking
water. The devising of comprehensive and far-seeing plans,
or programmes of procedure, is for park commissions, as for
all other executive bodies, the most necessary, arduous, and
responsible labor which they are called upon to perform.

It is sometimes said that the following of "general plans"
will induce a regrettable formalizing of the scenery of the
reservations now in question, or a lamentable taming and
smoothing of what is now wild and rough. That will, however, depend on the nature of the plans adopted, and the
desires of the Commission which directs the planting, precisely as the style of the architecture of a church or library
depends on the desires and taste of the trustees in charge of
the work. If it is desired to preserve wildness, and enhance
the natural beauty of reservations accessible to multitudinous
populations, that is precisely the thing that requires the most
considerate and prophetic planning.

It is sometimes said that the mere existence of general
plans tends to an extravagantly rapid prosecution of active
work. There is, however, no more real danger of excess of
expenditure when following a definite and comprehensive programme than there is when proceeding hap-hazard, while the
following of plans gives assurance that every dollar will count
toward worthy results. This, also, is a matter which lies
entirely in the control of the directing body.

Our survey of the present condition of the reservations has
brought out this fact, among others, — that the most pleasing
existing scenery is a product of men's work in making clearings and thinnings, pasturing large areas, encouraging seedling growths, and so on ; and that, if even the present meagre
degree of variety in the landscape is to be merely preserved,
intelligent attention will need to be continually given to the
control of the tree growth and the ground cover. The constant care which will be required for the preservation and
encouragement of the most appropriate types of vegetation
has been touched upon in previous reports. It is sufficient to
say here that the studies of this year have only confirmed us
in the belief that to leave the woods alone would be only to

lose scenery and develop monotony, and that to preserve and enrich this scenery a well-considered programme of work must be devised for controlling and guiding the vegetation of the reservations. Whatever is attempted ought, however, to be related to the prospective roads and other points of view, from which the scenery of the future is to be commanded. . . . To proceed to "improve" the woods without reference to the positions designed to be occupied by the permanent roads will plainly result either in much double expenditure, or else in failure to secure that varied and beautiful scenery which the public has a right to expect the reservation roads to exhibit.

Conversely, it is just as true that the placing of roads ought to be largely governed by the plans adopted for the control of vegetation. If roads are devised independently, there is danger that they will either seriously mar the landscape or else not effectively exhibit it. The existing preliminary roads of the reservations, opened on lines which served well the wood-choppers' commercial purposes, fail to meet the present purpose of the reservations in both of the two ways just mentioned; and for this reason, and because they have bad lines and grades, they ought to continue to be regarded as in great part temporary. To spend money in widening them or in improving their grades, to build permanent roads without regard to any programme for developing the forest scenery, or to attempt woodmen's work without reference to any road plans, will be to fix, without consideration, permanent features which will only obstruct the people of the metropolitan district in obtaining from these reservations that measure of refreshing and uplifting enjoyment which alone can justify their great cost and their excision from the taxable area.[1] . . .

The Lake, Brook, and River Reservations.

. . . The boundaries of Charles River Reservation were discussed in our report of last year, and no changes have been made during the present year, except that the line has been

[1] See the previous annual reports of the landscape architects, p. 502 for 1894, and p. 531 for 1895.

improved at one place close to Watertown village by moving it inland to coincide with the line of Wheeler Street. Plans have been made and submitted for a desirable, though narrow, additional acquisition of land on the Newton bank below Lemon Brook, but no action on this plan has been taken. Several abandonments have been proposed at different times, for present economy's sake. In our opinion, however, none can be made without too great a sacrifice of the essential value of the whole reservation. Private industrial frontages, interspersed between the irremovable Albany Railroad yards near Cottage Farm and the Abattoir in Brighton, would greatly detract from the effectiveness and value of the remaining river-bank parkways, which must depend upon their continuity for their appearance, as well as for their usefulness for travel. We have from the first maintained that all the purchasable frontage should be purchased, and then that such portions as may be rentable should be rented to private persons during the years which may intervene before the construction of the river-bank roads or parkways may be demanded. Should occasion require, public freight landings may be provided, as above remarked, when construction is once undertaken.

On the Cambridge side of the river, between the Cambridge Hospital and Boylston Street, the construction of the North Charlesbank Road, as it may perhaps be called, is already begun. The natural river-bank was here a salt marsh, subject to occasional flooding by the tide, as illustrated in the uppermost of the typical cross-sections in the drawing on p. 592. Not knowing whether the river will eventually have to be sea-walled, as in the second section, or whether, following the building of a dam, it may be green-banked, as in the third section, the Cambridge Park Commission has adopted the temporary mode of grading the bank, illustrated in the fourth cross-section. When it is remembered that there are, above Cottage Farm, some ten miles of salt-marsh river-bank which must sooner or later be made usable, the obvious economy, as well as the greater usefulness and beauty, to be secured by the scheme which substitutes a short crosswise wall or dam near the river's mouth for ten miles of wall lead-

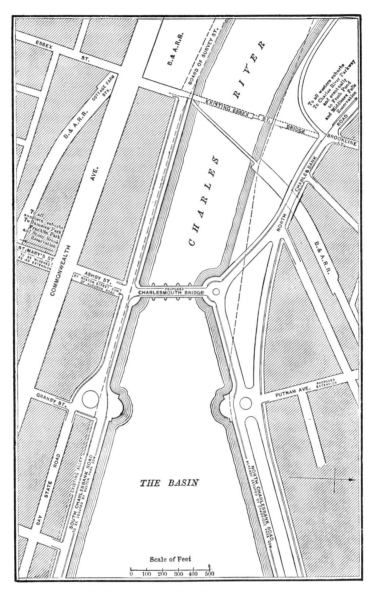

THE LOCATION OF CHARLESMOUTH BRIDGE

And the design for the head of Charles River Basin

ing upstream and back again cannot be questioned or disguised. Watertown, and part of Newton, with Brighton, and especially Cambridge, are now positively suffering for a decision of the question of dam or no dam. If there is to be no dam, the river ought to be dredged; if there is to be a dam, much of the dredging may be safely omitted; and so on. It is to be regretted that the Joint Commission which originally proposed the dam went out of existence with the filing of its report. A project, no matter how worthy, which requires the coöperation of four municipalities, three park commissions, the State, and the United States, cannot be expected to accomplish itself.

Meanwhile, and whether Charles River is to be relieved of the invading tides or not, at least the location for an adequate and handsome connection between the existing Muddy River Parkway and the proposed Charles River Parkway ought to be secured before the construction of buildings makes it too costly. As was pointed out in a report addressed to the Commission early in the year, such a connection would greatly enhance the value of the Metropolitan as well as the Boston and Cambridge parkways; and, as was then suggested, it can best be secured by widening St. Mary's Street and Ashby Street, as an extension to Charles River of the existing Audubon Road of the Boston Park System. It is about at the end of Ashby Street that the narrow Charles River empties into the broad and long Charles River basin; and here, and not at Cottage Farm, is the natural place for a bridge, to accommodate the travel which the great basin inevitably inconveniences. The accompanying diagram illustrates how such a Charlesmouth bridge might span the stream in a manner which would terminate the basin symmetrically and architecturally; while the same diagram makes it plain that such a bridge would be an improvement over the Cottage Farm bridge, not only for the users of the parkways, but also for ordinary traffic. It is already plain that this head of the basin is to be an important focal point of greater Boston, — a point from which broad parkways, not to speak of lines of traffic, will lead eastward along both banks of the basin and westward up the Charles to Watertown. It is also quite

within reason to expect that a branch from the Charles River
Parkway will lead northward by Fresh Pond to Middlesex
Fells Reservation, as the Boston and Brookline Parkway now
leads southward to Franklin Park and Stony Brook Reservation. So much the more reason, then, for an adequate bridge
at the head of the basin, and for the extension of Audubon
Road as a connecting link. . . .

The Bay and Seashore Reservations.

The two reservations of this most valuable class, thus far
acquired, both lie northeast of the State House. To the
comparatively remote and small King's Beach no attention
has been given by our office during the year ; but to Revere
Beach and the problem of its adaptation to public use much
study has, by direction of the Commission, been devoted. . . .

Concerning the boundaries of Revere Beach Reservation,
it is to be noted that the long land boundary, on which a
continuous row of buildings will eventually front, has from
the first been designed to be a curve, conforming as closely
as possible to the natural and singularly beautiful sweep of
the beach itself. The legal necessity of wiping out certain
public and semi-public streets and footways has resulted in
obscuring the desired curve for the present, but it ought to
be restored before any new buildings are built on lines not
in harmony with it. This is a case where some returning of
land to private ownership will distinctly improve the future
appearance of the reservation. Of the abandonment to its
former owners of the sea front of the Point of Pines — one
fifth of the original length of the reservation — there is nothing to be said, except that the Commission deemed it necessary, because of the lack of money wherewith to pay for the
property taken. It is not so much the loss of length of
sea-beach that is regrettable, as it is the possibility of the
occupation of the conspicuous point in question by disfiguring
industrial establishments. . . .

[The views of the landscape architects on the appropriate
constructions at Revere Beach have been expressed in the
preceding chapter, except on the proposal of subways from
the bath-houses to the beach.]

As a matter of fact, it is by no means impracticable to place the public bathing establishments, along with the hotels and private buildings, on the landward side of the road and sidewalk. The extension of the outlets from the stacks of dressing-rooms as subways running under the road and promenade is the only additional construction which this position would necessitate. By this arrangement bathers would enter the office of the bathing establishment, either directly from the electric cars in Ocean Avenue or from the reservation's sidewalk, and their passage to the beach through the airy (because open-ended) subways would involve only about forty additional footsteps in each direction. So entirely practicable is this scheme, and so little would it inconvenience bathers, that we are convinced that it ought to be adopted in preference to any structure projected on to the beach. . . .

It is sometimes said to be useless to spend time, pains, and money in making sure that public domains are made as beautiful as they can be made, because " ordinary people will never appreciate the difference." But what if fine results are not accurately valued and their causes discerned by the multitude? We all of us experience and enjoy sensations and emotions, the causes of which are unrecognized and even unknown. When he comes into the presence of unaccustomed beauty or grandeur, the average man does, as a matter of fact, consciously or unconsciously experience a reaction, which is of benefit to him. It is on this account, and not in order to satisfy competent students of æsthetics, that our democracy has ordered the setting apart of Revere Beach and the other reservations. It is precisely for the sake of " the common people " that these reservations ought to be made to exhibit their grand or beautiful scenery just as effectively as possible. The principle that the most effective arrangement is none too good for " the common people " already governs the trustees of our schools, libraries, and art museums. It has, also, been fully illustrated in many public parks. For example, Prospect Park, Brooklyn, includes a long and lovely meadow, made at large expense by joining fields together, and now extremely beautiful by reason of its great and unbroken expanse, its simplicity, and its unity. The Playstead in

Franklin Park, Boston, is another fine public meadow, which, like the Prospect Park meadow (and like Revere Beach), is chiefly valuable for its effective breadth, openness, and continuity. Both these fields are used by tennis, croquet, and ball players (as Revere Beach must be used by bathers); but are the buildings which are necessary for the convenience of the players allowed to intrude themselves so as to shatter the effect of the meadows? On the contrary, they are in each case pushed back into the edge of the bordering woods, where they are not quite as convenient as they might be, but where they are, nevertheless, reached easily enough. At Franklin Park the players pass to and from their lockers and wash-rooms by a subway which leads under the spectators' overlooking terrace, and by this means the convenience of all classes is well served, while the beautiful breadth of the meadow is preserved.

It seems to us that the preservation of the complete openness of Revere Beach is more important than the preservation of the openness of this meadow by as much as the ocean panorama and the view of the sea strand is rarer and grander than the landscape of a field. . . .

PART II. DESIRABLE RESERVATIONS.

[After an exposition of the equitable distribution of the acquired reservations, and a statement concerning three additional reservations which ought to be acquired (see pp. 594 and 597), the report proceeds : —]

It should be specially noted that the public ownership and control of non-commercial strips of land along river-banks and seashores is something very different from the public ownership of ordinary " parks." Parks like Franklin Park are valuable, indeed, but river-side and seashore strips provide access to great stores of fresh air and refreshing scenery without removing any large area from the tax lists. They do, indeed, quickly pay for themselves, because practically the whole value of the lands acquired is added to the next adjacent private lands. They, negatively, prevent the depreciation of the potential values of surrounding lands which is so generally caused by " cheap building " on fresh-water and tidal shores. They place the control of the trunk lines of surface drainage under public authority, and so forfend the public from such costly expenditures for the prevention of floods as Boston has been driven to along Stony Brook in Jamaica Plain and Roxbury. Reservations of this class are primarily desirable, not for æsthetic or sentimental, but for eminently practical, reasons; while their first cost is properly to be regarded as an intelligent investment, rather than an extravagant expenditure.

PART III. METROPOLITAN PARKWAYS.

. . . With respect to the general principles on which the routes of parkways to be paid for by the metropolitan district ought to be chosen, we see no reason to change the views expressed in previous annual reports. . . . [There are] several conspicuously desirable connections with and approaches to the reservations which it would profit the district to possess; for it is plain that the reservations cannot benefit the people as they ought to unless they can be made agreeably accessible. On the other hand, it is obvious that mandatory legislation, requiring the Commission to secure any particular parkways or any specifically mentioned reservations, would place the Commission in a very difficult situation as respects dealings with the owners of the lands directed to be bought, while it would probably upset such equitable and comprehensive schemes as commissions are established to devise and prosecute. If there are to be any additional Metropolitan Parkways, it is just as important that they should be placed and designed in accordance with some comprehensive scheme, as it is that the reservations should be chosen, bounded, and severally adapted to public use in accordance with rational and consistent general plans.

December 1, 1896.

CHAPTER XXXVII

SELECTED LETTERS OF JANUARY, FEBRUARY, AND MARCH, 1897

The works of man, bury them as we may, do not perish, cannot perish. What of heroism, what of Eternal Light was in a man and his life is with very great exactness added to the eternities, remains forever a divine portion of the sum of things. — CARLYLE.

In the fall of 1896 and the ensuing winter there was much criticism in the public prints of the condition of the plantations in the Boston parks and along the Boston parkways, some of which Charles thought to be well founded. The plantations had not been properly cared for; and in some instances the original designs of Mr. Olmsted had been departed from by subordinate agents of the Commission. In the next letter, which was addressed to the chairman of the Boston Park Commission, Charles states the fundamental principle, that the original treatment of the vegetation of a park, — trees, shrubs, and grass, or other ground-cover, — in order to develop and keep visible the scenery of the park, is properly chargeable to construction and not to maintenance — more properly even than the building of roads. He urges, therefore, that henceforth a much larger part of the money available for construction should be devoted to the woods and plantations. When the right conditions of vegetation have been once established, the preservation of those conditions may properly be charged to maintenance, just as the preservation of the roads and paths is so chargeable.

January 4, 1897.

THE TRUE DISTINCTION BETWEEN CONSTRUCTION AND MAINTENANCE. — The abolition at the last meeting of the Board of the office of " Landscape Gardener " and the proposed establishment of the office of " Superintendent " mark a step in the history of the parks which we hope means greater readiness to devote money to maintenance as distinguished from construction. There has always been money for construction, but never sufficient for maintenance. Roads and walks have been extended annually, and new planting has been done from time to time; but the money available for maintenance has barely sufficed to keep the constantly increasing mileage of roads in good repair. It has been argued that since roads cost so much, it would be shameful to allow them to deteriorate, and so the larger part of the appropriations for maintenance has been devoted to the roads, with the result that the care of grass and shrubberies has been sadly slighted, while the original trees and woods have received little or no attention.

That this is an anomalous condition of affairs is evident. Park roads and walks are merely means of approach to scenery; so that it would seem as if such work as may be most necessary for the preservation and improvement of the living elements of scenery ought by rights to be accomplished before, rather than after, the construction of roads. The "general plans" of parks contrived by our firm are always based on studies of the available scenery, and embody schemes for modifying preëxistent vegetation by clearing here and thinning there, planting trees or shrubs, and sowing grass, as well as schemes for making the resulting scenery agreeably accessible by roads. The vital element in a park design is indeed its suggestions concerning vegetation. It is only necessary to imagine a park without grass, bushes, or trees to realize that this is the case. The road lines of parks are chosen with reference to the scenery designed to be secured by modifications of the vegetation, and, conversely, the programme of work on the vegetation is devised with reference to the positions chosen for the roads and other points of view. Thus the "general plan" of a park is not a road plan only, and it is not a planting-plan, or a scheme for the treatment of old trees or roads. It is a closely related and logically combined design, requiring for its realization on the ground faithful work in all these different departments alike.

It follows that whatever work may be required for the complete realization of a "general plan," whether it be work of axe or pruning-hook, plough, spade, or steam-roller, may properly be charged to construction. The contrary assumption that while roads may be charged to construction, work in the preëxistent woods and all thinning of plantations after they are two years planted must be charged to maintenance, has naturally resulted in a partial and lop-sided development of the Boston parks, by no means representing the intents and plans of the designers. Roads and walks have been thoroughly well built in accordance with the general plans; but the vegetation of the Fens, for example, is not what it was designed to be, because it has not been properly thinned and readjusted from time to time. The desirable treatment of the original woods has also been too long postponed. We would recommend that a much larger part of the money available for construction should henceforth be devoted to the woods and plantations.

Assuming, for a moment, that this reform can be accomplished, permit us to briefly mention some of the more pressing items of work to be done. We will assume that the superintendent will have full charge of all the work of maintenance, including road repairs and watering, the care of buildings, finished lawns, shrubberies, and groves, and so on, and that the engineering department will continue to direct works of engineering construction in accordance with the same general plans.

After acquainting himself thoroughly with the intentions embodied in the general plans, the former officer ought to attend first to the rescue and readjustment of the plantations of the Fens. These plantations were rightly planted very thickly, both for immediate effect and because of the exposure of the place to the winds. Viewed from the water and from many of the paths, the resulting effects are generally pleasing, but radical thinning has for some time been needed for the encouragement of the longer-lived and finer sorts of trees and plants, which are choked by the quick-growing species of less permanent value. In addition, there are a few small areas, such as the triangle at the Boyle O'Reilly monument and the spaces near Westland Avenue, which, owing to changed circumstances, need to be thoroughly revised.

Throughout the parks, beyond the Fens, there is more or less old growth which needs to be removed or helped, as the

case may be, and there is much half-finished and more as
yet unattempted new planting, which will call for close and
faithful following of the intentions of the park designers.
For accomplishing the new planting, large stocks of suitable
species of trees and shrubs will need to be collected and
propagated, — much larger stocks of the more useful native
sorts than Mr. ——, with his leanings towards garden varieties, could be persuaded to gather and use. It was precisely because of Mr. ——'s increasing inability to keep in
mind the character of the simpler planting required by the
designs that we felt obliged some months ago to call the
attention of the Board to the matter. Fortunately there is
little of his recent work which cannot be easily recast to
accord with the spirit of the plans, and we may add that if
work in the original woods can now be taken up intelligently,
no one need much regret that it has been so long postponed.

PARK PLANTING DIFFERENT FROM GARDENING OR FOR-
ESTRY. — It is obvious that the work to be done cannot safely
be entrusted to a horticulturist or a gardener, nor can it be
left to an arboriculturist or forester. Good gardeners cannot
avoid working for the perfecting of individual plants — work
which is right in a garden, but wrong in a park, where the
general effect, or landscape, is of first importance. Good
foresters cannot avoid working for the development of individual trees — work which is right where a crop of timber is
desired, or where specimens are to be trained up, as in an
arboretum, but wrong in a park, where groups, masses, and
dense woods are more important in the landscape than single
trees. The planter to be appointed to carry out the designed
effect in the landscape should have as much knowledge of
trees and shrubs as possible, but should be young enough to
learn by study and experience to appreciate the various kinds
of landscape designed to be secured. We have found that
young men who have had experience in nurseries, provided
they have sufficient intelligence to shake off the nurseryman's
love of plants as novelties and curiosities, are far better fitted
to manage park planting than gardeners. . . .

Driveways for speeding horses have been regarded by an
influential class of citizens as legitimate parts of a city's park

system; and in the vicinity of Boston fast trotting has been habitually permitted on certain tolerably level highways, although they were but ill-adapted for that sport because of frequent cross-roads.   Both the Metropolitan and the Boston Commission have had to meet the demand for speedways.

THE BEST PLACES FOR SPEEDWAYS.

January 12, 1897.

MR. BENJAMIN WELLS, SUPT. OF STREETS, Boston.

Dear Sir, — I was happy to see some account the other day of your report in opposition to the building of speedways by the city of Boston on lines primarily intended for public streets.   At the time when it was first proposed that the Metropolitan Park Commission should acquire lands along Charles River, one of the arguments we used for the purchase of such lands was the fact that the level salt marshes furnished the only long stretches of absolutely level ground to be found in the neighborhood of Boston, and we pointed out at the time that these marshes were peculiarly well adapted to serve as the sites of speedways, because the infrequency of cross-roads and bridges makes it possible to have stretches without breaks where speed must be slackened.

I send you herewith one of the early lithographs of our scheme for the eventual development of the Charles River Reservation, on which you will find noted a desirable site for a speedway.[1]

To secure a handsome and symmetrical western end for the Charles River Basin by means of a new bridge and modifications of the adjacent shore lines was an object which Charles always had in mind.   Rumors of proposed expenditures on the existing bridge in continuation of Brookline Street, Cambridge, induced him to write as follows to the Mayor of Cambridge : —

January 23, 1897.

We are sending you, under separate cover, a copy of the new report of the Metropolitan Park Commission, asking your kind attention to that portion of our report to the Commission which is concerned with Charles River (see pp. 684–686).

[1] The speedway on the south bank of Charles River was finished in 1899.

You are doubtless already familiar with the main arguments for a dam. We have merely restated some of them very briefly at this time. The matter we desire to call to your particular attention is the suggestion for a substitute for the existing Essex Street or Brookline Street bridge. We think that there can be no doubt that the proposed change would greatly benefit Cambridge generally, however much it may be objected to in certain quarters. The suggestion is, of course, made on the assumption that a bridge will be eventually secured at Magazine Street, and it is also to be understood that the existing Brookline Street bridge would not be disturbed until the suggested bridge is completed, together with the parkway bridge over the railroad. On the other hand, the present Brookline Street bridge ought not to be so elaborated as to make it any harder to secure the proposed bridge. Among the advantages of the latter we may set down the following : —

1. More direct approach to Boston; in other words, a shorter line.

2. Better connection between Cambridge and all the southern suburbs of Boston.

3. Better service for all the Cambridge lands between Brookline Street, the Esplanade, and Massachusetts Avenue.

4. Direct connection between the Cambridge and Boston parkways by Audubon Road.

5. The fine view from the bridge of the great Basin; and, conversely, the handsome western end of the Basin which the proposed bridge would make.

Permit us to add that if the Beacon Street and other Boston people do not care to have the advantages of a tideless basin extended downstream to their doors, with its boating and skating privileges, etc., the proposed Charlesmouth bridge might well be made a dam. However this may be (the question is entirely a separate one), we have made the suggestion for a bridge at this time, not with a view to urging its construction at once, but solely in the hope that nothing may be done on the line of Brookline and Essex streets which would tend to defeat the future realization of the better project.

The great resort to Revere Beach during the summer of 1896 forced upon the attention of the Metropolitan Park Commission the question how to get an agreeable approach to the beach from the heart of the district and the northern suburbs. Early in February Charles carefully studied this difficult question on the ground, and made a preliminary suggestion for its solution in the following letter: —

February 10, 1897.

In obedience to a request of the Commission, conveyed to us by a letter from the Secretary, we submit herewith a preliminary sketch plan showing the outlines of lands which might advisedly be acquired for the extension of the Revere Beach Parkway towards the centre of population of the metropolitan district.

Beginning at the corner of Winthrop and Campbell avenues, where the taking already made for this parkway ends, the plan suggests the acquisition of the northern shore of Sales Creek, between Winthrop Avenue and the East Boston branch of the Boston and Maine Railroad. The parkway would here consist of but one broad roadway, and if electric cars should accompany this roadway, they would be placed on the southern side thereof.

Just west of the East Boston branch railroad is found a coal wharf at the head of navigation in Chelsea Creek; and the plan proposes that the parkway should pass in the rear of this property, though, if it is not too expensive, it might be advisable to purchase this property and lease it for the present. The view from this point down the length of Chelsea Creek is broad and fine, and it will make an interesting part of the scenery of the parkway.

Westward again, the main line of the eastern division of the Boston and Maine Railroad has to be crossed; but the necessary bridge will be founded upon upland, as indeed will be the case with the bridge over the East Boston branch. West of the railroad the plan proposes the acquisition of both banks of Mill or Snake Creek; and the suggestion is made that the main road of the parkway should follow the northern border of the lands to be acquired. As we understand it, it is the intention of the Chelsea Park Commission to approach the owners of the land along this creek, and to secure options or make purchases, as may prove possible.

West of the head of this creek there is found a somewhat crowded neighborhood, tributary to the electric cars which go to Boston over Washington Avenue and Broadway, Chelsea. There is, however, a passage still open through this district, one hundred and ten feet wide at the narrowest place. Unfortunately, the electric car line must be crossed in the immediate neighborhood of the terminal stables, which lie in a valley between two hills, and exactly in the midst of the most crowded quarter. It may be that these stables can eventually be removed to some other location, in which case the parkway could be greatly improved.

West of Washington Avenue open land not yet much built upon is met with, as well as a high ridge of rock and gravel lying along the so-called County Road, near the boundary between Chelsea and Everett. At the southern foot of this ridge is found the salt marsh which extends along Island End River, and west of the U. S. Marine Hospital to Mystic River. Consequently, this ridge commands broad views to the southward. The breadth and openness of these views will be preserved through the proposed acquirement by the Chelsea Park Commission of the large playground lying on the slope and at the foot of the ridge, and between it and Everett Avenue. It will require a detailed topographical survey to enable us to properly study the best way to overcome the difficult grades in this location and the best way of securing the view, but the accompanying sketch makes a suggestion which seems practicable at this time.

West of this interesting point, which, as before remarked, lies on the boundary between Chelsea and Everett, it is possible to continue the parkway across the marshes and other level lands of Everett in either of several different locations, which need not be discussed at this time. To enable us to determine which route would be the most advantageous on the whole, we would suggest that surveys should be made of the territory lying between Chelsea Street and the Eastern Division of the Boston and Maine Railroad, at least as far west as the Saugus Branch Railroad.

The equitable distribution of parks and parkways throughout the metropolitan district was a thought ever present to Charles's mind. Thirty-six municipalities had combined in the great work, and every one of them ought to get a fair proportion of the resulting benefits. There is, therefore, significance in the word "corresponding" in the second sentence of a letter which he wrote to the Metropolitan Park Commission on the 23d of February, 1897. The letter begins thus: "A fortnight ago we submitted a preliminary plan suggesting boundaries for the Revere Beach Parkway. Today we submit a similar preliminary sketch suggesting boundaries for a corresponding southern parkway between Milton station and the Old Colony Railroad on the way to Quincy Beach or Shore."

On the 3d of March he wrote another letter to the Commission, which begins thus: "We submit herewith preliminary plans for the acquisition of lands along the shore of Quincy Bay. between the existing road to Squantum and the existing Merrymount Park." He had steadily maintained that the population south of Boston should have a seashore reservation approximately equivalent to Revere Beach on the north of Boston.

A note from his father's friend, Professor William R. Ware of Columbia University, drew from Charles the following reply, in which he combatted the not uncommon opinion that the designs made by his firm were always of the informal, irregular, or picturesque type. He was the freer to express himself on this occasion, because he had not been intimately concerned with the designs for Jackson Park, Chicago.

January 4, 1897.

DEAR MR. WARE, — Your interesting, as well as entertaining, letter of January 2d is at hand, and I am sorry to say that you are too late with your suggestions for the Chicago park which once was the site of the World's Fair. Park Commissions in Chicago are extremely energetic bodies, and a very large part of the World's Fair site is already reshaped to park purposes in accordance with the general plan, a copy of which I send you herewith. This plan is a modification of Mr. F. L. Olmsted's original plan for this park, made many years before the World's Fair was thought of. In one corner of the drawing you will find the principal elements of the design briefly noted in type.

To show you that we work in the formal, or rectilinear, manner when circumstances or purpose seem to demand it, I send you with the Jackson Park plan our preliminary sketch for the new site of Washington University, St. Louis. This site is a very high and steep-sided ridge, extending eastward toward the city, and you will observe how the buildings of the college are proposed to be attached to the sides of the ridge in such a way as to leave a level campus between them. For the Methodist University at Washington we also, quite lately, prepared a preliminary plan on formal lines, and I could show you here many designs for rectangular and geometric gardens and terraces for the immediate surroundings of large private houses.

On the Jackson Park plan you will notice that the surroundings of the great Museum are designed to be formal; this formality extending even to the water basin and the bridge lying south of the Museum. The great avenue which the Midway has now become is also thoroughly formal throughout its length, having roads on either side, accompanied by walks and bridle-paths, and having in the middle a canal which affords a boating course in summer and skating in winter. In this way the Midway has become an avenue, accommodating travellers in carriages or sleighs, on cycles, on horseback, on foot, in boats, and on skates; and what a wonderful place for fêtes and carnivals it will be!

In the fall of 1896 Mr. Augustus Hemenway of Boston, a member of the Metropolitan Park Commission, asked Charles some questions about planting the islands of Boston Harbor. Charles answered in the following letter : —

November 5, 1896.

With respect to the possible and very desirable planting of the harbor islands, you will find a report of Mr. F. L. Olmsted's, published in the Thirteenth Annual Report of the Boston Park Department, under date of December 30, 1887. . . .

In order to catch up, so to speak, with the progress of building, and the establishment of new institutions on the harbor islands, a good deal of which has gone forward since

1887, it seems to me that a new investigation would be necessary, involving conferences with those in charge of the islands and of the institutions in question, and a compilation of sufficient maps to determine and estimate the areas which it might be agreed upon could be planted advantageously. A thorough study of the islands with reference to the kinds of plants to be used and the spaces or areas to be planted, so as not to incommode the occupants of the islands, while effecting the desired change in the appearance of the harbor, would be a matter of considerable difficulty, and it would involve the expenditure of more time than is ordinarily the case, because of the difficulty of getting about among the islands. A preliminary report, with an estimate of cost, but without detailed plans for executing the work, could, I think, be made for $500, expenses of all kinds included. If more detailed plans for the planting of the principal islands, with estimates of the number and cost of each kind of plant required, were desired, it would easily cost another $500, and more than this, if the planting-plans would need to be prepared in any fine detail.

It is only about a year ago that our firm discussed this question anew with the Boston Park Commission ; and we were then told that the work, in their opinion, would be more appropriately attempted by the Metropolitan Park Commission than by the Boston Department. We were also told that the Boston Department at that time had no $500 which could be properly devoted to the purpose. Probably, if some scheme of planting could be definitely outlined, and a fair estimate of the cost of the work prepared, some way could then be found to induce the different institutions now occupying the islands, or the Boston Park Department, or the Metropolitan Park Department, to undertake the work.

A little later, Mr. Henry Clarke Warren of Cambridge consulted Charles as to the cost and the pecuniary result of planting the whole of Bumkin Island in Boston Harbor, an island of about twenty-two acres in area, which then belonged to Harvard University, and was at the moment wholly unproductive. Mr. Warren indulged the hope that the planting of trees on this island might be shown to promise a profit in a

long term of years. Charles was unable to confirm this hope;
but the following extract from a letter to Mr. Warren shows
that he thought the re-foresting of the harbor islands and
headlands could be accomplished in a short term of years and
at a moderate expense : —

February 18, 1897.

. . . My own feeling as to what would be accomplished by
suitably planting the island is this: Supposing the island
were planted with broad belts of different kinds of the most
likely trees, with plenty of " nurse trees," and that an accurate scientific record should then be kept of the rate of growth
and product from thinnings during 25 or 50 years, data would
be obtained of the sort that by the end of 50 years will probably be much more highly valued than such data would be
to-day, were they at hand. It is as a scientific experiment
that it seems to me the proposed work would be valuable.   I
do not think it would profit the College treasury — though,
if well started, it might pay for its own keep afterwards.   It
strikes me that the College would get a better income from
the island if, for example, it leased lots on it for summer
camps or cottages. As to the cost of preparing the ground,
planting, weeding, and tending for, say five years, I think
$2500 would cover all that would be really necessary.   This
would not include providing any water ; and you know I
think the experiment would be more serviceable in the future
if water were not artificially supplied. . . .

   In 1896–97 plans were in preparation for a large Botanic
Garden in Bronx Park, New York, a park controlled by the
Commissioners of the Park Department of the city of New
York.   The Garden is a private institution with its own
Board of Managers ; but its land and most of its money
came from the city, and the plans for the Garden were, in
consequence, to be approved by the Park Commissioners.
Plans for the Garden had been prepared by a commission
appointed by the Managers and consisting of their Director-
in-chief, Engineer, Architect of the Museum Building, and
Gardener, with one of the seven Scientific Directors of the
Garden, and a representative of the architects of the glass-
houses. Their plans were not entirely acceptable to the Park
Commissioners, who thereupon asked the advice of four experts acting together as a commission to report on the plans ;

namely, Professor Charles S. Sargent of Harvard University, Samuel Parsons, Jr., Superintendent of Parks, Thomas Hastings, architect, and Charles Eliot, landscape architect.

Charles first heard of this invitation on the 11th of February, 1897, from his friend W. A. Stiles, editor of "Garden and Forest," who was one of the Park Commissioners. He gladly accepted the invitation; for he had imagined that a work might be done for New York City analogous to the Metropolitan Park work which he had seen done for Boston; and he welcomed any opportunity to study the park resources in the neighborhood of the great city. He ordered the best topographical maps of the vicinity of New York, and began to study the topography, the boundaries of the different municipalities, the unoccupied districts, the watercourses, the means of communication, and all the other elements of the problem, just as he had studied the similar elements of the metropolitan district problem. It was the end of the month before he could get to New York; but he then spent three days there, visiting Mulberry Bend and Bronx Park "to get the lay of the land," walking all over the ground from Bedford Park station and back, and conferring with Messrs. Stiles, Parsons, and Hastings at the Century Club, and with Mr. Hastings, and Messrs. Britton, Brinley, and Henshaw of the Managers' Plans Commission, on the ground. He was much impressed with the landscape possibilities of Bronx and Pelham Bay Parks, and wrote to his wife of Bronx Park: "I am glad to have had this afternoon's hours in the very beautiful park. Too bad it must become a Botanic Garden." He expressed his opinions informally to his friend Mr. Stiles before leaving New York, and was at his office in Brookline again on March 2d. The Commission of experts to report to the Park Commissioners on the plans of the Managers' Commission dissented from the proposals of that Commission in some respects; and as a result of the entire discussion between three Commissions and one Committee, some fine scenery was saved which the original plans would have marred. New York is now justly proud of both the parks and the Garden.

During the winter of 1896–97 Mr. Warren H. Manning consulted several persons, interested in landscape architecture as a profession, on the possibility and expediency of organizing a society of landscape designers, which should cover the United States, and endeavor to contribute by the selection of its members to a better comprehension of the nature of functions of the profession. He had obtained the assent of several leading practitioners when he wrote to Charles on the subject. Charles answered Mr. Manning's inquiry by the following letter written at Hartford while he was visiting the parks there : —

March 8, 1897.

Your letter of March 5 came to hand in due season, but really I have no time (or perhaps it is no energy) for anything more than the regular course of work which is always piled up ahead of me in a mass which I never can overlook. It is impossible for me to go into a discussion of the pros and cons of the association you propose ; but I can tell you frankly that I do not believe a league of professional men, covering the field of the United States and endeavoring to control admittance to the ranks of the profession, is worth attempting while the number of professional men concerned is only four or five, and while the profession is so generally unrecognized by the public.

It seems to me that if you have energy to spare for advancing the professional cause, and for cultivating a more general recognition of its usefulness and importance, it would be best to begin by organizing, not a professional, but a general association, to be made up of all who desire the advancement of landscape art, much as the Forestry Association is made up of those who hope for the advance of real forestry in our country.   In such a general association, amateurs, landed proprietors, writers, park superintendents, engineers, foresters, gardeners, and anybody interested might become members, and pay their two dollars or so a year.   A committee on publication might then print a sort of annual or quarterly report of progress with special papers.   A committee on membership would drum up new members among village improvement societies and elsewhere.   Your special point might even be gained by having a committee on fellowship who from time to time would designate as Fellows of the Association such professional men as might accomplish work worthy of being crowned with the approval of the association.   In brief, I think the proposed association, if attempted at all, should correspond more closely to the Association for the Advancement of Science than to any trades-union or professional league.

Please excuse the hasty composition of this note, which I would rather you would not copy or duplicate at present, except that I wish you would make one copy and send it to my address in Brookline.

Off now to a commission meeting.

Charles's idea of what the proposed Association should be was accepted by the persons most interested in the project, and the Park and Outdoor Art Association was duly organized at a meeting held at Louisville in the summer of 1897.

The following report — the last Charles wrote — is not in the form in which the report of the landscape architects appears in the printed report of the Boston Park Commission for 1896, for the reason that Charles did not have opportunity to revise his first draught in consultation either with his partners or with the Commission. The printed report appeared several months after Charles's death, and contains numerous sentences added by the firm, and does not contain several paragraphs and sentences which Charles actually wrote. These changes, whether by addition or subtraction, may all have been desirable or expedient, and very possibly Charles would have assented to them; but as he never had the opportunity to do so, it has seemed necessary to print here just what he wrote. The report is in his own handwriting. It was addressed to the chairman of the Boston Park Commission, but was never received by him in this form. The actual report made by the firm was dated March 23, 1897; it included what Charles had written, but there were some alterations and additions. This second draught was changed considerably before printing.

The following brief notes of our doings in connection with the work of the Boston Park Commission during the year 1896 are respectfully submitted.

GENERAL PLANS.

The last complete design or " general plan " officially adopted by the Park Commission was the plan for the small and peculiar pleasure grounds recently named North End Beach and Copps Hill Terrace.

A " general plan " for Dorchester Park has been prepared; but, though approved by the Commission, it has never been formally adopted, because certain agreements with the city departments controlling adjacent lands which ought to be joined to the park — namely, the City Hospital and the City Street Department — have not yet been entered into.

A "general plan" for the recently acquired West Roxbury Parkway, extending from the Arboretum to Bellevue Hill and Stony Brook Reservation, has been ordered by the Commission : it cannot, however, be satisfactorily finished until certain small additional areas of land are secured at two difficult places. When these two parcels are acquired, there will be no part of the Boston parks where boundary roads affording frontage for adjacent building land will not be obtainable when they are wanted.

It may be noted that the West Roxbury Parkway will presumably be the last large Boston park area for which a comprehensive design will be needed. Hereafter, or at least until the city shall take up in earnest the development of the remarkable opportunity presented by the Charles River Basin between Boston and Cambridge, it is to be presumed that the designing of small local recreation grounds will occupy the Commission's professional assistants.

DETAILS OF ADOPTED PLANS.

As has been the case in all recent years, the study of the details of previously submitted and adopted general plans has chiefly busied your landscape architects. In 1895 the grading plans for North End Beach, for the yacht club sites on the Strandway, for the neighborhood of the Franklin Park restaurant and carriage sheds, and the widening of Blue Hill Avenue, with a number of similar works, had close attention. During 1896 detailed construction designs have been prepared for a large part of West Roxbury Parkway, for several roadways in the Peters Hill section of the Arboretum, for a roadway in Jamaica Park between Prince Street and the Pond, for the peculiar bathing-place outside the Strandway at the foot of L Street, for a footpath entrance to Franklin Park from Blue Hill Avenue at the end of Wales Street, and so on.

The roads for the steep and difficult Peters Hill were first designed to have a maximum grade of six per cent. ; but the

Director of the Arboretum objected so seriously to the extensive grading of side slopes which was involved, that we were instructed to re-draw the plans in such a way as to reduce the side slopes to the narrowest possible limit. This was done; but the resulting roads will necessarily have maximum grades of eight per cent.; in other words, they will be steeper than any other roads of the Boston parks, and in our opinion steeper than any much-frequented pleasure driveways ought to be.

The new road planned for Jamaica Park will pass for the most part through gently sloping lands lying along that side of Jamaica Pond where the memorial to Francis Parkman is shortly to be built; but in another part of its course it must descend a hill along a very steep crosswise slope thick-set with fine trees; and just here the new road will also be so close to the existing border road called Prince Street, that it will inevitably appear unnecessary. The original design for Jamaica Park, indeed, proposed this road paralleling Prince Street; but this design was based on the underlying design for a continuous pleasure driveway, wholly separate from the border roads, and free from the traffic of their abutting buildings, which was to begin at Huntington Avenue, Brookline, and traverse Leverett Park, Jamaica Park, and the Arborway to Franklin Park. It was argued, and we think justly, that such a long, continuous, and separate park road, bordered by trees and shrubbery rather than by houses, would be more enjoyable than the border roads, which must in any event serve for pleasure driving all the way from the Public Garden to Leverett Park. As a matter of fact, the Leverett Park section of this separate road has been built, as well as that part of it which is included in the Arborway, but the land required to separate it from the border road along the northwest side of Jamaica Pond has never been secured. It seems to us that the placing of a road on the steep west bank of Jamaica Pond cannot be justified, unless the whole length of the originally proposed separate road is to be secured.

Among the most difficult details of park designs are the plans for the necessary buildings. The Commission has always employed good architects; but it has been necessary that we should define for the architects the purposes to be served by the buildings, and to sketch preliminary ground plans. Designs for the administration building, and for the men's and women's bath-houses at North End Beach, have been studied with Architect R. C. Sturgis during the past year. It is impossible to foretell how much this small bathing-beach may be frequented; but it seemed best not to make use of all the narrow space available for bathers' dressing-rooms at once. The buildings are ingeniously arranged so as to properly control the bathers, and so as to permit their passing to and from the beach without interfering with persons passing to or from the piers and boat-landings.

The bathing establishment at Marine Park was first opened last summer, and was much used; but it needs to be fenced off as originally designed; and it is to be hoped that the licensed manager may be a little more strictly controlled in some respects. We must needs regret that the restaurant, originally designed for the pier, was finally squeezed into the head-house to the ruin of its interior plan.

The restaurant in Franklin Park was also opened for the first time last summer, and was much visited in the evenings. For the sake of the health of the vines which are to cover the great arbor of the terrace, we were obliged to recommend a temporary flooring of boards. Brick will be substituted after the vines are well started. The circular carriage shed and a bicycle stand adjacent to this building have also been planned during the year in conjunction with Architects Hartwell and Richardson.

Among other buildings which are already needed are a house for players and skaters at Franklin Field, a boating and skating house at Jamaica Pond, and an administration building and stable in Franklin Park. A leading horticultural journal recently spoke of " useless buildings " in the Boston parks; but we know of none such. Those which have been built are essential to the realization of the adopted general plans. Whether their construction, or that of particular roads, bridges, or walls, might not have been postponed, or accomplished more cheaply, it is not for us to say. Having adopted a general plan, the Commission alone determines what part or parts thereof shall be executed from year to year.

Perhaps the most difficult of all the elements of a general plan to get carried out satisfactorily is such modification of existing vegetation, or such addition of new vegetation by planting, as may be required for the realization of the intended scenery. The lines and grades of roads and paths which make parks accessible can be described by drawings with great accuracy ; but not so the more essentially scenic work in the woods and fields. This work in the Boston parks has been, and indeed must be, entrusted to responsible specialists corresponding with the engineers in charge of the constructive works ; but if satisfactory results are to be secured, it is just as essential that these foresters or gardeners should be loyal to the general plans, as it is that the road-building engineers should be. The roads and paths of country parks are placed in certain positions so as to command certain landscapes, or bits of scenery, thus and so, and conversely the vegetation, which in this climate makes the scenery, must be controlled, encouraged, or modified accordingly. Unless the planting, thinning, and clearing are thus done sympathetically, the courses of the roads become meaningless, and their cost is wasted.

We feel obliged to say that, on account of circumstances which need not be detailed, this important department of work in the Boston parks has not, like the construction department, been uniformly faithful to the adopted general plans, as they have been described in the landscape architects' drawings, and in their reports on the designs for the Fens, for Franklin Park, and so on. With the appointment of a responsible superintendent of parks, we look forward to more thoroughly harmonious methods and results.

CHAPTER XXXVIII

LANDSCAPE FORESTRY IN THE METROPOLITAN RESER-
VATIONS

> Wherever Nature has herself glorified a country, and made a picture
> bounded only by the horizon, as in many parts of Switzerland, Italy,
> Southern Germany, and even our own Silesia, I am strongly of the
> opinion that park-works are superfluous. It seems to me like paint-
> ing a petty landscape in one corner of a beautiful Claude Lorraine.
> In these cases we should content ourselves with laying out good roads,
> to make the fine points more accessible, and here and there the cutting
> of a few trees, to open vistas which Nature has left closed. — PÜCKLER-
> MUSKAU.

By the time the metropolitan forest reservations had been
in possession of the Commission two years and a half, the
removal of dead wood had been accomplished, preliminary
roads on the lines of the old wood-roads had been opened to
give the public and the employees of the Commission access
to all parts of the reservations, and the topographical maps
on a scale of 100 feet to the inch had been completed (early
in 1896). Charles thought he saw in this state of things an
opportunity to procure some beginning of landscape forestry
work; and in January, 1896, he opened the subject to the
Commission in the following letter, which proposed a small
annual expenditure for supervision, and the diversion to
forestry work of some of the labor regularly employed. As
usual, his recommendations were moderate as regards expenditure — indeed, distinctly economical: —

January 8, 1896.

We beg leave to submit the following suggestions concerning the work in the three woodland reservations: —

From the date of the acquiring of these reservations to the
present time, the forces employed have been engaged in two
principal works: (1) removing dead wood, both standing
and fallen; (2) constructing preliminary roads on the lines
of the old woodpaths. Two winters have already been devoted to the first-named work, and two summers to the second.

The reservations have been opened to carriages and horse-back riders, and the preliminary roads are now quite sufficiently numerous. The work of the present winter ought to finally free the woods of the most dangerous part of the inflammable material. If the appropriations warrant the continuance of expenditure at the present rate, it would seem that some attention might soon be given to the restoration and betterment of the living vegetation, and we accordingly offer the following suggestions with respect to this delicate and most important work.

The existing forests of the reservations comprise both sprout and seedling woods; the former consisting of shoots sprung from the stumps of felled or fire-killed trees, and the latter consisting of woods which have grown from seeds sown without human aid in lands which once were completely cleared for pasturage or cultivation. The restoration of the burnt and sprout lands to an interesting and beautiful condition will require years of labor in accordance with a well-laid scheme of economical management. Such a scheme we may outline presently.

The work which calls for first attention is found in the reforested pastures. Here are to be seen most of the large trees and the only broad-spreading trees of the reservations. Around them press the seedling Oaks, Hickories, etc., which the birds and squirrels planted among the slow red Cedars, the short-lived gray Birches, and the beautiful wild shrubberies which were the first woody growths to appear in the old fields. If the lives of the older generation of spreading pasture trees are to be prolonged (as we hope they may be), it will be necessary to free them from the too close pressure of the trees of the younger generation, and at the same time to heal the most serious of the many wounds they have already received. The axe must be used to effect the first-named purpose, and the saw the second; but the axe must be used with discretion, and with care to retain enough of the vigorous young trees to fill the gaps when the veterans shall at last pass away.

In other smooth parts of the seedling woods, where the former pastures contained no old trees, and the present growth consists of mixed species too closely crowded, the axe ought likewise to be brought into play for the freeing of the most promising individuals, or the trees of the most desirable kinds. In valleys and glades where the surface is smooth enough and the soil good enough to grow grass when sufficient light has been admitted, it will generally, though not always, be advisable to take away all but a few trees, which will thus be encouraged to form noble individuals or groups. On rough, rocky, or steep ground where grass is unattainable, no such thinning for the development of individuals should be attempted. The axe may be used to eliminate incongruous or unsuitable kinds of trees and bushes, or to admit the sunlight necessary to the growth or increase of desirable species; but its use to produce a monotony of separated individuals regardless of soil and topography must be prohibited. Dense thickets will in many places be much more desirable than open glades.

Of the other good services in the cause of beauty which the axe may do among the seedling growths of the reservations, it is unnecessary to write at length. Among its good works may be the removal of trees for the encouragement of shrubby ground-cover at points where distant prospects would otherwise be shut out; the similar encouragement of low ground-cover on and among some of the finer crags which to-day are wrapped from sight by mantles of leaves; the removal of conflicting species for the encouragement of the white Dogwood on this southern slope, the Winterberry by this swamp, the Bearberry on this rocky summit, or the white Pine on this ridge. We are well aware that the axe is regarded with a sort of horror by many excellent people at this time; but we are equally convinced that with the help of no other instrument, the axe, if it be guided wisely, may gradually effect the desired rescue and enhancement of that part of the beauty of the scenery of the reservations which depends upon the seedling woods and shrubberies.

Concerning the large acreage of sprout-land within the reservations, it may be sufficient at this time to point out that inasmuch as sprouts from stumps form unnatural, comparatively short-lived, and generally monotonous and unbeautiful

woods, it ought to be the policy of the Commission to gradually replace the sprouts by seedlings. This work will
doubtless prove a somewhat slow and arduous undertaking ;
but, if it is not hurried, it need not prove expensive. Sprouts
which are large enough to be useful as poles, fence-posts, or
railroad sleepers are always salable as they stand. Such
salable sprouts should not, however, be all cut at once ; but
by felling a part of the crop one year and another part a few
years later, every inducement should be offered seedling trees
and a suitable undergrowth to take possession and obtain a
good start. On the other hand, sprouts which have sprung
from the stumps in the most recent clearings or since the
most recent killing fires, while unsalable, are still so small
that they may be cut rapidly and without undue expenditure
of time and money. If the cutting is done in August, most
of the stumps will at the same time be made incapable of
sprouting again ; and, if no valuable seedlings have yet come
in, sheep may be pastured in such places for a year or two to
complete the " killing." It is only in those places where the
sprouts are so large as to make it costly to cut them, and yet
so small as to be unsalable, that it seems as if it might be economical, and therefore advisable, to wait some years before the
seedlings can be offered their opportunity to possess the land.

It will be noticed that these proposed works in the living
woods demand uncommonly far-seeing and even artistic direction. Now that the preliminary roads have been roughed
out, and the topographical maps completed, it is to be presumed that the Commission's engineer will assume charge
and direction of whatever permanent works of construction
may be attempted. Similarly, whenever the clearing away of
dead wood shall have been practically completed, a trained
woodsman ought to be placed in charge of the work in the
living woods. The man who is thus placed in command of
the vegetation of parks is generally called a " landscape gardener ; " because he practises the operations of gardening for
the sake of developing " landscapes." Such a man employed
in the reservations of your Commission might more appropriately be called a " landscape forester ; " but, whatever he
may be called, he should be thoroughly acquainted with the

fauna and flora of the woods, competent to direct all woodland work, to devise economies, to discover sources of income, and eager, at the same time, to impart to the superintendents and to a succession of younger assistants something of his own enthusiasm, knowledge, and skill.   It will also be necessary that this woodsman, as well as the engineer, should be in complete sympathy with the landscape architects, and possess a good knowledge of their plans.   To make a beginning, we would suggest that we be authorized to supervise, through our assistants, such work as may be suitably entered upon before long, and at the same time to draw up a scheme of work to be executed in the order of its importance during a term of years.   This laying out of work and the accompanying supervising is something that we are accustomed to attend to for almost all our clients, both public and private. Our assistants (draughtsmen, plantsmen, and inspectors) take up, as we may direct, the office or field work of one client after another, the cost of their services being charged to different clients, according to the time given to the work of each.[1]   Whenever any work calling for special or novel service from our assistants is proposed, we, of course, ask for authority in advance.   Work done on the Metropolitan District Map, the Guide Maps of the Forest Reservations, and the Botanical Survey has thus been specially authorized.   The suggested supervision of work in the reservations is a new service, the cost of which we may estimate as $1000 for the first year.   Mr. Warren H. Manning, who has been connected with our office during eight years, would take charge of the supervising work.   A more competent man cannot be found.   To make his services as effective as possible, we would suggest the appointment by the Commission of at least two foremen of woodcraft, who should be men of some experience.   With the aid of these men, and such of the present foremen as may be competent or trainable, we feel sure that a good general scheme of work can be mapped out during the coming year, and that valuable beginnings in the more pressing work can be assured.

[1] Your Commission has been accustomed to settle these so-called expense accounts every three months.

It was, however, Charles's settled conviction that forestry work on a large scale, with a view to the improvement of landscape, could only be done safely after the preparation of general plans for each of the forest reservations; but the Commission was not yet ready to order such general plans. As soon as the completion of the topographical maps of the three forest reservations enabled him to get sun-prints from the full-scale tracings, he therefore organized a systematic mapping of the existing condition of the woods and ground-cover in these reservations. This work went on during the season of 1896; and Charles mentioned it in his report to the Commission for that year (see p. 680). It was in his mind a part of the desirable preparation for making general plans; and it also provided a permanent record of the deplorable state of the woods when the Commission took charge of them.

The completed "forest survey" was presented to the Commission on February 15, 1897. It consisted of seventy survey sheets in portfolios, accompanied by nine hundred numbered catalogue cards, each of which described the vegetation at a spot referred to by a number on one of the survey sheets. Flat tints were also used on the sheets to indicate the principal types of vegetation. The following letter accompanied this considerable piece of work : —

February 15, 1897.

We hand you herewith the field notes and maps of the "forest surveys" referred to in our last annual report, — the product of studies begun soon after the "taking" of the several reservations, and continued as opportunities have offered from time to time; also a list of the trees and shrubs of the reservations, with notes on their habits and distribution. Messrs. Warren H. Manning, Percival Gallagher, J. Fred Dawson, and Charles H. Wheeler have done most of this mapping and note-taking as our assistants.

A summary report of the principal ascertained facts, with photographic illustrations, is also submitted herewith, including some account of the origin of the commoner types of woodland scenery, and some suggestions as to that control of the vegetation of the reservations which will be necessary for the preservation and enhancement of the beauty and interest of the landscape.

The "summary report" referred to in the preceding letter was illustrated by 154 photographs, 6 sketches, and 3 maps, and as a piece of exposition and argument addressed to a small Board, all of whose members could examine the highly convincing illustrations, it certainly had remarkable merit. Charles wrote it between January 11 and February 12, 1897, in the midst of many other occupations, after assembling all the various contributions of his field and office assistants, and classifying them in his own mind with his usual discrimination and perspicuity. Although intended for the Park Commission as a business report indicating a long line of executive policy, the paper is much more than an argument addressed to one park board; it shows what the charming elements of park scenery really are, and how they may be preserved. Even genuine lovers of scenery are often quite unobservant of the constituent elements of the scenes they love. Here is a concise treatise on the different types of vegetation which, in addition to the fixed "lay of the land," make New England rural scenery, and on the ways of using these types to preserve and enhance the beauty of that characteristic scenery. It is reproduced here with only five of the illustrations which originally accompanied it.

VEGETATION AND SCENERY IN THE METROPOLITAN RESERVATIONS.

The Object of the Investigation.

The purpose of investing public money in the purchase of the several metropolitan reservations was to secure for the enjoyment of present and future generations such interesting and beautiful scenery as the lands acquired can supply; at all events, it is on the assumption that this was the purpose in view that the following report, with the investigation it describes, is based.

The scenery of the inland reservations may be considered as compounded of the varying forms of the ground, rocks, waters, and vegetation, and of a great variety of distant prospects, including views of the sea and of remote mountains, such as Wachusett and Monadnock. The more or less rock-ribbed masses of the Fells and the Blue Hills and the intricately carved or modelled hollows of Hemlock Gorge, Stony Brook, and Beaver Brook Reservations have life histories of their own ; but the processes of their evolution are so slow that for all human purposes these smooth, rough, concave, or convex surfaces may be regarded as changeless. It is, moreover, quite unlikely that there will ever be any need of artificially modifying them in any considerable degree. Such paths or roads as will be needed to make the scenery accessible will be mere slender threads of graded surfaces winding over and among the huge natural forms of the ground.

As to the waters of the reservations, they may, indeed, be artificially ponded here and there, as they already have been in the Fells and in Lynn Woods, where the reservoirs greatly enliven the general landscape ; but the numerous minor brooks and rivulets will doubtless continue to alternately dry up and rise in flood, as is their habit in our climate, without affecting more than the local scenery of the hollows or ravines in which they flow.

Thus the only changeful and changeable element in the general as well as the local landscape of the domains in question is the vegetation which clothes the surface everywhere, excepting only such bare areas as consist of naked rock or of water. Much of the most striking scenery of the world is almost or quite devoid of verdure ; but here in New England we cannot escape it, even if we would. Bulrushes insist upon crowding every undrained hollow, Bearberry carpets barren rocks, and a great variety of vigorous trees and shrubs have had to be continually and forcibly prevented from reoccupying such parts of the slopes between the rocks and the swamps as men have laboriously cleared at different times for the purpose of raising food crops or grass for the feeding of cattle. The original forests disappeared long ago. Where once stood towering Pines, there are to-day perhaps thickets of scrub Oak, and where great Hemlocks shaded damp, mossy cliffs, there may now be sun-baked ledges with clumps of Sweet Fern in their clefts. While seedlings have been pushing their way into the clearings at every opportunity, fire and the axe have made great changes in the vegetation of the wilder woodlands during the last two hundred years ; and all these changes have necessarily had their effect on the scenery.

The present investigation is not, however, an historical or

even a scientific inquiry.   Its purpose is simply to record the present condition of the verdure of the reservations, to note the effect in the landscape of the several predominant types of vegetation, and to inquire into the origins of these various types only so far as may be necessary to determine how best to encourage, control, or discourage the existing growth, with a view to the enrichment of that treasure of scenery which the reservations have been created to secure and preserve.

The Methods Pursued.

For the purpose of making a record of the present condition of the vegetation, sun-prints from the original tracings of the topographical maps of the several reservations were carried into the field, together with ordinary catalogue cards.   The maps used were drawn to the scale of one hundred feet to an inch, and showed roads, paths, stone walls, conspicuous rocks, and large trees, in addition to contour lines indicating every difference of five feet in elevation.   Each of the seventy separate survey sheets was designated by a letter and number (for example, Fells, B. 3), the dozen or more cards bearing notes referring to each separate sheet were also numbered (for example, $\frac{\text{Fells B. 3}}{13}$), and the card numbers were entered on the survey sheets at the several points to which the corresponding notes had reference.   Different observers engaged in different parts of the broad field have doubtless followed somewhat different standards in making notes ; but the endeavor of all has been to record every marked variation in the existing vegetation, together with such information as to the origin of each peculiar type as could be gathered either from study on the spot or from persons acquainted with the neighborhood.

The Principal Types of Vegetation.

On comparing and studying the returned map sheets and card notes, it gradually became clear that what at first seemed a hopeless confusion of isolated facts was after all resolvable into a rational order, and that the vegetation of the reservations can be truthfully said to be composed of some six principal landscape types or forms, the peculiarities of two of which depend chiefly on natural topographical conditions, while the distinguishing features of the other four types are principally derived from the work of men and of fire in the woodlands of the past. Perhaps the most interesting fact established by the inquiry is just this, — that the woods of these reservations, which are commonly thought of and spoken of as " wild," are really artificial in a high degree. The peculiar growth of dwarf trees and bushes which occupies the highest summits of the Blue Hills, and the equally peculiar growth of shrubs and herbs which fills the wetter swamps, have not been worth troubling with the axe, while the bare ledges of the hill-tops have defended the summit type of growth from fire almost as effectually as the presence of water has defended the swamp type. On the other hand, all the intervening slopes and plains of the reservations have been chopped over, or completely cleared, or pastured, or burnt over, time and again since the settlement of Massachusetts. Much of the resulting vegetation, and consequently much of the scenery of the reservations, is monotonous, insipid, and unlovely, but it must be added that those parts in which men have lived longest or worked hardest are often beautiful in a high degree.

The following are the principal types of the vegetation of the reservations which are about to be reviewed in the order here set down : —

Types dependent chiefly on topographical conditions : —
    The Summit,   The Swamp.

Types dependent chiefly on the interference of men : —
    The Coppice,   The Bushy Pasture,
    The Field and Pasture, The Seedling Forest.

It is, of course, to be understood that all these types, and particularly the last three, run together more or less, and that in sketching their distribution on the accompanying maps, all that is intended is to indicate to the observer's judgment as to which type predominates in each locality.

1. *The Summit Type.* — Whether the lofty or rocky summits of the Blue Hills were ever covered with high forest is

not quite clear, but that the scanty soil of these hill-tops is clothed to-day with an interesting and distinctive kind of vegetation is very noticeable. This vegetation is generally low, seldom exceeding five feet in height, except where wind-bent forms of pitch Pines, Hickories, Chestnut-Oaks, or other trees, occasionally rise above the dense mass of ground-covering shrubbery. This shrubbery consists for the most part of closely interlocking plants of scrub Oak, forming thickets almost as impenetrable as the chaparral of the Western States. Mixed with the scrub Oak are occasional patches of other bushes of kinds which are capable of withstanding adverse circumstances, such as Sweet Fern and Chokeberry; and where the gravelly soil is thinnest, broad mats of Bearberry are not uncommon. This growth has generally escaped destruction by fire, but where it has been killed so that raw soil has been exposed, the gray Birch has seeded itself and taken at least temporary possession. Many of the higher, steeper, and more naked crags have wholly escaped all recent fires and the axe as well; and here are found quaint stunted forms of pitch Pines and other hardy trees. The irregular upper edge of the ordinary forest in these hills (the "tree line," as it would be called in the mountains) also exhibits many more or less distorted growths of the hardier species of trees, and forms strong and sharp foregrounds for the panoramic views.

Speaking generally, this summit growth is altogether appropriate, interesting, and pleasing. It is generally low enough to enable the broad prospect of these hill-tops to be sufficiently well commanded. Its dwarfness also tends to increase the apparent height of the hills, and to set off the grand or picturesque forms of their ledges and crags. It ought to be the settled purpose of the administration of the reservations to foster the peculiar character of this vegetation by removing such few inappropriate species as may occasionally obtain a foothold on the heights, and by carefully refraining from any trimming or clearing of those crooked growths which give character to this type of scenery. It should be added that the type is in some measure imitated on even low-lying ledges and tracts of ledgy ground throughout the reservations, and that even where it is only a minor element of local scenery, it should be encouraged and helped. Rock scenery is indeed so interesting, and characteristic vegetation so enhances this interest, that it will be advisable (as is noted later) to remove much inappropriate and rock-concealing vegetation from the craggy parts of the reservations, and to induce the spreading therein of dwarf forms chiefly.

2. *The Swamp Type.* — In marked contrast to the vegetation of the prospect-commanding heights is the verdure of the many sheltered and secluded swamps and wet valleys. Small, roundish swamps, generally bordered, in part at least, by ledges, are very common in the three larger reservations. The ordinary forest presses close about these hollows, but owing to lack of drainage their level floors are too wet for most trees, although the stumps of white Pines are often found in them. Bulrushes are to-day the usual occupants of the deeper parts of these wet spots, while much beautiful shrubbery of Clethra, Azalea, Winterberry, and other sorts fringes their edges. The local scenery of these sunny openings in the monotonous woods is often extremely pleasing, as when some bold rock projects into the level of rushes, or when the encircling fringe of bushes is unbroken. It is evident that these places ought not to be meddled with, save for good reasons. Their peculiar beauty can be long preserved, if the natural drainage is not altered, and if such incongruous species as may from time to time appear are promptly removed.

According as these bowls or hollows of the surface are worse or better drained than in the typical cases just mentioned, the vegetation varies. Such high-lying or uncommonly large bowls as have not yet been completely filled by washings from the surrounding surfaces show open water in their centres, at least, and if the breadth of water is not so great as to generate waves, it is sometimes wholly or in part surrounded by a " floating or quaking bog " composed of matted roots of such low-growing woody plants as Cranberry, Cassandra, Andromeda, and the like. No shrubberies can be lovelier than some of these which, beginning with low bushes or rushes at the water's edge, increase irregularly in height as they recede from the water, until they finally merge into the margin

of the surrounding woods. It is noticeable that such shrubberies are best developed where the supply of water is most
constant; as at Turtle Pond in Stony Brook Reservation.
Where wetness alternates with dryness, the Button-bush
seems to feel at home, and covers large areas, almost without
companions. Again, where the conditions are just right and
men have not cut it out, the white Cedar still holds possession, with its exceedingly dense and dark growth.

On the other hand, such hollows and valleys as have better
drainage than the typical swamps first cited tend to clothe
themselves with trees in addition to the usual shrubs of wet
places. Where such trees thrive, the shrubs slowly disappear,
and a wood results much like the ordinary forest. In any
general view over the reservations these brook valleys are
easily traceable by the general coloring of the trees which fill
them. The gray Birch is frequent, but the characteristic tree
of such wet hollows is now the red Maple, which with its
haze of blossoms in early spring, its brilliant colors in early
autumn, and the peculiar gray of its twigs in winter, tints all
the valleys of the reservations and brings them out as on a
map.

In places where the conditions are suitable for the growth
of shrubs like high-bush Blueberry, Clethra, and the like, the
Maple often tends to intrude itself where it could well be
spared. The upland woods are quite sufficiently dense, continuous, and monotonous, without filling the wet bush-covered
openings with additional tree-trunks. The local scenery of
such bushy openings, the bounding ledges or slopes of rocky
débris, cannot be seen or appreciated, if Maples are to be
allowed to crowd in. On this account trees ought eventually
to be kept out of many of these places for the encouragement
of the bushy ground-cover, and particularly is this the case
where the removal or suppression of Maples will disclose
above the bushes and between the framing woods glimpses or
vistas of far blue distances.

3. *The Coppice Type.* — The summit and swamp types of
vegetation already reviewed have been but little molested or
changed in any recent years, but, with mention of the Maples
of the better drained lowlands, approach is made to the main

body of the woods which, modified past recognition by both axe and fire, still occupies the smooth or ragged uplands between the swamps and the highest summits. The transition from the lowland woods of Maples to the upland forest of Oaks, Chestnuts, and other species is generally quite sharply defined, whether the dry woods consist of seedling growth or sprout-growth. Sprout-growth or coppice greatly predominates in the woodlands under consideration. It consists of trees sprung, not from seed, but from the axed or burnt stumps of the trees of a previous generation. In some parts of the reservations, as many as six or eight crops have been taken by means of the axe from the same stumps ; twenty to thirty years having been allowed for the growth of each crop.

Much might be learned from study of this common practice of gathering periodical wood-crops from lands too rough for the nicer operations of husbandry ; how it tends to reduce the woods to masses of the few species which sprout with the greatest vigor and suffer the least from fire ; how the extremely rapid growth of the first sprouts from old stumps strangles the small seedling trees which may have started amid the undergrowth, and thus preserves the supremacy and continuity of the coppice ; and so on. Our present concern, however, is only with the appearance of coppice or sprout growth, and particularly with the part it plays in local and broad scenery.

The interior of a high coppice wood is seldom as beautiful as the interior of a seedling forest, not to speak of an open grove. It lacks the pleasing variety of natural woods, composed as they are of numerous competing kinds of trees and underwood. The crop-like or artificial nature of sprout-growth is obvious at a glance, and cannot be concealed by an occasional though rare luxuriance of undergrowth or pretty play of light and shade. Along paths and roads the monotonous effect of its crowded vertical lines is tedious in a high degree. It is only when some cause or condition introduces a little unwonted variety either of form or kind of tree or undergrowth, or when a distant vista catches the eye, that the paths of the sprout-lands are not comparatively dull. Along the edges of old or broad roads, clearings, swamps, or ponds, and where ledges or other impediments form a defence against too near neighbors, both masses and single specimens of sprout trees naturally send out low branches and take on more interesting forms; even remarkably striking forms in many cases. On the other hand, the general appearance of the ordinary sprout-growth, when it is seen from a distance in any broad view over the reservations, is as dull and tame as is its usual appearance close at hand. Its crowding swarms of nearly uniform trees press closely down to the swamps, climb close up to the summit ledges and invade their slopes of débris, crowd the hollows and notches between rocks, and generally tend to wrap both the softer and the bolder features of the general landscape in the same monotonous blanket of impenetrable twigs and leafage. A kind of vegetation which is so little beautiful in itself ought not to be permitted to take possession of those parts of public reservations which would be more interesting were the screens of close-set tree-trunks wholly or partly removed. Here, for example, is a hill on which the sprout-growth is not so thick as it often is, and yet it nevertheless conceals effectually the fine rock-buttresses of the slope, changes what would otherwise be a picturesque skyline into a level line of twigs, and in summer reduces the whole bold hillside to a soft bank of leaves. The opposing cliffs and talus slopes of the narrow valleys of the Blue Hills, many lesser knobs and ledges, and most of the elevated vista-commanding "notches" of the Hills and Fells are similarly smothered in curtains and veils of sprouts, which, in great measure, nullify the potential beauty of the scenery.

Fortunately, the one constant ally of the axe of the wood-chopper in the work of destroying the beauty of the wood-lands of the reservations is now presumably under control. Ground or leaf fires have ordinarily spread through the woods almost every spring and autumn, charring the base of the trees without killing them; but about once in every ten or twelve years the dry accumulations of chopped tree-tops and fallen wood have furnished material for conflagrations hot enough to kill trees as well as ground-cover over large areas. In such cases the dead or dying trees stand for a year or two, intact but naked, while new sprouts shoot up from their roots.

Later, the dead trees lose their now dry twigs and fall from time to time, forming almost impenetrable barriers of sticks, supremely well adapted to serve as kindling for new flames. The greater part of the woodland of Blue Hills Reservation was in this dead, dangerous, and unsightly condition at the time the reservation was acquired, and the woods of the Fells and Stony Brook Reservations were largely in the same miserable state. For the sake of the safety of the living growth, it was, therefore, necessary to clear away the accumulations of dead wood, and this has been done by burning it in heaps in winter.

When full-grown coppice is thus killed by fire or felled by the axe, the stumps, as has been noted, push out many vigorous and crowded shoots at the first seasonable opportunity. If care is taken to prevent such sprouting, for example, by bruising the shoots when tender, or by sending sheep to browse on them, the stumps can be eventually killed so that they will sprout no more, and clearings, pastures, or fields may be the result. If, however, the stumps are not killed, the ground is soon so thickly covered by the new sprouts that it cannot be seen and can hardly be traversed. It makes little difference whether such new sprout follows the killing of high sprout by fire, or whether it springs from the stumps of felled trees, its appearance is equally dreary and monotonous. If the fire-killed trees are not entirely removed (as they now have been throughout most of the reservations), or if they are allowed to slowly fall to pieces amid the tangle of new sprouts, the woodland scenery becomes still more dismal and squalid. It would, indeed, be hard to exaggerate the ruined appearance of such scenes; and yet they were met with on every hand when the reservations were first acquired.

As in the case of old sprout, the presence of young sprout is particularly unwelcome when it screens from sight any fine rocks or any richly verdurous swamp openings, as well as when it blots out possible vistas. It sometimes springs from the stumps of such deciduous trees as once were mixed with conifers on rocky hillsides, and in such cases it ought to be suppressed at once for the encouragement of seedling Pines, or other trees known to be long-lived and appropriate in such

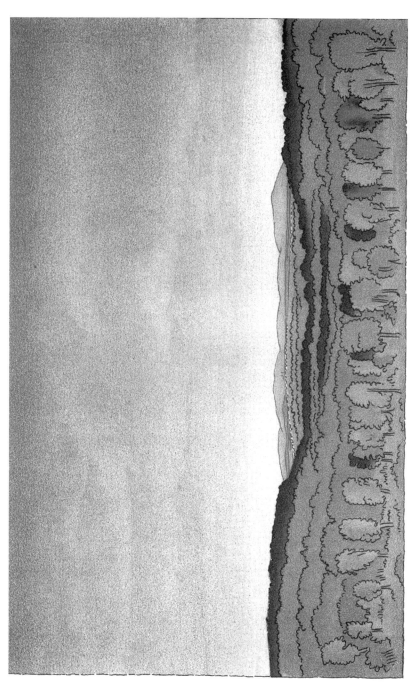

A BROAD VALLEY OF THE SOUTHEASTERN FELLS

Whose trees, about to hide the Blue Hill Range, have already hidden the valley of the Mystic

(see overleaf for open view)

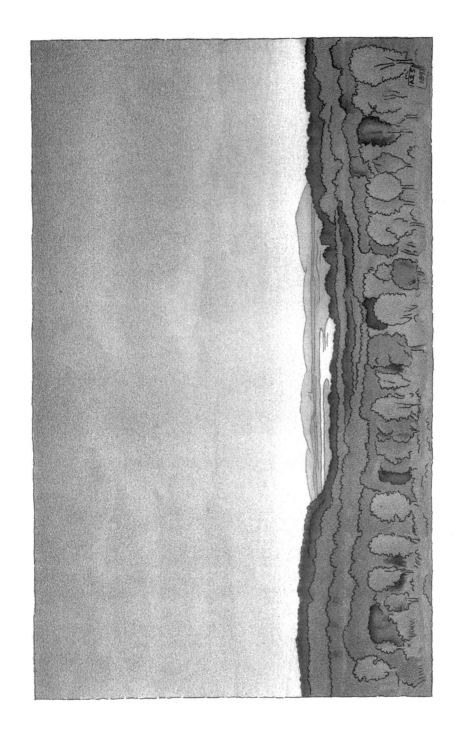

situations. The occasional broad views obtained from "clearings" made just previous to the acquisition of the reservations, or from areas from which fire-killed old sprout has been recently removed, are often fine, but they are generally only temporary, — the growth of the young sprout will obliterate most of these prospects in a very few years, together with many now pleasing glimpses of the ponds in the Fells, of the distant sea, or of the Great Blue Hill seen through some chance valley or ravine. The growth of the young sprout in other recent clearings will also once more shut out from view such bold hill-forms and foreground rock-masses as are temporarily visible and enjoyable just at present. Many of these chance and fleeting openings in the too continuous and too monotonous woods of high sprout ought certainly to be made more permanent, if only to illustrate how the removal of sprout-growth from large surfaces, and particularly from among the rocks, will enrich and vivify the scenery. To neither the old nor the young living coppice has any attention yet been given. The only care the previous private owners gave it was to cut the sprout-growth clean whenever the crop seemed ripe, that is, whenever most of the trees were large enough for cordwood, or sometimes for chestnut posts. To thin the sprout-growth so as to develop trees of more spreading habit was never worth while from the wood-lot owners' point of view; but such thinning has been practised at a few places within the limits of the reservations by persons desirous of making their lands more attractive in the eyes of purchasers of suburban house-lots, with results which, though startlingly ugly at first, serve the purpose after a few years. To treat the sprout-lands of the reservations in this manner throughout their length and breadth would, however, be inadvisable, since the result would be quite as monotonous and artificial in its way as is the present dense growth. Moreover, in most of the rough lands of the reservations no type of growth could be more inappropriate than that which consists of separated and spreading trees. In such lands there is not enough soil to grow really fine separate or specimen trees, and again there are few sprout trees which are sufficiently sound at their necessarily deformed bases to make them likely to thrive and live more than a comparatively small number of years. In view of the uninteresting quality of sprout-growth as an element of scenery, and of these grave objections to any general thinnings, it ought to be the settled policy of the management of the reservations to gradually effect the substitution of mixed seedling growth in place of the existing sprout-growth. Now that fires are prevented from spreading, seedlings of many species of trees will soon spring up wherever the sprout trees are not too thickly set; Pine seedlings here, Hemlocks and Beeches there, Birches among these rocks, Hickories, Chestnut-Oaks, and so on. Such seedling underwood is noticeable in many places to-day; and wherever it exists and wherever it appears, it can and ought to be given possession by gradually removing the sprout trees and killing their stumps. In such cases the high sprout trees should first be severely thinned, and then wholly removed perhaps two years later, so as not to expose the seedlings to new conditions with too great suddenness. In the high vista-commanding notches, as well as on the higher slopes and in other places where few trees, whether sprout or seedling, are really desirable, it will be best to fell all the sprout-growth at once and to kill the stumps. How beautifully a level or ledgy pasture will clothe itself with seedling shrubbery and trees will be illustrated later. It is sufficient to point out here that intelligent management will find it easy to gradually replace the crop-like coppice with vegetation much more beautiful in itself, and also more conducive to beauty of scenery.

4. *The Field and Pasture Type.* — The scenic value of even temporary clearings in woods has just been mentioned, but the importance and beauty of more lasting open places, such as fields and pastures, is incomparably greater. In this climate almost all treeless and grass-clothed areas, if not quite all, are due to the labor of men, supplemented by the browsing of domestic animals. For a year or two the stump-studded slopes or levels destined to be converted into pastures or fields are ugly enough in themselves, though they may open to view certain previously invisible prospects, but the more or less bare earth between the now dead stumps

soon springs to life and covers itself with plants of many sorts, — often with berry bushes, which will yield great crops of fruit so long as the bushes are not browsed down by animals, or overshaded by seedling plants of taller species. Much work devoted to dragging out stumps and stones is necessary before such lands can be called even rough fields. Most of the few smooth fields of the reservations are products of the slow labors of many generations, while the hard and close sod of the old pastures is the result of many years of continuous browsing.

After traversing long stretches of monotonous coppice, to emerge into grassy openings of this sort, set with occasional spreading trees, bordered or framed by hanging woods, beyond which rises perhaps some bold hill or ledge, is like coming to a richly interesting oasis in the midst of a bare desert, save that our desert is a close-ranked wood, and our oasis a sunny opening in it. Such man-made oases are specially lovely when they lie in hollow glades or intervales where there is moisture enough to keep them fresh and green in dry seasons; and even the still wetter meadows, from which crops of only the swamp grasses are obtainable, make welcome and interesting incidents in landscape.

It seems plain that few, if any, of the existing grassy areas of the reservations can be spared without loss of scenery, and they should, therefore, be maintained by systematic mowing and pasturing. In the future, some additional grassed openings will be desirable in smooth and hollow spots where provision will be needed for the gathering of people, or for the setting forth of some specially interesting local scenery; but as such grass-lands are troublesome to maintain, they ought not to be multiplied unduly. A ground-covering of bushes will serve as well as grass, when it is only a question of keeping a view open, and there is no need of providing strolling places for crowds or smooth playgrounds for boys or children.

5. *The Bushy Pasture Type.* — Of the several types of vegetation thus far mentioned, the coppice type occupies by far the largest part of the new reservations, while the summit, swamp, and field types cover approximately equal, but much smaller areas. It now appears that almost all the

remaining area of the reservations has been at one time or another either grass-land, field, or rough pasture land, and that the growth which now covers it more or less densely results from the more or less complete abandonment of the use and care of these lands by their owners. Why these considerable areas, cleared with great labor and situated near growing towns, should have been thus abandoned, it is not for us to ask, though the subject is one of considerable historical and economical interest. It is only to be noted here that the peculiar vegetation of these lands combines with their topography to form some of the most pleasing scenery of the reservations.

Even where cattle are still pastured, it is common enough to find plants of red Cedar starting up from seed here and there. Other seedlings are bitten off as fast as they appear, but the foliage of the red Cedar, prostrate Juniper, pitch Pine, and a few other species, is not edible, and so these plants survive and spread in pastures, unless they are burnt or rooted out by men. Sometimes, as at Bear Hill in the Fells, the red Cedar takes almost complete possession of the ground, often with striking effect, as when it stands up stiffly on bare rocks, or when it clothes a stony hillside. As soon as cattle cease to browse a piece of land, the common and fast-growing gray Birch mingles with the Cedar, or takes possession of large areas by itself. Abandoned ploughed land goes the same way in time, Cedars, pitch Pines, and Junipers forming the centres of many spreading islands of low or high shrubbery. The beautiful variety and intricacy of this bushy growth is often, and, indeed, generally remarkable and delightful. With time the bushes of Sweet Fern, Bayberry, Blueberry, Viburnum, and the like grow more and more numerous and entangled, and their combination with the dark Cedars and the white Birches often helps to form even broad landscape of rare beauty. Gradually, however, this type of landscape vanishes. From the midst, perhaps, of Junipers which browsing cattle have avoided, or from clumps of crowded bushes, slow-growing Oaks and other forest trees start up from seeds brought by the winds, birds, or squirrels. Slowly but surely, as the great trees grow in height and breadth, the low-growing

Birches, Cedars, Junipers, and bushes are overshadowed, and as it were suffocated, and in the end the forest of seedling trees takes full possession.

On the other hand, it is obvious that the bushy stage or type is so beautiful in itself that it ought to be preserved in many places for itself alone, while it is equally obvious that in such parts of the reservation as, command broad views which would be shut from sight by trees, this bushy ground-cover will need to be encouraged in every possible way; even, if need be, by going through the natural order of felling trees, killing the stumps, and pasturing the rough ground for a limited time.

6. *The Seedling Forest Type.* — That part of the total area of the reservations which is clothed with seedling woods is comparatively small. Here and there are found groups or patches of old seedling trees, like the Hemlocks of Hemlock Gorge, Hemlock Pool, or Breakneck Ledge, which appear to be direct descendants of innumerable generations occupying the same peculiarly rocky ground. Here and there are found clusters or groves of white Pines, apparently survivors of that generation of Pines which not so very many years ago clothed the major part of the reservations. Single specimens of such surviving Pines are not uncommon even in the midst of the sprout-lands. Like the Hemlocks, they have sometimes survived in positions from which it was thought too difficult to remove them. A few of the larger Pine groves have been leased by their owners as picnic grounds, and so have been more or less cleared of undergrowth and trampled. A few other woods, for example, the Wolcott Pines, have been in some measure cared for and encouraged, without destruction of low undergrowth, during one or two generations. Here conflicting deciduous trees have been cut out, and the Pines themselves thinned in some degree; while young seedlings from the parent trees have been protected both from fire and from too vigorous neighbors. The not unusual fate of the carelessly managed Pine woods has been their ruin by fire, and the subsequent surrender of the ground to coppice or scrub Oak. Here and there, again, are found crowded groves of deciduous trees, sprung from the small seedlings which,

after long struggling in the shade of Pines or Hemlocks, shot
up in vigorous competition with each other when the Pines or
Hemlocks were felled.   On the other hand, almost all such
deciduous seedling woods have long ago been cut down and
converted into that coppice which so shrouds the hills and
valleys, and which, on being cropped, again sprouts so vigorously as to suppress such seedlings, whether evergreen or
deciduous, as may have started in its shade.   Beech-trees
often seed the land around them very thickly ; Hemlocks and
Pines, also, when they have a chance ; and once in a while,
though by no means often, such seedlings compete successfully
with the surrounding coppice, and form colonies in the midst
thereof.

In spite, however, of these and other exceptions to the rule,
it is true that most of the now existing seedling woods of the
reservations owe their origin to the activity of the winds, and
of the seed and nut eating animals, in the fields and pastures
prepared by men for their own purposes, but afterwards
abandoned for one reason or another.   The trees which thus
eventually obliterate the fields and pastures are of many species, forms, and habits, and the resulting woods are often
varied, interesting, and beautiful, as no coppice can be.   The
varied appearance of these woods and groves has been increased also by the diversity of their history since they first
sprang up in the worn-out and abandoned pastures.   Where,
for example, all but the largest trees have at one time been
felled and removed, the sprout trees from the stumps now
form, with the old seedling trees, a mixed type of vegetation
common in the rougher parts of the Fells.   Where pasturing
has been resumed after certain trees have got a good start,
and then the animals have been again removed, a secondary
growth of seedling trees has subsequently mingled with the
primary trees, often to the injury of the latter, but as often
with pleasing effect.   If, on the other hand, pasturing is resumed and continued after well-spaced trees have been developed, the open groves which result present, perhaps, the most
lovely local scenery of the reservations.   The extreme rockiness and poverty of soil of most of the new domains makes
this preëminently " park-like " type of landscape impracticable,

BROAD-SPREADING TREES DEVELOPED IN OPEN LAND

And not yet surrounded by other trees or sprout-growths because pasturing has been continuous

as well as inappropriate. Intricacy, variety, and picturesqueness of detail of rock and vegetation, combined with numerous and varied openings, vistas, and broad prospects, must serve as the sources of interest and beauty throughout the larger part of the reservations; but where smooth grass-lands and broad-spreading trees exist, or are obtainable, they should certainly be preserved or secured. Compared with the sameness and dullness of the general scenery of the sprout-lands, the wealth of variety, character, and beauty presented by the relatively small area of fields, pastures, and seedling woods is indeed remarkable, and it is to be noted that this greater beauty counts in the broad scenery of the reservations as well as close at hand. The sky-lines and what may be called the profiles of the coppice woods are flat and nearly uniform. The masses of the seedling growths are bold in outline, as well as varied in detail, all of which only adds weight to the argument that the crop-like coppice should be forced to gradually give place to seedling shrubbery and seedling trees.

Conclusions.

With regard to the relation of the vegetation of the reservations to the present and future scenery, perhaps the most important conclusions to be derived from this investigation are the following: It is found that the vegetation of the reservations is an exceedingly important component part of the scenery. It is found, moreover, that the present vegetation — its variety and beauty, as well as its monotony and ugliness — has resulted from repeated or continuous interference with natural processes by men, fire, and browsing animals.

It follows that the notion that it would be wrong and even sacrilegious to suggest that this vegetation ought to be controlled and modified must be mistaken. The opposite is found to be the truth; namely, that as the beauty or ugliness and scenic appropriateness or inappropriateness of the present vegetation is due to the work of men, so also will the vegetation of the future be beautiful in itself and helpful or hurtful in the general scenery, according as it may or may not be skilfully restrained, encouraged, or modified during the next few years.

Simply to preserve the beauty of so much of this vegetation as is now beautiful, or the suitability of so much as is now suitable, — for example, the tree-fringed vales of grass, the open groves of great trees, the intricate shrubberies of old pastures, and the dwarf ground-cover of the hill-tops, — will necessarily require continual painstaking care. To restore variety and beauty in the now more or less degenerate or ruined woods will similarly demand intelligent attention. So to control, guide, and modify the vegetation generally that the reservations may be slowly but surely induced to present the greatest possible variety, interest, and beauty of landscape will particularly require skilled direction.

That such preservation, restoration, and enhancement of the beauty of vegetation and of scenery is only to be accomplished by the rightly directed labor of men is the principal lesson taught by this study of the present condition and the past history of the vegetation of the reservations. To preserve existing beauty, grass-lands must continue to be mowed or pastured annually, trees must be removed from shrubberies, competing trees must be kept away from veteran Oaks and Chestnuts, and so on. To restore beauty in such woods as are now dull and crop-like, large areas must be gradually cleared of sprout-growth by selling the standing crop, or otherwise, the stumps must be subsequently killed, and seedling trees encouraged to take possession. To prepare for increasing the interest and beauty of scenery, work must be directed to removing screens of foliage, to opening vistas through "notches," to substituting low ground-cover for high woods in many places, and other like operations which are, in some measure, illustrated by the accompanying diagrammatic sketches. The sooner all these kinds of work are entered upon systematically, the finer will be the scenery of twenty and fifty years hence, and the more economically will that scenery have been obtained.

Eight days after the above report was presented, Charles wrote to the Commission making a definite proposition on behalf of his firm for beginning forest work in the reserva-

TREE-CLOGGED NOTCH, NEAR THE SOUTHEASTERN ESCARPMENT OF THE FELLS

Which might command the Malden-Melrose valley and the Saugus hills

(see overleaf for open view)

tions, and continuing it three years. If the following letter
is from one point of view an asking for employment by the
Commission, from another it is a public-spirited offer of
valuable service. The Olmsted firm had at this time so much
well-paid work on hand that, from the strictly pecuniary point
of view, the less work they did for the Metropolitan Park
Commission, the better. Charles's interest in that work was
so keen that he would always give time to it altogether in
excess of the time which the Commission paid for. The firm
never took the view that their services were to be measured
carefully by the amount of compensation they received ; they
wanted the personal satisfaction and the professional credit
of contributing to the success of a superb and beneficent
public enterprise.

February 23, 1897.

. . . We have prepared and submitted a report on the
existing vegetation of the reservations, together with some
account of the kind of work in the living woods, which, as it
seems to us, ought to be begun at once if the reservations
are to serve their purpose in a manner to justify their cost.

A few reasons for making an early start in this work are
these : 1st. There is a great deal of this work to be done ;
but as the nature of the work is so peculiar, it will be advisable to make haste slowly, and to train men to prosecute it
rightly. This will take time. 2d. The " young sprout "
which now covers large areas, while easily controllable to-day,
will soon be too large to be easily handled. It already begins
to obliterate many valuable prospects, as well as much local
scenery. The small stature of the present growth also makes
it possible to discover scenic possibilities to-day which would
never be dreamed of if the trees were some years older. 3d.
Much of the work we have called " rescue work " (the saving
of fine or promising trees in smooth or good land from too
pressing neighbors, and the like) will not be worth attempting if it is not begun soon. Of course, the first-named reason
is fundamentally the most important.

There seems to us to be a strange incongruity in the provision by the Commission of elaborate approaches to the
reservations, like the Fellsway, while no attention is directed
to even preparing for the work of preserving and restoring
the scenery of the reservations themselves.

Accordingly, and in order that a beginning in this work may be made in an orderly way and under responsible direction, we beg leave to suggest that, in addition to such force as the superintendents of the reservations may be authorized to employ under the appropriation for maintenance, and in addition to such force as they may employ in the construction of boundary roads, they be also authorized to engage one or more foremen and one or more gangs of laborers to be assigned to work in the living woods; and that just as their work on roads is now guided by inspectors representing the Commission's engineer, so the new work in the woods should be guided by inspectors representing the Commission's landscape architects. These inspectors will not themselves be foremen — they will correspond to the men who set the line and grade stakes for the road-builders. It will not be necessary that they should give all their time to the work. Unless the work is begun on a grand scale (as we cannot recommend that it should be), the Commission would not be warranted in engaging the whole time of trained inspectors. To avoid this difficulty, we will lend inspectors from our office as often or as seldom as may be necessary, and will charge the Commission with just the cost to us of their time and travelling expenses. Our own professional and semi-annual fee, covering the responsible selection and laying out of the work which the inspectors will guide in detail, would certainly not exceed the reasonable amount which we have heretofore charged for advice and suggestions respecting the location and boundaries of the acquired reservations.

As the Commission is directed to, in some sense, complete its work by January, 1900, we would suggest that a certain part of the money now available be specially appropriated for labor in the living woods between the present time and the date named. If entrusted with the direction of the work as above suggested, we would do our best to secure the expenditure of whatever appropriation is made to the best advantage; but it would greatly assist us to lay out the work aright, if the amount to be spent in the three years, rather than that to be spent in one year, could be named at the outset.

As reported by us a year ago, and again in our last annual
report, we believe the only logical and truly economical way
of going about the slow development of the reservations is to
begin with a general scheme for each, and then to carry out
such parts of the work called for by the adopted plans as may
be most pressingly demanded from time to time. It is always
our custom, when we are engaged to suggest general plans, to
throw in advice and guidance during the period of study
without extra charge, and we should be happy to take up the
planning of one or more of the Commission's reservations,
with this understanding, at any time. The foregoing proposals as to the guidance of woodland work in advance of all
plan-making are submitted only because it seems wrong to
allow the present fleeting opportunities to accomplish valuable
results in the woods to pass unused.

On March 3, 1897, the Metropolitan Commission made an
appropriation of $500 for forestry inspection; and Charles
welcomed the chance to begin improving the woods in well-
selected spots, although he had failed to induce the Commission to order general landscape designs for the three forest
reservations.

The following letter to Mr. Hemenway, who was the Committee on Blue Hills Reservation, explains the principle on
which he proceeded in Marigold Valley : —

March 13, 1897.

Let me report to the Committee on Blue Hills Reservation
that I have (under the vote of the Board) asked the Superintendent to begin forest work at the extreme head of Marigold Valley, and to proceed southward along the eastern side
of the valley as far as the Plains. I have marked with him
a large number of trees for felling, most of which are to be
removed (1) for the sake of seedling Beeches in one place
and Hickories in another; (2) for the sake of freeing from
too near neighbors certain already well-established spreading
trees, and (3) for the sake of breaking up certain straight
rows of trees which followed walls now removed.

Some additional trees have been marked for the sake of
opening two vistas which it seemed desirable to open while we
were working in the neighborhood.

I shall, of course, be glad to have your suggestions and comments on the work proposed and executed.

On the same date Charles wrote also to Mr. de las Casas, who took special interest in the Middlesex Fells, explaining where he proposed to set the Superintendent at work in that reservation. It will be noticed that all the places he mentions for forestry work are on roads sure to be permanent, — that is, existing highways and border roads.

March 13, 1897.

The extent of the forest work will, I suppose, depend on the number of men employed and the length of time they keep at it. The place for beginning the work in the Fells is a matter of choice, of course. I have proposed to Price that he should begin on Ravine Road, where Pines and Hemlocks have begun to spring up on the slope once cleared by Mr. Butterfield. This is a hillside one would like to have clothed again with evergreen, and the process can be assisted by some chopping. It is a slope practically free from ledges; so that it does not call for the nice discrimination between trees which will be required among ledges.

Beyond this I would propose to attack similar work in a few spots along Pond and Woodland streets, where young evergreens are suffering, and after that I would suggest working round the east and southeast borders of the Fells for the purpose of ensuring the better appearance of the reservation as seen from the border roads, even as far round as Highland Avenue.

There is so much work to do that it seems to me it matters little where our small beginning is made, so long as it is arranged to be as educative as possible for the foreman and laborers employed.

Charles's letters to the Commission were invariably signed Olmsted, Olmsted & Eliot; but these two letters, addressed personally to members of the Commission, were signed, Yours sincerely, Charles Eliot. They were his last words on Metropolitan work.

CHAPTER XXXIX

METROPOLITAN PARKS AND PARKWAYS IN 1902

God Almighty first planted a Garden. And indeed, it is the purest of Human Pleasures. · It is the greatest Refreshment to the Spirits of Man; without which, Buildings and Palaces are but gross Handyworks: And a Man shall ever see, that when Ages grow to Civility and Elegancy, Men come to Build Stately, sooner than to Garden finely: As if Gardening were the greater Perfection. — BACON.

The Design and its Execution.

CHARLES'S project of December, 1892, for public reserva tions in the metropolitan district was a bold and comprehensive one. How much of it has been carried into execution in nine years? A comparison of his recommendations with the accompanying map of the public open spaces of the district in December, 1901 [1] (see the pocket of the right-hand cover), will bring out the extraordinary proportion of fulfilled proposals.

Rock-Hills. — The map of December, 1892 (see the pocket of the left-hand cover), proposed an enlargement of the Lynn Woods on the west; and Charles subsequently advocated the acquisition of the Woods by the Metropolitan Commission. The western boundary of the Woods has been much improved, and a spur has been carried out to Lynnfield, but not at the expense of the district; and as yet the Woods remain the charge of Lynn.

The Middlesex Fells have been secured as he proposed, with the exception of the Langwood Hotel property on the eastern side of Spot Pond, and of two areas on the southern side of the reservation, one of which was too costly, while the other was kept private property by act of the legislature. Through the action of the Metropolitan Water Board in converting Spot Pond, much enlarged but not injured as an element of the landscape, into a storage reservoir, the district has acquired a new interest in the Fells as a valuable water preserve.

West of Boston, and overlooking the valley of Charles River to the east, are Prospect, Bear, and Doublet hills, the

[1] In this edition the map of 1901 has been replaced by a map brought down to 1909; but the text of this chapter has not been changed, because it records the remarkable accomplishment of the first eight years.

acquisition of which Charles proposed. He pointed out, indeed, that Prospect and Bear hills lay entirely within the bounds of Waltham, so that they could be secured as public open spaces by local action. The two summits of Prospect Hill have been taken by Waltham as a city park, though with disadvantageous boundaries which do not regard the lay of the land. Bear Hill and Doublet Hill still remain in private hands.

Stony Brook Reservation, or Muddy Pond Woods, another of the rough forest reservations, has the length, but not the full breadth, which Charles originally suggested for it. He himself advocated, however, after the original taking was made, a narrowing of this forest tract for the sake of economy, and of equity in the distribution of the public open spaces.

The Blue Hills Reservation is much larger than Charles proposed in 1892, and includes all that he suggested taking at that date. Its 4858 acres with the 464 acres of Stony Brook exceed by 306 acres the entire forest reservations on the north side of Boston, including therein two large tracts which were not acquired by the Metropolitan Park Commission, namely, the 1145 acres of Water Works reservations in Middlesex Fells and the 2000 acres of the Lynn Woods.

Ponds and Streams. — Charles proposed in the rough that the shores and marshes of the Mystic, Charles, and Neponset rivers should become public property. It is astonishing to see on the map how much of this sweeping recommendation has been already carried out. The shores and marshes of the Mystic have been secured down to the Fellsway bridge to Somerville, the reservation covering 290 acres. Below that point the borders of the river have been claimed, as Charles foresaw, by railroads, factories, and wharves. He thought it desirable that the shores of Malden River and the valley and mouth of Island End Creek should be secured; but these were subordinate proposals. Nothing has as yet been done about Malden River, and the Island End tract is now occupied by huge commercial structures. Two salt creeks in this neighborhood, — Snake Creek and a branch of Belle Isle Creek, — which Charles proposed should be rescued for public use, have been saved by the construction of the Revere Beach Parkway. Only the eastern shores of the two Mystic ponds have become public property; the western shores, the possession of which Charles thought essential to the preservation of the beauty of these ponds, still remain in private hands.

The banks of Charles River have been "resumed" by the public to an extent which Charles did not venture to propose

BOSTON, 1892

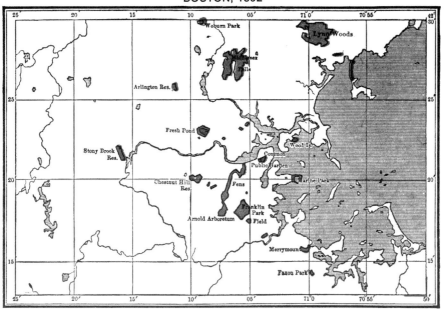

BOSTON, 1902

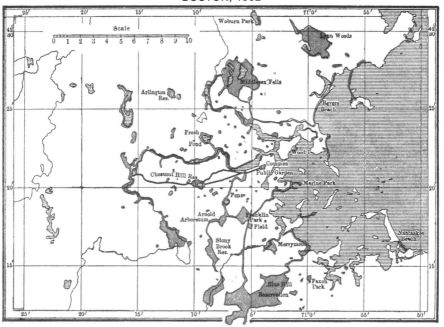

THE OPEN SPACES OF BOSTON IN 1892 AND 1902 COMPARED

in 1892, although the takings along the banks of the river have all been made in strict accordance with the principles he then laid down. With the exception of the properties of the Boston and Albany Railroad and the Brookline Gas Works on the south bank, both banks of the river have been secured for the public, or restricted against all objectionable uses, as far as Newton Upper Falls; and above that point the Brookline and Newton Water Works have large holdings on the stream.

On the Neponset River, the Fowl Meadows above Readville and the banks and salt marshes below have been secured, with small exceptions, down to a point in Milton Lower Mills within two miles of Dorchester Bay. The area of the Neponset River Reservation in charge of the Metropolitan Park Commission is 929 acres, against 563 acres on Charles River and 290 acres on the Mystic. Here, as well as in regard to the extent of its forest reservations and the serviceableness of its parkways, the south side of the district has been more fortunate than the north side. There remains to be preserved some of the charming scenery of the tidal Neponset on its way to Squantum.

The Bay and the Sea. — Under this head the recommendation in the text of Charles's report of December, 1892, is as follows: "When such a commission [Metropolitan Park] is established, what should be its first work upon the shore? The answer is, — the acquirement of the title to the foreshore and the beach from Winthrop Great Head to the Point of Pines." The map which accompanied the report contained another recommendation; for, proposed open spaces being colored brown, the shore of Quincy Bay from Moswetusset Hummock on the peninsula of Squantum to Nut Island off Great Hill at the extremity of Hough's Neck was so colored. The seven miles of foreshore and beach between Winthrop Great Head and the Point of Pines are now public property, except the Point of Pines itself and about a mile and one third of shore between Grover's Cliff and Crescent Beach. The westerly half of the shore of Quincy Bay, two miles in length, is also public property.

Two detached reservations were recommended in the text and map of the report to the preliminary Metropolitan Park Commission, namely, Beaver Brook with its group of ancient Oaks, and Hemlock Gorge at Newton Upper Falls. Both these beautiful spots have been acquired by the Commission.

The Commission has acquired three reservations which were not recommended by Charles in December, 1892, namely,

King's Beach, and Lynn Shore at the northeastern extremity of the district, and a part of Nantasket Beach outside of the district towards the southeast, the latter under a special act of the legislature. King's Beach and Lynn Shore were intended to form a continuous reservation as far as Nahant Long Beach; but the Commission has still a half mile of shore to acquire just beyond the northern end of Nahant Beach. The Commission now holds both Nahant beaches by transfer from the town of Nahant, which owned them in 1892.

The scale of operations of the Commission has been larger than was at first contemplated; for the work proved to be popular, and the legislature readily made liberal appropriations in every year down to 1900. The rapid development of the work of construction and maintenance in the reservations has fulfilled the prophecy with which Charles's report of December, 1892, closes: "In conclusion, it may be well to point out that the cost of the maintenance of all the metropolitan open spaces need not, for many years at least, exceed the expense of guarding them from forest fires, and other forms of depredation; on the other hand, if the community should wish to clean the streams, build paths or roads, or do any other proper work within the reservations, it would find in the Park Commission an instrument to do its bidding."

To December 1, 1901, the total expenditure for metropolitan reservations, including Nantasket Beach, was $7,049,256, of which sum more than two thirds ($5,087,237.40) was paid for land, the rest being paid for construction, maintenance, care, interest, and sinking-fund assessments during eight years. The expensive reservations have proved to be Revere Beach and Charles River, the land for these two having cost nearly half ($2,439,307.75) of the sum paid for the land of all the reservations taken together. It is altogether probable, however, that these two public properties will prove to be the most valuable of all in promoting the health and wholesome pleasures of the district population.

The distinct work of constructing parkways, which was imposed on the Metropolitan Park Commission in 1894, has cost to December 1, 1901, $2,848,328.06, of which sum less than one third ($923,546.70) has been paid for land.

The district, having spent ten millions of dollars on reservations and parkways since the summer of 1893, now needs to spend four or five millions more within a few years, in order to come into the full enjoyment of the investment already made. As Charles repeatedly pointed out, the two most important constructive designs still awaiting execution are the design for the improvement of Charles River and its Basin, and the design for a parkway from Broadway Park, Somerville, to Boston Common. These two designs, however, are by no means of equal consequence, and are supported by different considerations. The first will provide, beside enjoyable water parks, a much-needed sanitary improvement, and a great enlargement of the valley areas available for wholesome and pleasant human occupation; the second will furnish the inhabitants of central Boston with agreeable access to the northern reservations, and the inhabitants of the northern suburbs with a pleasant route into Boston, — something which they have never had, and greatly need. The briefest study of the map of December, 1901, will reveal other gaps or deficiencies in the park and parkway system, but none which compare in importance, or in costliness, with the Charles River Improvement and the Northern Parkway.

The taking of the 9248 acres of open public space, and the 23.6 miles of parkway (to 1902) was eminently timely. In the main, the reservation lands were secured at reasonable prices, as appears in the average price per acre — $550.11. Considering that the lands taken were all within eleven miles of the State House, and that Revere Beach cost $16,925.47, King's Beach and Lynn Shore [1] $10,197.83, and Nantasket Beach $23,350.19 per acre, it seems very improbable that the reservations as a whole could ever in the future have been obtained on more favorable terms. Their annual dividend in health and pleasure to the metropolitan population (about 1,000,000 people) ought easily to surpass the annual charges for interest, sinking fund, and maintenance (about $520,000).

Whatever the metropolitan parks and parkways have cost, or may hereafter cost, it is impossible to imagine a more purely beneficent expenditure of public money, or one more productive of genuine well-being and healthy happiness. The last years of the nineteenth century and the first years of the twentieth have seen three great securities taken for the welfare, through many generations, of the Boston group of municipalities, — the Metropolitan Sewage, Water, and Park Works.

[1] With two claims unsettled which will slightly raise the average.

CHAPTER XL

THE LAST DAYS

He who, from zone to zone,
Guides through the boundless sky thy certain flight,
In the long way that I must tread alone,
Will lead my steps aright.
                                                BRYANT.

CHARLES'S last days of work were given to the Keney Park in Hartford, Conn. He had been much interested in the Hartford parks since the fall of 1895, and had frequently conferred on the spot with the Commissioners or Trustees and their agents. He transformed a neglected and unsightly piece of open ground of irregular shape in the heart of the city, since called Barnard Park, into a tidy, well-planted, and attractive public enclosure. The name commemorates Henry Barnard, the veteran educationist, whose house stood near by. Most of his attention had been given, however, to the Keney Park, which was being developed on the north side of Hartford by a Board of Trustees, at the head of which was Rev. Francis Goodwin. Here is a little note to his wife from Hartford : —

31 October, 1895, 5 P. M. It rains now and the dark has come, so I am housed. I rode comfortably last evening, and dined properly in the dining-car. Between 8 and 9 I concocted an epistle to Mr. Goodwin which contained matter of importance ! . . . To-day I began by getting my important letter typewritten. Then left it at Mr. Goodwin's office, and departed for the woods, where I rambled until 2, lunching on chocolate and crackers. I got my mind pretty well made up. . . . To-morrow ought to be clear, to suit me ; but I shall go out even if it is wet. I finished with the thickets to-day, and open fields are not bad. . . .

Early in 1896 the firm made a contract with the Trustees of the Keney estate at Hartford (see Appendix V.), covering a term of five years, under which they were to prepare a general plan for the laying out of certain lands in and near Hartford to be known as Keney Park, and to give such advice and make such detailed drawings as would enable competent experts on the spot to order the materials and services needed to execute the general plan, and to lay out and direct the works; these experts, whether engineers, architects, or gardeners, to act under the general supervision of the firm. As compensation the firm was to receive a stated semi-annual payment, and their travelling and other expenses. This was precisely the kind of contract under which Charles best liked to work. It gave the firm the whole work of designing, and provided adequate security for the intelligent and faithful execution of their designs. The selection in detail of the fields and woods which make up this park, and of the lines of its main roads, was entrusted to Charles. He soon formed in his own mind a series of pictures of the park which was to be, recommended the acquisition of the essential parts of these pictures, rejected all unessential elements, however attractive in themselves, carried the roads to the points whence the most pleasing prospects, near or remote, were to be obtained, discerned and marked the future vistas through glades and woods, and the glimpses of distant hills, and in general showed how to utilize for the future enjoyment of the public all the natural advantages of the site. Some of the open areas which are finest to-day were then crowded with pasture fences and farm rubbish. Charles did not seem to notice these existing obstacles and blots; he saw the broad fields and meadows as they would appear when finished. He was always happy in the Hartford work. A postal card from Hartford to his wife in the summer of 1896 says: "July 7. Things and problems here are very complex and very interesting. I was out all day yesterday, and at a meeting of the Board until 11 P. M., and out again most of to-day. You see I am still pretty tough!"

The last word he wrote to her was from Hartford: "March 15, 1897. A great long day out in the sun and wind and snow! Went out of town on one electric car at 9 A. M. and got back on another at 5.30 P. M. Lunched with the Superintendent. Another such day to-morrow if all goes well, and a return to Brookline Hills station at 10.27 P. M. . . . My love to all those very dear little girls." . . .

On the 15th and 16th of March he was determining the course of the main road through the wooded tract called the Ten Mile Woods. With a map in hand on which the contour lines and the principal trees were shown, he walked back and forth through the woods searching for that line which would give the best grades and vistas, and save and exhibit the best trees. There was a light snow on the ground ; but the woods were pleasant in their winter dress. On the 16th, to save time, luncheon for Charles and the Superintendent, Mr. George A. Parker, was brought to a hut in the heart of the woods, which had been built and furnished for the sur-veyors. There Charles ate a hearty meal — his last in the woods he loved. That evening he returned to Brookline.

On the 17th he remained in the house, feeling as if he had taken cold. In the night of the 17th he was wakened by severe pains in the head and back. At first the disease was supposed to be the grippe ; but the consulting physician sum-moned on the third day immediately recognized it as cerebro-spinal meningitis, an inflammation of the lining of the brain and spinal cord. He had seen six cases of this rare disease [1] in his private and hospital practice within a fortnight. No treatment is known for it ; and complete recovery from it, even in mild cases, is rare. Charles lingered for seven days, ap-parently without much suffering after the first fierce onset of the disease, and most of the time in a condition suggesting sleep or unconsciousness. On the sixth day the physician held out a little hope ; but on the seventh all the symptoms became suddenly worse, and soon he quietly ceased to breathe.

So ended abruptly, and to human vision prematurely, a life simple, natural, happy, and wholly beneficent. The qualities and powers which gave such happiness and success are easily discerned.

Physically, Charles was tall and slight, and never seemed robust, or capable of any unusual amount of labor. His digestion was easily disturbed, and he was not infrequently kept from his work for a day or two. When he was four years old, he had a terrible typhoid pneumonia in Paris, and lay at the point of death for three weeks ; but he never was seriously ill again until his mortal sickness. In spite of a certain bodily delicacy, being light and long of limb, he could outwalk many people of apparently greater vigor; and he could travel by night-trains and work by day with surprising endurance — even with enjoyment. He was comparatively indifferent to heat and cold, provided he were in the open air. Long walks across country, through woods, bogs, and thickets, were always delightful to him, summer or winter.

---

[1] Epidemic in Massachusetts in 1873, when 747 deaths from it occurred; and next in 1897, when 355 deaths occurred, the average annual number of deaths from it during the five years preceding 1897 having been 106.

He rode well; but walking was what he most enjoyed; because so he could best see the prospects, and the vegetation. His sports were walking, riding, rowing, and sailing, in all of which he was proficient. The occasional, inevitable risks encountered in these pursuits he met without the least perturbation; but the source of his pleasure was not in the risks. Both in Europe and America he would wander alone in any wilderness, or rough, solitary place, without a thought of possible danger. He never had occasion to hurt or kill any living creature in the pursuit of his own pleasures. On the contrary, the animal life in the woods and thickets was to him a source of genuine delight; and he wanted to have it all preserved unmolested, except creatures indubitably noxious. He liked to be driven in open vehicles; but he was a bad driver himself, because his attention constantly wandered to the scenery or to the objects by the roadside. He could work all day in his office, or in the field, and in the evening speak at a hearing in Cambridge or Watertown on the improvement of Charles River, or at some Citizens' Association or Trade Club which wished to hear something about parks. In short, although rather frail in aspect, and never fit for any of the severe athletic sports, he had an available kind of toughness which served well his intellectual life.

Mentally, his constitution was of the best. His school life was not so happy as it should have been, because the traditional subjects of instruction — at that time the only road to college — were uncongenial to him ; but as soon as he reached subjects he was fit to master, study became an enjoyment. He worked intently and rapidly, but not at long stretches, unless in the open air. His observation was quick and decided, and his inferences from what he observed were unerring. In writing or speaking he was clear, concise, and consecutive, never wandering about, or amplifying unnecessarily, or missing the main point. The pictures with which observation and reading had filled his mind were distinct, and he recalled them distinctly at will. Moreover, his style in narrative or description has occasionally a charming imaginative, or poetic touch. His memory was not remarkable for languages or history; but for places, scenes, and roads, for ledges, harbor approaches, and landings, for spots where Rhodora, Linnæa, or Clethra grows, or for a grove of thrifty Pines or a mass of hardy Magnolias, his mental memoranda were indelible. These faculties stood him in good stead during the ten years of his active professional life; but there was another gift which presided over them all — the artistic sense of fitness, perspective, and proportion. He had from his mother the artist's imagination, which makes new combinations out of familiar elements, foresees beauty, and through prophetic designs ultimately reveals to ordinary eyes the artist's visions.

The most serviceable of Charles's powers, however, were neither physical nor mental, but spiritual. He brought to pass in ten crowded, youthful years an astonishing number of good things very difficult of attainment, because requiring legislation and the consent of many minds and wills. He succeeded in these enterprises because of his moral qualities. He was obviously thorough in knowledge of his subject, disinterested, reasonable, and fair-minded. He was also gentle though persistent, and modest though confident. In most of his undertakings he had to do with men much older than himself, who had achieved distinction in other fields than his, and were comparatively ignorant of his own. His relations with these older men were invariably pleasant, even when he could not bring them immediately to his views. Thus, the Metropolitan Park Commission, in the resolution passed after his death, spoke not only of his skill, knowledge, and constant connection with their work, but also of his character and temper, " which made him a delightful companion and co-laborer." Before popular audiences he was singularly persuasive, although his way of speaking was quiet and unadorned. It made no difference whether his audience was composed of Provincetown fishermen and traders, or dwellers in a rich suburb like Newton, or the well-to-do members of a trade association, or the interested men and women that gather in the committee-rooms of the Massachusetts legislature, — all alike were impressed with the reasonableness of the measures he advocated, and the soundness of the arguments by which he supported them. Dr. Walcott, chairman of the Joint Board of 1893–94 on the Improvement of Charles River, who accompanied Charles to many hearings and public meetings on that subject at the State House and in the cities and towns on the river, said that Charles was the most persuasive speaker he had ever listened to ; and during his long public service he had listened to many speakers, famous and obscure, who needed and wished to be persuasive. This persuasiveness was just as apparent in a small company, like the Metropolitan Park Commission, or a board of selectmen, or a committee of the legislature, as in a large assemblage, and often more immediately influential. It resulted from mastery of his subject and clearness in presenting it, from fairness in argument, and from a pleasantness, modesty, and gentleness in which there was no trace of weakness. He had plenty of firm insistence, but was never party to a quarrel or a bitter controversy. He was equally happy in dealing with men and women who were under his authority or supervision. In the last four years of his life these were numerous. They all felt that he was considerate, friendly, and gentle; that he knew what he wanted; and that their time and labor would not be wasted while working under his direction. He inspired them with something of his own enthusiasm and devotion, and made them feel that their work served high ends.

Such were the sources of Charles's professional success. Here was an active, interesting, and productive career, whose methods and fruits were all good; in it all, no evil preliminary to good, nothing harsh or coarse on the way to the sweet and fine, no selfishness or injustice as preparation for love and equity. Nothing but good, and much good, came of his labors.

The Standing Committee of the Trustees of Public Reservations, at a meeting held the day after Charles's death, summed up his services to Massachusetts in these words: " Charles Eliot found in this community a generous but helpless sentiment for the preservation of our historical and beautiful places. By ample knowledge, by intelligent perseverance, by eloquent teaching, he created organizations capable of accomplishing his great purposes, and inspired others with a zeal approaching his own."

In domestic life the same good sense and good feeling developed pure happiness, unalloyed except by inevitable external vicissitudes. He was habitually somewhat reticent and self-contained; but at home, or among intimates, a look, a word or two, or a touch, could suddenly express quiet content, or pleased satisfaction, or the warmest love and devotion. Nothing could exceed the serenity and unity of the family life into which death broke so suddenly on the 25th of March, 1897.

Charles was by temperament reflective, sympathetic, and affectionate, and he had an inquiring mind, which sought causes and uniform sequences; he was, therefore, naturally religious, but not in any emotional, conventional, or ecclesiastical sense. The institutions of religion, as a whole, he thought indispensable to society; but many of the forms and observances which he saw were grateful to others, he himself merely endured with patience, for they were to him unprofitable. His religious affiliations — like those of all his near kindred for three generations — were with the Unitarian Church. His creed was short and simple. He believed that a loving God rules the universe, that the path to loving and serving Him lies through loving and serving men, and that the way to worship Him is to reverence the earthly beauty, truth, and goodness He has brought forth.

The character which shines through these pages is of a kind seldom described in poetry or fiction, — perhaps because it is transparent, natural, and harmonious. It was not passionate — calm, rather, and reserved ; yet it had all the fire needed to warm mind and heart to great work and the sweetest affections.

APPENDIX

APPENDIX

I

MR. ELIOT offers his services to owners of suburban and country estates, trustees of institutions, park commissions, hotel proprietors, and persons or corporations desiring to lay out or improve suburban neighborhoods and summer resorts. He consults with owners, architects, engineers, and gardeners respecting the placing of buildings, the laying out of roads, the grading of surfaces, and the treatment of old and new plantations. He designs and revises the arrangement and planting of public squares and parks, of private grounds and gardens, of house-lots and streets. He assists in works of " scenery preservation," both public and private.

A visit and consultation on the ground is the first step in all cases. This visit binds neither party to any further dealings with each other. It is necessary simply to enable Mr. Eliot to acquaint himself with his client's wishes and with the physical and financial conditions of the case, to the end that he may suggest the most suitable method of procedure. It sometimes happens that verbal suggestions or rough sketches can be made on the spot to the satisfaction of the client. Sometimes a series of consultations on the ground may prove advisable. Sometimes a few rough measurements will serve as the basis of a suggestive sketch to be sent later from the office. Sometimes a written report is called for. Sometimes the employment of a surveyor is recommended, and instructions as to the elaborateness of the survey will then be prepared for him. A survey of some sort is a prerequisite to the making of a plan drawn to a scale.

Since the problems which present themselves differ greatly in complexity and importance, and may require for their comprehension anywhere from a few minutes to a few days, the fee for a visit varies in a like manner, and may be ten, fifty, or a hundred dollars. In similar cases this consultation fee is similar, no matter where the place of consultation may be ; but railroad and hotel expenses from and to Boston are to be added to the fee, and if the place of consultation is more than one night's journey from Boston, there is another additional charge of twenty-five dollars for every business day lost in travelling. If visits to two or more clients are made in one neighborhood, these time and travel charges are equally divided.

When distant clients are not in such haste as to require an immediate visit involving a special journey from Boston, a visit in the
course of a tour can generally be arranged. Tours are made as
often as any considerable number of calls are received from any
given part of the country, and the time and travel charges for visits
made in the course of a tour are dated as from and to the most
convenient of the great cities on the route. Thus, clients situated
at any distance from Buffalo, Washington, Atlanta, Cincinnati, St.
Louis, or Chicago are in these cases charged no more than they would
be if they were situated the same distance from Boston.

When a visit develops the need of a design based upon a survey,
Mr. Eliot usually submits first a Preliminary Plan, and when this
is approved, a finished General Plan. The General Plan can be
staked out by any surveyor, and carried out by day's work under
a qualified superintendent. If the work is to be done by contract,
working drawings, written specifications, and such supervision as
architects are accustomed to furnish will be provided, if required.
Planting-plans for both large and small areas and in any degree
of detail are also supplied when needed. Order Lists are made
up from reliable nursery catalogues, and lowest prices are always
obtained for the client's benefit. No commissions are taken on purchases ; neither is any responsibility assumed for miscarriages or
failures.

II

50 STATE STREET, BOSTON, April 14, 1890.

DEAR SIR, — A Committee of the Council of the Appalachian
Mountain Club proposes to call in May a conference of persons
interested in the preservation of scenery and historical sites in Massachusetts.

Can you not oblige this Committee by sending us a list of names
of persons of influence or zeal who ought to be invited to this conference from your part of the State — leaders in " village improvement," " country gentlemen," public-spirited lovers of out-of-doors
or of scenes associated with history or old times, leaders in horticultural or historical societies ?

We already have good lists from many places, and we shall be
much indebted to you if you will send us one for your neighborhood, before May 1st.

Yours truly,

CHARLES ELIOT,
for the Committee.

III

July 18, 1890.

AT a meeting of the Committee organized to promote the "Preservation of Beautiful and Historical Places in Massachusetts," held at 9 Park Street, Boston, July 17, 1890, Chairman Walcott presiding, and twelve members being present, the following votes were passed : —

Voted : That the report of the Sub-Committee, appointed at the last meeting, be taken from the table and referred to the Sub-Committee on Legislation. [Messrs. Shurtleff of Springfield, Parker of Worcester, and Williams of Brookline.]

Voted : That the report of the Sub-Committee be printed and distributed by the Secretary to the members of the Committee.

Voted : That the Chairman appoint a Sub-Committee of three to draw up a circular for early publication, and to issue the same as from the Committee. [Messrs. Parker of Worcester, Baxter of Malden, and Eliot of Cambridge, appointed.]

Voted : That the Treasurer be authorized to pay from moneys in the Treasury such bills as may be audited by the Chairman and Secretary of the Committee.

Voted : That the President, Treasurer, and Secretary be an Executive Committee, with power to add not more than twelve new members to the Committee.

In accordance with the second of the above votes, the report there referred to is printed below.

CHARLES ELIOT, *Secretary*,
50 State Street, Room 50, Boston.

To THE CHAIRMAN OF THE GENERAL COMMITTEE. — The undersigned Sub-Committee beg leave to report as follows : —

The General Committee was appointed by the Conference of May 24th "to promote the establishment of a Board of Trustees," whose powers and duties were only loosely sketched in the resolution adopted by the Conference. The duty of this Sub-Committee, as we have understood it, has been to define these powers in greater detail, and to devise the organization of the Board itself.

Upon consideration, we have concluded to recommend the establishment, beside the incorporated Board of Trustees, of a second body with the powers of a Board of Visitors. One Board will be a small and almost close corporation of the class which has been proved best able to manage invested funds well. The second Board will represent those associations of citizens which are vitally interested in the preservation of the memorable and beautiful places of the State. Without the one Board there would be no sufficient confidence in the safety of the property; without the other there would be no sufficiently vital connection with the interested citizenship of the Commonwealth. Our undertaking will not be likely to succeed if the historical and out-of-door societies of the State are not ready to coöperate in establishing and assisting a Board of Trustees capable of acting in behalf of all.

We recommend, then, that the Committee proceed to promote the incorporation of the "Trustees of Massachusetts Reservations," and the establishment of the "Delegates of the Affiliated Societies of Massachusetts," and we further suggest that these two Boards be organized and empowered as follows: —

A. *The Trustees.*

Two persons to be appointed by the Governor and Council: their successors to be appointed in the same manner, as vacancies occur.

Five persons to be named in the act of incorporation: their successors to be elected by the full Board, as vacancies occur.

The Trustees to be empowered: —

1. To elect annually by ballot a President and Treasurer from their number, and a Secretary, who may or may not be a member of the Board; and to provide for the appointment of all servants of the corporation.

2. To acquire, with the approval of the Delegates, by gift, devise, or purchase, parcels of real estate possessing natural beauty or historical interest; and to hold the same exempt from taxation and assessment.

3. To assume, with the approval of the Delegates, the care of permanent funds, the income of which shall be devoted to the general or special purposes of their incorporation as the donors may prescribe; and to hold the same exempt from taxation.

4. To assume direction of the expenditure of such moneys as may be offered them for immediate use in promoting the general or special objects of their incorporation.

5. To accept gifts of useful, artistic, or historically interesting objects.

6. To arrange with towns and cities for the admission of the public to the reservations in return for police protection.

B. *The Delegates.*

The President and Treasurer of the Trustees *ex-officiis.* Not less than seven nor more than twenty-three other persons to be appointed by the governing bodies of as many incorporated societies; vacancies to be filled as they occur by said governing bodies. Seven societies to be named in the act incorporating the Trustees, and the body of Delegates to admit, if they see fit, other societies to the privilege of appointing Delegates, provided that the total number of societies shall not exceed twenty-three.

The Delegates to be empowered: —

1. To elect annually by ballot a President and Secretary.

2. To confirm such acts of the Trustees as involve the assumption of permanent trusts. (See A., 2 and 3.)

3. To discuss ways and means, to devise methods, to propose new undertakings, and, in general, to promote the enlightened self-interest of the Commonwealth in respect to landscape beauty and historical memorials.

If the Committee shall in a general way approve the foregoing recommendations as to the organization and powers of the proposed Boards, the next step will be the reference of this report to a Sub-Committee to draught an act for presentation to the Legislature. Many of the above proposals should be embodied in By-Laws, rather than in an act of the Legislature.

Lastly we may be permitted to illustrate our scheme by a few imaginary cases: —

A., during his lifetime, offers the Trustees five acres of land, situated so and so, with a fund of five thousand dollars for maintenance purposes. The Trustees vote to accept the gift, and their vote is transmitted to the Delegates. The latter body appoints a Committee to inspect the property, and, upon a favorable report, votes to confirm the acceptance of the Trust by the Trustees. (See A., 2 and 3.)

B. offers the Trustees a similar property, the site of an Indian stronghold, but no fund for maintenance. The Trustees decline the gift with thanks; but the Delegate from the local historical society succeeds in raising by subscription a suitable fund, and Trustees and Delegates then unite in accepting the separate gifts. (See A., 2 and 3.)

C. offers the Trustees a thousand dollars to be spent in certain ways upon a designated reservation, and the Trustees may or may not accept the gift without reference to the Delegates. (See A., 4.)

D. offers seats, or a fountain, or a hundred young trees for a particular reservation, and the Trustees may or may not accept the gift without reference to the Delegates. (See A., 5.)

E. offers the sum of ten thousand dollars, the whole to be spent for a designated object which the Trustees have never before undertaken to promote. The Trustees may accept or reject the gift without reference to the Delegates; but the novelty of the proposed object makes them hesitate, and they ask advice of the Delegates, and act accordingly.

F., being a Delegate, reports to the Board that his society is contemplating raising a subscription for the purchase of a particular locality; and asks for a vote of encouragement and approval, which is granted.

It will be perceived that the possible variety of gifts is very great, and that it has been the endeavor of the Sub-Committee to draw up a general scheme which shall be broad enough to cover all probable cases and all varieties of conditions. We believe in giving the Trustees great liberty of action, and leaving them to decide, as each gift is presented to them, whether or not they shall accept it.

Sub-Committee,
{
J. EVARTS GREENE.
CHARLES ELIOT.
MOSES WILLIAMS.
FREDK. LAW OLMSTED.
GEORGE WIGGLESWORTH.
}

IV

April 29, 1896.

DRAUGHT OF A GENERAL ORDER RESPECTING THE GOVERNMENT
OF THE METROPOLITAN RESERVATIONS

1. THE superintendents of the several reservations shall receive the following monthly salaries, a suitable deduction being made whenever a superintendent is furnished with a house: —

Revere Beach	$100.00	$1200.00
Blue Hills	100.00	1200.00
Fells	100.00	1200.00
Stony Brook	60.00	720.00
Charles River	60.00	720.00
Beaver Brook	60.00	720.00
Hemlock Gorge	60.00	720.00
Annually		$6480.00

2. The superintendents of the reservations are to conduct themselves, under the direction of the Secretary, as the general managers of the public estates placed in their care. Their salaries are to be derived from the annual appropriation for "care and maintenance," and they will accordingly give first attention to (a) the guidance and assistance of visitors; (b) the checking of misuse of the reservations; (c) the suppression of disorder; (d) the protection of the woods from fire; (e) the maintenance of fields, pastures, roads, paths, guide-boards, fences, buildings, etc.; (f) the collection of rents and receipts from sales. To enable the superintendents to perform these several duties, they are to be authorized to employ as many "keepers," "extra keepers," and laborers as the Commission may from time to time determine. Keepers will report for duty daily, and will be assigned to "patrol duty," to "post duty," or to "special duty," as the superintendent may determine. Extra keepers will be similarly assigned to duty on those holidays or other special occasions when they may be called into service. Keepers and extra keepers will wear a uniform when on duty, and will be armed with police powers. Laborers will be called into service simply as occasion may demand and the Commission may determine. The pay of the keepers and extra keepers will be $1.75 per day, and laborers $1.50. At the beginning, the number of employees of each grade attached to each reservation shall not exceed the following : —

	Keepers.	Extra Keepers.	Laborers.
Revere Beach	2	4	20
Blue Hills	2	4	20
Fells	2	4	20
Stony Brook	1	1	10
Charles River	0	2	5
Beaver Brook	0	1	5
Hemlock Gorge	0	1	5

3. The superintendents of the reservations are furthermore to have charge and direction of whatever forest improvement works or path or road construction works the Commission may authorize from time to time, and for the prosecution of such work they will employ foremen, laborers, horses, carts, etc., as may be required.

DRAUGHT OF RULES FOR THE CONDUCT OF KEEPERS.

Wearing the uniform will signify that a keeper is on duty, and subject to the rules and discipline of duty in all respects. No outer clothing is to be worn on duty except the prescribed uniform. No part of the uniform is to be worn without all parts. From the time a keeper comes on active duty, including all the time in which he shall be in uniform, he is to carry and deport himself in a vigilant, decorous, and soldier-like way. When proceeding to a post, or when on patrol duty, he is to move at a quick march ; or if there is special need to move slowly for observation, he is to carefully avoid any appearance of sauntering or listlessness. He is to seek no shelter, and to occupy no position or locality unfavorable to his duty of preventing the misuse of the park, and aiding and giving confidence to visitors in its proper use. Nor is he, without special necessity, to enter any building, or take any position or action, in which he may appear to others to be seeking his own ease or comfort, or disengagement from activity and vigilance. He is not to try to surprise visitors ; is not to play the detective ; is not to move furtively or use slyness, in any way, for any purpose. He is not to suffer himself to be drawn into private conversation. He is not to engage in disputes or discussions on questions of his duty or that of visitors, or other matters. To lessen the liability of falling into conversation not required by his duty, and of an appearance of neglect of duty, he will, while in necessary communication with others, stand in the position of "attention," or, if in movement, will take special care to maintain a brisk and vigilant carriage. He is not to address visitors in a loud voice, when occasion for doing so can be avoided by his own activity. He is not to exhibit ill-temper, vexation, impatience, or vindictiveness in manner, tone of voice, words, or acts. The authority to make arrests is to be used with extreme caution ; only when to refrain from using it will bring the law, as represented by the keeper, into disrespect, or be followed by other results harmful to general public interests. Persons to be arrested, and while under arrest, must be saved from all unnecessary indignity. When the keeper is obliged, for the vindication of the law, to use force, he must be cautious to avoid unnecessary violence or harshness. The worst criminal having a right to a hearing by a magistrate before condemnation to punishment, the punishment of offenders can be no business of the keeper. No conduct or language toward a visitor, which conveys an intention of punishment, is, therefore, under any circumstances, to be justified.

V

ARTICLES OF AGREEMENT entered into by and between the Trustees
of the Keney Estate, Hartford, Connecticut, party of the first part,
and Frederick Law Olmsted, John Charles Olmsted, and Charles
Eliot, copartners doing business as Landscape Architects under
the firm name of Olmsted, Olmsted & Eliot, in Brookline, Massachusetts, for themselves, their executors, administrators, and
assigns, parties of the second part.

Whereas, The party of the first part wishes to obtain from the
parties of the second part a design or "general plan" for the
improvement of certain lands lying within and without the city of
Hartford to be known as Keney Park, and also such professional
advice and instruction, written or verbal, as may be necessary to
enable competent engineers, superintendents, and gardeners in the
employ of the party of the first part to elaborate working drawings
and to carry out the said general plan, now, therefore, the said
parties mutually agree as follows : —

The said parties of the second part, for the consideration hereinafter mentioned, shall devise and prepare a "general plan" for
the laying out and improvement of the said lands, and shall from
time to time during the continuance of this agreement give such
advice, written and verbal, and shall supervise the preparation in
their office of such detailed drawings and diagrams as will enable
competent experts to elaborate working plans, to set out the same,
and to order such material and services as may be required for
realizing the intents and designs of said "general plan." The said
parties of the second part shall also, during the continuance of this
agreement, visit the said property at intervals, according to their
custom, to review the working plans and the setting out of the
design, and to give such advice and instructions as they shall find
occasion for.

In order to secure good work of its kind in all that is to be
undertaken under this agreement, men of good standing and competent in the opinion of the parties of the second part shall be
employed by the party of the first part in each of the several departments of Engineering, Architecture, Forestry, and Gardening, who,
with suitable assistants, shall act coöperatively with, and under the
general direction and supervision of, the parties of the second part.

It is agreed that work affecting the appearance or landscape of
said lands to be known as Keney Park shall not be ordered by the
said party of the first part, unless it is in accordance with the

advice or plans of the said parties of the second part, until after they have been given a reasonable opportunity to submit their opinion of the same in writing, and it is further agreed that said written opinion shall be kept with the records of the Board of Park Commissioners.

The said party of the first part shall furnish, without expense to the said parties of the second part, adequate surveys, maps, and all other means, aid, and service required for the information of the said parties of the second part, and for the elaboration and setting out upon the ground of the intended plans.

It is agreed that the compensation hereinafter stated shall be for the personal services and advice of the said parties of the second part as designers and for the drawing hereinafter referred to as the " general plan," and it is agreed that the said party of the first part shall refund to the said parties of the second part the actual cost to them of the materials used and of the services of their assistants while engaged in the preparation of all drawings and sun-prints other than the " general plan " aforesaid, while engaged in inspecting the works, or in advising or conferring with the said party of the first part or the employees thereof, and in general while occupied with the business of the said party of the first part.

It is agreed that all expenses incurred by said parties of the second part or their assistants for travelling or subsistence while away from Brookline on the business of the said party of the first part, such as conferences, examinations of the ground, and inspections of the work, shall be refunded to said parties of the second part.

The party of the first part hereby agrees to pay to the parties of the second part, in consideration of the performance on the part of the parties of the second part of the services herein agreed upon to be performed, the sum of —— dollars, to be paid in ten semi-annual payments.

INDEX

KEY TO LETTERS AND FIGURES ON THE MAP OF DECEMBER 1901.

METROPOLITAN HOLDINGS.

A. King's Beach and Lynn Shore.
B. Revere Beach.
C. Revere Beach Parkway.
D. Fellsway.
E. Fellsway East.
F. Fellsway West.
G. Middlesex Fells Reservation.
H. Mystic Valley Parkway.
J. Beaver Brook Reservation.
K. Charles River Reservation.
L. Hemlock Gorge Reservation.
M. Stony Brook Reservation.

N. Neponset River Parkway.
O. Blue Hills Parkway.
P. Blue Hills Reservation.
Q. Nantasket Beach Reservation.
R. Quincy Shore Reservation.
S. Fowl Meadows.
T. Neponset River Reservation.
U. Mystic River Reservation.
V. Fresh Pond Parkway.
W. Whitmore Brook Entrance.
X. Furnace Brook Parkway.

OPEN SPACES.	CONTROLLED BY
1. Boston Common	Boston Department of Public Grounds.
2. Public Garden	" " "
3. Commonwealth Avenue	Boston Park Commission.
4. Charlesbank	" " "
5. Back Bay Fens	" " "
6. Blackstone Sq.	Boston Department of Public Grounds.
7. Franklin Square	" " "
8. Monument Sq.	Bunker Hill Monument Association.
9. Charlestown Hts.	Boston Park Comm'n.
10. Charlestown Playground	" " "
11. Wood Island Park	" " "
12. Commonwealth Park	Boston Department of Public Grounds.
13. Telegraph Hill	" " "
14. Independence Sq.	" " "
15. Marine Park	Boston Park Comm'n.
16. Castle Island	" " "
17. Rogers Park	Boston Department of Public Grounds.
18. Chestnut Hill Reservoir	Metropolitan Water Board.
19. Longwood Playground	Brookline Park Commission.
20. Brookline Avenue Playground	" " "
21. Cypress Street Playground	" " "
22. Muddy River Parkway	Boston and Brookline Park Commission.

OPEN SPACES.	CONTROLLED BY
23. Old Brookline Reservoir	Boston Water Board.
24. Brookline Res'vr	Brookline Water Department
25. Fisher Hill Res'vr	Boston Water Board.
26. Madison Square	Boston Department of Public Grounds.
27. Orchard Park	" " "
28. Parker Hill Reservoir	Boston Water Board.
29. Highland Park	Boston Department of Public Grounds.
30. Washington Park	" " "
31. Fountain Square	" " "
32. Jamaica Pond	Boston Park Comm'n.
33. Arnold Arboretum	" " "
34. Franklin Park	" " "
35. Franklin Field	" " "
36. Dorchester Park	" " "
37. Squaw Rock	Boston Sewage Dept.
38. Moon Island	" " "
39. Merrymount Park	Quincy Park Comm'n.
40. Faxon Park	" " "
41. Quincy Water Reserve	Quincy Water Commission.
42. French's Com'n.	Braintree Selectmen.
43. Webb Park	Weymouth Park Commission.
44. Beals Park	" " "
45. Hull Common	Hull Park Comm'n.
46. Dedham Com'n	Dedham Selectmen.
47. Boston Parental School	Trustees.

768

OPEN SPACES.	CONTROLLED BY	OPEN SPACES.	CONTROLLED BY
48. Brookline Water Works	Brookline Water Dept.	88. Eastern Common	Melrose Park Commission.
49. Brookline Water Reserve	" " "	89. Waitt's Mount	Malden Park Comm'n.
50. Brookline Water Reserve	" " "	90. Malden Water Works	Malden Water Board.
51. Newton Water Reserve	Newton Water Board.	91. Union Park	Chelsea Park Comm'n.
52. Needham Com'n	Needham Selectmen.	92. United States Marine and Naval Hospital	National Government.
53. Waban Hill Res'vr	Newton Water Board.	93. United States Battery	National Government.
54. Farlow Park	Newton Street Com'n.	94. United States Battery	" "
55. Newton Centre Playground & Green	" " "	95. Lynn Common	Lynn Park Comm'n.
56. River Park, Weston	Weston Park Comm'n.	96. Lynn Woods	" " "
57. Auburndale Park	Newton Street Com'n.	97. Lynn Water Reserve	Lynn Water Board.
58. River Park, Auburndale	" " "	98. Meadow Park	Lynn Park Comm'n.
59. Stony Brook Storage Basin	Cambridge Water B'rd.	99. Oceanside Terrace	" " "
60. Waltham Water Works	Waltham Water B'rd.	100. Nahant Long Beach	Transferred to Metropolitan Park Com'n.
61. Waltham Common	Waltham Department of Public Grounds.	101. Nahant Short Beach	" " "
62. Saltonstall Park	Watertown Park Commission.	102. Devereux Beach	Marblehead Selectmen.
63. United States Arsenal	National Government.	103. Marblehead Park	Marblehead Park Commission.
64. Fresh Pond Park.	Cambridge Water B'rd.	104. Crocker Rock	" " "
65. Cambridge Common	Cambridge Park Commission.	105. Fort Sewall	Marblehead Selectmen.
66. Broadway Park	" " "	106. Fort Glover	" "
67. The Esplanade	" " "	107. Prospect Hill	Waltham Department of Public Grounds.
68. Central Hill Park	Somerville Department of Public Grounds.	108. Rindge Field	Cambridge Park Commission.
69. Broadway Park	" " "	109. Winthrop Square	" " "
70. Nathan Tufts Park	" " "	110. Cambridge Field	" " "
71. Mystic Res'vr	Boston Water Board.	111. The Front	" " "
72. Mystic Water Works	" " "	112. Charles River Parkway	" " "
73. Arlington Hts.	Arlington Water Commission.	113. Hastings Square	" " "
74. Arlington Water Reserve	" " "	114. North Brighton Playground	Boston Park Commission.
75. Lexington Common	Lexington Selectmen.	115. Billings Field	" " "
76. Boston Water Reserve	Boston Water Board.	116. Milton Playground	Milton Selectmen.
77. Winchester Common	Winchester Selectmen.	117. Milton Hill.	Trustees of Public Reservations.
78. Woburn Park	Woburn Park Comm'n.	118. Neponset Playground	Boston Park Commission.
79. Cotymore Lea	Malden Park Comm'n.	119. Christopher Gibson Playground	" " "
80. Sheridan Park	" " "	120. M Street Playground	" " "
81. Fellsmere	" " "	121. Mystic Playground	" " "
82. Craddock Field	" " "	122. North End Park	" " "
83. Ferryway Green	" " "	123. West Roxbury Parkway	" " "
84. Playground	Stoneham Selectmen.	124. Watertown Water Works	Watertown Water B'rd
85. Wakefield Common	Wakefield Selectmen.	125. Bullough Pond Park	Newton Street Commission.
86. Lake Park	" "	126. Crystal Lake	" " "
87. Sewall's Wood	Melrose Park Commission.		

OPEN SPACES.	CONTROLLED BY
127. Islington Park	Newton Street Commission.
128. Wolcott Park	" " "
129. Lincoln Park	" " "
130. Linwood Avenue Park	" " "
131. Elmwood Park	" " "
132. Washington P'rk	" " "
133. Cabot Park	" " "
134. Boyd's Pond P'rk	" " "
135. Walnut Park	" " "
136. Kenrick Park	" " "
137. Loring Park	" " "
138. Lower Falls P'rk	" " "
139. Hobbs Brook Storage Basin	Cambridge Water B'rd.
140. Adams Park	Weymouth Park Commission.
141. Ward 4 Playground	Quincy Park Commission.
142. Heath Street Lot	Brookline Park Com'n.
143. Dudley Street Triangle	" " "
144. Newton Street Reserve	Brookline Water Department, Street Department, and Overseers of Poor.
145. Payson Park Reservoir	Cambridge Water B'rd.
146. Dana Square	Cambridge Park Commission.
147. Fort Washington	" " "
148. Clifton Grove	Malden Park Comm'n.
149. Menotomy Rock Park	Arlington Park Commission.
150. Russell Park	" " "
151. Meadow Park	" " "
152. Great Meadows	Arlington Water Commission.
153. Belmont	Belmont Selectmen.
154. How Park	Watertown Park Commission.
155. Whitney Hill Park	Watertown Park Commission.
156. Highway Lot	Watertown Highway Department.
157. Irving Park	Watertown Park Commission.
158. Knowles Delta	" " "
159. Wellesley Water Works	Wellesley Water B'rd.
160. Maugus Hill Reservoir	" " "
161. Stone Park Playground	Dedham Park Commission.

OPEN SPACES.	CONTROLLED BY
162. Hamilton Park	Hyde Park Comm'n.
163. Little Pond Reservation	Braintree Water B'rd.
164. Standpipe	" " "
165. City Park	Everett Park Comm'n.
166. Brooks Park	Medford Park Com'n.
167. Magoun Park	" " "
168. Logan Park	" " "
169. Public Common	" " "
170. Governor Avenue	" " "
171. Hastings Park	" " "
172. Brooks Playstead	" " "
173. Prospect Hill Park	Somerville Department of Public Grounds.
174. Lincoln Park	" " "
175. Playground, and High-service Pumping Station	Somerville Department of Public Grounds and Water Board.
176. Everett Avenue Park and Playground	Chelsea Park Commission.
177. Washington P'rk	" " "
178. Powder Horn Park	Chelsea Park Commission, Water Board, and Soldiers' Home.
179. Willow Street Park	Chelsea Park Commission.
180. Leased Common	Nahant Selectmen.
181. Dover Common	Dover Park Commis'n.
182. Water Reservation	Needham Water Commission.
183. Ryan's Hill Standpipe	" " "
184. Highlandville Common	Needham Selectmen.
185. Dedham Avenue Triangle	" "
186. Ward 3 Playground	Quincy Park Commission.
187. Ward 6 Playground	" " "
188. Sewerage Land	Quincy Sewerage Commission.
189. Reservoir	Metropolitan Water Board.
190. Quincy Standpipe	Quincy Water Commission.
191. Pumping Station	" " "
192. Ward 2 Playground	Quincy Park Commission.
193. Blaney's Beach	Swampscott Park Commission.
194. Lyman's Hill Standpipe	Brookline Water Department.

770